KAPLAN

Other Kaplan Books for College-Bound Students

College Admissions and Financial Aid

Kaplan/*Newsweek* College Catalog

Guide to the Best Colleges in the U.S.

Scholarships

What to Study: 101 Fields in a Flash

Yale Daily News Guide to Succeeding in College

Test Preparation

ACT

ACT Essential Review

SAT & PSAT

SAT & PSAT Essential Review

SAT Math Workbook

SAT Verbal Workbook

SAT or ACT? Test Your Best

SAT II: Biology E/M

SAT II: Chemistry

SAT II: Mathematics IC and IIC

SAT II: Writing

SAT Math Mania

SAT Verbal Velocity

YOU CAN AFFORD COLLEGE

The Family Guide to Meeting College Costs

By Alice Murphey and
the Staff of Kaplan, Inc.

Simon & Schuster

New York · London · Singapore · Sydney · Toronto

Kaplan Publishing
Published by Simon & Schuster
1230 Avenue of the Americas
New York, NY 10020

For bulk sales to schools, colleges, and universities, please contact: Order Department, Simon and Schuster, 100 Front Street, Riverside, NJ 08075. Phone: 1-800-223-2336. Fax: 1-800-943-9831.

Contributing Editor: Trent Anderson
Editor: Donna Ratajczak
Cover Designer: Cheung Tai
Database Administrator: Jessica Shapiro
Production Editor: Maude Spekes
Desktop Publishing Manager: Michael Shevlin
Managing Editor: Dave Chipps
Executive Editor: Del Franz

Thanks to Jude Bond, Eileen Mager, and Sara Pearl.

Manufactured in the United States of America
Published Simultaneously in Canada

September 2000

10 9 8 7 6 5 4 3 2 1

ISBN 0-684-87348-6
ISSN 1082-6017

CONTENTS

Introduction: How This Book Will Help You Pay for College 1

PART ONE: THE FINANCIAL AID PROCESS

Step 1: Make a Reality Check 9
College Financing in the '00s

Step 2: Figure Out the *Real* Cost 13
Beyond the College's Sticker Price

Step 3: Learn Where the Money Will Come From 21
Your Financial Resources

Step 4: Get Your Share of Student Aid 25
Financial Aid Programs

Step 5: Navigate the Process 39
Your Financial Aid Applications

Step 6: Get an Inside Look at How You're Evaluated 79
Your Calculated Financial Need

Step 7: Compare and Negotiate Aid Packages 121
Aid Awards for Sample Dependent Students

Step 8: Meet Your Share of Expenses 139
Borrowing and Money Management

Step 9: Solidify Your Plan 153
Personalized Financing Strategies

Step 10: Review Important Last-Minute Advice 163
Quick and Easy Tips

Steps for Independent Students 167
Financing College on Your Own

PART TWO: FINANCIAL AID RESOURCES

Regional Resources 189

Grant and Loan Tables 199

Glossary 211

PART THREE: SCHOOL-BY-SCHOOL INFORMATION

How Much Will It Cost? 221
Basic Data for Over 1,000 Schools

ABOUT THE AUTHOR

Alice Murphey has been counseling students regarding financial aid since 1977. She is currently the assistant director of financial aid for systems management at the City University of New York. In this position, she is responsible for training other financial aid personnel at City University. She is the former director of financial aid at the New York University Stern School of Business/Graduate Division. Prior to her tenure at NYU, she held financial aid positions at the University of Southern California and Fordham University.

Alice Murphey has acted as both a presenter and a trainer for a variety of financial aid organizations. She has been a trainer of new financial aid counselors in New York state for three years. She is the coauthor of Kaplan's *Business School Admissions Adviser* and also served as editor of *The Official Guide to Financing Your MBA*, published by GMAC. Murphey is currently active in both undergraduate and graduate financial aid organizations, and is a member of the National Association of Student Financial Aid Administrators (NASFAA) Graduate and Professional Interest Committee.

HOW THIS BOOK WILL HELP YOU PAY FOR COLLEGE

Introduction

It's probably not news to you that college* costs are skyrocketing. The total cost of four years at many private colleges is already over $100,000, and the cost could be over $150,000 in four or five years. These numbers are enough to make parents and students wonder how they'll ever afford college. Well, that's why you've turned to this guide, and that's exactly what we intend to address.

THE HARSH TRUTH

Most readers will not qualify for much scholarship or grant assistance. The bulk of costs will be paid by the student or the student's family, either from current income and assets or through long-term loans and financing strategies.

You Can Afford College reveals strategies for getting your share of available aid and gives you the real story of financial aid—trends, important programs, and changes. Also, since it's forecasted that the financial aid you're relying on may not be there for you, we supply money management techniques—borrowing, budgeting—and discuss how you can finance your share of the costs.

We show you, step-by-step, how your family can pay for college, and we bring the process to life with four sample dependent students and two independent students. Much of the information in this book, however, applies equally to dependent and independent students.

TEN EASY STEPS

Just thinking about college financial planning, let alone actually gathering information and completing paperwork, can induce a hair-pulling episode. Let's face it, the process is complicated.

Don't panic. These ten steps will ease you through the financial aid application process, the forms, and your financing options.

STEP 1: Make a Reality Check

Begin with a wake-up call to the current state of college financing and aid. This is your chance to evaluate how great a factor money will be in your choice of a college, to reevaluate your financial aid expectations in light of recent trends, and to learn to what extent you can rely on financial aid.

*The word *college* in this book refers generically to colleges and universities, unless otherwise indicated.

ARE YOU PAYING FOR COLLEGE ON YOUR OWN?

If you're financing your own college education without support from your parents, you will want to read the chapter called "Steps for Independent Students" in addition to the chapters outlining the 10 steps.

STEP 2: Figure out the *Real* Cost

Check out the costs beyond the sticker price, the expenses that may be hidden or buried. Worksheets help you estimate how much college is going to cost now and, in case you're planning long-term, down the road.

STEP 3: Learn Where the Money Will Come From

Survey the financial resources available to pay for this estimated cost, and see the value of early planning.

STEP 4: Get Your Share of Student Aid

Become an educated consumer. Explore the range of student financial aid programs and the important criteria for comparing them. Find the program that meets your needs.

STEP 5: Navigate the Process

Follow an outline of how the application process works and of how you can make it work for you. Examine the forms you may need to use, the important elements of each application, and the deadlines you must meet.

STEP 6: Get an Inside Look at How You're Evaluated

We demystify the methods by which your application is judged. Get a handle on how your financial need is determined. Estimate the share of college expenses that will be paid with financial aid awards and the share that will ultimately be paid by you.

STEP 7: Compare and Negotiate Aid Packages

When you receive your aid packages (the total amount of aid offered by schools), you need to compare them and decide which best meets your needs. Learn how to assess the offers and how to negotiate a better offer. Our sample students' aid packages will give you a point of reference.

STEP 8: Meet Your Share of Expenses

Once it's determined how much student financial aid will be awarded, you're left to come up with the balance of the college costs. Figure out how much money you'll be required to pay each month and over the course of the four years, and figure out how you're going to manage this expense. Explore key financing options, including borrowing and loans, money management, and budgeting.

STEP 9: Solidify Your Plan

It's important not only that you find financing opportunities that meet your needs, but that these programs and options work together to form a unified plan. Review the detailed strategies formulated for our sample students' families, and apply relevant approaches to your own situation.

STEP 10: Review Important Last-Minute Advice

If you're planning at the last minute or are looking for easy, quick ways to make college more affordable, this list of tips will prove useful. You don't want to miss out on any opportunities.

In addition to these ten steps, you'll find lists of other valuable resources, grant and loan tables, additional blank forms and worksheets, and a comprehensive glossary. There's also a helpful data section with aid and cost information on over 1,000 schools.

STUDENT CASE STUDIES

These steps may seem to add up to a long, hard process, but you're not going through it alone. You'll have expert advice to guide you, and six sample students to go before you. The six students that we've created act as case studies. The students not only go through and illustrate every step of the financing process, but they also receive sample financial aid awards. (These awards are comparable to actual financial aid offers from a variety of schools.)

As we progress through the book, you'll hear from the students and you'll learn a lot about them, their families, and their finances. They may be fictional, but their situations are quite common. While we don't expect you to fully identify with just one of the students, it is likely that you and your family will be able to relate to a combination. Let's meet them:

DEPENDENT STUDENTS

Frances

"I'll be the first in my family to graduate from high school, let alone go to college. My parents always push me to do well in school. It's very important to them, because they want me to make something of my life. I just hope I don't disappoint them."

TRIAL BY OTHERS' ERRORS

The sample students will illustrate not only what you should do, but what you should not do.

Angela

"My mom's been both a father and a mother to me for as long as I can remember. I want to make her proud. After graduation, a lot of my friends are going to get jobs or go to our community college. I know it's going to be tough for me and my mom, but I really want something more for myself. And I know she does, too."

"The admissions representatives recruit students; the financial aid administrators recruit parents."
—Catherine Thomas,
Director of Financial Aid,
Univ. of Southern California

James

"There's always been a lot of pressure on me to excel, and I've always assumed I would go to a prestigious college. I know my father makes a lot of money, so I never thought about how my parents would pay for my college education or about whether they could even afford it. When I saw how much it costs, though, I wondered if there was something I could do to help."

David

"My parents split up a long time ago, but they've both been good parents. I know it's hard to maintain two households and two families, so I don't know how much my parents can afford to help me. I guess I could have worked a little harder in high school so I could have gotten a scholarship. I just hope we'll figure out a way for me to go to one of my three college choices."

INDEPENDENT STUDENTS

Mary

"I always knew I wanted to go to college but I wanted to earn some money first so I wouldn't have to borrow so much. Time sort of got away from me but I really think that this is the right time for me to go to college. I just hope that I can find a way to afford it."

Michael

"When I graduated from high school, I never figured that I needed to go to college. Over the last couple of years, I've found that the only way that I can move up in my job is to have a degree. Even though it never seemed important before, I see that I need the additional training to advance. But, how am I going to do it when I'm married and we already have a child?"

By offering advice on how our six students and their families can finance their college costs, we hope to guide *you* through the process. Adapt these illustrations to your own lives and situations as much as you need to.

It's a Family Affair

The six students are especially valuable because they offer the student perspective. It's the student, after all, who actually applies for financial aid from colleges. However, since the burden of financing the total cost usually falls upon the parents, the bulk of this book is written to and for parents of prospective college students. As we said before, most of the information will still apply to an independent student who will be financing her degree herself. In any case, college financing almost always becomes a family matter.

Let's get started.

Part One:
THE FINANCIAL AID PROCESS

"Sheesh! If I'd known college was going to be this *expensive, I wouldn't have read to you so much."*

MAKE A REALITY CHECK

College Financing in the '00s

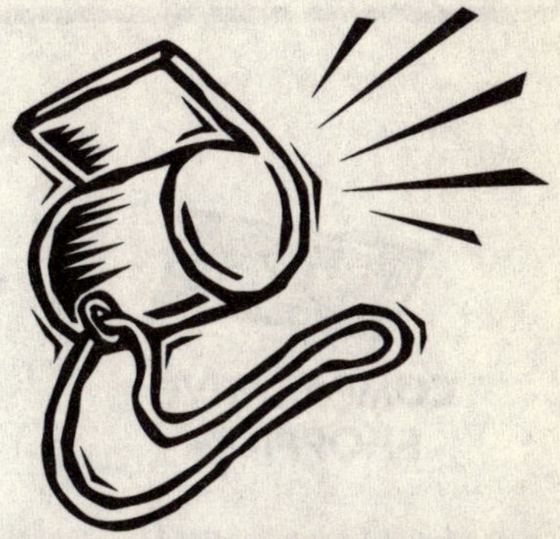

Step 1

Not long ago, the two most expensive purchases in a person's life were a house and a car. Now, for most families, the cost of putting a child through college has become the single most expensive purchase they'll ever make. The total cost of attending many private, independent colleges has already exceeded $100,000 for four years (and many students go for five years). By the year 2007, the total cost probably will be more than $150,000. Even at lower-cost, state-supported colleges, the total can be staggering. Furthermore, the cost of college tuition and fees continues to rise at rates greater than inflation. Until recently, these costs were rising at two or three times the inflation rate. This rate of increase has begun to slow down, and some colleges are holding tuition rates steady.

We'll break down college costs in the next step, and you'll see how to determine your own expenses. For now, before you jump into action, let's get a handle on what you're up against.

"There may be something rising faster than the price of going to college . . . the price of not going."
—Wall Street Journal

WILL COST LIMIT YOUR CHILD'S COLLEGE CHOICES?

You want the best for your child, and this certainly includes the best in education. Therefore, you want your child to be able to choose the school that is most suited to him or her and that allows him or her to excel. For some, this most suitable place may be one of the top-rated, most competitive schools, where students can meet and work with many of the brightest young minds in the world. For others, it may be a small, liberal arts school, where students can experiment in a supportive environment. The right place for others may be a technical or art school that uses a conservatory approach to teach students who are committed to working professionally in a discipline. Or it might be a local school that allows students to remain near home and find their life direction before venturing out on their own, or a state-supported, low-cost school that lets students get their feet wet and demonstrate responsibility.

The point is, you want your child to choose the college that's best for all the right reasons, and in an ideal world, money would not be one of them. But let's be realistic. Money is almost always a significant factor.

"For a long time, my mom has wanted to move to a nicer house. We stay put, though, because she says she just can't swing the cost. Needless to say, she freaked out when she realized college could cost more than a new home."

COMPARATIVE SHOPPING

What would you rather spend $100,000 on? Roughly:

- *2,000 performances of an Elvis impersonator*
- *4,000 ThighMasters*
- *30,000 cans of Spam*
- *One four-year college education for your son or daughter*

It's easy to see why spiraling college costs can affect a student's college choice. This being acknowledged, your child's choices need not be limited by cost considerations. If you get nothing else out of this guide, we hope you gain the knowledge that you do have financing options, that there are steps you can take to keep any college within your ability to pay.

Remember, while cost is a very real concern for most families, an investment in higher education is an investment for a lifetime. A wise choice will return far more than just the dollar value of the initial investment.

The Financial Safety School

College costs and financial assistance are now two of the most important factors students and families consider when choosing colleges. When students apply to a number of colleges, they generally include one "safety" school, one they're pretty sure will accept them. Now, many students regularly include a financial "safety" school, one they know they can afford—often a state school or one they know will give them very close to a full tuition scholarship, or one within commuting distance where they can save on housing costs.

ARE YOU RELYING ON FINANCIAL AID?

Data show that before World War II almost two-thirds of the cost of sending children to college were borne by the family. By 1989, this figure had dropped to below 40 percent. The balance of the costs was paid by federal and state governments and colleges themselves.

"Sure, my parents have money saved. They also have a lot of educational expenses, beyond mine. First off, there's my older brother, who is in an expensive university. Then there's my younger brother, who goes to a private school that helps with his learning disability. And it won't be too long before my younger sister starts thinking about college. It's not exactly going to be painless coming up with the dollars."

Higher education professionals worry that parents are increasingly adopting the following philosophy: "Hey, no average person can pay this much money for a kid's education. I'll kick in what I can, but it's up to the government and the schools themselves to make up the difference."

The truth is, parents and students are considered to have the primary responsibility for funding the cost of a college education to the extent they're able. This is the basic principle of the financial aid system. If you have a child going to college, at least a portion of your family's current income is expected to go toward his or her educational expenses. This portion is referred to as your *family contribution.*

The problem is, even parents who do want to accept primary responsibility for college expenses find themselves incapable of rising to the task. Too many of them are caught trying to do three things at once. They're trying to save for their own retirement, pay for their children's education, and help their elderly parents with nursing home or medical expenses. As many parents have discovered, meeting all of these costs can be the biggest financial challenge of their lives.

CAN YOU RELY ON FINANCIAL AID?

The existing system of financial aid is based on the fundamental concepts of access and choice. All students, regardless of ethnic origin, gender, or financial status, can choose to pursue a college education knowing that financial assistance is available to those who qualify based on need.

This is the way the system *should* work. Unfortunately, the foundation of student financial assistance is showing signs of serious deterioration. The reality is that federal and state financial aid programs have not kept pace with today's increasing costs. The HOPE Scholarship and Lifelong Learning Tax Credit are examples of the federal government's attempts to help families with the rising cost of college attendance. Still, it will take a major influx of federal dollars to make a dent in the rising cost of higher education.

"A college education will be the foundation for a lifetime of learning and personal growth, well beyond graduation. Make sure you're making a sound investment."

—Michael Steidel,
Director of Admission,
Carnegie Mellon University

THE BOTTOM LINE

As a result of federal aid's inability to keep up with the rise in college costs, many colleges and universities have been making up the difference by tapping into their own financial resources. In an attempt to continue helping students who demonstrate financial need, many colleges have raised tuition, only to channel a significant portion of the tuition increase back into their student financial aid budgets. Because this practice stretches resources, many colleges are forced to defer maintenance needed on existing campus facilities, to postpone new research initiatives and building projects, and sometimes to reduce or eliminate existing academic programs, faculty, staff, and services. While this has worked in the past, this strategy can't continue much longer.

Colleges and universities are struggling to find the middle ground between maintaining or improving the quality of the collegiate experience while enrolling the most qualified freshman class. And while they agree in principle with the concepts of access and choice, some colleges have been forced by limited financial resources to depart from the standard practice of meeting every student's financial need.

To enroll the most qualified freshman class using limited institutional funds, an increasing number of colleges have increased the number of scholarships they award based on merit, rather than on need. Other institutions now meet only a portion of each student's financial need. And a small but growing number of colleges consider a family's financial ability to afford the college's costs before they make their admission decision.

?$

GO FOR DOOR #3

You don't have to settle. Yes, a college's cost is probably going to be a factor in your decision. But it doesn't have to be the deciding factor.

IN A PERFECT WORLD . . .

Ideally, financial aid should be there to fill any financial gaps. Realistically, the aid may not be there for you.

How You're Affected

It's no wonder that financing a college education has become so complex. What was once a fairly straightforward, standardized process has now become a rather tedious one, often full of inconsistencies. Students who apply for aid at a number of comparably priced institutions often receive a vastly different financial aid award from each.

The students are often the losers. Paying for college is like buying an airplane ticket: everyone seems to be paying a different price. Like the airplane passenger, students and their families have no idea whether the price they paid to go to that school was more or less than that paid by any other family, or whether they could have received a better "deal" at another school or even by negotiating with the financial aid administrator or admissions director.

The good news is that by using this guide you'll make an informed decision.

"It seems like colleges try really hard to get good students. I just hope my college tries as hard to keep me happy once I'm actually there."

WHAT'S NEXT

Now that you're more aware of the system that you're about to enter, you can start taking control. Let's explore the real costs—traditional and hidden—of college, and develop a picture of your personal financial challenge.

FIGURE OUT THE *REAL* COST

Beyond the College's Sticker Price

Step 2

THE BIG PICTURE

When evaluating college costs, the first numbers people usually turn to are tuition and room and board. While the tuition figures listed in most financial aid guides are fairly accurate (the amounts may have gone up since the survey was printed, or there may be some additional fees), the average room and board figures can sometimes be off. Also, there are many expenses that aren't always discussed and that you might not consider.

In the back of this book you'll find a helpful section entitled, "Just the Facts." It's a list of more than 1,000 schools, with a breakdown of important data such as in-state and out-of-state tuition, room and board, and required fees. Use this section to estimate the cost of specific schools.

In this step, you'll review all the real costs of sending your son or daughter to college. We provide worksheets to help you determine what your child's expenses will be, so that you'll be able to compare college price tags effectively. And we discuss not just the new costs you'll have to deal with, but also those costs that you may already be paying for that must also be considered part of your child's total college expenses. Financial aid administrators usually speak of the costs as either "direct" or "indirect."

HUH?

If you forget the meaning of any of the terms used in this book, check the glossary in the back.

DIRECT COSTS

Direct costs are those expenses that generally are paid to the college and are specifically education related. As you review the following direct costs, plug your estimates into the College Costs worksheet that's on page 19.

DIRECT COSTS

- *Tuition*
- *Fees*
- *Books and supplies*

Tuition

Tuition is fairly simple to understand; it's the amount the college requires from you for your child to attend class. At some colleges, there's a flat tuition amount, regardless of how many credit hours are taken (except if your child attends less than full time). At others, the amount you pay depends on how many credit hours your child takes on.

FULL-TIMER

Full time = 12 credits or more per term
Three-quarter time = Nine credits per term
Half time = Six credits per term (assuming three credits per class)

The first thing you'll want to do when adding up your total cost, then, is to put down the exact tuition amount. If the school bases the amount on number of credit hours, assume 15 hours per term.

COLLEGE COSTS: PUBLIC VERSUS PRIVATE

- **In 1999–2000, the average cost of tuition and fees for a four-year private college was $15,380; adding in room, board, supplies, books, transportation, and other expenses brought the total to $23,651.**
- **In 1999–2000, the average cost of tuition and fees for a four-year public college was $3,356 per year. Adding in room, board, supplies, books, transportation, and other expenses brought the total to $10,319.**
- **About 51 percent of the students who attend four-year colleges go to schools that charge less than $3,000 in tuition and fees. Another 14 percent of the students go to schools that cost $16,000 or more in tuition and fees alone.**

The cost of attendance for the three schools that Frances has selected are very similar. College A's costs total $26,411, College B's total $25,894, and College C's total $28,246.

The data listed above may help you estimate your tuition figure, but for more exact numbers turn to the School-by-School Information section and admissions catalogs.

Fees

There are some fees required of all students and some you may have to pay simply because of the major your child has chosen. For example, science majors may have to pay a refundable lab breakage deposit of $50 to $100 per lab course. Assume that you'll get none of this amount refunded, since even the most careful student breaks a beaker occasionally. Some colleges may also have an optional student services fee, depending upon whether your child chooses to participate in certain activities. The point is, you should add $100 or more in fees to your College Costs worksheet.

"My older brother is a total klutz. In his first week of chem lab, he broke two beakers and three petri dishes and nearly blew up the lab. His lab deposit wasn't enough to cover the damages, so they made him deposit more. I just hope clumsiness isn't genetic."

Books and Supplies

Here again, this figure will vary according to the major. For example, science books can be extraordinarily expensive ($75 or more for some), and there could be ten or more books required for one English literature course. In addition, there may be lab workbooks, photocopied articles, and study guides that don't always get figured in. While the financial aid office usually provides an average annual amount, this figure is apt to be low. We suggest adding 10 to 15 percent more to the figure the college provides, particularly if your child will be taking science or art courses. For our purposes, estimate between $500 and $700 per year.

INDIRECT COSTS

- *Room*
- *Board*
- *Transportation and travel*
- *Personal*
- *Medical and dental*
- *Miscellaneous*

INDIRECT COSTS

Although somewhat of a misnomer, indirect costs include all other costs of attending college. As you did with direct costs, plug your estimate of each indirect cost into the College Costs worksheet that's on page 19.

Room

This expense is dependent on whether the student lives in a dorm, off-campus apartment, group house, relative's home, etcetera. The dorm costs may also vary depending on whether your child lives in a single, double, triple, or quad bedroom. You won't know the actual amount until after your child has been assigned a dorm spot. For purposes of calculating the amount, however, you won't go wrong using the average figure the college provides. Unfortunately, many colleges lump room and board charges together, which can be misleading, but the cost of dorm rooms or rent usually can be calculated accurately. The range is typically between $3,000 and $4,500 a year.

"My parents are thinking about buying a condo near the college. They figure I could live there, get a roommate or two, and they could sell the condo after I graduate. That may be a great idea for somebody else, but I really want to live on campus."

Board

Board is otherwise known as food. Keep in mind that the amount the school estimates will include only meal plans, not optional eating habits, dates, or splurges. Board costs can vary widely based on the meal plan the student chooses, diet, number of late-night snacks, etcetera. One thing worth noting is that board figures don't include beer and liquor. Legality and morality aside, most families should include a reasonable amount if they want to have a relatively accurate total of their college costs.

Only you and your child will be able to fill in the appropriate amount. We're not considering whether the parents or the students will pay; we're only trying to calculate how much college will cost. When you total the board costs, use the figure provided by the college or the School-by-School Information section and add another 10 to 15 percent. The range is usually $2,000 to $2,500 a year.

"Hope I have a kitchen in my dorm. If I can do some of my own cooking, I won't need the school's expensive three-meals-a-day plan. More important, I won't be forced to scarf as much mystery meat."

Transportation and Travel

This expense includes both the cost of commuting back and forth from the local residence to classes and the cost of getting to and from home during vacations and breaks. For a student living on campus, the transportation or commuting amount is probably zero, unless he or she has a car. If a car is involved, there are parking fees, insurance payments, and gas, oil, and maintenance costs. And don't forget to add in an amount for

"I'll be the first member of my family to go to college, so when I go, the whole family will go along to help me move in. It will cost a lot, but my family wouldn't miss this for anything."

campus tickets when he or she is late for class and there are no legal spots around. Again, we're not concerned here with who's paying, we're just trying to come up with a total. The average cost of transportation for a commuting student ranges from $2,100 to $2,400 per year.

The other transportation amount, referred to here as "travel," has to do with going between your home and the college. Every family will have a different amount, depending on whether the college is clear across the country or next door, whether the student comes home once, twice, or a dozen times, and whether the distance can be driven or not. We can't provide you with averages, but we will say that there are ways to make this figure lower, such as student discounts, public transportation, and ride-shares. This amount usually averages $500 to $700 per year.

Personal

These expenses include incidental expenditures such as laundry and entertainment. Use the space below to organize your child's personal budget for the school year. We'll get you started, but you know your child, so you should be able to come up with your own elements and estimates.

PERSONAL

Expense	Amount
Phone	$
Entertainment	$
Toiletries	$
Laundry	$
Clothing	$
Grooming	$
	$
	$
	$
	$
	$
TOTAL	$

The range is typically about $150 to $200 per month, but recognize that this could vary enormously.

KNOW THE LINGO

TUITION: The amount of money that colleges charge for instruction and for the use of some facilities

ROOM: The amount of money that goes toward living arrangements (e.g., a dormitory)

BOARD: The amount of money that goes toward food (e.g., a meal plan)

Medical and Dental Expenses

Your child probably will be able to remain on your health insurance plan while a student, even when living away from home. So you can assume health expenses will be similar to those of recent years. Don't discount a few extra expenses, though. If your child is away from home, some options may not be available.

Miscellaneous

Miscellaneous expenses are those beyond the basic cost of attending college. This isn't to say that they're unnecessary or insignificant. As with personal expenses, use the space below to organize your predictions for the school year. Use your best judgment when estimating.

HOMESICK FRESHMEN PHONE HOME

Don't forget telephone (or online service) charges, especially if homesickness and/or long-distance relationships are factors.

MISCELLANEOUS

Expense	Amount
Fraternity/Sorority Dues	$
Tutoring	$
Extra Books and Supplies	$
Summer Programs	$
Expenses for Students with Disabilities	$
	$
	$
	$
	$
	$
TOTAL	$

COLLEGE COSTS WORKSHEET

To total the college expenses your child probably will incur the first year, use the worksheet on page 19.

Sample Worksheet for Dependent Student

For the sake of comparison, let's first dissect a sample worksheet for one of our dependent students, Angela.

COLLEGE COSTS

Tuition	$21,031

For this purpose, we'll use "College B," which is one of Angela's college choices in Step 07.

Fees	$ 100

We've estimated $100 to cover any class or activity fees she might encounter.

Books and Supplies	$ 600

Angela is considering becoming an English major, which means a lot of books, including costly anthologies. We'll figure about $300 a semester, or $600 total.

Room	$ 4,292
Board	$ 2,146

These figures assume that Angela will take advantage of standard on-campus dorm living and a three-a-day meal plan.

Transportation and Travel	$ 580

Assuming, again, that Angela attends a university in her home state, and she does not have the expense of a car, transportation and travel expenses will be relatively low. Ride shares will especially help keep the number to a minimum.

Personal	$ 1,800

Aside from anticipated phone bills because of a soon-to-be long-distance relationship, her personal expenses will be pretty typical, so we'll use $200 per month here, or $1,800 per year.

HI, I'M DISCOUNTED. FLY ME.

Yes, take advantage of travel discounts when you can. Unfortunately, low-cost flights and use of frequent-flyer miles are not safe bets during the holidays, which is when your child probably would be traveling.

Medical and Dental	$ 150

Barring unforeseen medical emergencies, Angela's dental, doctor, and prescription expenses will probably remain in the $100–$200 range.

Miscellaneous	$ 400

Angela is considering joining a sorority. So, adding about $300 per year in sorority dues to $100 in typical miscellaneous expenses, we get an estimate of $400 a year.

TOTAL	$31,099

If we were to look at only the tuition figure, we'd have two-thirds of the picture. That's why it's important to break down the cost.

Your Worksheet

As we've done with the sample worksheet, total your direct and indirect costs below.

COLLEGE COSTS

Tuition	$
Fees	$
Books and Supplies	$
Room	$
Board	$
Transportation and Travel	$
Personal	$
Medical and Dental	$
Miscellaneous	$
Other	$
TOTAL	$

Is the total a bit more than you anticipated? Is it significantly greater than the number for tuition alone? That's because now you're seeing the whole picture. Keep this figure in mind as we progress through the next steps. It will come into play when we discuss how much of this total you'll be able to pay from your own resources and how much you'll require from outside assistance. We'll also see how you can reduce the individual expenses.

College Costs for Independent Students

If you're an independent student, there are some additional factors you'll need to consider when you're estimating how much you'll need to pay for your education. Check out the section on college costs in the chapter called "Steps for Independent Students."

The important result of this exercise is that now you have a real sense of the financial challenge you face.

BUT WAIT . . . HOW MUCH WILL IT COST *THEN*?

What if college isn't coming next year, but farther down the road? Most people are concerned about the costs of college right now. For those readers who are planning ahead (or for those who may have one child going to college next year and another in a few years), the following table shows how much costs have risen over the last few years and how much you can figure they'll rise over the next few years.

AVERAGE COLLEGE COSTS*

Year	Average Public College	Average Private College
1999	$43,505	$93,737
2000	$45,245	$97,487
2001	$47,055	$101,386
2002	$48,938	$105,442
2003	$50,895	$109,659
2004	$52,931	$114,046
2005	$55,048	$118,608
2006	$57,250	$123,352

**Based on a 4 percent annual rate of inflation, which is applied to the College Board's average annual expenses (tuition, room, board, books, and supplies). Data reprinted with permission of the College Board.*

Keep in mind that these are just average costs; expensive private college costs might add up to $50,000 onto the average private college costs.

WHAT'S NEXT

So, now you have a clear picture of the kinds of expenses and the total cost you can expect, and you see how the numbers will rise in the future. Where is this money supposed to come from? In the next step, you'll explore your available resources: your past, present, and future income.

LEARN WHERE THE MONEY WILL COME FROM

Your Financial Resources

Step 3

Like financing your home, paying for your child's college education should be thought of as a long-term project. Very few people would think of paying for a house in just four years. Yet, how many of us have really done our homework on college costs and how to meet them? How many of us had the discipline to start saving on the day our child was born (which is what most experts advise)?

While many families are indeed saving, most of us are hoping that by the time our children are college age our financial picture will have improved enough for us to pay, our family will qualify for financial aid, our children will be so gifted they'll win a full scholarship, or we'll be able to borrow as much as we have to and pay it back down the road.

Well, paying for your child's education is not just about saving and borrowing as much money as you can while praying for a full scholarship. It's about planning. It's about sacrifice. It's about hard work.

It's no great secret where people get money for college. People pay from three sources: past income, current income, and future income. Most pay from a combination of all three. Let's look at an overview of these sources; we'll get into more detail in later steps, as we take you through your options.

"People think that if you save for your child's education you'll be penalized, that you won't qualify for financial aid. Well, that may be the way it used to be, but now it's a different world. Now, if you don't save, your kids will need to borrow more."

—Natala Hart, Director of Financial Aid, Ohio State University

PAST INCOME

Your past income is reflected in your savings. You probably have some money in the bank (for a rainy day); you may own some stock, a certificate of deposit (CD), a retirement account, or a complicated portfolio. The purpose of these assets is to give you and your family financial strength and the freedom that comes with it. The more savings you have, the more you and your family are able to do what they want. Well, your son or daughter wants to attend college. And that's one of the reasons you saved.

FUNDING THEIR FUTURE

- *Past income*
- *Present income*
- *Future income*

"My parents were always told that they shouldn't save for my education because then they'd miss out on all the government financial aid. Wrong!"

Saving Money

Setting aside a certain amount of money each month or each payday will help build up a fund for college. If you and your child begin saving early, the amount you have to set aside each month will be smaller.

The following table shows you how much you'd have to set aside each month, depending on when you start, to have $10,000 available when your child starts college.

MONTHLY INVESTMENT REQUIRED TO SAVE $10,000 FOR YOUR CHILD'S EDUCATION

Investment Period	Monthly Contribution	Total Contributions	Interest Earned*	Total Saved
18 years	$32	$6,912	$3,187	$10,099
14 years	$45	$7,560	$2,552	$10,112
10 years	$68	$8,160	$1,853	$10,013
6 years	$124	$8,928	$1,144	$10,072
2 years	$401	$9,624	$378	$10,002

*assumes 4% interest

THE DIAPER SAVINGS THEORY

Natala Hart, Director of Financial Aid at Ohio State University, used her "Diaper Savings Plan" in saving for her child's education. When her daughter stopped wearing disposable diapers, Natala saved a significant amount of money. So, she put that savings into her daughter's college fund.

As the table demonstrates, if you start saving when your child is born, you have 18 years to save. Each month you have to deposit $32 in order to save $10,000 by the time your child turns 18 years old. However, if you wait until your child is 12, you have to save $124 each month.

Another factor that determines how long, and how much, you need to save is the *type* of savings plan. With a typical plan, you can regularly set aside small amounts of money and the money will earn interest or dividends. By using savings plans with higher interest rates, however, you can put aside smaller amounts and save more money in less time. Of course, be sure to examine the risks involved in any kind of investment. Make sure you'll be able to get the money out easily when you need it. If terms such as *dividend* and *risk* are familiar but not clear, refer to the following definitions.

BANKING 101

DIVIDENDS: Payments of part of a company's earnings to people who hold stock in the company.

INTEREST: The amount that your money earns when it's kept in a savings instrument. The interest rate refers to the rate at which the saved money increases over a certain period of time.

LIQUIDITY: How quickly you can gain access to the money.

PRINCIPAL: Face value, or the amount of money (on which interest is earned) you place in savings.

RETURN: The amount of money you earn on the savings or investment through interest or dividends.

RISK: The danger that the money you set aside could be worth less in the future.

TIME FRAME: The number of years you'll need to save or invest.

BORROWING FROM THE FUTURE

Loans may seem like current income, but you're actually paying for a loan out of your future earnings.

Here are some savings options to discuss with your financial planner or bank representative:

- Saving accounts
- CDs
- Money market accounts/money market mutual funds
- U.S. savings bonds
- Mutual funds
- Individual corporate bonds or stocks
- U.S. treasury securities (treasury bills, notes, or bonds)

To be fair, you've also been saving for some other important reasons, such as your retirement. And with all the talk about whether the social security system will have sufficient funds when you retire, saving is even more important than it used to be.

"My mom and I figured we could save about $200 a month for college. After using some financial aid worksheets, though, it looks like we could be expected to contribute over $600 a month. I don't know how my mom will pull it off, since she only has about $3,000 in the bank. I guess she'll need to borrow."

PRESENT INCOME

The second way people pay for their children's education is out of their current income. Current income includes all your wages, return on investments, and all other taxable and nontaxable income, whether or not you use it for education.

Present income also includes any financial aid in the form of scholarships and grants your child receives and any tuition benefit you receive from an employer.

In later steps, we'll estimate how much money you can expect to receive in financial aid, and how much of the college cost will indeed be paid from your present income.

FUTURE EARNINGS

The third way parents pay for their children's education is out of future earnings, through loans. A loan, whether for school, home mortgage, or credit card purchases, is simply a way to pay for something out of future income.

A loan may be a frightening option, particularly for people who have made it their business to stay out of debt. However, most people don't think twice about borrowing money to purchase a house. And it's still possible in many areas of the country to buy a house for about the same price as a private college education, that is, in the neighborhood of $100,000. Almost no one would think about buying a house for this price and paying it off in just four years. Yet that's how people often approach the cost of their children's education, believing they must pay out of savings and current earnings.

Paying for your child's education is much like buying a house. You borrow from an outside source to make a large expenditure and spread out the repayments over time (as long as 30 years now, with consolidated loans). You assume that your earnings will increase in time. This predicted increase makes the monthly mortgage or college loan payments easier to swallow, and allows more of your income to be saved for your retirement (or for a second or third child's education). Obviously, in times of recession and downsizing, this doesn't always pan out and, just as if you had a mortgage, you may find you're unable to keep up with the payments.

Here's where a college loan and a home mortgage differ. If you can't pay your mortgage, ultimately you'll lose your house. But you (or your child) will never lose that college education.

A loan is a reasonable way of paying later for something you get now. It's also an investment, when you look at the salary differences between high school grads and college grads.

We'll review loans and parent and student borrowing in great detail in later steps, after you get an idea of how much aid you'll receive. Then you'll have a sense of how much money you're going to have to derive from current income and loans.

WHAT'S NEXT

Now that you've surveyed your basic resources, let's look at the role that financial aid will play. In the next step, you'll review the financial aid system and specific programs, so that you'll be an educated participant and get the aid that you need.

GET YOUR SHARE OF STUDENT AID

Financial Aid Programs

Step 4

If you expect your child to receive financial aid, you're not alone. In fact, about 60 percent of the students in this country receive financial aid to varying degrees. This percentage includes students who are attending private, expensive colleges as well as students going to more affordable, state-supported public colleges. At private colleges, with costs running as high as $30,000, two-thirds to three-quarters of the students are receiving some assistance. Refer to the Just the Facts section for a clearer picture of what percentage of first-year students receive aid—and how much—at specific schools.

When we think of financial aid, we think of money provided by the federal government to help pay for a college education. And much of financial aid does, in fact, come from the federal government—more than $40 billion per year. But another $3 billion comes from state grant programs, and more than $10.5 billion from the colleges themselves, agencies, foundations, clubs, and individuals that award private scholarships.

In this step, you'll review different types of financial aid, the criteria you use to determine which financial aid programs meet your needs, the specific programs and their terms, and your rights and responsibilities.

NEED VERSUS MERIT

Some aid programs are based solely on your need, and some are based solely on merit. There are also some programs based on a combination of need and merit.

CRASH COURSE IN FINANCIAL AID BASICS

Programs have myriad eligibility and repayment requirements. These requirements depend on the program's general classification. The general classifications are gift aid (both merit based and need based) and self-help aid.

Need-Based and Merit-Based Aid

The first thing you should be aware of is that some aid programs are awarded based solely on your need, and some are based solely on merit. Need-based programs evaluate, by looking at the family's resources, how much money the student needs to attend the college. Merit-based programs evaluate a student's ability and/or potential—based on a student's academic records, athletic or artistic ability, good citizenship, or ethnicity.

NEED A LIFT?

Total Cost of College – Expected Family Contribution = Your Need

COST – EFC = NEED

There are also some programs based on a combination of need and merit (e.g., for some scholarships, selection of the recipient may be based on merit, but the award amount will depend upon need).

How Is Need Determined?

Financial aid administrators use federal and state or individual college guidelines to figure out how much money your family can contribute (your expected family contribution) to the cost of college. Once your expected family contribution (or EFC) is calculated, they know how much aid money you'll need to meet the rest of the total cost. The EFC, then, establishes your eligibility for need-based financial aid programs.

This whole process is known as *need analysis.* Need analysis is calculated based on the information (e.g., income, home equity, number of family members) you provide on your financial aid applications. Your need, simply put, is the total cost of a college (as published by the college or as estimated in Step 2) less the amount of your EFC (as determined by specific guidelines). If your estimates are higher than the costs published by the college, realize that the college will use its own estimates.

Need analysis is one of the most complicated aspects of financial aid. We'll go into great detail in later steps, when we examine the guidelines used to evaluate your financial aid applications, your ability to pay, your need, and your eligibility for specific programs.

"I've been doing some library research, to see if there are private scholarships for me. There's an organization for Chinese Americans that awards scholarships of up to $1,000. Also, my parents belong to a local service club that I'm hoping will award me a scholarship. I have to write essays for both scholarships, and there will probably be a lot of competition. Maybe I'll get lucky."

How Is Merit Determined?

Most colleges award at least some scholarships based on merit, but not everybody who gets one is a genius or star athlete. Yes, if a college is looking to recruit an exceptional athlete, musician, physicist, etcetera, it will offer that student thousands of dollars regardless of whether the family has demonstrated need. But some colleges, particularly colleges that are trying to maintain or increase their enrollment, and the so-called second- or third-tier schools that are trying to better their reputations, may award scholarships to students with grades or SAT/ACT scores that are not stratospheric. Also, instead of offering money to desired students, sometimes schools will offer to reduce the amount of tuition.

While many of the highest-ranked and most selective schools—the so-called first-tier schools—claim that they don't offer merit-based aid, that's often not quite true (even some of the Ivies award athletic scholarships). And many states award merit-based scholarships—Cal Grants, Garden State Scholarships, to name a few—for which only decent grades are required, not financial need.

Bottom line: Give it a shot. If your child's grades and/or test scores are high, or if your child has a specific talent, you should think about a merit-based scholarship to help fund his or her education. Even if your child's grades are not spectacular, however, you may be surprised at how many colleges will offer merit scholarships to students as an enticement.

Better Awards for Better Students

Most families, specifically more than two-thirds of families at private colleges, have some demonstrated need for financial aid. Merit-based scholarships are playing an increasingly important role in meeting that need and in attracting students to certain colleges. Many schools award greater amounts of grant and scholarship money to students they most want to attract. This doesn't usually apply to state-supported colleges, which generally have less flexibility in making merit-based awards. Also, many colleges are willing to match financial aid offers your child receives from competing colleges.

Gift Aid and Self-Help Aid

Another important difference among financial aid programs is gift aid versus self-help aid. Gift aid doesn't have to be earned or repaid by the student. Self-help aid must be earned or repaid. Scholarships and grants are considered gift aid. Self-help aid includes loans and work-study programs.

Most students pay for their schooling using a combination of gift aid, self-help aid, and the EFC. Naturally, students will want to maximize the gift portion so that neither the students nor the families will be saddled with debt, and the student won't have to work too many hours during school.

The most recent data available (for the 1998–99 year) show that over 58 percent of all aid awarded is in the form of loans. The ratio of loans to grants in a student's aid package has been increasing practically every year for the last 10 years.

You and your child should be careful to put the ratio of gift to self-help aid into perspective. With regard to the work-study portion, studies repeatedly show that working part time while attending college not only does no harm to most students, it can actually help them. Most of these studies show that students with part-time jobs are better organized and more focused and, as a result, achieve better grades. Of course, students are the only ones who can determine if this result will be the same for them. But students should not be afraid of working a little in order to attend the college of their choice.

The same can be said of having to borrow more in order to attend the college of their choice. Given the fact that college graduates earn much more even the first year out of school than do their colleagues who don't go to college, a little debt shouldn't deter you or your child from choosing the right college. We'll go further into this subject when we compare the financial aid awards of our six sample students.

FAMILY TITHES

Expected family contribution, or EFC, is the amount of a family's financial resources that should be available to help pay for college. EFC determines your need and your eligibility for federal aid.

GOVERNMENT TREND ALERT

Chances are that families will be relying more heavily on loans, or self-help aid, to fund college expenses, and that these loans will not be as heavily subsidized by the government.

THE THREE TYPES OF FINANCIAL AID

To find a financial aid program that meets your needs (immediate and long-term), you need to review all your options. We'll walk you through the key programs, starting with grants and scholarships, and moving on to loans and work-study programs.

THREE TYPES OF FINANCIAL ASSISTANCE

- *Grants and scholarships*
- *Loans*
- *Work-study programs*

1. Grants and Scholarships

Grants and scholarships are considered gift aid, in that they don't require repayment. As such, the following programs are the most desirable.

Institutional Grants and Scholarships

Most colleges offer some gift aid (merit-based, need-based, or both) from their own resources. This money from their own resources is referred to as *institutional aid* or *institutional funds,* and colleges may call this gift aid either grants or scholarships. The criteria for eligibility vary from college to college, but if a student has demonstrated need and is eligible for federal financial aid, the amount of these institutional funds is tied into the amount of federal aid your child is awarded. Institutional grants and scholarships can be very competitive, particularly if they are merit based. They may be awarded only to full-time students and to those who apply by a published deadline, and applicants with higher grades mat get a bigger piece of the pie. You should note that many colleges require an additional application for some scholarships.

MONEY IS MONEY

At some colleges, a grant is awarded based on need and a scholarship based on merit. At other colleges, the terms grant *and* scholarship *are used interchangeably.*

State Grants

All fifty states have grant programs, some of which are jointly funded by the federal and state governments through the Leveraging Educational Assistance Partnership (LEAP) Program. Your child usually has to be a resident of the state awarding the grant, and most programs require that your child attend a college in the state of residency. For more information, check with your state's higher education agency (see the Additional Resources section for a list of state agencies).

LOOK BEYOND THE PRICE TAGS

To help offset their higher costs, the private, expensive colleges tend to have more gift aid available than the low-cost, publicly supported colleges.

Federal Pell Grant

The single largest grant program is the Federal Pell Grant, which in 1998–99 went to almost 3.9 million students. The total dollars spent was more than $7.2 billion, with an average award of $1,869. The maximum award for 2000–2001 is $3,300, and the amount students receive will depend on the cost of the school, eligibility based on need, and full-time/part-time status. While millions of students receive Federal Pell Grants, most middle-income families do not qualify.

On the next page, you'll find a schedule of estimated Pell Grants for 1999–2000. The Federal Pell Grant amount your child will receive is a function of your expected family contribution based on the federal need-analysis formula, the cost of education at the school, and whether your child enrolls full or part time. The chart uses your total family assets and your adjusted gross income. Assets, different from income, are anything of value that you've accumulated, such as cash or property. Adjusted gross income is the income figure supplied on your federal tax return, less any allowable deductions.

ESTIMATED FEDERAL PELL GRANTS

Adjusted Gross Income	Total Family Assets*							
	$25,000	$30,000	$35,000	$40,000	$45,000	$50,000	$55,000	$60,000
$ 5,000	$3,300	$3,300	$3,300	$3,300	$3,300	$3,300	$3,300	$3,300
$10,000	$3,300	$3,300	$3,300	$3,300	$3,300	$3,300	$3,300	$3,300
$15,000	$3,300	$3,300	$3,300	$3,300	$3,300	$3,300	$3,300	$3,300
$20,000	$3,300	$3,300	$3,300	$3,300	$3,300	$3,300	$3,300	$3,300
$25,000	$2,850	$2,850	$2,850	$2,850	$2,850	$2,650	$2,550	$2,450
$30,000	$1,850	$1,850	$1,850	$1,850	$1,850	$1,750	$1,550	$1,450
$35,000	$950	$950	$950	$950	$950	$750	$650	$450
$40,000	$0	$0	$0	$0	$0	$0	$0	$0

**Assets before deduction of asset protection allowance. Assumes family of three with one child in college and one 45-year-old parent working in a state with 6 percent tax.*

Federal Supplemental Educational Opportunity Grant (FSEOG)

The Federal Supplemental Educational Opportunity Grant is generally referred to by its acronym or by the term *Supplemental Grant.* It's awarded by the colleges themselves, and since colleges have to award these funds to the neediest students, the grant is directed to Federal Pell Grant recipients. The total dollars available in 1998–99 (the most recent year for which data is available) was about $614 million, which went to approximately 1.1 million students (an average of about $553 per student with a maximum award of $4,000 a year). The future of FSEOG is always somewhat uncertain.

Other Federal Grants

There are a handful of other federal grants available in such programs as the Robert C. Byrd Honors Scholarship, science scholarships, nursing scholarships, and a few programs targeted to graduate students. The total amount awarded in all of these programs in 1998–99 (the last year for which data is available) was $290 million. These grants and scholarships are specifically targeted and are generally merit based. Although these are federal grants, state scholarship agencies select the winners. See the Additional Resources section for a list of the state agencies.

GRANTS AND SCHOLARSHIPS

- *Institutional grants and scholarships*
- *State grants*
- *Federal Pell Grant*
- *Federal Supplemental Educational Opportunity Grant (FSEOG)*
- *Other federal grants*

"We're not exactly loaded. My mom earns about $39,000, and we have just a few thousand dollars in the bank. Yet, we don't even come close to qualifying for a Pell Grant. You're eligible only if your family can contribute less than $2,500 to the cost of college. It's a good thing I qualify for a lot of other financial aid, or I'd never be able to go to college."

"I didn't think I would qualify for any financial assistance, since my dad makes a lot of money. But I figured I should at least apply. If nothing else, I thought maybe I'd get a student loan so my parents wouldn't have to pay the whole thing. You can imagine how surprised I was when I was awarded a grant by one of the colleges."

2. Loans

Loan terms are more complex than grant, scholarship, and work-study terms. For that reason, we'll go into greater detail on this type of financial assistance than on the others. First, we'll review important loan terminology, so you'll know what you're looking for in a loan program. Next, we'll examine the specific loan programs, applying your new understanding of the terms. Finally, we'll review elements of student borrowing—where does the money come from, should students borrow, etcetera. For tables that detail repayment provisions for many of these programs, turn to the Grant and Loan Tables section near the end of this book.

Loan Terms

All of these factors—interest rate, fees, repayment terms, monthly payment, deferment options, prepayment penalties, and consolidation—are important in determining how affordable a loan will be.

Interest Rate

Interest is a fee charged for the use of borrowed money. It's calculated as a percentage of the amount borrowed. In addition to comparing the basic rates, consider whether you want a fixed or a variable rate. The interest rate may be constant throughout the life of a loan (fixed rate) or it may change at specified times (variable rate). While some people think a fixed rate is safer, a variable rate lets you take advantage of low interest rates.

Fees

Make sure you understand exactly what fees you'll be charged. Education loans may include an application fee, a guarantee fee, and an origination fee, among others. An application fee covers the cost of processing the application, a guarantee fee is an insurance premium, and an origination fee is a fee charged by a bank to process the student loan. Make sure you ask about these fees before you borrow, so you won't be surprised later. In most cases, the fees are deducted directly from your loan amount, which means that the amount you receive will be less than the amount you borrowed. But interest will accrue on the total amount you borrowed.

Repayment Terms

Find out what the maximum length of repayment is, and when repayment starts. Repayment can run anywhere from 10 to 30 years. The length of repayment is one of the key factors in determining how affordable your monthly payments will be.

NEED MORE INFO?

The Kaplan/American Express Student Loan Information Program can help you get information and guidance about educational loans for college. For free assistance, call the program at 1-888-KAP-LOAN.

Monthly Payment
Make sure you know approximately what your monthly payment will be, so you'll be able to assess how this loan will impact your lifestyle when you leave college. Most education loan lenders will provide you with repayment examples in their application materials, making it easy to figure out what your monthly payment would be.

Deferment Options
A deferment is an authorized period of time during which a borrower may postpone principal and interest payments. Find out what deferment options are available, if any. Some loans allow you to defer payments of principal while the student is in school. For example, students can defer principal and interest on unsubsidized Federal Stafford Loans while they're in school. Some nongovernment programs allow borrowers to defer payment of principal and make interest-only payments while the student is in school.

Prepayment Penalty
Make certain the loan(s) you choose allows you to repay early without penalty. This feature offers the potential of great savings. If you decide to pay off your loan ahead of time, you'll save on some of the financing costs that accumulate over the life of the loan.

Consolidation
When a borrower has multiple loans, either from one lender or several, the monthly payment of each separate loan can sometimes add up to more than the monthly payment if all the loans were combined. This is true even if the interest rate for the combined loan is higher than for the other loans. This is because there may be a minimum repayment amount for one or more of the loans.

If you plan to borrow each year, it's generally better to borrow from the same lender each time, so that the total amount borrowed can be added together and your monthly payment is based on the one total.

To make it easier for students with multiple loans or lenders to pay back their loans, the Federal Consolidation Loan Program was established. Under the terms of this program, Federal Stafford and Federal Perkins loans can be combined under one lender with one interest rate and one monthly payment. In addition, the length of time allowed for repayment may be extended, lowering the monthly payments.

Loan Programs
The following federal education loans are considered self-help aid and must be repaid.

Federal Perkins Loan
Eligibility for this program is based on demonstrated need (using the federal need-analysis formula). Each participating college has a pool of money from which they

I'M LATE ... I'M LATE ...

The repayment period and monthly payments are designed so you'll be able to meet your monthly payments. If you don't meet these payments, you're defaulting on the loan. Lenders will employ various methods (e.g., garnishing wages) to recoup the money, and your credit rating probably will be hurt.

For James's family, as for most families with more than one child in college, affordable monthly payments are far more important than the financing cost over the life of the loan.

LOAN PROGRAMS

- *Federal Perkins Loan*
- *Federal Family Education Loan Programs (FFELP):*
  - *–Subsidized Federal Stafford Loan*
  - *–Unsubsidized Federal Stafford Loan*
  - *–Federal PLUS Loan*
- *William D. Ford Federal Direct Student Loan*

OFF THE TRADITIONAL CAREER PATH?

All or part of a Federal Perkins Loan can be canceled if the borrower teaches handicapped children, teaches in a designated school that serves low-income students, or serves in selected areas of the armed forces, VISTA, the Peace Corps, or a specified Head Start program.

make these 5 percent loans directly to students. The college decides the amount of the loan and chooses the recipient. Interest does not accrue while you're in school, and you don't begin repayment until nine months after graduation. The maximum award is $3,000 per year for undergraduates with a maximum total undergraduate borrowing amount of $15,000, but the average loan is about $1,350.

Federal Family Education Loan Programs (FFELP)

Under this umbrella title, there are three similar loan programs for students and their parents: the Subsidized Federal Stafford Loan, the Unsubsidized Federal Stafford Loan, and, for the parents of dependent undergraduate students only, the Federal PLUS Loan (Parental Loans for Undergraduate Students).

Subsidized Federal Stafford Loan This is a need-based loan made by a bank, savings and loan, credit union, or some other lender. Eligibility for this loan is determined by each college using the federal need-analysis formula, and the college financial aid office must certify the student's eligibility on the loan application. First-year students can borrow up to $2,625 per year, sophomores up to $3,500, and juniors and seniors up to $5,500.

The loan has a one-year adjustable interest rate set in June of each year based on the bond equivalent rate of either 91-day Treasury Bills or 52-week Treasury Bills plus 1.7 percent while you are in school, during your grace period, or deferment. The rate increases to the 91-day Treasury Bills or the 52-week Treasury Bills rate plus 2.3 percent during repayment. The maximum rate is capped at 8 percent (through June 30, 2000 the rate is 6.32 percent). Check with your school or lender for the most recent rate information. Like the Perkins Loan, interest doesn't accrue while students are in school and borrowers don't begin repayment until six months after graduation.

All first-time borrowers must go through an entrance interview in which all the terms and obligations are explained. All cancellation and deferment terms are included in the loan promissory note.

Borrowers pay an origination fee plus an insurance premium totaling 4 percent. These fees are subtracted from the loan and the balance is sent to the college.

Unsubsidized Federal Stafford Loan This program has basically the same terms as the Subsidized Federal Stafford Loan, except that eligibility is not based on need, and interest accrues even while the borrower is in school. Although students may choose to defer any payments while still in school, interest will accrue, and when repayment begins, they will owe considerably more than the amount they first borrowed. Independent students have increased borrowing limits for the unsubsidized Stafford Loan beyond what dependent students can borrow. Undergraduate independent students have the same subsidized Stafford Loan limits but may borrow an additional $4,000 for each of their first and second years, and an additional $5,000 for their third year and beyond.

Federal PLUS Loan This is an unsubsidized, non-need-based loan program for parents of undergraduate dependent students. The interest rate is set once a year in

June; the variable interest rate is based on the 52-week treasury bill plus 3.10%, not to exceed 9 percent. Eligibility is not based on need, and repayment begins 60 days after the money is loaned. There is no annual limit; parents can borrow up to the cost of education at the college, minus any financial aid (including loans) the student receives. Like the Federal Stafford Loan, an origination fee and an insurance premium totaling 4 percent are subtracted from the loan. A lender will check your credit record to see if there is any negative history; if there is, you may not be eligible unless you have taken care of the problem (or get someone to cosign the loan).

The Federal PLUS Loan is within this discussion of student financial aid and in the later discussion of parent borrowing, since it's a common element of a student's financial aid package and it's a financing option for parents.

William D. Ford Federal Direct Student Loan

A college will participate in either the Federal Direct Student Loan program or the Federal Stafford Loan program, and the terms of the two loans are similar. One major difference is that under the Federal Direct Loan, the U.S. Department of Education, rather than a bank, is the lender. Approximately 33 percent of all Federal Stafford Loans certified in 1998–99 were done through the Federal Direct Loan program.

There are four repayment choices in either program:

- A *standard repayment plan,* for which you have a fixed monthly payment of at least $50 over ten years.
- An *extended repayment plan,* which allows lower, fixed monthly payments that extend up to 30 years, based on the loan amount.
- A *graduated repayment plan,* where your payments will be lower at first and then increase generally every two years over a repayment period of 12 to 30 years.
- An *income contingent repayment plan,* with two options:
  — Option 1, which is based on debt level, allows payments for up to 25 years of 4 to 15 percent of income, with adjustments for dependents other than a spouse; and
  — Option 2, which is based on debt level, allows payments for up to 12 years of 4 to 15 percent of income, with payments not to exceed the amount that would be calculated using standard amortization and with no family size adjustment.

Student Borrowing

Unlike parents, who use current income to estimate monthly loan payments, students have to go by future income and estimate their *potential* to pay back a loan.

How can you predict what a student's income will be after college, graduate school, or postgraduate school? The answer is, you can't. But there are averages you can use.

"None of the schools I've applied to have decided to participate in the Federal Direct Loan Program, at least so far. I asked one of the schools what happens if I start out with a Stafford Loan in my first year and then switch over to Direct Loans later on. They told me not to worry, that I'd be able to consolidate the loans into one Direct Loan before I even left college."

AMORTIZATION

Amortization is the reduction of debt by monthly payments of interest and principal.

As a general guideline, here is a chart of the estimated starting salaries for new college graduates 1996–97 based on their academic majors.

STARTING SALARIES BY COLLEGE MAJOR (BACHELOR'S DEGREE)

Major	Starting Salary Range
Humanities/Social Science (all)	$26,100–29,300
Any major	$27,300–30,100
Liberal Arts – any major	$27,700–31,100
Psychology	$23,300–26,200
Social Work	$25,500–28,200
Sciences	$37,800–40,600
Mathematics	$39,700–43,700
Business (all)	$31,600–35,100
Business – any major	$28,400–32,500
Accounting	$33,000–36,200
Business Administration	$30,600–33,900
Economics	$34,300–36,500
Finance	$35,000–39,100
Hospitality	$29,100–33,200
Human Resources	$32,900–34,200
Logistics/Supply Chain Mgt.	$32,700–35,200
Marketing	$30,100–34,400
Engineering (all)	$41,700–44,400
Technical – any major	$33,000–38,200
Civil	$37,000–39,500
Chemical	$47,300–49,200
Computer	$45,200–48,000
Electrical	$42,500–45,600
Engineering Tech.	$40,400–44,600
Industrial	$39,200–41,600
Mechanical	$41,400–43,900
Computer Sciences (all)	$42,500–45,900
Computer Science	$43,200–46,800
Information Sciences	$44,100–47,200
Management Info. Systems	$40,500–44,100
Programming	$42,400–46,900
Communications/Telecomm.	$25,600–30,500
Allied Health	$31,700–35,000
Agriculture/Construction	$33,300–34,900
All Reported Salaries	$35,900–39,100

Source: *Recruiting Trends 1999–2000.* Copyright © Michigan State University. Reprinted by permission.

"I'm not sure what I want to do after college. I just know I'll need a college degree. I may major in history, which means if I get a job right after college I'll probably make only $22,000 or $23,000. If I have to pay a couple hundred dollars a month for student loans, it won't leave me very much money for anything else. Guess it means I need to be really careful about how much I borrow."

Should Students Take Out Loans?

For most students, it's generally a good idea to keep borrowing at a minimum. This is particularly true for the early part of students' educations, since it is likely that the level of debt will increase as students progress through their academic programs.

If it's possible to complete the first year without borrowing, it may be wise to delay the first Federal Stafford, Direct, or Perkins loan until the loan is absolutely necessary. If the money is needed, it can always be borrowed up until the last few months of the academic year, and it may turn out that less needs to be borrowed. Naturally, you don't want to wait until the rent is past due, but many students find that they're able to make do with less than they thought they needed.

When estimating how much to borrow, be realistic. Both overborrowing and underborrowing can hurt you in the long run. Overborrowing for college expenses can have a lasting effect on future borrowing ability. For example, your credit history could be ruined, and as a bad risk you'd have a hard time securing loans. On the other hand, underborrowing or overscrimping can be equally deleterious. While reducing debt is a worthy goal, borrowing to pay for an education is an excellent investment.

Below is a table that shows the income necessary to repay a student loan comfortably.

LOAN REPAYMENT GUIDE*

Loan Amount	Monthly Payment	Suggested Minimum Monthly Income	Suggested Gross Annual Income	Years to Repay	Total Interest	Total Amount Paid
$5,000	$63	$420	$5,040	10	$2,600	$7,600
$10,000	$126	$840	$10,080	10	$5,201	$15,201
$15,000	$190	$1,267	$15,200	10	$7,801	$22,801
$20,000	$253	$1,687	$20,240	10	$10,402	$30,402
$25,000	$316	$2,106	$25,280	10	$13,002	$38,002
$30,000	$380	$2,533	$30,340	10	$15,603	$45,603
$35,000	$443	$2,953	$35,440	10	$18,203	$53,203
$40,000	$506	$3,373	$40,480	10	$20,804	$60,804
$45,000	$570	$3,800	$45,600	10	$23,405	$68,405
$50,000	$633	$4,220	$50,640	10	$26,005	$76,005

**Assumes 15 percent of monthly income is available for loan payments and 9 percent interest.*

For example, in order to repay loans totaling $25,000 in ten years, in monthly payments of $316, your minimum salary should be just over $25,000 a year, or just over $2,000 a month. The interest on this loan would be over $13,000.

YOUR NEED TO BORROW MAY SUBSIDE

Sometimes parents find they're able to contribute more than what is expected or, occasionally, a grandparent or close relative makes a significant gift that allows the student to borrow less. Also, students often find that working at a job does not jeopardize their studies, and they're able to work and earn more, thereby reducing the amount they need to borrow.

DON'T BELIEVE THE HYPE

Despite the media hype, about 85 percent of borrowers repay their student loans.

A Word about Repaying a Student Loan

For the last several years there has been a great deal of media attention paid to student-loan defaulters. The media plays up stories about how deadbeats don't pay back their student loans (it's especially attention grabbing when the defaulter is a doctor or lawyer). Loan defaults are certainly a problem; it costs taxpayers billions of dollars. The truth is, though, most borrowers do pay back their loans. And the majority of student loan defaulters are people who are in financial difficulty and unable to pay.

3. Work-Study Programs

The following employment opportunities are considered self-help aid.

WORK-STUDY PROGRAMS

- *Federal Work-Study (FWS)*
- *State work-study programs*
- *Part-time jobs*

Federal Work-Study (FWS) Program

The Federal Work-Study Program is a need-based program in which students are awarded an amount of money that they earn through employment. Many FWS jobs are on campus, and FWS recipients work with other student workers (at the same rate of pay). The only difference is that a portion of the student's salary is paid through federal funds, so FWS recipients are very much in demand by employers. Eligibility for FWS is determined through the federal need-analysis formula. Who receives FWS and in what amount is determined by each college. This program is popular with the federal government and additional funds are beomg added to it every year.

State Work-Study Programs

A few states offer work-study programs that are similar to the Federal Work-Study Program. For more information about these programs, refer to the state agencies listed in the Additional Resources section of this guide or to the financial aid offices at colleges.

"I was offered a Federal Work-Study award at two colleges. My dad says he'll talk to some friends who have offices nearby, to see if they'll hire me part-time and pay me a lot more than a campus job would pay. I told him it's worth a phone call, but to remember that I can't earn more than the $4,000 self-help amount they awarded without losing my grant."

Part-Time Jobs

Although this is not a financial aid program in the traditional sense, many students help finance their education through part-time employment on campus and off. Virtually every college offers part-time jobs to students. These jobs are not need-based in the official sense, because no need-analysis or financial aid application is necessary. However, how students present their need for the job to the prospective employer or to the job placement office staff that refers them may go a long way toward their being hired.

Working on campus for the college can have some benefits that aren't available from off-campus employers. Typically, college employers are more sensitive to peak study and class times (e.g., finals and midterms) and may give time off for studying. There's no time lost for commuting; sometimes students can even work an hour or two, go to class for an hour or two, and go back to work. Sometimes students can work in the department in which they are majoring. This provides valuable experience and an opportunity to work closely with the professors and staff.

On the other hand, off-campus employers may pay more and offer jobs that have long-term potential.

Students should check with the job placement office or career center about potential jobs, whether or not they're awarded a FWS job. You never know when the right opportunity will come along.

RÉSUMÉ ENHANCEMENT

Part-time jobs, like summer jobs and internships, can give you relevant work experience and impress prospective employers.

YOUR RIGHTS AND RESPONSIBILITIES

When it comes to student financial aid, you have the following rights and responsibilities. Use the following list as your guide as you investigate financial aid programs.

You Have the Right To:

- Privacy—all records and data submitted with financial aid applications are treated as confidential information
- Accept or decline any offer of financial aid
- Be notified before cancellation of aid and to be notified of the reason for cancellation

You Have the Right to Know:

- The cost of attendance
- The refund policy for students who withdraw
- What financial assistance is available from federal, state, and institutional resources
- Procedures and deadlines for submitting applications for financial aid
- How financial aid recipients are selected
- How your eligibility is determined, including all resources considered available to you by the financial aid office
- How and when funds will be disbursed to you
- Full details of each type of award you receive
- For any student loan you receive: the interest rate, total amount you must repay, when your repayment begins, the length of your repayment period, and the cancellation or deferment provisions of your loan
- For any Federal Work-Study job: a description of the job, the hours you must work, the rate of pay, and how and when you will be paid
- The criteria used to determine satisfactory academic progress for financial aid purposes
- How to appeal a decision by the financial aid office concerning your aid award

You Have the Responsibility To:

- Read and understand all financial aid documents
- Read directions thoroughly, complete all application forms accurately, and comply with any deadlines
- Read, understand, and keep copies of any forms your are required to sign
- Provide correct information on all financial aid applications and forms (misrepresentation may be considered a criminal offense)
- Provide documentation supporting your financial aid application
- Repay any student loans you may receive
- Report any change in your enrollment status or financial status, including any scholarships or grants received from outside sources, and personal status, including address, name, and marital changes
- Report to your lender any changes in personal or enrollment status
- Attend an entrance and exit interview if you receive a student loan
- Satisfactorily perform the work agreed upon in a Federal Work-Study job
- Know and comply with all requirements for continuation of financial aid, including maintaining satisfactory academic progress as defined by the college
- Use financial aid funds only for educationally related expenses

WHAT'S NEXT

Now that we've explored the programs, let's talk about exactly how you'll apply for this financial aid. The next step is the heart of the book, and the heart of the entire process. You'll walk through the financial aid process, including applications and worksheets.

NAVIGATE THE PROCESS

Your Financial Aid Applications

Step 5

Applying for financial aid is a daunting prospect to a family facing it for the first time. The forms seem to be ever changing and each college seems to want you to provide something different.

There are two forms you need to become familiar with in order to navigate the process. The basic required form for all federal aid is called the Free Application for Federal Student Aid (FAFSA). This form must be filed by any student who wishes to be considered for the federal financial aid programs—a Federal Pell Grant, federal work-study, a Federal Perkins Loan, a Federal Stafford Loan, and the other federal programs that were described in Step Four. Students must file this form after January 1 of the year that they intend to attend college (and every year thereafter).

The other form you may need to file is called the CSS/Financial Aid PROFILE form. This form first became available in October 1995 when the College Scholarship Service (CSS) of the College Board developed a new application process, which is now used by some institutions. This process was designed to provide information to colleges that wanted more information (and earlier information) than the federal government was providing from the FAFSA. Usually, these colleges have their own funds to award and the PROFILE process gives them the additional information that they need for the award process.

In this step, we'll take you through every stage of the financial aid application processes—both the federal process and the institutional process used by some schools. You'll familiarize yourself with the information on the applications, as well as with deadlines and actual forms. This step is to give you a sense of the overall procedure, of how you get from here to there. In the next steps, we'll go behind the scenes and see how your application is evaluated and how your share of financial aid is determined.

Since it's the student, not the parent, who applies for financial aid, this stage-by-stage discussion will address the student.

UNCLE SAM'S PROGRAMS

- *Federal Pell Grant*
- *Federal Supplemental Educational Opportunity Grant (FSEOG)*
- *Federal Work-Study*
- *Federal Perkins Loan*
- *Federal Stafford Loan*
- *Federal Direct Loan*

OFA: OUR FAVORITE ACRONYMS

EFC: Expected family contribution

FAFSA: Free Application for Federal Student Aid

FAFSA? PROFILE? THE RIGHT TRACK FOR YOU

Which application form should you fill out—the FAFSA or the PROFILE? Or should you fill out both forms? How do you figure this out?

Which form(s) you file depends somewhat on which schools you are planning on applying to. All of the government programs require the FAFSA. Since these programs are the basis of any financial aid package you may receive, all schools eventually will require that you complete the FAFSA.

Some of the schools' programs also require the PROFILE. So, you'll be completing either the FAFSA only, or both the FAFSA and the PROFILE. You'll virtually never be filing the PROFILE only.

Decision 1

Which colleges will you be applying to for admission and financial aid? As soon as you know that, you can start the financial aid process.

Decision 2

Will you be filling out the FAFSA alone or do some of the schools you are applying to also require the PROFILE form?

The free FAFSA is available at high school guidance offices and colleges late in the fall. You should not file it until after January 1. You can choose up to six colleges to receive your completed FAFSA results.

The PROFILE registration packet is available in most high school guidance offices and in the college financial aid offices at those schools that require you to file this form. This form is available much earlier than the FAFSA, usually in the early fall. To find out which colleges do or don't want you to use the PROFILE, check the colleges' literature, call the colleges' financial aid offices, or check the PROFILE registration packet.

As a general rule, more of the private colleges (particularly those that have a significant amount of their own financial aid money) and fewer of the state-supported colleges (which often have limited financial aid resources beyond the government programs) will want you to use the PROFILE. In addition, some private scholarship programs, such as the National Merit Scholarship Program, will require the PROFILE. Make sure that each college you list on the PROFILE registration form actually wants the PROFILE, since the cost of filing this form depends on how many schools you list.

If you are applying only to schools that require you to file the FAFSA, you should follow Track B. If you are applying to any school that requires the PROFILE, you need to follow *both* Track A and Track B.

WHEN IT'S TIME TO CHANGE, YOU'VE GOT TO REARRANGE

When you apply for institutional aid (funds controlled by the schools), you'll use a customized application called the Financial Aid PROFILE.

OFA: OUR FAVORITE ACRONYMS

CSS: College Scholarship Service, the arm of the College Board that handles financial aid and processes the Financial Aid PROFILE

FAFSA: The Free Application for Federal Student Aid, the federal financial aid application that establishes eligibility for all federal programs, including loan programs, and for some institutional aid

FROM HERE TO THERE

TRACK A

1. Fill out PROFILE registration.
2. Complete/submit PROFILE.

TRACK B

1. Pick up a FAFSA.
2. Complete/submit FAFSA.

3. Review acknowledgment letter.
4. Verify reported income.
5. Examine your award letter.

MAKING TRACKS

TRACK A: At least one school requires the PROFILE

TRACK B: None of the schools requires the PROFILE

Track A usually will begin before you need to start on Track B, but these can occur simultaneously. Many students file the PROFILE form during the fall of their senior year, but must wait to file the FAFSA until after January 1 of the calendar year they will attend college. For this reason, we will discuss the PROFILE process before the FAFSA process, even though fewer students will need to follow this track.

TRACK A

For students applying to at least one college that requires the PROFILE.

October

Stage 1: Fill out the PROFILE Registration

The PROFILE Registration is primarily a worksheet that initiates this financial aid process. You provide some basic information, and CSS generates your own customized financial aid application. Many schools use the PROFILE form specifically for their early decision candidates. If you have access to the World Wide Web, you can submit an online request for a registration form or you can complete the actual PROFILE registration process right there. The URL for the site is www.collegeboard.org.

PROFILE Registration Form

On the next page is a sample of the PROFILE Registration Worksheet that you will use. This is just for your review, and shouldn't be submitted.

CSS's PROFILE Registration Worksheet

SAMPLE. DO NOT USE.

Worksheet Help

Additional information for the worksheet at right.

Be certain you have the student's social security number before you register.

Give the CSS Code Number and Housing Code for up to 10 schools and programs to which the student wants CSS to send information. CSS will send the student a customized PROFILE Application packet based on the requirements of the schools and programs listed in this question. At least one code number must be given.

Don't list a code for a school or program unless it is included on the CSS Code List or unless the school or program has told the student to do so.

Write in the Housing Code that best describes where the student plans to live while attending school during 2000–2001. If the student is considering more than one school, provide a Housing Code for each school the student lists. Answer "Campus housing" if the student will live in housing controlled by the school the student will attend. Answer "Off-campus housing" if the student will not be living with parents, in campus housing, or with relatives (other than a spouse or children). Answer "With parents" if the student will live with one or both parents while attending school. Answer "With relatives" if the student will live with relatives other than parents, spouse, or children.

If you are requesting the optional express delivery service (see Question 16), a street address must be given. **Do not enter a P.O. box number.**

If you live in Canada, be sure to include your province.

Mark the student's year in school from July 1, 2000, through June 30, 2001. If the student is currently a senior in high school or will be a first-time, entering freshman, check "1st year (never previously attended college)."

Worksheet

Complete this worksheet before calling CSS to register for your customized PROFILE Application.

1 Student's social security number:

☐☐☐-☐☐-☐☐☐☐

2 Student's name:

Last

First M.I.

3 Student's title (optional):

☐ Mr. ☐ Miss, Ms., or Mrs.

4 Colleges, universities, and programs to receive PROFILE information. Write in the Code Number and Housing Code for up to 10 schools to which the student wants CSS to send information. Use only the CSS Code List. At least one code must be entered.

	CSS Code No.	Housing Code*
1.		
2.		
3.		
4.		
5.		
6.		
7.		
8.		
9.		
10.		

*Housing Codes for 2000–2001.
(Enter only one code per school.)
1=Campus housing
2=Off-campus housing
3=With parents
4=With relatives

5 Student's permanent mailing address (mail will be sent to this address):

Number, street, and apartment number

City State Zip

Postal Code (outside U.S. and Puerto Rico only)

Country (outside U.S. and Puerto Rico only)

6 Student's home telephone number:

Area code

7 Student's date of birth:

Month Day Year

8 What will be the student's year in school during 2000–2001? (check one)

- ☐ 1st year (never previously attended college)
- ☐ 1st year (previously attended college)
- ☐ 2nd year
- ☐ 3rd year
- ☐ 4th year
- ☐ 5th year or more undergraduate
- ☐ first-year graduate/professional (beyond a bachelor's degree)
- ☐ second-year graduate/professional
- ☐ third-year graduate/professional
- ☐ fourth-year or more graduate/professional

(continued on back)

CSS's PROFILE Registration Worksheet (cont.)

SAMPLE. DO NOT USE.

Worksheet (continued)

9 What will be the student's 2000–2001 financial aid status?

- ☐ First-time applicant, entering student (including transfer student)
- ☐ Renewal applicant, continuing student
- ☐ First-time applicant, continuing student

10 What is the student's current marital status? (check one)

- ☐ unmarried (single, divorced, widowed)
- ☐ married
- ☐ separated

11 Is the student a veteran of the U.S. Armed Forces?

☐ Yes ☐ No

12 Is the student an orphan, or a ward of the court, or was the student a ward of the court until age 18?

☐ Yes ☐ No

13 Does the student have legal dependents (other than a spouse) that fit the definition in the instructions?

☐ Yes ☐ No

14 Are the student's biological or adoptive parents separated or divorced, or were they never married?

☐ Yes ☐ No

15 Do the student's parents own all or a part of a business, corporation, partnership, or farm, or is either parent self-employed?

☐ Yes ☐ No

16 Fee and type of payment

A. Registration Fee **(nonrefundable)** $ 7.00

B. Schools' and Programs' Processing Fee (Multiply number from Question 4 by $16.00. Enter result. Must be at least $16.00) $______

C. Express Delivery Service (optional)
Express delivery fees are:
$16 – U.S., Puerto Rico, Canada
$25 – Central and South America, Europe, Mexico, the Caribbean
$39 – All other $______

D. *Meeting College Costs* (optional) $11.95 (nonrefundable) $______

Total (Add amounts on lines A through D) $______

If you are paying by credit card, have the following information available when you call CSS.

Check one: ☐ MasterCard ☐ VISA ☐ American Express

Credit Card Number ☐☐☐☐☐☐☐☐☐☐☐☐☐☐☐☐ Expiration Date (Month/Year) ☐☐/☐☐

Worksheet Help

(9) If the student is a high school senior or has never attended college before, mark the first box. If the student is planning to transfer to another institution, mark the first box.

(11) Mark "Yes" if the student was released from active military service under a condition other than dishonorable, or if the student is not a veteran now, but will be one by June 30, 2001.

(12) Mark "Yes" if both of the student's parents are dead and the student doesn't have an adoptive parent or legal guardian. Also check "Yes" if the student is currently a ward of the court or was a ward of the court until age 18.

(13) Mark "Yes" if the student has any children who get more than half of their support from the student. Also mark "Yes" if other people (not the student's spouse) live with the student and get more than half of their support from the student and will continue to get that support through June 30, 2001.

(14) Mark "Yes" if the student's biological or adoptive parents have separated or divorced, even if one or both have since remarried. Also mark "Yes" if the student's biological parents were never married to each other.

(15) Mark "Yes" if the student's parents own all or part of a business, corporation, partnership, or are a farm or ranch owner, operator, or farm tenant. Also mark "Yes" if either parent is self-employed.

(16) The PROFILE Registration Fee covers the cost of preparing and mailing the PROFILE Application packet. The fee for schools and programs covers processing and reporting the student's PROFILE information to the schools and programs that have been requested. CSS's responsibility to the student in this regard does not extend beyond the amount of the student's fee.

The CSS representative who handles your phone registration will give you your CSS ID.

Write it here______________________________

It is your confirmation that you completed the registration process.

CSS cannot accept the 2000–2001 PROFILE Registration before September 15, 1999, or after November 15, 2000.

"My mom, also known in our family as Digit-head, worships computers. She's pretty excited that she'll be able to do some of this financial aid application stuff electronically."

On your PROFILE Registration Worksheet, you list all the schools you've applied to that want you to use the PROFILE service (list only those schools that want the PROFILE, even if you've applied for admission at other schools that don't use the PROFILE). Once you have completed the PROFILE Registration Worksheet, you may register in one of two ways:

- By calling the toll-free PROFILE telephone registration service at (800) 778-6888
- By connecting to College Board Online at www.collegboard.org

Students and parents can get answers to their questions about PROFILE by sending an email message to help@cssprofile.org, or by calling (305) 829-9793.

November

Stage 2: Complete and Submit the Financial Aid PROFILE

A few weeks after submitting the registration form, you'll receive in the mail a customized financial aid application called the Financial Aid PROFILE. With this form you'll be able to apply for institutional aid at the colleges you've designated. These colleges will get the information you've reported and also be able to estimate your eligibility for federal aid. This estimate is not binding and cannot be used to apply for actual federal aid. You'll eventually have to fill out the FAFSA in order to receive federal aid (including student loans).

The Financial Aid PROFILE is customized for you, your family, and the schools you've designated. It includes questions that every PROFILE applicant has to fill out, questions that only the colleges you've designated want you to fill out, and relevant supplemental forms.

The PROFILE Application for Institutional Aid

Your customized PROFILE packet will include your financial aid application for institutional aid at the colleges you designated. On the following pages you'll see a sample of the application you'll receive. This application collects student information, parent information, and some other detailed information.

SAMPLE. DO NOT USE.

CSS/FINANCIAL AID PROFILE® 2000–2001

3328593-3

Basic Application 1

Section A — Student's Information

1. Student's name Last / First / M.I.

2. Student's permanent mailing address (Mail will be sent to this address. See instructions.)
Number, street, and apartment number
City / State / Zip
For students outside the U.S. and Puerto Rico only → Postal Code → Country

3. Student's home telephone number Area Code

4. Title (optional) 1 ○ Mr. 2 ○ Miss, Ms., or Mrs.

5. Student's date of birth Month Day Year

6. Student's social security number

7. What will be the student's year in school during 2000–2001? (Fill in only one oval.)
1 ○ 1st year (never previously attended college)
2 ○ 1st year (previously attended college)
3 ○ 2nd year
4 ○ 3rd year
5 ○ 4th year
6 ○ 5th year or more undergraduate
7 ○ first-year graduate/professional (beyond a bachelor's degree)
8 ○ second-year graduate/professional
9 ○ third-year graduate/professional
10 ○ fourth-year or more graduate/professional

8. What is the student's current marital status? (Fill in only one oval.)
1 ○ unmarried (single, divorced, widowed) 2 ○ married 3 ○ separated

9. Is the student an orphan, or a ward of the court, or was the student a ward of the court until age 18?
Yes ○ 1 No ○ 2

10. Does the student have legal dependents (other than a spouse) that fit the definition in the instructions?
Yes ○ 1 No ○ 2

11. How many people are in the student's (and spouse's) household? Always include the student (and spouse). List their names and give information about them in Section M. See instructions.

12. Of the number in 11, how many will be college students between July 1, 2000, and June 30, 2001? Include yourself.

13. What is the student's state of legal residence?

14. What is the student's citizenship status?
a. 1 ○ U.S. citizen (Skip to Question 15.)
2 ○ Eligible noncitizen—see instructions (Skip to Question 15.)
3 ○ Neither of the above (Answer "b" and "c" below.)
b. Country of citizenship?
c. Visa classification?
1 ○ F1 2 ○ F2 3 ○ J1 4 ○ J2 5 ○ G 6 ○ Other

Section B — Student's 1999 Income & Benefits

If married, include spouse's information in Sections B, C, D, and E.

15. The following 1999 U.S. income tax return figures are (Fill in only one oval.)
1 ○ estimated. Will file IRS Form 1040EZ, 1040A, or 1040 TEL. Go to 16.
2 ○ estimated. Will file IRS Form 1040. Go to 16.
3 ○ from a completed IRS Form 1040EZ, 1040A, or 1040 TEL. Go to 16.
4 ○ from a completed IRS Form 1040. Go to 16.
5 ○ a tax return will not be filed. Skip to 20.

Tax Filers Only

16. 1999 total number of exemptions (IRS Form 1040, line 6d or 1040A, line 6d or 1040EZ — see instructions)

17. 1999 Adjusted Gross Income from IRS Form 1040, line 33 or 1040A, line 18 or 1040EZ, line 4 $ .00

18. a. 1999 U.S. income tax paid (IRS Form 1040, line 49 or 1040A, line 32 or 1040EZ, line 10) $ .00

b. 1999 Education Credits—Hope and Lifetime Learning (IRS Form 1040, line 44 or 1040A, line 29) $ .00

19. 1999 itemized deductions (IRS Form 1040, Schedule A, line 28. Write in "0" if deductions were not itemized.) $ .00

20. 1999 income earned from work by student (See instructions.) $ .00

21. 1999 income earned from work by student's spouse $ .00

22. 1999 dividend and interest income $ .00

23. 1999 untaxed income and benefits (Give total amount for year.)
a. Social security benefits (See instructions.) $ .00
b. AFDC/ADC or TANF (See instructions.) $ .00
c. Child support received for all children $ .00
d. Earned Income Credit (IRS Form 1040, line 59a or 1040A, line 37a or 1040EZ, line 8a) $ .00
e. Other – write total from instruction worksheet, page 4 $ .00

24. 1999 earnings from Federal Work-Study or other need-based work programs plus any grant and scholarship aid required to be reported on your U.S. income tax return $ .00

Page 1

SAMPLE. DO NOT USE.

PROFILE Application (cont.)

Section C — Student's Assets – Include trust accounts only in Section D.

25. Cash, savings, and checking accounts $ .00

26. Total value of IRA, Keogh, 401(k), 403(b), etc. accounts as of December 31, 1999 $ .00

	What is it worth today?	What is owed on it?
27. Investments (Including Uniform Gifts to Minors—see instructions)	$ .00	$ .00
28. Home (Renters write in "0.")	$ .00	$ .00
29. Other real estate	$ .00	$ .00
30. Business and farm	$ .00	$ .00

31. If a farm is included in 30, is the student living on the farm? Yes ○ 1 No ○ 2

32. If student owns home, give a. year purchased ☐☐☐☐ b. purchase price $ .00

Section D — Student's Trust Information

33. a. Total value of all trust(s) $ .00

b. Is any income or part of the principal currently available? Yes ○ 1 No ○ 2

c. Who established the trust(s)? 1 ○ Student's parents 2 ○ Other

Section E — Student's 1999 Expenses

34. 1999 child support paid because of divorce or separation $ .00

35. 1999 medical and dental expenses not covered by insurance (See instructions.) $ .00

Section F — Student's Expected Summer/School-Year Resources for 2000–2001

36. a. Is the student a veteran of the U.S. Armed Forces? Yes ○ 1 No ○ 2

	Amount per month	Number of months
b. If yes, write in student's veterans benefits (July 1, 2000 – June 30, 2001)	$ .00	☐☐

37. Student's (and spouse's) resources (Don't enter monthly amounts.)	Summer 2000 (3 months)	School Year 2000–2001 (9 months)
a. Student's wages, salaries, tips, etc.	$ .00	$ .00
b. Spouse's wages, salaries, tips, etc.	$ .00	$ .00
c. Other taxable income	$ .00	$ .00
d. Untaxed income and benefits	$ .00	$ .00
e. Grants, scholarships, fellowships, etc. from sources other than the colleges or universities to which the student is applying (List sources in Section Q.)		$ .00
f. Tuition benefits from the parents' and/or the student's or spouse's employer		$ .00
g. Amount the student's parent(s) think they will be able to pay for the student's 2000–2001 college expenses		$ .00
h. Amounts expected from other relatives, spouse's parents, and all other sources (List sources in Section Q.)		$ .00

Complete the worksheet on page 5 of the instructions, which will tell you whether or not parents' information is required.

Section G — Parents' Household Information – See page 5 of the instruction booklet.

38. How many people are in your parents' household? ☐☐
Always include the student and parents.
List their names and give information about them in Section M. (See instructions.)

39. Of the number in 38, how many will be college students between July 1, 2000, and June 30, 2001? Include the student. ☐

40. How many parents will be in college at least half-time in 2000–2001? (Fill in only one oval.)
1 ○ Neither parent 2 ○ One parent 3 ○ Both parents

41. What is the current marital status of your parents? (Fill in only one oval.)
1 ○ single 3 ○ separated 5 ○ widowed
2 ○ married 4 ○ divorced

42. What is your parents' state of legal residence? ☐☐

Section H — Parents' Expenses

		1999	Expected 2000
43. Child support paid because of divorce or separation	43.	$ .00	$ .00
44. Repayment of parents' educational loans (See instructions.)	44.	$ .00	$ .00
45. Medical and dental expenses not covered by insurance (See instructions.)	45.	$ .00	$ .00
46. Total elementary, junior high, and high school tuition paid for dependent children			
a. Amount paid (Don't include tuition paid for the student.)	46.	$ .00	$ .00
b. For how many dependent children? (Don't include the student.)		☐	☐

Page 2

PROFILE Application (cont.)

SAMPLE. DO NOT USE.

Section I — Parents' Assets – If parents own all or part of a business or farm, write in its name and the percent of ownership in Section Q.

47. Cash, savings, and checking accounts $ .00

48. Total value of assets held in the names of the student's brothers and sisters who are under age 19 and not college students $ .00

	What is it worth today?	What is owed on it?
49. Investments	$ .00	$ .00
50. a. Home (Renters write in "0." Skip to 50d.)	$ .00	$ .00

b. Year purchased ____ c. Purchase price $ .00

d. Monthly home mortgage or rental payment (If none, explain in Section Q.) $ .00

	What is it worth today?	What is owed on it?
51. Business	$ .00	$ .00
52. a. Farm	$ .00	$ .00

b. Does family live on the farm? Yes ◯ 1 No ◯ 2

53. a. Other real estate	$ .00	$ .00

b. Year purchased ____ c. Purchase price $ .00

Section J — Parents' 1998 Income & Benefits

54. 1998 Adjusted Gross Income (IRS Form 1040, line 33 or 1040A, line 18 or 1040EZ, line 4) $ .00

55. 1998 U.S. income tax paid (IRS Form 1040, line 49 or 1040A, line 32 or 1040EZ, line 10) $ .00

56. 1998 itemized deductions (IRS Form 1040, Schedule A, line 28. Write "0" if deductions were not itemized.) $ .00

57. 1998 untaxed income and benefits (Include the same types of income and benefits that are listed in 65a – k.) $ .00

Section K — Parents' 1999 Income & Benefits

58. The following 1999 U.S. income tax return figures are (Fill in only one oval.)
1◯ estimated. Will file IRS Form 1040EZ, 1040A, or 1040 TEL. Go to 59.
2◯ estimated. Will file IRS Form 1040. Go to 59.
3◯ from a completed IRS Form 1040EZ, 1040A, or 1040 TEL. Go to 59.
4◯ from a completed IRS Form 1040. Go to 59.
5◯ a tax return will not be filed. Skip to 63.

Tax Filers Only

59. 1999 total number of exemptions (IRS Form 1040, line 6d or 1040A, line 6d or 1040EZ—see instructions) 59. ___

60. 1999 Adjusted Gross Income (IRS Form 1040, line 33 or 1040A, line 18 or 1040EZ, line 4) 60. $ .00

Breakdown of income in 60

a. Wages, salaries, tips (IRS Form 1040, line 7 or 1040A, line 7 or 1040EZ, line 1) 60. a. $ .00

b. Interest income (IRS Form 1040, line 8a or 1040A, line 8a or 1040EZ, line 2) b. $ .00

c. Dividend income (IRS Form 1040, line 9 or 1040A, line 9) c. $ .00

d. Net income (or loss) from business, farm, rents, royalties, partnerships, estates, trusts, etc. (IRS Form 1040, lines 12, 17, and 18) If a loss, enter the amount in (parentheses). d. $ .00

e. Other taxable income such as alimony received, capital gains (or losses), pensions, annuities, etc. (IRS Form 1040, lines 10, 11, 13, 14, 15b, 16b, 19, 20b, and 21 or 1040A, lines 10b, 11b, 12, and 13b or 1040EZ, line 3) e. $ .00

f. Adjustments to income (IRS Form 1040, line 32 or 1040A, line 17—see instructions) f. $ .00

61. a. 1999 U.S. income tax paid (IRS Form 1040, line 49, 1040A, line 32 or 1040EZ, line 10) 61. a. $ .00

b. 1999 Education Credits—Hope and Lifetime Learning (IRS Form 1040, line 44 and 1040A, line 29) b. $ .00

62. 1999 itemized deductions (IRS Form 1040, Schedule A, line 28. Write in "0" if deductions were not itemized.) 62. $ .00

63. 1999 income earned from work by father/stepfather 63. $ .00

64. 1999 income earned from work by mother/stepmother 64. $ .00

65. 1999 untaxed income and benefits (Give total amount for the year. Do not give monthly amounts.)

a. Social security benefits received	$ .00	g. Earned Income Credit (IRS Form 1040, line 59a or 1040A, line 37a or 1040EZ, line 8a)	$ .00
b. AFDC/ADC or TANF (See instructions.)	$ .00	h. Housing, food, and other living allowances (See instructions.)	$ .00
c. Child support received for all children	$ .00	i. Tax-exempt interest income (IRS Form 1040, line 8b or 1040A, line 8b)	$ .00
d. Deductible IRA and/or Keogh payments (See instructions.)	$ .00	j. Foreign income exclusion (IRS Form 2555, line 43 or Form 2555EZ, line 18)	$ .00
e. Payments to tax-deferred pension and savings plans (See instructions.)	$ .00	k. Other – write total from worksheet, page 7	$ .00
f. Amounts withheld from wages for dependent care and medical spending accounts	$ .00		

Section L — Parents' 2000 Expected Income & Benefits
(If the expected total income and benefits will differ from the 1999 total income and benefits by $3,000 or more, explain in Section Q.)

66. 2000 income earned from work by father	$ .00	68. 2000 other taxable income	$ .00
67. 2000 income earned from work by mother	$ .00	69. 2000 untaxed income and benefits (See 65a – k.)	$ .00

Page 3

PROFILE Application (cont.)

SAMPLE. DO NOT USE.

33285933

Section M — Family Member Listing – Give information for all family members entered in question 11 or 38. List up to seven family members in addition to the student. If there are more than seven, list first those who will be in school or college at least half-time. List the others in Section Q. Leave shaded sections blank.

70.

	Full name of family member	Use codes from below	Age (Req'd)	Claimed by parents as tax exemption in 1999? Yes? No?	1999–2000 school year				2000–2001 school year		
					Name of school or college	Year in school	Scholarships and grants	Parents' contribution	Attend college at least one term full-time half-time	College or university Type	Name
1	You — the student applicant			O O			$	$			
2				O O			$	$	1O 2O		
3				O O			$	$	1O 2O		
4				O O			$	$	1O 2O		
5				O O			$	$	1O 2O		
6				O O			$	$	1O 2O		
7				O O			$	$	1O 2O		
8				O O			$	$	1O 2O		

Write in the correct code from the right. 1 = Student's parent, 2 = Student's stepparent, 3 = Student's brother or sister, 4 = Student's husband or wife, 5 = Student's son or daughter, 6 = Student's grandparent, 7 = Student's stepbrother or stepsister, 8 = Other

Write in the correct code from the instructions on page 8.

Section N — Parents' Information (to be answered by the parent(s) completing this form)

71. Fill in one: O Father O Stepfather O Legal guardian O Other (Explain in Q.)

a. Name ____________ **Age** ⎵⎵

b. Fill in if: O Self-employed O Unemployed – Date: ______

c. Occupation ____________

d. Employer ____________ **No. years** ___

e. Work telephone ⎵⎵⎵-⎵⎵⎵-⎵⎵⎵⎵

f. Retirement plans: O Social security O Civil service/state O Military O Union/employer O IRA/Keogh/tax-deferred O Other

72. Fill in one: O Mother O Stepmother O Legal guardian O Other (Explain in Q.)

a. Name ____________ **Age** ⎵⎵

b. Fill in if: O Self-employed O Unemployed – Date: ______

c. Occupation ____________

d. Employer ____________ **No. years** ___

e. Work telephone ⎵⎵⎵-⎵⎵⎵-⎵⎵⎵⎵

f. Retirement plans: O Social security O Civil service/state O Military O Union/employer O IRA/Keogh/tax-deferred O Other

Section O — Information About Noncustodial Parent (to be answered by the parent who completes this form if the student's biological or adoptive parents are divorced, separated, or were never married to each other)

73. a. Who last claimed the student as a tax exemption? ____________ **Year?** ⎵⎵⎵⎵

b. How much does the noncustodial parent plan to contribute to the student's education for the 2000–2001 school year? $ ________.00

Section P — Student's Schools & Programs

74. Schools and programs to receive PROFILE information (See instructions.)

*Housing Plans: 1 = Campus housing 3 = With parents 2 = Off-campus 4 = With relatives

	CSS Code No.	Housing Plans*
1	⎵⎵⎵⎵	⎵
2	⎵⎵⎵⎵	⎵

75. What will be the student's 2000–2001 financial aid status?

1 O First-time applicant, entering student (including transfer students) 2 O Renewal applicant, continuing student 3 O First-time applicant, continuing student

76. Fee and type of payment

O $20 for 1 CSS® Code Number

O $36 for 2 CSS Code Numbers

Enclose a check or money order for either $20 or $36. Make payable to College Scholarship Service®. Write the number from the top of page 1 on your payment.

A check or money order must be included with this form. If you fail to do so, the form will be returned unprocessed.

CSS Use Only	
	W
	B
	G
	S

Section Q — Explanations/Special Circumstances – Use this space to explain any unusual expenses such as high medical or dental expenses, educational and other debts, child care, elder care, or special circumstances. Also, give information for any outside scholarships you have been awarded. **If more space is needed, use sheets of paper and send them directly to your schools and programs.** Please print.

Certification: All the information on this form is true and complete to the best of my knowledge. I agree to pay all appropriate fees and, if asked, to give proof of the information that I have given on this form. I realize that this proof may include a copy of my U.S., state, or local income tax returns. I certify that all information is correct at this time, and that I will send timely notice to my schools/programs of any significant change in family income or assets, financial situation, college plans of other children, or the receipt of other scholarships or grants.

1 **Student's signature** 2 **Student's spouse's signature**

3 **Father's (stepfather's) signature** 4 **Mother's (stepmother's) signature**

Date completed: Month ⎵⎵ Day ⎵⎵ Year 1 O 1999 2 O 2000

Page 4

When a College Wants More Information

In addition to the customized application, the PROFILE packet will include additional questions colleges want addressed in order to award their own funds. There will also be codes to tell you which colleges want which questions answered.

TRACK B

For students applying to schools requiring the FAFSA (which will probably be all of your schools).

December

Stage 1: Pick up a Free Application for Federal Student Aid (FAFSA)

Since many schools do not ask their students to use the PROFILE, the financial aid application process is often initiated using the FAFSA. This is the form that every financial aid applicant must eventually fill out to establish eligibility for federal aid and, for many schools, for institutional and state aid as well. The form is available in November or December from your guidance office. You cannot send it in until after January 1.

The FAFSA is the only form allowed to establish eligibility for federal financial aid programs, which include the Federal Pell Grant, Federal Supplemental Educational Opportunity Grant (FSEOG), Federal Work-Study, Federal Perkins Loan, Federal Stafford Loan, and Federal Direct Loan programs. The FAFSA is also used by many state agencies and colleges to award their own funds.

CyberFAFSA

The FAFSA Express is an electronic version of the FAFSA form. Available from the federal government, this software program allows you to complete the FAFSA on your computer and electronically transmit your information to the federal processor by modem. You can also dowload the software from the Department of Education's Web site at http://www.ed.gov/offices/OPE/express.html

FAFSA on the Web

Over the last several years, the U.S. Department of Education has begun to put much more information on the Web and, for the 1998-1999 academic year, the Department created a web application for the FAFSA. Many students and parents still feel more comfortable using the paper process, but there are some pretty positive advantages to completing the FAFSA on the Web. These include a narrative question style that directs you through the FAFSA and eliminates questions that don't apply to your situation, an automatic checking process that basically does not allow you to make any mistakes, and a speedier response from the federal processor.

To access FAFSA on the Web, just get onto any computer with Internet access and type www.fafsa.ed.gov. This will take you directly to the FAFSA on the Web site and you can get started. Just a quick warning. If you have a lot of experience with the Web, you may be used to assuming that every Web address ends with ".com". Be careful to type in the correct address as we have given it above. The address www.fafsa.com will get you to a private Web site that charges for help in completing the FAFSA. If you want to make use of this service, we're not saying that it is not a reputable company. We're just warning you that filing the FAFSA is free and you don't need to pay to have it done.

If you are filing a FAFSA on the Web, you should follow these steps to complete the application process once you have signed www.fafsa.ed.gov:

Step 1: Choose 2000-2001 FAFSA

Step 2: Complete the FAFSA

Step 3: After you finish, check your FAFSA for missing information and inconsistent answers

Step 4: Print and sign (and have your parents sign, if necessary) your signature page

Step 5: Submit your FAFSA to the Department of Education through the Internet

Step 6: Receive and print your confirmation

Step 7: Mail your signature page to the Department of Education

FAFSA

On the following pages you'll find a blank copy of the four-page FAFSA for your perusal. We've placed more blank forms in the Additional Forms and Worksheets section, so you can draft your applications. You cannot submit these actual forms. You'll need to use original, current applications (not photocopies).

If you have any questions about FAFSA, you can contact any of the colleges that you are applying to or call the Federal Student Aid Information Center at (800) 4-FED-AID. This phone number tends to be very busy, so you should usually start with the college.

SAMPLE. DO NOT USE.

Free Application for Federal Student Aid

OMB 1845-0001

July 1, 2000 — June 30, 2001 school year

Step One: For questions 1-36, leave blank any questions that do not apply to you (the student).

1-3. Your full name (as it appears on your Social Security card) — 1. LAST NAME — 2. FIRST NAME — 3. M.I.

4-7. Your permanent mailing address — 4. NUMBER AND STREET (INCLUDE APARTMENT NUMBER) — 5. CITY (AND COUNTRY, IF NOT U.S.) — 6. STATE — 7. ZIP CODE

8. Your Social Security Number ___ – __ – ____

9. Your date of birth — MONTH / DAY / YEAR 19__

10. Your permanent telephone number — AREA CODE

11. Do you have a driver's license? Yes ○ 1 No ○ 2

12-13. Driver's license number and state — 12. LICENSE NUMBER — 13. STATE

14. Are you a U.S. citizen? Pick one. **See Page 2.**

a. Yes, I am a U.S. citizen. ○ 1

b. No, but I am an eligible noncitizen. **Fill in question 15.** ○ 2

c. No, I am not a citizen or eligible noncitizen. ○ 3

15. ALIEN REGISTRATION NUMBER A________

16. Marital status as of today

I am single, divorced, or widowed. ○ 1

I am married. ○ 2

I am separated. ○ 3

17. Month and year you were married, separated, divorced, or widowed — MONTH / YEAR

For each question (18 - 22), please mark whether you will be full time, 3/4 time, half time, less than half time, or not attending. Mark "Full time" if you are not sure. See page 2.

18.	Summer 2000	Full time ○ 1	3/4 time ○ 2	Half time ○ 3	Less than half time ○ 4	Not attending ○ 5
19.	Fall semester or quarter 2000	Full time ○ 1	3/4 time ○ 2	Half time ○ 3	Less than half time ○ 4	Not attending ○ 5
20.	Winter quarter 2000-2001	Full time ○ 1	3/4 time ○ 2	Half time ○ 3	Less than half time ○ 4	Not attending ○ 5
21.	Spring semester or quarter 2001	Full time ○ 1	3/4 time ○ 2	Half time ○ 3	Less than half time ○ 4	Not attending ○ 5
22.	Summer 2001	Full time ○ 1	3/4 time ○ 2	Half time ○ 3	Less than half time ○ 4	Not attending ○ 5
23.	Highest school your father completed	Middle school/Jr. High ○ 1	High school ○ 2	College or beyond ○ 3	Other/unknown ○ 4	
24.	Highest school your mother completed	Middle school/Jr. High ○ 1	High school ○ 2	College or beyond ○ 3	Other/unknown ○ 4	

25. What is your state of legal residence? STATE

26. Did you become a legal resident of this state before January 1, 1995? Yes ○ 1 No ○ 2

27. If the answer to question 26 is **"No,"** give month and year you became a legal resident. MONTH / YEAR

28. If you have **never** been convicted of any illegal drug offense, enter "1" in the box and go to question 29. A drug-related conviction does not necessarily make you ineligible for aid; call 1-800-433-3243 or go to http://www.fafsa.ed.gov/q28 to find out how to fill out this question.

29. Most male students must register with Selective Service to get federal aid. Are you male? Yes ○ 1 No ○ 2

30. If you are male (age 18-25) and not registered, do you want Selective Service to register you? Yes ○ 1 No ○ 2

31. What degree or certificate will you be working towards during 2000-2001? **See page 2** and enter the correct number in the box.

32. What will be your grade level when you begin the 2000-2001 school year? **See page 2** and enter the correct number in the box.

33. Will you have a high school diploma or GED before you enroll? Yes ○ 1 No ○ 2

34. Will you have your first bachelor's degree before July 1, 2000? Yes ○ 1 No ○ 2

35. In addition to grants, are you interested in student loans (which you must pay back)? Yes ○ 1 No ○ 2

36. In addition to grants, are you interested in "work-study" (which you earn through work)? Yes ○ 1 No ○ 2

FAFSA (cont.)

Step Two: For 37-51, if you (the student) are now married (even if you were not married in 1999), report both your and your spouse's income and assets. Ignore references to "spouse" if you are currently single, separated, divorced, or widowed.

37. For 1999, have you filed your IRS income tax return or another tax return listed in **question 38**?

a. I have already filed. ○ 1 **b.** I will file, but I have not yet filed. ○ 2 **c.** I'm not going to file. **(Skip to question 44.)** ○ 3

38. What income tax return did you file or will you file for 1999?

a. IRS 1040 ○ 1
b. IRS 1040A, 1040EZ, 1040Telefile ○ 2
c. A foreign tax return. **See Page 2.** ○ 3
d. A tax return for Puerto Rico, Guam, American Samoa, the Virgin Islands, the Marshall Islands, the Federated States of Micronesia, or Palau. **See Page 2.** ○ 4

39. If you have filed or will file a 1040, were you eligible to file a 1040A or 1040EZ? **See page 2.** Yes ○ 1 No/don't know ○ 2

For questions 40-53, if the answer is zero or the question does not apply to you, enter 0.

40. What was your (and spouse's) adjusted gross income for 1999? Adjusted gross income is on IRS Form 1040–line 33; 1040A–line 18; 1040EZ–line 4; or Telefile–line I. $ ___,___

41. Enter the total amount of your (and spouse's) income tax for 1999. Income tax amount is on IRS Form 1040–line 49 plus 51; 1040A–line 32; 1040EZ–line 10; or Telefile–line K. $ ___,___

42. Enter your (and spouse's) exemptions. Exemptions are on IRS Form 1040–line 6d, or on Form 1040A–line 6d. For Form 1040EZ or Telefile, **see page 2.** ___

43. Enter your Earned Income Credit from IRS Form 1040–line 59a; 1040A–line 37a; 1040EZ–line 8a; or Telefile–line L. $ ___,___

44-45. How much did you (and spouse) earn from working in 1999? Answer this question whether or not you filed a tax return. This information may be on your W-2 forms, or on IRS Form 1040–lines 7, 12, and 18; 1040A–line 7; or 1040EZ–line 1. Telefilers should use their W-2's.
You (44) $ ___,___
Your Spouse (45) $ ___,___

46. Go to page 8 of this form; complete the column on the left of **Worksheet A**; enter student total here. $ ___,___

47. Go to page 8 of this form; complete the column on the left of **Worksheet B**; enter student total here. $ ___,___

48. Total current balance of cash, savings, and checking accounts $ ___,___

For 49-51, if net worth is one million or more, enter $999,999. If net worth is negative, enter 0.

49. Current net worth of investments (investment value minus investment debt) **See page 2.** $ ___,___

50. Current net worth of business (business value minus business debt) **See page 2.** $ ___,___

51. Current net worth of investment farm (Don't include a farm that you live on and operate.) $ ___,___

52-53. If you receive veterans education benefits, for **how many months** from July 1, 2000 through June 30, 2001 will you receive these benefits, and **what amount** will you receive per month? Do not include your spouse's veterans education benefits.
Months (52) ___
Amount (53) $ ___

Step Three: Answer all six questions in this step.

54. Were you born before January 1, 1977? Yes ○ 1 No ○ 2

55. Will you be working on a degree beyond a bachelor's degree in school year 2000-2001? Yes ○ 1 No ○ 2

56. As of today, are you married? (Answer yes if you are separated, but not divorced.) Yes ○ 1 No ○ 2

57. Answer **"Yes"** if: (1) You have children who receive more than half of their support from you; **or**
(2) You have dependents (other than your children or spouse) who live with you and receive more than half of their support from you, now and through June 30, 2001. Yes ○ 1 No ○ 2

58. Are you an orphan or ward of the court or were you a ward of the court until age 18? Yes ○ 1 No ○ 2

59. Are you a veteran of the U.S. Armed Forces? **See page 2.** Yes ○ 1 No ○ 2

If you (the student) answer "No" to every question in Step Three, go to Step Four.

If you answer "Yes" to any question in Step Three, skip Step Four and go to Step Five.

(If you are a graduate health profession student, you may be required to complete Step Four even if you answered "Yes" to any question in Step Three.)

Page 4

SAMPLE. DO NOT USE.

FAFSA (cont.)

Step Four: Complete this step if you (the student) answered "No" to all questions in Step Three. Please tell us about your parents. **See page 7 for who is considered a parent.**

60. Parents' marital status as of today? (Pick one.) Married ○ 1 Single ○ 2 Divorced/Separated ○ 3 Widowed ○ 4

61. FATHER'S/STEPFATHER'S SSN 62. FATHER'S/STEPFATHER'S LAST NAME

61-62. Your father's Social Security Number and last name

63. MOTHER'S/STEPMOTHER'S SSN 64. MOTHER'S/STEPMOTHER'S LAST NAME

63-64. Your mother's Social Security Number and last name

65. How many people are in your parents' household? **See page 7.**

66. How many in question 65 **(exclude your parents)** will be college students between July 1, 2000, and June 30, 2001? **See page 7.**

STATE

67. What is your parents' state of legal residence?

68. Did your parents become legal residents of the state in question 67 before January 1, 1995? **Yes** ○ 1 **No** ○ 2

MONTH YEAR

69. If the answer to question 68 is "No," give the month and year legal residency began for the parent who has lived in the state the longest. /

70. What is the age of your older parent?

71. For 1999, have your parents filed their IRS income tax return or another tax return listed in **question 72**?

a. My parents have already filed. ○ 1 **b.** My parents will file, but they have not yet filed. ○ 2 **c.** My parents are not going to file. **(Skip to question 78.)** ○ 3

72. What income tax return did your parents file or will they file for 1999?

a. IRS 1040 ○ 1

b. IRS 1040A, 1040EZ, 1040Telefile ○ 2

c. A foreign tax return. **See Page 2.** ○ 3

d. A tax return for Puerto Rico, Guam, American Samoa, the Virgin Islands, the Marshall Islands, the Federated States of Micronesia, or Palau. **See Page 2.** ○ 4

73. If your parents have filed or will file a 1040, were they eligible to file a 1040A or 1040EZ? **See page 2.** **Yes** ○ 1 **No/don't know** ○ 2

For 74 - 85, if the answer is zero or the question does not apply, enter 0.

74. What was your parents' adjusted gross income for 1999? Adjusted gross income is on IRS Form 1040–line 33; 1040A–line 18; 1040EZ–line 4; or Telefile–line I. $,

75. Enter the total amount of your parents' income tax for 1999. Income tax amount is on IRS Form 1040–line 49 plus 51; 1040A–line 32; 1040EZ–line 10; or Telefile–line K. $,

76. Enter your parents' exemptions. Exemptions are on IRS Form 1040–line 6d or on Form 1040A–line 6d. For Form 1040EZ or Telefile, **see page 2.**

77. Enter your parents' Earned Income Credit from IRS Form 1040–line 59a; 1040A–line 37a; 1040EZ–line 8a; or Telefile–line L. $,

78-79. How much did your parents earn from working in 1999? Answer this question whether or not your parents filed a tax return. This information may be on their W-2 forms, or on IRS Form 1040–lines 7, 12, and 18; 1040A–line 7; or 1040EZ–line 1. Telefilers should use their W-2's. **Father/Stepfather (78)** $, **Mother/Stepmother (79)** $,

80. Go to page 8 of this form; complete the column on the right of **Worksheet A**; enter parent total here. $,

81. Go to page 8 of this form; complete the column on the right of **Worksheet B**; enter parent total here. $,

82. Total current balance of cash, savings, and checking accounts $,

For 83–85, if net worth is one million or more, enter $999,999. If net worth is negative, enter 0.

83. Current net worth of investments (investment value minus investment debt) **See page 2.** $,

84. Current net worth of business (business value minus business debt) **See page 2.** $,

85. Current net worth of investment farm (Don't include a farm that your parents live on and operate.) $,

Now go to Step Six. **Page 5**

SAMPLE. DO NOT USE.

FAFSA (cont.)

SAMPLE. DO NOT USE.

Step Five: Complete this step only if you (the student) answered "Yes" to any question in Step Three.

86. How many people are in your (and your spouse's) household? **See page 7.**

87. How many in question 86 will be college students between July 1, 2000, and June 30, 2001? **Do not include your parents. See page 7.**

Step Six: Please tell us which schools should receive your information.

For each school (up to six), please provide the federal school code and your housing plans **(enter "1" for on campus, "2" for off campus, and "3" for with parents)**. Look for the federal school codes on the Internet at **http://www.ed.gov/studentaid**, at your college financial aid office, at your public library, or by asking your high school guidance counselor. If you cannot get the federal school code, write in the complete name, address, city, and state of the college.

	Federal school code OR	Name of college	College street address and city	State	Housing Plans
88.	FIRST SCHOOL CODE				89.
90.	SECOND SCHOOL CODE				91.
92.	THIRD SCHOOL CODE				93.
94.	FOURTH SCHOOL CODE				95.
96.	FIFTH SCHOOL CODE				97.
98.	SIXTH SCHOOL CODE				99.

Step Seven: Please read, sign, and date.

By signing this application, you agree, if asked, to provide information that will verify the accuracy of your completed form. This information may include a copy of your U.S. or state income tax form. Also, you certify that you (1) will use federal and/or state student financial aid only to pay the cost of attending an institution of higher education, (2) are not in default on a federal student loan or have made satisfactory arrangements to repay it, (3) do not owe money back on a federal student grant or have made satisfactory arrangements to repay it, (4) will notify your school if you default on a federal student loan, and (5) understand that **the Secretary of Education has the authority to verify income reported on this application with the Internal Revenue Service.** If you purposely give false or misleading information, you may be fined $10,000, sent to prison, or both.

100. Date this form was completed.

MONTH / DAY / 2000 ○ or 2001 ○

101. Student signature (Sign in box)

1

Parent signature (one parent whose information is provided in Step Four.) (Sign in box)

2

If this form was filled out by someone other than you, your spouse, or your parent(s), that person must complete this part.

Preparer's Name and Firm ____________________

Address ____________________

102. Social Security # ___ – __ – ____

OR

103. Employer ID # __ – _______

104. Signature and Date 1 ____________________

SCHOOL USE ONLY

D/O ○ 1 Federal School Code

FAA SIGNATURE

1

MDE USE ONLY

Special Handle

Page 6

Stage 2: Complete and Submit Your Completed FAFSA

The FAFSA asks questions about your family, the income and assets of you and your parents, and your college plans. It's relatively straightforward. Here are some important tips for completing the application:

January/February

1. Before starting, have your and your parents' financial records handy.
2. To avoid errors, read all instructions carefully.
3. Complete only those sections you're required to complete.
4. Print neatly, so your application(s) will be easy to read.
5. Use a No. 2 black pencil with a good point.
6. Do not cross out. Erase mistakes.
7. Round off all figures to the nearest dollar (do not use cents).
8. Write only in the spaces provided. Do not write in the margins.
9. If checking off a box, use an "x."
10. When writing dates, use numbers. For example, February 3, 1999 should be written 02-03-99.
11. Estimate income tax figures. You will have the opportunity to amend figures when you receive your Student Aid Report (SAR).
12. Make sure you and your parents sign the form(s).
13. Double- and triple-check your responses for accuracy (especially make sure your social security number is correct).
14. Make a photocopy of your completed form(s).
15. Send the original, completed form in the envelope provided.
16. Don't enclose anything other than the application itself.
17. Use first class mail, but ask for a postal receipt.

DON'T DELAY

Do not procrastinate. If you don't request and submit your forms on time, you'll edge yourself out of important financial aid opportunities.

On the following pages, you'll find completed FAFSAs for each of our four dependent students.

In the next step, you'll get a closer look at the role each element plays in determining the students' (and your) financial need.

SAMPLE FAFSA FORM FOR FRANCES

Free Application for Federal Student Aid

OMB 1845-0001

July 1, 2000 — June 30, 2001 school year

Step One: For questions 1-36, leave blank any questions that do not apply to you (the student).

1-3. Your full name (as it appears on your Social Security card) — 1. LAST NAME: LIU; 2. FIRST NAME: FRANCES; 3. M.I.: A

4-7. Your permanent mailing address — 4. NUMBER AND STREET (INCLUDE APARTMENT NUMBER): 16 MOTT STREET; 5. CITY (AND COUNTRY, IF NOT U.S.): NEW YORK; 6. STATE: NY; 7. ZIP CODE: 10001

8. Your Social Security Number: 111-11-1111

9. Your date of birth: MONTH 04 / DAY 19 / YEAR 1982

10. Your permanent telephone number: AREA CODE 212 555-6594

11. Do you have a driver's license? Yes ○ 1 No ○ 2

12-13. Driver's license number and state — 12. LICENSE NUMBER; 13. STATE

14. Are you a U.S. citizen? Pick one. **See Page 2.**
- **a.** Yes, I am a U.S. citizen. ● 1
- **b.** No, but I am an eligible noncitizen. **Fill in question 15.** ○ 2
- **c.** No, I am not a citizen or eligible noncitizen. ○ 3

15. ALIEN REGISTRATION NUMBER: A

16. Marital status as of today
- I am single, divorced, or widowed. ● 1
- I am married. ○ 2
- I am separated. ○ 3

17. Month and year you were married, separated, divorced, or widowed: MONTH / YEAR

For each question (18 - 22), please mark whether you will be full time, 3/4 time, half time, less than half time, or not attending. Mark "Full time" if you are not sure. See page 2.

	Full time	3/4 time	Half time	Less than half time	Not attending
18. Summer 2000	○ 1	○ 2	○ 3	○ 4	○ 5
19. Fall semester or quarter 2000	● 1	○ 2	○ 3	○ 4	○ 5
20. Winter quarter 2000-2001	● 1	○ 2	○ 3	○ 4	○ 5
21. Spring semester or quarter 2001	● 1	○ 2	○ 3	○ 4	○ 5
22. Summer 2001	○ 1	○ 2	○ 3	○ 4	○ 5

	Middle school/Jr. High	High school	College or beyond	Other/unknown
23. Highest school your father completed	○ 1	● 2	○ 3	○ 4
24. Highest school your mother completed	○ 1	● 2	○ 3	○ 4

25. What is your state of legal residence? STATE: NY

26. Did you become a legal resident of this state before January 1, 1995? Yes ● 1 No ○ 2

27. If the answer to question 26 is **"No,"** give month and year you became a legal resident. MONTH / YEAR

28. If you have **never** been convicted of any illegal drug offense, enter "1" in the box and go to question 29. A drug-related conviction does not necessarily make you ineligible for aid; call 1-800-433-3243 or go to http://www.fafsa.ed.gov/q28 to find out how to fill out this question. 1

29. Most male students must register with Selective Service to get federal aid. Are you male? Yes ○ 1 No ● 2

30. If you are male (age 18-25) and not registered, do you want Selective Service to register you? Yes ○ 1 No ○ 2

31. What degree or certificate will you be working towards during 2000-2001? **See page 2** and enter the correct number in the box. 1

32. What will be your grade level when you begin the 2000-2001 school year? **See page 2** and enter the correct number in the box. 1

33. Will you have a high school diploma or GED before you enroll? Yes ● 1 No ○ 2

34. Will you have your first bachelor's degree before July 1, 2000? Yes ○ 1 No ● 2

35. In addition to grants, are you interested in student loans (which you must pay back)? Yes ● 1 No ○ 2

36. In addition to grants, are you interested in "work-study" (which you earn through work)? Yes ● 1 No ○ 2

(continued on next page)

SAMPLE FAFSA FORM FOR FRANCES (CONT.)

Step Two: For 37-51, if you (the student) are now married (even if you were not married in 1999), report both your and your spouse's income and assets. Ignore references to "spouse" if you are currently single, separated, divorced, or widowed.

37. For 1999, have you filed your IRS income tax return or another tax return listed in **question 38**?

a. I have already filed. ○ 1   **b.** I will file, but I have not yet filed. ○ 2   **c.** I'm not going to file. **(Skip to question 44.)** ● 3

38. What income tax return did you file or will you file for 1999?

a. IRS 1040 ○ 1
b. IRS 1040A, 1040EZ, 1040Telefile ○ 2
c. A foreign tax return. **See Page 2.** ○ 3
d. A tax return for Puerto Rico, Guam, American Samoa, the Virgin Islands, the Marshall Islands, the Federated States of Micronesia, or Palau. **See Page 2.** ○ 4

39. If you have filed or will file a 1040, were you eligible to file a 1040A or 1040EZ? **See page 2.** Yes ○ 1 No/don't know ○ 2

For questions 40-53, if the answer is zero or the question does not apply to you, enter 0.

40. What was your (and spouse's) adjusted gross income for 1999? Adjusted gross income is on IRS Form 1040–line 33; 1040A–line 18; 1040EZ–line 4; or Telefile–line I. $ ___,__0

41. Enter the total amount of your (and spouse's) income tax for 1999. Income tax amount is on IRS Form 1040–line 49 plus 51; 1040A–line 32; 1040EZ–line 10; or Telefile–line K. $ ___,__0

42. Enter your (and spouse's) exemptions. Exemptions are on IRS Form 1040–line 6d, or on Form 1040A–line 6d. For Form 1040EZ or Telefile, **see page 2.** __

43. Enter your Earned Income Credit from IRS Form 1040–line 59a; 1040A–line 37a; 1040EZ–line 8a; or Telefile–line L. $ ___,__0

44-45. How much did you (and spouse) earn from working in 1999? Answer this question whether or not you filed a tax return. This information may be on your W-2 forms, or on IRS Form 1040–lines 7, 12, and 18; 1040A–line 7; or 1040EZ–line 1. Telefilers should use their W-2's.
You (44) $ 2,100
Your Spouse (45) $ ___,__0

46. Go to page 8 of this form; complete the column on the left of **Worksheet A**; enter student total here. $ ___,__0

47. Go to page 8 of this form; complete the column on the left of **Worksheet B**; enter student total here. $ ___,__0

48. Total current balance of cash, savings, and checking accounts $ 1,200

For 49-51, if net worth is one million or more, enter $999,999. If net worth is negative, enter 0.

49. Current net worth of investments (investment value minus investment debt) **See page 2.** $ ___,__0

50. Current net worth of business (business value minus business debt) **See page 2.** $ ___,__0

51. Current net worth of investment farm (Don't include a farm that you live on and operate.) $ ___,__0

52-53. If you receive veterans education benefits, for **how many months** from July 1, 2000 through June 30, 2001 will you receive these benefits, and **what amount** will you receive per month? Do not include your spouse's veterans education benefits.
Months (52) __
Amount (53) $ __0

Step Three: Answer all six questions in this step.

54. Were you born before January 1, 1977? Yes ○ 1 No ● 2
55. Will you be working on a degree beyond a bachelor's degree in school year 2000-2001? Yes ○ 1 No ● 2
56. As of today, are you married? (Answer yes if you are separated, but not divorced.) Yes ○ 1 No ● 2
57. Answer **"Yes"** if: (1) You have children who receive more than half of their support from you; **or**
(2) You have dependents (other than your children or spouse) who live with you and receive more than half of their support from you, now and through June 30, 2001. Yes ○ 1 No ● 2
58. Are you an orphan or ward of the court or were you a ward of the court until age 18? Yes ○ 1 No ● 2
59. Are you a veteran of the U.S. Armed Forces? **See page 2.** Yes ○ 1 No ● 2

If you (the student) answer "No" to every question in Step Three, go to Step Four.
If you answer "Yes" to any question in Step Three, skip Step Four and go to Step Five.
(If you are a graduate health profession student, you may be required to complete Step Four even if you answered "Yes" to any question in Step Three.)

Page 4

(continued on next page)

SAMPLE FAFSA FORM FOR FRANCES (CONT.)

Step Four: Complete this step if you (the student) answered "No" to all questions in Step Three. Please tell us about your parents. **See page 7 for who is considered a parent.**

60. Parents' marital status as of today? (Pick one.) Married ● 1 Single ○ 2 Divorced/Separated ○ 3 Widowed ○ 4

61-62. Your father's Social Security Number and last name
61. FATHER'S/STEPFATHER'S SSN: 111-11-1112
62. FATHER'S/STEPFATHER'S LAST NAME: LIU

63-64. Your mother's Social Security Number and last name
63. MOTHER'S/STEPMOTHER'S SSN: 111-11-1113
64. MOTHER'S/STEPMOTHER'S LAST NAME: LIU

65. How many people are in your parents' household? **See page 7.** 05

66. How many in question 65 **(exclude your parents)** will be college students between July 1, 2000, and June 30, 2001? **See page 7.** 1

67. What is your parents' state of legal residence? STATE: NY

68. Did your parents become legal residents of the state in question 67 before January 1, 1995? Yes ● 1 No ○ 2

69. If the answer to question 68 is "No," give the month and year legal residency began for the parent who has lived in the state the longest. MONTH ☐☐ / YEAR ☐☐☐☐

70. What is the age of your older parent? 61

71. For 1999, have your parents filed their IRS income tax return or another tax return listed in **question 72**?
a. My parents have already filed. ● 1
b. My parents will file, but they have not yet filed. ○ 2
c. My parents are not going to file. **(Skip to question 78.)** ○ 3

72. What income tax return did your parents file or will they file for 1999?
a. IRS 1040 ● 1
b. IRS 1040A, 1040EZ, 1040Telefile ○ 2
c. A foreign tax return. **See Page 2.** ○ 3
d. A tax return for Puerto Rico, Guam, American Samoa, the Virgin Islands, the Marshall Islands, the Federated States of Micronesia, or Palau. **See Page 2.** ○ 4

73. If your parents have filed or will file a 1040, were they eligible to file a 1040A or 1040EZ? **See page 2.** Yes ○ 1 No/don't know ● 2

For 74 - 85, if the answer is zero or the question does not apply, enter 0.

74. What was your parents' adjusted gross income for 1999? Adjusted gross income is on IRS Form 1040–line 33; 1040A–line 18; 1040EZ–line 4; or Telefile–line I. $56,300

75. Enter the total amount of your parents' income tax for 1999. Income tax amount is on IRS Form 1040–line 49 plus 51; 1040A–line 32; 1040EZ–line 10; or Telefile–line K. $5,250

76. Enter your parents' exemptions. Exemptions are on IRS Form 1040–line 6d or on Form 1040A–line 6d. For Form 1040EZ or Telefile, **see page 2.** 05

77. Enter your parents' Earned Income Credit from IRS Form 1040–line 59a; 1040A–line 37a; 1040EZ–line 8a; or Telefile–line L. $0

78-79. How much did your parents earn from working in 1999? Answer this question whether or not your parents filed a tax return. This information may be on their W-2 forms, or on IRS Form 1040–lines 7, 12, and 18; 1040A–line 7; or 1040EZ–line 1. Telefilers should use their W-2's.
Father/Stepfather (78) $32,000
Mother/Stepmother (79) $24,000

80. Go to page 8 of this form; complete the column on the right of **Worksheet A**; enter parent total here. $0

81. Go to page 8 of this form; complete the column on the right of **Worksheet B**; enter parent total here. $0

82. Total current balance of cash, savings, and checking accounts $5,000

For 83–85, if net worth is one million or more, enter $999,999. If net worth is negative, enter 0.

83. Current net worth of investments (investment value minus investment debt) **See page 2.** $0

84. Current net worth of business (business value minus business debt) **See page 2.** $200,000

85. Current net worth of investment farm (Don't include a farm that your parents live on and operate.) $0

Now go to Step Six.

Page 5

(continued on next page)

SAMPLE FAFSA FORM FOR FRANCES (CONT.)

Step Five: Complete this step only if you (the student) answered "Yes" to any question in Step Three.

86. How many people are in your (and your spouse's) household? **See page 7.** [ ][ ]

87. How many in question 86 will be college students between July 1, 2000, and June 30, 2001? **Do not include your parents. See page 7.** [ ]

Step Six: Please tell us which schools should receive your information.

For each school (up to six), please provide the federal school code and your housing plans **(enter "1" for on campus, "2" for off campus, and "3" for with parents)**. Look for the federal school codes on the Internet at **http://www.ed.gov/studentaid,** at your college financial aid office, at your public library, or by asking your high school guidance counselor. If you cannot get the federal school code, write in the complete name, address, city, and state of the college.

	Federal school code	OR Name of college	College street address and city	State		Housing Plans
88.	FIRST SCHOOL CODE 002130	BOSTON UNIVERSITY	121 BAY STATE ROAD BOSTON	MA	89.	1
90.	SECOND SCHOOL CODE 003242	CARNEGIE MELLON UNIVERSITY	5000 FORBES AVENUE PITTSBURGH	PA	91.	1
92.	THIRD SCHOOL CODE 001445	GEORGETOWN UNIVERSITY	37TH & O STREET, N.W. WASHINGTON	DC	93.	1
94.	FOURTH SCHOOL CODE				95.	
96.	FIFTH SCHOOL CODE				97.	
98.	SIXTH SCHOOL CODE				99.	

Step Seven: Please read, sign, and date.

By signing this application, you agree, if asked, to provide information that will verify the accuracy of your completed form. This information may include a copy of your U.S. or state income tax form. Also, you certify that you (1) will use federal and/or state student financial aid only to pay the cost of attending an institution of higher education, (2) are not in default on a federal student loan or have made satisfactory arrangements to repay it, (3) do not owe money back on a federal student grant or have made satisfactory arrangements to repay it, (4) will notify your school if you default on a federal student loan, and (5) understand that **the Secretary of Education has the authority to verify income reported on this application with the Internal Revenue Service.** If you purposely give false or misleading information, you may be fined $10,000, sent to prison, or both.

100. Date this form was completed.

MONTH 01 / DAY 31 / **2000** ● **or 2001** ○

101. Student signature (Sign in box)

1 Frances Liu

Parent signature (one parent whose information is provided in Step Four.) (Sign in box)

2 Edward Liu

If this form was filled out by someone other than you, your spouse, or your parent(s), that person must complete this part.

Preparer's Name and Firm ______________________

Address ______________________

102. Social Security # [ ][ ][ ]–[ ][ ]–[ ][ ][ ][ ]

OR

103. Employer ID # [ ][ ]–[ ][ ][ ][ ][ ][ ][ ]

104. Signature and Date 1 ______________________

SCHOOL USE ONLY

D/O ○ 1 Federal School Code [ ][ ][ ][ ][ ][ ]

FAA SIGNATURE

1

MDE USE ONLY

Special Handle [ ]–[ ][ ][ ][ ][ ][ ][ ]

Page 6

SAMPLE FAFSA FORM FOR ANGELA

Free Application for Federal Student Aid

OMB 1845-0001

July 1, 2000 — June 30, 2001 school year

Step One: For questions 1-36, leave blank any questions that do not apply to you (the student).

1-3. Your full name (as it appears on your Social Security card) — 1. LAST NAME: MARTIN; 2. FIRST NAME: ANGELA; 3. M.I.: E

4-7. Your permanent mailing address — 4. NUMBER AND STREET (INCLUDE APARTMENT NUMBER): 11443 DEANZA BLVD; 5. CITY (AND COUNTRY, IF NOT U.S.): SUNNY VALE; 6. STATE: CA; 7. ZIP CODE: 94086

8. Your Social Security Number: 222-22-2222

9. Your date of birth: MONTH 11 / DAY 19 / YEAR 1982

10. Your permanent telephone number: AREA CODE 408 555-1299

11. Do you have a driver's license? Yes ● 1 No ○ 2

12-13. Driver's license number and state — 12. LICENSE NUMBER: 222222222; 13. STATE: CA

14. Are you a U.S. citizen? Pick one. **See Page 2.**
- **a.** Yes, I am a U.S. citizen. ● 1
- **b.** No, but I am an eligible noncitizen. **Fill in question 15.** ○ 2
- **c.** No, I am not a citizen or eligible noncitizen. ○ 3

15. ALIEN REGISTRATION NUMBER: A

16. Marital status as of today
- I am single, divorced, or widowed. ● 1
- I am married. ○ 2
- I am separated. ○ 3

17. Month and year you were married, separated, divorced, or widowed: MONTH / YEAR

For each question (18 - 22), please mark whether you will be full time, 3/4 time, half time, less than half time, or not attending. Mark "Full time" if you are not sure. See page 2.

	Full time	3/4 time	Half time	Less than half time	Not attending
18. Summer 2000	○ 1	○ 2	○ 3	○ 4	○ 5
19. Fall semester or quarter 2000	● 1	○ 2	○ 3	○ 4	○ 5
20. Winter quarter 2000-2001	● 1	○ 2	○ 3	○ 4	○ 5
21. Spring semester or quarter 2001	● 1	○ 2	○ 3	○ 4	○ 5
22. Summer 2001	○ 1	○ 2	○ 3	○ 4	○ 5

	Middle school/Jr. High	High school	College or beyond	Other/unknown
23. Highest school your father completed	○ 1	○ 2	○ 3	● 4
24. Highest school your mother completed	○ 1	○ 2	● 3	○ 4

25. What is your state of legal residence? STATE: CA

26. Did you become a legal resident of this state before January 1, 1995? Yes ● 1 No ○ 2

27. If the answer to question 26 is **"No,"** give month and year you became a legal resident. MONTH / YEAR

28. If you have **never** been convicted of any illegal drug offense, enter "1" in the box and go to question 29. A drug-related conviction does not necessarily make you ineligible for aid; call 1-800-433-3243 or go to http://www.fafsa.ed.gov/q28 to find out how to fill out this question. 1

29. Most male students must register with Selective Service to get federal aid. Are you male? Yes ○ 1 No ● 2

30. If you are male (age 18-25) and not registered, do you want Selective Service to register you? Yes ○ 1 No ○ 2

31. What degree or certificate will you be working towards during 2000-2001? **See page 2** and enter the correct number in the box. 1

32. What will be your grade level when you begin the 2000-2001 school year? **See page 2** and enter the correct number in the box. 1

33. Will you have a high school diploma or GED before you enroll? Yes ● 1 No ○ 2

34. Will you have your first bachelor's degree before July 1, 2000? Yes ○ 1 No ● 2

35. In addition to grants, are you interested in student loans (which you must pay back)? Yes ● 1 No ○ 2

36. In addition to grants, are you interested in "work-study" (which you earn through work)? Yes ● 1 No ○ 2

Page 3

(continued on next page)

SAMPLE FAFSA FORM FOR ANGELA (CONT.)

Step Two: For 37-51, if you (the student) are now married (even if you were not married in 1999), report both your and your spouse's income and assets. Ignore references to "spouse" if you are currently single, separated, divorced, or widowed.

37. For 1999, have you filed your IRS income tax return or another tax return listed in **question 38**?

a. I have already filed. ○ 1 **b.** I will file, but I have not yet filed. ○ 2 **c.** I'm not going to file. **(Skip to question 44.)** ● 3

38. What income tax return did you file or will you file for 1999?

a. IRS 1040 ○ 1
b. IRS 1040A, 1040EZ, 1040Telefile ○ 2
c. A foreign tax return. **See Page 2.** ○ 3
d. A tax return for Puerto Rico, Guam, American Samoa, the Virgin Islands, the Marshall Islands, the Federated States of Micronesia, or Palau. **See Page 2.** ○ 4

39. If you have filed or will file a 1040, were you eligible to file a 1040A or 1040EZ? **See page 2.** Yes ○ 1 No/don't know ○ 2

For questions 40-53, if the answer is zero or the question does not apply to you, enter 0.

40. What was your (and spouse's) adjusted gross income for 1999? Adjusted gross income is on IRS Form 1040–line 33; 1040A–line 18; 1040EZ–line 4; or Telefile–line I. $ 0

41. Enter the total amount of your (and spouse's) income tax for 1999. Income tax amount is on IRS Form 1040–line 49 plus 51; 1040A–line 32; 1040EZ–line 10; or Telefile–line K. $ 0

42. Enter your (and spouse's) exemptions. Exemptions are on IRS Form 1040–line 6d, or on Form 1040A–line 6d. For Form 1040EZ or Telefile, **see page 2.**

43. Enter your Earned Income Credit from IRS Form 1040–line 59a; 1040A–line 37a; 1040EZ–line 8a; or Telefile–line L. $ 0

44-45. How much did you (and spouse) earn from working in 1999? Answer this question whether or not you filed a tax return. This information may be on your W-2 forms, or on IRS Form 1040–lines 7, 12, and 18; 1040A–line 7; or 1040EZ–line 1. Telefilers should use their W-2's.

You (44) $ 2,700

Your Spouse (45) $ 0

46. Go to page 8 of this form; complete the column on the left of **Worksheet A**; enter student total here. $ 0

47. Go to page 8 of this form; complete the column on the left of **Worksheet B**; enter student total here. $ 0

48. Total current balance of cash, savings, and checking accounts $ 1,100

For 49-51, if net worth is one million or more, enter $999,999. If net worth is negative, enter 0.

49. Current net worth of investments (investment value minus investment debt) **See page 2.** $ 0

50. Current net worth of business (business value minus business debt) **See page 2.** $ 0

51. Current net worth of investment farm (Don't include a farm that you live on and operate.) $ 0

52-53. If you receive veterans education benefits, for **how many months** from July 1, 2000 through June 30, 2001 will you receive these benefits, and **what amount** will you receive per month? Do not include your spouse's veterans education benefits.

Months (52)

Amount (53) $ 0

Step Three: Answer all six questions in this step.

54. Were you born before January 1, 1977? Yes ○ 1 No ● 2

55. Will you be working on a degree beyond a bachelor's degree in school year 2000-2001? Yes ○ 1 No ● 2

56. As of today, are you married? (Answer yes if you are separated, but not divorced.) Yes ○ 1 No ● 2

57. Answer **"Yes"** if: (1) You have children who receive more than half of their support from you; **or**
(2) You have dependents (other than your children or spouse) who live with you and receive more than half of their support from you, now and through June 30, 2001. Yes ○ 1 No ● 2

58. Are you an orphan or ward of the court or were you a ward of the court until age 18? Yes ○ 1 No ● 2

59. Are you a veteran of the U.S. Armed Forces? **See page 2.** Yes ○ 1 No ● 2

If you (the student) answer "No" to every question in Step Three, go to Step Four.

If you answer "Yes" to any question in Step Three, skip Step Four and go to Step Five.

(If you are a graduate health profession student, you may be required to complete Step Four even if you answered "Yes" to any question in Step Three.)

Page 4

(continued on next page)

SAMPLE FAFSA FORM FOR ANGELA (CONT.)

Step Four: Complete this step if you (the student) answered "No" to all questions in Step Three. Please tell us about your parents. **See page 7 for who is considered a parent.**

60. Parents' marital status as of today? (Pick one.) Married ◯ 1 Single ● 2 Divorced/Separated ◯ 3 Widowed ◯ 4

61-62. Your father's Social Security Number and last name
61. FATHER'S/STEPFATHER'S SSN: ___-__-____
62. FATHER'S/STEPFATHER'S LAST NAME: ____

63-64. Your mother's Social Security Number and last name
63. MOTHER'S/STEPMOTHER'S SSN: 222-22-2220
64. MOTHER'S/STEPMOTHER'S LAST NAME: MARTIN

65. How many people are in your parents' household? **See page 7.** 03

66. How many in question 65 **(exclude your parents)** will be college students between July 1, 2000, and June 30, 2001? **See page 7.** 1

67. What is your parents' state of legal residence? STATE: CA

68. Did your parents become legal residents of the state in question 67 before January 1, 1995? **Yes** ● 1 **No** ◯ 2

69. If the answer to question 68 is "No," give the month and year legal residency began for the parent who has lived in the state the longest. MONTH __ / YEAR ____

70. What is the age of your older parent? 45

71. For 1999, have your parents filed their IRS income tax return or another tax return listed in **question 72**?
a. My parents have already filed. ◯ 1
b. My parents will file, but they have not yet filed. ● 2
c. My parents are not going to file. **(Skip to question 78.)** ◯ 3

72. What income tax return did your parents file or will they file for 1999?
a. IRS 1040 .... ● 1
b. IRS 1040A, 1040EZ, 1040Telefile ..... ◯ 2
c. A foreign tax return. **See Page 2.** .... ◯ 3
d. A tax return for Puerto Rico, Guam, American Samoa, the Virgin Islands, the Marshall Islands, the Federated States of Micronesia, or Palau. **See Page 2.** ...... ◯ 4

73. If your parents have filed or will file a 1040, were they eligible to file a 1040A or 1040EZ? **See page 2.** **Yes** ◯ 1 **No/don't know** ● 2

For 74 - 85, if the answer is zero or the question does not apply, enter 0.

74. What was your parents' adjusted gross income for 1999? Adjusted gross income is on IRS Form 1040–line 33; 1040A–line 18; 1040EZ–line 4; or Telefile–line I. $ 48,400

75. Enter the total amount of your parents' income tax for 1999. Income tax amount is on IRS Form 1040–line 49 plus 51; 1040A–line 32; 1040EZ–line 10; or Telefile–line K. $ 4,232

76. Enter your parents' exemptions. Exemptions are on IRS Form 1040–line 6d or on Form 1040A–line 6d. For Form 1040EZ or Telefile, **see page 2.** 03

77. Enter your parents' Earned Income Credit from IRS Form 1040–line 59a; 1040A–line 37a; 1040EZ–line 8a; or Telefile–line L. $ 0

78-79. How much did your parents earn from working in 1999? Answer this question whether or not your parents filed a tax return. This information may be on their W-2 forms, or on IRS Form 1040–lines 7, 12, and 18; 1040A–line 7; or 1040EZ–line 1. Telefilers should use their W-2's.
Father/Stepfather (78) $ ____
Mother/Stepmother (79) $ 48,400

80. Go to page 8 of this form; complete the column on the right of **Worksheet A**; enter parent total here. $ 0

81. Go to page 8 of this form; complete the column on the right of **Worksheet B**; enter parent total here. $ 0

82. Total current balance of cash, savings, and checking accounts $ 3,000

For 83–85, if net worth is one million or more, enter $999,999. If net worth is negative, enter 0.

83. Current net worth of investments (investment value minus investment debt) **See page 2.** $ 4,000

84. Current net worth of business (business value minus business debt) **See page 2.** $ 0

85. Current net worth of investment farm (Don't include a farm that your parents live on and operate.) $ 0

Now go to Step Six. **Page 5**

(continued on next page)

SAMPLE FAFSA FORM FOR ANGELA (CONT.)

Step Five: Complete this step only if you (the student) answered "Yes" to any question in Step Three.

86. How many people are in your (and your spouse's) household? **See page 7.**

87. How many in question 86 will be college students between July 1, 2000, and June 30, 2001? **Do not include your parents. See page 7.**

Step Six: Please tell us which schools should receive your information.

For each school (up to six), please provide the federal school code and your housing plans **(enter "1" for on campus, "2" for off campus, and "3" for with parents)**. Look for the federal school codes on the Internet at **http://www.ed.gov/studentaid**, at your college financial aid office, at your public library, or by asking your high school guidance counselor. If you cannot get the federal school code, write in the complete name, address, city, and state of the college.

	Federal school code	OR Name of college	College street address and city	State		Housing Plans
88.	FIRST SCHOOL CODE 001238	MILLS COLLEGE	5000 MACARTHUR BLVD. OAKLAND	CA	89.	1
90.	SECOND SCHOOL CODE 003797	UNIVERSITY OF PUGET SOUND	1500 N. WARNER STREET TACOMA	WA	91.	1
92.	THIRD SCHOOL CODE 001328	UNIVERSITY OF SOUTHERN CALIFORNIA	UNIVERSITY PARK CAMPUS LOS ANGELES	CA	93.	1
94.	FOURTH SCHOOL CODE				95.	
96.	FIFTH SCHOOL CODE				97.	
98.	SIXTH SCHOOL CODE				99.	

Step Seven: Please read, sign, and date.

By signing this application, you agree, if asked, to provide information that will verify the accuracy of your completed form. This information may include a copy of your U.S. or state income tax form. Also, you certify that you (1) will use federal and/or state student financial aid only to pay the cost of attending an institution of higher education, (2) are not in default on a federal student loan or have made satisfactory arrangements to repay it, (3) do not owe money back on a federal student grant or have made satisfactory arrangements to repay it, (4) will notify your school if you default on a federal student loan, and (5) understand that **the Secretary of Education has the authority to verify income reported on this application with the Internal Revenue Service.** If you purposely give false or misleading information, you may be fined $10,000, sent to prison, or both.

100. Date this form was completed.

MONTH 02 / DAY 02 / 2000 ● or 2001 ○

101. Student signature (Sign in box)

1 Angela Martin

Parent signature (one parent whose information is provided in Step Four.) (Sign in box)

2 Suzanne Martin

If this form was filled out by someone other than you, your spouse, or your parent(s), that person must complete this part.

Preparer's Name and Firm ____________

Address ____________

102. Social Security # ___ - __ - ____

OR

103. Employer ID # __ - _______

104. Signature and Date 1 ____________

SCHOOL USE ONLY

D/O ○ 1 Federal School Code

FAA SIGNATURE

1

MDE USE ONLY

Special Handle

Page 6

SAMPLE FAFSA FORM FOR JAMES

Free Application for Federal Student Aid

OMB 1845-0001

July 1, 2000 — June 30, 2001 school year

Step One: For questions 1-36, leave blank any questions that do not apply to you (the student).

1-3. Your full name (as it appears on your Social Security card) — 1. LAST NAME: GARWOOD — 2. FIRST NAME: JAMES — 3. M.I.: R

4-7. Your permanent mailing address — 4. NUMBER AND STREET (INCLUDE APARTMENT NUMBER): 612 JEFFERSON PLACE — 5. CITY (AND COUNTRY, IF NOT U.S.): ROANOKE — 6. STATE: VA — 7. ZIP CODE: 24001

8. Your Social Security Number: 333-33-3333

9. Your date of birth (MONTH / DAY / YEAR): 02 / 17 / 1982

10. Your permanent telephone number: AREA CODE 703 555-1629

11. Do you have a driver's license? Yes ○ 1 No ○ 2

12-13. Driver's license number and state — 12. LICENSE NUMBER: 333333333GA — 13. STATE: VA

14. Are you a U.S. citizen? Pick one. **See Page 2.**

- a. Yes, I am a U.S. citizen. ● 1 (filled)
- b. No, but I am an eligible noncitizen. **Fill in question 15.** ○ 2
- c. No, I am not a citizen or eligible noncitizen. ○ 3

15. ALIEN REGISTRATION NUMBER: A

16. Marital status as of today

- I am single, divorced, or widowed. ● 1 (filled)
- I am married. ○ 2
- I am separated. ○ 3

17. Month and year you were married, separated, divorced, or widowed (MONTH / YEAR): ___ / ____

For each question (18 - 22), please mark whether you will be full time, 3/4 time, half time, less than half time, or not attending. Mark "Full time" if you are not sure. See page 2.

	Full time (1)	3/4 time (2)	Half time (3)	Less than half time (4)	Not attending (5)
18. Summer 2000	○	○	○	○	○
19. Fall semester or quarter 2000	●	○	○	○	○
20. Winter quarter 2000-2001	●	○	○	○	○
21. Spring semester or quarter 2001	●	○	○	○	○
22. Summer 2001	○	○	○	○	○

	Middle school/Jr. High (1)	High school (2)	College or beyond (3)	Other/unknown (4)
23. Highest school your father completed	○	○	●	○
24. Highest school your mother completed	○	○	●	○

25. What is your state of legal residence? STATE: VA

26. Did you become a legal resident of this state before January 1, 1995? Yes ● 1 No ○ 2

27. If the answer to question 26 is **"No,"** give month and year you became a legal resident. (MONTH / YEAR): ___ / ____

28. If you have **never** been convicted of any illegal drug offense, enter "1" in the box and go to question 29. A drug-related conviction does not necessarily make you ineligible for aid; call 1-800-433-3243 or go to http://www.fafsa.ed.gov/q28 to find out how to fill out this question. — 1

29. Most male students must register with Selective Service to get federal aid. Are you male? Yes ● 1 No ○ 2

30. If you are male (age 18-25) and not registered, do you want Selective Service to register you? Yes ● 1 No ○ 2

31. What degree or certificate will you be working towards during 2000-2001? **See page 2** and enter the correct number in the box. — 1

32. What will be your grade level when you begin the 2000-2001 school year? **See page 2** and enter the correct number in the box. — 1

33. Will you have a high school diploma or GED before you enroll? Yes ● 1 No ○ 2

34. Will you have your first bachelor's degree before July 1, 2000? Yes ○ 1 No ● 2

35. In addition to grants, are you interested in student loans (which you must pay back)? Yes ● 1 No ○ 2

36. In addition to grants, are you interested in "work-study" (which you earn through work)? Yes ● 1 No ○ 2

Page 3

(continued on next page)

SAMPLE FAFSA FORM FOR JAMES (CONT.)

Step Two: For 37-51, if you (the student) are now married (even if you were not married in 1999), report both your and your spouse's income and assets. Ignore references to "spouse" if you are currently single, separated, divorced, or widowed.

37. For 1999, have you filed your IRS income tax return or another tax return listed in **question 38**?

a. I have already filed. ○ 1 b. I will file, but I have not yet filed. ○ 2 c. I'm not going to file. **(Skip to question 44.)** ● 3

38. What income tax return did you file or will you file for 1999?

a. IRS 1040 ○ 1
b. IRS 1040A, 1040EZ, 1040Telefile ○ 2
c. A foreign tax return. **See Page 2.** ○ 3
d. A tax return for Puerto Rico, Guam, American Samoa, the Virgin Islands, the Marshall Islands, the Federated States of Micronesia, or Palau. **See Page 2.** ○ 4

39. If you have filed or will file a 1040, were you eligible to file a 1040A or 1040EZ? **See page 2.** Yes ○ 1 No/don't know ○ 2

For questions 40-53, if the answer is zero or the question does not apply to you, enter 0.

40. What was your (and spouse's) adjusted gross income for 1999? Adjusted gross income is on IRS Form 1040–line 33; 1040A–line 18; 1040EZ–line 4; or Telefile–line I. $, 0

41. Enter the total amount of your (and spouse's) income tax for 1999. Income tax amount is on IRS Form 1040–line 49 plus 51; 1040A–line 32; 1040EZ–line 10; or Telefile–line K. $, 0

42. Enter your (and spouse's) exemptions. Exemptions are on IRS Form 1040–line 6d, or on Form 1040A–line 6d. For Form 1040EZ or Telefile, **see page 2.**

43. Enter your Earned Income Credit from IRS Form 1040–line 59a; 1040A–line 37a; 1040EZ–line 8a; or Telefile–line L. $, 0

44-45. How much did you (and spouse) earn from working in 1999? Answer this question whether or not you filed a tax return. This information may be on your W-2 forms, or on IRS Form 1040–lines 7, 12, and 18; 1040A–line 7; or 1040EZ–line 1. Telefilers should use their W-2's.
You (44) $, 0
Your Spouse (45) $, 0

46. Go to page 8 of this form; complete the column on the left of **Worksheet A**; enter student total here. $, 0

47. Go to page 8 of this form; complete the column on the left of **Worksheet B**; enter student total here. $, 0

48. Total current balance of cash, savings, and checking accounts $, 0

For 49-51, if net worth is one million or more, enter $999,999. If net worth is negative, enter 0.

49. Current net worth of investments (investment value minus investment debt) **See page 2.** $ 4,000

50. Current net worth of business (business value minus business debt) **See page 2.** $, 0

51. Current net worth of investment farm (Don't include a farm that you live on and operate.) $, 0

52-53. If you receive veterans education benefits, for **how many months** from July 1, 2000 through June 30, 2001 will you receive these benefits, and **what amount** will you receive per month? Do not include your spouse's veterans education benefits.
Months (52)
Amount (53) $ 0

Step Three: Answer all six questions in this step.

54. Were you born before January 1, 1977? Yes ○ 1 No ● 2
55. Will you be working on a degree beyond a bachelor's degree in school year 2000-2001? Yes ○ 1 No ● 2
56. As of today, are you married? (Answer yes if you are separated, but not divorced.) Yes ○ 1 No ● 2
57. Answer **"Yes"** if: (1) You have children who receive more than half of their support from you; **or**
(2) You have dependents (other than your children or spouse) who live with you and receive more than half of their support from you, now and through June 30, 2001. Yes ○ 1 No ● 2
58. Are you an orphan or ward of the court or were you a ward of the court until age 18? Yes ○ 1 No ● 2
59. Are you a veteran of the U.S. Armed Forces? **See page 2.** Yes ○ 1 No ● 2

If you (the student) answer "No" to every question in Step Three, go to Step Four.
If you answer "Yes" to any question in Step Three, skip Step Four and go to Step Five.
(If you are a graduate health profession student, you may be required to complete Step Four even if you answered "Yes" to any question in Step Three.)

Page 4

(continued on next page)

SAMPLE FAFSA FORM FOR JAMES (CONT.)

Step Four: Complete this step if you (the student) answered "No" to all questions in Step Three. Please tell us about your parents. **See page 7 for who is considered a parent.**

60. Parents' marital status as of today? (Pick one.) Married ● 1 Single ○ 2 Divorced/Separated ○ 3 Widowed ○ 4

61-62. Your father's Social Security Number and last name — 61. FATHER'S/STEPFATHER'S SSN: 333-33-3331 — 62. FATHER'S/STEPFATHER'S LAST NAME: GARWOOD

63-64. Your mother's Social Security Number and last name — 63. MOTHER'S/STEPMOTHER'S SSN: 333-33-3332 — 64. MOTHER'S/STEPMOTHER'S LAST NAME: GARWOOD

65. How many people are in your <u>parents' household</u>? **See page 7.** 06

66. How many in question 65 **(exclude your parents)** will be <u>college students</u> between July 1, 2000, and June 30, 2001? **See page 7.** 2

67. What is your parents' state of legal residence? STATE: VA

68. Did your parents become legal residents of the state in question 67 before January 1, 1995? Yes ● 1 No ○ 2

69. If the answer to question 68 is "No," give the month and year legal residency began for the parent who has lived in the state the longest. MONTH __ / YEAR ____

70. What is the age of your older parent? 55

71. For 1999, have your parents filed their IRS income tax return or another tax return listed in **question 72**?

a. My parents have already filed. ● 1 **b.** My parents will file, but they have not yet filed. ○ 2 **c.** My parents are not going to file. **(Skip to question 78.)** ○ 3

72. What income tax return did your parents file or will they file for 1999?

a. IRS 1040 ● 1
b. IRS 1040A, 1040EZ, 1040Telefile ○ 2
c. A foreign tax return. **See Page 2.** ○ 3
d. A tax return for Puerto Rico, Guam, American Samoa, the Virgin Islands, the Marshall Islands, the Federated States of Micronesia, or Palau. **See Page 2.** ○ 4

73. If your parents have filed or will file a 1040, were they <u>eligible to file a 1040A or 1040EZ</u>? **See page 2.** Yes ○ 1 No/don't know ● 2

For 74 - 85, if the answer is zero or the question does not apply, enter 0.

74. What was your parents' adjusted gross income for 1999? Adjusted gross income is on IRS Form 1040–line 33; 1040A–line 18; 1040EZ–line 4; or Telefile–line I. $119,800

75. Enter the total amount of your parents' income tax for 1999. Income tax amount is on IRS Form 1040–line 49 plus 51; 1040A–line 32; 1040EZ–line 10; or Telefile–line K. $18,200

76. Enter your parents' exemptions. Exemptions are on IRS Form 1040–line 6d or on Form 1040A–line 6d. For Form 1040EZ or Telefile, **see page 2.** 06

77. Enter your parents' Earned Income Credit from IRS Form 1040–line 59a; 1040A–line 37a; 1040EZ–line 8a; or Telefile–line L. $0

78-79. How much did your parents earn from working in 1999? Answer this question whether or not your parents filed a tax return. This information may be on their W-2 forms, or on IRS Form 1040–lines 7, 12, and 18; 1040A–line 7; or 1040EZ–line 1. Telefilers should use their W-2's. **Father/Stepfather (78)** $150,000 **Mother/Stepmother (79)** $0

80. Go to page 8 of this form; complete the column on the right of **Worksheet A**; enter parent total here. $9,000

81. Go to page 8 of this form; complete the column on the right of **Worksheet B**; enter parent total here. $0

82. Total current balance of cash, savings, and checking accounts $20,000

For 83–85, if net worth is one million or more, enter $999,999. If net worth is negative, enter 0.

83. Current <u>net worth</u> of <u>investments</u> (<u>investment value</u> minus <u>investment debt</u>) **See page 2.** $120,000

84. Current <u>net worth</u> of business (<u>business value</u> minus <u>business debt</u>) **See page 2.** $0

85. Current <u>net worth</u> of investment farm (Don't include a farm that your parents live on and operate.) $0

Now go to Step Six. **Page 5**

(continued on next page)

SAMPLE FAFSA FORM FOR JAMES (CONT.)

Step Five: Complete this step only if you (the student) answered "Yes" to any question in Step Three.

86. How many people are in your (and your spouse's) household? **See page 7.** [ ][ ]

87. How many in question 86 will be college students between July 1, 2000, and June 30, 2001? **Do not include your parents. See page 7.** [ ]

Step Six: Please tell us which schools should receive your information.

For each school (up to six), please provide the federal school code and your housing plans **(enter "1" for on campus, "2" for off campus, and "3" for with parents)**. Look for the federal school codes on the Internet at **http://www.ed.gov/studentaid**, at your college financial aid office, at your public library, or by asking your high school guidance counselor. If you cannot get the federal school code, write in the complete name, address, city, and state of the college.

	Federal school code	*OR* Name of college	College street address and city	State		Housing Plans
88.	FIRST SCHOOL CODE 002920	DUKE UNIVERSITY	2138 CAMPUS DRIVE DURHAM	NC	89.	1
90.	SECOND SCHOOL CODE 001564	EMORY UNIVERSITY	3000 B. JONES CENTER ATLANTA	GA	91.	1
92.	THIRD SCHOOL CODE 002974	UNIVERSITY OF NORTH CAROLINA	CB 2200 JACKSON HALL CHAPEL HILL	NC	93.	1
94.	FOURTH SCHOOL CODE				95.	
96.	FIFTH SCHOOL CODE				97.	
98.	SIXTH SCHOOL CODE				99.	

Step Seven: Please read, sign, and date.

By signing this application, you agree, if asked, to provide information that will verify the accuracy of your completed form. This information may include a copy of your U.S. or state income tax form. Also, you certify that you (1) will use federal and/or state student financial aid only to pay the cost of attending an institution of higher education, (2) are not in default on a federal student loan or have made satisfactory arrangements to repay it, (3) do not owe money back on a federal student grant or have made satisfactory arrangements to repay it, (4) will notify your school if you default on a federal student loan, and (5) understand that **the Secretary of Education has the authority to verify income reported on this application with the Internal Revenue Service.** If you purposely give false or misleading information, you may be fined $10,000, sent to prison, or both.

100. Date this form was completed.

MONTH 02 / DAY 01 / **2000** ● **or 2001** ○

101. **Student** signature (Sign in box)

1 James Garwood

Parent signature (one parent whose information is provided in Step Four.) (Sign in box)

2 Margo Garwood

If this form was filled out by someone other than you, your spouse, or your parent(s), that person must complete this part.

Preparer's Name and Firm ______________________

Address ______________________

102. Social Security # [ ][ ][ ]–[ ][ ]–[ ][ ][ ][ ]

OR

103. Employer ID # [ ][ ]–[ ][ ][ ][ ][ ][ ][ ]

104. Signature and Date 1 ______________________

SCHOOL USE ONLY

D/O ○ 1 Federal School Code [ ][ ][ ][ ][ ][ ]

FAA SIGNATURE

1

MDE USE ONLY

Special Handle [ ]–[ ][ ][ ][ ][ ][ ]

Page 6

SAMPLE FAFSA FORM FOR DAVID

Free Application for Federal Student Aid

OMB 1845-0001

July 1, 2000 — June 30, 2001 school year

Step One: For questions 1-36, leave blank any questions that do not apply to you (the student).

1-3. Your full name (as it appears on your Social Security card)
1. LAST NAME: BARNES
2. FIRST NAME: DAVID
3. M.I.: E

4-7. Your permanent mailing address
4. NUMBER AND STREET (INCLUDE APARTMENT NUMBER): 421 WOODLAWN AVENUE
5. CITY (AND COUNTRY, IF NOT U.S.): HOUSTON
6. STATE: TX
7. ZIP CODE: 77040

8. Your Social Security Number: 444-44-4444

9. Your date of birth: MONTH 07 / DAY 12 / YEAR 1982

10. Your permanent telephone number: AREA CODE 713 555-4291

11. Do you have a driver's license? Yes ● 1 No ○ 2

12-13. Driver's license number and state
12. LICENSE NUMBER: 44444BAD01
13. STATE: TX

14. Are you a U.S. citizen? Pick one. **See Page 2.**
- **a.** Yes, I am a U.S. citizen. ● 1
- **b.** No, but I am an eligible noncitizen. **Fill in question 15.** ○ 2
- **c.** No, I am not a citizen or eligible noncitizen. ○ 3

15. ALIEN REGISTRATION NUMBER: A

16. Marital status as of today
- I am single, divorced, or widowed. ● 1
- I am married. ○ 2
- I am separated. ○ 3

17. Month and year you were married, separated, divorced, or widowed: MONTH __ / YEAR ____

For each question (18 - 22), please mark whether you will be full time, 3/4 time, half time, less than half time, or not attending. Mark "Full time" if you are not sure. See page 2.

	Full time	3/4 time	Half time	Less than half time	Not attending
18. Summer 2000	○ 1	○ 2	○ 3	○ 4	○ 5
19. Fall semester or quarter 2000	● 1	○ 2	○ 3	○ 4	○ 5
20. Winter quarter 2000-2001	● 1	○ 2	○ 3	○ 4	○ 5
21. Spring semester or quarter 2001	● 1	○ 2	○ 3	○ 4	○ 5
22. Summer 2001	○ 1	○ 2	○ 3	○ 4	○ 5

	Middle school/Jr. High	High school	College or beyond	Other/unknown
23. Highest school your father completed	○ 1	○ 2	● 3	○ 4
24. Highest school your mother completed	○ 1	○ 2	● 3	○ 4

25. What is your state of legal residence? STATE: TX

26. Did you become a legal resident of this state before January 1, 1995? Yes ● 1 No ○ 2

27. If the answer to question 26 is **"No,"** give month and year you became a legal resident. MONTH __ / YEAR ____

28. If you have **never** been convicted of any illegal drug offense, enter "1" in the box and go to question 29. A drug-related conviction does not necessarily make you ineligible for aid; call 1-800-433-3243 or go to http://www.fafsa.ed.gov/q28 to find out how to fill out this question. 1

29. Most male students must register with Selective Service to get federal aid. Are you male? Yes ● 1 No ○ 2

30. If you are male (age 18-25) and not registered, do you want Selective Service to register you? Yes ● 1 No ○ 2

31. What degree or certificate will you be working towards during 2000-2001? **See page 2** and enter the correct number in the box. 1

32. What will be your grade level when you begin the 2000-2001 school year? **See page 2** and enter the correct number in the box. 1

33. Will you have a high school diploma or GED before you enroll? Yes ● 1 No ○ 2

34. Will you have your first bachelor's degree before July 1, 2000? Yes ○ 1 No ● 2

35. In addition to grants, are you interested in student loans (which you must pay back)? Yes ● 1 No ○ 2

36. In addition to grants, are you interested in "work-study" (which you earn through work)? Yes ● 1 No ○ 2

Page 3

(continued on next page)

SAMPLE FAFSA FORM FOR DAVID (CONT.)

Step Two: For 37-51, if you (the student) are now married (even if you were not married in 1999), report both your and your spouse's income and assets. Ignore references to "spouse" if you are currently single, separated, divorced, or widowed.

37. For 1999, have you filed your IRS income tax return or another tax return listed in **question 38**?

- **a.** I have already filed. ○ 1
- **b.** I will file, but I have not yet filed. ○ 2
- **c.** I'm not going to file. **(Skip to question 44.)** ● 3

38. What income tax return did you file or will you file for 1999?

- **a.** IRS 1040 ○ 1
- **b.** IRS 1040A, 1040EZ, 1040Telefile ○ 2
- **c.** A foreign tax return. **See Page 2.** ○ 3
- **d.** A tax return for Puerto Rico, Guam, American Samoa, the Virgin Islands, the Marshall Islands, the Federated States of Micronesia, or Palau. **See Page 2.** ○ 4

39. If you have filed or will file a 1040, were you eligible to file a 1040A or 1040EZ? **See page 2.** Yes ○ 1 No/don't know ○ 2

For questions 40-53, if the answer is zero or the question does not apply to you, enter 0.

40. What was your (and spouse's) adjusted gross income for 1999? Adjusted gross income is on IRS Form 1040–line 33; 1040A–line 18; 1040EZ–line 4; or Telefile–line I. $ 0

41. Enter the total amount of your (and spouse's) income tax for 1999. Income tax amount is on IRS Form 1040–line 49 plus 51; 1040A–line 32; 1040EZ–line 10; or Telefile–line K. $ 0

42. Enter your (and spouse's) exemptions. Exemptions are on IRS Form 1040–line 6d, or on Form 1040A–line 6d. For Form 1040EZ or Telefile, **see page 2.**

43. Enter your Earned Income Credit from IRS Form 1040–line 59a; 1040A–line 37a; 1040EZ–line 8a; or Telefile–line L. $ 0

44-45. How much did you (and spouse) earn from working in 1999? Answer this question whether or not you filed a tax return. This information may be on your W-2 forms, or on IRS Form 1040–lines 7, 12, and 18; 1040A–line 7; or 1040EZ–line 1. Telefilers should use their W-2's.

You (44) $ 2,520

Your Spouse (45) $ 0

46. Go to page 8 of this form; complete the column on the left of **Worksheet A**; enter student total here. $ 0

47. Go to page 8 of this form; complete the column on the left of **Worksheet B**; enter student total here. $ 0

48. Total current balance of cash, savings, and checking accounts $ 2,400

For 49-51, if net worth is one million or more, enter $999,999. If net worth is negative, enter 0.

49. Current net worth of investments (investment value minus investment debt) **See page 2.** $ 0

50. Current net worth of business (business value minus business debt) **See page 2.** $ 0

51. Current net worth of investment farm (Don't include a farm that you live on and operate.) $ 0

52-53. If you receive veterans education benefits, for **how many months** from July 1, 2000 through June 30, 2001 will you receive these benefits, and **what amount** will you receive per month? Do not include your spouse's veterans education benefits.

Months (52)

Amount (53) $ 0

Step Three: Answer all six questions in this step.

54. Were you born before January 1, 1977? Yes ○ 1 No ● 2

55. Will you be working on a degree beyond a bachelor's degree in school year 2000-2001? Yes ○ 1 No ● 2

56. As of today, are you married? (Answer yes if you are separated, but not divorced.) Yes ○ 1 No ● 2

57. Answer **"Yes"** if: (1) You have children who receive more than half of their support from you; **or**
(2) You have dependents (other than your children or spouse) who live with you and receive more than half of their support from you, now and through June 30, 2001. Yes ○ 1 No ● 2

58. Are you an orphan or ward of the court or were you a ward of the court until age 18? Yes ○ 1 No ● 2

59. Are you a veteran of the U.S. Armed Forces? **See page 2.** Yes ○ 1 No ● 2

If you (the student) answer "No" to every question in Step Three, go to Step Four.

If you answer "Yes" to any question in Step Three, skip Step Four and go to Step Five.

(If you are a graduate health profession student, you may be required to complete Step Four even if you answered "Yes" to any question in Step Three.)

Page 4

(continued on next page)

SAMPLE FAFSA FORM FOR DAVID (CONT.)

Step Four: Complete this step if you (the student) answered "No" to all questions in Step Three. Please tell us about your parents. **See page 7 for who is considered a parent.**

60. Parents' marital status as of today? (Pick one.) Married ○ 1 Single ○ 2 Divorced/Separated ● 3 Widowed ○ 4

61-62. Your father's Social Security Number and last name
61. FATHER'S/STEPFATHER'S SSN: ___-__-____
62. FATHER'S/STEPFATHER'S LAST NAME: ____

63-64. Your mother's Social Security Number and last name
63. MOTHER'S/STEPMOTHER'S SSN: 444-44-4442
64. MOTHER'S/STEPMOTHER'S LAST NAME: SMITH

65. How many people are in your parents' household? **See page 7.** [03]

66. How many in question 65 **(exclude your parents)** will be college students between July 1, 2000, and June 30, 2001? **See page 7.** [1]

67. What is your parents' state of legal residence? STATE [TX]

68. Did your parents become legal residents of the state in question 67 before January 1, 1995? Yes ● 1 No ○ 2

69. If the answer to question 68 is "No," give the month and year legal residency began for the parent who has lived in the state the longest. MONTH __ / YEAR ____

70. What is the age of your older parent? [47]

71. For 1999, have your parents filed their IRS income tax return or another tax return listed in **question 72**?
a. My parents have already filed. ● 1
b. My parents will file, but they have not yet filed. ○ 2
c. My parents are not going to file. **(Skip to question 78.)** ○ 3

72. What income tax return did your parents file or will they file for 1999?
a. IRS 1040 .... ● 1
b. IRS 1040A, 1040EZ, 1040Telefile ..... ○ 2
c. A foreign tax return. **See Page 2.** .... ○ 3
d. A tax return for Puerto Rico, Guam, American Samoa, the Virgin Islands, the Marshall Islands, the Federated States of Micronesia, or Palau. **See Page 2.** ...... ○ 4

73. If your parents have filed or will file a 1040, were they eligible to file a 1040A or 1040EZ? **See page 2.** Yes ○ 1 No/don't know ● 2

For 74 - 85, if the answer is zero or the question does not apply, enter 0.

74. What was your parents' adjusted gross income for 1999? Adjusted gross income is on IRS Form 1040–line 33; 1040A–line 18; 1040EZ–line 4; or Telefile–line I. $ 39,200

75. Enter the total amount of your parents' income tax for 1999. Income tax amount is on IRS Form 1040–line 49 plus 51; 1040A–line 32; 1040EZ–line 10; or Telefile–line K. $ 3,889

76. Enter your parents' exemptions. Exemptions are on IRS Form 1040–line 6d or on Form 1040A–line 6d. For Form 1040EZ or Telefile, **see page 2.** [03]

77. Enter your parents' Earned Income Credit from IRS Form 1040–line 59a; 1040A–line 37a; 1040EZ–line 8a; or Telefile–line L. $ 0

78-79. How much did your parents earn from working in 1999? Answer this question whether or not your parents filed a tax return. This information may be on their W-2 forms, or on IRS Form 1040–lines 7, 12, and 18; 1040A–line 7; or 1040EZ–line 1. Telefilers should use their W-2's.
Father/Stepfather (78) $ ___,___
Mother/Stepmother (79) $ 38,600

80. Go to page 8 of this form; complete the column on the right of **Worksheet A**; enter parent total here. $ 14,400

81. Go to page 8 of this form; complete the column on the right of **Worksheet B**; enter parent total here. $ 0

82. Total current balance of cash, savings, and checking accounts $ 8,000

For 83–85, if net worth is one million or more, enter $999,999. If net worth is negative, enter 0.

83. Current net worth of investments (investment value minus investment debt) **See page 2.** $ 0

84. Current net worth of business (business value minus business debt) **See page 2.** $ 0

85. Current net worth of investment farm (Don't include a farm that your parents live on and operate.) $ 0

Now go to Step Six. **Page 5**

(continued on next page)

Step Five: Complete this step only if you (the student) answered "Yes" to any question in Step Three.

86. How many people are in your (and your spouse's) household? **See page 7.** [ ][ ]

87. How many in question 86 will be college students between July 1, 2000, and June 30, 2001? **Do not include your parents. See page 7.** [ ]

Step Six: Please tell us which schools should receive your information.

For each school (up to six), please provide the federal school code and your housing plans **(enter "1" for on campus, "2" for off campus, and "3" for with parents)**. Look for the federal school codes on the Internet at **http://www.ed.gov/studentaid**, at your college financial aid office, at your public library, or by asking your high school guidance counselor. If you cannot get the federal school code, write in the complete name, address, city, and state of the college.

	Federal school code *OR*	Name of college	College street address and city	State		Housing Plans
88.	FIRST SCHOOL CODE 003647	TRINITY UNIVERSITY	715 STADIUM DRIVE SAN ANTONIO	TX	89.	1
90.	SECOND SCHOOL CODE 003613	SOUTHEN METHODIST UNIVERSITY	P.O. BOX 750196 DALLAS	TX	91.	1
92.	THIRD SCHOOL CODE 002978	WAKE FOREST UNIVERSITY	BOX 7305 REYNOLDA STATION WINSTON SALEM	NC	93.	1
94.	FOURTH SCHOOL CODE				95.	
96.	FIFTH SCHOOL CODE				97.	
98.	SIXTH SCHOOL CODE				99.	

Step Seven: Please read, sign, and date.

By signing this application, you agree, if asked, to provide information that will verify the accuracy of your completed form. This information may include a copy of your U.S. or state income tax form. Also, you certify that you (1) will use federal and/or state student financial aid only to pay the cost of attending an institution of higher education, (2) are not in default on a federal student loan or have made satisfactory arrangements to repay it, (3) do not owe money back on a federal student grant or have made satisfactory arrangements to repay it, (4) will notify your school if you default on a federal student loan, and (5) understand that **the Secretary of Education has the authority to verify income reported on this application with the Internal Revenue Service.** If you purposely give false or misleading information, you may be fined $10,000, sent to prison, or both.

100. Date this form was completed.

MONTH 02 / DAY 15 / 2000 ● or 2001 ○

101. **Student** signature (Sign in box)

1 David Barnes

Parent signature (one parent whose information is provided in Step Four.) (Sign in box)

2 Melissa Smith

If this form was filled out by someone other than you, your spouse, or your parent(s), that person must complete this part.

Preparer's Name and Firm ____________

Address ____________

102. Social Security # [ ][ ][ ]-[ ][ ]-[ ][ ][ ][ ]

OR

103. Employer ID # [ ][ ]-[ ][ ][ ][ ][ ][ ][ ]

104. Signature and Date 1 ____________

SCHOOL USE ONLY

D/O ○ 1 Federal School Code [ ][ ][ ][ ][ ][ ]

FAA SIGNATURE

1

MDE USE ONLY

Special Handle [ ]-[ ][ ][ ][ ][ ][ ][ ]

Page 6

SAMPLE FAFSA FORM FOR DAVID (CONT.)

THE FINAL STAGES (TRACK A OR B)

FEBRUARY/MARCH

Stage 3: Review Your Acknowledgment Letters

Here's where the two tracks merge, although there are still different requirements for federal and institutional funds.

A few weeks after you submit your PROFILE and/or FAFSA, you'll receive an acknowledgment letter in the mail, confirming the information you reported. If you complete only the FAFSA, the acknowledgment will take the form of a Student Aid Report (SAR). Review all the material to make sure that the information is accurate. If the information is not accurate, check the letter or report for details on how to submit the necessary corrections to the processor.

WAIT UNTIL YOU'RE TOLD

Presumably, if it appears you will be eligible for some federal aid, the school will eventually ask you to fill out a FAFSA. We suggest waiting until you've been told to fill it out, since some colleges may want you to wait until they are sure you will be using the correct numbers.

The most important element of both your PROFILE acknowledgment letter and your SAR will be the calculated expected family contribution (EFC). As discussed, EFC is the amount of money it's been determined that you and your family can pay. As such, the EFC establishes your financial need, and therefore your eligibility for federal programs. Although only the FAFSA leads to official results, the PROFILE will provide your college with enough information to estimate your federal eligibility. The colleges you designated on your application receive this information about your EFC and use it to put together your total financial aid offer.

We'll get into how exactly your EFC is calculated, and how colleges use this figure, in the next chapter, Step 6.

Stage 4: Verify Your Reported Income

Often, you'll be asked to send a copy of both your and your parents' income tax returns directly to the financial aid office at each college. These documents are used to verify the income reported on the application.

Some families must also send documents that verify the amount of untaxed income a family received, statements from banks and investment accounts that verify the amount of a family's assets, a supplemental form that details the assets and income from a farm or business, information from a divorced or separated parent, and any other documentation that a college financial aid office determines is required to establish eligibility.

MARCH

Verification Worksheet

Approximately 30 percent of all FAFSAs submitted are selected for a verification process. You can tell if you were selected by whether there is an "*" next to the EFC number on the top right of your Student Aid Report (SAR). This does not mean that you made any mistakes on the original FAFSA, only that your application was randomly selected to be verified. This verification process involves the financial aid office's getting documentation from you to support the information that you provided on your application. You must fill out the Verification Worksheet and submit it to the colleges you are applying to with the appropriate documentation (usually completed tax forms). This is not a process to worry about but you should complete it as soon as possible after you receive your SAR in order to give the college time to make a financial aid offer. Colleges will not make an offer of financial aid that includes any federal funds until the verification process is complete.

A sample Verification Worksheet is included here for your review.

SAMPLE. DO NOT USE.

Dependent

U.S. Department of Education

2000-2001 Verification Worksheet

Federal Student Aid Programs

FORM APPROVED
OMB NO. 1840-0570
EXP. DATE 12/31/2001

Your application was selected for review in a process called "Verification." In this process, your school will be comparing information from your application with signed copies of your and your parent(s)' 1999 Federal tax forms, or with W-2 forms or other financial documents. The law says we have the right to ask you for this information before awarding Federal aid. If there are differences between your application information and your financial documents, you may need to send in corrections on your Student Aid Report (SAR), or your school may send corrections electronically, to have your information reprocessed.

Try to complete verification as soon as possible, so that your financial aid won't be delayed. Your financial aid administrator will help you.

What you should do

1. Collect your and your parent(s)' financial documents (signed Federal income tax forms, W-2 forms, etc.).
2. Talk to your financial aid administrator if you have questions about completing this worksheet.
3. Fill in and sign the worksheet—you and at least one parent.
4. Take the completed worksheet, tax forms, and any other documents your school needs to your financial aid administrator.
5. Your financial aid administrator will compare information on the documents. You may need to make corrections on your SAR and send it back to the application processor.

Your school must review the requested information, under the financial aid program rules (CFR Title 34, Part 668).

A. Student Information

Last name ______ First name ______ M.I. ______ Social Security Number ______

Address (include apt. no.) ______ Date of birth ______

City ______ State ______ ZIP code ______ Phone number (include area code) ______

B. Family Information

List the people in your parents' household; include:

- yourself and your parent(s) you live with (including stepparent), and
- your parents' other children, even if they don't live with your parent(s), if (a) your parents provide more than half of their support from July 1, 2000 through June 30, 2001, or (b) the children would be required to provide parental information when applying for Federal Student Aid, and
- other people if they now live with your parents, and your parents provide more than half of their support and will continue to provide more than half of their support from July 1, 2000 through June 30, 2001.

Write the names of all household members. Also write in the name of the college for any household member, excluding your parent(s), who will be attending college at least half-time between July 1, 2000 and June 30, 2001, and will be enrolled in a degree or certificate program. If you need more space, attach a separate page.

Full Name	Age	Relationship	College
Missy Jones (example)	18	Sister	Central University
		Self	

According to the Paperwork Reduction Act of 1995, no persons are required to respond to a collection of information unless it dsplays a valid OMB control number. The valid OMB control number for this information collection is 1840-0570. The time required to complete this information collection is estimated to average twelve minutes, including thetime to review instructions, search existing data resources, gather the data needed, and complete and review the information collection. If you have any comments concerning the accuracy of the time estimate(s) or suggestions forimproving this form, please write to: U.S. Department of Education, Washington, DC 20202-4651. If you have comments or concerns regarding the status of your individual submission of this form, write directly to: Applicatin and Pell Processing Systems Division, U.S. Department of Education, 400 Maryland Avenue, S.W.,

(continued on next page)

Verification Worksheet (cont.)

C. Student's Tax Forms and Income Information (all applicants) Dependent

1. Check one box only. Tax returns include the 1999 IRS Form 1040, 1040A, 1040EZ, TeleFile Tax Record, a tax return from Puerto Rico or a foreign income tax return. If you did not keep a copy of the tax return, request a copy from your tax preparer or a copy of an Internal Revenue Service form that lists tax account information.

☐ Check and attach signed tax return.

☐ Check and complete: signed tax return will be submitted to the school by ____________________(date).

☐ Check here if you will not file and are not required to file a 1999 U.S. Income Tax Return.

2. Amounts received for child support and other untaxed income. (See Worksheet A of the Free Application for Federal Student Aid)

Sources of Untaxed Income	**Amount**	Sources of Untaxed Income	**Amount**
a. Child Support		d.	
b. Social Security (non-taxed)		e.	
c. Welfare (including TANF)		f.	

3. If you did not file and are not required to file a 1999 Federal income tax return, list below your employer(s) and any income received in 1999.

Sources (Use the W-2 form or other earnings statements.)	Amount

D. Parent(s)' Tax Forms and Income Information

1. Check one box only. Tax returns include the 1999 IRS Form 1040, 1040A, 1040EZ, TeleFile Tax Record, a tax return from Puerto Rico or a foreign income tax return. If your parent(s) did not keep a copy of the tax return, request a copy from the tax preparer or a copy of an Internal Revenue Service form that lists tax account information.

☐ Check and attach signed tax return(s).

☐ Check and complete: signed tax return(s) will be submitted to the school by ____________________(date).

☐ Check here if your parent(s) will not file and are not required to file a 1999 U.S. Income Tax Return.

2. Amounts received for child support and other untaxed income. (See Worksheet A of the Free Application for Federal Student Aid)

Sources of Untaxed Income	**Amount**	Sources of Untaxed Income	**Amount**
a. Child Support		d.	
b. Social Security (non-taxed)		e.	
c. Welfare (including TANF)		f.	

3. If your parent(s) did not file and are not required to file a 1999 Federal income tax return, list below your parent(s)' employer(s) and any income they received in 1999.

Sources (Use the W-2 form or other earnings statements.)	Amount

E. Sign this Worksheet

By signing this worksheet, we certify that all the information reported on this worksheet is complete and correct. At least one parent must sign.

WARNING: If you purposely give false or misleading information on this worksheet, you may be fined, be sentenced to jail, or both.

____
Student Date

____
Parent Date

Do not mail this worksheet to your application processor. Take it to your Financial Aid Administrator at your school. Don't forget to sign your tax forms.

Stage 5: Examine Your Financial Aid Award Letter

After your file is completed, the financial aid office of each college that accepted you will send an award letter. This letter details your eligibility for specific financial aid programs.

Most students are awarded aid from a combination of programs and from the different sources available to the college, hence the term *package.*

The Financial Aid Package

APRIL

A financial aid package is the total amount of financial aid a student receives. Federal and nonfederal grants, loans, and work-study are combined in a package to help meet the student's need. Using available resources to give each student the best possible package of aid is one of the major responsibilities of a school's financial aid administrator.

The financial aid award letter will often tell you how much the school estimates it will cost in the next year, what aid you will receive if you attend that school, and how much you and your family will have to pay out of your own pocket. For first-year students, this letter is often sent with, or soon after, the letter of admission. Ideally, this package will supply the amount of money you need in order to pay for college (the amount of money that you and your family can't afford to pay). Realistically, there may still be financial need that is not met with financial aid awards.

In Step 7, you'll learn how these packages are put together, how to compare them, and how to negotiate a better aid offer. We'll also evaluate sample packages for each of our four students. In Step 8, you'll learn what to do if the aid package, even when negotiated, doesn't meet your need.

TIMETABLE

Financial aid applications are generally based on the traditional academic year, September through June, not on the calendar year. This means that you apply for aid for an entire academic year that generally crosses into the next calendar year. As a result, if you're filling out only the FAFSA, you'll apply in the beginning of 2000 (as soon after January 1 as possible) for the 2000–2001 academic year. The FAFSA must be submitted after January 1 for the coming fall entrance so it reflects income and asset information from the year just ended.

The Financial Aid PROFILE and applications for admission to the college are submitted earlier, in the preceding fall, for entrance the next fall. So, if you're required to fill out the PROFILE, you'll complete the PROFILE registration in October, your admission application between November and February by the college's application deadline, and the individual PROFILE and the FAFSA as instructed by the college.

If you're initiating the financial aid process with a FAFSA, note that many colleges impose financial aid application deadlines, some as early as the February 1 preceding

"Some financial aid counselors told us to wait to fill in our EAFSA until at least the end of January or early February, when my parents would have their financial records available and they wouldn't have to use estimates. But, most recommended that we file as soon as possible after January 1 and just use estimates."

enrollment in the fall (remember, you may not apply until after January 1). Students who apply for aid after these college-determined dates may still be eligible for some financial aid, but may not be eligible for college-based aid. Often, students who apply after these deadlines receive only loans and, if eligible, a Pell Grant (the deadline to apply for a Pell Grant is not until much later).

If you're initiating the financial aid process with a PROFILE, your customized packet will tell you the deadlines for each college. Make sure you file your PROFILE before the earliest deadline listed.

And, of course, if you're required to fill out the PROFILE for one school, but must initiate the process with the FAFSA for another school, you must do both.

LOAN APPLICATIONS

Thought you were done? Well, not yet, at least for about half of the aid recipients.

If you're awarded a Federal Stafford Loan, you'll need to complete a supplemental loan application as well as complete an "entrance" interview. The loan application is fairly simple (one page) and, in addition to basic name and address information, it asks you for names and addresses of relatives and friends (so you can be found years later if you default on the loan). Once you complete this, the financial aid office must complete its section certifying you are eligible.

When you are filling out the loan application, one of the question asks which bank you wish to have as your lender. The application will be sent by the college to the lender you've chosen. This lender can be your local bank, a national bank, a savings-and-loan, or a credit union. There are some other lending organizations that participate in the FFELP programs, and you may want to investigate them as well. For example, Kaplan can help you find ways to pay for college through KapLoan, the Kaplan Student Loan Information Program. Through an association with one of the largest providers of federal student loans, the KapLoan program can provide you with information about the various types of loan programs available and offers a number of free services to help you complete the student loan process.

It's up to you and your family to decide which lender to use. If you're unsure, check with the financial aid office. While they don't usually recommend specific lenders, they may steer you away from some with whom they've had problems in the past.

If you've been awarded either a Federal Ford Direct Loan or a Perkins Loan, the lender is either the federal government or the college itself, for which you've already applied with the FAFSA. You won't need a supplemental loan application, but there are other papers you'll have to complete (such as a promissory note, with which you promise to repay the money you borrow). You may also have to undergo a counseling session of sorts, referred to as an "entrance" interview, at which your borrower's rights and responsibilities will be reviewed.

NEED HELP?

To find out more about how the Kaplan/American Express Student Loan Information program can help you get information on financing your college education, call 1-888-KAP-LOAN.

FINANCIAL AID APPLICATIONS IN NINE STEPS

Step 1
In late September of your senior year in high school, visit your guidance office and find out whether the college(s) you're applying to want you to fill out the PROFILE. If at least one college does, complete PROFILE Registration with CSS in one of the ways discussed here. You must also pick up a copy of the FAFSA (usually in November).

Step 2
If you registered for PROFILE, you'll receive your customized Financial Aid PROFILE (usually a few weeks later). Read it carefully to find out when you're supposed to send it in. Complete it and send it in as instructed. Complete and submit the FAFSA after January I of your senior year, but before any college deadlines. List on the FAFSA all colleges you will be applying to, regardless of whether they use the PROFILE or not. Even if all of the colleges you're applying to use the PROFILE, you still will need to eventually fill out the FAFSA.

VERIFICATION

A process of review to determine the accuracy of the information on a student's financial aid application.

Step 3
When you receive an acknowledgment after submitting either or both of your financial aid applications (either the FAFSA or the PROFILE *and* the FAFSA), review what's sent you and make sure the information is accurate. If incorrect, you'll have to make the necessary corrections, and both forms will provide instructions on how to do so.

Step 4
In late winter or early spring (or sooner if instructed to do so by a college), send copies of your and your parents' income tax returns to each college you've applied to. You may have to send other verifying documents. If a college requests something, send it as soon as possible. It's a good idea to keep a copy of everything you send.

Step 5
You'll receive an award letter from each college, generally along with or soon after you receive your letter of admission.

Step 6
Compare award letters to make sure they reflect accurate information and to know how much you and your family are going to be expected to pay.

Step 7
Send in your nonrefundable deposit, confirming your plans to attend.

Step 8
If required to do so, complete any and all paperwork for your student loan, parent loan, tuition payment plan, etcetera.

Step 9
Finally, pay the tuition and fees as required by the college.

WHAT'S NEXT

Now you know your role in the application process. But what happens to your application when you send it to the processing service? How are your financial need and your family contribution calculated? How do colleges determine how much money they'll award you? Let's go behind the scenes. In the next step, you'll go beyond merely filling in the blanks and following prompts. You'll become an active player in the game.

GET AN INSIDE LOOK AT HOW YOU'RE EVALUATED

Your Calculated Financial Need

Step 6

You spend all this time gathering information and completing forms, dutifully completing every application requirement, staying in control of the whole process. Then what happens? The application processing service sends you a figure, the expected family contribution (EFC), which represents the amount of money you're supposed to be able to pay for college. What happens in between the time you mail your application and you receive this important number? How is all that information you provided on your application used? How is this EFC determined? What happened to your control?

Let's explore the formulas that determine your EFC, see how your income and assets are really assessed, and walk through estimates of your contribution. We'll also revisit our sample students and learn from their situations.

"Believe me, I'm glad this whole application process is over. I turned into a total squid, spending Friday nights writing essays and adding numbers. But where did all my hard work go?"

YOUR RESPONSIBILITY

As discussed, the fundamental principle of financial aid is that parents and students have the primary responsibility of paying, to the extent that they're able, the cost of a college education. If you have a child going to college, at least a portion of your family's income and assets is expected to go toward his or her educational expenses.

For that reason, your income and assets are assessed to see exactly how much you can afford to pay. Only when colleges know this can they figure out how much aid money you'll need to meet the total cost of college.

HOW YOUR ASSETS AND INCOME ARE ASSESSED

Your current family income available to pay for college education includes not only your wages, interest, and dividends, but all nontaxed income. Your assets are anything of value that you've accumulated, such as home and other real estate equity, checking and savings accounts, stocks, bonds, trusts and other securities, loan receivables, business equipment, and business inventory.

GIVE ME SHELTER

Some tax shelters are added into the financial aid formulas by many colleges.

It's Not Like the Tax System

The system for assessing a family's ability to pay for education is not like the tax system. In the tax system, there are certain incentives built in to encourage investments and national policy. For example, the tax law encourages people to save for their retirement by not counting income you set aside in a 401(k) retirement account. When you calculate your total income to determine your taxes, your contributions to this 401(k) fund are not included.

For financial aid, though, what's being measured is your need for funds to pay for an education. These tax shelters must be added back in so that the financial aid funds available go to the families that have a demonstrated need for them. Many people feel angry about the discrepancy between the tax formulas and the financial aid formulas, but they're very different animals and have different purposes. They only happen to use some overlapping numbers.

Allowances

The need-analysis formulas are realistic. They take into account that you've been saving for things other than education, such as your retirement, so they permit certain allowances. This way you're not punished for responsibly saving and planning. You're allowed to exclude a certain amount of your assets. Then, based on what's left, it's determined how much you can pay.

Furthermore, the older you are, the greater the asset protection allowance, in recognition of the fact that more of your assets should be available as you get closer to retirement age. As the following chart illustrates, using Federal Methodology (explained on page 83), the federal asset protection allowance for 2000–2001 is $44,400 when the older parent is 45 years old, and it increases to $67,200 when the older parent is 60 years old.

Education Savings and Asset Protection Allowance (Parents and Independent Students)

Age of Older Parent*	Allowance if there are Two Parents	Allowance if there is only One Parent	Age of Older Parent*	Allowance if there are Two Parents	Allowance if there is only One Parent
25 or less	$0	$0	51	$51,900	$31,400
26	2,600	1,600	52	53,200	32,200
27	5,200	3,300	53	54,800	33,000
28	7,800	4,900	54	56,200	33,800
29	10,500	6,600	55	57,900	34,700
30	13,100	8,200	56	59,700	35,600
31	15,700	9,800	57	61,500	36,400
32	18,300	11,500	58	63,400	37,500
33	20,900	13,100	59	65,300	38,500
34	23,500	14,800	60	67,200	39,400
35	26,100	16,400	61	69,600	40,600
36	28,700	18,000	62	71,600	41,700
37	31,400	19,700	63	74,100	42,900
38	34,000	21,300	64	76,600	44,100
39	36,600	23,000	65 or over	78,900	45,500
40	39,200	24,600			
41	39,900	25,200			
42	40,900	25,800			
43	42,000	26,300			
44	43,100	26,900			
45	44,400	27,400			
46	45,600	28,100			
47	46,700	28,700			
48	47,900	29,300			
49	49,100	30,000			
50	50,300	30,700			

***Age of Older Parent is FAFSA/SAR #70; if blank, use age 45 on the table.**

Reprinted from The EFC Formula Book, 2000–01, *by the U.S. Department of Education.*

In the need-analysis formula to determine your EFC, which we'll examine next, subtraction of the asset protection allowance yields a figure referred to as your *discretionary net worth.* Discretionary net worth is the amount that you have discretion over, the amount that you could use to buy a car, home furnishings, a boat, etcetera. It could also be the amount you're saving for a rainy day. The members of the U.S. Congress who put the federal need-analysis formula into legislation believe that at least a portion of this savings should go toward education.

The portion of your assets that's assessed for financial aid purposes depends on how large your discretionary net worth is. The maximum is 47 percent of 12 percent, or 5.6 percent. This means that if you have $100,000 in the bank, are married, have one child going to college, earn more than about $20,000, and are 45 years old, only $3,136 of that $100,000 asset is assessed for financial aid eligibility (the reason it's not $5,600 is that we subtracted the asset protection allowance before assessing the discretionary net worth).

DOUBLE YOUR FUN

If you have two kids in college at the same time, your financial contribution is divided in half.

Let's illustrate this:

CONTRIBUTION FROM ASSETS FORMULA

TOTAL ASSETS (not counting your home)		$100,000
Minus	asset protection allowance (age 45)	– $ 44,400
Equals	discretionary net worth	= $ 55,600
Times	conversion percentage	× 12%
Equals	income supplement	= $ 6,672
Times	contribution percentage	× 47%
Equals	**contribution from assets**	= $ **3,136**

If this were your situation, with $100,000 in assets, just think how many options you'd be giving your child knowing that, in the worst case scenario, you'd have almost four years of a private college education already in the bank.

But, say you have two children, and both of them will be in college at the same time. The formula also takes that into consideration. If there are two in college, the EFC figure is divided in half. And if there are three in college, in thirds. Four in college? Well, you get the idea.

The need-analysis formula also takes into account that you have certain nondiscretionary expenses, such as federal and state taxes, FICA, employment expenses, etcetera, and there is an allowance for basic needs that takes into account family size. When the analysis is done to determine your EFC, which ultimately determines your eligibility for need-based financial aid, these items are accounted for.

We talk more about how assets are treated later on, when we walk through the need analyses for our sample students.

THE MAGIC FORMULAS

To see how large your EFC should be, the application processing service reviews your income and assets. And they permit certain allowances, so your savings aren't drained. But what exactly are the formulas used to calculate your EFC?

The EFC listed on the Student Aid Report generated by your FAFSA is calculated using a formula called the Federal Methodology. The Federal Methodology (FM) is a need-analysis method developed by Congress to determine your eligibility for federal student aid programs.

On the PROFILE acknowledgment, you'll find an estimated EFC figure based on this Federal Methodology, as well as an EFC based on something called the Institutional Methodology. The Institutional Methodology (IM) is an alternate method of need analysis used by some colleges to determine eligibility for institutional and nonfederal aid. The PROFILE lists both because some colleges use the FM number, instead of the IM, to award their own aid.

Students qualify for federal aid if the total cost to attend a college exceeds the calculated EFC using the FM. If the institution is awarding its own need-based money using the IM and not the FM, students qualify for institutional aid if the total cost to attend college exceeds the calculated EFC using the IM. The two formulas overlap somewhat, but in general, the FM is considerably more lenient. For example, in the FM the equity you have in your home is not assessed. All else being equal, this gives homeowners an advantage over renters.

FM AND YOUR HOME

Unlike the Institutional Methodology, the Federal Methodology does not include your home equity as part of your assets.

CALCULATING YOUR EFC BASED ON FEDERAL METHODOLOGY

The FM formula takes into account:

- Parents' and student's income from the previous year (the base year)
- Total income tax paid
- Number of family members
- Number of family members attending college
- Assets (excluding the equity in the family's primary residence)
- Parents' ages

FEDERAL METHODOLOGY (FM)

A need-analysis method, developed by Congress, used to calculate the family contribution, which determines eligibility for federal student aid programs.

Here's a table to give you a rough idea of your expected EFC based on the FM.

ESTIMATED FAMILY CONTRIBUTION* BASED ON THE FEDERAL METHODOLOGY (FM)

Annual Income	Number in Family	Total Family Assets** $25,000	$50,000	$75,000	$100,000
$20,000	3	$0	$386	$1,046	$1,706
	4	$0	$0	$337	$997
	5	$0	$0	$0	$300
$40,000	3	$2,924	$3,755	$4,736	$5,901
	4	$2,156	$2,867	$3,688	$4,658
	5	$1,490	$2,150	$2,860	$3,681
$60,000	3	$8,252	$9,662	$11,072	$12,482
	4	$6,828	$8.238	$9,648	$11,058
	5	$5,507	$6,815	$8,225	$9,635
$80,000	3	$13,736	$15,146	$16,556	$17,966
	4	$12,388	$13,798	$15,208	$16.618
	5	$11,133	$12,543	$13.953	$15.343
$100,000	3	$19,221	$20,631	$25,397	$23,451
	4	$17,872	$19,282	$20,692	$22,102
	5	$16,618	$18,028	$19,438	$20,848

Note: For parents and students who file or are eligible to file IRS 1040A or EZ forms or who aren't required to file, no assets are included in the methodology if parents' taxable income is less than $50,000. All these families would have greater than $400 interest income and would be required to file the IRS 1040 form.

* *These numbers assume two adults in one family, with one parent employed, in a state with 6 percent taxation, and the older parent 45 years of age.*

***Assets before deduction of asset protection allowance.*

OH, GIVE ME A HOME

In preparing for the financial aid application process, you might take note of the edge given to homeowners who pay down their mortgage rather than putting excess cash in other investments. Their children's chances of qualifying for financial aid are increased, since home equity is not assessed for federal eligibility, and it's easier to borrow against your home for college expenses.

Following is a blank need-analysis worksheet, along with instructions and the tables for 2000–2001, so you can calculate your EFC using the FM. If you'd like more blank worksheets, photocopy this form. The IM and FM worksheets are for your own use. At no point do they have to be submitted. The tables will change for the 2000–2001 year, but using these tables should give you a good estimate of your calculated EFC for the next year. Remember, your contribution for 2000–2001 will be based on your 1999 income and on your assets as of the day you complete the applications. If your income doesn't increase, your contribution will actually decrease because the formula and tables are adjusted annually for inflation.

SAMPLE. DO NOT USE.

2000-01 EFC FORMULA: DEPENDENT STUDENT

PARENT'S INCOME IN 1999	
1. Parents' Adjusted Gross Income (FAFSA #74)	
2. a. Father's income earned from work (FAFSA #78) ____	
b. Mother's income earned from work (FAFSA #79) ____	
Total parents' income earned from work	
3. Parents' Taxable Income (If tax files, enter the amount from line 1 above. If non-tax files, enter the amount from line 2.	
4. Untaxed income and benefits Earned Income Credit (tax filers only) (FAFSA #77) ____ Total from FAFSA Worksheet A (FAFSA #80) ____	
Total untaxed income and benefits	
5. Taxable and untaxed income Sum of line 3 and line 4)	
6. Total from FAFSA Worksheet B (FAFSA #81) -	
7. TOTAL INCOME (line 5 minus line 6) May be a negative number =	

ALLOWANCES AGAINST PARENTS' INCOME	
8. 1999 U.S. income tax paid (FAFSA #75) (tax filers only); If negative, enter zero.	
9. State and other tax allowance (Table A1. If negative, enter zero. +	
10. Father's Social Security tax (Table A2) +	
11. Mother's Social Security tax (Table A2) +	
12. Income protection allowance (Table A3) +	
13. Employment expense allowance: Two working parents: 35% of the lesser of the earned incomes, or $2,800, whichever is less ____ One parent families: 35% of earned income, or $2,800, whichever is less ____	
Two-parent families, one working parent: zero +	
14. **TOTAL ALLOWANCES** =	

AVAILABLE INCOME	
Total Income (from line 7)	
Total Allowances (from line 14) -	
15. **AVAILABLE INCOME (AI)** May be a negative number. =	

PARENTS' CONTRIBUTION FROM ASSETS	
16. Cash, savings, & checking (FAFSA #82)	
17. Net worth of investments** (FAFSA #83) If negative, enter zero.	
18. Net worth of business (FAFSA #84) ____ If negative, enter zero.	
19. Net worth of investment farm (FAFSA #85) ____ If negative, enter zero. If the family resides on the farm, enter zero.	
20. Net worth of business/farm (sum of lines 18 and 19)	
21. Adjusted net worth of business/farm (Calculate using Table A4) +	
22. Net Worth (sum of lines 16, 17, and 21) =	
23. Education savings and asset protection allowance (Table A5) -	
24. Discretionary net worth (line 22 minus line 23) =	
25. Asset conversion rate x	
26. **CONTRIBUTION FROM ASSETS** If negative, enter zero. =	

PARENTS' CONTRIBUTION	
Available Income (AI) (from line 15)	
Contribution from assets (from line 26) +	
27. **Adjusted Available Income (AAI)** May be a negative number. =	
28. **Total parents' contribution from AAI** (Calculate using Table A6)	
29. **Number in college in 2000-01** (exclude parents) (FAFSA #66) div	
30. **PARENTS' CONTRIBUTION** (standard contribution for 9-month enrollment) =	

** Do not include the family's home.

(continued next page)

2000-01 EFC FORMULA: DEPENDENT STUDENT

STUDENT'S INCOME IN 1999	
31. Adjusted Gross Income (FAFSA #40)	
32. Income earned from work (FAFSA #44)	
33. Taxable Income (If tax filer, enter the amount from line 31 above. If non-tax filer, enter the amount from line 32.	
34. Total from FAFSA Worksheet A (FAFSA #46)	
35. Taxable and untaxed income (sum of line 33 and line 34)	
36. Total from FAFSA Worksheet B (FAFSA #47) -	
37. TOTAL INCOME (line 35 minus line 36) May be a negative number =	

ALLOWANCES AGAINST STUDENTS' INCOME	
38. 1999 U.S. income tax paid (FAFSA #41) (tax filers only); if negative, enter zero.	
39. State and other tax allowance (Table A7. If negative, enter zero. +	
40. Social Security tax allowance (Table A2) +	
41. Income protection allowance +	
42. Allowance for parent's negative Adjusted Available Income (if line 27 isnegative, enter line 27 as a positive number in line 42. If line 27 is positive, enter zero in line 42. +	
43. **TOTAL ALLOWANCES** =	

STUDENT'S CONTRIBUTION FROM INCOME	
TOTAL INCOME	
TOTAL ALLOWANCES -	
44. **Available Income (AI)** =	
45. **Assessment of AI** x	
46. **STUDENT CONTRIBUTION FROM AI** If negative, enter zero. =	

STUDENT'S CONTRIBUTION FROM ASSETS	
47. Cash, savings, & checking (FAFSA #48)	
48. Net worth of investments** (FAFSA #49) If negative, enter zero. +	
49. Net worth of business (FAFSA #50) If negative, enter zero. +	
50. Net worth of investment farm (FAFSA #51) If negative, enter zero. If the family resides on the farm, enter zero. +	
51. Net Worth (sum of lines 47 through 50) =	
52. Assessment rate x	
53. **CONTRIBUTION FROM ASSETS** =	

EXPECTED FAMILY CONTRIBUTION	
PARENTS' CONTRIBUTION (from line 30)	
STUDENT'S CONTRIBUTION FROM AI (from line 46)	
STUDENT'S CONTRIBUTION FROM ASSETS (from line 53) +	
54. **EXPECTED FAMILY CONTRIBUTION** =	

SAMPLE. DO NOT USE.

Instructions for Completing the Federal Methodology Worksheet

- On the Federal Methodology (FM) Worksheet, enter your income data on Lines 1 and/or 2a and 2b and then transfer the appropriate amount to Line 3. Complete the bullets under Line 4 and total your entries. Add Lines 3 and 4, enter the result on Line 5, then subtract line 6, and enter your total income in Line 7.
- You will need to use the following FM Computation Tables to complete Lines 8–13. Be careful to calculate Social Security taxes separately for each wage earner based on the income earned from work. You should also have only one entry in the three bullets under Line 13. Total your allowances on Line 14.
- Add your total income from Line 7 to your total allowances from Line 14 to calculate your available income.

Note:

If the taxable income in Line 3 is less than $50,000, and you file or are eligible to file the IRS 1040A or 1040EZ forms, skip Lines 16 through 26 (the asset information section). If the adjusted gross income (AGI) on Line 1 is $12,000 or less, and you're eligible to file the 1040A or 1040EZ forms, skip the rest of the form and put a zero on line 30.

- Enter your asset data on Lines 16–19. Use Table A4 to calculate Line 20 (if necessary). Add Lines 16, 17, and 21 to get your total net worth. Subtract the education savings and asset protection allowance from Table 5 to get your discretionary net worth, and multiply the result by 12 percent to get your contribution from assets.
- Add your available income from Line 15 to your contribution from assets from Line 26 to get your adjusted available income (AAI). Calculate your contribution using Table 6. Divide this number by the number in college to get your contribution for each child in college.
- The number on Line 30 is an estimate of your parents' contribution (EFC), the amount you're expected to pay for college.
- Go on to complete items 31–52 to calculate the student contribution.
- Add the parents' contribution to the student's contribution to get the Expected Family Contribution (EFC).

Remember these special circumstances:

- For parents and students who file or are eligible to file IRS 1040A or 1040EZ forms or who aren't required to file, no assets are included in the methodology if parents' taxable income is less than $50,000.
- Federal need analysis provisions provide a zero EFC variant for families with parents' AGI of $12,000 or less. The parents must file or be eligible to file the 1040A or 1040EZ federal income tax return, or do not file taxes. In such cases, no contribution would be expected.

Federal Methodology Computation Tables, 2000–2001

Tables are from *The EFC Formula Book, 2000–2001,* published by the U.S. Department of Education. These tables change every year, so the calculations will be estimates only.

Table A1: State and Other Tax Allowance

for EFC Formula Worksheet A (parents only)

STATE	PERCENT OF TOTAL INCOME		STATE	PERCENT OF TOTAL INCOME	
	$0-14,999	$15,000 or more		$0-14,999	$15,000 or more
Alabama	5%	4%	Missouri	6%	5%
Alaska	3%	2%	Montana	8%	7%
American Samoa	4%	3%	Nebraska	8%	7%
Arizona	6%	5%	Nevada	3%	2%
Arkansas	6%	5%	New Hampshire	7%	6%
California	8%	7%	New Jersey	8%	7%
Canada	4%	3%	New Mexico	6%	5%
Colorado	7%	6%	New York	11%	10%
Connecticut	6%	5%	North Carolina	8%	7%
Delaware	8%	7%	North Dakota	6%	5%
District of Columbia	10%	9%	Northern Mariana Islands	4%	3%
Federated States of Micronesia	4%	3%	Ohio	8%	7%
Florida	4%	3%	Oklahoma	6%	5%
Georgia	7%	6%	Oregon	10%	9%
Guam	4%	3%	Palau	4%	3%
Hawaii	8%	7%	Pennsylvania	7%	6%
Idaho	7%	6%	Puerto Rico	4%	3%
Illinois	6%	5%	Rhode Island	9%	8%
Indiana	6%	5%	South Carolina	8%	7%
Iowa	8%	7%	South Dakota	4%	3%
Kansas	7%	6%	Tennessee	3%	2%
Kentucky	7%	6%	Texas	3%	2%
Louisiana	4%	3%	Utah	8%	7%
Maine	9%	8%	Vermont	8%	7%
Marshall Islands	4%	3%	Virgin Islands	4%	3%
Maryland	9%	8%	Virginia	8%	7%
Massachusetts	9%	8%	Washington	4%	3%
Mexico	4%	3%	West Virginia	6%	5%
Michigan	9%	8%	Wisconsin	10%	9%
Minnesota	9%	8%	Wyoming	3%	2%
Mississippi	5%	4%	Blank or invalid State	4%	3%
			OTHER	4%	3%

Multiply parents' total income (from EFC formula Worksheet A, line 7) by the appropriate rate from the table above to get the "state and other tax allowance" (line 9 of Worksheet A). Use the parents' *state of legal residence* (FAFSA/SAR #67). If this item is blank or invalid, use the student's *state of legal residence* (FAFSA/SAR #25). If both items are blank or invalid, use the *state* in the student's mailing address (FAFSA/SAR #6). If all three items are blank or invalid, use the rate for a blank or invalid state above.

Federal Methodology Computation Tables, 2000–2001 (cont.)

Table A2: Social Security Tax

Calculate separately the Social Security tax of father, mother, and student.

Income Earned from Work *	Social Security Tax
$0 - $72,600	7.65% of income
$72,601 or greater	$5,553.90 + 1.45% of amount over $72,600

* Father's 1999 income earned from work is FAFSA/SAR #78.
Mother's 1999 income earned from work is FAFSA/SAR #79.
Student's 1999 income earned from work is FAFSA/SAR #44.
Social Security tax will never be less than zero.

Table A3: Income Protection Allowance

Number in parents' household, including student (FAFSA/SAR #65)	Number of college students in household (FAFSA/SAR #66) Exclude parents from number in college				
	1	2	3	4	5
2	$12,450	$10,320	——	——	——
3	15,500	13,380	$11,250	——	——
4	19,140	17,010	14,890	$12,760	——
5	22,580	20,450	18,340	16,210	$14,090
6	26,420	24,290	22,170	20,040	17,920

NOTE: For each additional family member, add $2,980.
For each additional college student (except parents), subtract $2,120.

Table A4: Business/Farm Net Worth Adjustment

for EFC Formula Worksheet A (parents only)

If the net worth of a business or farm is—	Then the adjusted net worth is—
Less than $1	$0
$1 to $90,000	40% of net worth of business & farm
$90,001 to $265,000	$ 36,000 + 50% of excess over $90,000
$265,001 to $445,000	$123,500 + 60% of excess over $265,000
$445,001 or more	$231,500 + 100% of excess over $445,000

Federal Methodology Computation Tables, 2000–2001 (cont.)

Table A5: Education Savings and Asset Protection Allowance
for EFC Formula Worksheet A (parents only)

age of older parent *	Allowance if there are two parents	Allowance if there is only one parent	*age of older parent* *	Allowance if there are two parents	Allowance if there is only one parent
25 or less	0	0	45	44,400	27,400
26	2,600	1,600	46	45,600	28,100
27	5,200	3,300	47	46,700	28,700
28	7,800	4,900	48	47,900	29,300
29	10,500	6,600	49	49,100	30,000
30	13,100	8,200	50	50,300	30,700
31	15,700	9,800	51	51,900	31,400
32	18,300	11,500	52	53,200	32,200
33	20,900	13,100	53	54,800	33,000
34	23,500	14,800	54	56,200	33,800
35	26,100	16,400	55	57,900	34,700
36	28,700	18,000	56	59,700	35,600
37	31,400	19,700	57	61,500	36,400
38	34,000	21,300	58	63,400	37,500
39	36,600	23,000	59	65,300	38,500
40	39,200	24,600	60	67,200	39,400
41	39,900	25,200	61	69,600	40,600
42	40,900	25,800	62	71,600	41,700
43	42,000	26,300	63	74,100	42,900
44	43,100	26,900	64	76,600	44,100
			65 or more	78,900	45,500

**age of older parent* is FAFSA/SAR #70; if blank, use age 45 on the table

Table A6: Parents' Contribution From AAI

If parents' AAI is—	The parents' contribution from AAI is—
Less than -$3,409	-$750
-$3,409 to $11,100	22% of AAI
$11,101 to $14,000	$2,442 + 25% of AAI over $11,100
$14,001 to $16,800	$3,167 + 29% of AAI over $14,000
$16,801 to $19,600	$3,979 + 34% of AAI over $16,800
$19,601 to $22,500	$4,931 + 40% of AAI over $19,600
$22,501 or more	$6,091 + 47% of AAI over $22,500

Federal Methodology Computation Tables, 2000–2001 (cont.)

Table A7: State and Other Tax Allowance
for EFC Formula Worksheet A (student only)

State	Allowance
Alabama	3%
Alaska	0%
American Samoa	2%
Arizona	3%
Arkansas	4%
California	5%
Canada	2%
Colorado	4%
Connecticut	2%
Delaware	5%
District of Columbia	7%
Federated States of Micronesia	2%
Florida	1%
Georgia	4%
Guam	2%
Hawaii	6%
Idaho	5%
Illinois	2%
Indiana	4%
Iowa	5%
Kansas	4%
Kentucky	5%
Louisiana	2%
Maine	5%
Marshall Islands	2%
Maryland	6%
Massachusetts	5%
Mexico	2%
Michigan	4%
Minnesota	6%
Mississippi	3%
Missouri	3%
Montana	5%
Nebraska	4%
Nevada	0%
New Hampshire	1%
New Jersey	3%
New Mexico	4%
New York	7%
North Carolina	5%
North Dakota	2%
Northern Mariana Islands	2%
Ohio	5%
Oklahoma	4%
Oregon	6%
Palau	2%
Pennsylvania	3%
Puerto Rico	2%
Rhode Island	4%
South Carolina	5%
South Dakota	0%
Tennessee	0%
Texas	0%
Utah	5%
Vermont	4%
Virgin Islands	2%
Virginia	4%
Washington	0%
West Virginia	4%
Wisconsin	5%
Wyoming	0%
Blank or Invalid State	2%
OTHER	2%

Multiply the total income of student (EFC Formula Worksheet A, line 37) by the appropriate rate from the table above to get the "state and other tax allowance" (line 39 of Worksheet A). Use the student's *state of legal residence* (FAFSA/SAR #25). If this item is blank or invalid, use the *state* in student's mailing address (FAFSA/SAR #6). If both items are blank or invalid, use the parents' *state of legal residence* (FAFSA/SAR #67). If all three items are blank or invalid, use the rate for a blank or invalid state above.

SIMPLE NEEDS TEST

If your family income is less than $50,000, you may be eligible for a Simple Needs Test, in which none of your assets are counted in calculating your family contribution. To qualify for this Simple Needs Test, parents must either have filed or be eligible to file IRS 1040A or 1040EZ forms.

Sample Students' EFCs Based on Federal Methodology

Here and on the next few pages, you'll find completed FM worksheets for our sample dependent students.

Sample Students' EFCs Based on Federal Methodology

2000-01 EFC FORMULA: DEPENDENT STUDENT

PARENT'S INCOME IN 1999		
1. Parents' Adjusted Gross Income (FAFSA #74)		56,300
2. a. Father's income earned from work (FAFSA #78)	32,000	
b. Mother's income earned from work (FAFSA #79)	24,000	
Total parents' income earned from work		56,000
3. Parents' Taxable Income (If tax files, enter the amount from line 1 above. If non-tax files, enter the amount from line 2.		56,300
4. Untaxed income and benefits Earned Income Credit (tax filers only) (FAFSA #77)	0	
Total from FAFSA Worksheet A (FAFSA #80)	0	
Total untaxed income and benefits		0
5. Taxable and untaxed income Sum of line 3 and line 4)		56,300
6. Total from FAFSA Worksheet B (FAFSA #81)	-	0
7. TOTAL INCOME (line 5 minus line 6) May be a negative number	=	56,300

ALLOWANCES AGAINST PARENTS' INCOME		
8. 1999 U.S. income tax paid (FAFSA #75) (tax filers only); if negative, enter zero.		5,250
9. State and other tax allowance (Table A1. If negative, enter zero.	+	5,630
10. Father's Social Security tax (Table A2)	+	2,448
11. Mother's Social Security tax (Table A2)	+	1,836
12. Income protection allowance (Table A3)	+	22,580
13. Employment expense allowance:		
Two working parents: 35% of the lesser of the earned incomes, or $2,800, whichever is less	2,800	
One parent families: 35% of earned income, or $2,800, whichever is less	0	
Two-parent families, one working parent:	zero +	
14. TOTAL ALLOWANCES	=	40,544

AVAILABLE INCOME		
Total Income (from line 7)		56,300
Total Allowances (from line 14)	-	40,544
15. AVAILABLE INCOME (AI) May be a negative number.	=	15,756

PARENTS' CONTRIBUTION FROM ASSETS		
16. Cash, savings, & checking (FAFSA #82)		5,000
17. Net worth of investments** (FAFSA #83) If negative, enter zero.		0
18. Net worth of business (FAFSA #84) If negative, enter zero.	200,000	
19. Net worth of investment farm (FAFSA #85) If negative, enter zero. If the family resides on the farm, enter zero.	0	
20. Net worth of business/farm (sum of lines 18 and 19)	200,000	
21. Adjusted net worth of business/farm (Calculate using Table A4)	+	91,000
22. Net Worth (sum of lines 16, 17, and 21)	=	96,000
23. Education savings and asset protection allowance (Table A5)	-	69,600
24. Discretionary net worth (line 22 minus line 23)	=	26,400
25. Asset conversion rate	x	12%
26. CONTRIBUTION FROM ASSETS If negative, enter zero.	=	3,168

PARENTS' CONTRIBUTION		
Available Income (AI) (from line 15)		15,756
Contribution from assets (from line 26)	+	3,168
27. Adjusted Available Income (AAI) May be a negative number.	=	18,924
28. Total parents' contribution from AAI (Calculate using Table A6)		4,701
29. Number in college in 2000-01 (exclude parents) (FAFSA #66)	div	1
30. PARENTS' CONTRIBUTION (standard contribution for 9-month enrollment)	=	4,701

** Do not include the family's home.

(continued on next page)

2000-01 EFC FORMULA: DEPENDENT STUDENT

STUDENT'S INCOME IN 1999		
31. Adjusted Gross Income (FAFSA #40)		0
32. Income earned from work (FAFSA #44)		2,100
33. Taxable Income (If tax filer, enter the amount from line 31 above. If non-tax filer, enter the amount from line 32.		2,100
34. Total from FAFSA Worksheet A (FAFSA #46)		0
35. Taxable and untaxed income (sum of line 33 and line 34)		2,100
36. Total from FAFSA Worksheet B (FAFSA #47)	-	0
37. TOTAL INCOME (line 35 minus line 36) May be a negative number	=	2,100

ALLOWANCES AGAINST STUDENTS' INCOME		
38. 1999 U.S. income tax paid (FAFSA #41) (tax filers only); if negative, enter zero.		0
39. State and other tax allowance (Table A7. If negative, enter zero.	+	147
40. Social Security tax allowance (Table A2)	+	161
41. Income protection allowance	+	2,200
42. Allowance for parent's negative Adjusted Available Income (if line 27 isnegative, enter line 27 as a positive number in line 42. If line 27 is positive, enter zero in line 42.	+	0
43. TOTAL ALLOWANCES	=	2,508

STUDENT'S CONTRIBUTION FROM INCOME		
TOTAL INCOME		2,100
TOTAL ALLOWANCES	-	2,508
44. Available Income (AI)	=	-408
45. Assessment of AI	x	50%
46. STUDENT CONTRIBUTION FROM AI If negative, enter zero.	=	0

STUDENT'S CONTRIBUTION FROM ASSETS		
47. Cash, savings, & checking (FAFSA #48)		1,200
48. Net worth of investments** (FAFSA #49) If negative, enter zero.	+	0
49. Net worth of business (FAFSA #50) If negative, enter zero.	+	0
50. Net worth of investment farm (FAFSA #51) If negative, enter zero. If the family resides on the farm, enter zero.	+	0
51. Net Worth (sum of lines 47 through 50)	=	1200
52. Assessment rate	x	35%
53. CONTRIBUTION FROM ASSETS	=	420

EXPECTED FAMILY CONTRIBUTION		
PARENTS' CONTRIBUTION (from line 30)		4,701
STUDENT'S CONTRIBUTION FROM AI (from line 46)	+	0
STUDENT'S CONTRIBUTION FROM ASSETS (from line 53)	+	420
54. EXPECTED FAMILY CONTRIBUTION	=	5,121

SAMPLE FM WORKSHEET FOR FRANCES (cont.)

Frances's family owns a restaurant that they estimate is worth $200,000, from which they pay themselves annual salaries of $32,000 and $24,000. They have only $5,000 in a savings account; all other accumulated savings have gone into purchasing and building the business. Frances has accumulated $1,200 in her savings account through part-time work in the restaurant. Notice that her entire income is protected by the student income protection allowance. She will not be expected to contribute anything from her earnings and only $420 from her savings. The calculated family contribution for 2000–2001 is $5,121.

SAMPLE FM WORKSHEET FOR ANGELA

2000-01 EFC FORMULA: DEPENDENT STUDENT

PARENT'S INCOME IN 1999			
1. Parents' Adjusted Gross Income (FAFSA #74)			48,400
2. a. Father's income earned from work (FAFSA #78)		0	
b. Mother's income earned from work (FAFSA #79)		48,400	
Total parents' income earned from work			48,400
3. Parents' Taxable Income (If tax files, enter the amount from line 1 above. If non-tax files, enter the amount from line 2.			48,400
4. Untaxed income and benefits Earned Income Credit (tax filers only) (FAFSA #77)		0	
Total from FAFSA Worksheet A (FAFSA #80)		0	
Total untaxed income and benefits			0
5. Taxable and untaxed income Sum of line 3 and line 4)			48,400
6. Total from FAFSA Worksheet B (FAFSA #81)	-		0
7. TOTAL INCOME (line 5 minus line 6) May be a negative number	=		48,400

ALLOWANCES AGAINST PARENTS' INCOME			
8. 1999 U.S. income tax paid (FAFSA #75) (tax filers only); if negative, enter zero.			4,232
9. State and other tax allowance (Table A1. If negative, enter zero.	+		3,388
10. Father's Social Security tax (Table A2)	+		0
11. Mother's Social Security tax (Table A2)	+		3,703
12. Income protection allowance (Table A3)	+		15,500
13. Employment expense allowance:			
Two working parents: 35% of the lesser of the earned incomes, or $2,800, whichever is less		0	
One parent families: 35% of earned income, or $2,800, whichever is less		2,800	
Two-parent families, one working parent:	zero +		
14. TOTAL ALLOWANCES	=		29,623

AVAILABLE INCOME		
Total Income (from line 7)		48,400
Total Allowances (from line 14)	-	29,623
15. AVAILABLE INCOME (AI) May be a negative number.	=	18,777

PARENTS' CONTRIBUTION FROM ASSETS			
16. Cash, savings, & checking (FAFSA #82)			3,000
17. Net worth of investments** (FAFSA #83) If negative, enter zero.			4,000
18. Net worth of business (FAFSA #84) If negative, enter zero.		0	
19. Net worth of investment farm (FAFSA #85) If negative, enter zero. If the family resides on the farm, enter zero.		0	
20. Net worth of business/farm (sum of lines 18 and 19)		0	
21. Adjusted net worth of business/farm (Calculate using Table A4)	+		0
22. Net Worth (sum of lines 16, 17, and 21)	=		7,000
23. Education savings and asset protection allowance (Table A5)	-		27,400
24. Discretionary net worth (line 22 minus line 23)	=		-20,400
25. Asset conversion rate	x		12%
26. CONTRIBUTION FROM ASSETS If negative, enter zero.	=		0

PARENTS' CONTRIBUTION		
Available Income (AI) (from line 15)		18,777
Contribution from assets (from line 26)	+	0
27. Adjusted Available Income (AAI) May be a negative number.	=	18,777
28. Total parents' contribution from AAI (Calculate using Table A6)		4,651
29. Number in college in 2000-01 (exclude parents) (FAFSA #66)	div	1
30. PARENTS' CONTRIBUTION (standard contribution for 9-month enrollment)	=	4,651

** Do not include the family's home.

(continued on next page)

2000-01 EFC FORMULA: DEPENDENT STUDENT

STUDENT'S INCOME IN 1999		
31. Adjusted Gross Income (FAFSA #40)		0
32. Income earned from work (FAFSA #44)		2,700
33. Taxable Income (If tax filer, enter the amount from line 31 above. If non-tax filer, enter the amount from line 32.		2,700
34. Total from FAFSA Worksheet A (FAFSA #46)		0
35. Taxable and untaxed income (sum of line 33 and line 34)		2,700
36. Total from FAFSA Worksheet B (FAFSA #47)	-	0
37. TOTAL INCOME (line 35 minus line 36) May be a negative number	=	2,700

ALLOWANCES AGAINST STUDENTS' INCOME		
38. 1999 U.S. income tax paid (FAFSA #41) (tax filers only); if negative, enter zero.		0
39. State and other tax allowance (Table A7. If negative, enter zero.	+	135
40. Social Security tax allowance (Table A2)	+	207
41. Income protection allowance	+	2,200
42. Allowance for parent's negative Adjusted Available Income (if line 27 isnegative, enter line 27 as a positive number in line 42. If line 27 is positive, enter zero in line 42.	+	0
43. TOTAL ALLOWANCES	=	2,542

STUDENT'S CONTRIBUTION FROM INCOME		
TOTAL INCOME		2,700
TOTAL ALLOWANCES	-	2,542
44. Available Income (AI)	=	158
45. Assessment of AI	x	50%
46. STUDENT CONTRIBUTION FROM AI If negative, enter zero.	=	79

STUDENT'S CONTRIBUTION FROM ASSETS		
47. Cash, savings, & checking (FAFSA #48)		1,100
48. Net worth of investments** (FAFSA #49) If negative, enter zero.	+	0
49. Net worth of business (FAFSA #50) If negative, enter zero.	+	0
50. Net worth of investment farm (FAFSA #51) If negative, enter zero. If the family resides on the farm, enter zero.	+	0
51. Net Worth (sum of lines 47 through 50)	=	1100
52. Assessment rate	x	35%
53. CONTRIBUTION FROM ASSETS	=	385

EXPECTED FAMILY CONTRIBUTION		
PARENTS' CONTRIBUTION (from line 30)		4,651
STUDENT'S CONTRIBUTION FROM AI (from line 46)	+	79
STUDENT'S CONTRIBUTION FROM ASSETS (from line 53)	+	385
54. EXPECTED FAMILY CONTRIBUTION	=	5,115

SAMPLE FM WORKSHEET FOR ANGELA (cont.)

Angela, her younger brother, and their mother live just outside of San Jose, California. Angela's mother is the sole supporter of the family, earning $48,400 as a computer programmer. They have no other income, but managed to save $3,000 in the bank and $4,000 in her company's stock. Angela also works part time and earned $2,700, of which she was able to save $1,100. Her mother's calculated family contribution is $4,701, and there's an expected contribution of $464 from Angela's earnings and savings.

"I paid for all of my own expenses this year out of my part-time job, but we just never have enough. With a first and second mortgage on our house, my mom said she wouldn't be able to borrow from a bank to come up with an expected contribution of over $5,000, because she's already maxed out on her borrowing power. It's a good thing there's that loan program for parents (PLUS loan)."

SAMPLE FM WORKSHEET FOR JAMES

2000-01 EFC FORMULA: DEPENDENT STUDENT

PARENT'S INCOME IN 1999			
1. Parents' Adjusted Gross Income (FAFSA #74)			119,800
2. a. Father's income earned from work (FAFSA #78)		150,000	
b. Mother's income earned from work (FAFSA #79)		0	
Total parents' income earned from work			150,000
3. Parents' Taxable Income (If tax files, enter the amount from line 1 above. If non-tax files, enter the amount from line 2.			119,800
4. Untaxed income and benefits			
Earned Income Credit (tax filers only) (FAFSA #77)		0	
Total from FAFSA Worksheet A (FAFSA #80)		9,000	
Total untaxed income and benefits			9,000
5. Taxable and untaxed income Sum of line 3 and line 4)			128,800
6. Total from FAFSA Worksheet B (FAFSA #81)	-		0
7. TOTAL INCOME (line 5 minus line 6) May be a negative number	=		128,800

ALLOWANCES AGAINST PARENTS' INCOME			
8. 1999 U.S. income tax paid (FAFSA #75) (tax filers only); if negative, enter zero.			18,200
9. State and other tax allowance (Table A1. If negative, enter zero.	+		9,016
10. Father's Social Security tax (Table A2)	+		6,676
11. Mother's Social Security tax (Table A2)	+		0
12. Income protection allowance (Table A3)	+		24,290
13. Employment expense allowance:			
Two working parents: 35% of the lesser of the earned incomes, or $2,800, whichever is less		0	
One parent families: 35% of earned income, or $2,800, whichever is less		0	
Two-parent families, one working parent:	zero +		
14. TOTAL ALLOWANCES	=		58,182

AVAILABLE INCOME		
Total Income (from line 7)		128,800
Total Allowances (from line 14)	-	58,182
15. AVAILABLE INCOME (AI) May be a negative number.	=	70,618

PARENTS' CONTRIBUTION FROM ASSETS			
16. Cash, savings, & checking (FAFSA #82)			20,000
17. Net worth of investments** (FAFSA #83) If negative, enter zero.			120,000
18. Net worth of business (FAFSA #84) If negative, enter zero.		0	
19. Net worth of investment farm (FAFSA #85) If negative, enter zero. If the family resides on the farm, enter zero.		0	
20. Net worth of business/farm (sum of lines 18 and 19)		0	
21. Adjusted net worth of business/farm (Calculate using Table A4)	+		0
22. Net Worth (sum of lines 16, 17, and 21)	=		140,000
23. Education savings and asset protection allowance (Table A5)	-		57,900
24. Discretionary net worth (line 22 minus line 23)	=		82,100
25. Asset conversion rate	x		12%
26. CONTRIBUTION FROM ASSETS If negative, enter zero.	=		9,852

PARENTS' CONTRIBUTION		
Available Income (AI) (from line 15)		70,618
Contribution from assets (from line 26)	+	9,852
27. Adjusted Available Income (AAI) May be a negative number.	=	80,470
28. Total parents' contribution from AAI (Calculate using Table A6)		33,337
29. Number in college in 2000-01 (exclude parents) (FAFSA #66)	div	2
30. PARENTS' CONTRIBUTION (standard contribution for 9-month enrollment)	=	16,669

** Do not include the family's home.

(continued on next page)

SAMPLE FM WORKSHEET FOR JAMES (cont.)

2000-01 EFC FORMULA: DEPENDENT STUDENT

STUDENT'S INCOME IN 1999		
31. Adjusted Gross Income (FAFSA #40)		0
32. Income earned from work (FAFSA #44)		0
33. Taxable Income (If tax filer, enter the amount from line 31 above. If non-tax filer, enter the amount from line 32.		0
34. Total from FAFSA Worksheet A (FAFSA #46)		0
35. Taxable and untaxed income (sum of line 33 and line 34)		0
36. Total from FAFSA Worksheet B (FAFSA #47)	-	0
37. TOTAL INCOME (line 35 minus line 36) May be a negative number	=	0

ALLOWANCES AGAINST STUDENTS' INCOME		
38. 1999 U.S. income tax paid (FAFSA #41) (tax filers only); if negative, enter zero.		0
39. State and other tax allowance (Table A7. If negative, enter zero.	+	0
40. Social Security tax allowance (Table A2)	+	0
41. Income protection allowance	+	2,200
42. Allowance for parent's negative Adjusted Available Income (if line 27 isnegative, enter line 27 as a positive number in line 42. If line 27 is positive, enter zero in line 42.	+	0
43. TOTAL ALLOWANCES	=	2,200

STUDENT'S CONTRIBUTION FROM INCOME		
TOTAL INCOME		0
TOTAL ALLOWANCES	-	2,200
44. Available Income (AI)	=	-2,200
45. Assessment of AI	x	50%
46. STUDENT CONTRIBUTION FROM AI If negative, enter zero.	=	0

STUDENT'S CONTRIBUTION FROM ASSETS		
47. Cash, savings, & checking (FAFSA #48)		0
48. Net worth of investments** (FAFSA #49) If negative, enter zero.	+	4,000
49. Net worth of business (FAFSA #50) If negative, enter zero.	+	0
50. Net worth of investment farm (FAFSA #51) If negative, enter zero. If the family resides on the farm, enter zero.	+	0
51. Net Worth (sum of lines 47 through 50)	=	4000
52. Assessment rate	x	35%
53. CONTRIBUTION FROM ASSETS	=	1400

EXPECTED FAMILY CONTRIBUTION		
PARENTS' CONTRIBUTION (from line 30)		16,669
STUDENT'S CONTRIBUTION FROM AI (from line 46)	+	0
STUDENT'S CONTRIBUTION FROM ASSETS (from line 53)	+	1,400
54. EXPECTED FAMILY CONTRIBUTION	=	18,069

James's father is a successful attorney in a small law firm in Roanoke, Virginia, while his mother stays home to take care of the four children, two of whom (James and his older brother) will be in college next year. The father's income is $150,000 per year, from which he contributes $9,000 to a 401(K) supplemental retirement plan. They have $20,000 in a savings account and own stocks and property with a net worth of about $120,000. James has $4,000 in stocks that were gifts from his grandparents. The total FM parent contribution is $33,337, which divided by the two family members in college comes to $16,669 per child. James did not work during the 1999 calendar year, although he expects to find a job during the summer before college. This income will not appear until next year's application. James's assets yield an FM contribution of $1,400.

"Last year my grandparents gave me some stock worth about $4,000, and it cost me $1,400 in a student contribution. If they had given that stock to my parents to hold for me, it would have been assessed for only about $240. And, if my grandparents had waited until I started school, it wouldn't have appeared at all on my financial aid application for this year (although it would show up on next year's application)."

SAMPLE FM WORKSHEET FOR DAVID

2000-01 EFC FORMULA: DEPENDENT STUDENT

PARENT'S INCOME IN 1999			
1. Parents' Adjusted Gross Income (FAFSA #74)			39,200
2. a. Father's income earned from work (FAFSA #78)		0	
b. Mother's income earned from work (FAFSA #79)		38,600	
Total parents' income earned from work			38,600
3. Parents' Taxable Income (If tax files, enter the amount from line 1 above. If non-tax files, enter the amount from line 2.			39,200
4. Untaxed income and benefits Earned Income Credit (tax filers only) (FAFSA #77)		0	
Total from FAFSA Worksheet A (FAFSA #80)		14,400	
Total untaxed income and benefits			14,400
5. Taxable and untaxed income Sum of line 3 and line 4)			53,600
6. Total from FAFSA Worksheet B (FAFSA #81)	-		0
7. TOTAL INCOME (line 5 minus line 6) May be a negative number	=		53,600

ALLOWANCES AGAINST PARENTS' INCOME			
8. 1999 U.S. income tax paid (FAFSA #75) (tax filers only); if negative, enter zero.			3,889
9. State and other tax allowance (Table A1. If negative, enter zero.	+		1,072
10. Father's Social Security tax (Table A2)	+		0
11. Mother's Social Security tax (Table A2)	+		2,953
12. Income protection allowance (Table A3)	+		15,500
13. Employment expense allowance:			
Two working parents: 35% of the lesser of the earned incomes, or $2,800, whichever is less		0	
One parent families: 35% of earned income, or $2,800, whichever is less		2,800	
Two-parent families, one working parent:	zero +		
14. TOTAL ALLOWANCES	=		26,214

AVAILABLE INCOME		
Total Income (from line 7)		53,600
Total Allowances (from line 14)	-	26,214
15. AVAILABLE INCOME (AI) May be a negative number.	=	27,386

PARENTS' CONTRIBUTION FROM ASSETS			
16. Cash, savings, & checking (FAFSA #82)			8,000
17. Net worth of investments** (FAFSA #83) If negative, enter zero.			0
18. Net worth of business (FAFSA #84) If negative, enter zero.		0	
19. Net worth of investment farm (FAFSA #85) If negative, enter zero. If the family resides on the farm, enter zero.		0	
20. Net worth of business/farm (sum of lines 18 and 19)		0	
21. Adjusted net worth of business/farm (Calculate using Table A4)	+		0
22. Net Worth (sum of lines 16, 17, and 21)	=		8,000
23. Education savings and asset protection allowance (Table A5)	-		28,700
24. Discretionary net worth (line 22 minus line 23)	=		-20,700
25. Asset conversion rate	x		12%
26. CONTRIBUTION FROM ASSETS If negative, enter zero.	=		0

PARENTS' CONTRIBUTION		
Available Income (AI) (from line 15)		27,386
Contribution from assets (from line 26)	+	0
27. Adjusted Available Income (AAI) May be a negative number.	=	27,386
28. Total parents' contribution from AAI (Calculate using Table A6)		8,387
29. Number in college in 2000-01 (exclude parents) (FAFSA #66)	div	1
30. PARENTS' CONTRIBUTION (standard contribution for 9-month enrollment)	=	8,387

** Do not include the family's home.

(continued on next page)

SAMPLE FM WORKSHEET FOR DAVID

2000-01 EFC FORMULA: DEPENDENT STUDENT

PARENT'S INCOME IN 1999			
1. Parents' Adjusted Gross Income (FAFSA #74)			39,200
2. a. Father's income earned from work (FAFSA #78)	0		
b. Mother's income earned from work (FAFSA #79)	38,600		
Total parents' income earned from work			38,600
3. Parents' Taxable Income (If tax files, enter the amount from line 1 above. If non-tax files, enter the amount from line 2.			39,200
4. Untaxed income and benefits			
Earned Income Credit (tax filers only) (FAFSA #77)	0		
Total from FAFSA Worksheet A (FAFSA #80)	7,200		
Total untaxed income and benefits			7,200
5. Taxable and untaxed income Sum of line 3 and line 4)			46,400
6. Total from FAFSA Worksheet B (FAFSA #81)		-	0
7. TOTAL INCOME (line 5 minus line 6) May be a negative number		=	46,400

ALLOWANCES AGAINST PARENTS' INCOME			
8. 1999 U.S. income tax paid (FAFSA #75) (tax filers only); if negative, enter zero.			3,889
9. State and other tax allowance (Table A1. If negative, enter zero.		+	928
10. Father's Social Security tax (Table A2)		+	0
11. Mother's Social Security tax (Table A2)		+	2,953
12. Income protection allowance (Table A3)		+	15,500
13. Employment expense allowance:			
Two working parents: 35% of the lesser of the earned incomes, or $2,800, whichever is less	0		
One parent families: 35% of earned income, or $2,800, whichever is less	2,800		
Two-parent families, one working parent:	zero	+	
14. TOTAL ALLOWANCES		=	26,070

AVAILABLE INCOME		
Total Income (from line 7)		46,400
Total Allowances (from line 14)	-	26,070
15. AVAILABLE INCOME (AI) May be a negative number.	=	20,330

PARENTS' CONTRIBUTION FROM ASSETS			
16. Cash, savings, & checking (FAFSA #82)			8,000
17. Net worth of investments** (FAFSA #83) If negative, enter zero.			0
18. Net worth of business (FAFSA #84) If negative, enter zero.	0		
19. Net worth of investment farm (FAFSA #85) If negative, enter zero. If the family resides on the farm, enter zero.	0		
20. Net worth of business/farm (sum of lines 18 and 19)	0		
21. Adjusted net worth of business/farm (Calculate using Table A4)		+	0
22. Net Worth (sum of lines 16, 17, and 21)		=	8,000
23. Education savings and asset protection allowance (Table A5)		-	28,700
24. Discretionary net worth (line 22 minus line 23)		=	-20,700
25. Asset conversion rate		x	12%
26. CONTRIBUTION FROM ASSETS If negative, enter zero.		=	0

PARENTS' CONTRIBUTION		
Available Income (AI) (from line 15)		20,330
Contribution from assets (from line 26)	+	0
27. Adjusted Available Income (AAI) May be a negative number.	=	20,330
28. Total parents' contribution from AAI (Calculate using Table A6)		5,223
29. Number in college in 2000-01 (exclude parents) (FAFSA #66)	div	1
30. PARENTS' CONTRIBUTION (standard contribution for 9-month enrollment)	=	5,223

** Do not include the family's home.

(continued on next page)

SAMPLE FM WORKSHEET FOR DAVID (cont.)

2000-01 EFC FORMULA: DEPENDENT STUDENT

STUDENT'S INCOME IN 1999		
31. Adjusted Gross Income (FAFSA #40)		0
32. Income earned from work (FAFSA #44)		2,520
33. Taxable Income (If tax filer, enter the amount from line 31 above. If non-tax filer, enter the amount from line 32.		2,520
34. Total from FAFSA Worksheet A (FAFSA #46)		0
35. Taxable and untaxed income (sum of line 33 and line 34)		2,520
36. Total from FAFSA Worksheet B (FAFSA #47)	-	0
37. TOTAL INCOME (line 35 minus line 36) May be a negative number	=	2,520

ALLOWANCES AGAINST STUDENTS' INCOME		
38. 1999 U.S. income tax paid (FAFSA #41) (tax filers only); if negative, enter zero.		0
39. State and other tax allowance (Table A7. If negative, enter zero.	+	0
40. Social Security tax allowance (Table A2)	+	193
41. Income protection allowance	+	2,200
42. Allowance for parent's negative Adjusted Available Income (if line 27 isnegative, enter line 27 as a positive number in line 42. If line 27 is positive, enter zero in line 42.	+	0
43. TOTAL ALLOWANCES	=	2,393

STUDENT'S CONTRIBUTION FROM INCOME		
TOTAL INCOME		2,520
TOTAL ALLOWANCES	-	2,393
44. Available Income (AI)	=	127
45. Assessment of AI	x	50%
46. STUDENT CONTRIBUTION FROM AI If negative, enter zero.	=	64

STUDENT'S CONTRIBUTION FROM ASSETS		
47. Cash, savings, & checking (FAFSA #48)		2,400
48. Net worth of investments** (FAFSA #49) If negative, enter zero.	+	0
49. Net worth of business (FAFSA #50) If negative, enter zero.	+	0
50. Net worth of investment farm (FAFSA #51) If negative, enter zero. If the family resides on the farm, enter zero.	+	0
51. Net Worth (sum of lines 47 through 50)	=	2400
52. Assessment rate	x	35%
53. CONTRIBUTION FROM ASSETS	=	840

EXPECTED FAMILY CONTRIBUTION		
PARENTS' CONTRIBUTION (from line 30)		8,387
STUDENT'S CONTRIBUTION FROM AI (from line 46)	+	64
STUDENT'S CONTRIBUTION FROM ASSETS (from line 53)	+	840
54. EXPECTED FAMILY CONTRIBUTION	=	9,291

** 8,387*

** This total contribution is based on father's child support being included. If father's child support is eliminated, the expected family contribution (EFC) is reduced to $6,127.*

"We didn't think it was fair to include money in the expected contribution that won't continue to roll in when I turn eighteen. Given how little we have, there was no way we could have saved any of it for my college expenses. I mean, isn't our contribution supposed to reflect what we have now, not what we had a year ago?"

David lives with his mother and his brother in their small home in Houston, Texas. His mother teaches in a middle school. In addition to her $38,600 salary, she receives $14,400 a year in child support from her ex-husband. As soon as the children turn 18, the child support payments are eliminated, and David just turned 18. His mother has $8,000 in savings, and David has another $4,000 of his own that he plans on using for college. Their calculated EFC is $8,387. David worked full time during the summer after his junior year as a camp counselor. Note how all but $64 of his earnings are protected by the income allowance. David's contribution is $904 from his earnings and savings. If the child support for David is eliminated from the formula, which may be done at the discretion of the financial aid administrator, the EFC is reduced to $6,127 ($5,223 from David's mom, and $904 from David).

CALCULATING YOUR OWN EFC

If all of these charts and calculations make you want to do your own FM calculations right now, you can get started. However, you might want to do a "quick and dirty" FM calculation without having a calculator in hand. For this purpose, we've done some research on the World Wide Web and found several sources that allow you to do an estimate of your family contribution online. The two best sites are:

www.finaid.org—select Calculators, then select Financial Aid Estimation under the Need Analysis section

www.kaplan.com—select College, then select Financial Aid, then select Aid Calculators and use the Undergraduate EFC Calculator

INSTITUTIONAL METHODOLOGY (IM)

An alternative method of need analysis used by individual colleges to calculate a family contribution, which is used to determine eligibility for institutional and nonfederal aid.

These two sites each have EFC calculators that will do the job for you. You don't need to do all the calculations manually or have access to all the FM charts because it's all automatic. What you do need is your most recent tax form and some idea of the value of your assets. All you have to do is enter the financial information they ask for and your EFC will be calculated. You can even print out the results for reference. These results represent what the federal government considers to be the money you have available for your education. We can't guarantee that the figure you arrive at using the worksheet will exactly match the figure used in the financial aid office or your longhand calculations, but it should give you a reasonable estimate. You can use this estimated FM figure in your financial planning.

The next step in the process is to look at Institutional Methodology (IM).

CALCULATING YOUR EFC BASED ON THE IM

Major changes in the calculation of the Institutional Methodology (IM) were introduced for the 2000-2001 year. The revised formula changes the allowances that are subtracted from assets by creating two new allowances—the Emergency Reserve Allowance and Cumulative Education Savings Protection. The Emergency Reserve Allowance (ERA) protects assets for unanticipated expenses such as illness or unemployment. The amount is based on family size and represents six months of average family expenses as reported in the federal Consumer Expenditure Survey. The Cumulative Education Savings Protection Allowance (CESA) recognizes a family's need to save to finance their children's college expenses. The CESA protects an amount of assets equal to the amount the family would have accumulated if they had saved a specified percentage of their income each year for each child. The CESA is designed to prevent a family's expected contribution from increasing as a result of saving conscientiously for college.

Low income families are provided additional asset protection. The Low Income Asset Allowance recognizes that a family with very low income needs additional asset protection because that family may need to draw on assets to cover basic living expenses.

In addition, the new formula allows parents' negative available income as a further allowance against assets. In cases where the parents' available income is negative, an increased amount of their assets should be protected from assessment, since they need to draw on assets to cover basic living expenses.

The IM includes other variables such as home equity, medical and dental expenses, and elementary and secondary school tuition. As with the FM calculation, following is a blank need analysis worksheet and the tables for 2000–2001, so that you can calculate your EFC using the IM. You'll find more blank worksheets in the Additional Forms and Worksheets section, and sample worksheets for each of the four students later in this step. These worksheets don't need to be submitted; they're just for your use. The tables will change for the 2000–2001 year, but using the need-analysis tables for 2000–2001 should give you a good estimate of your calculated EFC for the next year. Remember, your contribution for 2001–2002 will be based on your 2000 income and on your assets as of the day you complete the applications.

Instructions for Completing Your IM Worksheet

Fill in your AGI/taxable income in Line 1. Some colleges add to income any business losses claimed. If you claim business losses on your income tax, you may wish to calculate your IM EFC twice, once with business losses included, once with them added back in. Add any untaxed income/benefits from Line 2, any child support paid from Line 3, and place the total in Line 4. Fill in Lines 5–11 (allowances), referring to the IM Computation Tables that follow.

Total the allowances and subtract from the total income. Then complete Lines 17–22 to calculate the net worth. This figure may be a negative number. Subtract the asset protection allowance from the appropriate tables. Add the parents' contribution from income to the parent's contribution from assets to get the total parent's contribution.

The worksheet itself will explain which tables to use and the calculations that need to be made.

Sample Students' EFC Based on Institutional Methodology

Following the blank IM worksheet, you'll find completed IM worksheets for our four dependent sample students.

College Scholarship Service (CSS)

2000-2001 Institutional Methodology (IM Worksheet)

Computational Model **Parent(s) of dependent student**			
Student's name:			
INCOME OF PARENT(S)			
1.	AGI/taxable income		$
1a.	Add back losses from business, farm, etc., and capital losses		+
2.	Untaxed income and benefits		+
3.	Child support paid		-
4.	**Total parents' income (sum of lines 1, 1a, 2, minus 3)**		=
ALLOWANCES			
5.	U.S. income tax		
6.	State and other taxes (% from Table 1 X line 4)		+
7.	F.I.C.A. (Table 2)		+
8.	Medical/dental expense allowance (Table 2)		+
9.	Employment allowance (Table 2)		+
10.	Annual education savings allowance (AESA) (Table 4)		
a.	Annual savings goal (1.5% X line 4, up to $1,670)	=	
b.	Number of precollege children, excluding student	=	
c.	Total AESA (line 10a X 10b)		+
11.	Income protection allowance (Table A3a)		+
12.	Total allowances (sum of lines 5 - 11)		=
13.	Calculated available income (line 4 minus line 12)		=
14.	Total PC from income (calculate using line 13 and Table 5 - may not be negative)		=
15.	Number in college adjustment (Table 10)		x
16.	**Parents; contribution from income (line 14 X line 15)**		=
ASSETS			
17.	Cash, Savings, and checking accounts		
18.	Home equity		+
19.	Investment equity		+
20.	Other real estate equity		+
21.	Adjusted business/farm equity (Table 7)		+
22.	Assets in siblings' names		+
23.	Net worth (sum of lines 17 - 22)		=
24.	Asset protection allowances:		
a.	Emergency reserve allowance (Table 8):	=	
b.	Cumulative education savings allowance (CESA) (Table 4)	=	
c.	Low income asset allowance (amount from line 13, if negative)	=	
d.	Total asset allowances (sum of a + b + c)		-
25.	Discretionary net worth (line 23 minus line 24d - may not be negative)		=
26.	Total PC from assets (calculate using line 25 and Table 9)		=
27.	Number in college adjustment (Table 10)		x
28.	**Parents' contribution from assets (line 26 X line 27)**		=
CONTRIBUTION			
29.	**Parent contribution for student (sum of line 16 and line 28)**		=

College Scholarship Service (CSS)

2000-2001 Institutional Methodology (IM Worksheet)

Computational Model **Dependent Student**		
INCOME OF STUDENT (& SPOUSE)		
1.	AGI/taxable income	$
2.	Untaxed income/benefits	+
3.	Taxable student aid	-
4.	**Total Income (sum of lines 1 and 2, minus 3)**	=
ALLOWANCE		
5.	U.S. Income Tax	
6.	State and other taxes (% from Table 1 X line 1)	+
7.	F.I.C.A. (Table 2)	+
8.	Total allowances (sum of lines 5 - 7)	=
9.	Calculated available income (line 4 minus line 8)	=
10.	**SC from income (line 9 X 50%) or minimum student contribution (Table 11), whichever is greater**	=
ASSETS		
11.	Cash, savings, and checking accounts	
12.	Home equity	+
13.	Investment equity	+
14.	Other real estate equity	+
15.	Business/farm equity	+
16.	Trust value	+
17.	Net worth (sum of lines 11 - 16)	=
18.	**SC from assets (line 17 X .25)**	=
CONTRIBUTION		
19.	**Total contribution (sum of line 10 and line 18)**	=

2000–2001 CSS Institutional Methodology (IM) Computation Tables

2000-2001 CSS Institutional Methodology (IM) Computation Tables

TABLE 1. ALLOWANCES FOR STATE AND OTHER TAXES

State/Territory/Country of Residence	Parents of Dependent Students — Total Income: $0–30,000	30,001–40,000	40,001–50,000	50,001–60,000	60,001–70,000	70,001–80,000	80,001–or more	Students — Taxable Income: $0–20,000	20,001 or more
Alabama (AL)	9.0%	8.5%	8.0%	7.5%	7.0%	6.5%	6.5%	2.5%	3.0%
Alaska (AK)	4.5	4.0	3.5	3.0	2.5	2.0	2.0	0.0	0.0
American Samoa (AS)	4.5	4.0	3.5	3.0	2.5	2.0	2.0	0.0	0.0
Arizona (AZ)	8.0	7.5	7.0	7.0	7.0	6.5	6.5	0.5	1.0
Arkansas (AR)	9.0	8.5	8.0	8.0	8.0	8.0	8.0	1.5	2.0
California (CA)	8.C	8.0	7.5	7.5	8.0	8.0	8.0	0.5	1.0
Canada (CN)	4.5	4.0	3.5	3.0	2.5	2.0	2.0	4.0	5.0
Colorado (CO)	8.0	8.0	7.5	7.5	7.5	7.5	7.0	1.5	2.0
Connecticut (CT)	10.0	9.5	9.0	9.0	9.5	9.5	9.5	0.5	1.0
Delaware (DE)	6.0	6.0	6.0	6.0	6.5	7.0	7.0	2.5	3.0
District of Columbia (DC)	8.5	8.5	8.5	9.0	9.0	9.0	9.0	3.5	4.0
Federated States of Micronesia (FM)	4.5	4.0	3.5	3.0	2.5	2.0	2.0	0.0	0.0
Florida (FL)	7.5	7.0	6.5	6.0	5.5	5.0	4.5	0.0	0.0
Georgia (GA)	9.0	8.5	8.5	8.5	8.0	8.0	8.0	1.5	2.0
Guam (GU)	4.5	4.0	3.5	3.0	2.5	2.0	2.0	0.0	0.0
Hawaii (HI)	9.0	9.0	9.0	9.0	8.5	8.5	8.5	3.0	3.5
Idaho (ID)	8.5	8.5	8.5	8.5	8.5	8.5	8.5	1.0	1.5
Illinois (IL)	10.0	9.5	9.0	8.5	8.0	8.0	7.5	1.5	2.0
Indiana (IN)	9.5	9.0	8.5	8.0	7.5	7.5	7.5	2.5	3.0
Iowa (IA)	10.0	9.5	9.0	9.0	9.0	9.0	9.0	2.0	2.5
Kansas (KS)	9.0	8.5	8.5	8.5	8.5	8.0	8.0	1.5	2.0
Kentucky (KY)	9.5	9.5	9.5	9.5	9.5	9.5	9.5	3.0	3.5
Louisiana (LA)	9.0	8.5	8.0	7.5	7.0	7.0	6.5	1.0	1.5
Maine (ME)	9.0	9.0	9.0	9.5	9.5	9.5	9.5	1.0	1.5
Marshall Islands (MH)	4.5	4.0	3.5	3.0	2.5	2.0	2.0	0.0	0.0
Maryland (MD)	11.0	10.5	10.5	10.5	10.5	10.5	10.5	3.5	4.0
Massachusetts (MA)	10.5	10.0	9.5	9.5	9.5	9.5	9.5	3.0	3.5
Mexico (MX)	4.5	4.0	3.5	3.0	2.5	2.0	2.0	4.0	5.0
Michigan (MI)	11.0	10.5	10.0	9.5	9.0	9.0	8.5	2.5	3.0
Minnesota (MN)	9.0	9.0	9.0	9.0	9.0	9.0	9.0	1.5	2.0
Mississippi (MS)	8.0	8.0	8.0	8.0	8.0	7.5	7.0	0.5	1.0
Missouri (MO)	9.0	9.0	9.0	8.5	8.5	8.5	8.0	2.0	2.5
Montana (MT)	6.0	6.0	6.0	6.0	6.5	6.5	6.5	1.5	2.0
Nebraska (NE)	9.0	9.0	9.0	9.0	9.0	9.0	9.0	1.0	1.5
Nevada (NV)	6.0	5.5	5.0	4.5	4.0	3.5	3.5	0.0	0.0
New Hampshire (NH)	7.5	7.0	6.5	6.0	5.5	5.5	5.5	0.0	0.0
New Jersey (NJ)	12.0	11.5	11.0	10.5	10.0	9.5	9.0	1.0	1.5
New Mexico (NM)	9.0	9.0	8.5	8.5	8.0	8.0	8.0	0.5	1.0
New York (NY)	12.5	12.5	12.5	12.5	12.5	12.5	12.5	1.5	2.0
North Carolina (NC)	8.5	8.5	8.5	8.5	8.5	8.5	8.5	1.5	2.0
North Dakota (ND)	7.5	7.0	6.5	6.5	6.5	6.0	6.0	0.5	1.0
Northern Mariana Islands (MP)	4.5	4.0	3.5	3.0	2.5	2.0	2.0	0.0	0.0
Ohio (OH)	9.5	9.0	9.0	9.0	9.0	9.0	9.0	2.5	3.0
Oklahoma (OK)	8.5	8.5	8.5	8.5	8.0	8.0	8.0	1.0	1.5
Oregon (OR)	9.5	9.5	9.5	10.0	10.0	10.0	10.0	3.0	3.5
Palau (PW)	4.5	4.0	3.5	3.0	2.5	2.0	2.0	0.0	0.0
Pennsylvania (PA)	10.5	10.0	9.5	9.0	9.0	8.5	8.5	2.5	3.0
Puerto Rico (PR)	4.5	4.0	3.5	3.0	2.5	2.0	2.0	1.0	1.0
Rhode Island (RI)	10.5	10.0	9.5	9.5	9.5	9.5	9.5	1.0	1.5
South Carolina (SC)	6.5	6.5	7.0	7.5	7.5	7.5	7.5	0.5	1.0
South Dakota (SD)	7.5	7.0	6.5	6.0	5.5	5.0	5.0	0.0	0.0
Tennessee (TN)	7.5	7.0	6.5	6.0	5.5	5.0	4.5	0.0	0.0
Texas (TX)	7.5	7.0	6.5	6.0	5.5	5.5	5.0	0.0	0.0

TABLE 1., *continued*

State/Territory/Country of Residence	Parents of Dependent Students — Total Income: $0–30,000	30,001–40,000	40,001–50,000	50,001–60,000	60,001–70,000	70,001–80,000	80,001–or more	Students — Taxable Income: $0–20,000	20,001 or more
Utah (UT)	10.0%	10.0%	10.0%	9.5%	9.0%	9.0%	8.5%	1.5%	2.0%
Vermont (VT)	8.0	8.0	8.0	8.0	8.0	8.0	8.0	0.5	1.0
Virgin Islands (VI)	4.5	4.0	3.5	3.0	2.5	2.0	2.0	0.0	0.0
Virginia (VA)	8.0	8.0	8.0	8.0	8.0	8.0	8.0	2.0	2.5
Washington (WA)	10.0	9.5	9.0	8.5	8.0	7.5	7.0	0.0	0.0
West Virginia (WV)	8.0	7.5	7.5	7.5	7.5	7.5	7.5	2.0	2.5
Wisconsin (WI)	11.5	11.5	11.5	11.5	11.5	11.0	10.5	1.5	2.0
Wyoming (WY)	5.5	5.0	4.5	4.0	4.0	3.5	3.0	0.0	0.0
Not Reported (NR)	9.5	9.0	8.5	8.5	8.0	8.0	8.0	1.5	2.0

TABLE 2. ALLOWANCES AGAINST INCOME

FICA: *Wages*	
$1 to $72,600	7.65% of income earned by each wage earner (maximum $5,553.90 per person)
$72,601 or more	$5,553.90 + 1.45% of income earned above $72,600 by each wage earner
Elementary/secondary tuition allowance	Reported tuition paid to maximum $8,390 per eligible child
Employment allowance	32% of lesser earned income to maximum $2,880 (single parent: 32% of earned income to maximum of $2,880)
Medical/dental expense allowance	Unreimbursed expenses in excess of 4% of total income

TABLE 3a. INCOME PROTECTION ALLOWANCE (IPA)
(Parents of Dependent Students)

Family Size (including student)*	*Number in College***: *1*	*2*	*3*	*4*	*5*
2	$ 12,660	$ 11,760			
3	15,110	14,210	$ 13,310		
4	18,890	17,990	17,090	$ 16,190	
5	22,670	21,770	20,870	19,970	$ 19,070
6	26,260	25,360	24,460	23,560	22,660

** For each additional family member, add $3,400.*
***For each additional college student, subtract $900.*

2000-2001 CSS Institutional Methodology (IM) Computation Tables

TABLE 3b. MONTHLY MAINTENANCE ALLOWANCE
(Independent Students)

Single Student	$1,330 per month during period of nonenrollment
Married Student	$820 per month during period of nonenrollment (calculated for student and spouse)
Children of Independent Students	$410 per month during period of nonenrollment for each child

TABLE 4. EDUCATION SAVINGS ALLOWANCES

Annual Savings Goal (ASG) =
1.5% of Total Income, to a maximum of $1,670

Annual Education Savings Allowance (AESA) =
ASG × number of pre-college children, excluding the student applicant

Cumulative Education Savings Allowance (CESA) =
[(Number of college students × ASG × 18 × .625) + (ASG × total ages of pre-college children)]

OR

$13,840, whichever is greater

TABLE 5. CONTRIBUTION FROM AVAILABLE INCOME (AI)
(Parents of Dependent Students)

Available Income (AI)	*Total Contribution from Income*
Less than $ 10,700	22% of AI
$ 10,701 to 15,970	$ 2,354 + 26% of AI over $ 10,700
$ 15,971 to 19,970	$ 3,724 + 30% of AI over $ 15,970
$ 19,971 to 23,960	$ 4,924 + 34% of AI over $ 19,970
$ 23,961 to 27,960	$ 6,281 + 38% of AI over $ 23,960
$ 27,961 to 31,950	$ 7,801 + 42% of AI over $ 27,960
$ 31,951 or more	$ 9,477 + 46% of AI over $ 31,950

TABLE 6. STUDENT INCOME ASSESSMENT RATES

Dependent Students	50 % of Available Income (AI)
Independent Students	70 % of Available Income (AI)

TABLE 7. ADJUSTED NET WORTH OF A BUSINESS OR FARM

Net Worth (NW)	*Adjusted Net Worth*
Less than $1	$ 0
$ 1 to 90,000	$ 0 + 40% of NW
$ 90,001 to 265,000	$ 36,000 + 50% of NW over $ 90,000
$265,001 to 445,000	$123,500 + 60% of NW over $ 265,000
$445,001 or more	$231,500 + 100% of NW over $ 445,000

TABLE 8. EMERGENCY RESERVE ALLOWANCE (ERA)

Parents of Dependents and Independent Students with Dependents:

Family Size	*ERA*
2	$ 9,900
3	11,820
4	14,770
5	17,720
6	20,530
Each additional family member	+ 2,810

Single Independent Students without Dependents:	$ 1,330
Married Independent Students without Dependents:	$ 1,640

TABLE 9. ASSET CONVERSION RATE

Parents of Dependent Students:

Discretionary Net Worth	*Total Contribution From Assets*
Up to $ 25,000	3%
25,001 to 50,000	$ 750 + 4% of DNW over $ 25,000
50,001 or more	$ 1,750 + 5% of DNW over $ 50,000

All Students:

Asset conversion rate is 25% of discretionary net worth.

TABLE 10. NUMBER IN COLLEGE ADJUSTMENT

Number of Children in College	*Adjustment Rate*
1	100 % of PC
2	60 %
3	45 %
4 or more	35 %

For independent students, the adjustment rate is determined by the total number in college, including the student, spouse, and dependent children.

TABLE 11. STUDENT'S MINIMUM STANDARD CONTRIBUTION

$1,150	Freshman: Dependent/Independent with Dependents
1,400	All Other Students: Dependent/Independent with Dependents
1,900	Independent Students with NO Dependents

College Scholarship Service (CSS)

2000-2001 Institutional Methodology (IM Worksheet)

Computational Model					
Parent(s) of dependent student					
Student's name:	Frances Liu				
INCOME OF PARENT(S)					
1.	AGI/taxable income			$	56,300
1a.	Add back losses from business, farm, etc., and capital losses			+	0
2.	Untaxed income and benefits			+	0
3.	Child support paid			-	0
4.	**Total parents' income (sum of lines 1, 1a, 2, minus 3)**			=	56,300
ALLOWANCES					
5.	U.S. income tax				5,250
6.	State and other taxes (% from Table 1 X line 4)			+	7,038
7.	F.I.C.A. (Table 2)			+	4,284
8.	Medical/dental expense allowance (Table 2)			+	0
9.	Employment allowance (Table 2)			+	2,880
10.	Annual education savings allowance (AESA) (Table 4)				
a.	Annual savings goal (1.5% X line 4, up to $1,670)	=	845		
b.	Number of precollege children, excluding student	=	2		
c.	Total AESA (line 10a X 10b)			+	1,690
11.	Income protection allowance (Table A3a)			+	22,670
12.	Total allowances (sum of lines 5 - 11)			=	43,812
13.	Calculated available income (line 4 minus line 12)			=	12,488
14.	Total PC from income (calculate using line 13 and Table 5 - may not be negative)			=	2,819
15.	Number in college adjustment (Table 10)			x	100%
16.	**Parents; contribution from income (line 14 X line 15)**			=	2,819
ASSETS					
17.	Cash, Savings, and checking accounts				5,000
18.	Home equity			+	40,000
19.	Investment equity			+	0
20.	Other real estate equity			+	0
21.	Adjusted business/farm equity (Table 7)			+	91,000
22.	Assets in siblings' names			+	0
23.	Net worth (sum of lines 17 - 22)			=	136,000
24.	Asset protection allowances:				
a.	Emergency reserve allowance (Table 8):	=	17,720		
b.	Cumulative education savings allowance (CESA) (Table 4)	=	30,631		
c.	Low income asset allowance (amount from line 13, if negative)	=	0		
d.	Total asset allowances (sum of a + b + c)			-	48,351
25.	Discretionary net worth (line 23 minus line 24d - may not be negative)			=	87,649
26.	Total PC from assets (calculate using line 25 and Table 9)			=	3,632
27.	Number in college adjustment (Table 10)			x	1
28.	**Parents' contribution from assets (line 26 X line 27)**			=	3,632
CONTRIBUTION					
29.	**Parent contribution for student (sum of line 16 and line 28)**			=	6,451

SAMPLE IM WORKSHEETS FOR FRANCES

College Scholarship Service (CSS)

2000-2001 Institutional Methodology (IM Worksheet)

Computational Model Dependent Student			
INCOME OF STUDENT (& SPOUSE)			
1.	AGI/taxable income	$	0
2.	Untaxed income/benefits	+	0
3.	Taxable student aid	-	0
4.	**Total Income (sum of lines 1 and 2, minus 3)**	=	2,100
ALLOWANCE			
5.	U.S. Income Tax		0
6.	State and other taxes (% from Table 1 X line 1)	+	32
7.	F.I.C.A. (Table 2)	+	161
8.	Total allowances (sum of lines 5 - 7)	=	193
9.	Calculated available income (line 4 minus line 8)	=	1,907
10.	**SC from income (line 9 X 50%) or minimum student contribution (Table 11), whichever is greater**	=	1,150
ASSETS			
11.	Cash, savings, and checking accounts		1,200
12.	Home equity	+	0
13.	Investment equity	+	0
14.	Other real estate equity	+	0
15.	Business/farm equity	+	0
16.	Trust value	+	0
17.	Net worth (sum of lines 11 - 16)	=	1,200
18.	**SC from assets (line 17 X .25)**	=	300
CONTRIBUTION			
19.	**Total contribution (sum of line 10 and line 18)**	=	1450

"My parents own a great restaurant, but they work twelve to fourteen hours almost every day. I wanted to work more in the restaurant last year to help them out and to earn more money for college. But my parents insisted I spend as much time as I could on my studies. So, I'd stay home to study and take care of the younger kids while my parents were working."

The IM contribution for Frances's parents is $1,750 more than the FM contribution ($6,451 versus $4,701), due mostly to the additional assets of $40,000 in home equity. This increase is also due to the fact that IM tables use higher state tax allowances than the FM tables (the IM New York state tax allowance is 12.5 percent, whereas the FM allowance is 10 percent) and all assets are treated differently than in FM. Another difference in the family contribution results from the minimum contribution from income of $1,050 expected from Frances. With these two main differences, the outcome of the IM is $7,901 versus the FM result of $5,121, a difference of $2,780.

SAMPLE IM WORKSHEETS FOR ANGELA

College Scholarship Service (CSS)

2000-2001 Institutional Methodology (IM Worksheet)

Computational Model					
Parent(s) of dependent student					
Student's name:	Angela Martin				
INCOME OF PARENT(S)					
1.	AGI/taxable income			$	48,400
1a.	Add back losses from business, farm, etc., and capital losses			+	0
2.	Untaxed income and benefits			+	0
3.	Child support paid			-	0
4.	**Total parents' income (sum of lines 1, 1a, 2, minus 3)**			=	48,400
ALLOWANCES					
5.	U.S. income tax				4,232
6.	State and other taxes (% from Table 1 X line 4)			+	3,630
7.	F.I.C.A. (Table 2)			+	3,703
8.	Medical/dental expense allowance (Table 2)			+	1,064
9.	Employment allowance (Table 2)			+	2,880
10.	Annual education savings allowance (AESA) (Table 4)				
a.	Annual savings goal (1.5% X line 4, up to $1,670)	=	726		
b.	Number of precollege children, excluding student	=	1		
c.	Total AESA (line 10a X 10b)			+	726
11.	Income protection allowance (Table A3a)			+	15,110
12.	Total allowances (sum of lines 5 - 11)			=	31,345
13.	Calculated available income (line 4 minus line 12)			=	17,055
14.	Total PC from income (calculate using line 13 and Table 5 - may not be negative)			=	4,050
15.	Number in college adjustment (Table 10)			x	100%
16.	**Parents; contribution from income (line 14 X line 15)**			=	4,050
ASSETS					
17.	Cash, Savings, and checking accounts				3,000
18.	Home equity			+	45,000
19.	Investment equity			+	4,000
20.	Other real estate equity			+	0
21.	Adjusted business/farm equity (Table 7)			+	0
22.	Assets in siblings' names			+	0
23.	Net worth (sum of lines 17 - 22)			=	52,000
24.	Asset protection allowances:				
a.	Emergency reserve allowance (Table 8):	=	11,820		
b.	Cumulative education savings allowance (CESA) (Table 4)	=	18,332		
c.	Low income asset allowance (amount from line 13, if negative)	=	0		
d.	Total asset allowances (sum of a + b + c)			-	30,152
25.	Discretionary net worth (line 23 minus line 24d - may not be negative)			=	21,849
26.	Total PC from assets (calculate using line 25 and Table 9)			=	655
27.	Number in college adjustment (Table 10)			x	1
28.	**Parents' contribution from assets (line 26 X line 27)**			=	655
CONTRIBUTION					
29.	**Parent contribution for student (sum of line 16 and line 28)**			=	4,705

College Scholarship Service (CSS)

2000-2001 Institutional Methodology (IM Worksheet)

Computational Model **Dependent Student**			
INCOME OF STUDENT (& SPOUSE)			
1.	AGI/taxable income	$	0
2.	Untaxed income/benefits	+	0
3.	Taxable student aid	-	0
4.	**Total Income (sum of lines 1 and 2, minus 3)**	=	2,700
ALLOWANCE			
5.	U.S. Income Tax		0
6.	State and other taxes (% from Table 1 X line 1)	+	14
7.	F.I.C.A. (Table 2)	+	207
8.	Total allowances (sum of lines 5 - 7)	=	221
9.	Calculated available income (line 4 minus line 8)	=	2,479
10.	**SC from income (line 9 X 50%) or minimum student contribution (Table 11), whichever is greater**	=	1,240
ASSETS			
11.	Cash, savings, and checking accounts		1,100
12.	Home equity	+	0
13.	Investment equity	+	0
14.	Other real estate equity	+	0
15.	Business/farm equity	+	0
16.	Trust value	+	0
17.	Net worth (sum of lines 11 - 16)	=	1,100
18.	**SC from assets (line 17 X .25)**	=	275
CONTRIBUTION			
19.	**Total contribution (sum of line 10 and line 18)**	=	1515

The difference in parents' contribution from FM to IM is only $54 and results from Angela's family's home equity. If Angela's mother didn't already have two mortgages on the house, and her income were high enough to qualify for a loan, she would be able to borrow against this equity. A renter in a comparable situation wouldn't have this option, and this is one of the key differences between the two methodologies. Angela's contribution through the IM is more than $1,000 higher, since more of her earned income is considered available for school. The IM family contribution is calculated to be $6,220 compared to a total family contribution from FM of $5,115. The resulting $1,105 difference will be difficult for this family to handle.

SAMPLE IM WORKSHEETS FOR JAMES

College Scholarship Service (CSS)

2000-2001 Institutional Methodology (IM Worksheet)

Computational Model **Parent(s) of dependent student**				
Student's name: James Garwood				
INCOME OF PARENT(S)				
1.	AGI/taxable income		$	119,800
1a.	Add back losses from business, farm, etc., and capital losses		+	0
2.	Untaxed income and benefits		+	9,000
3.	Child support paid		-	0
4.	**Total parents' income (sum of lines 1, 1a, 2, minus 3)**		=	128,800
ALLOWANCES				
5.	U.S. income tax			18,200
6.	State and other taxes (% from Table 1 X line 4)		+	10,304
7.	F.I.C.A. (Table 2)		+	6,676
8.	Medical/dental expense allowance (Table 2)		+	0
9.	Employment allowance (Table 2)		+	0
10.	Annual education savings allowance (AESA) (Table 4)			
a.	Annual savings goal (1.5% X line 4, up to $1,670)	= 1670		
b.	Number of precollege children, excluding student	= 2		
c.	Total AESA (line 10a X 10b)		+	3,340
11.	Income protection allowance (Table A3a)		+	25,360
12.	Total allowances (sum of lines 5 - 11)		=	63,880
13.	Calculated available income (line 4 minus line 12)		=	64,920
14.	Total PC from income (calculate using line 13 and Table 5 - may not be negative)		=	24,643
15.	Number in college adjustment (Table 10)		x	60%
16.	**Parents; contribution from income (line 14 X line 15)**		=	14,786
ASSETS				
17.	Cash, Savings, and checking accounts			20,000
18.	Home equity		+	100,000
19.	Investment equity		+	0
20.	Other real estate equity		+	120,000
21.	Adjusted business/farm equity (Table 7)		+	0
22.	Assets in siblings' names		+	0
23.	Net worth (sum of lines 17 - 22)		=	240,000
24.	Asset protection allowances:			
a.	Emergency reserve allowance (Table 8):	= 20,530		
b.	Cumulative education savings allowance (CESA) (Table 4)	= 79,325		
c.	Low income asset allowance (amount from line 13, if negative)	= 0		
d.	Total asset allowances (sum of a + b + c)		-	99,855
25.	Discretionary net worth (line 23 minus line 24d - may not be negative)		=	140,145
26.	Total PC from assets (calculate using line 25 and Table 9)		=	6,257
27.	Number in college adjustment (Table 10)		x	1
28.	**Parents' contribution from assets (line 26 X line 27)**		=	3,754
CONTRIBUTION				
29.	**Parent contribution for student (sum of line 16 and line 28)**		=	18,540

SAMPLE IM WORKSHEETS FOR JAMES

The calculated IM contribution for James's parents is $18,540 almost $1,900 more than the FM, primarily because of the $100,000 in home equity. Some colleges may disallow the deduction his parents took off their adjusted gross income (for investment real estate depreciation) and/or subtract from the available income the deduction of $5,700 for private school tuition (for James's youngest brother). If a college includes the private school tuition, the parents' IM contribution is reduced to $16,967.

College Scholarship Service (CSS)

2000-2001 Institutional Methodology (IM Worksheet)

Computational Model				
Parent(s) of dependent student				
Student's name:	James Garwood			
INCOME OF PARENT(S)				
1.	AGI/taxable income		$	119,800
1a.	Add back losses from business, farm, etc., and capital losses		+	0
2.	Untaxed income and benefits		+	9,000
3.	Child support paid		-	0
4.	**Total parents' income (sum of lines 1, 1a, 2, minus 3)**		=	128,800
ALLOWANCES				
5.	U.S. income tax			18,200
6.	State and other taxes (% from Table 1 X line 4)		+	10,304
7.	F.I.C.A. (Table 2)		+	6,676
8.	Medical/dental expense allowance (Table 2)		+	0
9.	Employment allowance (Table 2)		+	0
10.	Annual education savings allowance (AESA) (Table 4)			
a.	Annual savings goal (1.5% X line 4, up to $1,670)	= 1670		
b.	Number of precollege children, excluding student	= 2		
c.	Total AESA (line 10a X 10b)		+	3,340
11.	Income protection allowance (Table A3a)		+	25,360
12.	Total allowances (sum of lines 5 - 11)		=	69,580
13.	Calculated available income (line 4 minus line 12)		=	59,220
14.	Total PC from income (calculate using line 13 and Table 5 - may not be negative)		=	22,021
15.	Number in college adjustment (Table 10)		x	60%
16.	**Parents; contribution from income (line 14 X line 15)**		=	13,213
ASSETS				
17.	Cash, Savings, and checking accounts			20,000
18.	Home equity		+	100,000
19.	Investment equity		+	0
20.	Other real estate equity		+	120,000
21.	Adjusted business/farm equity (Table 7)		+	0
22.	Assets in siblings' names		+	0
23.	Net worth (sum of lines 17 - 22)		=	240,000
24.	Asset protection allowances:			
a.	Emergency reserve allowance (Table 8):	= 20,530		
b.	Cumulative education savings allowance (CESA) (Table 4)	= 79,325		
c.	Low income asset allowance (amount from line 13, if negative)	= 0		
d.	Total asset allowances (sum of a + b + c)		-	99,855
25.	Discretionary net worth (line 23 minus line 24d - may not be negative)		=	140,145
26.	Total PC from assets (calculate using line 25 and Table 9)		=	6,257
27.	Number in college adjustment (Table 10)		x	1
28.	**Parents' contribution from assets (line 26 X line 27)**		=	3,754
CONTRIBUTION				
29.	**Parent contribution for student (sum of line 16 and line 28)**		=	16,967

In addition, James will have to provide a minimum contribution from income even though he has not worked. The IM formula has a minimum contribution for income for freshmen of $1,150. This is added to James's $1,000 contribution from his assets to give him a total contribution of $2,150

College Scholarship Service (CSS)

2000-2001 Institutional Methodology (IM Worksheet)

Computational Model			
Dependent Student			
INCOME OF STUDENT (& SPOUSE)			
1.	AGI/taxable income	$	0
2.	Untaxed income/benefits	+	0
3.	Taxable student aid	-	0
4.	**Total Income (sum of lines 1 and 2, minus 3)**	=	0
ALLOWANCE			
5.	U.S. Income Tax		0
6.	State and other taxes (% from Table 1 X line 1)	+	0
7.	F.I.C.A. (Table 2)	+	0
8.	Total allowances (sum of lines 5 - 7)	=	0
9.	Calculated available income (line 4 minus line 8)	=	0
10.	**SC from income (line 9 X 50%) or minimum student contribution (Table 11), whichever is greater**	=	1,150
ASSETS			
11.	Cash, savings, and checking accounts		0
12.	Home equity	+	4000
13.	Investment equity	+	0
14.	Other real estate equity	+	0
15.	Business/farm equity	+	0
16.	Trust value	+	0
17.	Net worth (sum of lines 11 - 16)	=	4,000
18.	**SC from assets (line 17 X .25)**	=	1000
CONTRIBUTION			
19.	**Total contribution (sum of line 10 and line 18)**	=	2150

SAMPLE IM WORKSHEETS FOR DAVID

College Scholarship Service (CSS)

2000-2001 Institutional Methodology (IM Worksheet)

Computational Model					
Parent(s) of dependent student					
Student's name:	David Barnes				
INCOME OF PARENT(S)					
1.	AGI/taxable income			$	39,200
1a.	Add back losses from business, farm, etc., and capital losses			+	0
2.	Untaxed income and benefits			+	14,400
3.	Child support paid			-	0
4.	**Total parents' income (sum of lines 1, 1a, 2, minus 3)**			=	53,600
ALLOWANCES					
5.	U.S. income tax				3,889
6.	State and other taxes (% from Table 1 X line 4)			+	3,216
7.	F.I.C.A. (Table 2)			+	2,953
8.	Medical/dental expense allowance (Table 2)			+	0
9.	Employment allowance (Table 2)			+	2,880
10.	Annual education savings allowance (AESA) (Table 4)				
a.	Annual savings goal (1.5% X line 4, up to $1,670)	=	804		
b.	Number of precollege children, excluding student	=	1		
c.	Total AESA (line 10a X 10b)			+	804
11.	Income protection allowance (Table A3a)			+	15,110
12.	Total allowances (sum of lines 5 - 11)			=	28,852
13.	Calculated available income (line 4 minus line 12)			=	24,748
14.	Total PC from income (calculate using line 13 and Table 5 - may not be negative)			=	6,580
15.	Number in college adjustment (Table 10)			x	100%
16.	**Parents; contribution from income (line 14 X line 15)**			=	6,580
ASSETS					
17.	Cash, Savings, and checking accounts				8,000
18.	Home equity			+	33,000
19.	Investment equity			+	0
20.	Other real estate equity			+	0
21.	Adjusted business/farm equity (Table 7)			+	0
22.	Assets in siblings' names			+	0
23.	Net worth (sum of lines 17 - 22)			=	41,000
24.	Asset protection allowances:				
a.	Emergency reserve allowance (Table 8):	=	11,820		
b.	Cumulative education savings allowance (CESA) (Table 4)	=	19,497		
c.	Low income asset allowance (amount from line 13, if negative)	=	0		
d.	Total asset allowances (sum of a + b + c)			-	31,317
25.	Discretionary net worth (line 23 minus line 24d - may not be negative)			=	9,683
26.	Total PC from assets (calculate using line 25 and Table 9)			=	290
27.	Number in college adjustment (Table 10)			x	1
28.	**Parents' contribution from assets (line 26 X line 27)**			=	290
CONTRIBUTION					
29.	**Parent contribution for student (sum of line 16 and line 28)**			=	6,870

David's situation is complex. The IM parent contribution depends on how a college treats the child support payments and the noncustodial parent's income. The calculated parent's IM contribution is $6,870, and includes the child support. If that support is subtracted, the IM contribution drops to $4,659, as you see below.

College Scholarship Service (CSS)

2000-2001 Institutional Methodology (IM Worksheet)

Computational Model					
Parent(s) of dependent student					
Student's name:	David Barnes				
INCOME OF PARENT(S)					
1.	AGI/taxable income			$	39,200
1a.	Add back losses from business, farm, etc., and capital losses			+	0
2.	Untaxed income and benefits			+	7,200
3.	Child support paid			-	0
4.	**Total parents' income (sum of lines 1, 1a, 2, minus 3)**			=	46,400
ALLOWANCES					
5.	U.S. income tax				3,889
6.	State and other taxes (% from Table 1 X line 4)			+	3,016
7.	F.I.C.A. (Table 2)			+	2,953
8.	Medical/dental expense allowance (Table 2)			+	0
9.	Employment allowance (Table 2)			+	2,880
10.	Annual education savings allowance (AESA) (Table 4)				
a.	Annual savings goal (1.5% X line 4, up to $1,670)	=	696		
b.	Number of precollege children, excluding student	=	1		
c.	Total AESA (line 10a X 10b)			+	696
11.	Income protection allowance (Table A3a)			+	15,110
12.	Total allowances (sum of lines 5 - 11)			=	28,544
13.	Calculated available income (line 4 minus line 12)			=	17,856
14.	Total PC from income (calculate using line 13 and Table 5 - may not be negative)			=	4,290
15.	Number in college adjustment (Table 10)			x	100%
16.	**Parents; contribution from income (line 14 X line 15)**			=	4,290
ASSETS					
17.	Cash, Savings, and checking accounts				8,000
18.	Home equity			+	33,000
19.	Investment equity			+	0
20.	Other real estate equity			+	0
21.	Adjusted business/farm equity (Table 7)			+	0
22.	Assets in siblings' names			+	0
23.	Net worth (sum of lines 17 - 22)			=	41,000
24.	Asset protection allowances:				
a.	Emergency reserve allowance (Table 8):	=	11,820		
b.	Cumulative education savings allowance (CESA) (Table 4)	=	16,878		
c.	Low income asset allowance (amount from line 13, if negative)	=	0		
d.	Total asset allowances (sum of a + b + c)			-	28,698
25.	Discretionary net worth (line 23 minus line 24d - may not be negative)			=	12,302
26.	Total PC from assets (calculate using line 25 and Table 9)			=	369
27.	Number in college adjustment (Table 10)			x	1
28.	**Parents' contribution from assets (line 26 X line 27)**			=	369
CONTRIBUTION					
29.	**Parent contribution for student (sum of line 16 and line 28)**			=	4,659

Some colleges may expect David's noncustodial father to continue to contribute the $7,200 or a calculated contribution based on his income and assets (in this case, David's father earns $59,000 and his IM contribution is $2.959). See the worksheet below. If the $14,400 child support payment is reduced to $7,200 (since David is in college), David's father's IM contribution is increased to $4,906.

College Scholarship Service (CSS)

2000-2001 Institutional Methodology (IM Worksheet)

Computational Model					
Parent(s) of dependent student					
Student's name:	David Barnes				
INCOME OF PARENT(S)					
1.	AGI/taxable income			$	59,000
1a.	Add back losses from business, farm, etc., and capital losses			+	0
2.	Untaxed income and benefits			+	0
3.	Child support paid			-	14,400
4.	**Total parents' income (sum of lines 1, 1a, 2, minus 3)**			=	44,600
ALLOWANCES					
5.	U.S. income tax				5,500
6.	State and other taxes (% from Table 1 X line 4)			+	2,899
7.	F.I.C.A. (Table 2)			+	4,514
8.	Medical/dental expense allowance (Table 2)			+	0
9.	Employment allowance (Table 2)			+	2,880
10.	Annual education savings allowance (AESA) (Table 4)				
a.	Annual savings goal (1.5% X line 4, up to $1,670)	=	669		
b.	Number of precollege children, excluding student	=	1		
c.	Total AESA (line 10a X 10b)			+	669
11.	Income protection allowance (Table A3a)			+	15,110
12.	Total allowances (sum of lines 5 - 11)			=	31,572
13.	Calculated available income (line 4 minus line 12)			=	13,028
14.	Total PC from income (calculate using line 13 and Table 5 - may not be negative)			=	2,959
15.	Number in college adjustment (Table 10)			x	100%
16.	**Parents; contribution from income (line 14 X line 15)**			=	2,959
ASSETS					
17.	Cash, Savings, and checking accounts				10,000
18.	Home equity			+	15,000
19.	Investment equity			+	0
20.	Other real estate equity			+	0
21.	Adjusted business/farm equity (Table 7)			+	0
22.	Assets in siblings' names			+	0
23.	Net worth (sum of lines 17 - 22)			=	25,000
24.	Asset protection allowances:				
a.	Emergency reserve allowance (Table 8):	=	11,820		
b.	Cumulative education savings allowance (CESA) (Table 4)	=	16,223		
c.	Low income asset allowance (amount from line 13, if negative)	=	0		
d.	Total asset allowances (sum of a + b + c)			-	28,043
25.	Discretionary net worth (line 23 minus line 24d - may not be negative)			=	0
26.	Total PC from assets (calculate using line 25 and Table 9)			=	0
27.	Number in college adjustment (Table 10)			x	1
28.	**Parents' contribution from assets (line 26 X line 27)**			=	0
CONTRIBUTION					
29.	**Parent contribution for student (sum of line 16 and line 28)**			=	2,959

College Scholarship Service (CSS)

2000-2001 Institutional Methodology (IM Worksheet)

Computational Model **Parent(s) of dependent student**				
Student's name: David Barnes				
INCOME OF PARENT(S)				
1.	AGI/taxable income		$	59,000
1a.	Add back losses from business, farm, etc., and capital losses		+	0
2.	Untaxed income and benefits		+	0
3.	Child support paid		-	7,200
4.	**Total parents' income (sum of lines 1, 1a, 2, minus 3)**		=	51,800
ALLOWANCES				
5.	U.S. income tax			5,500
6.	State and other taxes (% from Table 1 X line 4)		+	3,108
7.	F.I.C.A. (Table 2)		+	4,514
8.	Medical/dental expense allowance (Table 2)		+	0
9.	Employment allowance (Table 2)		+	2,880
10.	Annual education savings allowance (AESA) (Table 4)			
a.	Annual savings goal (1.5% X line 4, up to $1,670)	= 777		
b.	Number of precollege children, excluding student	= 1		
c.	Total AESA (line 10a X 10b)		+	777
11.	Income protection allowance (Table A3a)		+	15,110
12.	Total allowances (sum of lines 5 - 11)		=	31,889
13.	Calculated available income (line 4 minus line 12)		=	19,911
14.	Total PC from income (calculate using line 13 and Table 5 - may not be negative)		=	4,906
15.	Number in college adjustment (Table 10)		x	100%
16.	**Parents; contribution from income (line 14 X line 15)**		=	4,906
ASSETS				
17.	Cash, Savings, and checking accounts			10,000
18.	Home equity		+	15,000
19.	Investment equity		+	0
20.	Other real estate equity		+	0
21.	Adjusted business/farm equity (Table 7)		+	0
22.	Assets in siblings' names		+	0
23.	Net worth (sum of lines 17 - 22)		=	25,000
24.	Asset protection allowances:			
a.	Emergency reserve allowance (Table 8):	= 11,820		
b.	Cumulative education savings allowance (CESA) (Table 4)	= 18,842		
c.	Low income asset allowance (amount from line 13, if negative)	= 0		
d.	Total asset allowances (sum of a + b + c)		-	30,662
25.	Discretionary net worth (line 23 minus line 24d - may not be negative)		=	0
26.	Total PC from assets (calculate using line 25 and Table 9)		=	0
27.	Number in college adjustment (Table 10)		x	1
28.	**Parents' contribution from assets (line 26 X line 27)**		=	0
CONTRIBUTION				
29.	**Parent contribution for student (sum of line 16 and line 28)**		=	4,906

Whatever the college does with this case, David's mother can talk to the financial aid officer about her situation. She should make sure that the college understands that David's support from his father has stopped and that her income appears substantially higher than it actually is. A situation like this is not unusual; financial aid officers often make adjustments

College Scholarship Service (CSS)

2000-2001 Institutional Methodology (IM Worksheet)

Computational Model Dependent Student			
INCOME OF STUDENT (& SPOUSE)			
1.	AGI/taxable income	$	0
2.	Untaxed income/benefits	+	0
3.	Taxable student aid	-	0
4.	**Total Income (sum of lines 1 and 2, minus 3)**	=	2,520
ALLOWANCE			
5.	U.S. Income Tax		0
6.	State and other taxes (% from Table 1 X line 1)	+	0
7.	F.I.C.A. (Table 2)	+	193
8.	Total allowances (sum of lines 5 - 7)	=	193
9.	Calculated available income (line 4 minus line 8)	=	2,327
10.	**SC from income (line 9 X 50%) or minimum student contribution (Table 11), whichever is greater**	=	1,164
ASSETS			
11.	Cash, savings, and checking accounts		2,400
12.	Home equity	+	0
13.	Investment equity	+	0
14.	Other real estate equity	+	0
15.	Business/farm equity	+	0
16.	Trust value	+	0
17.	Net worth (sum of lines 11 - 16)	=	2,400
18.	**SC from assets (line 17 X .25)**	=	600
CONTRIBUTION			
19.	**Total contribution (sum of line 10 and line 18)**	=	1764

to deal with cases like this. David's mother just needs to make sure that someone carefully looks at David's application so that appropriate steps can be taken before the college has no funding left for the academic year.

David's mother also needs to talk to David's father to tell him that the college that David decides to attend might ask him for a contribution even though his legal responsibility ended when David turned 18. Sometimes the college will ask for a copy of the divorce decree to verify that there is nothing in it dealing with Dabid's college expenses. Discussing this possibility before it occurs will make David's application process go more smoothly.

COLLEGE FINANCIAL AID AND YOUR EFC

Now that you see how your EFC is calculated, and you have a fair estimate of what your EFC will be, how is this number used by colleges?

This EFC information in the report and/or acknowledgment letters is also sent to the colleges that you selected on your applications. Schools use your EFC to figure out how much financial aid they'll award, and from what sources. In other words, they use it to put together your financial aid package. We'll cover financial aid packages in-depth in the next step.

Since each school's total cost is different, a family's need for aid will be different at each school. The EFC derived from your application is supposed to remain the same regardless of which school the student will be attending. In practice, however, the EFC does, in fact, differ quite significantly from school to school.

As we've seen with our sample students, college financial aid administrators are permitted to change any of the elements that go into either methodology. They'll do so in individual cases based on their professional judgment or additional information. While this permission is written into the law, in practice many financial aid administrators shy away from making too many changes. Nevertheless, if there are extenuating circumstances that you believe warrant a change, you should write or call the financial aid office at each college and make your appeal.

Many financial aid offices have set up elaborate appeals committees and processes. Your appeal should include documentation as well as a clear explanation. Often, when an exception is made, the student is awarded additional loan money, not grant money, to meet the additional need.

There is no provision on the FAFSA to indicate any special or extenuating circumstances that would warrant a change in either the need analysis or the student budget. Therefore, you have to notify the college directly. On the PROFILE, however, there is a small section in which you can explain special circumstances.

PLEASE, SIR, MAY I HAVE SOME MORE?

Successful appeals are usually based on such things as high medical or dental expenses, educational and other debts, child care, elder care, or special circumstances.

A Student Example

David's situation is a classic example in which a successful appeal could be made. The need analysis was based on the family's previous year's income, which included child support payments for David. However, those payments will end in July, when David turns eighteen. This means that David's mother will receive only about half the annual child support income for David. The financial aid administrator may decide to recalculate the FM family contribution using the lower amount if the family appeals the calculated contribution. They'll probably want to keep a file copy of the divorce agreement that spells out David's father's obligation, so that this professional judgment can be justified to an auditor.

The More They Want You, the More You Get

It's no great secret that the more a college wants your child to attend, the more willing they are to do what they can for you. This is particularly true for private colleges, which compete for students more than publicly supported colleges do. With some justification, colleges will alter elements of the need analysis or make an adjustment in the student budget so that there is greater eligibility for aid. And, again, the more attractive the student, the more willing the school is to bend the rules. It's not always the case that more grant assistance is offered, especially later in the cycle when most of the aid has been promised already. Often, when adjustments are made, students are permitted to borrow or work more.

WHAT'S NEXT

In the next step, we'll go into greater detail about what colleges do with your EFC and about the different ways colleges award financial aid to students. Then we'll analyze the awards for our students and give you tips to compare and negotiate your awards.

COMPARE AND NEGOTIATE AID PACKAGES

Aid Awards for Sample Dependent Students

Step 7

Colleges use your family contribution, based on either the FM or the IM, to figure out exactly how much aid they're going to offer you. As discussed, financial aid packaging is the process colleges use to determine how much to award an eligible student from each of its financial aid programs (scholarships and grants, loans, and work-study). It's called packaging because money from a variety of financial aid programs is usually combined to cover the amount the student needs. The total amount of the financial package as well as each of its elements will be detailed in your award letter.

In this step, you'll review the elements of a financial aid package and learn how to evaluate and negotiate your package. Our four dependent students and their sample packages will provide helpful examples.

FM VS. IM

Federal Methodology = FM

Institutional Methodology = IM

PACKAGING AND YOUR NEED

Ideally, the financial aid package will cover the entire amount you need to pay for college. Unfortunately, this isn't always the case. When a package does not meet the calculated need (the difference between the cost of attendance and the Family Contribution), the amount left is called *unmet need.* In the next step, you'll review what other financing options are available to you, beyond the student financial aid programs, to make up the difference.

Because packaging is based on many variables, the approach each college takes will be different. Very few colleges, if any, offer only grants and scholarships in financial aid awards. As college costs have risen, students and their families have found that they must rely more and more on loans to finance college expenses.

Colleges use different approaches to award financial aid for a number of reasons. Colleges do so to recruit the best students, to minimize the use of loans by needier students, to target students with the most need for grants or scholarships, and to

ARE YOU INDEPENDENT?

Sample financial aid packages for our two independent students can be found in the chapter called "Steps for Independent Students."

control college resources. The more you understand about the colleges' policies, the better you'll be able to understand your child's financial aid award.

BAIT AND SWITCH?

It may sound like a scam. Schools recruit students with attractive offers, then a year or two down the road, when the students are committed to attending the schools, change the terms of their offers. In most cases, though, this approach benefits the students as well as the colleges, because the students won't be burdened with huge loans until they have the potential to repay them.

PACKAGE ELEMENTS

You examined some of these elements when you explored the different types of financial aid and how to get your share of student financial aid. Let's take another look, with an eye to how the colleges combine the aid in your overall package.

Self-Help and Gift Aid

As discussed, loans and work-study programs are considered self-help aid because the recipient must earn the money or pay it back later. Grants and scholarships are considered gift aid because the money doesn't have to be earned or repaid. Most colleges try to balance the amount of loan and work-study money with grant aid, so that no student is overburdened with debt after graduation.

Some colleges will not award a loan to a first-year student or will increase the size of a loan in later years. In the latter case, a student is recruited with an attractive offer, but the offer changes after the student has attended one or more years. In other words, when the school no longer needs to attract the student, because the student is already committed, the terms become less attractive. Some responsible financial aid administrators view this practice in a less cynical light. They feel, often rightly so, that it's unfair to burden a student with a big loan in the early years, especially since some students don't go on to complete their educations. Those students who stay on will have a better chance of getting higher paying jobs and will be in a better position to pay back their student loans.

This is the same thinking used by many colleges that award more grant aid to students with lower parent contributions. The idea here is that students shouldn't be burdened with more debt just because their families can't contribute as much as other families.

While some may disagree with these concepts, each college decides on its own packaging policies. There are guidelines and regulations that must be adhered to, particularly when the funds come from sources other than the college itself, but there's no rule about packaging.

ALL THE RIGHT MOVES

Athletic scholarships, a type of merit-based aid, have gone a long way in helping colleges recruit students.

Merit-Based Aid

Using merit-based aid to attract the best students is a good example of what some might call unfair awarding practices. While most federal and state funds are awarded based on need, many colleges have their own funds that they award based on other criteria. Those other criteria are generally lumped together as "merit-based aid."

Merit-based aid is used by colleges to attract students who are academically gifted or have special talents. The idea here is that colleges use this aid to attract students who might otherwise go somewhere else. Many colleges, for example, award more grant money to students who have scored high on national tests such as the SAT, or who have excelled in sports.

Essentially, these colleges are trying to buy some of the best students, possibly to raise the level of the college's reputation. Colleges that become well known—for sports, academics, or some other element—receive a greater number of entrance applications from which they can choose a top-notch freshman class. Some colleges have been quite successful in this practice and now rank in what is often called the "highly competitive" college category. For other colleges, this practice has seriously eroded their financial stability.

NO SURPLUS

If you receive any need- or merit-based aid, including federal or state funds, the total amount you receive from all sources cannot exceed the cost of attendance at the college.

Merit-based aid is also widely used to target certain populations. For example, while it's a controversial issue, many colleges offer students from minority groups more grant aid. In doing so, administrators hope to increase the campus' diversity, thereby improving the overall education *all* the students receive.

The Controversy

In financial aid circles, the use of merit-based aid is probably the most controversial issue (other than lack of funding). Those who support it believe that high achievement should be rewarded, and that the "best and the brightest" should be spurred on to greater heights. For example, there are many state programs that award tax dollars to high-achieving students, based on the concept that it is a good societal practice to reward excellence.

Those who oppose merit-based aid believe that there's just not enough money, particularly grant aid, for students who have financial need. After that need is met, they argue, *then* merit-based aid can be used. All students, they've reasoned, should have an equal opportunity to attend the colleges they choose, regardless of their families' financial status.

Outside Scholarships

Outside scholarships are any scholarships awarded by high schools, local community organizations, service clubs, private companies, or any other sponsors not specifically connected with a college. These outside scholarships are currently getting a lot of attention.

SCHOLARSHIPS ON THE NET

The Internet is a great place to search for scholarship information. Try the fastWEB, a searchable database of more than 375,000 scholarships, fellowships, grants, and loans. (www.studentservices.com/fastweb)

Scholarship Search Companies

Many companies have sprung up that guarantee to find you a certain number of scholarships.

The best advice we can give you is to beware of these companies. While some are quite legitimate, others are nothing more than scams. Most scholarship search firms are run by people with little or no experience in financial aid. They tend to charge a lot of money (between $45 and $200) for information that can be found, free of charge, in libraries, guidance offices, college financial aid offices, and on the Internet.

MILLIONS OF DOLLARS GO UNUSED—DON'T MISS OUT

The old cliché applies here. If an advertising claim (like the one above) sounds too good to be true, it probably is.

IS IT *REALLY* A SCHOLARSHIP?

Some "scholarships" listed by search firms aren't really scholarships, but low-interest loans.

SNEAK PREVIEW

You have the right to see a sample report from a scholarship search company before signing up.

Most firms don't tell you that all they do is provide a list of scholarships for which you may be eligible. You still have to apply. And the chance of being one of the winners is often quite small. For some of these scholarships, there are over 100,000 applicants for just a few hundred awards ranging in value from one hundred to a few thousand dollars. The competition can be fierce, requiring very high grades or very high scores on tests. Also, the application requirements may be overwhelming, often requiring original essays and letters of recommendation.

Furthermore, some of the "scholarships" that some search companies list are federal and state programs; others may be scholarships or grant aid awarded by individual colleges if you attend (which colleges award as part of your financial aid package anyway).

There is a page on the World Wide Web (www.finaid.org) that contains information on some of these operations. The listings are updated regularly and are a good source of information about bad scholarship companies.

Buyer Beware

Here are seven important questions to ask a scholarship search company:

1. **Is the company for-profit?** Business is business. These companies are capitalizing on people's desire to go to college, while giving questionable services in return.

2. **Is the company a franchise?** Many franchises use a national database with listings of thousands of awards, but it's likely that an overwhelming number of them will not apply to your personal situation.

3. **How much experience does this person have in the financial aid field?** Anyone can buy into these franchises, whether or not they know anything about financial aid, scholarships, grants, loans, etcetera.

4. **Can I believe the guarantee?** It's impossible for search companies to guarantee that you'll receive a scholarship. All they can guarantee is that they'll find you a certain number of sources to which you still have to apply.

5. **How complete will the information be?** Scholarship reports may not contain vital information such as deadlines, contacts, or eligibility requirements.

6. **Does the company have a list of past clients I can contact?** Any company worth its salt will be able to give you a list of satisfied clients.

7. **Is it necessary to pay for this information?** Much of this information can be found in public sources, which takes only time and effort (not money).

How Colleges Treat Outside Scholarships

For many families, an important issue is how outside scholarships will affect their financial aid packages, or how colleges treat outside scholarships. The question is, "Is it worth it for me to do the research and work required to win an outside scholarship if it's just going to reduce the amount of aid I get?"

First of all, you must report outside scholarships to the financial aid office. Most scholarship-awarding agencies and organizations send the actual checks to the college itself, so you can't get the money unless you report it. Also, recipients of student aid are required to sign a statement declaring that they have reported all income.

Most students who receive outside scholarships receive other aid, including aid from federal and state governments (remember, a student loan is aid and often costs taxpayers more than a grant). It is possible that a student who is awarded a private scholarship may have his or her other aid reduced, or even eliminated. Whether the amount of aid your child will receive will be changed as a result of an outside scholarship depends on several factors.

PLAY FAIR OR PAY

Thinking of lying on the signed statement that declares you've reported all income? Penalties can be quite stiff.

Will Other Awards Be Affected by Scholarships?

The number one factor is whether the student's total financial need has been met and whether any aid received is need based. If financial need has been met, then the college is required to reduce the need-based award. If the total need has *not* been fully met, however, additional outside scholarships usually can be applied toward the remaining need level. Since most colleges are not able to meet the full need level, most packages are not reduced by outside scholarship awards.

For a student whose complete need has been met (minus the family contribution, of course), outside scholarships will reduce the package. Typically, colleges try to reduce the self-help portion of the package (loans and work-study) before touching grants or other scholarships. A handful of colleges will reduce their own grant assistance, particularly if they have awarded this grant based on merit criteria in addition to need. Obviously, in the rare cases in which the outside scholarship is substantial, it may wind up covering more than just the loan portion and the unmet need, so other grants may have to be reduced as well.

DO YOU WANT THE BAD NEWS FIRST?

Bad news: Most colleges cannot meet a student's full need level. Good news: In that case, an outside scholarship usually will not affect other need-based awards.

The two graphs that follow show how outside scholarships could affect your financial picture. As discussed, outside scholarships could be used to fulfill any unmet need, with or without affecting your self-help financial aid. Whether your aid is reduced or not is decided by the college. (These students are not our sample students.)

TO TELL THE TRUTH

If you've applied for aid, it's required that you report any scholarship you receive to the financial aid office.

ORIGINAL FINANCIAL AID AWARDS

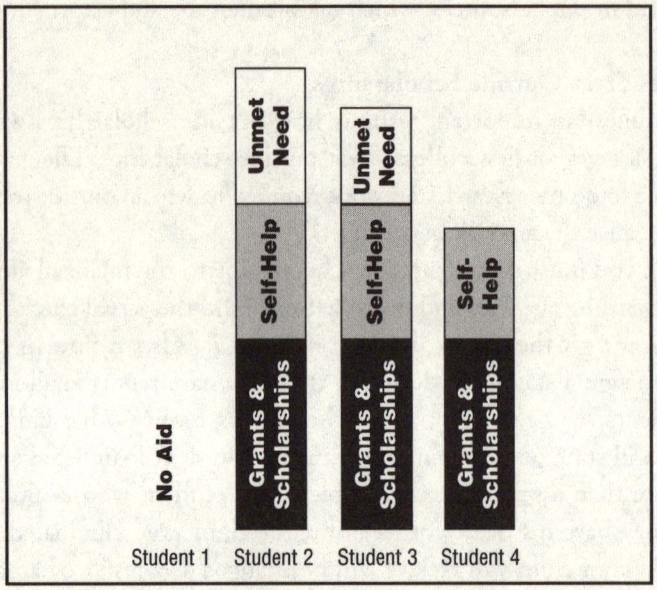

POSSIBLE FINANCIAL AID AWARDS AFTER OUTSIDE SCHOLARSHIP IS REPORTED

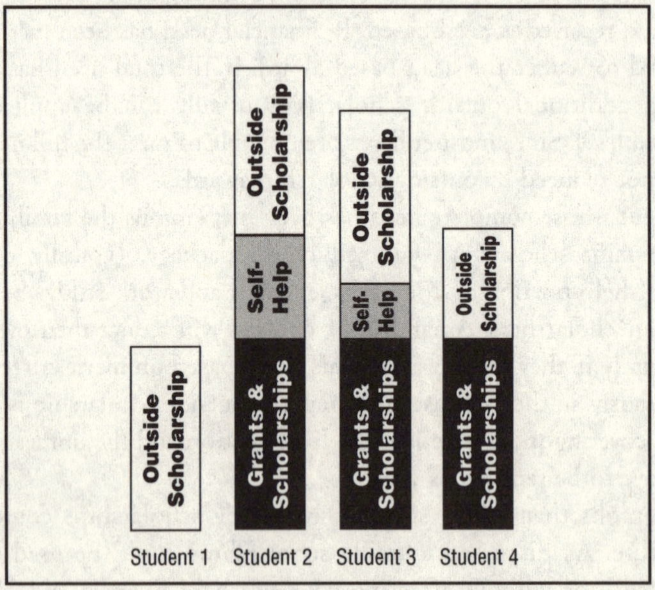

The bottom line: Outside scholarships can be well worth pursuing, as long as they don't take so much time and effort that the awards are less than what a student would have earned in a part-time job, or if it takes a student away from schoolwork.

Employee Tuition Benefits

A large source of aid, and perhaps one of the largest, is the tuition stipend that a company pays its employee for dependents attending college. In most cases, this assistance is treated by colleges as an outside scholarship. (This aid accounts for a great deal of the money referred to when headlines say "millions go unused." The fact is, it goes unused because not every employee who has access to this benefit has a child going to college.)

AFTER DRESS CODE, BEFORE VACATION

Next time you're checking out your employee handbook, look to see if your company offers employee tuition benefits.

Employees of Colleges and Reciprocal Tuition Benefits

Most private colleges offer their employees free or reduced tuition for their dependents attending the college. Sometimes a parent takes a position with a private college a year or two preceding their child's college years, knowing that this benefit adds thousands of dollars to the base salary (without having to pay taxes on it).

Even if your child is not bound for the college that employs you, there are often reciprocal arrangements with other private colleges for a reduced tuition. If you or another member of your family works in higher education or is thinking about working in higher education, this is an important benefit that should be investigated.

COMPARING FINANCIAL AID AWARDS

Here are important tips on how to evaluate the combination of elements in your package:

- Don't assume that the package offering the highest amount of grant aid is the most attractive financial aid award. Rather, add up the total self-help aid offered. You may find, to your surprise, that you could graduate from an expensive college with less debt than if you graduated from a low-cost school.
- Compare the unmet need and expected family contribution from each college. A college offering more grant aid while expecting a greater family contribution could be less attractive financially. Students needing to borrow funds to meet a high family contribution could graduate with more debt.
- How realistic is the budget used to determine your package? If it's low and will need to be increased to meet your actual expenses, chances are you'll have to borrow or earn more to meet that additional need.
- The farther away a college is from your home, the higher your travel expenses. A budget revision may be necessary to incorporate this additional expense.
- If you expect to receive a scholarship from an outside source, find out if the scholarship is renewable and if it will affect the rest of your financial package.

- Compare the terms of the different loans within your financial aid package. Borrowing a smaller amount from a loan program with less attractive terms could end up costing more than borrowing a larger amount from a loan program with more attractive terms.
- Borrowing smaller amounts from multiple loan programs can also end up costing you more. Although you can sometimes combine payments by consolidating loans, the terms for a consolidated loan may end up being less attractive.
- Find out if financial aid awards for continuing students remain consistent with first-year packages. Some colleges award more grant aid for freshman year and increase the loan or work portion in the upper-class years.
- Keep in mind that the short-term cost of a college education is only one criterion for choosing a college. If a school meets your educational needs, and you're convinced it can launch you to an exciting career, a significant investment may turn out to be a bargain over the long run.

NEGOTIATING YOUR FINANCIAL AID AWARD

Many families have taken to negotiating with financial aid administrators to improve their aid packages (much to the chagrin of the financial aid administrators). After deciding on policy and sweating over how best to use their limited funds, administrators are faced with families armed with financial aid awards from competing colleges.

Not only are more families asking for better offers, but more colleges are improving their offers, particularly to students with impressive academic credentials. Some colleges, in fact, actually invite families to show a competing college's offer, so that they can try to equal or surpass it. While these colleges don't guarantee that they'll change anything, the implication is clear: Feel free to negotiate. The college admitted you, believes you can succeed, and doesn't want to lose you without having the opportunity to change your financial aid award.

Our advice is that you can negotiate, but do it with honest intentions and without making a big deal of it. When you receive your financial aid award letter (or your no-need letter), call or write a nice note reiterating your interest in the college and asking whether there's a chance you can get a bit more help (in particular, in the form of grant money) with the expenses. Be careful here not to be too aggressive. Demanding additional grant and scholarship money will not work. You need to have some reason for asking for a review of the financial aid package—change in circumstances, errors on the application, or even a better offer from another school.

WHAT YOUR FINANCIAL AID OFFICE MAY NOT WANT YOU TO KNOW

Your financial aid package is negotiable. It's becoming more likely that, after negotiation, a college will enhance its original offer.

Let's Make a Deal

Here's how a phone negotiation might work:

PARENT: *My daughter is very interested in attending your college. In fact, it's probably her number-one choice. But I have some questions about her financial aid.*

FINANCIAL AID OFFICER: *What would you like to know?*

PARENT: *There are a couple of things, actually. First, I'm a bit concerned about the family contribution that was calculated. I don't know how I can possibly come up with that amount. As it is, our income barely meets our expenses. Is there anything you can do to lower that expected contribution?*

FINANCIAL AID OFFICER: *First, why don't you review the numbers you reported on your application. If there are any errors, let us know and we'll recalculate. Second, if there are any unusually high expenses that aren't reflected in these numbers—high medical bills, for example—let us know. We may have some flexibility there. Third, as you know, you can always take out a PLUS loan to meet your family share.*

PARENT: *Thanks. I'll let you know. But there's something else that bothers us. As I said, your school is probably my daughter's first choice, but frankly the financial aid award isn't as attractive as some others she's received. She's going to have to borrow an awful lot to make it through. Is there any possibility of increased scholarships or grants?*

FINANCIAL AID OFFICER: *Well, you know, we spend a great deal of time working up packaging guidelines for students. I'll be happy to review hers to make sure we didn't make any errors. Also, if there are any special expenses that she'll have that are not usually considered in our budgets, let me know so we can consider whether the budget we used for her is appropriate.*

PARENT: *We don't have any unusual expenses. We're just concerned that the two other colleges that have accepted her have made significantly better offers in terms of how much she'll have to borrow or work. If it were just a few dollars difference, I wouldn't say anything. But these are pretty big differences. Big enough that we may have to recommend that she go to one of those other schools. Are you sure you can't do something?*

FINANCIAL AID OFFICER: *Tell you what. Why don't you send me a copy of the offer letters from those other schools. I'll look at them and see what I can do. No guarantees, you understand. But we'd very much like your daughter to come here so I promise I'll give her every possible consideration.*

PARENT: *Thanks. That's all I can ask.*

As discussed earlier, if the college wants to be competitive, they'll let you know right away. If they don't negotiate, you'll also be told, and you'll be in a position to make an informed admission decision. With negotiating financial aid awards, there's no harm in asking. But be prepared to accept no for an answer. And don't harass the financial aid office if the change in offer is minimal or if no change is made.

DOES IT MAKE A DIFFERENCE?

One of the colleges that does negotiate reports that of the students whose packages they improve, slightly more than half attend. Ironically, this figure is only a little better than the figure for students whose packages are not improved.

OUR SAMPLE PACKAGES

With this basic understanding of packaging, next we'll look at the packages our four sample students were awarded. First, though, we must point out a few critical things:

- These awards are samples. While similar to awards made to students with similar financial and academic profiles, they are not real and are presented to give you a rough idea of what you may expect.

- These awards were made more than a year before any student would be applying for the 2001–2002 year. The college costs and aid amounts are 2000–2001 figures.

- The analyses that follow the packages are provided to give you a format against which to compare your own awards. We use the concept of "total cost to the family" as one key element. This cost includes the family's contributions (parent and student, with student contribution being 35 percent of his or her assets) plus all self-help aid (loans and work-study) and any unmet need. This sum is the amount your family will really have to come up with in order to send your child to each college.

With these qualifiers, following are three packages for each of our students.

FRANCES'S PACKAGES

	College A	College B	College C
Cost of Attendance	$26,411	$25,894	$28,246
Family Contribution	[$6,451]	[$4,701]	[$6,451]
Student Contribution	[$1,450]	[$420]	[$1,450]
Need	**$18,510**	**$20,773**	**$20,345**
AWARD:			
Institutional Grant	$14,000	$11,700	$15,220
Federal Stafford Loan	$2,625	$2,625	$2,625
Federal Perkins Loan	$0	$1,500	$0
Federal Work-Study	$1,800	$2,000	$2,500
Federal PLUS	$0	$2,940	$0
Unmet Need	**$5**	**$8**	**$0**

Analysis of Frances's Packages

As you can see, all three colleges have similar budgets. (Frances's college choices are all private schools away from home.) A striking difference here is that College B chooses to use the Federal Methodology (FM) rather than the Institutional Methodology (IM). For Frances, this difference is over $2,780, with the difference evenly split between an increased contribution from Frances and from her parents.

The key here is to look at what the total cost would be to the family. This includes the family and student contributions, all self-help awards (loans and work-study), and unmet need.

At College A, the total cost to Frances's family would be $12,406:

$6,451	(IM family contribution)
$1,450	(minimum student contribution plus contribution from assets)
$2,625	(Federal Stafford Loan)
$1,880	(Federal Work-Study)
$12,406	

At College B, the total cost to the family would be $14,186. This is almost $1,800 more than at College A, despite use of the lower FM and a slightly lower cost of attendance.

$4,701	(FM family contribution)
$ 420	(minimum student contribution plus contribution from assets)
$2,625	(Federal Stafford Loan)
$2,000	(Federal Work-Study)
$1,500	(Federal Perkins Loan)
$2,940	(Federal PLUS)
$14,186	

SEMANTICS

College C's grant offer is called a University Scholarship, *while both College A and College B use the term* grant.

College B offers packages based on the strength of the applicant. For Frances, they assumed she was an average applicant to the School of Humanities and Social Sciences (they award women and underrepresented minorities in the sciences higher grants). If she had had a high GPA and high SAT scores, her grant would have increased, which might have made her total family cost about the same as for College A.

At College C, the family's total cost comes to $13,026, also higher than at College A. This is basically the result of slightly higher costs, although the school tries to make up for it with a more generous grant offer.

In terms of total indebtedness, Frances would end her first year owing $2,625 at College A, $2,625 at College C, and a whopping $7,026 at College B (although, again, if she were a strong applicant, her total indebtedness for her first year would drop).

None of the schools leaves much unmet need, although College C's Federal Work-Study award of $2,500 is higher than the award at either of the other two schools. If Frances earned $6 per hour, to use up her award she would have to work over 200 hours each semester. At College A and College B, she would have to work fewer hours. For some students, these three or four additional hours a week can be quite significant. For others, it may have little or no effect on their studies.

THE WORK-STUDY COCKTAIL

Most studies show that, on the average, students who work while attending school do at least as well as, if not better than, students who do not work.

Bottom Line

Which college should Frances attend? Well, if it's strictly a monetary issue, there's no question that College A would be less costly, but only if she's an "average" student at College B and only if her award doesn't change as a result of negotiation.

The big question here is, "Does one or two thousand dollars a year make a difference?" If Frances really loved College C or B, or if one of those two schools had the ideal program for her, would a few thousand dollars make a difference?

Suppose, for example, Frances wanted to major in computer science, a field in which College B is ranked as one of the top two or three schools in the world. Would a few thousand dollars a year make a difference? Is this sum relatively insignificant, considering her opportunities after graduation?

Suppose Frances intended to major in political science and had government work in mind. Wouldn't it make sense for her to go to College C, located in Washington, DC, where she would be able to live (and make contacts) in the very heart of government? Would a thousand dollars or so a year be too much to pay for that opportunity?

When you total your costs and compare financial aid packages, these are the types of questions we hope you'll ask.

ANGELA'S PACKAGES

	College A	College B	College C
Cost of Attendance	$22,188	$27,569	$12,008
Family Contribution	[$4,705]	[$4,705]	[$4,651]
Student Contribution	[$1,515]	[$1,515]	[$464]
Need	**$15,968**	**$21,349**	**$6,893**
AWARD:			
Institutional Grant	$5,890	$8,970	$0
Cal. State Grant	$5,250	$5,250	$3,800
Federal Stafford Loan	$2,625	$2,625	$2,625
Federal Perkins Loan	$0	$2,000	$460
Federal Work-Study	$2,200	$2,500	$0
Federal PLUS	$0	$0	$0
Unmet Need	**$3**	**$4**	**$8**

Analysis of Angela's Packages

Here we get to compare the cost of attending a publicly supported college (College C) to the cost of private schools. At College C, with its low tuition and fees for residents of California, the total cost to Angela's family would be $8,208. This is the sum of her family contribution based on Federal Methodology ($4,651), her student contribution ($464), the loan awarded to her ($2,625), her Federal Perkins loan of $350, and her unmet need of $3. If Angela were not a California resident, her total cost would jump another $9,000, and she wouldn't be eligible for a Cal Grant.

College B and College A use the Institutional Methodology for determining eligibility. The larger student contribution is due to the student minimum standard contribution expected along with Angela's contribution from her savings.

GO WHERE YOU LIVE

It may sound like a New Age philosophy, but it's actually a practical recommendation. Savings due to in-state residency can be large enough to be a deciding factor.

Allowing for all of these differences, the total family cost at College B would be $13,345, or just over $5,100 more than at College C. Angela's total indebtedness for the year would be over $4,600 in two loan programs plus a substantial Federal Work-Study award.

If Angela were to attend College A, the total cost would be $11,045, or $2,300 less than College B and over $2,800 more than College C. She would also have a substantial Federal Work-Study award, allowing her to earn money over the course of the year.

Bottom Line

Which college should Angela attend? The difference in cost between the least expensive school, College C, and the most expensive, College B, is over $5,000. College A is in the middle. If money is the prime consideration, College C would be the least expensive and the first choice. However, there are other important differences to consider. College C is a large public university, College B is a large private university in the heart of Los Angeles, and College A is a small, private women's college. Considering that the difference in cost can be met with an additional loan, Angela should choose a college to attend based on the criteria most important to her.

JAMES'S PACKAGES

	College A	College B	College C
Cost of Attendance	$26,850	$26,370	$15,700
Family Contribution	[$18,540]	[$18,540]	[$16,669]
Student Contribution	[$2,150]	[$1,400]	[$1,400]
Need	**$6,160**	**$6,430**	**$0**
AWARD:			
Institutional Grant	$0	$1,800	$0
Federal Stafford Loan	$2,625	$2,625	$0
Federal Perkins Loan	$1,000	$0	$0
Federal Work-Study	$2,500	$2,000	$0
Federal PLUS	$0	$0	$0
Unmet Need	**$35**	**$5**	**$0**

Analysis of James's Packages

The most obvious thing to note is that the total cost at College C is only $15,700, even for an out-of-state student (which James would be). For James's family, with their expected contribution of about $1,800, this means he would not qualify for aid at College C. He would receive a gentle "no-aid letter," with the suggestion that he apply for an Unsubsidized Federal Stafford Loan, which is not a need-based program.

To assist in the recruiting effort, the letter may also indicate that by attending College C, James "would have an opportunity for an outstanding education without having to borrow or stretch family resources." And, of course, the total family cost for James to attend College C would be the cost of attendance, $15,700.

At College A, James would not be offered any grant aid, although he would be offered $6,125 in a combination of loan and work awards. This means that the total cost of $26,850 would be borne by James and his family.

College B uses a student contribution that is different from College A's. While College A uses "straight" IM, assuming a contribution from student income even when the student hasn't worked, College B uses only James's assets to calculate his contribution. This reduces the overall family contribution by $1,150. James would receive a $4,625 self-help award (a combination of Federal Stafford Loan and Federal Work-Study), and a grant of $1,800. The total cost to the family for James to attend College B would be $24,570.

James illustrates that even a fairly wealthy family could qualify for some need-based aid, albeit mostly self-help. It's amazing to think that an annual income of $150,000 and a quarter of a million dollars in assets is not enough to bear the entire cost of two children in college.

DOUBLE WHAMMY

A major reason James qualifies for aid is that there are two family members in college, and so the total family contribution is divided in half.

Bottom Line

Which college should James attend? The difference in total cost is about $11,000 or so per year. For most families, this can be a significant amount. But for this family, it's a relatively small sum given their financial strength and income. So, James gets to decide which school he wants to attend based on the other criteria he believes are important.

DAVID'S PACKAGES

	College A	College B	College C
Cost of Attendance	$21,500	$16,245	$21,035
Family Contribution	[$4,659]	[$6,870]	[$6,870]
Student Contribution	[$1,764]	[$1,764]	[$2,927]
Need	**$15,077**	**$7,511**	**$11,238**
AWARD:			
Merit Scholarship	$4,000	$2,000	$3,900
Institutional Grant	$3,950	$0	$0
State Grant	$2,000	$2,000	$0
Federal Stafford Loan	$2,625	$2,625	$2,625
Federal Perkins Loan	$0	$880	$2,500
Federal Work-Study	$2,500	$0	$2,200
Federal PLUS	$0	$0	$0
Unmet Need	**$2**	**$6**	**$13**

Analysis of David's Packages

David's family situation is considerably more complicated than any of our other students, and his packages reflect this complexity.

First of all, David's parents are divorced, and his father's child support payments for him end when David turns eighteen (which occurs just before David goes to college). College B and College C require a contribution from the noncustodial parent, while College A adjusted for the loss of child support for David. This is not necessarily how it's handled at all colleges, and the only way to know is to ask. In general, colleges that use only the Federal Methodology don't require a noncustodial parent contribution, and would likely recalculate the FM parent contribution without including the child support payments for David. College C uses the FM calculation when awarding federal aid to students, but uses an IM calculation to determine how much of the school's own funds to award. College A and College B use the IM calculated student contribution of $1,753, while College C uses the actual $2,327 available student income plus $600 from student assets (totaling $2,927), rather than the $1,164 student's contribution from income.

THE CONTRIBUTION OF DAVID'S FATHER

Some colleges require that the noncustodial parent pay a share of the expenses. Ask each college about its policy.

At College A, the cost to David's family is the combined contributions plus David's Federal Stafford Loan and Federal Work-Study, or a total of $11,550. Based on David's test scores and grades, he would qualify for an institutional scholarship. This scholarship would be promised to him in his letter of admission, even before a financial aid package was calculated. If David did not qualify for the state grant portion, College A would expect David's parents to borrow a PLUS loan.

At College B, the total cost to David's family would be the total cost of education minus the $2,000 state grant and $2,000 scholarship, or a total of $12,145. Of that amount, $2,625 would be in a low-interest, unsubsidized loan; the balance would be in either an unsubsidized loan or additional parent and student contribution.

College C's packaging guidelines give David the maximum eligibility for federal loans, with the subsidy intact (Perkins and Stafford), and eligibility for a Federal Work-Study award. While the total cost to David's family is $17,135, the loan programs he is awarded are the two lowest-cost programs available (the interest rates are low, and no interest accrues while David is in school) and he can earn $2,200 through a work-study job.

LOOK AT THE BIG PICTURE

If it comes down to a difference of a couple thousand dollars, try to step back from the numbers and consider the long-term benefits.

Bottom Line

Which college should David attend? The difference between the most and least expensive is about $5,500, an amount that can be paid by a combination of a summer job and an additional loan. This being considered, David has the freedom to make his decision based on additional factors.

SUMMARY

Our sample families are all facing significant financial commitments, despite being awarded grants of as much as $15,000. Unfortunately, this is often the case. Very few students receive scholarships and grants that cover the entire cost. How families and students come up with their contributions is an important issue.

WHAT'S NEXT

In the next step, you'll look at alternate ways a family can meet the expected family contribution and other college expenses. We'll review different loans, credit guidelines, and basic money management principles, and we'll provide budget hints for students.

MEET YOUR SHARE OF EXPENSES

Borrowing and Money Management

Step 8

"Even with grants and student loans, my family's expected contribution will be more than what we have available in savings."

Let's assume the financial aid application process is over. You know the exact amount of financial aid that you'll be receiving from student financial aid programs, and you know the exact amount of money that will be coming out of your own pocket. Now what do you do? Like most families (including our four sample families), you face the daunting task of securing significant sums of money.

It may be that you have the resources to pay your share of college expenses, but can't pay all at once without using all your assets or experiencing severe cash-flow problems. The good news is that there are alternatives for families in this situation. These financing alternatives include tuition payment plans, federal loans that are not based on need and are not subsidized, home equity loans, lines of credit, and private loans from banks and other lenders.

In this step, we'll show you how to take advantage of these alternatives. We'll highlight when you'll be expected to pay your share and how you can pay your share over time. You'll learn important money-management techniques, such as budgeting monthly loan or tuition payments. And we'll help you find the loan terms and parent loan program that meet your particular needs.

WHEN WILL I BE EXPECTED TO PAY?

Key times in the payment cycle include the beginning of September and midyear at the start of the second semester. Sometimes, if the college is on a quarter system rather than a semester system, payments are required three times per academic year.

Here we'll revisit the elements of Step 2's College Costs Worksheet and look at when each expense (if it applies to your child) will typically hit your checkbook.

Frances's college will set up a student account, and at the beginning of each term the college will credit her account with one-half of the grant and student loan.

By Fall Registration

- One-half of the year's tuition
- One-half of the cost of room and board

On Arrival

- Cost of transporting student and parents to the college
- Setup expenses associated with relocation (phone, utilities, etcetera)
- Personal expenses associated with relocation (room decorations, clothing, etcetera)

By the Start of Classes

- One-half to two-thirds the cost of the year's books and supplies

By Spring Semester

- Balance of the year's tuition
- Balance of the room-and-board fee
- Balance of the books and supplies expense

As Required over the Course of the Year

- Activities, lab, and miscellaneous fees
- Phone/utility bills
- Clothing/laundry/dry cleaning expenses
- Transportation costs
- Medical/dental bills
- Recreation allowance
- Personal expenses
- Savings allotments
- Child care payments
- Credit card bills

The cost of tuition, fees, dorm, and board for one year at Angela's College A is about $26,000, and Angela's been awarded $10,200 in grant money, plus the Federal Stafford Loan of $2,625. Angela's mother's contribution toward these expenses will be more than $6,500, which uses up all of her savings.

As you've learned, these costs can add up to substantial amounts, regardless of whether the student has qualified for financial aid. The thought of making such large payments at one time is sobering, to say the least. Fortunately, you can spread out your payments.

YOU DON'T HAVE TO PAY EVERYTHING UP FRONT

Many schools offer extended payment plans, called tuition payment plans, to help families meet their expected contribution. These plans let you pay the tuition, fees, and dormitory room and board contract *over time*, rather than at the beginning of each term. A typical tuition payment plan begins the May or June preceding enrollment and extends to February or March. There are usually 10 or 12 monthly payments, rather than one large one in September and another large one in January.

When a Tuition Payment Plan *Is Not* a Solution

In Angela's case, her family will owe more than $2,500 in September and again in January. They could spread the annual cost over ten months and make ten equal payments of more than $500 each. It seems unlikely that Angela's mother would be able to accomplish this solely with her income, so she'll probably have to look at alternatives, particularly at long-term loans. On the other hand, since Angela is the older of two children and her brother is likely to go to college, Angela's mother may want to keep their borrowing to a minimum at this point and stretch her limited income as far as it can go. Later on, for the other child, she may not have any choice but to borrow.

"The need analysis says we have to come up with a contribution of about $8,200, plus all of the other costs of starting school. There's no way we can afford to pay more than $800 a month from what my mom earns, and she doesn't have that much in the bank. It looks like a tuition payment plan is not going to help us very much."

When a Tuition Payment Plan *Is* a Solution

James's parents are expected to contribute about $10,000 per semester, a whopping bill, to say the least. But they also have a significant income, so a tuition payment plan may be an excellent program for them. This would be especially attractive if they were unable or chose not to tap into their assets, or preferred not to borrow against their home. A tuition payment plan would allow James's family to pay about $2,000 a month. This is still a large sum, but by itself it's within their budget. However, James's brother is also in college, and he'll require about the same amount. It's likely, then, that James's parents will take advantage of a monthly tuition payment plan for both children and tap into some of their assets.

Is a Tuition Payment Plan a Loan?

A tuition payment plan is *not* a loan, even though it looks like one. Families pay no interest, and eligibility is not strictly based on credit history or your ability to pay. The only cost to the family is a nominal fee to administer the program and, with some plans, a charge for life insurance on the unpaid balance.

To enroll in a tuition payment plan, the college itself must either contract with an outside organization or have its own plan. If the plan is with an outside organization, once your participation is approved, the organization notifies the school and sets up a monthly plan.

"With my brother in college, too, my parents are expected to come up with 40 grand for the year. I know my family is pretty wealthy, but that's still a lot of money. Even if they sell some stock or something, it's not going to be easy."

So, how can any organization afford to offer this service? The answer is "the interest float." The organization holds on to your payment for a period of time before sending it to the school, thereby earning interest on it. Because you begin paying prior to the semester, the organization has most of the money before it has to pay the college, so there's very little concern about your not paying the balance.

The best part of a tuition payment plan is that it allows you to work tuition payments into your family's budget, and it reduces your need to borrow. Payment plans can be used alone or to supplement financial aid and savings. You benefit because you don't have to come up with large sums at once and you don't have to pay any interest. The college benefits because it receives a portion of its tuition funds before the academic year begins. Of course, you could put aside the same amount of money each month as you would be pay-

EVERYBODY'S HAPPY

With a tuition payment plan:

- *You're happy, because you get to pay the tuition over time.*
- *The provider of the plan is happy, because it earns interest on your money.*
- *The school is happy, because it gets its money.*

ing into the tuition payment plan. But most of us are not able to do that without the structure of an outside plan. The nominal cost is worth the structure that it offers.

Outside Organizations

In addition to many colleges that offer their own plans, the following organizations offer tuition payment plans. These organizations may also offer private loan programs, which are not to be confused with tuition payment plans.

Academic Management Services, Inc.
One AMS Place, P.O. Box 100
Swansea, MA 02777-0100
(800) 531-4300

Key Education Resources
Insured Tuition Payment Plan
745 Atlantic Avenue
Boston, MA 02111-2735
(800) 225-6783

HOW MUCH CAN YOU PAY EACH MONTH?

An extremely hot topic in higher education is debt management. Students and families must decide how much they can afford in regular payments. This issue comes into play when you're determining how much you can afford to pay each month toward your tuition payment plan, as discussed above. It's more important, however, when you're figuring out how much you can afford to pay each month in *loan* payments. We'll explore loan payments and programs later in this step, after you've evaluated your borrowing and repayment potential.

When deciding how much to borrow to pay for your child's education, a good rule of thumb is to use the criteria lenders use when they consider an applicant's ability to repay a loan. The total monthly payments for housing (mortgage and home equity loans) should be no more than 28 percent of your gross monthly income. The total payments for all other loans, including education loans, credit card payments, and all other installment loans (car, furniture, etcetera), should not exceed 8 percent of your gross monthly income. So, adding these figures, your total monthly payments, for all loans should not be more than 37 percent of your gross monthly income.

For a quick estimate of your monthly loan payments, based on lender criteria, use the following chart. The chart lists your yearly income and monthly income, and based on these numbers estimates the amount you can make toward mortgage, car, student loan, and recurring debt payments. Take a look at how much of your monthly income can be eaten up by monthly payments.

LENDER STANDARDS FOR BORROWING

Income		Suggested Mortgage Payment	Maximum Payments for All Other Debts	Maximum Total Debt Payments
YEARLY	MONTHLY			
$20,000	$1,667	$466	$133	$600
$25,000	$2,083	$583	$167	$750
$30,000	$2,500	$700	$200	$900
$35,000	$2,917	$817	$233	$1,050
$40,000	$3,333	$933	$267	$1,200
$45,000	$3,750	$1,050	$300	$1,350
$50,000	$4,166	$1,167	$333	$1,500
$55,000	$4,583	$1,283	$367	$1,650
$60,000	$5,000	$1,400	$400	$1,800

REMEMBER THIS?

In deciding how much to borrow, it's a good idea to reevaluate the estimate of your total costs, the amount of your family contribution, and the total financial aid package offered. You've explored these factors in earlier steps, but it's a good idea to take another look.

Let's use Frances's situation as an example. With a gross monthly income of about $5,000, the suggested monthly mortgage payment is $1,400 (28 percent). Frances's parents are already paying more than that, $1,700 including property taxes. This figure is just $100 less than the total suggested monthly debt payment for them, $1,800 (37 percent of their gross income), so they would have difficulty qualifying for any additional loans or credit.

Clearly, these percentages are just guidelines. These numbers are not fixed in stone. For example, if your rent or mortgage payment is less than 28 percent, you may be able to reasonably afford a more expensive car or make a large purchase that you plan to finance over several years.

For a more exact estimate of your monthly payments, again based on lender criteria, the following debt-to-income ratio worksheet should prove helpful. First let's review a completed worksheet for Angela's family.

"When my mom needed to buy a new car, she asked the bank how much they would lend her. They told her that based on her income, home mortgage, and credit card payments, the maximum she could pay was about $440 per month. But that would mean she wouldn't be able to borrow for my education. So she found a good used car that cost her only $200 a month and now she can still take out a parent loan."

DEBT-TO-INCOME RATIO

■ **Step 1**		
	Current monthly gross income	$4,000
×	.37 industry standard for manageable debt	
=	Portion of monthly gross available for debt payments	= $1,480
■ **Step 2**		
	Monthly rent or mortgage payments	$ 900
+	Monthly car payment	$ 200
+	Minimum monthly payment on installment loan(s)	$ 100
+	Minimum monthly payment on all credit cards	$ 0
=	Total monthly payments	= $1,200
■ **Step 3**		
	37 percent of monthly gross (result from Step 1)	$1,480
–	Total monthly payments (result from Step 2)	$1,200
=	Available for additional monthly debt payment	= $ 280

Now, fill in your own amounts:

DEBT-TO-INCOME RATIO

■ **Step 1**		
	Current monthly gross income	$____
×	.37 industry standard for manageable debt	
=	Portion of monthly gross available for debt payments	= $____
■ **Step 2**		
	Monthly rent or mortgage payments	$____
+	Monthly car payment	$____
+	Minimum monthly payment on installment loan(s)	$____
+	Minimum monthly payment on all credit cards	$____
=	Total monthly payments	= $____
■ **Step 3**		
	37 percent of monthly gross (result from Step 1)	$____
–	Total monthly payments (result from Step 2)	$____
=	Available for additional monthly debt payment	= $____

The key is to keep the total debt at or below the total 37 percent figure. The amount available for additional monthly debt payment determines not only the size of the loan you'll be able to take on, obviously, but also the type of loan you should take on, as we'll discuss later in this chapter.

HOW TO EVALUATE STUDENT LOANS

Before we get into specific loans for parents, let's review the important loan terms. We covered most of these in detail in Step 4, but they're certainly worth reviewing at this point, too. Don't go into the loan process blind. Determine what loan terms and features are important to you.

Interest Rate

In addition to comparing the basic rates, consider whether you want a fixed or a variable rate. While some people think a fixed rate is safer, a variable rate lets you take advantage of low-interest rates.

PUT IT IN WRITING

A repayment schedule, provided by the lender, will list your monthly payment, interest rate, total repayment obligation, and length of time for repaying the loan.

Fees

In most cases, the fees (application fee, origination fee, guarantee fee) are deducted directly from your loan amount, which means that the amount you receive will be less than the amount you borrowed. But interest will accrue on the total amount you borrowed.

Repayment Terms

Find out what the maximum length of repayment is, and when repayment starts. Repayment can run anywhere from ten to 30 years.

Monthly Payment

Make sure you know approximately what your monthly payment will be, so you'll be able to assess how this loan will impact your lifestyle. Having completed the debt-to-income ratio worksheet, you should already have a fair estimate.

Deferment Options

As noted in our discussion of repaying student loans, some loans allow you to defer, or postpone, payments of principle while the student is in school.

Prepayment Penalty

Make sure the loan you choose allows you to repay early without penalty. If you can pay off your loan ahead of time, you'll save on some of the financing costs that accumulate over the life of the loan.

Consolidation

When a borrower has multiple loans, either from one lender or several, the monthly payment of each separate loan can sometimes add up to more than the monthly payment if all the loans were combined. This is true even if the interest rate for the combined loan is higher than for the other loans. This is because there may be a minimum repayment amount for one or more of the loans.

WHICH LOAN IS RIGHT FOR YOU?

Now that you know which terms are particularly relevant to your financial situation and you have an estimate of affordable monthly payments, you can take an educated tour of the following loan programs. Earlier in this guide we reviewed *student* loan programs. The loan programs that follow are for parents, because you're faced with meeting the costs that financial aid and your contributions could not meet.

Home Equity Loans

A home equity loan is a fixed loan for a defined term. You take the entire amount right away and make payments for an agreed upon number of months.

Borrowing against the equity in your home can be an excellent source of income, particularly if one of the following points applies to your situation:

- The college doesn't offer a tuition payment plan.
- The monthly payments with a tuition payment plan would be too much.
- You need to borrow funds to meet the other costs of education (books and supplies, transportation, etcetera).
- You need to borrow your entire family contribution.

A home equity loan has the double advantage of being the least expensive loan available (it has the lowest interest rate and best terms available) and of being tax deductible for most borrowers. A home equity loan at 9 percent actually costs the family closer to 6 percent, because the interest can be written off the income taxes. In some cases, however, a family may not be able to deduct this interest, so check with your tax advisor about whether you're permitted this deduction.

WHY SO INEXPENSIVE?

The lender of a home equity loan has collateral against the money, and that collateral is your home.

The major downside of a home equity loan is, obviously, the possibility that a family unable to make payments could lose their home.

Most families looking to finance a college education will want to look at a home equity line of credit, rather than a straight home equity loan. A line of credit is like a credit card with a credit limit. It allows borrowers to borrow what they need when they need it, up to the maximum they've been approved.

Federal PLUS Loans

The Federal PLUS Loan is a non-need-based loan for parents of undergraduate students. It was discussed in the student financial aid chapter because, as reviewed, it can be included in part of a student's award letter. With this loan, parents may borrow up to the entire cost of education, as determined by the college, minus the total financial aid eligibility, whether or not the aid is accepted.

The interest rate is adjusted annually and is based on the treasury bill (T-bill) rate. The maximum interest rate is 9 percent. Borrowers begin paying back the loan within 60 days of receipt of the funds and the repayment period is up to ten years, depending on the amount borrowed. In addition to the interest, borrowers pay a fee of up to 4 percent deducted proproportionally each time a loan payment is made.

In James's case, the family's share of his expenses is about $20,000 per year. There is little reason to borrow the entire four-year total of $80,000 at once. It would be much better to borrow $20,000 per year (or even smaller amounts more often).

Private Loans

A number of nongovernment sources can also help offset the cost of your child's college education. Privately sponsored loan programs have been around since the mid-1980s, when it became apparent that financial aid was not keeping up with tuition increases and middle-income families needed more help than what was available. Some of these private loans are the lowest-cost loans available.

Many organizations allow credit-worthy students and parents to borrow up to the total cost of education, less any financial aid received. They also allow up to thirty years to repay, which makes monthly payments more affordable. Most private loans offer competitive interest rates, low fees, and generous repayment terms. This makes these privately funded loans a popular and affordable alternative for families.

The terms of private loans vary from lender to lender, and comparing terms requires reading all the fine print. For example, some lenders may allow you to pay only the interest while your child is in school; others may set up a gradually increasing payment plan. Some loans have adjustable interest rates, while others have fixed rates.

Eligibility for Private Loan Approval

There are general debt and credit history requirements to qualify for a private loan.

Debt-to-Income Ratio

As discussed earlier, your payment on all debts should not exceed 37 percent of your total gross monthly income, including the payment required for the new loan. Depending on the amount of income you have available, exceptions may be granted when the ratio is in excess of 37 percent.

NEED MORE LOAN INFO?

For more information about federal PLUS or private loans, call the Kaplan/American Express Student Loan Program toll-free at 1-888-KAP-LOAN.

Self-Employment

If you're self-employed, you must have been in business at least one full year before filing an application, or have other verifiable sources of income.

Credit History

All applicants must have a satisfactory credit history and at least one of the applicants must have a minimum credit history of two years (based on a credit bureau report).

A satisfactory credit history is defined as making continual and prompt payments on all credit obligations such as mortgages, personal loans, credit cards, auto loans, and especially education loans.

You can't have charged off loans within the past five years, have a record of foreclosure, repossession, open judgment or suit, unpaid tax lien, unpaid prior education loan defaults, or other negative public record items in the past seven years. Also, you can't have a record of bankruptcy within the past ten years.

The Kaplan/American Express student loan program offers a credit reevaluation program called The Second Look™. This program guides previously denied borrowers through the process of clearing incorrect and/or outdated credit report listings and, if possible, reverses a credit-denied status.

MONEY-MANAGEMENT TIPS FOR REDUCING COSTS

"My best friend and I are applying to some of the same schools, so we might try to room together. It could save us money, but I wonder if it would ruin our friendship."

In addition to payment plans and loans, there's the old money-management standby of budgeting. There are budgeting strategies students can implement that won't affect the quality of the college experience, but will definitely help make payments less troublesome. When college expenses are reduced, the amount required for a loan decreases and the amount you and your student can afford each month increases.

Let's revisit the college costs worksheet. We've already explored the various college expenses, and determined when each expense would hit your checkbook. Now, let's see how some of these costs can be lowered. When relevant or possible, students should consider the following budgeting tips:

Books and Supplies

- Buy used books, if possible.
- Sell books back to the bookstore if no longer needed or wanted.

Room

- Share a dorm room, apartment, or house with a roommate or two (or three). It may even be possible to rent a room in a private home.
- Live with parents or a relative.

- If off-campus living is preferable, check the college's housing office for reasonably priced apartments.
- Exchange services for a portion of the rent (by gardening, doing home maintenance, babysitting, etcetera).

Board

- If not on a meal plan, eat at home as much as possible and pack a lunch instead of eating out.
- Plan meals and use a shopping list.
- Avoid impulse buying, and never go shopping when hungry.
- Use money-saving coupons.
- Avoid gourmet specialty shops and convenience markets.
- Buy in bulk.
- Avoid "convenience" foods.

Transportation and Travel

- Unless absolutely essential, do not own a car. If it's a necessity, perform do-it-yourself maintenance and use the car as sparingly as possible.
- Try to stay on your parents' car insurance plan.
- Take advantage of public transportation, a carpool, or a bicycle.
- For long-distance travel, make reservations early to get the lowest fares. Use the services of a good travel agent who is sensitive to students' needs and who looks for the least expensive fares.

Personal

- Put off buying any luxury items.
- Shop in outlet/discount stores.
- Consider shopping in thrift and "previously owned" clothing shops.

"I prefer wearing vintage clothes. They have a real history. Luckily, these clothes are usually a lot cheaper than what's available at the mall."

Miscellaneous

- Conserve energy and save money. Turn off appliances and lights when not in use. In winter, lower the thermostat overnight and during the day.
- Keep a record of all long-distance calls, particularly if there are roommates. Check that the phone bill is accurate.
- Make long-distance calls during discount times.
- If a checking account is needed, choose a bank with low-cost or free accounts.
- Avoid bouncing checks, as it can ruin credit history and cost a fee of $20 or more.
- Choose a credit card with low interest, or pay the balance every month.
- Have only one credit card, and keep it for emergencies only.

NO GRACE PERIOD

If you don't pay off your entire balance on a credit card, you pay interest not only on that balance, but also on every charge made from the date it is posted. You get no grace period. If you have a zero balance, then you get the 25-day (approximately) grace period before a payment is due.

A Note About Credit Cards

Many students receive credit card solicitations from banks very early on in their college years, sometimes before they've even left high school. We suggest students apply for one or two major cards, since it may be tougher to get one later on, but choose and use them very carefully. Pay close attention to which bank is offering the card, because terms can vary widely. For example, some banks require that the total charges are paid off each month, while some let a balance carry forward. Some banks also offer affinity cards, for which benefits such as airline miles are offered.

The basic rule is, if the balance is going to be paid off every month, choose one of the cards with no annual fee. Inversely, if a balance is going to be carried over from month to month, choose the card with the lowest annual percentage.

Using a credit card to pay for tuition can make sense if the card provides additional benefits, such as airline miles. This is true only if the account starts with a zero balance and the entire balance is paid when the statement comes. Remember, if any balance is carried forward, interest is charged from the date a purchase is posted—there's no grace period.

Having a credit card is excellent insurance. You can't even rent a car without one. And, in an emergency, it's a way to get cash. Here again, though, use this privilege only as a last resort. There's a transaction fee to get cash, and interest is added the moment the cash is withdrawn. Cash advances, though a terrific convenience and wonderful in an emergency, can be very, very expensive.

1997 TAX CUTS FOR EDUCATION

The federal balanced budget signed into law in August 1997 offers new tax benefits for parents who are sending or planning to send their children to college. There are two tax credits that could directly affect you.

The "HOPE Scholarship" Tax Credit

This tax credit allows you to receive a 100 percent tax credit for the first $1,000 of tuition and required fees and a 50 percent credit on the second $1,000 for a maximum credit of $1,500. This credit is available for tuition and required fees less grants, scholarships, and other tax-free educational assistance. This credit is phased out for joint filers who have between $80,000 and $100,000 of adjusted gross income. The credit can be claimed for students who are in their first two years of college and who are enrolled on at least a half-time basis in a degree or certificate program for any part of the year.

The Lifetime Learning Tax Credit

This tax credit is targeted for college juniors and seniors. The family will receive a 20 percent tax credit for the first $5,000 of tuition and required fees paid each year through 2002, and for the first $10,000 thereafter. Just like the "HOPE Scholarship," this credit is available for tuition and required fees less grants, scholarships, and other tax-free educational assistance.

These tax credits wont help you up-front putting together the funds to pay for the first year of college, but they should help you free up some money for subsequent years. Further information on these tax credits is available through the IRS or on the World Wide Web at www.ed.gov.

WHAT'S NEXT

You're in the home stretch. Now you know all the pieces of the story—the types and amount of aid you and your student will receive, the amount you'll be expected to pay, and your financing options. It's time to see the *whole* story. By using our sample families again, let's learn how to put all these financing elements together to pay for college. In the next step we'll use the College Money Planner™ Report, a service available from the College Board, to bring together what we've covered.

[illegible]

[illegible]

[illegible]

[illegible]

SOLIDIFY YOUR PLAN

Personalized Financing Strategies

Step 9

In this step, you'll review the financing scenarios that we've put together for each of our students and their families. These scenarios and strategies will help you figure out which financial strategies will work for *your* family. While this kind of analysis is somewhat complicated, you can see how valuable it is in helping you determine the best way to meet your child's college costs.

A NOTE ABOUT ONE OF OUR SOURCES

When this book was originally written in 1995, some of the following information reflected the results of the College Money Planner™ Report generated by the College Scholarship Service of the College Board. Over the last three editions of *You Can Afford College*, this information has been edited and updated by the author. Only the information, not the financing suggestions, are from the College Board.

Information on the College Money Planner can be requested by calling the College Board at (212) 713-8000 or by writing:

College Scholarship Service
College Money Planner Report
45 Columbus Avenue
New York, NY 10023-6992

KEY STRATEGIES

1. *Pay as you go from current income and assets.*
2. *Borrow your share from the Federal PLUS Program.*
3. *Pay your share by a combination of saving and borrowing through PLUS.*
4. *Borrow your share using a home equity loan or line of credit.*

Only the information, not the financing suggestions, are from the College Board. Check with your financial advisor or attorney before undertaking any major financial, tax, or legal strategy.

FRANCES

Frances's parents' wages (income from their restaurant) from the previous year totaled $56,300. The family's monthly income is about $4,000 after taxes, out of which they pay $1,700 for mortgage and property taxes and $600 for insurance and medical deductibles. This leaves them with approximately $1,700 per month for all other expenses. They also have $5,000 in savings, which they dip into occasionally, but want to keep as a cushion.

As we learned in Step 7, Frances's family's share of her college costs (including Frances's contribution) would be about $7,900 per year, or about $658 per month, at any of the three colleges she has applied to. These figures don't include the loans Frances would have to repay herself.

Strategy 1: Pay as You Go from Current Income and Assets

It would be extremely difficult for Frances's family to pay $658 per month, for four years, out of their current earnings. Their savings wouldn't even cover one year's expenses. The advantage of paying their share out of current earnings and savings, of course, is that Frances's family wouldn't have to take on more debt (and pay more interest in the long term). The disadvantage, however, is that this option would require making large and potentially unaffordable monthly payments for the four years that Frances is in college.

"During high school my parents didn't want me working too hard at the restaurant. For college summer and winter breaks, though, I'm going to push them for more hours or try to get a higher-paying job. The more I can earn and save, the less my parents will have to borrow."

Strategy 2: Borrow Your Share from the Federal PLUS Program

A second option is for the family to borrow their contribution from the Federal PLUS Program, beginning in Frances's freshman year, and repaying the loans over a ten-year period.

Seven years after Frances graduates, when the first PLUS loan is repaid, their monthly payment would begin to decline. It would continue to drop until their last payment, nine years following Frances's graduation.

However, Frances is the oldest of three children, and both of her siblings are planning to go to college (one in three years, when Frances is a senior, and the second three years later). This means that for one year, Frances and her sister both will be in college. As we saw in the need-analysis discussion, their parents' share of the costs would remain the same, and the contribution for each child would be divided in half.

Two years after Frances graduates, her parents would still be paying for Frances's four PLUS loans, and would have to pay also for the second daughter's expenses. If they chose to borrow again to meet their share of the costs, their PLUS loan payments would double. While this is the same as if they paid their share of Frances's costs without borrowing, hopefully their income will increase enough in the six years to make those payments more affordable.

Strategy 3: Pay Your Share by a Combination of Saving and Borrowing Through PLUS

A third strategy is for Frances's parents to start saving now, putting aside as much as possible each month until she begins college one year from now. They could then borrow the balance they need to pay their share of college costs through the PLUS program. Unfortunately, given their total income and expenses, Frances's family would be able to save very little of their income. Therefore, this strategy is probably not appropriate for them.

Strategy 4: Borrow Your Share Using a Home Equity Loan or Line of Credit

Many parents choose to use their home equity to finance their share of college costs. While Frances's family has about $40,000 in home equity, they would qualify only for a very small home equity line of credit based on their income. To qualify for a home equity loan or line of credit, most lenders require that borrowers have less than 36 percent of their gross monthly income going toward all debts. Thirty-four percent of Frances's parents' gross income goes toward their mortgage, leaving only about $100 a month available to pay any other loan. Furthermore, many lenders would include required insurance payments in this formula, thereby making Frances's family unable to qualify for a home equity loan. And even those lenders that don't include these payments might not feel it worthwhile to lend so little money.

Recommendation

In Frances' situation, the only viable option for her family is Strategy 2 (borrow your share from the Federal PLUS Loan Program). If they manage to save anything out of their current income, or if their income increases, it probably would be wise for them to limit the amount they borrow, since they'll also have to borrow to pay for Frances's sister's education.

FEDERAL PLUS LOAN

A nongovernment subsidized loan program for parents of undergraduate students. It falls under the Federal Family Education Loan Program or William D. Ford Federal Direct Loan umbrella.

"I can't imagine my parents paying more than $600 a month for my education. So, I guess they'll need to take out a PLUS Loan. I hate having to ask them to do that, but they've already told me that they consider my education an appropriate reason to take out a loan. Hope I can make it up to them."

ANGELA

Angela's mother's net income is just over $3,000 per month. With this income, she supports herself and her two children, and the younger child still has three years before he applies to college. The mortgage payment and property taxes are about $1,500, or almost half of the net income. Her employer, a software manufacturing company in Silicon Valley, contributes to a retirement plan, but only in company stock, and the asset is not available until retirement.

The family's calculated contribution is $4,651 based on Federal Methodology and $4,705 based on Institutional Methodology. There's also a student contribution of $385 from Angela's $1,100 assets plus an amount between $79 and $1,200 in a student contribution from Angela's income.

"My mom checked with her employer about tuition reimbursement benefits. She works for a pretty small company, so they don't have a plan. They said they'd consider starting one, though. We'll keep our fingers crossed for next year."

Strategy 1: Pay as You Go from Current Income and Assets

Twelve monthly payments per year of up to $518 would be necessary for Angela's family to pay their expected share. This amount is well beyond their means. If they were somehow able to do so, their family contribution for four undergraduate years would be about $24,864. One option is an employer tuition reimbursement plan. Over half of Fortune 1000 companies offer financial assistance to employees going to school, and many of these extend this benefit to an employee's dependents.

Strategy 2: Borrow Your Share from the Federal PLUS Program

A second strategy is for Angela's mother to borrow the family share from the PLUS program, beginning Angela's freshman year, and to repay the loans over a ten-year period.

In the seventh year after Angela's graduation, when the first PLUS loan is repaid, the payment would begin to decline and would continue to drop until the last payment, nine years following graduation.

Strategy 3: Pay Your Share by a Combination of Saving and Borrowing Through PLUS

With only about $1,500 per month remaining after the mortgage and property tax payments, it would be difficult for Angela's mother to save anything for Angela's schooling. Furthermore, her $3,000 cash savings and $4,000 in company stock would cover only the first year's expected contribution. This would leave the family with no assets and, therefore, no cushion.

Nevertheless, Angela's mother feels that by scrimping and being extra careful, she would be able to save almost $100 per month, which she would put toward Angela's college expenses. This means that Angela's mother would have to borrow only the rest from the PLUS program.

"I don't know why my mom says she could save $100 a month out of her current income. It seems we're always looking for every extra penny at the end of the month."

Strategy 4: Borrow Your Share Using a Home Equity Loan or Line of Credit

Although Angela's mother has $45,000 in home equity, she already has a first and second mortgage on her home. Furthermore, her $48,000 salary would likely make her ineligible to borrow against the equity, since already 35 percent of her salary goes to the mortgage payment. Combined with her car payment of $350, this totals $1,750, or almost 44 percent of her gross income. As we said earlier, most lenders require that no more than 36 percent go to outstanding debts.

Recommendation

Like Frances's parents, Angela's mother probably would be unable to contribute much either from her current income or from a home equity loan. Therefore, she'll probably have to borrow her entire share using a Federal PLUS Loan. If she's able to scrimp and save, as she said she would do, any amount she saves could lower the amount she would need to borrow.

HOME ADVANTAGE

HOME EQUITY LOAN: A fixed loan for a defined term. You take the entire amount right away and make payments for an agreed-upon number of months.

HOME EQUITY LINE OF CREDIT: This is like a credit card with a credit limit. You can use it as you need to, and pay only the amount you use.

JAMES

James is the second of four children. His older brother is currently a sophomore at a private, expensive university, his sister is in high school, and his younger brother attends a private school that costs $7,000 in tuition. James's father is an attorney in a small law firm, making $150,000 per year. James's mother has been staying home taking care of the children, but has started to go to the local community college part time to complete her education. They own their own home, with about $100,000 of equity, and pay $2,600 per month for mortgage and property taxes. They also own and manage rental property that has a net value of $80,000 for which they take $8,000 off their income tax in depreciation. They have stocks and bonds worth $40,000 and approximately $20,000 in savings.

By working part time during the school year and by saving some money given to him as a gift, James has accumulated $4,000. He plans to use this money for his college expenses.

His parents' family contribution using the Federal Methodology is $16,669, and the EFC using the Institutional Methodology is $16,967. However, if the $8,000 in rental property depreciation is added back in to income, and $5,770 of the $7,000 private secondary school tuition is taken out (the maximum permitted in the IM formula), the IM parent contribution is $18,540. This contribution is for each of the family's two children (James's mother takes only one or two classes each term at the local community college, at a minimal cost, so no allowance is made for her college expenses). James's IM student contribution is the $1,400 from his assets plus at least $1,150 in minimum student contributions from his income.

Strategy 1: Pay as You Go from Current Income and Assets

If James's family decided to pay the college expenses for him and for his brother out of current income and assets, it would be about $1,600 per month for each of the two children in college (two years of James's contribution could almost be covered by the amount he has in savings, which he planned to use anyway). After taxes and retirement are deducted, James's father's net monthly income comes to around $8,800, $2,600 of which goes to housing and almost $600 toward the private secondary school tuition for James's younger brother. Out of the remaining $5,600, it would be impossible to pay the total $30,900 EFC, but they could pay a portion out of income and the balance from savings. The EFC for the four years of both children in college would be about $160,000.

"I was thinking how great it would be to spend one or two semesters in Europe on a study-abroad program. The colleges told me that the costs would be just about the same as studying here, so my parents said I should consider it for my sophomore or junior year."

With two other children coming along who will likely go to college, one after James's brother has graduated and the second after James graduates, it may be wise for the family to pay as much as they can for the two current college students out of their assets, while still maintaining a reasonable amount of their savings for protection. By doing so, they have the added benefit of reducing their future expected family contribution.

Strategy 2: Borrow Your Entire Share from the PLUS Program

If James's parents chose to borrow from the PLUS program to meet their share of James's college costs, their payments for James's first year would be about $250 per month, plus the same amount for James's brother. For the two years James and his brother are both in school, this would grow to $1,000 per month. James's brother would then graduate, but his sister would begin school, so James's parents would continue to pay James's brother's PLUS loans for another eight years, then begin another series of PLUS loans for their daughter. The total amount of PLUS loan for James would be over $80,000, monthly payments for which would be close to $1,000 per month. If they used this strategy for each child, their monthly payments would max out at close to $4,000 per month for the years when they're still paying on James's older brother's PLUS loans and borrowing for James's younger brother.

Strategy 3: Pay Your Share by a Combination of Saving and Borrowing Through PLUS

James's parents could also put aside as much as possible each month until James begins college and then borrow the balance through the PLUS program. Although they have a high income, they have high expenses in their current mortgage, outstanding loan repayments, and secondary school tuition payments. These expenses will not allow them to save much before James begins college.

However, James's parents believe they can save about $2,000 per month, or almost one-fourth of their after-tax income. This is more than the amount required to meet one child's college family contribution. If they saved this amount during James's high school senior year, they would accumulate another $20,000 or so. Combined with the $20,000 they have in savings, they could reduce the amount they needed to borrow from PLUS or a private loan. Assuming they were unable to continue saving, because of James's expenses, and wanted to borrow the balance they needed, they would still have to borrow for James's last two years, for James's older brother's two years of college expenses, and James's sister's four years.

Strategy 4: Borrow Your Share Using a Home Equity Loan or Line of Credit

Based on their home value of $100,000 and their income, James's family would qualify for a home equity line of credit of just under $7,000 per year. If they used this line of credit to finance their share of college costs, their principal and interest payment—assuming an interest rate of 8.38 percent—would be about $25 per month for the first year, growing to about $100 per month during James's senior year. Payments would continue at this level for six years following James's graduation, after which they would begin to decline. James's family could not continue to use a home equity line of credit for the college expenses of the other two children until the principal owed was under approximately $28,000 (or 28 percent of the home equity most banks use as a limit).

One advantage of using their home equity to finance their college costs is that it's likely the interest payments would be tax deductible. This reduces their costs of borrowing by more than 30 percent, given James's family's tax bracket. Of course, they should check with their tax advisor to make sure they qualify to deduct interest payments and to determine how much their federal taxes could be reduced.

"I can't believe how much my parents will need to borrow. I always thought my dad made so much money it wouldn't matter how much college cost. I guess I was wrong."

Recommendation

Once again, given the financial strength of the family, and the fact that there are two children who will be going to college after James, it's probably advisable the family use some of their assets for the two older children's college expenses and take out a home equity line of credit for the maximum they're permitted. They should have that maximum increase as the equity in the home increases (through mortgage payments and, possibly, an increase in the value), pay the $2,000 or so per month they felt they could afford out of their current income, and either borrow or dip into their savings for the two later children as needed.

DAVID

David's parents have been divorced for a number of years, and David's father has been paying $7,200 per year in child support for each of the two children, David and his younger sister. The child support for David is scheduled to end when David turns eighteen, at the end of his senior year in high school. David's mother takes home just under $2,500 per month from her job, out of which she must pay $520 for their mortgage and property taxes, and $600 for her car loan, credit card debts, and other obligations. She has $8,000 in savings. Their home is worth about $100,000, and she still owes $67,000, leaving her with an equity of $33,000.

"I know it's pretty hard for my dad to keep paying for my education. He still pays for our house plus the child support for my sister, and he has his own apartment to pay for. There's no way my mom can handle the whole thing herself, though."

The calculated FM contribution is about $8,287. If, however, the financial aid office agrees to recalculate the package based on the fact that the $7,200 in child support payments will end on David's eighteenth birthday (and, as we saw, this is a definite possibility), then the FM contribution would be about $5,223.

The IM contribution for David's mother is either $6,870, if the child support is in the equation, or $4,659, if the child support payment is taken out of the equation. David's noncustodial parent contribution (his father's) is calculated at about $3,000. Many colleges will insist that the noncustodial parent make a contribution.

David's student contribution of $840 is based on 35 percent of his assets (plus he may have to make a minimum contribution from his income).

Strategy 1: Pay as You Go from Current Income and Assets

If the college expects contributions from both parents, his mother's IM contribution would be about $573 per month, considerably more than what she could afford to pay. David's father's expected contribution would be less than one-half of what he had been paying, although, legally, he would no longer be required to make any contribution.

With only $8,000 in savings, David's mother would be unable to pay her entire contribution from either savings or a combination of savings and assets. In fact, she reported that she thought she could afford only $200 per month toward David's education.

Strategy 2: Borrow Your Entire Share from the PLUS Program

If David's mother chose to borrow her entire share from the PLUS program every year and repaid the loans over a ten-year period, by David's senior year, the payments would be more than she feels she could afford. However, any pay raise she received would make up some of that difference. Her payments would continue at this same level until six years after David graduated.

In the seventh year, when the first PLUS loan is repaid, her monthly payment would begin to decline and would continue to drop until her last payment, nine years following graduation. If David's sister, who is four years younger, went to college, and everything else remained the same and David's mother paid for the daughter's college expenses with PLUS loans, the monthly payments would rise each year.

"I wanted to pay for college myself, but I'm not allowed to borrow more than what I've been awarded. So I told my parents I would pay them back for whatever they need to borrow for my education. They wouldn't agree to that, and told me to save the money for my kid's college fund."

Strategy 3: Pay Your Share by a Combination of Saving and Borrowing Through PLUS

David's mother could start saving early, putting aside as much as possible each month until David began college, and then borrow the balance she would need from the PLUS program. If she started saving the $200 per month that she reported she could put towards David's education, she would be able to reduce the amount she needs to borrow. If she used most of this increased savings, especially early in David's college career, and borrowed from the PLUS program as needed, she would reduce the amount she needed to borrow significantly.

Since David's mother's total PLUS eligibility for David's four years of college is about $28,000, using all or part of her savings could reduce the total loan to $20,000 or less. If she were able to continue saving before her daughter started school, she could both increase her savings and reduce the amount she would have to borrow for her daughter's education.

Strategy 4: Borrow Your Share Using a Home Equity Loan or Line of Credit

With a net home value of $33,000 and her current income (including the child support payments, which she would report since it would increase her loan eligibility), she would qualify for a home equity line of credit of about $18,000. Most lenders would permit her to borrow 80 percent of the value of the home, minus the outstanding debt, since her income is sufficient to repay the amount. This amounts to almost two-thirds of her expected contribution, and has the added benefit of probably being tax deductible for her. In her tax bracket, this could save another $50 or $60 per month, which she also could use for David's expenses. She would also have to dip into her savings or use more of her current income to make up the difference of $10,000, or $208 per month for David's four years. This is just a bit more than the $200 per month she reported she'd be able to save.

"No matter which school I go to, I know that my mom and I are both going to have to borrow to pay for it. My mom told me that she could afford the payments as long as she didn't lose her job. She also reminded me that with a college degree I'll be able to get a higher-paying job."

Recommendation

A combination of strategies is the likely choice for David's family. We assume that David's father would continue to support David at the same level he has, although he might prefer to make the calculated noncustodial parent's contribution. David's mother, then, could meet her share by contributing the $200 per month she said she could ($2,400 per year) and getting a home equity line of credit for $4,500 per year. The $18,000 credit she would qualify for (which will save her $50 a month because it will lower her taxes), in combination with the $200 per month from her income and the father's contribution, would carry David through his four years.

WHAT'S NEXT

Whether you're late thinking about paying for college, or you're approaching the final stages of the financial aid process, there are still strategies available to you. In the next step, you'll review important last-minute advice on how to pay for your child's college education.

REVIEW IMPORTANT LAST-MINUTE ADVICE

Quick and Easy Tips

Step 10

If you're like most parents, you've put away some money for your child's education. And whether you've read straight through this book or you've skipped right to this chapter, you probably realize that the saved amount may not be enough.

If your child is already a junior or senior in high school, you may think there aren't many planning steps left to help finance his or her upcoming college education.

This isn't the case. Although it would have been better if you had started planning earlier, it's definitely not too late to start planning now.

In this step, review these useful suggestions for last-minute or short-term planning. Some of these tips have been discussed in other steps of this guide, but they should also prove helpful at this stage.

Attend "College Nights" Throughout the Fall and Spring, and Speak Directly to College Representatives

Keep in mind, though, that colleges are often represented by alumni, not college staff. The alumni mean well, but may not have enough information to be of much help. Also, these nights are often quite frenetic, so getting to speak with a college representative for more than a few moments may be difficult. Questions you might ask are:

- Does the college offer any merit-based aid?
- Does the college leave any unmet need?
- Does the college award more grant aid to students with higher grades or higher SAT/ACT scores in high school?

Ensure That You and the Other Members of Your Family Have Good Credit Ratings

Since you may have to borrow to finance an education, you should request a copy of your credit report from one of the national credit bureaus to make sure there are no

Credit Insecurity?

Some lenders will help you address your particular credit situation. For example, one lender will do a pre-approval of your credit by fax, and try to help you solve credit problems through a "second look" process. Call 1-888-KAP-LOAN for more information.

errors. If there are any delinquencies or defaults, try to make amends with your creditors. There are three major credit bureaus in the United States:

Equifax
www.equifax.com
(800) 685-1111

Experian Information Solutions, Inc. (formerly TRW Consumer Assistance)
www.experian.com
(888) 397-3742

Trans Union Corp.
wwww.transunion.com
(800) 888-4213

Confer with a Personal Financial Advisor Who Can Help You with Your Financial Planning

Securing a home equity line of credit, refinancing your home mortgage, repositioning your assets, and obtaining loans against life insurance policies or stock and bond portfolios are all options to consider. Few, however, should tackle these sorts of financing strategies without the assistance of a trained professional. In choosing a financial advisor, you'll want to ask these questions:

- What experience do you have in financial planning?
- What experience do you have in helping families pay for college expenses?
- What kind of services can you offer?
- What does it cost for these services?
- Do you offer recommendations for specific investments or investment products? If so, do you get a commission and what percentage?

Transfer Any Assets Currently in Your Child's Name to Your Name

If you're applying for financial aid, and after you've discussed the tax consequences with your tax advisor, transfer any assets currently in your child's name to your name. Assets in the student's name are assessed for financial aid at 35 percent; assets in the parent's name are assessed at less than 6 percent. In other words, 35 percent of students' assets are expected to be used for their education, but less than 6 percent of parents' assets are added to the Family Contribution for their children.

Investigate Living Arrangements Outside of the School's Board System

Consider purchasing an apartment or small house near the college your child will attend. Your child can live there instead of in a dorm, and you can rent the additional rooms to classmates. This strategy probably won't cost you any less, but at least the money you pay for living expenses will go toward your investment. As an alternative, your child could live at home or at a relative's home and commute to a local school.

THE VOCABULARY OF BAD CREDIT

DELINQUENT: When a scheduled payment is not made by the date required.

DEFAULT: Failure to make required installment payments for a specified period.

BAD CREDIT: When a borrower is delinquent for 90 days on any financial obligation, including previous student loan, credit card payment, auto loan, revolving loan, rent, and even telephone bill.

Check with Your Employer About Tuition Reimbursement or Employee Educational Benefits for Dependents

More than half of the Fortune 1000 companies offer tuition benefits to employees; many of these extend benefits to dependents of employees. The benefits can be substantial, paying as much as half of the tuition. On the other hand, the benefit may pay only a few hundred dollars. Either way, it's money you're entitled to, and it takes nothing more than a phone call to your human resources department.

Apply for Scholarships from All Local Service Clubs and Fraternal Organizations

While the awards from these organizations rarely are great, neither is the amount of competition and the application work. If you're a member of the club or organization, your child stands a much greater chance of receiving an award. Service clubs include Rotary International, Elks, Lions, Knights of Columbus, and Knights of Pythias.

Learn Everything You Can About College Financing Strategies

You'll probably have to use a combination of financing strategies—student financial aid programs and parent loan programs, for example. Explore all of the options and their benefits, limitations, and requirements, so you'll be an educated consumer. While this book has explained many of your options, you should also check out college catalogs, which are valuable resources for information on general and school-specific programs.

DON'T GO INTO THE PROCESS BLIND

You have a right to know how the financial aid system works, and a responsibility to make it work for you.

Get a Handle on the Financial Aid Application Process and the Application Deadlines

If you overlook deadlines, neglect required forms, or fail to send appropriate documentation at the right time, you miss out on thousands of dollars in aid. While the process is confusing, especially with the continual changes, familiarity will ensure your timeliness and accuracy.

Consider Seeking the Advice of a Private Financial Aid Counselor

A private financial aid counselor will take you through the process and forms. Remember, these people charge a fee, and the fee can be fairly hefty. As a general rule, most people can do just as well by reading this guide and talking to the financial aid office staff at any college (your local community college is an excellent resource).

STEPS FOR INDEPENDENT STUDENTS

FINANCING COLLEGE ON YOUR OWN

This chapter contains advice and strategies for students who are financing college without assistance from their parents. If you're an independent student, be sure to check out the preceding chapters, in addition to this chapter, if you haven't done so already. The step-by-step information in the earlier chapters, especially regarding financial aid programs, budgets, and some of the financing strategies will be useful to you.

As an independent student, you probably have two primary financial aid questions: how you'll be evaluated and how to secure the funds to attend college. This chapter will concentrate on those two concerns. Then we'll explore some financial aid issues that independent students need to be aware of.

ARE YOU REALLY INDEPENDENT?

Before you go any further with this chapter, make sure you'll really be considered independent when you apply for financial aid. Your status as an independent student will be assessed according to the federal government's standards. Your view of independence might differ from the government's.

Many students consider themselves independent solely because they no longer live at home. According to the federal government, that is not an adequate criteria for being considered independent. If you refer to the FAFSA (the Free Application for Federal Student Aid), you will find that there are six questions that the government uses to ascertain whether you are independent. They are the six questions in Step Two of the FAFSA:

FOLLOW THE STEPS

The first five steps in this book provide an overview of the financial aid process. The information in those chapters applies equally to dependent and independent students.

FEDERAL FORM

The basic required form for all federal aid is called the Free Application for Federal Student Aid (FAFSA). See Step 5 for more information.

1. Were you born before January 1, 1977?

2. Will you be working on a degree beyond a bachelor's degree in school year 2000–2001?

3. As of today, are you married?

4. Are you an orphan or ward of the court or were you a ward of the court until age 18?

5. Are you a *veteran* of the U.S. Armed Forces?

6. Do you have *legal dependents* (children who receive more than half of their support from you); *or* do you have dependents (other than your children or spouse) who live with you and receive more than half of their support from you, now and through June 30, 2001?

TERMS USED IN THE DEFINITION OF AN INDEPENDENT STUDENT

VETERAN: A student who has engaged in active service in the U.S. Army, Navy, Air Force, Marines or Coast Guard and was released under a condition other than dishonorable—including a student who attended a U.S. military academy but withdrew in good standing—or a student who is not a veteran now but will be a veteran by June 30, 2001.

LEGAL DEPENDENT: Any child of the student who receives more than half support from the student (the child does not have to live with the student), including a natural or adopted child, or a child for whom the student is legal guardian. Also, any person who lives with the student and receives more than half of his or her support from the student and will continue to receive more than half support from the student during the award year.

The federal government has determined that in order to be considered independent, you must have established your independence by one of the six criteria above. Simply moving away from home and getting a job to support yourself is not enough until you have achieved a minimum age. Remember that one of the basic tenets of financial aid is that financing college is the responsibility of the family to the extent that they are able to contribute. Your feeling that you don't want to make your parents pay, or your parents' reluctance to pay is not sufficient reason to declare yourself independent.

Some students who do not meet the federal criteria might still be considered independent under special circumstances. If your situation is exceptional, speak with the financial aid officer at the school you're planning to attend. Financial aid officers are allowed by law to make some exceptions. They will do so if they are convinced that your case is unique. Each case is viewed on its own merits; there are no general criteria guaranteed to make a financial aid officer override your dependency status. Sometimes one college will override the student's dependency status when another college will refuse to change it. It's up to the college to determine whether a particular student's case is valid.

Remember, as long as you meet any one of the above criteria, you will be considered independent and your parents' financial information will not be used to determine your eligibility for federal financial aid. Some colleges (especially those with large amounts of scholarship money available) will still request that you provide your parent's information to determine your eligibility for their own scholarship funds. This practice is perfectly legal. If you refuse to provide the requested information, these schools will just award you federal funds, eliminating you from consideration for their own scholarship money.

EVALUATING INDEPENDENT STUDENTS: TWO PATHS

Once you have determined that you are actually an independent student, you must understand how your need analysis might differ from the analysis of dependent students and their parents. Your need analysis will follow one path of two paths. You'll follow one path if anyone is financially dependent upon you (other than your spouse) and another path if you're responsible only for yourself. Depending on your status, the analysis uses different formulas and tables to calculate your estimated family contribution (EFC). We'll continue to call the contribution by that generic name even though, as an independent student, your family just consists of you (and your spouse, if you're married).

In Step 6 we discussed allowances taken against income based on your age. There are allowances taken based on age for independent students too. Independent students use basically the same Asset Protection Allowance deduction that parents of dependent students are eligible for. Independent students are expected to be saving for retirement just like everybody else.

ALL IN THE FAMILY

Expected family contribution, or EFC, is the amount of a family's resources that should be available to help for college. EFC determines your need and your eligibility for federal aid.

Asset Protection Allowance		
Age of student as of 12/31/00	Allowance for —	
	Married Student	Unlimited Student
25 or less	0	0
26	2,600	1,600
27	5,200	3,300
28	7,800	4,900
29	10,500	6,600
30	13,100	8,200
31	15,700	9,800
32	18,300	11,500
33	20,900	13,100
34	23,500	14,800
35	26,100	16,400
36 or more	For additional information, check online at http://ifap.ed.gov/csb_html/efcform.htm	

Independent Student Case Studies

Let's reintroduce our independent students. These two students might not exactly mirror your situation, but they will give you an idea of how the independent student need analysis works and how your situation might be addressed.

Mary

"I thought about going to college right after high school but I felt that I needed to get a job first. The cost of college just seemed overwhelming when I was 18. I'm 24 now and I've discovered that I really want to go to college and get my degree in teaching. I've been on my own so long that I don't want to ask my parents for help. They're older now anyway and it would be a hardship for them to assume my college costs. I'm independent of them and they shouldn't be expected to contribute."

Michael

"My wife and I have decided that I need to go to college and get my degree so that I can increase my earning power and be able to move up in my profession. We've been married for a couple of years and have a two-year-old daughter. My wife is only working part time but I would like to go to school full time so that it won't take me forever to finish. We've agreed that I can work part time and attend college full time, but we'll definitely need some financial help to make ends meet and pay my tuition."

These two scenarios are common among part-time students. Many high school students put off attending for several years and then realize that they need a degree in order to either increase their income or pursue a new career.

ARE YOU READY TO CHANGE YOUR LIFE?

It is not impossible to return to school after an absence of several years although you'll probably have to make some sacrifices. Your lifestyle is no longer the same as it was when you were 18 and willing to forgo a lot of the comforts that you've grown accustomed to. In addition, you are used to having a steady paycheck to feed your bank account.

This will change. One of the biggest problems that you'll face when returning to school is learning to budget your money while you adjust to the loss of that steady paycheck. It usually takes a semester or two to get a handle on your altered financial situation. For example, you can expect to receive much of your financial aid at the beginning of the semester. Often, this is everything that you'll have to live on for the next four months, unless you have a federal work-study job or a part-time job off campus. You need to learn to budget your funds so that you don't run out of money before the next semester begins and your financial aid is available again. As an independent student you might find yourself living very close to the line between solvency and being broke. And you probably can't count on a handout from your family. So, the point is to plan accordingly: Have a small financial cushion for any unforeseen expenditures.

This doesn't mean that you can never go out to eat or go to the movies. It just means that you need to set up a reasonable budget and stick to it.

Step 2 Review: Figure Out the Real Cost

In Step 2 we talked about direct and indirect college costs. Your direct costs are basically the same as those of a dependent student. The big difference is in some of your indirect costs.

Let's review the basic components of the student expense budget:

Direct Costs:	Tuition
	Fees
	Books and Supplies
Indirect Costs:	Room
	Board
	Transportation and Travel
	Personal Expenses (including phone, entertainment, toiletries, laundry, clothing, etcetera)

DIRECT COSTS

- *Tuition*
- *Fees*
- *Books and supplies*

You also need to add in the following items:

- Medical and Dental Expenses
- Miscellaneous expenses (such as child care)

While your tuition and fees and books and supplies should be the same as that of a dependent student, your indirect costs could be substantially more. Often on-campus housing is subsidized so that it is cheaper than the cost of living off-campus. Most independent students don't live in the dorms. Many student have families; others might feel that they would be uncomfortable in that setting based on their age. Living off-campus might substantially increase a student's housing costs especially if housing in the area of the college is expensive.

As an independent student, you have higher personal expenses since you are responsible for all your costs yourself. While a dependent student can go home for a weekend to get some laundry done, you must pay for everything yourself. In addition, medical and dental expenses are your responsibility rather than your family's. This can add a substantial amount to the budget, along with any child care expenses. You need to look very carefully at your current expenses to see if there is anything we might have missed that you need to build into your budget.

Remember that the student expense budget is only valid for the semesters that you will be attending school. That means that, if you are going to attend school for the fall and spring semesters, your budget will cover nine months (since you will not be attending during the summer). If you plan to attend year round, your student expense budget will be for the entire twelve months. You need to plan accordingly.

Another important concept behind the student expense budget is that it covers the costs of the student only. That means that, if you are married, only your housing and food costs are included; your spouse's expenses are excluded. Although this may not seem to make sense at first, the federal government stresses that financial aid is for the student, not the family. Although food costs can be separated, housing is just one cost. Still, the student expense budget will estimate the cost of your portion of housing. The policy on this will differ greatly between schools. Some schools will fund your living alone off-campus, while others will only build in the cost of your portion of a shared apartment.

INDIRECT COSTS

- *Room*
- *Board*
- *Transportation and travel*
- *Personal*
- *Medical and dental*
- *Miscellaneous*

Fill out the following chart to help you estimate what your actual expenses will be:

COLLEGE COSTS

Tuition	$
Fees	$
Books and Supplies	$
Room	$
Board	$
Transportation and Travel	$
Personal	$
Medical and Dental	$
Miscellaneous	$
Other	$
TOTAL	$

CALCULATING YOUR EFC: TWO SAMPLES

Now you are ready to look into how you are going to meet these estimated college costs.

Let's use our sample independent students to illustrate what you might be expected to pay.

SAMPLE EFC WORKSHEET FOR MARY

2000-01 EFC FORMULA: INDEPENDENT STUDENT
Without Dependent(s) Other Than A Spouse

STUDENT/SPOUSE INCOME IN 1999			
1.	Student's and spouse's Adjusted Gross Income (FAFSA #40)		23,175
2. a.	Student's income earned from work (FAFSA #44)	23,000	
b.	Spouse's income earned from work (FAFSA #45)	0	
	Total student/spouse income earned from work		23,000
3.	Student/spouse Taxable Income (If tax filers, enter the amount from line 1 above. If non-tax files, enter the amount from line 2.		23,175
4.	Untaxed income and benefits:		
	Earned Income Credit (tax filers only) (FAFSA # 43)	0	
	Total from FAFSA Worksheet A (FAFSA #46)	0	
	Total untaxed income and benefits		0
5.	Taxable and untaxed income Sum of line 3 and line 4)		23,175
6.	Total from FAFSA Worksheet B (FAFSA #47)	-	0
7.	TOTAL INCOME (line 5 minus line 6) May be a negative number	=	23,175

ALLOWANCES AGAINST STUDENT/SPOUSE INCOME			
8.	1999 U.S. income tax paid (FAFSA #41) (tax filers only); if negative, enter zero.		3,476
9.	State and other tax allowance (Table B1. If negative, enter zero.)	+	464
10.	Student's Social Security tax (Table B2)	+	1,760
11.	Spouse's Social Security tax (Table B2)	+	0
12.	Income protection allowance (Table A3) $5,000 for unmarried student; $5,000 for married student if the spouse is enrolled at least 1/2 time $8,000 for married student if the spouse isn't enrolled at least 1/2 time	=	5,000
13.	Employment expense allowance: If student is not married, allowance is zero. If student is married but only one person is working (the student If student is married and both student and spouse are working, the allowance is 35% of the lesser of the earned incomes or $2,800, whichever is less.		0
14.	TOTAL ALLOWANCES	=	10,700

AVAILABLE INCOME		
Total Income (from line 7)		23,175
Total Allowances (from line 14)	-	10,700
15. AVAILABLE INCOME (AI)	=	12,475
16. Assessment rate	x	.50
17. CONTRIBUTION FROM AI May be a negative number.	=	12,475

STUDENT/SPOUSE CONTRIBUTION FROM ASSETS			
18. Cash, savings, & checking (FAFSA #48)			3500
19. Net worth of investments* (FAFSA #49) If negative, enter zero.			0
20. Net worth of business (FAFSA #50) If negative, enter zero.		0	
21. Net worth of investment farm (FAFSA #51) If negative, enter zero, If the family resides on the farm, enter zero.		0	
22. Net worth of business/farm (sum of lines 20 and 21)		0	
23. Adjusted net worth of business/farm (Calculate using Table A4)	+		0
24. Net Worth (sum of lines 18, 19, and 23)	=		3500
25. Asset protection allowance (Table B4)	-		0
26. Discretionary net worth (line 24 minus line 25)	=		3500
27. Asset conversion rate	x		35%
28. CONTRIBUTION FROM ASSETS If negative, enter zero.	=		1225

EXPECTED FAMILY CONTRIBUTION		
Contribution from AI (from line 17) May be a negative number.		6238
Contribution from assets (from line 28)	+	1225
29. Contribution from AI and assets	=	7463
30. Number in college in 2000-01 (FAFSA #87)	div	1
31. EXPECTED FAMILY CONTRIBUTION for 9-month enrollment (if negative, enter zero)		7,463

* Do not include the student's home.

Mary lives in Chicago, Illinois in a two-bedroom apartment with a roommate. She is 25 years old and moved out of her parents' house when she was 19. She earns $23,000 as a personnel assistant at a large corporation. She has managed to save $3,500 over the last several years but she is worried that her car might need to be replaced. Her salary is her only source of income. Her calculated family contribution is $7,463 from her earnings and savings. This figure may seem high until you realize that this contribution is used for both tuition and fees and her living expenses. Looking at it this way, her contribution works out to $829 per month, which basically covers her rent, food, and transportation expenses. She still has a large financial need.

DO THE MATH

If you have Internet access you can find the information you need to do your own calculations at http://ifap.ed.gov/csb_html/efcform.htm

SAMPLE EFC WORKSHEET FOR MICHAEL

2000-01 EFC FORMULA: INDEPENDENT STUDENT
With Dependent(s) Other Than A Spouse

STUDENT/SPOUSE INCOME IN 1999		
1. Student's and spouse's Adjusted Gross Income (FAFSA #40)		34,200
2. a. Student's income earned from work (FAFSA #44)	28,000	
b. Spouse's income earned from work (FAFSA #45)	6,000	
Total student/spouse income earned from work		34,000
3. Student/spouse Taxable Income (If tax filers, enter the amount from line 1 above. If non-tax files, enter the amount from line 2.)*		34,200
4. Untaxed income and benefits:		
Earned Income Credit (tax filers only) (FAFSA # 43)	0	
Total from FAFSA Worksheet A (FAFSA #46)	0	
Total untaxed income and benefits		0
5. Taxable and untaxed income Sum of line 3 and line 4)		34,200
6. Total from FAFSA Worksheet B (FAFSA #47)	-	0
7. TOTAL INCOME (line 5 minus line 6) May be a negative number	=	34,200

ALLOWANCES AGAINST STUDENT/SPOUSE INCOME		
8. 1999 U.S. income tax paid (FAFSA #41) (tax filers only); if negative, enter zero.		5,126
9. State and other tax allowance (Table C1. If negative, enter zero.)		2,052
10. Student's Social Security tax (Table C2)	+	2,142
11. Spouse's Social Security tax (Table C2)	+	459
12. Income protection allowance (Table C3)	+	15,500
13. Employment expense allowance: If student is not married, allowance is zero. If student is married but only one person is working (the ... If student is married and both student and spouse are working, the allowance is 35% of the lesser of the earned incomes or $2,800, whichever is less.		2,100
14. TOTAL ALLOWANCES	=	27,379

AVAILABLE INCOME		
Total Income (from line 7)		34,200
Total Allowances (from line 14)	-	27,379
15. AVAILABLE INCOME (AI) May be a negative n	=	6,821

STUDENT/SPOUSE CONTRIBUTION FROM ASSETS			
16. Cash, savings, & checking (FAFSA #48)			4000
17. Net worth of investments* (FAFSA #49) If negative, enter zero.			0
18. Net worth of business (FAFSA #50) If negative, enter zero.	0		
19. Net worth of investment farm (FAFSA #51) If negative, enter zero, If the family resides on the farm, enter zero.	0		
20. Net worth of business/farm (sum of lines 18 and 19)	0		
21. Adjusted net worth of business/farm (Calculate using Table C4)		+	0
22. Net Worth (sum of lines 16, 17, and 21)		=	4000
25. Asset protection allowance (Table C5)		-	10500
26. Discretionary net worth (line 22 minus line 23)		=	-6500
27. Asset conversion rate		x	12%
28. CONTRIBUTION FROM ASSETS If negative, enter zero.		=	0

EXPECTED FAMILY CONTRIBUTION		
Contribution from AI (from line 15) May be a negative number.		6821
Contribution from assets (from line 26)	+	0
27. Adjusted Available Income (AAI) May be a negative number	=	6821
28. Total Contribution from AAI (Use Table C6; if negative, enter zero.)		1,501
29. Number in college in 2000-01 (FAFSA #87)	div	1
31. EXPECTED FAMILY CONTRIBUTION for 9-month enrollment	=	1,501

* Do not include the student's home.

Michael and his wife, Melanie, live in Atlanta, Georgia in a townhouse that his parents helped them to purchase. Michael is 29 years old and works as a skilled machinist in a factory. He and Melanie have a daughter, Elizabeth, who is two years old. Michael earns $28,000 but the union has been trading off benefits in order to keep salaries up. He now has to contribute to his medical plan, and his family's dental and eye care are not covered. Melanie made $6,000 working part time in a day care center, an arrangement which allows her to save on child care while still bringing in additional income for the family. They have a small savings of $4,000. Michael's calculated family contribution is $1,501 from the family's earnings and savings.

Two Different Stories

Looking at the two EFCs for these students, you can see where there are some major differences in how the contribution is calculated. You can see that the single independent student (Mary) is expected to contribute a greater percentage of her income Michael, on the other hand, is treated in the need analysis like the parent of a dependent student even though he is the student. The assumption is that the single independent student has only her living and school expenses while the married student with a child has many other expenses to handle.

Some colleges are willing to use an estimated year income to calculate your contribution but you shouldn't count on that (especially if you are looking primarily at public institutions).

You should also note that Mary shows a greater contribution from her assets since she is under 26 years of age and doesn't have any of her assets protected. Even with the age difference, Michael's contribution would be much less since his assets are only assessed at 12 percent while Mary's savings are assessed at 35 percent. You can see how this compares with the dependent student model where the parent's assets are assessed at 12 percent while the student's assets are assessed at 35 percent.

Although there is not an example of a married student with no dependents in this chapter, you need to know that a student in this position is looked at in the same manner as the single independent student with a higher percentage of both the student's income and assets considered available to fund his or her education.

Will My EFC Ever Change?

Independent students' contributions often differ greatly from the first two years of that they apply for financial aid to their last two years. This is because their income level was much higher before they started to attend college. Whereas a dependent student's family income will not change substantially from year to year, you will show a much higher income on your FAFSA in the first two years as opposed to the last two years. To illustrate this point, let's look at Mary's situation.

	Tax Year	Income	EFC
1st year	1999	$23,000	$7,463
2nd year	2000	$15,333	$5,317 (est)
3rd year	2001	$0	$0 (est)
4th year	2002	$0	$0 (est)

Her first-year income reflects her working 12 months. In 2000, she will work for only 8 months since she will quit her job and go to school in September. Her contribution will drop $2,146 for the 2002–2003 academic year. If she has used all her savings in the first semester (which she might do), her 2nd year contribution goes down to $4,092. Assuming that her only income from then on is federal work-study or that she makes $4,250 or less per year and she has used up her savings, her EFC will drop to $0 in her last two years. This will increase her overall eligibility and make her eligible for Federal Pell Grants (currently $3,300 per year). The same type of reduction will occur for Michael and his family although it won't be as dramatic since his contribution is low to start with.

CALCULATING THE EFC ANOTHER WAY

Let's go on to see how these students would be treated in the Institutional Methodology analysis.

SAMPLE IM WORKSHEET FOR MARY

College Scholarship Service (CSS)

2000-2001 Institutional Methodology (IM Worksheet)

Computational Model					
Independent student					
Student's name:	Mary Williams				
INCOME OF STUDENT(& SPOUSE)					
1.	AGI/taxable income			$	23,175
2.	Untaxed income/benefits			+	0
3.	Income adjustments (child support paid + taxable student aid)			-	0
4.	**Total family income (sum of lines 1 and 2, minus 3)**			=	23,175
ALLOWANCES					
5.	U.S. income tax				3,476
6.	State and other taxes (% from Table 1 X line 1)			+	464
7.	F.I.C.A. (Table 2)			+	1,760
8.	Medical/dental expense allowance (Table 2)			+	0
9.	Employment allowance (Table 2)			+	0
10.	Annual education savings allowance (AESA) (Table 4)				
a.	Annual savings goal (Line 4 X 1.5%, up to $1,670)	=	348		
b.	Number of precollege children	=	0		
c.	Total AESA (line 10a X 10b)			+	348
11.	Monthly maintenance allowance (Table 3b)			+	3,990
12.	Total allowances (sum of lines 5 - 11)			=	9,690
13.	Calculated available income (line 4 minus line 12)			=	13,485
14.	**SC from income [(line 13 X 70%) X number in college adjustment (Table 10)] or minimum student contribution (Table 11), whichever is greater**			=	9,440
ASSETS					
15.	Cash, Savings, and checking accounts				3,500
16.	Home equity			+	0
17.	Investment equity			+	0
18.	Other real estate equity			+	0
19.	Adjusted business/farm equity (Table 7)			+	0
20.	Value of Trusts			+	0
21.	Net worth (sum of lines 15 - 20)			=	3,500
22.	Asset protection allowances:				
a.	Emergency reserve allowance (Table 8):	=	0		
b.	Cumulative education savings allowance (CESA) (Table 4 dependent children only)	=	0		
c.	Total asset allowances (Sum of a + b)			-	0
23.	Discretionary net worth (line 21 minus line 22c - may not be negative)			=	3,500
24.	Total SC from assets (line 23 X .25)			=	875
25.	**SC from assets [line 24 X number in college adjustment (Table 10)]**			=	875
CONTRIBUTION					
29.	**Total contribution (sum of line 14 and line 25)**			=	10,315

As you can see, the FM and IM analysis differ in the amount that Mary is expected to contribute from her income (based on a nine-month academic year). The federal need analysis uses a set offset against a student's income of $4,250 while the IM uses $1,330 per month for any months of nonenrollment. If the college Mary chooses to attend has two four-month semesters, leaving her with four months of nonenrollment, her contribution would be closer to the FM calculation. With the changes in the IM for the 2000-2001 year, the difference between Mary's FM and IM is $2,852, mostly because the IM uses 70% of available income while the FM only uses 50%. Her financial aid package may be very different depending on which methodology the colleges decide to use.

SAMPLE IM WORKSHEET FOR MICHAEL

College Scholarship Service (CSS)

2000-2001 Institutional Methodology (IM Worksheet)

Computational Model Independent student				
Student's name: Michael Jones				
INCOME OF STUDENT(& SPOUSE)				
1.	AGI/taxable income		$	34,200
2.	Untaxed income/benefits		+	0
3.	Income adjustments (child support paid + taxable student aid)		-	0
4.	**Total family income (sum of lines 1 and 2, minus 3)**		=	34,200
ALLOWANCES				
5.	U.S. income tax			5,126
6.	State and other taxes (% from Table 1 X line 1)		+	684
7.	F.I.C.A. (Table 2)		+	2,601
8.	Medical/dental expense allowance (Table 2)		+	0
9.	Employment allowance (Table 2)		+	2,100
10.	Annual education savings allowance (AESA) (Table 4)			
a.	Annual savings goal (Line 4 X 1.5%, up to $1,670)	= 513		
b.	Number of precollege children	= 1		
c.	Total AESA (line 10a X 10b)		+	513
11.	Monthly maintenance allowance (Table 3b)		+	3,690
12.	Total allowances (sum of lines 5 - 11)		=	14,714
13.	Calculated available income (line 4 minus line 12)		=	19,486
14.	**SC from income [(line 13 X 70%) X number in college adjustment (Table 10)] or minimum student contribution (Table 11), whichever is greater**		=	13,640
ASSETS				
15.	Cash, Savings, and checking accounts			4,000
16.	Home equity		+	10,000
17.	Investment equity		+	0
18.	Other real estate equity		+	0
19.	Adjusted business/farm equity (Table 7)		+	0
20.	Value of Trusts		+	0
21.	Net worth (sum of lines 15 - 20)		=	14,000
22.	Asset protection allowances:			
a.	Emergency reserve allowance (Table 8):	= 11,820		
b.	Cumulative education savings allowance (CESA) (Table 4 dependent children only)	= 13,840		
c.	Total asset allowances (Sum of a + b)		-	25,660
23.	Discretionary net worth (line 21 minus line 22c - may not be negative)		=	0
24.	Total SC from assets (line 23 X .25)		=	0
25.	**SC from assets [line 24 X number in college adjustment (Table 10)]**		=	0
CONTRIBUTION				
29.	**Total contribution (sum of line 14 and line 25)**		=	13,640

The difference between the FM and IM analyses is even more pronounced in Michael's case. On the income side, while the income is the same, there is no income protection allowance for independent students in IM. Instead, there is a monthly maintenance allowance for periods of non-enrollment and an Annual Education Savings Allowance (AESA) deducted from Michael's family income. While the FM deduction is $15,500 against income, the IM deduction is only $4,203. This leaves Michael with a much larger contribution from his income ($13,640 vs. $6,821 in FM). His $10,000 in home equity doesn't affect the contribution because it is all protected by the Asset Protection Allowances. If he had more equity in his house, it might add something onto the contribution, but it will have to be greater than $21,660 before it will have any effect.

The decision of any college Michael is planning to attend to use IM rather than FM will reduce the amount of financial aid he will be able to secure.

HOW WILL YOU BE PACKAGED?

Now that you know how you are going to be evaluated, the next question is, what type of financial aid package can you expect from colleges?

Actually, financial aid packaging is no different for an independent student than for a dependent student. The only real difference is that the budget tends to be higher and the package may include more self-help funds. (In other words, loans and work-study.) This is not because the colleges discriminate against independent students. Rather it's because the needs are often so high that the only way that the college can meet the need is to include a lot of self-help funds.

Anything Extra?

There is one difference in the money available to you. Independent students are automatically eligible for additional federal loan funds. While a dependent undergraduate student may receive a maximum of $2,625 in subsidized and unsubsidized federal Stafford loans, you may receive up to $6,625 in subsidized and unsubsidized federal Stafford loans. The chart on the next page illustrates the difference in the amounts available.

Maximum Annual Loan Amounts
Federal Stafford Loan Program and Federal Direct Stafford Loan Program

Borrower's Academic Level	Dependent Student Total Subsidized & Unsubsidized	Independent Student Subsidized Limit	Independent Student Unsubsidized Limit *Less Subsidized Amount Borrowed*
First Year Undergraduate Student	$2,625	$2,625	$6,625
Second Year Undergraduate Student	$3,500	$3,500	$7,500
Third Year and Beyond Undergraduate Student	$5,500	$5,500	$10,500

MARY'S PACKAGES

	College A	College B	College C
Cost of Attendance	$15,411	$14,894	$28,246
Student Contribution	$7,463	$7,463	$10,315
Need	$7,948	$7,431	$17,931
AWARD:			
Federal Pell Grant	$0	$0	$0
State Award	$0	$0	$0
Institutional Grant	$1,000	$0	$7,500
Federal Perkins Loan	$0	$0	$1,300
Federal Work-Study	$2,400	$2,000	$2,500
Federal Stafford Loan	$4,548	$5,431	$6,625
Unmet Need	$0	$0	$6

Analysis of Mary's Packages

As you can see, Mary will need to take on a substantial loan wherever she decides to attend. This often happens to independent students in their first two years because of their income level before leaving work to attend college. Remember our example earlier in this step that showed how her contribution will go down over the four years that she attends college. She needs to do her budgeting over the four years of attendance and project her loan burden based on her changing EFC.

The financial aid packages as they appear may not show Mary's actual loan burden since she may not be able to come up with her contribution. Remember the chart earlier in this step that showed how much additional Unsubsidized Federal Stafford Loan you can borrow at each academic level? You're allowed to borrow the Unsubsidized Federal Stafford Loan to replace part or all of your EFC. If Mary finds that she needs additional money to meet her expenses, she has some eligibility left in the Federal Stafford Loan to help her out.

College C is a private college which is able to offer her a substantial Institutional Grant. Even with this large grant, Mary much take on more debt than at the other two public colleges if she decides to attend here. Her cost (including Federal Work-study) is $10,425 for her first year, as opposed to $6,948 at College A and $7,431 at College B.

All of the colleges have offered her Federal Work-Study funds which she might want to decline if she can find a better paying job off-campus. She needs to be careful, though. She should avoid working too many hours off-campus when she is readjusting to the rigors of academic life. Unfortunately, this is a mistake that many returning students make.

Mary's Bottom Line

Which college should Mary attend? It all depends on her goals. If one college offers a better teaching program, that could sway her decision. Also, since Mary is a commuter student, the location of the school might have a greater effect on her decision than it would for a student living in the dorms.

A final consideration for Mary is how flexible the school is in allowing students to switch from full-time to part-time status. If Mary runs into financial or academic difficulty she might need to take a smaller load of classes in one or more semesters. How amenable is the college to this type of change?

Mary must consider these issues before she commits to any of the schools. Whichever college she chooses will give her a good education, but she needs to weigh the different factors carefully before making a final decision.

MICHAEL'S PACKAGES

	College A	College B	College C
Cost of Attendance	$15,410	$28,870	$17,000
Student Contribution	$1,501	$13,640	$1,501
Need	$13,909	$15,230	$15,499
AWARD:			
Federal Pell Grant	$1,750	$1,750	$1,750
State Award	$0	$0	$0
Institutional Grant	$0	$10,000	$2,500
Federal Perkins Loan	$1,500	$0	$2,120
Federal Work-Study	$2,500	$0	$2,500
Federal Stafford Loan	$6,625	$3,480	$6,625
Unmet Need	$1,534	$0	$4

Analysis of Michael's Packages

Michael is not eligible for the Georgia Hope Scholarship because he graduated from high school before the program was begun. Therefore, it is much more difficult for the colleges in his home state to find the funding for him since so much of the state money is aimed at the Hope Scholarship.

Michael's contribution is calculated at $1,501, but he will probably have to come up with more than that to fund his education. His wife might need to work additional hours in order to help fund his education. In addition, Michael will have to work, whether it's at the Federal Work-Study job offered or at an outside job. Most likely, he will need to work outside of the college in order to earn more than the $2,500 offered. This award probably cannot be increased: Work-study funds are spread across many applicants. Also, FWS jobs tend to pay less than jobs outside the college environment.

Michael is also being expected to borrow the maximum Subsidized and Unsubsidized Federal Stafford Loan at two of the colleges. This means Michael doesn't have any flexibility here for additional borrowing. He may find that he needs to make use of one of the private loan programs discussed earlier in this book. Although they have higher interest rates, they might be Michael's only option.

Note that Michael is not being asked to borrow the maximum federal loan at College B but his cost to attend here will still exceed the other two schools due to the high student contribution. Michael should make sure that he calculatees the real cost to him of each of the colleges rather than just look at the high institutional grant and the lower loan.

One of Michael's colleges has left him with unmet need (which we haven't really seen before for any of the dependent students). This is due to Michael's high level of financial need and where he is applying to school. Many public institutions do not have substantial amounts of their own institutional scholarship funds to allocate to students. When a high-need student like Michael applies, there is just not enough money available to fund his full need. It's not that the schools don't want to; they simply lack the funds.

Michael's Bottom Line

Michael needs to make some serious decisions with his wife before he commits to any of these colleges. He may want to consider attending part time in the beginning and then switching to full time once he gets closer to his degree. Starting college full time and then switching to part time makes it more difficult to complete your degree for many students. The work typically gets harder and you just run out of energy.

If Michael and Melanie are committed to Michael's attending full time, they might need to discuss Melanie's getting a full-time job and putting Elizabeth into child care. This solution is feasible only if her salary is high enough to justify the cost of full-time child care. Melanie may be able to increase the number of hours she works at her current job, which would result in more income without the additional cost of child care. Michael can investigate the possibility of staying part time at his current job. He might also be able to negotiate medical benefits which would reduce the family's costs.

There's another possibility: Michael could always ask his family for financial assistance. This is usually difficult, and in Michael's case it would be especially difficult since his parents have already helped him to purchase a home. If Michael is paying his parents back, they might be willing to defer the payments until Michael finishes school, as an alternative to giving Michael more money. Another possibility is borrowing funds from parents rather than going to a private loan fund. All these possibilities need to be investigated.

WHAT'S NEXT

If you haven't already done so, refer to Step 10 for some last-minute strategies. Financing for independent students is not impossible but it does present challenges, especially if you're thinking of returning to college full time. Still, the rewards are there; you'll just need to work out a strategy. In the end, your college education will be worth the sacrifices.

Part Two: FINANCIAL AID RESOURCES

"Honey . . . your muffled, demented laughter is starting to frighten me. I'm calling 911."

REGIONAL RESOURCES

State Loan Agencies 190

U.S. Department of Education Regional Offices 196

STATE LOAN AGENCIES

ALABAMA

Alabama Students contact:

Kentucky Higher Education Assistance Authority
1050 U.S. 127 South
West Frankfort Office Complex
Frankfort, KY 40601-4323
(502) 696-7200, (800) 928-8926
http://www.kheaa.com

ALASKA

Alaska Commission on Postsecondary Education
Alaska Student Loan Corporation
3030 Vintage Boulevard
Juneau, AK 99801-7109
(907) 465-2962
http://www.usagroup.com

ARIZONA

USA Funds, Inc.
P.O. Box 6180
Indianapolis, IN 46206-6180
(317) 849-6510, (800) 382-4506
http://www.usagroup.com

ARKANSAS

Student Loan Guarantee Foundation of Arkansas
219 South Victory Street
Little Rock, AR 72201-1884
(501) 372-1491, (800) 622-3446
http://www.slgfa.org

CALIFORNIA

California Student Aid Commission
P.O. Box 419032
Rancho Cordova, CA 95741
(916) 445-0880
(800) 367-1589 (defaulted loans)
(916) 322-9277 (billing problems)
http://www.edfund.org

COLORADO

Colorado Student Loan Program
Suite 425
999 18th Street
Denver, CO 80202-2471
(303) 294-5050, (800) 727-9834
http://www.cslp.org

CONNECTICUT

Connecticut Student Loan Foundation
P.O. Box 1009
Rocky Hill, CT 06067
(860) 257-4001, (800) 237-9721
http://www.cslf.com

DELAWARE

Pennsylvania Higher Education Assistance Agency
1200 North 7th Street
Harrisburg, PA 17102-1444
(717) 720-2850, (800) 692-7392
http://www.pheaa.org

DISTRICT OF COLUMBIA

American Student Assistance
P.O. Box 9154
Boston, MA 02205-9154
(617) 426-9434, (800) 999-9080
http://www.amsa.com

FLORIDA

Florida Department of Education
Office of Student Financial Assistance
325 W. Gaines Street
Collins Building, Rm. 255
Tallahassee, FL 32399-0400
(850) 488-4095, (800) 366-3475 (loans)
http://www.firn.edu/doe/bin00065

GEORGIA

Georgia Higher Education Assistance Corporation
2082 East Exchange Place, Suite 200
Tucker, GA 30084
(770) 414-3000; (800) 776-6878
http://www.gsfc.org

HAWAII

USA Funds, Inc.
P.O. Box 6180
Indianapolis, IN 46206-6180
(317) 849-6510, (800) 382-4506, (800) 428-9250
http://www.usagroup.com

IDAHO

Northwest Education Loan Association.
500 Coleman Building
811 First Avenue
Seattle, WA 98104
(206) 461-5300, (800) 562-3001
http://www.nela.net

ILLINOIS

Illinois Student Assistance Commission
1755 Lake Cook Road
Deerfield, IL 60015
(847) 948-8500, (800) 477-4411 (preclaims)
(800) 934-3572 (defaulted loans)
http://www.isac1.org

INDIANA

USA Funds, Inc.
P.O. Box 6180
Indianapolis, IN 46206-6180
(317) 849-6510, (800) 824-7044, (800) 428-9250
http://www.usagroup.com

IOWA

Iowa College Student Aid Commission
200 10th Street, 4th floor
Des Moines, IA 50309-3609
(515) 281-3501, (800) 383-4222
http://www.state.ia.us/government/icsac

KANSAS

USA Funds, Inc.
P.O. Box 6180
Indianapolis, IN 46206-6180
(317) 849-6510, (800) 428-9250, (800) 824-7044
http://www.usagroup.com

KENTUCKY

Kentucky Higher Education Assistance Authority
1050 U.S. 127 South
West Frankfort Office Complex
Frankfort, KY 40601-4323
(502) 564-7990, (800) 928-8926
http://www.kheaa.com

LOUISIANA

Louisiana Office of Student Financial Assistance
P.O. Box 91202
Baton Rouge, LA 70821-9202
(225) 922-1012, (800) 259-5626
http://www.osfa.state.la.us

MAINE

Finance Authority of Maine
1 Weston Court
State House Station 119
Augusta, ME 04333
(207) 626-8200, (800) 228-3734 (in Maine)
http://www.usagroup.com

MARYLAND

USA Funds, Inc.
P.O. Box 6180
Indianapolis, IN 46206-6180
(317) 849-6510, (800) 428-9250, (800) 824-7044
htytp://www.usagroup.com

MASSACHUSETTS

American Student Assistance
330 Stuart Street
Boston, MA 02116-5292
(617) 426-9434, (800) 999-9080
http://www.amsa.com

MICHIGAN

Michigan Higher Education Assistance Authority
P.O. Box 30047
Lansing, MI 48909
(517) 373-0760, (800) 642-5626
http://www.state.mi.us

MINNESOTA

Great Lakes Higher Education Corporation
P.O. Box 7859
Madison, WI 53707
(608) 246-1800
(800) 236-4300,
(800) 354-6980 (defaulted loans)
http://www.glhec.org

MISSISSIPPI

USA Funds, Inc.
P.O. Box 6180
Indianapolis, IN 46206-6180
(317) 849-6510, (800) 428-9250, (800) 824-7044
http://www.usagroup.com

MISSOURI

Coordinating Board for Higher Education
3515 Amazonas Drive
Jefferson City, MO 65109-5717
(573) 751-2361, (800) 473-6757 (in Missouri)
http://www.mocbhe.gov

MONTANA

Montana Guaranteed Student Loan Program
P.O. Box 203101
Helena, MT 59620-3101
(406) 444-6594, (800) 537-7508
(800) 322-3086 (defaulted loans)
http://www.mgslp.state.mt.us

NEBRASKA

Nebraska Student Loan Program
P.O. Box 82507
Lincoln, NE 68501-2507
(402) 475-8686, (800) 735-8778
http://www.nslp.org

NEVADA

USA Funds, Inc.
P.O. Box 6180
Indianapolis, IN 46206-6180
(317) 849-6510, (800) 428-9250, (800) 382-4506
http://www.usagroup.com

NEW HAMPSHIRE

New Hampshire Higher Education Assistance Foundation
P.O. Box 877
Concord, NH 03302-0877
(603) 225-6612, (800) 525-2577
http://www.nhheaf.org

NEW JERSEY

New Jersey Higher Education Assistance Authority
4 Quakerbridge Plaza, CN 540
Trenton, NJ 08625
(609) 588-3200, (800) 792-8670
http://www.state.nj.us/treasury/osa

NEW MEXICO

New Mexico Student Loan Guarantee Corporation
P.O. Box 25136
Albuquerque, NM 87125
(505) 345-3371, (800) 279-3070
http://www.nmslgc.org

NEW YORK

New York State Higher Education Services Corporation
99 Washington Avenue
Albany, NY 12255
(888) 697-4372, (800) 642-6234
http://www.hesc.state.ny.us

NORTH CAROLINA

North Carolina State Education Assistance Authority
P.O. Box 14103
Research Triangle Park, NC 27709
(919) 549-8614
http://www.ncseaa.edu

NORTH DAKOTA

Student Loans of North Dakota Guarantor
P.O. Box 5524
Bismarck, ND 58506-5524
(701) 328-5662, (800) 472-2166
http://www.banknd.com/slnd

OHIO

Great Lakes Higher Education Corporation
P.O. Box 7858
Madison, WI 53707
(608) 246-1800, (800) 236-4300,
(800) 944-0904 (defaulted loans)
http://www.glhec.org

OKLAHOMA

Oklahoma Guaranteed Student Loan Program
P.O. Box 3000
Oklahoma City, OK 73101-3000
(800) 247-0420
http://www.ogslp.org

OREGON

Oregon State Scholarship Commission
1500 Valley River Drive, Suite 100
Eugene, OR 97401
(541) 687-7400, (800) 452-8807
http://www.ossc.state.or.us

PENNSYLVANIA

Pennsylvania Higher Education Assistance Agency
1200 N. 7th Street
Harrisburg, PA 17102-1444
(717) 720-2860, (800) 692-7392
http://www.pheaa.org

RHODE ISLAND

Rhode Island Higher Education Assistance Authority
560 Jefferson Boulevard
Warwick, RI 02886-1320
(401) 736-1100; (800) 922-9855
http://www.rieaa.org

SOUTH CAROLINA

South Carolina State Education Assistance Authority
Interstate Center, Suite 210
P.O. Box 210219
Columbia, SC 29221
(803) 798-0916, (800) 347-2752
http://www.slc.sc.edu

SOUTH DAKOTA

Education Assistance Corporation
115 First Avenue, S.W.
Aberdeen, SD 57401
(605) 225-6423, (800) 592-1802
http://www.eac-easci.org

TENNESSEE

Tennessee Student Assistance Corporation
404 James Robertson Parkway
Parkway Towers, Suite 1950
Nashville, TN 37243-0820
(615) 741-1346, (800) 257-6526 (out-of-state)
(800) 342-1663, (800) 447-1523 (in Tennessee)
http://www.state.tn.us/tsac

TEXAS

Texas Guaranteed Student Loan Corporation
P.O. Box 201725
Austin, TX 78720-1725
(512) 219-5700, (800) 252-9743
http://www.tgslc.org/tgslc

UTAH

Utah Higher Education Assistance Authority
P.O. Box 45202
Salt Lake City, UT 84145-0202
(801) 321-7200, (800) 418-8757
http://www.uheaa.org

VERMONT

Vermont Student Assistance Corporation
P.O. Box 2000
Winooski, VT 05404-2601
(802) 655-9602, (800) 642-3177 (in Vermont)
http://www.vsac.org

VIRGINIA

Educational Credit Managment Corporation
American Bank Building
101 East 5th Street
Suite 2400
St. Paul, MN 55101
(612) 221-0566
http://www.ecmc.org

WASHINGTON

Northwest Education Loan Association
500 Coleman Building
811 First Avenue
Seattle, WA 98104
(206) 461-5300, (800) 562-3001
http://www.nela.net

WEST VIRGINIA

Pennsylvania Higher Education Assistance Agency
1200 N. 7th Street
Harrisburg, PA 17102-1444
(717) 720-2860, (800) 692-7392
http://www.pheaa.org

WISCONSIN

Great Lakes Higher Education Corporation
P.O. Box 7858
Madison, WI 53707
(608) 246-1800, (800) 236-5900
(800) 354-6980 (defaulted loans)
http://www.glhec.org

WYOMING

USA Funds, Inc.
P.O. Box 6180
Indianapolis, IN 46206-6180
(317) 849-6510, (800) 428-9250, (800) 382-4506
http://www.usagroup.com

PUERTO RICO, VIRGIN ISLANDS

Great Lakes Higher Education Corporation
P.O. Box 7858
Madison, WI 53707
(608) 246-1800, (800) 236-5900,
(800) 354-6980 (defaulted loans)
http://www.glhec.org

GUAM, AMERICAN SAMOA, NORTHERN MARIANAS, PALAU

USA Funds, Inc.
P.O. Box 6180
Indianapolis, IN 46206-6180
(317) 849-6510, (800) 428-9250, (800) 382-4506
http://www.usagroup.com

U.S. DEPARTMENT OF EDUCATION REGIONAL OFFICES

REGION	STATES IN REGION	OFFICE ADDRESS
1	Connecticut, Maine, Massachusetts, New Hampshire, Rhode Island, Vermont	FOS Regional Office U.S. Department of Education 10 Causeway St. 3rd Floor - Rm. 341 Boston, MA 02222 (617) 565-6911
2	New Jersey, New York, Puerto Rico, Virgin Islands	FOS Regional Office U.S. Department of Education 75 Park Place, 12th Floor New York, NY 10007 (212) 264-8012
3	Delaware, District of Columbia, Maryland, Pennsylvania, Virginia, West Virginia	FOS Regional Office U.S. Department of Education 3535 Market Street, Room 2304 Philadelphia, PA 19104 (215) 596-1716
4	Alabama, Florida, Georgia, Kentucky, Mississippi, North Carolina, South Carolina, Tennessee	FOS Regional Office U.S. Department of Education 61 Forsyth Street SW Rm. 18T20 - A Atlanta, GA 30303 (404) 562-6259
5	Illinois, Indiana, Michigan, Ohio, Wisconsin	FOS Regional Office U.S. Department of Education 111 North Canal Street, Room 830 Chicago, IL 60606 - 7206 (312) 886-8766

REGION	STATES IN REGION	OFFICE ADDRESS
6	Arkansas, Louisiana, New Mexico, Oklahoma, Texas	FOS Regional Office U.S. Department of Education 1999 Bryan St. Suite 2735 Dallas, TX 75201
7	Iowa, Kansas, Missouri, Nebraska	FOS Regional Office U.S. Department of Education 7505 Tiffany Springs Parkway Suite 500 Kansas City, MO 64153 - 1367 (816) 880-4090
8	Colorado, Minnesota Montana, North Dakota, South Dakota, Utah, Wyoming	FOS Regional Office U.S. Department of Education 1391 North Speer Blvd., Suite 800-A Denver,CO 80204-2512 (303) 844-3677
9	Arizona, California, Hawaii, Nevada, American Samoa, Guam, Federated States of Micronesia, Republic of Palau, Republic of Marshall Islands, the Northern Marianas	FOS Regional Office U.S. Department of Education 50 United Nations Plaza Rm. 121 San Francisco, CA 94102-4987 (415) 437-8843
10	Alaska, Idaho, Oregon, Washington	FOS Regional Office U.S. Department of Education 1000 Second Avenue Suite. 1200 Seattle, WA 98104 - 1023 (206) 287-9840

Also, for general federal financial aid info, call the Federal Student Aid Information Center at (800) 4-FED-AID.

GRANT AND LOAN TABLES

Federal Pell Grant Program Payment Schedule 200

Federal Perkins Loan Deferment Provisions. 201

Federal Perkins Loan Cancellation Provisions 202

Direct Loan Program and FFEL Program Limits 203

Grace Periods for Direct Loans and FFEL Program Loans 204

Direct Loan Program and FFEL Program
Interest Rate Provisions. 205

Direct Loan Program Repayment Plans 206

FFEL Program Deferment Provisions 207

Direct Loan Program/FFEL Program Loan
Cancellation and Payment by ED 208

William D. Ford Federal Direct Loan Program
Repayment Plan Choices 209

Full Time

Federal Pell Grant Program

Regular Payment Schedule for Determining
Full-Time Scheduled Awards in the 2000-2001 Award Period
December 1999

Cost of Attendance	Expected Family Contribution																																
	0 To 0	1 To 100	101 To 200	201 To 300	301 To 400	401 To 500	501 To 600	601 To 700	701 To 800	801 To 900	901 To 1000	1001 To 1100	1101 To 1200	1201 To 1300	1301 To 1400	1401 To 1500	1501 To 1600	1601 To 1700	1701 To 1800	1801 To 1900	1901 To 2000	2001 To 2100	2101 To 2200	2201 To 2300	2301 To 2400	2401 To 2500	2501 To 2600	2601 To 2700	2701 To 2800	2801 To 2900	2901 To 3000	3001 To 3100	3101 To 9999
0 - 199	0	0	0	0	0	0	0	0	0	0	0	0	0	0	0	0	0	0	0	0	0	0	0	0	0	0	0	0	0	0	0	0	0
200 - 299	400	400	0	0	0	0	0	0	0	0	0	0	0	0	0	0	0	0	0	0	0	0	0	0	0	0	0	0	0	0	0	0	0
300 - 399	400	400	400	0	0	0	0	0	0	0	0	0	0	0	0	0	0	0	0	0	0	0	0	0	0	0	0	0	0	0	0	0	0
400 - 499	450	400	400	400	0	0	0	0	0	0	0	0	0	0	0	0	0	0	0	0	0	0	0	0	0	0	0	0	0	0	0	0	0
500 - 599	550	500	400	400	400	0	0	0	0	0	0	0	0	0	0	0	0	0	0	0	0	0	0	0	0	0	0	0	0	0	0	0	0
600 - 699	650	600	500	400	400	400	0	0	0	0	0	0	0	0	0	0	0	0	0	0	0	0	0	0	0	0	0	0	0	0	0	0	0
700 - 799	750	700	600	500	400	400	400	0	0	0	0	0	0	0	0	0	0	0	0	0	0	0	0	0	0	0	0	0	0	0	0	0	0
800 - 899	850	800	700	600	500	400	400	400	0	0	0	0	0	0	0	0	0	0	0	0	0	0	0	0	0	0	0	0	0	0	0	0	0
900 - 999	950	900	800	700	600	500	400	400	400	0	0	0	0	0	0	0	0	0	0	0	0	0	0	0	0	0	0	0	0	0	0	0	0
1000 - 1099	1050	1000	900	800	700	600	500	400	400	400	0	0	0	0	0	0	0	0	0	0	0	0	0	0	0	0	0	0	0	0	0	0	0
1100 - 1199	1150	1100	1000	900	800	700	600	500	400	400	400	0	0	0	0	0	0	0	0	0	0	0	0	0	0	0	0	0	0	0	0	0	0
1200 - 1299	1250	1200	1100	1000	900	800	700	600	500	400	400	400	0	0	0	0	0	0	0	0	0	0	0	0	0	0	0	0	0	0	0	0	0
1300 - 1399	1350	1300	1200	1100	1000	900	800	700	600	500	400	400	400	0	0	0	0	0	0	0	0	0	0	0	0	0	0	0	0	0	0	0	0
1400 - 1499	1450	1400	1300	1200	1100	1000	900	800	700	600	500	400	400	400	0	0	0	0	0	0	0	0	0	0	0	0	0	0	0	0	0	0	0
1500 - 1599	1550	1500	1400	1300	1200	1100	1000	900	800	700	600	500	400	400	400	0	0	0	0	0	0	0	0	0	0	0	0	0	0	0	0	0	0
1600 - 1699	1650	1600	1500	1400	1300	1200	1100	1000	900	800	700	600	500	400	400	400	0	0	0	0	0	0	0	0	0	0	0	0	0	0	0	0	0
1700 - 1799	1750	1700	1600	1500	1400	1300	1200	1100	1000	900	800	700	600	500	400	400	400	0	0	0	0	0	0	0	0	0	0	0	0	0	0	0	0
1800 - 1899	1850	1800	1700	1600	1500	1400	1300	1200	1100	1000	900	800	700	600	500	400	400	400	0	0	0	0	0	0	0	0	0	0	0	0	0	0	0
1900 - 1999	1950	1900	1800	1700	1600	1500	1400	1300	1200	1100	1000	900	800	700	600	500	400	400	400	0	0	0	0	0	0	0	0	0	0	0	0	0	0
2000 - 2099	2050	2000	1900	1800	1700	1600	1500	1400	1300	1200	1100	1000	900	800	700	600	500	400	400	400	0	0	0	0	0	0	0	0	0	0	0	0	0
2100 - 2199	2150	2100	2000	1900	1800	1700	1600	1500	1400	1300	1200	1100	1000	900	800	700	600	500	400	400	400	0	0	0	0	0	0	0	0	0	0	0	0
2200 - 2299	2250	2200	2100	2000	1900	1800	1700	1600	1500	1400	1300	1200	1100	1000	900	800	700	600	500	400	400	400	0	0	0	0	0	0	0	0	0	0	0
2300 - 2399	2350	2300	2200	2100	2000	1900	1800	1700	1600	1500	1400	1300	1200	1100	1000	900	800	700	600	500	400	400	400	0	0	0	0	0	0	0	0	0	0
2400 - 2499	2450	2400	2300	2200	2100	2000	1900	1800	1700	1600	1500	1400	1300	1200	1100	1000	900	800	700	600	500	400	400	400	0	0	0	0	0	0	0	0	0
2500 - 2599	2550	2500	2400	2300	2200	2100	2000	1900	1800	1700	1600	1500	1400	1300	1200	1100	1000	900	800	700	600	500	400	400	400	0	0	0	0	0	0	0	0
2600 - 2699	2650	2600	2500	2400	2300	2200	2100	2000	1900	1800	1700	1600	1500	1400	1300	1200	1100	1000	900	800	700	600	500	400	400	400	0	0	0	0	0	0	0
2700 - 2799	2750	2700	2600	2500	2400	2300	2200	2100	2000	1900	1800	1700	1600	1500	1400	1300	1200	1100	1000	900	800	700	600	500	400	400	400	0	0	0	0	0	0
2800 - 2899	2850	2800	2700	2600	2500	2400	2300	2200	2100	2000	1900	1800	1700	1600	1500	1400	1300	1200	1100	1000	900	800	700	600	500	400	400	400	0	0	0	0	0
2900 - 2999	2950	2900	2800	2700	2600	2500	2400	2300	2200	2100	2000	1900	1800	1700	1600	1500	1400	1300	1200	1100	1000	900	800	700	600	500	400	400	400	0	0	0	0
3000 - 3099	3050	3000	2900	2800	2700	2600	2500	2400	2300	2200	2100	2000	1900	1800	1700	1600	1500	1400	1300	1200	1100	1000	900	800	700	600	500	400	400	400	0	0	0
3100 - 3199	3150	3100	3000	2900	2800	2700	2600	2500	2400	2300	2200	2100	2000	1900	1800	1700	1600	1500	1400	1300	1200	1100	1000	900	800	700	600	500	400	400	400	0	0
3200 - 3299	3250	3200	3100	3000	2900	2800	2700	2600	2500	2400	2300	2200	2100	2000	1900	1800	1700	1600	1500	1400	1300	1200	1100	1000	900	800	700	600	500	400	400	400	0
3300 - 99999	3300	3250	3150	3050	2950	2850	2750	2650	2550	2450	2350	2250	2150	2050	1950	1850	1750	1650	1550	1450	1350	1250	1150	1050	950	850	750	650	550	450	400	400	0

I Important: schools with tuitions and fees lower than $300 must use the alternate schedule for students in the cells outlined above.

Federal Perkins Loan Deferment Provisions

DEFERMENT CONDITION	Federal Perkins/NDSL Disbursed on or after 07/01/93	Federal Perkins Disbursed before 07/01/93 & on or after 07/01/87	NDSL Dispersed before 07/01/93 & on or after 10/01/80	NDSL Disbursed before 10/01/80
Half-time enrollment	No limit*	No limit*	No limit*	No limit*
Rehabilitation Training	No limit*	No limit*	No limit*	No limit*
Graduate fellowship study	No limit*	No limit*	No limit*	No limit*
Eligible internship or residency program	N/A	2 years**	2 years*	N/A
Inability to secure full-time employment	3 years*	3 years*	3 years*	3 years*
Economic hardship	3 years*	3 years*	3 years*	3 years*
Hardship as determined by school	N/A	No limit*	No limit*	No limit*
Law enforcement/correction officer	see footnote 5*	see footnote 5*	see footnote 5*	see footnote 5*
Peace Corps/ACTION program volunteer	see footnote 5*	3 years*	3 years*	3 years*
Full-time volunteer for tax-exempt organization in service comparable to Peace Corps or ACTION	N/A	3 years*	3 years*	N/A
U.S. Armed Service	see footnote 5*	3 years*	3 years*	3 years*
Officer in Commissioned Corps of U.S. Public Health Service	N/A	3 years*	3 years*	N/A
National Oceanic and Atmospheric Admin Corps	N/A	3 years*	N/A	N/A
Nurse/medical technician providing health services	see footnote 5*	see footnote 5*	see footnote 5*	see footnote 5*
Temporary total disability or care for temporarily totally disabled spouse/dependent	N/A	3 years*	3 years*	N/A
Pregnancy, care of newborn or newly adopted child*	N/A	6 months*	N/A	N/A
Mother of pre-schooler working or returning to work*	N/A	1 year*	N/A	N/A
Employment in Head Start Program	see footnote 5*	see footnote 5*	see footnote 5*	see footnote 5*
Teacher in designated low-income school	see footnote 5*	see footnote 5*	see footnote 5*	see footnote 5*
Teacher of special education, including teacher of infants, toddlers, children, or youth with disabilities*	see footnote 5*	see footnote 5*	see footnote 5*	see footnote 5*
Provider of early intervention services	see footnote 5*	see footnote 5*	see footnote 5*	see footnote 5*
Teacher of mathematics, science, foreign languages, bilingual education, or other field of expertise determined by the state education agency to have a shortage of qualified teachers	see footnote 5*	see footnote 5*	see footnote 5*	see footnote 5*
Provider or supervisor of provision of services to high-risk children from low income communities and their families	see footnote 5*	see footnote 5*	see footnote 5*	see footnote 5*

*** Principal need not be paid, and interest does not accrue**
**** Principal and interest may be deferred, but interest continues to accrue**

NOTE: The numbered footnotes for this table have not been listed here, since they refer to current deferment provisions. These change regularly, so you would have to check the latest provisions at the time of deferment.

Federal Perkins Loan Cancellation Conditions

CANCELLATION CRITERIA	Federal Perkins/ National Direct Loans Made on or after 07/23/92	Federal Perkins Loans Made Prior to 07/23/92	National Direct Loan Made Prior to 07/23/92	National Defense Loan
Total and permanent disability or death of borrower	100%	100%	100%	100%
Full-time employment in a Head Start Program[1]	100%	100%	100%	N/A
Full-time law enforcement or correction officer[2]	100%	100%[3]	100%[3]	N/A
Full-time teaching in low-income school eligible for funding under Chaper 1 of the Education Consolidation and Improvement Act of 1981[2/5]	100%	100%	100%	100%[6]
Full-time special education teacher, including teacher of infants, toddlers, children, or youth with disabilities[4/7]	100%	N/A	N/A	N/A
Provider of early intervention services in a public or nonprofit program under public supervision[2/8]	100%	N/A	N/A	N/A
Full-time teacher of handicapped services in a public or nonprofit elementary/secondary school	N/A	100%[4]	100%[4]	100%[6]
Full-time teacher of mathematics, science, foreign languages bilingual education, or any field of expertise determined by the state education agency to have a shortage of qualified teachers[4]	100%	N/A	N/A	N/A
Provider or supervisor of provision of services to high-risk children from low-income communities and their families[2/9]	100%	N/A	N/A	N/A
Nurse or medical technician providing health care service[4]	100%	N/A	N/A	N/A
Peace Corps or ACTION Program volunteer[10]	70% - Perkins (N/A - Natl. Direct Loan)	70%	N/A	N/A
Service in U.S. Armed Forces	50%[11]	50%[11]	50%[11]	50%[11]
Full-time teaching in public/nonprofit elementary/secondary school, institution of higher education or overseas U.S. Department of Defense elementary/secondary school	N/A	N/A	N/A	50%[13]
Bankruptcy[14]	in some cases	in some cases	in some cases	in some cases

NOTE: The numbered footnotes for this table have not been listed here, since they refer to current deferment provisions. These change regularly, so you would have to check the latest provisions at the time of deferment.

Direct Subsidized and Unsubsidized Combined Annual and Aggregate Loan Limits

Student Year	Annual Limit	Aggregate Limit
Dependent Undergraduates		
1st year	$2,625	
2nd year	$3,500	
3rd, 4th, and 5th years	$5,500	$23,000
Independent Undergraduates		
1st year	$6,625[1]	
2nd year	$7,500[2]	
3rd, 4th, and 5th years	$10,500[3]	$46,000[4]
Graduate Students	$18,500[5]	$138,500[6]

1. No more than $2,625 of this amount may be in subsidized loans.
2. No more than $3,500 of this amount may be in subsidized loans.
3. No more than $5,500 of this amount may be in subsidized loans.
4. No more than $23,000 of this amount may be in subsidized loans.
5. No more than $8,500 of this amount may be in subsidized loans.
6. No more than $65,500 of this amount may be in subsidized loans.

Grace Periods for Direct Loan Program and FFEL Program		
Federal (Subsidized) Stafford Loan and Direct Subsidized Loan	Federal Unsubsidized Loan and Direct Unsubsidized Loan	Federal PLUS Loan and SLS and Direct PLUS Loan
6 months for all loans for periods of enrollment 01/01/81 and after. 9-12 months for all loans for periods of enrollment before 01/01/81.	6 months on repaying principal. Interest may be paid or accrued and capitalized during in-school and grace periods.	None. The repayment period begins on the date the loan is fully disbursed. Interest begins to accrue on the date of the loans' first disbursement. For Federal PLUS Loans on or after 07/01/93, repayment may be deferred while the students for whom the funds are borrowed are enrolled at least half time. Interest may be capitalized.

1. If the grace period has not already been used, the loan's grace period begins on the data the student ceased to be enrolled at least half-time.
2. Also applied to Federal SLS loans, which were discontinued on 07/01/94.
3. Combined Federal SLS/federal sub/unsub borrowers have the option to defer Federal SLS repayment for up to 6 months after at least half-time enrollment ceases. This provision applies only when the borrower's loans have not entered repayment.
4. Paying accrued interest is postponed by adding it to the loan principal as the interest comes due. (This is called "capitalization.")
5. Not all loans made after 1/1/81 have 6 months grace period. If a student received a 7% loan prior to 1/1/81 with a 9–12 month grace period, the student continued to receive the 7% interest rate and the 9–12 month grace period on subsequent loans up until 7/1/94. Beginning 7/1/94 all loans had variable intersest rates and 6 months grace period.

Direct Loan Program and FFEL Program Interest-Rate Provisions as of 1998

	Subsidized and Unsubsidized Loans	PLUS Loans
Interest Rate	Variable rate; maximum annual rate 8.25%	Variable rate; max. annual rate 9%
Interest Rate Formula	For loans first disbursed on or after 07/01/94 through 06/30/95: • 91-day Treasury bills plus 3.1% For loans first disbursed on or after 07/01/95 through 06/30/98: • In-school, grace, or deferment: 91-day Treasury bills plus 2.5% • In repayment: 91-day Treasury plus 3.1% For loans first disbursed on or after 10/01/98 through 06/30/2003: • In-school, grace, or deferment: 91-day Treasury bills plus 1.7% • In repayment: 91-day Treasury plus 2.3%	For loans first disbursed on or after 07/01/94 through 06/30/98: • 52-week Treasury bills plus 3.1% For loans first disbursed on or after 10/01/98 through 06/30/2003: • 91-day Treasury bills plus 3.1%

Note: When this book was published, the interest rate for Direct Loans and FFELP loans was under consideration. As of July 1, 1998, the borrower interest rate on student loans will be based on the 91-day Treasury Bill plus 2.3%, with an 8.25% cap. For the coming academic year, that rate would be 7.43%. This rate is only guaranteed until 10/1/98 and may change again after that date. Please contact your college or lending institution to find out what the rate is when you plan to borrow.

Direct Loan Program Repayment Plans[1]

Standard Repayment Plan	• Fixed annual repayment amount paid over a fixed period of time[2] • Maximum repayment period 10 years[3] • $50 minimum monthly payment
Extended Repayment Plan	• Fixed annual repayment amount paid over an extended period of time[2] • Maximum repayment period varies depending on total amount of borrower's Direct Loans[3, 4] • $50 minimum monthly payment
Graduated Repayment Plan	• Two or more graduated levels of repayment[2] • Maximum repayment period varies depending on total amount of borrower's Direct Loans[3, 4] • Minimum monthly payments may not be less than 50%, nor more than 150%, of the payment if loan were repaid under the Standard Repayment Plan • Minimum monthly payment must at least cover interest that accrues monthly
Income Contingent Repayment Plan	• Not available for Direct PLUS Loans or Direct PLUS Consolidation Loans • Maximum repayment period may not exceed 25 years[5, 6] • Varying annual payment amounts generally based on AGI of borrower (and spouse) and total amount of Direct Loans but will never exceed 20% of discretionary income

1 This chart does not include the alternative repayment plan, which will vary from borrower to borrower.

2 The monthly amount a borrower pays will reflect changes in the variable interest rate, unless the borrower requests that the maximum number of monthly payments be extended.

3 Excludes any period of authorized deferment or forbearance.

4
- 12-year maximum repayment period if total amount of Direct Loans is less than $10,000
- 15-year maximum repayment period if total amount of Direct Loans is between $10,000 and $19,999.99
- 20-year maximum repayment period if total amount of Direct Loans is between $20,000 and $39,999.99
- 25-year maximum repayment period if total amount of Direct Loans is between $40,000 and $59,999.99
- 30-year maximum repayment period if total amount of Direct Loans is equal to or greater than $60,000

5 If the loan is not repaid within the maximum repayment period, the remaining portion of the loan is canceled. Any canceled loan amount is currently considered taxable income.

6 Excludes any periods of authorized deferments or forbearance. Also, if a borrower has made payments under the Standard Plan or the 12-year Extended Plan and then switches to ICR, the earlier payment periods are counted toward the 25-year repayment period. Earlier payment periods in other plans do not count toward the 25-year period.

Federal Family Education Loan Program Deferment Provisions

Deferment Condition*	Time Limit	Federal Stafford Loans (subsidized & unsubsidized) & Federal Supplemental Loans for Students (SLS)			Federal PLUS Loans				Federal Consolidation Loans	
		Refinanced and Prior Borrowers[1] of Loans (before 7/1/87)	Prior Borrowers[2] (7/1/87- 6/30/93)	New Borrowers[3]	Loans Made Before 8/15/83	Refinanced and Prior Borrowers of Loans (before 7/1/87)	Prior Borrowers[2] (7/1/87- 6/30/93)	New Borrowers[3]	Prior Borrowers (before 7/1/93)	New Borrowers[4] (after 7/1/93)
Full-time study	None	Y	Y	Y	Y	Y	Y	Y	Y	Y
Half-time study[5]	None	N	Y	Y	N	N	Y	Y	Y	Y
Graduate fellowship study[6]	None	Y	Y	Y	Y	Y	Y	Y	Y	Y
Rehabilitation training	None	Y	Y	Y	Y	Y	Y	Y	Y	Y
U.S. Armed Forces[7] or Public Health Service, or	3 years	Y	Y	N	Y	N	N	N	N	N
Nat'l Oceanic & Atmospheric Admin. (including Military and Public Health Service)	3 years	N	Y	N	N	N	N	N	N	N
Peace Corps	3 years	Y	Y	N	Y	N	N	N	N	N
ACTION	3 years	Y	Y	N	Y	N	N	N	N	N
Temporary total disability (borrower, spouse, or dependent)	3 years	Y	Y	N	Y	Y	Y	N	Y	N
Tax-exempt organization	3 years	Y	Y	N	Y	N	N	N	N	N
Teaching in teacher shortage area	3 years	N	Y	N	N	N	N	N	N	N
Eligible internship or residency program[8]	2 years	Y	Y	N	Y	N	N	N	N	N
Unemployment	2 years	Y	Y	N	Y	Y	Y	N	Y	N
Mother entering work force[9]	1 year	N	Y	N	N	N	N	N	N	N
Inability to secure full-time employment[10]	3 years	N	N	Y	N	N	N	Y	N	Y
Economic hardship[11]	3 years	N	N	Y	N	N	N	Y	N	Y
Parental leave[12]	6 months	Y	Y	N	N	N	N	N	N	N
PLUS borrower/dependent student in-school[13]	.....	N/A	N/A	N/A	Y	Y	Y	N	N/A	N/A

* Y: Deferment Applies N: Deferment Does Not Apply

Cancellation and Loan Forgiveness

Borrower	Direct and FFEL Loans
Loan Cancellation	• Death of borrower • Death of student on whose behalf a parent borrowed a PLUS Loan • Permanent and total disability of borrower • Discharge of loan in bankruptcy • Some teaching and childcare provider provisions [1]
Loan Forgiveness	• Students unable to complete their programs of study because their schools closed [2] • Students whose schools falsely certified their loans

1. For loans made on or after October 1, 1998.

2. These students are only eligible for forgiveness if their schools do not provide them with an alternate way to complete their program. This may include attendance at another nearby school that has an agreement in place with the closing school.

Examples of Debt Levels, Beginning Monthly Payments, and Total Amounts Repaid for All Direct Loan Repayment Plans[1]

Initial Debt When Loan Enters Repayment	Standard		Extended		Graduated		Income Contingent[2]											
							Income = $15,000				Income = $25,000				Income = $45,000			
							Single		Married/HOH[3]		Single		Married/HOH[3]		Single		Married/HOH[3]	
	Per Month	Total	Per Month	Total	Per Month	Total	Per Month	Total	Per Month	Total	Per Month	Total	Per Month	Total	Per Month	Total	Per Month	Total
$2,500	$50	$3,074	$50	$3,074	$25	$4,029	$17	$5,927	$17	$5,910	$23	$4,462	$22	$4,514	$28	$3,799	$28	$3,808
5,000	61	7,359	55	7,893	35	8,655	35	11,853	34	11,820	46	8,925	44	9,028	56	7,599	56	7,616
7,500	92	11,039	82	11,839	53	12,982	52	17,780	50	17,730	69	13,387	66	13,541	84	11,398	84	11,425
10,000	123	14,718	97	17,463	70	19,085	70	23,707	67	23,640	92	17,850	88	18,055	112	15,197	111	15,233
15,000	184	22,077	146	26,194	105	28,628	105	35,560	73	34,461	137	26,775	131	27,083	168	22,796	167	22,849
20,000	245	29,437	170	40,899	140	44,115	119	46,910	73	43,268	183	35,700	175	36,111	225	30,395	223	30,465
25,000	307	36,796	213	51,124	175	55,144	119	56,511	73	50,414	229	44,625	219	45,138	281	37,994	278	38,082
30,000	368	44,155	256	61,349	210	66,173	119	64,529	73	56,058	275	53,549	240	55,316	337	45,592	334	45,698
40,000	491	58,873	315	94,614	280	100,567	119	76,330	73	63,300	285	78,460	240	88,857	449	60,790	445	60,931
50,000	613	73,592	394	118,268	350	125,708	119	83,149	73	65,814	285	119,127	240	133,007	562	75,987	557	76,164
75,000	920	110,387	563	202,842	526	212,324	119	85,647	73	65,814	285	172,253	240	157,204	619	127,816	573	133,802
100,000	1,227	147,183	751	270,456	701	283,098	119	85,647	73	65,814	285	181,099	240	161,266	619	214,977	573	231,471

Notes: [1] Payments are calculated using the maximum interest rate for student borrowers, 8.25 percent.
[2] Assumes a 5 percent annual income growth (Census Bureau).
[3] HOH is Head of Household. Assumes a family size of two.

GLOSSARY

Academic Year
A period of at least 30 weeks of instructional time that usually consists of two semesters or three quarters.

Accrued Interest
Interest that accumulates on loans and must be paid at a later date.

Adjusted Gross Income (AGI)
The income figure taken from the federal income tax form. AGI is the total of wages, interest, and dividend income minus certain adjustments.

Aid to Families with Dependent Children (AFDC)
Also called welfare, AFDC is federal grant money administered by state departments of social services.

Asset Protection Allowance
An allowance, subtracted from a family's total assets, that's used to determine the expected family contribution. This allowance increases with age, recognizing that more assets should be available as you get closer to retirement age.

Assets
Financial holdings such as checking and savings accounts, stocks, bonds, trusts and other securities, loan receivables, home and other real estate equity, business equipment, and business inventory.

Award Letter
A college's notification of financial aid qualification. The award letter usually gives information about the types and amounts of aid offered, specific program information, and the conditions that govern the award.

Base Year
The 12-month period ending on December 31 preceding the award year. For example, calendar year 1995 is the base year for the 1996–97 award year.

Billing Servicer
A company that manages billing and loan collection for lenders.

Business/Farm Supplement
A form required of parents and students who own a business or farm. This form is processed by the College Scholarship Service as a supplement to the Financial Aid PROFILE.

Campus-Based Programs
The three federal financial aid programs administered by eligible colleges include the Federal Supplemental Educational Opportunity Grant, Federal Work Study, and Federal Perkins Loan.

Cancellation of Loan
A portion or all of some student loans can be canceled if the borrower performs service in certain geographic or academic fields. Some loans will be canceled upon the death of the borrower. Promissory notes outline the circumstances under which loans can be canceled.

Collection Agency
An agency that specializes in collecting payment on default or delinquent loans. Collection agencies usually receive a percentage of the amount they collect from borrowers whose payments are overdue.

College Board
A nonprofit membership organization of about 3,000 colleges, secondary schools, and education associations. It administers the SAT, Financial Aid PROFILE applications, and other education-related services.

College Scholarship Service (CSS)
The arm of the College Board that deals with financial aid information and the processing of applications.

Compound Interest
Interest that is computed on the sum of an original principal and any accrued interest.

Cooperative Education
A program offered by some colleges in which students alternate periods of enrollment with periods of employment, usually paid employment.

Cost of Attendance (Cost of Education)
The costs that are usually associated with attending college for one academic year. Costs are determined by colleges themselves and usually include tuition and fees, room and board, books and supplies, transportation, personal, and miscellaneous expenses.

Credit Bureau
An agency that keeps credit histories and other financial information and reports this information to lenders.

Default
When a borrower fails to make payments on a loan for a certain time, or has failed to comply with other terms of a promissory note.

Deferment
A specified period during which a borrower does not have to repay a loan. Depending on the type of loan, interest may or may not continue to accrue during a deferment period.

Dependent Student
Any undergraduate student under the age of 24 who is not a veteran of the U.S. Armed Forces, not married, not a ward of the court, and who does not have legal dependents (other than a spouse).

Delinquency
When a borrower fails to make an installment payment when it's due.

Direct Costs
Education-related expenses (tuition, fees, books, supplies) a family generally pays to a college.

Disbursement
The process by which financial aid monies are paid through either check distribution or crediting a student's account.

Disclosure Statement
A statement from a lender to a borrower that provides the borrower with information about the terms of the loan and the consequences of defaulting on that loan.

Discretionary Income
In the Institutional Methodology (IM) of need analysis, the income that is available to a family after taxes, medical expenses, and employment, income protection and elementary/secondary tuition allowances have been subtracted.

Documentation
Proof of the accuracy of statements made on your financial aid applications. May include any of the following: signed copies, with appropriate schedules, of federal and state tax returns; proof of citizenship status;

Social Security benefit statement; proof of unemployment benefits; completed form required by the financial aid office; any other data needed to verify information submitted on your financial aid applications.

Eligible Noncitizen
A student aid applicant who is not a U.S. citizen, but is eligible to receive federal financial aid because he or she is a permanent resident, noncitizen national, or a resident of the Trust Territory of the Pacific Islands or Micronesia.

Enrollment Status
Either full-time, half-time, part-time, etcetera, based on the number of credit hours in which a student is enrolled.

Entrance Interview
A required counseling session at which a college must inform student borrowers about their rights and responsibilities.

Exit Interview
A counseling session conducted when the student is leaving school (similar to an entrance interview). At the interview, a student's loan obligation and responsibilities are reviewed.

Expected Family Contribution (EFC)
The figure that indicates how much of a family's financial resources should be available to help pay for educational expenses. The figure is calculated using a government-approved formula and determines eligibility for financial aid.

Federal Direct Loan
A family of federal loan programs for which the lender is the federal government. Included in these programs are government-subsidized loans for students and unsubsidized loans for both students and parents of undergraduate students.

Federal Family Educational Loan Programs (FFELP)
A family of federal loan programs for which the lender is a bank, savings and loan, credit union, or other private lender. Included in these programs are government-subsidized loans for students and unsubsidized loans for both students and parents of undergraduate students.

Federal Methodology (FM)
A need analysis method developed by Congress and used to calculate the expected family contribution (EFC), which determines eligibility for federal student aid programs.

Federal Pell Grant
A federal grant awarded to undergraduate students based on need as determined using a federal need analysis formula.

Federal Perkins Loan
A 5 percent loan awarded by colleges to undergraduate and graduate students based on need as determined using a federal need analysis formula.

Federal PLUS Loan
A nongovernment subsidized loan program for parents of undergraduate students. It falls under either the Federal Family Education Loan Program or William D. Ford Federal Direct Loan umbrella.

Federal Stafford Loan
A Federal Family Education Loan Program for students. The Federal Stafford Loan can either be government-subsidized, for which the government pays any interest while the borrower is attending college, or an unsubsidized loan, for which interest accrues when the loan is made.

Federal State Student Incentive Grant
Federal funds that are pooled with state money and used for state grant programs.

Federal Supplemental Educational Opportunity Grant (FSEOG)
A federal grant awarded by colleges to the most needy undergraduate students as determined by a federal need analysis formula.

Federal Work-Study
A federal need-based financial aid program through which eligible students can earn a portion of their college expenses. Work-study is awarded by colleges, and a portion of the funding comes from the federal government. Several states also have work-study programs that are similar to the federal programs.

Financial Aid Award
A specific amount of financial assistance offered to a student through financial aid programs.

Financial Aid PROFILE
A financial aid application developed by the College Scholarship Service (CSS). Colleges can use this application to award institutional funds.

Financial Aid Transcript
A form used by colleges to collect data about financial aid received at any previously attended college.

Financial Need
The difference between the college's cost of attendance and the family's ability to pay, as measured by the family contribution.

Fixed Interest
Rate of interest that does not change during the life of a loan.

Forbearance
When a lender allows a borrower to stop paying a loan temporarily or agrees to accept smaller payments than previously scheduled. Usually, forbearance is given only when personal problems such as short-term unemployment or hospitalization prevents a borrower from making loan payments.

Free Application for Federal Student Aid (FAFSA)
The official application used to apply and establish eligibility for federal aid.

Full-Time
Usually when a student is enrolled in twelve semester or quarter hours per academic term.

General Education Development Certificate (GED)
The General Education Development Certificate is given if you have passed a high school equivalency test.

Gift Aid
Grant and scholarship money that does not have to be repaid or earned by the student.

Grace Period
The period of time that begins when a student loan borrower graduates (or ceases to be enrolled at least half-time) and ends when repayment must begin. The grace period for most student loans is six months.

Grant
Financial aid that does not have to be repaid. Financial aid grants can take the form of tuition assistance paid directly to the college on the student's behalf or a direct disbursement of money to the student to help cover other educational or living expenses. Grants can be awarded on the basis of financial need or academic merit.

Guarantee Agency
A state agency or private, not-for-profit organization that insures lenders against losses due to a borrower's default, death, disability, or bankruptcy.

Guarantee Fee
An insurance fee that the guarantee agency charges a lender. This fee is usually paid by the borrower. The

insurance or guarantee fee for a Federal Stafford Loan is 1 percent.

Half-Time
Usually when a student is enrolled in six to eight semester or quarter hours per academic term.

Immigration and Naturalization Service (INS)
The federal agency responsible for citizenship status and immigration.

Independent Student
Any student who meets any one of the following criteria: is at least 24 years old, is enrolled in a graduate or professional school, has legal dependents other than a spouse, is a ward or orphan of the court, is a veteran of the U.S. Armed Forces, or is married.

Indirect Costs
All nondirect costs of attending college, including room, board, transportation, medical, and personal expenses.

Institutional Methodology (IM)
An alternate method of need analysis used by individual colleges to calculate a family contribution used to determine eligibility for institutional and nonfederal aid.

Insurance Fee
A fee (charged on certain loans) that is deducted from the principal and is used to cover defaults (see *guarantee fee*).

Interest Subsidy
Interest payments made by the federal government to the lender on a Subsidized Federal Stafford Loan while the borrower is enrolled at least half-time or is in a grace period.

Internal Revenue Service (IRS)
The federal agency responsible for collecting income taxes. Student aid applications are verified using IRS forms.

KapLoan
Through an affiliation with one of the nation's largest providers of federal student loans, KapLoan, the Kaplan Student Loan Information Program, can provide students and families with information about the various types of loan programs available and offers a number of free services to help students complete the student loan process. Kaplan is not a lender and does not participate in determinations of loan eligibility.

Merit-Based Aid
Any form of financial aid awarded on the basis of personal achievement or individual characteristics and not based on demonstrated financial need.

Need-Analysis Formula
A formula used to determine the amount a family is expected to contribute to college expenses. This formula takes into account the family's financial strength and includes both income and assets.

Office of Student Financial Assistance (OSFA)
The Department of Education branch responsible for administering federal student financial aid programs and developing policies and procedures.

Origination Fee
A processing fee charged to a borrower by a lender to make the loan. This fee, like the guarantee or insurance fee, is usually subtracted from the amount of the loan proceeds.

Overaward
A situation that occurs when a student's family contribution plus any financial aid awarded exceeds the cost of attendance. Overawards result most often when a student's enrollment status changes or when additional resources become available to a student (such as an outside scholarship).

Package
Awards from a combination of two or more financial aid programs (e.g., grants plus work plus loans equal package).

Principal
The face value of a loan, or the total amount you borrow. Also, it's the amount on which the interest is charged.

Professional Judgment
The law allows a financial aid administrator to change the calculated family contribution or any of the elements used in the calculation based on additional information or individual circumstances that would lead to a more accurate assessment of the family's financial condition.

Promissory Note
The legal document that a borrower must sign when obtaining a loan. It lists the conditions under which the loan is made and the terms under which the borrower agrees to repay the loan.

Repayment Schedule
A plan that sets forth the interest rate on a loan, the frequency of payments, the principal and interest due in each installment, the number of payments required to pay back the loan in full, and the due date of each payment.

Satisfactory Academic Progress
A term defined by each college that describes a satisfactory rate of course completion as well as individual term performance. Regulations require that a student make satisfactory progress in order to receive any federal aid.

Scholarship
A financial aid grant based on either scholastic achievement or financial need.

Secondary Market
Institutions that buy loans from lenders. This provides more capital for lenders to make additional loans. If your loan is sold, the secondary market is responsible for managing and servicing it. The sale of a loan does not affect the borrower, since the terms of the loan remain the same.

Self-Help Aid
Funds from work and loan programs. Federal self-help programs include Federal Perkins Loan, Federal Stafford Loans, Federal Work-Study, and Federal Direct Loans.

Self-Help Expectation
The principle that students have an obligation to help pay for a portion of their education. A standard self-help expectation is frequently computed in the analysis of a student's resources.

Simplified Needs Test
A formula under the Federal Methodology (FM) for those families whose Adjusted Gross Income (AGI) is less than $50,000 and who file either the 1040A or 1040EZ IRS forms. When using this formula, the family's assets are not included.

Skiptracing
The attempt to file a valid address for a borrower who cannot be located. Any information from the borrower's loan application, the alumni or registrar's office, the U.S. Department of Education, or a commercial skiptracing service may be used to find a borrower.

Student Aid Report (SAR)
An official document that colleges use to award federal aid. The SAR shows the calculated family contribution as determined using the federal need analysis formula and based on information reported on the Free Application for Federal Student Aid (FAFSA).

Subsidized Loan
A loan for which the borrower is not responsible for all of the interest payments. For Subsidized Federal Stafford Loans, the government pays interest to the lender on behalf of the borrower while the student is in school and during approved grace periods.

Unmet Need
When a student's financial aid package (award) does not meet the calculated need (the difference between the cost of attendance and the family contribution).

Variable Interest
Rate of interest that changes during the life of a loan on a regular basis and is generally tied to an index. Some student and parent loan programs have variable interest rates that change annually based on the one-year treasury bill rate.

Verification
The process of substantiating data that a financial aid applicant reports on a financial aid application.

Part Three:
SCHOOL-BY-SCHOOL INFORMATION

"Congratulations, Zorgon! You've won the Marv J. Smmelton Memorial Scholarship for ostrich-necked, six-eyed, slug-eating sentient beings with a 4.0 grade point average."

HOW MUCH WILL IT COST?

Basic Data for Over 1,000 Schools

In this section, you'll find information on tuition, fees, and room and board at over 1,000 colleges and universities (most figures are from the 1999–2000 academic year). Tuition figures are estimated for the 2000–01 academic year, except where noted. Using this data, you'll be able to compare the schools that interest you and estimate your college costs. We've also included information you will need on each school's process for applying for financial aid. Finally, to make it easy to contact the schools you're interested in, you'll find the mailing address, phone number, fax number, and e-mail address for the admissions office at each school.

Note: Schools marked with an asterisk (*) did not respond to our request for updated information for the 2000–01 academic year.

ALABAMA

Alabama State University

Office of Admissions and Recruitment, 915 South Jackson Street, Montgomery, AL 36104. Phone: (334) 229-4291, (800) 253-5031. Fax: (334) 229-4984. E-mail: dlamar@asunet.alasu.edu. Web Site: alasu.edu. In-State Tuition and Fees: $2,520. Out-of-State Tuition and Fees: $5,040. Room and Board: $3,700. Students Receiving Some Form of Aid: 90%. Students Receiving Non-Need-Based Aid: 23%. Average Aid Package: $7,788. Required Financial Aid Forms: FAFSA. Deadline to Apply for Financial Aid: none.

Auburn University

Admissions Office, 202 Mary Martin Hall, Auburn University, AL 36849-5145. Phone: (334) 844-4080, (800) AUBURN9 (in-state). Fax: (334) 844-6179. E-mail: admissions@auburn.edu. Web Site: auburn.edu. In-State Tuition and Fees: $2,976. Out-of-State Tuition and Fees: $8,766. Room and Board: $1,911. Students Receiving Some Form of Aid: 25%. Students Receiving Non-Need-Based Aid: 5%. Average Aid Package: $5,233. Required Financial Aid Forms: FAFSA. Deadline to Apply for Financial Aid: 30 days prior to enrollment; April 15 (priority).

Auburn University—Montgomery

Admissions Office, P.O. Box 244023, Montgomery, AL 36124-4023. Phone: (334) 244-3614, (800) 227-2649. Fax: (334) 244-3795. E-mail: mmoore@mickey.aum.edu. Web Site: aum.edu. In-State Tuition and Fees: $2,577. Out-of-State Tuition and Fees: $7,731. Room and Board: $5,034. Required Financial Aid Forms: FAFSA. Deadline to Apply for Financial Aid: rolling.

Birmingham-Southern College

Office of Admission, 900 Arkadelphia Road, Box 549008, Birmingham, AL 35254. Phone: (205) 226-4696, (800) 523-5793, ext. 4696. Fax: (205) 226-3074. E-mail: admission@bsc.edu. Web Site: bsc.edu. Tuition and Fees: $15,498. Room and Board: $5,460. Students Receiving Some Form of Aid: 32%. Students Receiving Non-Need-Based Aid: 28%. Average Aid Package: $8,521. Required Financial Aid Forms: FAFSA. Deadline to Apply for Financial Aid: March 1 (priority).

Faulkner University

Office of Admissions, 5345 Atlanta Highway, Montgomery, AL 36109. Phone: (334) 386-7200, (800) 879-9186. Fax: (334) 386-7137. E-mail: kmock@faulkner.edu. Web Site: faulkner.edu. Tuition and Fees: $260. Room and Board: $3,950. Students Receiving Non-Need-Based Aid: 3%. Average Aid Package: $4,000. Required Financial Aid Forms: FAFSA.

Huntingdon College

Admissions Office, 1500 East Fairview Avenue, Montgomery, AL 36106-2148. Phone: (334) 833-4497, (800) 763-0313. Fax: (334) 833-4347. E-mail: admiss@huntingdon.edu. Web Site: huntingdon.edu. Tuition and Fees: $11,910. Room and Board: $5,500. Students Receiving Some Form of Aid: 94%. Students Receiving Non-Need-Based Aid: 46%. Average Aid Package: $10,079. Required Financial Aid Forms: FAFSA. Deadline to Apply for Financial Aid: April 15.

Jacksonville State University

Admissions and Records, 700 Pelham Road North, Jacksonville, AL 36265-1602. Phone: (256) 782-5268, (800) 231-5291. Fax: (256) 782-5291. E-mail: jsmith@jsucc.edu. Web Site: jsu.edu/home.html. In-State Tuition and Fees: $2,440. Out-of-State Tuition and Fees: $4,880. Room and Board: $3,080. Deadline to Apply for Financial Aid: March 15.

Oakwood College

Admissions Office, 7000 Adventist Boulevard, Huntsville, AL 35816. Phone: (256) 726-7030, (256) 726-7346. Fax: (256) 726-7154. E-mail: admission@oakwood.edu. Web Site: oakwood.edu. Tuition and Fees: $8,628. Room and Board: $5,040. Required Financial Aid Forms: FAFSA, institutional form. Deadline to Apply for Financial Aid: April 15.

Samford University

Admissions Office, 800 Lakeshore Drive, Birmingham, AL 35229. Phone: (205) 726-2901, (800) 888-7218. Fax: (205) 726-2171. E-mail: admiss@samford.edu. Web Site: samford.edu. Tuition and Fees: $10,300. Room and Board: $4,560. Students Receiving Some Form of Aid: 37%. Average Aid Package: $8,748. Required Financial Aid Forms: FAFSA, state aid form. Deadline to Apply for Financial Aid: March 1 (priority).

Spring Hill College

Admissions Office, 4000 Dauphin Street, Mobile, AL 36608. Phone: (334) 380-3030, (800) 742-6704. Fax: (334) 460-2186. E-mail: admit@shc.edu. Web Site: shc.edu. Tuition and Fees: $16,254. Room and Board: $5,768. Students Receiving Some Form of Aid: 52%. Students Receiving Non-Need-Based Aid: 6%. Average Aid Package: $14,654. Required Financial Aid Forms: FAFSA, institutional form. Deadline to Apply for Financial Aid: March 1 (priority).

Talladega College

Admissions Office, 627 West Battle Street, Talladega, AL 35160. Phone: (256) 761-6219, (800) 762-2168 (in-state), (800) 633-2440 (out-of-state). Fax: (256) 362-2268. E-mail: be2long@talladega.edu. Web Site: talladega.edu. Tuition and Fees: $5,949. Room and Board: $2,964. Students Receiving Some Form of Aid: 80%. Students Receiving Non-Need-Based Aid: 11%. Average Aid Package: $8,676. Required Financial Aid Forms: FAFSA. Deadline to Apply for Financial Aid: rolling; March 15 (priority).

Troy State University

Admissions Office, Adams Administration 134, Troy, AL 36082. Phone: (334) 670-3179, (800) 551-9716. Fax: (334) 670-3733. E-mail: bstar@trojan.troyst.edu. Web Site: troyst.edu. In-State Tuition and Fees: $2,900. Out-of-State Tuition and Fees: $5,560. Room and Board: $3,854. Average Aid Package: $1,732. Required Financial Aid Forms: FAFSA. Deadline to Apply for Financial Aid: May 1.

Tuskegee University

Admissions Office, 102 Old Administration Building, Tuskegee, AL 36088. Phone: (334) 727-8500, (800) 622-6531. Fax: (334) 724-4402. E-mail: Admi@acd.tusk.edu. Web Site: tusk.edu. Tuition and Fees: $9,500. Required Financial Aid Forms: FAFSA. Deadline to Apply for Financial Aid: March 31.

University of Alabama

Admissions Office, Box 870132, Tuscaloosa, AL 35487-0132. **Phone:** (205) 348-5666, (800) 933-BAMA. **Fax:** (205) 348-9046. **E-mail:** uaadmit@enroll.ua.edu. **Web Site:** ua.edu. **In-State Tuition and Fees:** $2,872. **Out-of-State Tuition and Fees:** $7,722. **Room and Board:** $4,154. **Students Receiving Some Form of Aid:** 55%. **Students Receiving Non-Need-Based Aid:** 11%. **Average Aid Package:** $3,866. **Required Financial Aid Forms:** FAFSA. **Deadline to Apply for Financial Aid:** March 1 (priority).

University of Alabama—Birmingham

Office of Undergraduate Admissions, HUC 260, 1530 Third Avenue South, Birmingham, AL 35294-1150. **Phone:** (205) 934-8221, (800) 421-8743. **Fax:** (205) 975-7114. **E-mail:** UndergradAdmit@uab.edu. **Web Site:** uab.edu. **In-State Tuition and Fees:** $3,240. **Out-of-State Tuition and Fees:** $5,970. **Room Only:** $2,438. **Students Receiving Some Form of Aid:** 32%. **Students Receiving Non-Need-Based Aid:** 13%. **Average Aid Package:** $8,498. **Required Financial Aid Forms:** FAFSA, UAB's form. **Deadline to Apply for Financial Aid:** May 1 (priority).

University of Alabama—Huntsville

Office of Admissions, 301 Sparkman Drive, Huntsville, AL 35899. **Phone:** (256) 890-6070, (800) 824-2255. **Fax:** (256) 894-6073. **E-mail:** admitme@email.uah.edu. **Web Site:** uah.edu. **In-State Tuition and Fees:** $3,112. **Out-of-State Tuition and Fees:** $6,516. **Room and Board:** $3,780. **Students Receiving Some Form of Aid:** 22%. **Students Receiving Non-Need-Based Aid:** 7%. **Average Aid Package:** $6,145. **Required Financial Aid Forms:** FAFSA, institutional form. **Deadline to Apply for Financial Aid:** April 1.

University of Mobile

Admissions Office, P.O. Box 13220, 5437 Parkway Drive, Mobile, AL 36663-0220. **Phone:** (334) 442-2287, (334) WIN-RAMS. **Fax:** (334) 442-2498. **E-mail:** adminfo@mail.umobile.edu. **Web Site:** umobile.edu. **Tuition and Fees:** $7,830. **Room and Board:** $4,280. **Students Receiving Some Form of Aid:** 55%. **Average Aid Package:** $8,250. **Required Financial Aid Forms:** FFS, Institutional forms. **Deadline to Apply for Financial Aid:** rolling; March 13 (priority).

University of Montevallo

Admissions Office, Station 6030, Montevallo, AL 35115-6030. **Phone:** (205) 665-6030, (800) 292-4349. **Fax:** (205) 665-6032. **E-mail:** admissions@um.montevallo.edu. **Web Site:** montevallo.edu. **In-State Tuition and Fees:** $3,290. **Out-of-State Tuition and Fees:** $6,440. **Room and Board:** $3,354. **Students Receiving Some Form of Aid:** 35%. **Students Receiving Non-Need-Based Aid:** 12%. **Average Aid Package:** $2,984. **Required Financial Aid Forms:** FAFSA. **Deadline to Apply for Financial Aid:** April 15 (priority).

University of North Alabama

Admissions Office, UNA Box 5011, Florence, AL 35632-0001. **Phone:** (256) 765-4608, (800) TALK-UNA. **Fax:** (256) 765-4329. **E-mail:** admisl@unanov.una.edu. **Web Site:** una.edu. **In-State Tuition and Fees:** $2,372. **Out-of-State Tuition and Fees:** $4,604. **Room and Board:** $3,352. **Students Receiving Some Form of Aid:** 49%. **Required Financial Aid Forms:** FAFSA. **Deadline to Apply for Financial Aid:** April 1 (priority).

University of South Alabama*

Admissions Office, Administration Building Room 182, Mobile, AL 36688-0002. **Phone:** (334) 460-6141. **E-mail:** admiss@jaguan1.usouthal.edu. **Web Site:** usouthal.edu. **In-State Tuition and Fees:** $2,911. **Out-of-State Tuition and Fees:** $5,581. **Room and Board:** $3,081. **Required Financial Aid Forms:** FAFSA. **Deadline to Apply for Financial Aid:** rolling.

University of West Alabama

Admissions Office, Station 4, Livingston, AL 35470. **Phone:** (888) 621-7742 (in-state), (888) 621-8044 (out-of-state). **Fax:** (205) 652-3522. **E-mail:** admissions@univ.westal.edu. **Web Site:** westal.edu. **In-State Tuition and Fees:** $2,670. **Out-of-State Tuition and Fees:** $4,950. **Room and Board:** $1,110. **Students Receiving Some Form of Aid:** 69%. **Students Receiving Non-Need-Based Aid:** 9%. **Average Aid Package:** $2,505. **Required Financial Aid Forms:** FAFSA. **Deadline to Apply for Financial Aid:** April 1.

ALASKA

Alaska Pacific University

Admissions Office, 4101 University Drive, Anchorage, AK 99508. **Phone:** (907) 564-8248. **Fax:** (907) 564-8317. **Web Site:** alaskapacific.edu. **In-State Tuition and Fees:** $10,068. **Out-of-State Tuition and Fees:** $12,032. **Room and Board:** $5,090. **Required Financial Aid Forms:** FAFSA, institutional form. **Deadline to Apply for Financial Aid:** March 15.

Sheldon Jackson College

Admissions and Financial Aid Office, 801 Lincoln Street, Sitka, AK 99835. **Phone:** (800) 478-4556. **Fax:** (907) 747-6366. **E-mail:** yukonjohn@sj-alaska.edu. **Web Site:** sj-alaska.edu. **Tuition and Fees:** $7,220. **Room and Board:** $5,150. **Required Financial Aid Forms:** FAFSA. **Deadline to Apply for Financial Aid:** July 15.

University of Alaska—Anchorage

Office of Admissions- ADM 158, 3211 Providence Drive, Anchorage, AK 99508. **Phone:** (907) 786-1480. **Fax:** (907) 786-4888. **Web Site:** uaa.alaska.edu. **In-State Tuition and Fees:** $2,694. **Out-of-State Tuition and Fees:** $7,464. **Room and Board:** $5,680. **Students Receiving Some Form of Aid:** 11%. **Required Financial Aid Forms:** FAFSA, UAA financial aid application. **Deadline to Apply for Financial Aid:** April 1.

University of Alaska—Fairbanks

Admissions Office, P.O. Box 757480, Fairbanks, AK 99775-7480. **Phone:** (907) 474-7500, (800) 478-1823. **Fax:** (907) 474-5379. **E-mail:** fyapply@uaf.edu. **Web Site:** uaf.edu. **In-State Tuition and Fees:** $3,390. **Out-of-State Tuition and Fees:** $8,310. **Room and Board:** $4,150. **Students Receiving Some Form of Aid:** 59%. **Students Receiving Non-Need-Based Aid:** 5%. **Required Financial Aid Forms:** FAFSA.

ARIZONA

Arizona State University

Admissions Office, Box 870112, Tempe, AZ 85287-0112. **Phone:** (480) 965-7788. **Fax:** (480) 965-3610. **E-mail:**

ugradadm@asuvm.inre.asu.edu. Web Site: asu.edu. In-State Tuition and Fees: $2,261. Out-of-State Tuition and Fees: $9,413. Room and Board: $5,010. Students Receiving Some Form of Aid: 32%. Students Receiving Non-Need-Based Aid: 1%. Average Aid Package: $6,794. Required Financial Aid Forms: FAFSA. Deadline to Apply for Financial Aid: March 1 (priority).

Embry-Riddle Aeronautical University—Arizona

Admissions Office, 3200 Willow Creek Road, Prescott, AZ 86301-3720. Phone: (520) 708-6600. Fax: (520) 708-6606. E-mail: admit@pr.erau.edu. Web Site: pr.erau.edu. Tuition and Fees: $11,020. Room and Board: $4,426. Students Receiving Some Form of Aid: 52%. Average Aid Package: $5,198. Required Financial Aid Forms: FAFSA. Deadline to Apply for Financial Aid: June 30; April 15 (priority).

Grand Canyon University

Admissions Office, 3300 West Camelback Road, Phoenix, AZ 85017. Phone: (602) 589-2855, (800) 800-9776. Fax: (602) 589-2580. E-mail: admis@grand-canyon.edu. Web Site: grand-canyon.edu. Tuition and Fees: $8,380. Room and Board: $6,138. Students Receiving Some Form of Aid: 49%. Students Receiving Non-Need-Based Aid: 36%. Average Aid Package: $8,068. Required Financial Aid Forms: FAFSA. Deadline to Apply for Financial Aid: rolling.

Northern Arizona University

Admissions Office, P.O. Box 4084, Flagstaff, AZ 86011-4084. Phone: (520) 523-5511, (888) 667-3628. Fax: (520) 523-6023. E-mail: undergraduate.admissions@nau.edu. Web Site: nau.edu. In-State Tuition and Fees: $2,262. Out-of-State Tuition and Fees: $8,378. Room and Board: $3,802. Students Receiving Some Form of Aid: 45%. Students Receiving Non-Need-Based Aid: 16%. Average Aid Package: $8,222. Required Financial Aid Forms: FAFSA. Deadline to Apply for Financial Aid: April 15 (priority).

University of Arizona

Admissions and New Student Enrollment, P.O. Box 210040, Tucson, AZ 85721-0040. Phone: (520) 621-3237. Fax: (520) 621-9799. E-mail: appinfo@arizona.edu. Web Site: arizona.edu. In-State Tuition and Fees: $2,264. Out-of-State Tuition and Fees: $9,416. Room and Board: $5,548. Students Receiving Some Form of Aid: 45%. Required Financial Aid Forms: FAFSA. Deadline to Apply for Financial Aid: March 1.

ARKANSAS

Arkansas State University

Admissions Office, P.O. Box 1630, State University, AR 72467. Phone: (800) 382-3030 (in-state), (800) 643-0080 (out-of-state). Fax: (870) 910-8094. E-mail: admissions@chickasaw.astate.edu. Web Site: astate.edu. In-State Tuition and Fees: $2,972. Out-of-State Tuition and Fees: $6,644. Room and Board: $3,020. Students Receiving Some Form of Aid: 52%. Students Receiving Non-Need-Based Aid: 34%. Average Aid Package: $2,300. Required Financial Aid Forms: FAFSA, institutional form. Deadline to Apply for Financial Aid: July 1; February 15 (priority).

Arkansas Tech University

Office of Admission, 1605 Coliseum Drive, Russellville, AR 72801. Phone: (501) 968-0343, (800) 582-6953. Fax: (501) 964-0522. E-mail: tech.enroll@mail.atu.edu. Web Site: atu.edu. In-State Tuition and Fees: $2,462. Out-of-State Tuition and Fees: $4,814. Room and Board: $3,222. Students Receiving Some Form of Aid: 39%. Students Receiving Non-Need-Based Aid: 13%. Average Aid Package: $4,145. Required Financial Aid Forms: FAFSA. Deadline to Apply for Financial Aid: rolling; April 15 (priority).

Harding University

Admissions Office, 900 East Center, Box 12255, Searcy, AR 72149. Phone: (501) 279-4407, (800) 477-4407. Fax: (501) 279-4865. E-mail: admissions@harding.edu. Web Site: harding.edu. Tuition and Fees: $8,155. Room and Board: $4,250. Students Receiving Some Form of Aid: 58%. Students Receiving Non-Need-Based Aid: less than 1%. Average Aid Package: $8,349. Required Financial Aid Forms: FAFSA. Deadline to Apply for Financial Aid: rolling.

Henderson State University

Admissions, 1100 Henderson Street, Box 7560, Arkadelphia, AR 71999-0001. Phone: (870) 230-5028, (800) 228-7333. Fax: (870) 230-5144. E-mail: lancask@hsu.edu. Web Site: hsu.edu. In-State Tuition and Fees: $2,503. Out-of-State Tuition and Fees: $4,783. Room and Board: $2,976. Students Receiving Some Form of Aid: 45%. Students Receiving Non-Need-Based Aid: 16%. Average Aid Package: $5,426. Required Financial Aid Forms: FAFSA, Application for Admission. Deadline to Apply for Financial Aid: June 1.

Hendrix College

Office of Admission, 1600 Washington Avenue, Conway, AR 72032. Phone: (501) 450-1362, (800) 277-9017. Fax: (501) 450-3843. E-mail: adm@hendrix.edu. Web Site: hendrix.edu. Tuition and Fees: $12,638. Room and Board: $4,625. Students Receiving Some Form of Aid: 52%. Students Receiving Non-Need-Based Aid: 48%. Average Aid Package: $11,601. Required Financial Aid Forms: FAFSA, institutional form. Deadline to Apply for Financial Aid: February 15 (priority).

John Brown University

Admissions Office, 2000 West University, Siloam Springs, AR 72761. Phone: (501) 524-7157, (877) 528-4636. Fax: (501) 524-4196. E-mail: jbuinfo@acc.jbu.edu. Web Site: jbu.edu. Tuition and Fees: $11,492. Room and Board: $4,478. Students Receiving Some Form of Aid: 53%. Students Receiving Non-Need-Based Aid: 3%. Average Aid Package: $9,053. Required Financial Aid Forms: FAFSA. Deadline to Apply for Financial Aid: March 1.

Lyon College

Admissions Office, P.O. Box 2317, Batesville, AR 72503-2317. Phone: (870) 698-4250, (800) 423-2542. Fax: (870) 793-1791. E-mail: admissions@lyon.edu. Web Site: lyon.edu. Tuition and Fees: $10,955. Room and Board: $4,930. Students Receiving Some Form of Aid: 55%. Students Receiving Non-Need-Based Aid: 13%. Average Aid Package: $11,633. Required Financial Aid Forms: FAFSA. Deadline to Apply for Financial Aid: rolling; February15 (priority).

Ouachita Baptist University*

Admissions Office, Box 3776, Arkadelphia, AR 71998-0001. Phone: (870) 245-5110, (800) 342-5628. Fax: (870) 245-5500. E-mail: Berryk@alpha.obu.edu. Web Site: obu.edu. Tuition and Fees: $9,010. Room and Board: $3,450. Students Receiving Some Form of Aid: 54%. Students Receiving Non-Need-Based Aid: 49%. Average Aid Package: $10,382. Required Financial Aid Forms: FAFSA. Deadline to Apply for Financial Aid: May 1.

Southern Arkansas University

Office of Admissions, PO Box 9382, Magnolia, AR 71754-9382. Phone: (870) 235-4040, (800) 332-7286. Fax: (870) 235-4931. E-mail: addonna@saumag.edu. Web Site: saumag.edu. In-State Tuition and Fees: $2,208. Out-of-State Tuition and Fees: $3,336. Room and Board: $2,800. Students Receiving Some Form of Aid: 40%. Students Receiving Non-Need-Based Aid: 37%. Average Aid Package: $6,025. Required Financial Aid Forms: FAFSA. Deadline to Apply for Financial Aid: July 1.

University of Arkansas—Fayetteville

Admissions Office, 200 Silas Hunt Hall, Fayetteville, AR 72701. Phone: (501) 575-5346, (800) 377-8632. Fax: (501) 575-7515. E-mail: uafadmis@comp.uark.edu. Web Site: uark.edu. In-State Tuition and Fees: $3,334. Out-of-State Tuition and Fees: $8,318. Room and Board: $4,112. Students Receiving Some Form of Aid: 36%. Students Receiving Non-Need-Based Aid: 14%. Average Aid Package: $7,191. Required Financial Aid Forms: FAFSA, institutional application. Deadline to Apply for Financial Aid: rolling; March 15 (priority).

University of Arkansas—Little Rock*

UALR Office of Admissions and Records, 208 Administration South, 2801 University Avenue, Little Rock, AR 72204. Phone: (501) 569-3127, (800) 482-8892 (in-state). Fax: (510) 569-8956. E-mail: adminfo@uair.edu. Web Site: oir.ualr.edu. In-State Tuition and Fees: $2,724. Out-of-State Tuition and Fees: $6,540. Room and Board: $6,170. Required Financial Aid Forms: FAFSA. Deadline to Apply for Financial Aid: March 1 (priority), November 1 (final).

University of Central Arkansas*

Admissions Office, 201 Donaghey Avenue, Conway, AR 72035. Phone: (501) 450-3128, (800) 243-8245. Fax: (501) 450-5228. E-mail: admission@ecom.uca.edu. Web Site: uca.edu. In-State Tuition and Fees: $3,238. Out-of-State Tuition and Fees: $5,902. Room and Board: $3,150. Required Financial Aid Forms: FAFSA. Deadline to Apply for Financial Aid: February 15.

CALIFORNIA

Academy of Art College

Admissions Office, 79 New Montgomery Street, San Francisco, CA 94105. Phone: (415) 274-2222, (800) 544-ARTS. Fax: (415) 263-4130. E-mail: info@academyart.edu. Web Site: academyart.edu. Tuition and Fees: $10,860. Room Only: $7,000. Students Receiving Some Form of Aid: 44%. Average Aid Package: $4,750. Required Financial Aid Forms: FAFSA, school financial aid application. Deadline to Apply for Financial Aid: March 2.

Art Center College of Design

Admissions Office, 1700 Lida Street, Pasadena, CA 91103. Phone: (626) 396-2373. Fax: (626) 795-0578. Web Site: artcenter.edu. Tuition and Fees: $18,890. Students Receiving Some Form of Aid: 66%. Average Aid Package: $11,486. Required Financial Aid Forms: FAFSA, institutional form. Deadline to Apply for Financial Aid: rolling; March 1 (priority).

Azusa Pacific University

Office of Undergraduate Admission, 901 East Alosta Avenue P.O. Box 7000, Azusa, CA 91702-7000. Phone: (626) 812-3016, (800) 825-5278. Fax: (626) 812-3096. E-mail: admissions@apu.edu. Web Site: apu.edu. Tuition and Fees: $14,727. Room and Board: $4,880. Students Receiving Some Form of Aid: 13%. Students Receiving Non-Need-Based Aid: 7%. Average Aid Package: $9,477. Required Financial Aid Forms: FAFSA, institution's own aid form, Business/Farm Supplement. Deadline to Apply for Financial Aid: March 2.

Biola University

Office of Admissions, 13800 Biola Avenue, La Mirada, CA 90639-0001. Phone: (562) 903-4752. Fax: (562) 903-4709. E-mail: admissions@biola.edu. Web Site: biola.edu. Tuition and Fees: $16,630. Room and Board: $5,272. Required Financial Aid Forms: FAFSA, institutional form. Deadline to Apply for Financial Aid: March 1.

California Baptist University

Office of Admissions, 8432 Magnolia Avenue, Riverside, CA 92504. Phone: (909) 343-4212, (877) 228-8866. Fax: (909) 343-4525. E-mail: admissions@calbaptist.edu. Web Site: calbaptist.edu. Tuition and Fees: $10,696. Room and Board: $4,966. Students Receiving Some Form of Aid: 79%. Students Receiving Non-Need-Based Aid: 63%. Average Aid Package: $9,100. Required Financial Aid Forms: FAFSA, institutional form. Deadline to Apply for Financial Aid: rolling; March 2 (priority).

California College of Arts and Crafts

Office of Admissions, 1111 Eigth Street, San Francisco, CA 94107. Phone: (415) 703-9523, (800) 447-1ART. Fax: (415) 703-9539. E-mail: enroll@ccac-art.edu. Web Site: ccac-art.edu. Tuition and Fees: $18,368. Room and Board: $5,858. Students Receiving Some Form of Aid: 58%. Students Receiving Non-Need-Based Aid: 10%. Average Aid Package: $13,089. Required Financial Aid Forms: FAFSA, institutional application. Deadline to Apply for Financial Aid: rolling; March 2 (priority).

California Institute of Technology

Office of Admissions, Mail Code 55-63, Pasadena, CA 91125. Phone: (626) 395-6341. Fax: (626) 683-3026. E-mail: ugadmissions@caltech.edu. Web Site: admissions.caltech.edu. Tuition and Fees: $19,959. Room and Board: $6,180. Required Financial Aid Forms: FAFSA, CSS Profile. Deadline to Apply for Financial Aid: January 15.

California Institute of the Arts

Admissions Office, 24700 McBean Parkway, Valencia, CA 91355. Phone: (661) 255-1050, ext. 2185, (800) 545-2787. Fax: (661) 254-8352. E-mail: admiss@calarts.edu. Web Site: calarts.edu. Tuition and Fees: $19,950. Room and Board: $5,150. Students Receiving Some Form of Aid: 61%. Average Aid Package: $17,674. Required Financial Aid Forms: FAFSA. Deadline to Apply for Financial Aid: March 2 (priority).

California Lutheran University

Admissions Office, 60 West Olsen Road, #1350, Thousand Oaks, CA 91360. Phone: (877) 258-3678, (805) 493-3135. Fax: (805) 493-3114. Web Site: clunet.edu. Tuition and Fees: $16,200. Room and Board: $6,240. Required Financial Aid Forms: FAFSA. Deadline to Apply for Financial Aid: March 2 (priority).

California Maritime Academy*

Admissions Office, P.O. Box 1392, Vallejo, CA 94590-0644. Phone: (707) 654-1330, (800) 561-1945. Fax: (707) 654-1336. E-mail: enroll@csum.edu. Web Site: csum.edu. In-State Tuition and Fees: $2,138. Out-of-State Tuition and Fees: $9,518. Room and Board: $5,832. Students Receiving Some Form of Aid: 89%. Students Receiving Non-Need-Based Aid: 1%. Average Aid Package: $10,560. Required Financial Aid Forms: FAFSA. Deadline to Apply for Financial Aid: March 2.

California Polytechnic State University

Admissions Office. , San Luis Obispo, CA 93407. Phone: (805) 756-2311. Fax: (805) 756-5400. E-mail: admprosp@calpoly.edu. Web Site: calpoly.edu. In-State Tuition and Fees: $2,126. Out-of-State Tuition and Fees (add an additional $164 per quarter unit): $9,506. Room and Board: $5,554. Students Receiving Some Form of Aid: 41%. Students Receiving Non-Need-Based Aid: 8%. Average Aid Package: $6,527. Required Financial Aid Forms: FAFSA. Deadline to Apply for Financial Aid: June 30; March 2 (priority).

California State Polytechnic University—Pomona

Admissions Office, 801 West Temple Avenue, Pomona, CA 91768. Phone: (909) 869-7659. Fax: (909) 869-4529. E-mail: cppadmit@csupomona.edu. Web Site: csupomona.edu. In-State Tuition and Fees: $1,777. Out-of-State Tuition and Fees: $9,157. Room and Board: $6,278. Students Receiving Some Form of Aid: 40%. Students Receiving Non-Need-Based Aid: less than 1%. Average Aid Package: $6,884. Required Financial Aid Forms: FAFSA. Deadline to Apply for Financial Aid: March 2 (priority).

California State University—Bakersfield

Admissions Office, 9001 Stockdale Highway, Bakersfield, CA 93311. Phone: (661) 664-3036. Web Site: csub.edu. In-State Tuition and Fees: $1,795. Out-of-State Tuition and Fees: $9,175. Room and Board: $4,783. Students Receiving Some Form of Aid: 70%. Required Financial Aid Forms: FAFSA. Deadline to Apply for Financial Aid: March 2.

California State University—Chico

Admissions Office, 400 West First Street, Chico, CA 95929-0722. Phone: (800) 542-4426, (530) 898-4428. Fax: (530) 898-6456. E-mail: info@csuchico.edu. Web Site: csuchico.edu. In-State Tuition and Fees: $1,994. Out-of-State Tuition and Fees: $9,374. Room and Board: $5,860. Required Financial Aid Forms: FAFSA. Deadline to Apply for Financial Aid: March 2 (priority).

California State University—Dominguez Hills*

Admissions Office, 1000 East Victoria Street, Carson, CA 90747-9960. Phone: (310) 243-3613, (310) 243-3300. Fax: (310) 243-3609. Web Site: csudh.edu. In-State Tuition and Fees: $1,735. Out-of-State Tuition and Fees: $9,115. Room and Board: $5,626. Required Financial Aid Forms: FAFSA. Deadline to Apply for Financial Aid: April 16.

California State University—Fresno

Admissions Office, 5150 North Maple, Fresno, CA 93740-8026. Phone: (559) 278-2261, (559) 278-4240. Fax: (559) 278-4812. E-mail: vivian_franco@csufresno.edu. Web Site: csufresno.edu. In-State Tuition and Fees: $3,492. Out-of-State Tuition and Fees: $10,880. Room and Board: $6,288. Students Receiving Some Form of Aid: 55%. Students Receiving Non-Need-Based Aid: 9%. Average Aid Package: $4,869. Required Financial Aid Forms: FAFSA. Deadline to Apply for Financial Aid: March 2.

California State University—Fullerton

Admissions Office. , Fullerton, CA 92834-9480. Phone: (714) 278-2370. Fax: (714) 278-2356. E-mail: admissions@fullerton.edu. Web Site: fullerton.edu. In-State Tuition and Fees: $1,809. Out-of-State Tuition and Fees: $7,713. Room Only: $3,672. Students Receiving Some Form of Aid: 38%. Average Aid Package: $5,464. Required Financial Aid Forms: FAFSA. Deadline to Apply for Financial Aid: March 2 (priority).

California State University—Hayward*

Admissions Office, California State University—Hayward, Hayward, CA 94542. Phone: (510) 885-3811. Fax: (510) 885-3616. Web Site: csuhayward.edu. In-State Tuition and Fees: $1,680. Out-of-State Tuition and Fees: $9,060. Room and Board: $5,967. Required Financial Aid Forms: FAFSA. Deadline to Apply for Financial Aid: March 2.

California State University—Long Beach

Admissions Office, 1250 Bellflower Boulevard, Long Beach, CA 90840. Phone: (562) 985-4111. Fax: (562) 985-8887. E-mail: brady@csulb.edu. Web Site: csulb.edu. In-State Tuition and Fees: $1,702. Out-of-State Tuition and Fees: $9,082. Room and Board: $5,400. Students Receiving Some Form of Aid: 34%. Students Receiving Non-Need-Based Aid: less than 1%. Average Aid Package: $6,812. Required Financial Aid Forms: FAFSA. Deadline to Apply for Financial Aid: March 2.

California State University—Los Angeles

Admissions Office, 5151 State University Drive, Los Angeles, CA 90032. Phone: (323) 343-3901. Fax: (323) 343-3888. Web Site: calstatela.edu. In-State Tuition and Fees: $1,722. Out-of-State Tuition and Fees: $9,106. Room and Board: $6,165. Students Receiving Some Form of Aid: 49%. Average Aid Package: $6,950. Required Financial Aid Forms: FAFSA. Deadline to Apply for Financial Aid: March 2.

California State University—Northridge

Admissions Office, 18111 Nordhoff Street, Northridge, CA 91330. **Phone:** (818) 677-3700. **Fax:** (818) 677-3766. **E-mail:** admissions@csun.edu. **Web Site:** csun.edu. **In-State Tuition and Fees:** $1,814. **Out-of-State Tuition and Fees:** $9,194. **Room and Board:** $6,800. **Required Financial Aid Forms:** FAFSA. **Deadline to Apply for Financial Aid:** rolling.

California State University—Sacramento

Admissions Office, 6000 J Street, Sacramento, CA 95819-6048. **Phone:** (916) 278-6723. **Fax:** (916) 278-5603. **E-mail:** admissions@csus.edu. **Web Site:** csus.edu. **In-State Tuition and Fees:** $1,648. **Out-of-State Tuition and Fees:** $9,028. **Room and Board:** $5,510. **Students Receiving Some Form of Aid:** 35%. **Average Aid Package:** $6,847. **Required Financial Aid Forms:** FAFSA. **Deadline to Apply for Financial Aid:** rolling.

California State University—San Bernardino*

Admissions Office, 5500 University, San Bernardino, CA 92407. **Phone:** (909) 880-5188. **Fax:** (909) 880-7021. **Web Site:** csusb.edu. **In-State Tuition and Fees:** $1,747. **Out-of-State Tuition and Fees:** $9,127. **Room and Board:** $6,408. **Required Financial Aid Forms:** FAFSA. **Deadline to Apply for Financial Aid:** March 2.

California State University—San Marcos*

Office of Admissions, 333 South Twin Oaks Valley Road, San Marcos, CA 92096-0001. **Phone:** (760) 750-4848. **Fax:** (760) 750-3248. **Web Site:** ww2.csusm.edu. **In-State Tuition and Fees:** $1,706. **Out-of-State Tuition and Fees:** $9,322. **Students Receiving Some Form of Aid:** 35%. **Students Receiving Non-Need-Based Aid:** 2%. **Average Aid Package:** $6,000. **Required Financial Aid Forms:** FAFSA. **Deadline to Apply for Financial Aid:** March 2 (priority).

California State University—Stanislaus

Admissions Office, 801 West Monte Vista Avenue, Turlock, CA 95382. **Phone:** (209) 667-3151. **Fax:** (209) 667-3788. **E-mail:** outreach@stan.csustan.edu. **Web Site:** csustan.edu. **In-State Tuition and Fees:** $3,754. **Out-of-State Tuition and Fees:** $11,134. **Room and Board:** $6,480. **Students Receiving Some Form of Aid:** 19%. **Students Receiving Non-Need-Based Aid:** 1%. **Average Aid Package:** $6,425. **Required Financial Aid Forms:** FAFSA, state aid form. **Deadline to Apply for Financial Aid:** March 2 (priority).

Chapman University

Admissions Office, One University Drive, Orange, CA 92866. **Phone:** (714) 997-6711, (888) CU-APPLY. **Fax:** (714) 997-6713. **E-mail:** admit@chapman.edu. **Web Site:** chapman.edu. **Tuition and Fees:** $21,288. **Room and Board:** $7,044. **Students Receiving Some Form of Aid:** 78%. **Students Receiving Non-Need-Based Aid:** 3%. **Average Aid Package:** $17,047. **Required Financial Aid Forms:** FAFSA. **Deadline to Apply for Financial Aid:** March 2.

Christian Heritage College

Admissions Office, 2100 Greenfield Drive, El Cajon, CA 92019. **Phone:** (619) 590-1111, (800) 676-2242. **Fax:** (619) 440-0209. **E-mail:** chcadm@christianheritage.edu. **Web Site:** christianheritage.edu. **Tuition and Fees:** $12,264. **Room and Board:** $5,000. **Average Aid Package:** $3,000. **Required Financial Aid Forms:** FAFSA, institutional forms. **Deadline to Apply for Financial Aid:** March 2.

Claremont McKenna College

Office of Admission, 890 Columbia Avenue, Claremont, CA 91711-6425. **Phone:** (909) 621-8088. **Fax:** (909) 621-8516. **E-mail:** admission@mckenna.edu. **Web Site:** mckenna.edu. **Tuition and Fees:** $20,795. **Room and Board:** $7,420. **Students Receiving Some Form of Aid:** 72%. **Students Receiving Non-Need-Based Aid:** 19%. **Average Aid Package:** $18,980. **Required Financial Aid Forms:** FAFSA, CSS Profile. **Deadline to Apply for Financial Aid:** February 1.

Concordia University

Admissions Office, 1530 Concordia West, Irvine, CA 92612-3299. **Phone:** (949) 854-8002 ext. 1106, (800) 229-1200. **Fax:** (949) 854-6894. **Web Site:** cui.edu. **Tuition and Fees:** $15,700. **Room and Board:** $5,550. **Students Receiving Some Form of Aid:** 53%. **Students Receiving Non-Need-Based Aid:** 38%. **Average Aid Package:** $8,000. **Required Financial Aid Forms:** FAFSA, institutional form. **Deadline to Apply for Financial Aid:** March 2 (priority).

Fresno Pacific University*

Undergraduate Admissions, 1717 South Chestnut Avenue, Fresno, CA 93702-4709. **Phone:** (559) 453-2039, (800) 660-6089. **Fax:** (559) 453-2007. **E-mail:** ugadmis@fresno.edu. **Web Site:** fresno.edu. **Tuition and Fees:** $13,448. **Room and Board:** $4,212. **Required Financial Aid Forms:** FAFSA, institutional form. **Deadline to Apply for Financial Aid:** March 1.

Harvey Mudd College

Admissions Office, 301 East 12th Street, Claremont, CA 91711-5990. **Phone:** (909) 621-8011. **Fax:** (909) 607-7046. **E-mail:** admission@hmc.edu. **Web Site:** hmc.edu. **Tuition and Fees:** $22,069. **Room and Board:** $7,946. **Students Receiving Some Form of Aid:** 58%. **Students Receiving Non-Need-Based Aid:** 9%. **Average Aid Package:** $17,333. **Required Financial Aid Forms:** FAFSA, Profile. **Deadline to Apply for Financial Aid:** February 1.

Humboldt State University

Admissions Office, 1 Harpst Street, Arcata, CA 95521-8299. **Phone:** (707) 826-4402. **Fax:** (707) 826-6194. **E-mail:** hsuinfo@laurel.humboldt.edu. **Web Site:** humboldt.edu. **In-State Tuition and Fees:** $1,861. **Out-of-State Tuition and Fees:** $7,765. **Room and Board:** $5,845. **Students Receiving Some Form of Aid:** 48%. **Average Aid Package:** $6,794. **Required Financial Aid Forms:** FAFSA. **Deadline to Apply for Financial Aid:** March 2 (priority).

Loyola Marymount University*

Admissions Office, 7900 Loyola Boulevard, Los Angeles, CA 90045-8350. **Phone:** (310) 338-2750, (800) LMU-INFO. **Fax:** (310) 338-2797. **E-mail:** admissns@lmumail.lmu.edu.

Web Site: lmu.edu. Tuition and Fees: $17,932. Room and Board: $7,537. Average Aid Package: $16,180. Required Financial Aid Forms: FAFSA, CSS, Financial aid profile, state aid form. Deadline to Apply for Financial Aid: February 15, March 2.

Mills College

Admission Office, 5000 MacArthur Boulevard, Oakland, CA 94605. Phone: (510) 430-2135, (800) 87-MILLS. Fax: (510) 430-3314. E-mail: admission@mills.edu. Web Site: mills.edu. Tuition and Fees: $18,262. Room and Board: $7,296. Students Receiving Some Form of Aid: 73%. Students Receiving Non-Need-Based Aid: 11%. Average Aid Package: $18,246. Required Financial Aid Forms: FAFSA, Mills FAF. Deadline to Apply for Financial Aid: February 1 (freshwomen), March 2 (transfers).

National University

Admissions Office, 11255 N. Torrey Pines Road, La Jolla, CA 92037. Phone: (619) 563-7100, (800) 628-8648. Fax: (619) 563-7299. E-mail: advisor@nu.edu. Web Site: nu.edu. Tuition and Fees: $6,600. Room and Board: $6,256. Required Financial Aid Forms: FAFSA, institutional form. Deadline to Apply for Financial Aid: rolling.

Occidental College

Admissions Office, 1600 Campus Road, Los Angeles, CA 90041. Phone: (323) 259-2700, (800) 825-5262. Fax: (323) 341-4875. E-mail: admission@oxy.edu. Web Site: oxy.edu. Tuition and Fees: $22,518. Room and Board: $6,490. Students Receiving Some Form of Aid: 59%. Students Receiving Non-Need-Based Aid: 22%. Average Aid Package: $23,869. Required Financial Aid Forms: FAFSA, CSS/Financial Aid Profile, state aid form, noncustodial parent's statement, Business/Farm Supplement. Deadline to Apply for Financial Aid: February 1.

Pacific Union College

Office of Admissions, One Angwin Avenue, Angwin, CA 94508. Phone: (707) 965-6336, (800) 862-7080. Fax: (707) 965-6432. E-mail: enroll@puc.edu. Web Site: puc.edu. Tuition and Fees: $14,475. Room and Board: $4,425. Students Receiving Some Form of Aid: 62%. Students Receiving Non-Need-Based Aid: 1%. Average Aid Package: $11,110. Required Financial Aid Forms: FAFSA, FAA, parent and student tax returns. Deadline to Apply for Financial Aid: May 1.

Pepperdine University

Office of Admission, Seaver College, 24255 Pacific Coast Highway, Malibu, CA 90263-4392. Phone: (310) 456-4392. Fax: (310) 456-4861. Web Site: pepperdine.edu. Tuition and Fees: $23,070. Room and Board: $7,010. Students Receiving Some Form of Aid: 79%. Average Aid Package: $23,364. Required Financial Aid Forms: FAFSA, institutional form, Federal Income Tax form, W-2, state scholarship/grant form (CA residents), Financial Aid transcript (transfer students). Deadline to Apply for Financial Aid: April 1.

Pitzer College

Admissions Office, 1050 North Mills Avenue, Claremont, CA 91711. Phone: (909) 621-8129, (800) 748-9371. Fax: (909) 621-8770. E-mail: admission@pitzer.edu. Web Site: pitzer.edu. Tuition and Fees: $24,096. Room and Board: $6,240. Students Receiving Some Form of Aid: 48%. Students Receiving Non-Need-Based Aid: 2%. Average Aid Package: $22,648. Required Financial Aid Forms: FAFSA, Profile. Deadline to Apply for Financial Aid: February 1.

Point Loma Nazarene University

Admissions Office, 3900 Lomaland Drive, San Diego, CA 92106-2899. Phone: (619) 849-2273, (800) 733-7770. Fax: (619) 849-2222. E-mail: discover@ptloma.edu. Web Site: ptloma.edu. Tuition and Fees: $13,626. Room and Board: $5,480. Students Receiving Some Form of Aid: 60%. Students Receiving Non-Need-Based Aid: 57%. Average Aid Package: $11,493. Required Financial Aid Forms: FAFSA, institutional form. Deadline to Apply for Financial Aid: March 15 (priority).

Pomona College

Office of Admissions, 333 North College Way, Claremont, CA 91711. Phone: (909) 621-8134. Fax: (909) 621-8952. E-mail: admissions@pomona.edu. Web Site: pomona.edu. Tuition and Fees: $24,170. Room and Board: $8,170. Students Receiving Some Form of Aid: 55%. Average Aid Package: $22,032. Required Financial Aid Forms: FAFSA, CSS/Financial Aid Profile, State Aid Form, Noncustodial Parent's Statement, Business/Farm Supplement, Tax returns for both student and parents. Deadline to Apply for Financial Aid: February 1.

Saint Mary's College of California

Admissions Office, P.O. Box 4800, Moraga, CA 94575-4800. Phone: (925) 631-4224, (800) 800-4762. Fax: (925) 376-7193. E-mail: smcadmit@stmarys-ca.edu. Web Site: stmarys-ca.edu. Tuition and Fees: $18,320. Room and Board: $7,560. Students Receiving Some Form of Aid: 73%. Students Receiving Non-Need-Based Aid: 16%. Average Aid Package: $18,886. Required Financial Aid Forms: FAFSA. Deadline to Apply for Financial Aid: March 2.

San Diego State University

Admissions Office, 5500 Campanile Drive, San Diego, CA 92182-7455. Phone: (619) 594-7800, (619) 594-5200. Web Site: sdsu.edu. In-State Tuition and Fees: $1,776. Out-of-State Tuition and Fees: $10,932. Room and Board: $7,110. Students Receiving Some Form of Aid: 37%. Students Receiving Non-Need-Based Aid: 6%. Average Aid Package: $7,300. Required Financial Aid Forms: FAFSA. Deadline to Apply for Financial Aid: rolling.

San Francisco State University

Admissions Office, 1600 Holloway Avenue, San Francisco, CA 94132. Phone: (415) 338-6486. Fax: (415) 338-7196. E-mail: ugadmit@sfsu.edu. Web Site: sfsu.edu. In-State Tuition and Fees: $1,826. Out-of-State Tuition and Fees: $7,730. Room and Board: $6,754. Students Receiving Some Form of Aid: 33%. Students Receiving Non-Need-Based Aid: 2%. Average Aid Package: $6,693. Required Financial Aid Forms: FAFSA. Deadline to Apply for Financial Aid: rolling; March 2 (priority).

San Jose State University

Office of Enrollment Services, One Washington Square, San Jose, CA 95192-0011. Phone: (408) 924-2550, (408) 283-7500. Fax: (408) 924-2050. Web Site: sjsu.edu. In-State Tuition and Fees: $3,714. Out-of-State Tuition and Fees: $7,761. Room and Board: $6,454. Students Receiving Some Form of Aid: 27%. Students Receiving Non-Need-Based Aid: 2%.

Average Aid Package: $6,060. Required Financial Aid Forms: FAFSA. Deadline to Apply for Financial Aid: March 2 (priority).

Santa Clara University

Undergraduate Admissions Office, 500 El Camino Real, Santa Clara, CA 95053. Phone: (408) 554-4700. Fax: (408) 554-5255. Web Site: scu.edu. Tuition and Fees: $17,622. Room and Board: $7,323. Students Receiving Some Form of Aid: 46%. Students Receiving Non-Need-Based Aid: 20%. Average Aid Package: $15,872. Required Financial Aid Forms: FAFSA, Profile. Deadline to Apply for Financial Aid: February 1 (priority).

Scripps College

Office of Admission, 1030 Columbia Avenue, Claremont, CA 91711. Phone: (909) 621-8149, (800) 770-1333. Fax: (909) 607-7508. E-mail: admofc@ad.scrippscol.edu. Web Site: scrippscol.edu. Tuition and Fees: $21,130. Room and Board: $7,870. Students Receiving Some Form of Aid: 50%. Students Receiving Non-Need-Based Aid: 1%. Average Aid Package: $19,799. Required Financial Aid Forms: FAFSA, profile. Deadline to Apply for Financial Aid: February 1; November 15 (priority).

Sonoma State University

Admissions and Records, 1801 East Cotati Avenue, Rohnert Park, CA 94928-3609. Phone: (707) 664-2778. Fax: (707) 664-2060. E-mail: admitme@sonoma.edu. Web Site: sonoma.edu. In-State Tuition and Fees: $1,974. Out-of-State Tuition and Fees: $9,354. Room and Board: $6,246. Students Receiving Some Form of Aid: 39%. Students Receiving Non-Need-Based Aid: 8%. Average Aid Package: $8,520. Required Financial Aid Forms: FAFSA. Deadline to Apply for Financial Aid: January 31 (priority).

Stanford University

Undergraduate Admissions, Old Student Union, Stanford, CA 94305. Phone: (650) 723-2091. Fax: (650) 723-6050. E-mail: undergrad.admissions@forsythe.stanford.edu. Web Site: stanford.edu. In-State Tuition and Fees: $24,991. Out-of-State Tuition and Fees: $24,716. Room and Board: $8,030. Students Receiving Some Form of Aid: 45%. Students Receiving Non-Need-Based Aid: 2%. Average Aid Package: $20,926. Required Financial Aid Forms: FAFSA. Deadline to Apply for Financial Aid: February 1.

United States International University

Admissions Office, 10455 Pomerado Road, San Diego, CA 92131-1799. Phone: (858) 635-4772. Fax: (858) 635-4739. E-mail: admissions@usiu.edu. Web Site: usiu.edu. Tuition and Fees: $13,611. Room and Board: $5,775. Students Receiving Some Form of Aid: 25%. Students Receiving Non-Need-Based Aid: 13%. Average Aid Package: $16,800. Required Financial Aid Forms: FAFSA, institutional application. Deadline to Apply for Financial Aid: rolling.

University of California—Berkeley

Admissions Office, 110 Sproul Hall, Berkeley, CA 94720. Phone: (510) 642-3175, (510) 642-8396. Fax: (510) 642-7333. E-mail: ouars@uclink.berkeley.edu. Web Site: berkeley.edu. In-State Tuition and Fees: $4,046. Out-of-State Tuition and Fees: $13,850. Room and Board: $8,266. Students Receiving Some Form of Aid: 65%. Students Receiving Non-Need-Based Aid: 10%. Average Aid Package: $10,456. Required Financial Aid Forms: FAFSA. Deadline to Apply for Financial Aid: March 2.

University of California—Davis

Undergraduate Admissions and Outreach Services, 175 Mrak Hall, One Shields Avenue, Davis, CA 95616. Phone: (530) 752-2971. Fax: (530) 752-1280. E-mail: thinkucd@ucdavis.edu. Web Site: ucdavis.edu. In-State Tuition and Fees: $4,214. Out-of-State Tuition and Fees: $18,145. Room and Board: $7,163. Students Receiving Some Form of Aid: 44%. Students Receiving Non-Need-Based Aid: 5%. Average Aid Package: $9,651. Required Financial Aid Forms: FAFSA. Deadline to Apply for Financial Aid: March 1.

University of California—Irvine

Admissions Office, 204 Administration Building, Irvine, CA 92697-1075. Phone: (949) 824-6703. E-mail: oars@uci.edu. Web Site: ucap.edu/pathways. In-State Tuition and Fees: $3,871. Out-of-State Tuition and Fees: $14,193. Room and Board: $6,407. Students Receiving Some Form of Aid: 56%. Students Receiving Non-Need-Based Aid: 4%. Average Aid Package: $11,254. Required Financial Aid Forms: FAFSA. Deadline to Apply for Financial Aid: March 1.

University of California—Los Angeles

UCLA Undergraduate Admissions and Relations with Schools, 1147 Murphy Hall, Los Angeles, CA 90095-1436. Phone: (310) 825-3101. Fax: (310) 206-1206. E-mail: ugadm@saonet.ucla.edu. Web Site: ucla.edu. In-State Tuition and Fees: $3,698. Out-of-State Tuition and Fees: $13,872. Room and Board: $7,692. Required Financial Aid Forms: FAFSA. Deadline to Apply for Financial Aid: March 2.

University of California—Riverside

Admissions Office, 1120 Hinderaker Hall, Riverside, CA 92521. Phone: (909) 787-4531. Fax: (909) 787-6344. E-mail: discover@pop.ucr.edu. Web Site: ucr.edu. In-State Tuition and Fees: $3,757. Out-of-State Tuition and Fees: $13,561. Room and Board: $6,579. Students Receiving Some Form of Aid: 55%. Students Receiving Non-Need-Based Aid: 7%. Average Aid Package: $8,921. Required Financial Aid Forms: FAFSA. Deadline to Apply for Financial Aid: March 2 (priority).

University of California—San Diego

Office of Admissions and Outreach, 9500 Gilman Drive, 0337, La Jolla, CA 92093-0337. Phone: (858) 534-4831. Fax: (858) 534-5629. E-mail: admissionsinfo@ucsd.edu. Web Site: ucsd.edu. In-State Tuition and Fees: $3,847. Out-of-State Tuition and Fees: $14,021. Room and Board: $7,134. Students Receiving Some Form of Aid: 48%. Students Receiving Non-Need-Based Aid: 7%. Average Aid Package: $9,179. Required Financial Aid Forms: FAFSA. Deadline to Apply for Financial Aid: March 2.

University of California—Santa Barbara

Undergraduate Admissions Office, University of California, Santa Barbara, Santa Barbara, CA 93106. Phone: (805) 893-2881. Fax: (805) 893-2676. E-mail: appinfo@sa.ucsb.edu. Web Site: ucsb.edu. In-State Tuition and Fees:

$3,844. Out-of-State Tuition and Fees: $14,018. Room and Board: $7,156. Required Financial Aid Forms: FAFSA. Deadline to Apply for Financial Aid: March 2 (priority).

University of California—Santa Cruz

Admissions Office, Cook House, 1156 High Street, Santa Cruz, CA 95064. Phone: (831) 459-4008, (831) 459-2131. Fax: (831) 459-4163, (831) 459-4452. E-mail: admissions@cats.ucsc.edu. Web Site: admissions.ucsc.edu. In-State Tuition and Fees: $4,235. Out-of-State Tuition and Fees: $14,409. Room and Board: $7,337. Required Financial Aid Forms: FAFSA. Deadline to Apply for Financial Aid: March 2.

University of La Verne

Admissions Office, 1950 Third Street, La Verne, CA 91750. Phone: (909) 593-3511 ext. 4026, (800) 876-4858. Fax: (909) 392-2714. E-mail: admissions@ulv.edu. Web Site: ulv.edu. Tuition and Fees: $16,860. Room and Board: $5,650. Students Receiving Some Form of Aid: 74%. Students Receiving Non-Need-Based Aid: 40%. Average Aid Package: $13,896. Required Financial Aid Forms: FAFSA (UScitizens); international students need bank statements and financial statements. Deadline to Apply for Financial Aid: March 1 (priority).

University of Redlands

Admissions Office, 1200 East Colton Avenue, P.O. Box 3080, Redlands, CA 92373-0999. Phone: (800) 455-5064. Fax: (909) 335-4089. E-mail: admissions@uor.edu. Web Site: redlands.edu. Tuition and Fees: $20,581. Room and Board: $7,590. Students Receiving Some Form of Aid: 74%. Students Receiving Non-Need-Based Aid: 29%. Average Aid Package: $19,757. Required Financial Aid Forms: FAFSA. Deadline to Apply for Financial Aid: February 15.

University of San Diego

Admissions Office, 5998 Alcala Park, San Diego, CA 92110. Phone: (619) 260-4506, (800) 248-4873. Fax: (619) 260-6836. E-mail: admissions@is.acusd.edu. Web Site: acusd.edu. Tuition and Fees: $19,120. Room and Board: $7,000. Required Financial Aid Forms: FAFSA, FAA. Deadline to Apply for Financial Aid: February 20.

University of San Francisco

Admissions Office, 2130 Fulton Street, San Francisco, CA 94117-1080. Phone: (415) 422-6563, (800) CALL-USF. Fax: (415) 422-2217. Web Site: usfca.edu. Tuition and Fees: $19,060. Room and Board: $8,242. Students Receiving Some Form of Aid: 49%. Students Receiving Non-Need-Based Aid: 5%. Average Aid Package: $15,159. Required Financial Aid Forms: FAFSA. Deadline to Apply for Financial Aid: February 15.

University of Southern California

Office of Admission, 700 Childs Way, University Park, Los Angeles, CA 90089. Phone: (213) 740-1111. Fax: (213) 740-6364. Web Site: usc.edu. Tuition and Fees: $22,636. Room and Board: $7,282. Students Receiving Some Form of Aid: 53%. Students Receiving Non-Need-Based Aid: 13%. Average Aid Package: $22,090. Required Financial Aid Forms: FAFSA, CSS Profile. Deadline to Apply for Financial Aid: rolling.

University of the Pacific

Admissions Office, 3601 Pacific Avenue, Stockton, CA 95211. Phone: (209) 946-2211, (800) 959-2867. Fax: (209) 946-2413. E-mail: admissions@uop.edu. Web Site: uop.edu. Tuition and Fees: $20,725. Room and Board: $6,378. Students Receiving Some Form of Aid: 71%. Average Aid Package: $20,468. Required Financial Aid Forms: FAFSA. Deadline to Apply for Financial Aid: February 15 (priority).

Vanguard University of Southern California

Admissions Office, 55 Fair Drive, Costa Mesa, CA 92626. Phone: (714) 556-3610, (800) 722-6279. Fax: (714) 966-5471. E-mail: admissions@vanguard.edu. Web Site: vanguard.edu. Tuition and Fees: $13,868. Room and Board: $5,120. Required Financial Aid Forms: FAFSA. Deadline to Apply for Financial Aid: March 2.

Westmont College

Admissions Office, 955 La Paz Road, Santa Barbara, CA 93108. Phone: (805) 565-6200, (800) 777-9011. Fax: (805) 565-6234. E-mail: admissions@westmont.edu. Web Site: westmont.edu. Tuition and Fees: $20,964. Room and Board: $7,068. Students Receiving Some Form of Aid: 66%. Students Receiving Non-Need-Based Aid: 5%. Average Aid Package: $15,299. Required Financial Aid Forms: FAFSA. Deadline to Apply for Financial Aid: March 1 (priority).

Whittier College

Admissions Office, 13406 East Philadelphia Street, Whittier, CA 90608. Phone: (562) 907-4238. Fax: (562) 907-4870. E-mail: admissions@whittier.edu. Web Site: whittier.edu. Tuition and Fees: $20,758. Room and Board: $6,736. Students Receiving Some Form of Aid: 73%. Students Receiving Non-Need-Based Aid: 52%. Average Aid Package: $17,150. Required Financial Aid Forms: FAFSA, Profile. Deadline to Apply for Financial Aid: rolling; February 1 (priority).

COLORADO

Adams State College

Admissions Office, 208 Edgemont Blvd., Alamosa, CO 81102. Phone: (719) 587-7712, (800) 824-6494. Fax: (719) 589-7522. E-mail: ascadmit@adams.edu. Web Site: adams.edu. In-State Tuition and Fees: $1,530. Out-of-State Tuition and Fees: $5,740. Room and Board: $5,080. Students Receiving Some Form of Aid: 87%. Students Receiving Non-Need-Based Aid: 67%. Average Aid Package: $7,500. Required Financial Aid Forms: FAFSA. Deadline to Apply for Financial Aid: April 15.

Colorado Christian University

Admissions Office, 180 South Garrison Street, Lakewood, CO 80226. Phone: (303) 963-3200, (800) 44-FAITH. Fax: (303) 238-2191. E-mail: admissions@ccu.edu. Web Site: ccu.edu. Tuition and Fees: $10,790. Room and Board: $5,160. Required Financial Aid Forms: FAFSA, institutional form. Deadline to Apply for Financial Aid: March 15 (priority).

Colorado College

Admissions Office, 14 East Cache La Poudre Street, Colorado Springs, CO 80903-3298. Phone: (719) 389-6344, (800) 542-7214. Fax: (719) 389-6816. E-mail: admission@ColoradoCollege.edu. Web Site: ColoradoCollege.edu. Tuition and Fees: $22,800. Room and Board: $5,808. Students Receiving Some Form of Aid: 45%. Students Receiving Non-Need-Based Aid: 2%. Average

Aid Package: $18,764. Required Financial Aid Forms: FAFSA, CSS Profile. Deadline to Apply for Financial Aid: February 15.

Colorado School of Mines

Admissions, Weaver Towers, 1811 Elm Street, Golden, CO 80401-1842. Phone: (303) 273-3220, (800) 446-9488. Fax: (303) 273-3509. E-mail: admit@mines.edu. Web Site: mines.edu. In-State Tuition and Fees: $5,370. Out-of-State Tuition and Fees: $15,780. Room and Board: $4,920. Students Receiving Some Form of Aid: 66%. Students Receiving Non-Need-Based Aid: 37%. Average Aid Package: $10,300. Required Financial Aid Forms: FAFSA. Deadline to Apply for Financial Aid: March 1 (priority).

Colorado State University

Admissions Office, Spruce Hall, Fort Collins, CO 80523-0015. Phone: (970) 491-6909. Fax: (970) 491-7799. E-mail: admissions@vines.colostate.edu. Web Site: colostate.edu. In-State Tuition and Fees: $3,062. Out-of-State Tuition and Fees: $10,748. Room and Board: $5,142. Students Receiving Some Form of Aid: 40%. Average Aid Package: $6,929. Required Financial Aid Forms: FAFSA. Deadline to Apply for Financial Aid: rolling.

Mesa State College*

Admissions Office, P.O. Box 2647, Grand Junction, CO 81502-2647. Phone: (970) 248-1875. Fax: (970) 248-1973. E-mail: admissions@mesastate.edu. Web Site: mesastate.edu. In-State Tuition and Fees: $2,122. Out-of-State Tuition and Fees: $6,512. Room and Board: $5,078. Students Receiving Some Form of Aid: 40%. Students Receiving Non-Need-Based Aid: 20%. Average Aid Package: $5,918. Required Financial Aid Forms: FAFSA. Deadline to Apply for Financial Aid: rolling.

Metropolitan State College of Denver*

Admissions Office, Campus Box 16, P.O. Box 173362, Denver, CO 80217-3362. Phone: (303) 556-3058. Fax: (303) 556-6345. Web Site: mscd.edu. In-State Tuition and Fees: $2,113. Out-of-State Tuition and Fees: $7,443. Students Receiving Some Form of Aid: 45%. Required Financial Aid Forms: FAFSA. Deadline to Apply for Financial Aid: rolling.

United States Air Force Academy

HQ USAFA/RRS, 2304 Cadet Drive, Suite 200, USAF Academy, CO 80840-5025. Phone: (719) 333-2520. Fax: (719) 333-3012. E-mail: rrmail.rr@usafa.af.mil. Web Site: usafa.edu. Tuition, Fees, Room and Board: Paid for by the U.S. Government.

University of Colorado—Boulder

Office of Admissions, Campus Box 30, Boulder, CO 80309-0030. Phone: (303) 492-6301. Fax: (303) 492-7115. E-mail: apply@colorado.edu. Web Site: colorado.edu. In-State Tuition and Fees: $3,118. Out-of-State Tuition and Fees: $15,898. Room and Board: $5,202. Students Receiving Some Form of Aid: 30%. Students Receiving Non-Need-Based Aid: 7%. Average Aid Package: $8,470. Required Financial Aid Forms: FAFSA. Deadline to Apply for Financial Aid: April 1 (priority).

University of Colorado—Colorado Springs*

Office of Admissions and Records, P.O. Box 7150, Colorado Springs, CO 80933-7150. Phone: (719) 262-3383. Fax: (719) 262-3116. E-mail: admrec@mail.uccs.edu. Web Site: uccs.edu. In-State Tuition and Fees: $3,002. Out-of-State Tuition and Fees: $10,178. Room and Board: $5,400. Required Financial Aid Forms: FAFSA. Deadline to Apply for Financial Aid: April 1 (priority).

University of Colorado—Denver

Admissions Office, Box 173364, Campus Box 167, 1250 14th Street, Denver, CO 80217-3364. Phone: (303) 556-3287. Fax: (303) 556-4838. E-mail: admissions@carbon.cudenver.edu. Web Site: cudenver.edu. In-State Tuition and Fees: $2,443. Out-of-State Tuition and Fees: $11,569. Students Receiving Some Form of Aid: 26%. Students Receiving Non-Need-Based Aid: 8%. Average Aid Package: $5,268. Required Financial Aid Forms: FAFSA. Deadline to Apply for Financial Aid: March 1 (priority).

University of Denver

Undergraduate Admissions Office, 2199 South University Boulevard, Denver, CO 80208. Phone: (303) 871-2036, (800) 525-9495. Fax: (303) 871-3301. E-mail: admission@du.edu. Web Site: du.edu. Tuition and Fees: $19,440. Room and Board: $6,165. Students Receiving Some Form of Aid: 46%. Students Receiving Non-Need-Based Aid: 16%. Average Aid Package: $11,814. Required Financial Aid Forms: FAFSA. Deadline to Apply for Financial Aid: February 15 (priority).

University of Northern Colorado

Admissions Office. , Greeley, CO 80639. Phone: (970) 351-2881, (888) 700-4862. Fax: (970) 351-2984. E-mail: unc@mail.unco.edu. Web Site: unco.edu. In-State Tuition and Fees: $2,754. Out-of-State Tuition and Fees: $9,737. Room and Board: $4,796. Students Receiving Some Form of Aid: 45%. Students Receiving Non-Need-Based Aid: 15%. Average Aid Package: $6,170. Required Financial Aid Forms: FAFSA. Deadline to Apply for Financial Aid: March 1 (priority).

University of Southern Colorado

Admissions Office, 2200 Bonforte Blvd., Pueblo, CO 81001-4901. Phone: (719) 549-2461, (800) USC-WOLF. Fax: (719) 549-2419. E-mail: info@uscolo.edu. Web Site: uscolo.edu. In-State Tuition and Fees: $2,284. Out-of-State Tuition and Fees: $8,924. Room and Board: $4,768. Students Receiving Some Form of Aid: 27%. Students Receiving Non-Need-Based Aid: less than 1%. Average Aid Package: $6,891. Required Financial Aid Forms: FAFSA. Deadline to Apply for Financial Aid: March 1 (priority).

Western State College of Colorado

Admissions Office, College Heights, Gunnison, CO 81231. Phone: (970) 943-2119, (800) 876-5309. Fax: (970) 943-2212. E-mail: discover@western.edu. Web Site: western.edu. In-State Tuition and Fees: $2,203. Out-of-State Tuition and Fees: $7,713. Room and Board: $6,700. Required Financial Aid Forms: FAFSA. Deadline to Apply for Financial Aid: March 15.

CONNECTICUT

Albertus Magnus College*

Admissions Office, 700 Prospect St., New Haven, CT 06511-1189. Phone: , (800) 578-9160. Fax: (203) 785-8652. E-mail: admissions@albertus.edu. Web Site: albertus.edu. Tuition and Fees: $20,860. Room and Board: $6,324. Required Financial Aid Forms: none. Deadline to Apply for Financial Aid: February 15.

Central Connecticut State University

Admissions Office, 1615 Stanley St., New Britain, CT 06050. Phone: (860) 832-2278, (860) 832-2278. Fax: (860) 832-2295. E-mail: admissions@ccsu.edu. Web Site: ccsu.edu. In-State Tuition and Fees: $3,772. Out-of-State Tuition and Fees: $8,384. Room and Board: $5,652. Students Receiving Some Form of Aid: 33%. Students Receiving Non-Need-Based Aid: 15%. Average Aid Package: $5,652. Required Financial Aid Forms: FAFSA. Deadline to Apply for Financial Aid: April 22.

Connecticut College

Admissions Office, 270 Mohegan Avenue, New London, CT 06320. Phone: (860) 439-2200, (888) 553-8760. E-mail: admit@conncoll.edu. Web Site: camel.conncoll.edu. Tuition and Fees: $31,985. Students Receiving Some Form of Aid: 49%. Average Aid Package: $21,186. Required Financial Aid Forms: FAFSA, Profile. Deadline to Apply for Financial Aid: January 15.

Eastern Connecticut State University

Admissions Office, 83 Windham Street, Willimantic, CT 06226. Phone: (860) 465-5286, (877) 353-3278. Fax: (860) 465-5544. E-mail: ecsu.ctstateu.edu/admis/index.html. Web Site: ecsu.ctstateu.edu. In-State Tuition and Fees: $4,922. Out-of-State Tuition and Fees: $9,534. Room and Board: $5,544. Students Receiving Some Form of Aid: 40%. Students Receiving Non-Need-Based Aid: 26%. Average Aid Package: $4,965. Required Financial Aid Forms: FAFSA.

Fairfield University

Admissions Office, BLM 114, 1073 North Benson Road, Fairfield, CT 06430-5195. Phone: (203) 254-4100. Fax: (203) 254-4199. Web Site: fairfield.edu. Tuition and Fees: $19,935. Room and Board: $7,380. Students Receiving Some Form of Aid: 39%. Students Receiving Non-Need-Based Aid: 6%. Average Aid Package: $14,460. Required Financial Aid Forms: FAFSA, CSS Profile. Deadline to Apply for Financial Aid: February 15.

Quinnipiac University

Admissions Office, 275 Mount Carmel Avenue, Hamden, CT 06518-1908. Phone: (203) 281-8600, (800) 462-1944. Fax: (203) 281-8906. E-mail: admissions@quinnipiac.edu. Web Site: quinnipiac.edu. Tuition and Fees: $17,780. Room and Board: $8,170. Students Receiving Some Form of Aid: 58%. Students Receiving Non-Need-Based Aid: 13%. Average Aid Package: $10,947. Required Financial Aid Forms: FAFSA. Deadline to Apply for Financial Aid: rolling; March 1 (priority).

Sacred Heart University

Admissions Office, 5151 Park Avenue, Fairfield, CT 06432-1000. Phone: (203) 371-7880. Fax: (203) 365-7607. E-mail: enroll@sacredheart.edu. Web Site: sacredheart.edu. Tuition and Fees: $15,307. Room and Board: $7,530. Students Receiving Some Form of Aid: 47%. Students Receiving Non-Need-Based Aid: 26%. Average Aid Package: $10,900. Required Financial Aid Forms: FAFSA, CSS Profile. Deadline to Apply for Financial Aid: March 15; February 15 (priority).

Saint Joseph College*

Admissions Office, 1678 Asylum Avenue, West Hartford, CT 06117. Phone: (860) 232-4571, (800) 285-6565. Fax: (203) 233-5695. E-mail: infor@mercy.sjc.edu. Web Site: sjc.edu. Tuition and Fees: $15,900. Room and Board: $6,610. Students Receiving Some Form of Aid: 51%. Students Receiving Non-Need-Based Aid: 13%. Average Aid Package: $12,894. Required Financial Aid Forms: FAFSA. Deadline to Apply for Financial Aid: rolling.

Southern Connecticut State University

Admissions House, 131 Farnham Avenue, New Haven, CT 06515-1202. Phone: (203) 392-5656. Fax: (203) 392-5727. E-mail: adminfo@scsu.ctstateu.edu. Web Site: southernct.edu. In-State Tuition and Fees: $3,850. Out-of-State Tuition and Fees: $9,123. Room and Board: $6,062. Required Financial Aid Forms: FAFSA, institutional form, FAForm, Federal Tax forms. Deadline to Apply for Financial Aid: April 15.

Teikyo Post University

Admissions Office, 800 Country Club Road, Waterbury, CT 06723-2540. Phone: (203) 596-4520, (800) 345-2562. Fax: (203) 756-5810. E-mail: tpuadmis@teikyopost.edu. Web Site: teikyopost.edu. Tuition and Fees: $13,400. Room and Board: $5,900. Required Financial Aid Forms: FAFSA. Deadline to Apply for Financial Aid: March 15 (priority deadline).

Trinity College

Admissions Office, 300 Summit Street, Hartford, CT 06106. Phone: (860) 297-2180. Fax: (860) 297-2287. E-mail: admissions.office@trincoll.edu. Web Site: trincoll.edu. Tuition and Fees: $25,440. Room and Board: $7,160. Students Receiving Some Form of Aid: 43%. Average Aid Package: $22,495. Required Financial Aid Forms: FAFSA, Profile, federal income tax return, noncustodial parent statement. Deadline to Apply for Financial Aid: February 1.

United States Coast Guard Academy

Admissions Office, 31 Mohegan Avenue, New London, CT 06320-4195. Phone: (860) 444-8501, (800) 883-8724. Fax: (860) 701-6700. E-mail: uscgatr@dseg.uscga.edu. Web Site: cga.edu. Tuition, Fees, Room and Board: Paid for by the U.S. Government.

University of Bridgeport

Admissions Office, 126 Park Avenue, Bridgeport, CT 06601. Phone: (203) 576-4552, (800) 898-8278. Fax: (203) 576-4941. E-mail: admit@cse.bridgeport.edu. Web Site: bridgeport.edu. Tuition and Fees: $14,641. Room and Board: $6,970. Students Receiving Some Form of Aid: 73%. Students Receiving Non-Need-Based Aid: 43%. Average Aid Package: $14,270. Required Financial Aid Forms: FAFSA, UB form. Deadline to Apply for Financial Aid: April 15.

University of Connecticut

Admissions Office, 2131 Hillside Road, U-88, Storrs, CT 06268-3088. Phone: (860) 486-3137. Fax: (860) 486-1476. E-mail: beahusky@uconn.edu. Web Site: UConn.edu. In-State Tuition and Fees: $5,404. Out-of-State Tuition and Fees: $13,922. Room and Board: $5,694. Students Receiving Some Form of Aid: 34%. Students Receiving Non-Need-Based Aid: 14%. Average Aid Package: $6,904.

Required Financial Aid Forms: FAFSA, institutional form. Deadline to Apply for Financial Aid: rolling.

University of Hartford

Admissions Office, 200 Bloomfield Avenue, West Hartford, CT 06117. Phone: (860) 768-4296, (800) 947-4303. Fax: (860) 768-4961. E-mail: admission@mail.hartford.edu. Web Site: hartford.edu. Tuition and Fees: $18,980. Room and Board: $7,538. Students Receiving Some Form of Aid: 46%. Students Receiving Non-Need-Based Aid: 40%. Required Financial Aid Forms: FAFSA. Deadline to Apply for Financial Aid: February 1 (priority).

University of New Haven

Admissions Office, 300 Orange Avenue, New Haven, CT 06516. Phone: (203) 932-7319, (800) DIAL-UNH. Fax: (203) 931-6093. E-mail: adminfo@charger.newhaven.edu. Web Site: newhaven.edu. Tuition and Fees: $14,550. Room and Board: $6,560. Students Receiving Some Form of Aid: 40%. Students Receiving Non-Need-Based Aid: 3%. Average Aid Package: $12,800. Required Financial Aid Forms: FAFSA. Deadline to Apply for Financial Aid: March 1.

Wesleyan University

Admissions Office, The Stewart M. Reid House, 70 Wyllys Avenue, Middletown, CT 06459-0265. Phone: (860) 685-3000. Fax: (860) 685-3001. E-mail: admissions@wesleyan.edu. Web Site: wesleyan.edu. Tuition and Fees: $25,120. Room and Board: $6,510. Students Receiving Some Form of Aid: 47%. Average Aid Package: $22,563. Required Financial Aid Forms: FAFSA, financial aid profile form. Deadline to Apply for Financial Aid: February 1.

Western Connecticut State University

Undergraduate Admissions, 181 White Street, Danbury, CT 06810-6860. Phone: (203) 837-9000, (877) 837-WCSU. Fax: (203) 837-8338. E-mail: weasil@wcsu.edu. Web Site: wcsu.edu. In-State Tuition and Fees: $3,758. Out-of-State Tuition and Fees: $9,298. Room and Board: $5,434. Students Receiving Some Form of Aid: 29%. Students Receiving Non-Need-Based Aid: less than 1%. Average Aid Package: $4,732. Required Financial Aid Forms: FAFSA, institutional form. Deadline to Apply for Financial Aid: April 15; March 15 (priority).

Yale University

Office of Undergraduate Admissions, P.O. Box 208234, New Haven, CT 06520-8234. Phone: (203) 432-9300. Fax: (203) 432-9392. E-mail: undergraduate.admissions@yale.edu. Web Site: yale.edu. Tuition and Fees: $25,220. Room and Board: $7,660.

DELAWARE

Delaware State University

Office of Undergraduate Admissions, 1200 North DuPont Highway, Dover, DE 19901. Phone: (302) 857-6353. Fax: (302) 857-6352. E-mail: jwilliam@asc.edu. Web Site: dsc.edu. In-State Tuition and Fees: $3,256. Out-of-State Tuition and Fees: $7,248. Room and Board: $5,430. Students Receiving Some Form of Aid: 56%. Students Receiving Non-Need-Based Aid: 18%. Average Aid Package: $6,178. Required Financial Aid Forms: FAFSA. Deadline to Apply for Financial Aid: February 15.

Goldey-Beacom College

Admissions Office, 4701 Limestone Road, Wilmington, DE 19808. Phone: (302) 998-8814, (800) 833-4877. Fax: (302) 996-5408. E-mail: admissions@goldey.gbc.edu. Web Site: goldey.gbc.edu. Tuition and Fees: $7,950. Room and Board: $3,490. Required Financial Aid Forms: FAFSA. Deadline to Apply for Financial Aid: May 1.

University of Delaware

Admissions Office. , Newark, DE 19716-6210. Phone: (302) 831-8123. Fax: (302) 831-6905. E-mail: admissions@udel.edu. Web Site: udel.edu. In-State Tuition and Fees: $4,858. Out-of-State Tuition and Fees: $13,228. Room and Board: $5,132. Students Receiving Some Form of Aid: 32%. Students Receiving Non-Need-Based Aid: 8%. Average Aid Package: $8,200. Required Financial Aid Forms: FAFSA. Deadline to Apply for Financial Aid: March 15; February 1 (priority).

Wesley College

Admissions Office, 120 North State Street, Dover, DE 19901-3875. Phone: (302) 736-2400, (800) 937-5398. Fax: (302) 736-2382. E-mail: admissions@mail.wesley.edu. Web Site: wesley.edu. Tuition and Fees: $11,919. Room and Board: $5,017. Students Receiving Some Form of Aid: 49%. Students Receiving Non-Need-Based Aid: 36%. Average Aid Package: $6,000. Required Financial Aid Forms: FAFSA. Deadline to Apply for Financial Aid: April 15.

DISTRICT OF COLUMBIA

American University

Office of Admissions, 4400 Massachusetts Avenue N.W., Washington, DC 20016-8001. Phone: (202) 885-6000. Fax: (202) 885-1025. E-mail: afa@american.edu. Web Site: american.edu. Tuition and Fees: $21,399. Room and Board: $8,372. Students Receiving Some Form of Aid: 44%. Students Receiving Non-Need-Based Aid: 8%. Average Aid Package: $19,470. Required Financial Aid Forms: FAFSA, institutional forms. Deadline to Apply for Financial Aid: March 1.

Catholic University of America

Office of Undergraduate Admissions, 102 McMahon Hall, Washington, DC 20064. Phone: (202) 319-5305, (800) 673-2772. Fax: (202) 319-6533. E-mail: cua-admissions@cua.edu. Web Site: cua.edu. Tuition and Fees: $19,930. Room and Board: $8,073. Students Receiving Some Form of Aid: 57%. Students Receiving Non-Need-Based Aid: 11%. Average Aid Package: $16,859. Required Financial Aid Forms: FAFSA, FAF, school's form. Deadline to Apply for Financial Aid: February 1 (priority).

Gallaudet University

Director of Admissions, 800 Florida Avenue NE, Washington, DC 20002. Phone: (202) 651-5750, (800) 995-0550. Fax: (202) 651-5744. E-mail: admissions@gallaudet.edu. Web Site: gallaudet.edu. Tuition and Fees: $7,940. Room and Board: $7,130. Students Receiving Some Form of Aid: 63%. Students Receiving Non-Need-Based Aid: 14%. Average Aid Package: $10,324. Required Financial Aid Forms: FAFSA, institutional form. Deadline to Apply for Financial Aid: August 15.

George Washington University

Admissions Office, 2121 Eye Street NW, Suite 201, Washington, DC 20052. **Phone:** (202) 994-6040, (800) 447-3765. **Fax:** (202) 994-0325. **E-mail:** gwadm@gwis2.circ.gwu.edu. **Web Site:** gwu.edu. **Tuition and Fees:** $24,430. **Room and Board:** $8,538. **Students Receiving Some Form of Aid:** 33%. **Students Receiving Non-Need-Based Aid:** 2%. **Average Aid Package:** $20,900. **Required Financial Aid Forms:** FAFSA, CSS Profile. **Deadline to Apply for Financial Aid:** February 1.

Georgetown University

Undergraduate Admissions, 37th and O Streets, NW, Washington, DC 20057. **Phone:** (202) 687-3600. **Fax:** (202) 687-5084. **Web Site:** georgetown.edu. **Tuition and Fees:** $23,295. **Room and Board:** $8,693. **Students Receiving Some Form of Aid:** 40%. **Students Receiving Non-Need-Based Aid:** less than 1%. **Average Aid Package:** $19,048. **Required Financial Aid Forms:** FAFSA, CSS, FAF. **Deadline to Apply for Financial Aid:** February 1.

Howard University*

Admissions Office, 2400 6th Street NW, Washington, DC 20059. **Phone:** (202) 806-2752, (800) 822-6363. **Fax:** (202) 806-4465. **E-mail:** admission@howard.edu. **Web Site:** howard.edu. **Tuition and Fees:** $9,330. **Room and Board:** $5,714. **Students Receiving Some Form of Aid:** 84%. **Average Aid Package:** $10,939. **Required Financial Aid Forms:** FAFSA. **Deadline to Apply for Financial Aid:** April 1.

Trinity College

Admissions Office, 125 Michigan Avenue, NE, Washington, DC 20017. **Phone:** (202) 884-9400, (800) 492-6882. **Fax:** (202) 884-9403. **E-mail:** admissions@trinitydc.edu. **Web Site:** trinitydc.edu. **Tuition and Fees:** $14,440. **Room and Board:** $6,700. **Students Receiving Some Form of Aid:** 37%. **Students Receiving Non-Need-Based Aid:** 3%. **Average Aid Package:** $15,093. **Required Financial Aid Forms:** FAFSA. **Deadline to Apply for Financial Aid:** April 1 (priority).

University of the District of Columbia

Admissions Office, 4200 Connecticut Avenue Northwest, Washington, DC 20008. **Phone:** (202) 274-6069. **Fax:** (202) 274-5552. **In-State Tuition and Fees:** $1,935. **Out-of-State Tuition and Fees:** $4,575. **Required Financial Aid Forms:** FAFSA. **Deadline to Apply for Financial Aid:** rolling.

FLORIDA

Barry University

Division of Enrollment Services, 11300 NE Second Avenue, Miami Shores, FL 33161-6695. **Phone:** (305) 899-3100, (800) 695-2279. **Fax:** (305) 899-2971. **E-mail:** admissions@mail.barry.edu. **Web Site:** barry.edu. **Tuition and Fees:** $15,530. **Room and Board:** $6,220. **Students Receiving Some Form of Aid:** 36%. **Students Receiving Non-Need-Based Aid:** 36%. **Average Aid Package:** $14,430. **Required Financial Aid Forms:** FAFSA. **Deadline to Apply for Financial Aid:** rolling.

Bethune-Cookman College

Admissions Office, 640 Dr. Mary McLeod Bethune Boulevard, Daytona Beach, FL 32114. **Phone:** (904) 238-3803, (800) 448-0228. **Fax:** (904) 257-5338. **E-mail:** byrdw@cookman.edu. **Web Site:** bethune.cookman.edu. **Tuition and Fees:** $8,988. **Room and Board:** $5,534. **Students Receiving Some Form of Aid:** 84%. **Students Receiving Non-Need-Based Aid:** 49%. **Average Aid Package:** $9,855. **Required Financial Aid Forms:** FAFSA. **Deadline to Apply for Financial Aid:** April 1 (priority).

Eckerd College

Admissions Office, 4200 54th Avenue South, St. Petersburg, FL 33711. **Phone:** (727) 867-1166, (800) 456-9009. **Fax:** (727) 866-2304. **E-mail:** admissions@eckerd.edu. **Web Site:** eckerd.edu. **Tuition and Fees:** $18,220. **Room and Board:** $4,960. **Students Receiving Some Form of Aid:** 58%. **Students Receiving Non-Need-Based Aid:** 23%. **Average Aid Package:** $16,600. **Required Financial Aid Forms:** Federal Methodology. **Deadline to Apply for Financial Aid:** April 1.

Embry-Riddle Aeronautical University—Florida

Admissions Office, 600 South Clyde Morris Boulevard, Daytona Beach, FL 32114-3900. **Phone:** (904) 226-6100, (800) 862-2416. **Fax:** (904) 226-7070. **E-mail:** admit@db.erau.edu. **Web Site:** embryriddle.edu. **Tuition and Fees:** $14,820. **Room and Board:** $5,440. **Students Receiving Some Form of Aid:** 52%. **Students Receiving Non-Need-Based Aid:** 14%. **Average Aid Package:** $10,679. **Required Financial Aid Forms:** FAFSA. **Deadline to Apply for Financial Aid:** June 31; April 15 (priority).

Flagler College

Admissions Office, P.O. Box 1027, St. Augustine, FL 32085-1027. **Phone:** (904) 829-6481, (800) 304-4208. **Fax:** (904) 826-0094. **E-mail:** info@flagler.edu. **Web Site:** flagler.edu. **Tuition and Fees:** $6,320. **Room and Board:** $3,910. **Students Receiving Some Form of Aid:** 42%. **Students Receiving Non-Need-Based Aid:** 28%. **Average Aid Package:** $6,612. **Required Financial Aid Forms:** FAFSA, CSS Profile, institutional form. **Deadline to Apply for Financial Aid:** May 1.

Florida A&M University

Office of Admissions, Foote Hilyer Administration, G-9, Tallahassee, FL 32307-3200. **Phone:** (850) 599-3796. **Fax:** (850) 599-3069. **E-mail:** bcox2@famu.edu. **Web Site:** famu.edu. **In-State Tuition and Fees:** $2,336. **Out-of-State Tuition and Fees:** $9,324. **Room and Board:** $3,896. **Students Receiving Some Form of Aid:** 88%. **Students Receiving Non-Need-Based Aid:** 13%. **Average Aid Package:** $2,175. **Required Financial Aid Forms:** FAFSA. **Deadline to Apply for Financial Aid:** rolling.

Florida Atlantic University

Admissions Office, 777 Glades Road, P.O. Box 3091, Boca Raton, FL 33431-0991. **Phone:** (561) 297-3040, (800) 299-4FAU. **E-mail:** admisweb@fau.edu. **Web Site:** fau.edu. **In-State Tuition and Fees:** $2,253. **Out-of-State Tuition and Fees:** $9,242. **Room and Board:** $4,774. **Students Receiving Some Form of Aid:** 22%. **Average Aid Package:** $5,992. **Required Financial Aid Forms:** FAFSA. **Deadline to Apply for Financial Aid:** March 1 (priority).

Florida Institute of Technology

Admissions Office, 150 West University Boulevard, Melbourne, FL 32901-6975. Phone: (321) 674-8030. Fax: (321) 723-9468. E-mail: admissions@fit.edu. Web Site: fit.edu. Tuition and Fees: $18,450. Room and Board: $5,290. Required Financial Aid Forms: FAFSA. Deadline to Apply for Financial Aid: March 15.

Florida International University*

Admissions Office, University Park, PC 140, Miami, FL 33199. Phone: (305) 348-2363. Fax: (305) 348-3648. E-mail: admiss@fiu.edu. Web Site: fiu.edu. In-State Tuition and Fees: $2,322. Out-of-State Tuition and Fees: $9,311. Room and Board: $6,413. Students Receiving Some Form of Aid: 21%. Students Receiving Non-Need-Based Aid: 9%. Average Aid Package: $652. Required Financial Aid Forms: FAFSA. Deadline to Apply for Financial Aid: March 15.

Florida Southern College

Admissions Office, 111 Lake Hollingsworth Drive, Lakeland, FL 33801. Phone: (863) 680-4131, (800) 274-4131. Fax: (863) 680-4120. E-mail: fscadm@flsouthern.edu. Web Site: flsouthern.edu. Tuition and Fees: $11,810. Room and Board: $5,600. Students Receiving Some Form of Aid: 66%. Students Receiving Non-Need-Based Aid: 37%. Average Aid Package: $12,111. Required Financial Aid Forms: FAFSA, institutional application. Deadline to Apply for Financial Aid: August 1; April 1 (priority).

Florida State University

Office of Admissions, Florida State University, Tallahassee, FL 32306-2400. Phone: (850) 644-6200. Fax: (850) 644-0197. E-mail: admissions@admin.fsu.edu. Web Site: fsu.edu. In-State Tuition and Fees: $1,697. Out-of-State Tuition and Fees: $8,685. Room and Board: $4,951. Students Receiving Some Form of Aid: 33%. Students Receiving Non-Need-Based Aid: 17%. Average Aid Package: $3,127. Required Financial Aid Forms: FAFSA. Deadline to Apply for Financial Aid: February 15 (priority).

Jacksonville University

Office of Admissions, 2800 University Boulevard North, Jacksonville, FL 32211. Phone: (904) 745-7000, (800) 225-2027. Fax: (904) 745-7012. E-mail: admissions@ju.edu. Web Site: ju.edu. Tuition and Fees: $15,510. Room and Board: $5,400. Students Receiving Some Form of Aid: 49%. Students Receiving Non-Need-Based Aid: 43%. Average Aid Package: $13,358. Required Financial Aid Forms: FAFSA. Deadline to Apply for Financial Aid: rolling.

Johnson & Wales University—Florida

Admissions Office, 1701 NE 127th Street, North Miami, FL 33181. Phone: (305) 892-7600, (800) 232-2433. Fax: (305) 892-7020. E-mail: admissions@jwu.edu. Web Site: jwu.edu. Tuition and Fees: $16,890. Room Only: $4,815. Students Receiving Some Form of Aid: 74%. Students Receiving Non-Need-Based Aid: 41%. Average Aid Package: $11,831. Required Financial Aid Forms: FAFSA. Deadline to Apply for Financial Aid: rolling.

Lynn University

Admissions Office, 3601 North Military Trail, Boca Raton, FL 33431. Phone: (561) 237-7900, (561) 237-7000. Fax: (561) 237-7100. E-mail: admission@lynn.edu. Web Site: lynn.edu. Tuition and Fees: $19,250. Room and Board: $6,800. Required Financial Aid Forms: FAFSA. Deadline to Apply for Financial Aid: July 15.

New College of the University of South Florida

Admissions Office, 5700 North Tamiami Trail, Sarasota, FL 34243-2197. Phone: (941) 359-4269. Fax: (941) 359-4435. E-mail: ncadmissions@sar.usf.edu. Web Site: newcollege.usf.edu. In-State Tuition and Fees: $2,492. Out-of-State Tuition and Fees: $10,878. Room and Board: $4,663. Students Receiving Some Form of Aid: 36%. Students Receiving Non-Need-Based Aid: 28%. Average Aid Package: $9,962. Required Financial Aid Forms: FAFSA. Deadline to Apply for Financial Aid: March 1 (priority, processing is continuous).

Nova Southeastern University

Admissions Office, 3301 College Avenue, Fort Lauderdale, FL 33314. Phone: (954) 262-8000, (800) 338-4723, ext. 8000. Fax: (954) 262-3811. E-mail: ncsinfo@polaris.acast.nova.edu. Web Site: nova.edu. Tuition and Fees: $11,850. Room and Board: $6,200. Required Financial Aid Forms: FAFSA. Deadline to Apply for Financial Aid: April 1.

Palm Beach Atlantic College

Office of Enrollment Services, 901 South Flagler Avenue, P.O. Box 24708, West Palm Beach, FL 33416-4708. Phone: (561) 803-2100, (888) GO-TO-PBA. Fax: (561) 803-2186. E-mail: admit@pbac.edu. Web Site: pbac.edu. Tuition and Fees: $11,120. Room and Board: $4,470. Students Receiving Some Form of Aid: 33%. Students Receiving Non-Need-Based Aid: 33%. Average Aid Package: $10,152. Required Financial Aid Forms: FAFSA, student data form, state aid form. Deadline to Apply for Financial Aid: rolling, April 1 (priority).

Rollins College

Admissions Office, 1000 Holt Avenue, Winter Park, FL 32789-4499. Phone: (407) 646-2161. Fax: (407) 646-1502. E-mail: admission@rollins.edu. Web Site: rollins.edu. Tuition and Fees: $22,868. Room and Board: $7,000. Students Receiving Some Form of Aid: 45%. Students Receiving Non-Need-Based Aid: 9%. Average Aid Package: $23,356. Required Financial Aid Forms: FAFSA, institutional form. Deadline to Apply for Financial Aid: March 1.

Saint Thomas University

Admissions Office, 16400 Northwest 32nd Avenue, Miami, FL 33054. Phone: (305) 628-6546, (800) 367-9010 (out-of-state), (800) 367-9006 (in-state). Fax: (305) 628-6591. E-mail: signup@stu.edu. Web Site: stu.edu. Tuition and Fees: $14,082. Room and Board: $4,400. Average Aid Package: $8,142. Required Financial Aid Forms: FAFSA. Deadline to Apply for Financial Aid: April 3.

Stetson University

Admissions Office, 421 N. Woodland Blvd, Unit 8378, DeLand, FL 32720-3781. Phone: (904) 822-7100, (800) 688-0101. Fax: (904)

822-7112. **E-mail:** admissions@stetson.edu. **Web Site:** stetson.edu. **Tuition and Fees:** $18,385. **Room and Board:** $6,070. **Students Receiving Some Form of Aid:** 55%. **Students Receiving Non-Need-Based Aid:** 46%. **Average Aid Package:** $17,137. **Required Financial Aid Forms:** FAFSA. **Deadline to Apply for Financial Aid:** as soon after January 1 as possible.

University of Central Florida

Admissions Office, P.O. Box 16011, Orlando, FL 32816-0111. **Phone:** (407) 823-3000, (407) 823-2000. **Fax:** (407) 823-5625. **E-mail:** admission@mail.ucf.edu. **Web Site:** ucf.edu/admissions.html. **In-State Tuition and Fees:** $2,297. **Out-of-State Tuition and Fees:** $9,286. **Room and Board:** $5,279. **Students Receiving Some Form of Aid:** 28%. **Students Receiving Non-Need-Based Aid:** 11%. **Average Aid Package:** $3,310. **Required Financial Aid Forms:** FAFSA. **Deadline to Apply for Financial Aid:** rolling; March 1 (priority).

University of Florida

Admissions Office, 201 Criser Hall P.O. Box 114000, Gainesville, FL 32611-4000. **Phone:** (352) 392-1365. **Fax:** (352) 392-3987. **E-mail:** freshman@ufl.edu,transfer@ufl.edu. **Web Site:** ufl.edu. **In-State Tuition and Fees:** $2,141. **Out-of-State Tuition and Fees:** $9,130. **Room and Board:** $5,040. **Students Receiving Some Form of Aid:** 29%. **Students Receiving Non-Need-Based Aid:** 18%. **Average Aid Package:** $8,657. **Required Financial Aid Forms:** FAFSA, UF application for financial aid. **Deadline to Apply for Financial Aid:** March 15 (priority).

University of Miami

Office of Admission, P.O. Box 248025, Coral Gables, FL 33124-4616. **Phone:** (305) 284-4323. **Fax:** (305) 284-2507. **E-mail:** admission@miami.edu. **Web Site:** miami.edu. **Tuition and Fees:** $21,354. **Room and Board:** $7,782. **Students Receiving Some Form of Aid:** 53%. **Students Receiving Non-Need-Based Aid:** 6%. **Average Aid Package:** $19,537. **Required Financial Aid Forms:** FAFSA. **Deadline to Apply for Financial Aid:** Feb 15 (priority).

University of North Florida

Admissions Office, 4567 St. Johns Bluff Road, South, Jacksonville, FL 32224-2645. **Phone:** (904) 620-2624. **Fax:** (904) 620-2414. **E-mail:** osprey@unf.edu. **Web Site:** unf.edu. **In-State Tuition and Fees:** $2,145. **Out-of-State Tuition and Fees:** $8,492. **Room and Board:** $5,400. **Students Receiving Some Form of Aid:** 24%. **Students Receiving Non-Need-Based Aid:** 10%. **Average Aid Package:** $2,184. **Required Financial Aid Forms:** FAFSA. **Deadline to Apply for Financial Aid:** April 1 (priority).

University of South Florida

Admissions Office, 4202 East Fowler Avenue SVC 1036, Tampa, FL 33620-9915. **Phone:** (813) 974-3350. **Fax:** (813) 974-9689. **E-mail:** BULLSEYE@admin.usf.edu. **Web Site:** usfweb.usf.edu. **In-State Tuition and Fees:** $2,256. **Out-of-State Tuition and Fees:** $9,245. **Room and Board:** $4,896. **Required Financial Aid Forms:** FAFSA. **Deadline to Apply for Financial Aid:** April 15.

University of Tampa

Admissions Office, 401 West Kennedy Boulevard, Tampa, FL 33606-1490. **Phone:** (813) 253-6211, (800) 733-4773. **Fax:** (813) 258-7398. **E-mail:** admissions@alpha.utampa.edu. **Web Site:** utampa.edu. **Tuition and Fees:** $15,542. **Room and Board:** $5,175. **Required Financial Aid Forms:** FAFSA. **Deadline to Apply for Financial Aid:** rolling.

University of West Florida

UWF Admissions Office, 11000 University Parkway, Pensacola, FL 32514. **Phone:** (850) 474-2230. **Fax:** (850) 474-3360. **E-mail:** admiss@uwf.edu. **Web Site:** uwf.edu. **In-State Tuition and Fees:** $2,324. **Out-of-State Tuition and Fees:** $9,312. **Room and Board:** $4,532. **Students Receiving Some Form of Aid:** 48%. **Students Receiving Non-Need-Based Aid:** 16%. **Required Financial Aid Forms:** FAFSA, UWF. **Deadline to Apply for Financial Aid:** March 1.

GEORGIA

Agnes Scott College

Admission Office, 141 E. College Avenue, Atlanta/Decatur, GA 30030. **Phone:** (404) 471-6285, (800) 868-8602. **Fax:** (404) 471-6414. **E-mail:** admission@agnesscott.edu. **Web Site:** agnesscott.edu. **Tuition and Fees:** $16,745. **Room and Board:** $6,900. **Students Receiving Some Form of Aid:** 61%. **Students Receiving Non-Need-Based Aid:** 32%. **Average Aid Package:** $16,335. **Required Financial Aid Forms:** FAFSA, State aid form. **Deadline to Apply for Financial Aid:** May 1; March 1 (priority).

Armstrong Atlantic State University

Admissions Office, 11935 Abercorn Street, Savannah, GA 31419. **Phone:** (912) 927-5277. **Fax:** (912) 921-5462. **E-mail:** adm-info@mail.armstrong.edu. **Web Site:** armstrong.edu. **In-State Tuition and Fees:** $2,388. **Out-of-State Tuition and Fees:** $7,812. **Room and Board:** $4,460. **Required Financial Aid Forms:** FAFSA, institutional form. **Deadline to Apply for Financial Aid:** April 15.

Augusta State University

Admissions Office, 2500 Walton Way, Augusta, GA 30904-2200. **Phone:** (706) 737-1632, (800) 341-4373. **Fax:** (706) 667-4355. **E-mail:** admissio@aug.edu. **Web Site:** aug.edu. **In-State Tuition and Fees:** $2,082. **Out-of-State Tuition and Fees:** $7,506. **Students Receiving Some Form of Aid:** 50%. **Students Receiving Non-Need-Based Aid:** 13%. **Average Aid Package:** $6,280. **Required Financial Aid Forms:** FAFSA. **Deadline to Apply for Financial Aid:** rolling; April 15 (priority).

Berry College

Admissions Office, 2277 Martha Berry Boulevard, NE, Mt. Berry, GA 30149. **Phone:** (706) 236-2215, 800-237-7942. **Fax:** (706) 290-2178. **E-mail:** admissions@berry.edu. **Web Site:** berry.edu. **Tuition and Fees:** $12,500. **Room and Board:** $5,610. **Students Receiving Some Form of Aid:** 54%. **Students Receiving Non-Need-Based Aid:** 44%. **Average Aid Package:** $11,100. **Required Financial Aid Forms:** institutional form, state aid. **Deadline to Apply for Financial Aid:** April 1 (priority).

Clark Atlanta University

Admissions Office, 223 James P. Brawley Drive, SW, Atlanta, GA 30314. **Phone:** (404) 880-6605, (800) 688-3228. **Fax:** (404) 880-6174. **E-mail:** pmeadows@cau.edu. **Web Site:** cau.edu. **Tuition and Fees:** $10,450. **Room and Board:** $5,974. **Students Receiving Some Form of

Aid: 78%. Students Receiving Non-Need-Based Aid: 4%. Average Aid Package: $11,106. Required Financial Aid Forms: FAFSA or institution's own financial aid form. Deadline to Apply for Financial Aid: April 1.

Clayton College & State University

The Office of Admissions, 5900 North Lee Street, Morrow, GA 30260-0285. Phone: (770) 961-3500. Fax: (770) 961-3752. E-mail: ccsu-info@mail.clayton.edu. Web Site: clayton.edu. In-State Tuition and Fees: $2,702. Out-of-State Tuition and Fees: $8,126. Students Receiving Some Form of Aid: 20%. Students Receiving Non-Need-Based Aid: 11%. Required Financial Aid Forms: FAFSA, institutional form. Deadline to Apply for Financial Aid: three months prior to semester.

Columbus State University*

Admissions Office, 4225 University Avenue, Columbus, GA 31907-5645. Phone: (706) 568-2035. Fax: (706) 568-2462. E-mail: admissions@colstate.edu. Web Site: colstate.edu. In-State Tuition and Fees: $2,126. Out-of-State Tuition and Fees: $7,550. Room and Board: $3,870. Students Receiving Some Form of Aid: 126%. Students Receiving Non-Need-Based Aid: 45%. Average Aid Package: $6,900. Required Financial Aid Forms: FAFSA. Deadline to Apply for Financial Aid: 4-6 weeks before registration.

Emory University

Admissions Office, 200 B. Jones Center, Atlanta, GA 30322. Phone: (404) 727-6036, (800) 727-6036. E-mail: admiss@emory.edu. Web Site: emory.edu. Tuition and Fees: $23,130. Room and Board: $7,650. Students Receiving Some Form of Aid: 39%. Students Receiving Non-Need-Based Aid: 15%. Average Aid Package: $19,873. Required Financial Aid Forms: FAFSA. Deadline to Apply for Financial Aid: April 1.

Georgia College and State University

Office of Admissions, Campus Box 23, Milledgeville, GA 31061-0490. Phone: (912) 445-2774, (800) 342-0471 (in-state). Fax: (912) 445-1914. E-mail: gcsu@mail.gcsu.edu. Web Site: gcsu.edu. In-State Tuition and Fees: $2,214. Out-of-State Tuition and Fees: $7,638. Room and Board: $5,242. Students Receiving Some Form of Aid: 30%. Students Receiving Non-Need-Based Aid: 23%. Required Financial Aid Forms: FAFSA, institutional form. Deadline to Apply for Financial Aid: March 1 (priority date).

Georgia Institute of Technology

Office of Undergraduate Admission, 225 North Avenue, Atlanta, GA 30332-0320. Phone: (404) 894-4154. Fax: (404) 894-9511. E-mail: admissions@success.gatech.edu. Web Site: gatech.edu. In-State Tuition and Fees: $3,107. Out-of-State Tuition and Fees: $10,349. Room and Board: $4,976. Students Receiving Some Form of Aid: 30%. Students Receiving Non-Need-Based Aid: 7%. Average Aid Package: $5,890. Required Financial Aid Forms: FAFSA, institutional form. Deadline to Apply for Financial Aid: March 1 (priority).

Georgia Southern University

Admissions Office, P.O. Box 8024, Statesboro, GA 30460. Phone: (912) 681-5391. Fax: (912) 681-5635. E-mail: admissions@gasou.edu. Web Site: gasou.edu. In-State Tuition and Fees: $2,500. Out-of-State Tuition and Fees: $8,128. Room and Board: $4,154. Students Receiving Some Form of Aid: 47%. Students Receiving Non-Need-Based Aid: 5%. Average Aid Package: $5,306. Required Financial Aid Forms: FAFSA. Deadline to Apply for Financial Aid: March 17 (priority).

Georgia Southwestern State University

Admissions Office, 800 Wheatley Street, Americus, GA 31709. Phone: (912) 928-1273, (800) 338-0082. Fax: (912) 931-2983. E-mail: gswapps@canes.gsw.edu. Web Site: gsw.edu. In-State Tuition and Fees: $2,060. Out-of-State Tuition and Fees: $7,484. Room and Board: $3,540. Students Receiving Some Form of Aid: 53%. Students Receiving Non-Need-Based Aid: 34%. Average Aid Package: $6,832. Required Financial Aid Forms: FAFSA. Deadline to Apply for Financial Aid: April 1.

Georgia State University

Office of Admissions, P.O. Box 4009, Atlanta, GA 30302-4009. Phone: (404) 651-2365. Fax: (404) 651-4811. E-mail: admissions@gsu.edu. Web Site: gsu.edu. In-State Tuition and Fees: $2,886. Out-of-State Tuition and Fees: $10,128. Room and Board: $7,948. Students Receiving Non-Need-Based Aid: 10%. Average Aid Package: $3,522. Required Financial Aid Forms: FAFSA. Deadline to Apply for Financial Aid: April 1 (priority).

Kennesaw State University

Admissions Office, 1000 Chastain Road, Kennesaw, GA 30144-5591. Phone: (770) 423-6300. Fax: (770) 423-6541. E-mail: ksuadmit@kennesaw.edu. Web Site: kennesaw.edu. In-State Tuition and Fees: $2,526. Out-of-State Tuition and Fees: $7,746. Required Financial Aid Forms: FAFSA.

LaGrange College

Office of Admission, 601 Broad Street, LaGrange, GA 30240-2999. Phone: (706) 812-7260, (800) 593-2885. Fax: (706) 812-7348. E-mail: lgcadmis@lgc.edu. Web Site: lgc.edu. Tuition and Fees: $11,660. Room and Board: $4,485. Students Receiving Some Form of Aid: 55%. Students Receiving Non-Need-Based Aid: 22%. Average Aid Package: $16,831. Required Financial Aid Forms: FAFSA, institutional form, State aid form. Deadline to Apply for Financial Aid: June 1; May 1 (priority).

Mercer University

Admissions Office, 1400 Coleman Avenue, Macon, GA 31207-0001. Phone: (912) 301-2650, (800) 342-0841. Fax: (912) 301-2828. E-mail: admissions@mercer.edu. Web Site: mercer.edu. Tuition and Fees: $16,290. Room and Board: $5,380. Students Receiving Some Form of Aid: 79%. Students Receiving Non-Need-Based Aid: 33%. Average Aid Package: $11,892. Required Financial Aid Forms: FAFSA, institutional form, state form. Deadline to Apply for Financial Aid: May 1.

Morehouse College

Admissions Office, 830 Westview Drive, SW, Atlanta, GA 30314. Phone: (404) 681-2800, ext. 2632, (800) 851-1254. Fax: (404) 524-5635. E-mail: apattillo@morehouse.edu. Web Site: morehouse.edu. Tuition and Fees: $11,738. Room and Board: $6,970. Students Receiving Some Form of Aid: 85%. Students Receiving Non-Need-Based Aid: 21%. Required Financial Aid Forms: FAFSA, institutional form, financial aid profile, state aid forms. Deadline to Apply for Financial Aid: April 1.

Morris Brown College

Office of Admissions, 643 Martin Luther King, Jr. Drive, NW, Atlanta, GA 30314. Phone: (404) 739-1560. Fax: (404) 220-1565. E-mail: admissions@morrisbrown.edu. Web Site: morrisbrown.edu. Tuition and Fees: $9,253. Room and Board: $5,012. Students Receiving Some Form of Aid: 85%. Students Receiving Non-Need-Based Aid: 58%. Average Aid Package: $6,911. Required Financial Aid Forms: FAFSA. Deadline to Apply for Financial Aid: March 15 (priority).

North Georgia College and State University

Admissions Office, College Circle, Dahlonega, GA 30597. Phone: (706) 864-1800, (800) 498-9581. Fax: (706) 864-1478. E-mail: tdavis@ngcsu.edu. Web Site: ngcsu.edu. In-State Tuition and Fees: $2,210. Out-of-State Tuition and Fees: $7,644. Room and Board: $3,542. Required Financial Aid Forms: FAFSA, institutional form. Deadline to Apply for Financial Aid: May 1.

Oglethorpe University

Admissions Office, 4484 Peachtree Road NE, Atlanta, GA 30319. Phone: (404) 364-8307, (800) 428-4484. Fax: (404) 364-8500. E-mail: admission@oglethorpe.edu. Web Site: oglethorpe.edu. Tuition and Fees: $17,700. Room and Board: $5,300. Average Aid Package: $15,782. Required Financial Aid Forms: FAFSA, institution's own form, State Aid Form. Deadline to Apply for Financial Aid: March 1 (priority).

Savannah College of Art and Design

Admissions Office, 342 Bull Street, P.O. Box 3146, Savannah, GA 31402-3146. Phone: (912) 525-5100, (800) 869-7223. Fax: (912) 525-5981. E-mail: admissions@scad.edu. Web Site: scad.edu. Tuition and Fees: $16,200. Room and Board: $6,750. Required Financial Aid Forms: FAFSA. Deadline to Apply for Financial Aid: rolling.

Savannah State University

Admissions Office, P.O. Box 20209, Savannah, GA 31404. Phone: (912) 356-2181, (800) 788-0478. Fax: (912) 356-2256. E-mail: ssuadmissions@savstate.edu. Web Site: savstate.edu. In-State Tuition and Fees: $2,356. Out-of-State Tuition and Fees: $7,920. Room and Board: $4,084. Average Aid Package: $3,200. Required Financial Aid Forms: FAFSA. Deadline to Apply for Financial Aid: August 1; May 1 (priority).

Southern Polytechnic State University

Admissions Office, 1100 South Marietta Parkway, Marietta, GA 30060-2896. Phone: (770) 528-7281, (800) 635-3204. Fax: (770) 528-7292. E-mail: admissions@spsu.edu. Web Site: spsu.edu. In-State Tuition and Fees: $2,134. Out-of-State Tuition and Fees: $7,558. Room and Board: $4,452. Students Receiving Some Form of Aid: 26%. Students Receiving Non-Need-Based Aid: 8%. Average Aid Package: $4,082. Required Financial Aid Forms: FAFSA. Deadline to Apply for Financial Aid: March 15 (priority).

Spelman College

Office of Admissions, Box 277, 350 Spelman Lane, SW, Atlanta, GA 30314. Phone: (800) 982-2411. Fax: (404) 215-7788. E-mail: admiss@spelman.edu. Web Site: spelman.edu. Tuition and Fees: $9,260. Room and Board: $6,730. Students Receiving Some Form of Aid: 88%. Students Receiving Non-Need-Based Aid: 43%. Average Aid Package: $6,000. Required Financial Aid Forms: FAFSA.

State University of West Georgia

Admissions Office, 1600 Maple Street, Carrollton, GA 30117. Phone: (770) 836-6416. Fax: (770) 836-4659. Web Site: westga.edu. In-State Tuition and Fees: $3,154. Out-of-State Tuition and Fees: $8,578. Room and Board: $3,806. Students Receiving Some Form of Aid: 47%. Students Receiving Non-Need-Based Aid: 32%. Average Aid Package: $5,406. Required Financial Aid Forms: FAFSA. Deadline to Apply for Financial Aid: rolling; April 1 (priority).

Toccoa Falls College

Admissions Office, P.O. Box 800-899, Toccoa Falls, GA 30598. Phone: (800) 868-5380. Fax: (706) 282-6012. E-mail: admissions@toccoafalls.edu. Web Site: toccoafalls.edu. Tuition and Fees: $8,888. Room and Board: $4,012. Students Receiving Some Form of Aid: 77%. Students Receiving Non-Need-Based Aid: 60%. Average Aid Package: $6,800. Required Financial Aid Forms: FAFSA. Deadline to Apply for Financial Aid: March 1 (priority).

University of Georgia*

Admissions Office, 212 Terrell Hall, Athens, GA 30602-1633. Phone: (706) 542-2112. Fax: (706) 542-1466. E-mail: undergrad@admissions.uga.edu. Web Site: uga.edu. In-State Tuition and Fees: $3,034. Out-of-State Tuition and Fees: $10,276. Room and Board: $4,902. Students Receiving Some Form of Aid: 30%. Students Receiving Non-Need-Based Aid: 5%. Average Aid Package: $5,371. Required Financial Aid Forms: FAFSA, University forms. Deadline to Apply for Financial Aid: March 1.

Valdosta State University

Admissions Office, 1500 N. Patterson Street, Valdosta, GA 31698. Phone: (912) 333-5791, (800) 618-1878. Fax: (912) 333-5482. E-mail: admissions@valdosta.edu. Web Site: valdosta.edu. In-State Tuition and Fees: $2,290. Out-of-State Tuition and Fees: $7,714. Room and Board: $3,954. Students Receiving Some Form of Aid: 53%. Students Receiving Non-Need-Based Aid: 31%. Average Aid Package: $6,624. Required Financial Aid Forms: FAFSA, institutional form. Deadline to Apply for Financial Aid: ASAP.

Wesleyan College

Admissions Office, 4760 Forsyth Road, Macon, GA 31210. Phone: (912) 757-5206, (800) 447-6610. Fax: (912) 757-4030. E-mail: admissions@wesleyancollege.edu. Web Site: wesleyancollege.edu. Tuition and Fees: $16,310. Room and Board: $7,150. Required Financial Aid Forms: FAFSA, institutional form. Deadline to Apply for Financial Aid: March 1.

HAWAII

Brigham Young University—Hawaii

Admissions Office, Brigham Young University Hawaii, Oahu, HI 96762. Phone: (808) 293-3738. Fax: (808) 293-3741. E-mail: admissions@byuh.edu. Web Site: byuh.edu. Tuition and Fees (members of the Church of Latter Day Saints): $2,900. Tuition and Fees (non-members of the Church of Latter Day Saints): $4,350. Room and Board: $5,125.

Students Receiving Some Form of Aid: 73%. Students Receiving Non-Need-Based Aid: 56%. Required Financial Aid Forms: FAFSA. Deadline to Apply for Financial Aid: February 15.

Chaminade University of Honolulu

Admissions Office, 3140 Waialae Avenue, Honolulu, HI 96816. Phone: (808) 735-4735. Fax: (808) 739-4647. E-mail: cuhadm@lava.net. Web Site: chaminade.edu. Tuition and Fees: $11,700. Room and Board: $5,720. Required Financial Aid Forms: FAFSA. Deadline to Apply for Financial Aid: March 1 (priority).

Hawaii Pacific University

Office of Admission, 1164 Bishop Street, Honolulu, HI 96813. Phone: (808) 544-0238, (800) 669-4724. Fax: (808) 544-1136. E-mail: admissions@hpu.edu. Web Site: hpu.edu. Tuition and Fees: $8,920. Room and Board: $8,350. Students Receiving Some Form of Aid: 21%. Students Receiving Non-Need-Based Aid: 8%. Average Aid Package: $10,733. Required Financial Aid Forms: FAFSA. Deadline to Apply for Financial Aid: rolling.

University of Hawaii—Hilo

Admissions Office, 200 W Kawili St., Hilo, HI 96720-4091. Phone: (808) 974-7414. Fax: (808) 974-7691. E-mail: uhhadm@hawaii.edu. Web Site: www2.hawaii.edu/~uhhilo. In-State Tuition and Fees: $1,466. Out-of-State Tuition and Fees: $7,082. Room and Board: $4,989. Required Financial Aid Forms: FAFSA. Deadline to Apply for Financial Aid: March 1 (priority).

University of Hawaii—Manoa

Admissions Office, 2600 Campus Road, SSC Room 001, Honolulu, HI 96822. Phone: (808) 956-8975, (800) 823-9771. E-mail: ar-info@hawaii.edu. Web Site: uhm.hawaii.edu. In-State Tuition and Fees: $3,142. Out-of-State Tuition and Fees: $9,622. Room and Board: $4,435. Students Receiving Some Form of Aid: 26%. Students Receiving Non-Need-Based Aid: 5%. Average Aid Package: $5,686. Required Financial Aid Forms: FAFSA, institutional form. Deadline to Apply for Financial Aid: March 1.

IDAHO

Albertson College of Idaho

Admissions Office, 2112 Cleveland Boulevard, Caldwell, ID 83605-4432. Phone: (208) 459-5305, (800) 224-3246. Fax: (208) 454-2077. E-mail: admission@acofi.edu. Web Site: acofi.edu. Tuition and Fees: $16,600. Room and Board: $4,400. Students Receiving Some Form of Aid: 100%. Students Receiving Non-Need-Based Aid: 97%. Average Aid Package: $11,090. Required Financial Aid Forms: institutional form, FAFSA (federal programs only). Deadline to Apply for Financial Aid: February 15 (priority).

Boise State University

New Student Information Center, 1910 University Drive, Boise, ID 83725. Phone: (208) 426-1156, (800) 824-7017. Fax: (208) 426-3765. E-mail: businfo@boisestate.edu. Web Site: boisestate.edu. In-State Tuition and Fees: $2,644. Out-of-State Tuition and Fees: $8,524. Room and Board: $3,876. Students Receiving Some Form of Aid: 44%. Students Receiving Non-Need-Based Aid: 34%. Average Aid Package: $4,866. Required Financial Aid Forms: FAFSA. Deadline to Apply for Financial Aid: March 1 (priority).

Idaho State University

Admissions Office, Campus Box 8270, Pocatello, ID 83209-8270. Phone: (208) 282-2475. Fax: (208) 282-4231. E-mail: info@isu.edu. Web Site: isu.edu. In-State Tuition and Fees: $2,398. Out-of-State Tuition and Fees: $8,638. Room and Board: $3,780. Students Receiving Some Form of Aid: 35%. Students Receiving Non-Need-Based Aid: 25%. Average Aid Package: $9,030. Required Financial Aid Forms: FAFSA. Deadline to Apply for Financial Aid: June 30; March 15 (priority).

University of Idaho

Admissions Office, University of Idaho, Moscow, ID 83844-3133. Phone: (208) 885-6326. Fax: (208) 885-9061. E-mail: admappl@uidaho.edu. Web Site: uidaho.edu/index-ext.shtml. In-State Tuition and Fees: $2,348. Out-of-State Tuition and Fees: $8,348. Room and Board: $3,952. Students Receiving Some Form of Aid: 40%. Average Aid Package: $5,170. Required Financial Aid Forms: FAFSA. Deadline to Apply for Financial Aid: February 15 (priority).

ILLINOIS

Augustana College

Office of Admissions, 639 38th Street, Rock Island, IL 61201-2296. Phone: (309) 794-7341, (800) 798-8100. Fax: (309) 794-7422. E-mail: admissions@augustana.edu. Web Site: augustana.edu. Tuition and Fees: $17,187. Room and Board: $5,037. Students Receiving Some Form of Aid: 71%. Students Receiving Non-Need-Based Aid: 47%. Average Aid Package: $13,518. Required Financial Aid Forms: FAFSA, institutional form. Deadline to Apply for Financial Aid: April 1 (priority).

Benedictine University

Admissions Office, 5700 College Road, Lisle, IL 60532-0900. Phone: (630) 829-6300. Fax: (630) 829-6301. Web Site: ben.edu. Tuition and Fees: $12,600. Room and Board: $5,180. Required Financial Aid Forms: FAFSA, institutional form. Deadline to Apply for Financial Aid: April 15.

Bradley University

Admissions Office, 1501 West Bradley Avenue, Peoria, IL 61625. Phone: (309) 677-1000, (800) 447-6460. Fax: (309) 677-2797. E-mail: admissions@bradley.edu. Web Site: bradley.edu. Tuition and Fees: $13,960. Room and Board: $5,300. Students Receiving Some Form of Aid: 68%. Students Receiving Non-Need-Based Aid: 4%. Average Aid Package: $11,112. Required Financial Aid Forms: FAFSA. Deadline to Apply for Financial Aid: March 1.

Chicago State University*

Admissions Office, 9501 S. King Drive, Chicago, IL 60628. Phone: (773) 995-2513, (773) 995-2000. Fax: (773) 995-3820. Web Site: csu.edu. In-State Tuition and Fees: $3,177. Out-of-State Tuition and Fees: $7,697. Room and Board: $5,700. Required Financial Aid Forms: FAFSA. Deadline to Apply for Financial Aid: April 15.

Columbia College—Chicago

Office of Admissions, 600 South Michigan Avenue, Chicago, IL 60605. Phone: (312) 344-7129/7130/7131. Fax: (312) 344-8024. E-mail: admissions@popmail.colum.edu. Web Site: colum.edu. Tuition and Fees: $10,830. Room Only: $4,988. Required Financial Aid Forms: FAFSA.

Concordia University*

Admissions Office, 7400 Augusta Street, River Forest, IL 60305. Phone: (708) 209-3100, (800) 285-2668. Fax: (708) 209-3176. E-mail: crfadmis@curf.edu. Web Site: curf.edu. Tuition and Fees: $13,860. Room and Board: $5,365. Students Receiving Some Form of Aid: 59%. Students Receiving Non-Need-Based Aid: 33%. Average Aid Package: $10,000. Required Financial Aid Forms: FAFSA, institutional form. Deadline to Apply for Financial Aid: May 31; April 15 (priority).

DePaul University

Admissions Office, 1 East Jackson Boulevard, Suite 9100, Chicago, IL 60604. Phone: (312) 362-8300, (800) 4-DEPAUL. Fax: (312) 362-5749. E-mail: admitdpu@wppost.depaul.edu. Web Site: depaul.edu. Tuition and Fees: $14,700. Room and Board: $6,300. Students Receiving Some Form of Aid: 54%. Students Receiving Non-Need-Based Aid: 16%. Average Aid Package: $12,480. Required Financial Aid Forms: FAFSA. Deadline to Apply for Financial Aid: May 1.

Eastern Illinois University

Admissions Office, 600 Lincoln Avenue, Charleston, IL 61920-3099. Phone: (217) 581-2223, (800) 252-5711. Fax: (217) 581-7060. E-mail: admissns@eiu.edu. Web Site: eiu.edu. In-State Tuition and Fees: $4,092. Out-of-State Tuition and Fees: $9,912. Students Receiving Some Form of Aid: 44%. Students Receiving Non-Need-Based Aid: 17%. Average Aid Package: $6,866. Required Financial Aid Forms: FAFSA. Deadline to Apply for Financial Aid: April 15 (priority).

Elmhurst College

Admission Office, 190 Prospect Avenue, Elmhurst, IL 60126. Phone: (630) 617-3400, (800) 697-1871. Fax: (630) 617-5501. E-mail: admit@elmhurst.edu. Web Site: elmhurst.edu. Tuition and Fees: $13,900. Room and Board: $5,266. Students Receiving Some Form of Aid: 49%. Students Receiving Non-Need-Based Aid: 8%. Average Aid Package: $13,950. Required Financial Aid Forms: FAFSA, institutional form. Deadline to Apply for Financial Aid: April 15 (priority).

Eureka College

Office of Admissions, 300 E. College Avenue, Eureka, IL 61530-1500. Phone: (888) 4-EUREKA. Fax: (309) 467-6576. E-mail: admissions@eureka.edu. Web Site: eureka.edu. Tuition and Fees: $15,450. Room and Board: $4,860. Average Aid Package: $13,640. Required Financial Aid Forms: FAFSA. Deadline to Apply for Financial Aid: May 1.

Greenville College

Admissions Office, 315 East College Ave., P.O. Box 159, Greenville, IL 62246. Phone: (618) 664-2800, (800) 345-4440. Fax: (618) 664-9841. E-mail: admissions@greenville.edu. Web Site: greenville.edu. Tuition and Fees: $12,586. Room and Board: $4,850. Students Receiving Some Form of Aid: 67%. Students Receiving Non-Need-Based Aid: 7%. Average Aid Package: $13,021. Required Financial Aid Forms: FAFSA. Deadline to Apply for Financial Aid: May 1.

Illinois College*

Admissions Office, 1101 West College Avenue, Jacksonville, IL 62650. Phone: (217) 245-3030, (888) 595-3030. Fax: (217) 245-3034. E-mail: admissions@hilltop.ic.edu. Web Site: ic.edu. Tuition and Fees: $10,200. Room and Board: $4,500. Students Receiving Some Form of Aid: 73%. Students Receiving Non-Need-Based Aid: 38%. Average Aid Package: $10,043. Required Financial Aid Forms: FAFSA. Deadline to Apply for Financial Aid: May 1 (priority).

Illinois Institute of Technology

Undergraduate Admission, Room 101, Perlstein Hall, 10 W. 33rd St., Chicago, IL 60616-3793. Phone: (312) 567-3025, (800) 448-2329. Fax: (312) 567-6939. E-mail: admission@iit.edu. Web Site: iit.edu. Tuition and Fees: $17,600. Room and Board: $5,250. Students Receiving Some Form of Aid: 54%. Students Receiving Non-Need-Based Aid: 48%. Average Aid Package: $18,831. Required Financial Aid Forms: FAFSA. Deadline to Apply for Financial Aid: March 16.

Illinois State University

Admissions Office, Campus Box 2200, Normal, IL 61790-2200. Phone: (309) 438-2181, (800) 366-2478. Fax: (309) 438-3932. E-mail: ugradadm@ilstu.edu. Web Site: ilstu.edu. In-State Tuition and Fees: $4,340. Out-of-State Tuition and Fees: $10,778. Room and Board: $4,238. Students Receiving Some Form of Aid: 42%. Students Receiving Non-Need-Based Aid: 7%. Average Aid Package: $7,120. Required Financial Aid Forms: FAFSA. Deadline to Apply for Financial Aid: March 1(priority).

Illinois Wesleyan University

Admissions Office, P.O. Box 2900, Bloomington, IL 61702-2900. Phone: (309) 556-3031, (800) 332-2498. Fax: (309) 556-3411. E-mail: iwuadmit@titan.iwu.edu. Web Site: iwu.edu. Tuition and Fees: $20,410. Room and Board: $5,150. Students Receiving Some Form of Aid: 16%. Students Receiving Non-Need-Based Aid: less than 1%. Average Aid Package: $15,303. Required Financial Aid Forms: FAFSA, institutional form. Deadline to Apply for Financial Aid: March 1.

Knox College

Admissions Office, Box K-148, Galesburg, IL 61401. Phone: (309) 341-7100, (800) 678-KNOX. Fax: (309) 341-7070. E-mail: admission@knox.edu. Web Site: knox.edu. Tuition and Fees: $21,174. Room and Board: $5,436. Students Receiving Some Form of Aid: 76%. Students Receiving Non-Need-Based Aid: 4%. Average Aid Package: $17,313. Required Financial Aid Forms: FAFSA, institutional form, tax returns. Deadline to Apply for Financial Aid: March 1.

Lake Forest College

Office of Admissions, 555 North Sheridan Road, Lake Forest, IL 60045. Phone: (847) 735-5000, (800) 848-4751. Fax: (847) 735-6271. E-mail: admissions@lfc.edu. Web Site: lfc.edu. Tuition and Fees: $21,190. Room and Board: $5,000. Students Receiving Some Form of Aid: 71%. Average Aid Package: $16,875. Required Financial Aid Forms: FAFSA, profile. Deadline to Apply for Financial Aid: March 1.

Lewis University

Admissions Office, Route 53, Romeoville, IL 60446. Phone: (815) 836-5250, (800) 897-9000. Fax: (815) 836-5002. E-mail: admissions@lewisu.edu. Web Site: lewisu.edu. Tuition and Fees: $12,810. Room and Board: $5,730. Students Receiving Some Form of Aid: 43%. Students Receiving Non-Need-Based Aid: 19%. Average Aid Package: $12,039. Required Financial Aid Forms: FAFSA. Deadline to Apply for Financial Aid: May 1.

Loyola University of Chicago*

Admissions Office, 820 North Michigan Avenue, Chicago, IL 60611-9810. Phone: (312) 915-6500, (800) 262-2373. Fax: (312) 915-6449. E-mail: admission@luc.edu. Web Site: luc.edu. Tuition and Fees: $18,190. Room and Board: $7,200. Required Financial Aid Forms: FAFSA. Deadline to Apply for Financial Aid: rolling.

MacMurray College

Admissions Office, 447 E. College, Jacksonville, IL 62650. Phone: (217) 479-7056, (800) 252-7485. Fax: (217) 245-0405. E-mail: admiss@mac.edu. Web Site: mac.edu. Tuition and Fees: $13,240. Room and Board: $4,650. Students Receiving Some Form of Aid: 85%. Students Receiving Non-Need-Based Aid: 51%. Average Aid Package: $15,208. Required Financial Aid Forms: FAFSA. Deadline to Apply for Financial Aid: rolling.

McKendree College

Admissions Office, 701 College Road, Lebanon, IL 62254. Phone: (618) 532-6831, (800) 232-7228. Web Site: mckendree.edu. Tuition and Fees: $12,000. Room and Board: $4,250. Students Receiving Some Form of Aid: 48%. Students Receiving Non-Need-Based Aid: 38%. Average Aid Package: $10,369. Required Financial Aid Forms: FAFSA. Deadline to Apply for Financial Aid: May 31.

Millikin University

Admissions Office, 1184 West Main Street, Decatur, IL 62522-2084. Phone: (217) 424-6210, (800) 373-7733. Fax: (217) 425-4669. E-mail: admis@mail.millikin.edu. Web Site: millikin.edu. Tuition and Fees: $16,008. Room and Board: $5,593. Students Receiving Some Form of Aid: 77%. Students Receiving Non-Need-Based Aid: 18%. Average Aid Package: $14,497. Required Financial Aid Forms: FAFSA, MAFA. Deadline to Apply for Financial Aid: June 1; April 1 (priority).

Monmouth College

Admissions Office, 700 East Broadway, Monmouth, IL 61462. Phone: (309) 457-2131, (800) 747-2687. Fax: (309) 457-2141. E-mail: admit@monm.edu. Web Site: monm.edu. Tuition and Fees: $16,370. Room and Board: $4,450. Required Financial Aid Forms: FAFSA. Deadline to Apply for Financial Aid: rolling.

National-Louis University*

Enrollment Office, 2840 Sheridan Road, Evanston, IL 62201. Phone: (847) 475-1100, ext. 3039, (800) 443-5522, ext. 3039. E-mail: ppet@wheeling1.nl.edu. Web Site: nlu.nl.edu. Tuition and Fees: $13,095. Room and Board: $5,520. Required Financial Aid Forms: FAFSA. Deadline to Apply for Financial Aid: April 15 (priority).

North Central College

Office of Admission, 30 North Brainard Street P.O. Box 3063, Naperville, IL 60666-7063. Phone: (630) 637-5800, (800) 411-1861. Fax: (630) 637-5819. E-mail: ncadm@noctrl.edu. Web Site: noctrl.edu. Tuition and Fees: $15,096. Room and Board: $5,250. Students Receiving Some Form of Aid: 58%. Students Receiving Non-Need-Based Aid: 16%. Average Aid Package: $13,316. Required Financial Aid Forms: FAFSA, institutional verification form. Deadline to Apply for Financial Aid: rolling.

Northeastern Illinois University

Office of Admissions, 5500 North St. Louis Avenue, Chicago, IL 60625. Phone: (773) 794-2600. Fax: (773) 794-6246. E-mail: webteam@neiu.edu. Web Site: neiu.edu. In-State Tuition and Fees: $2,890. Out-of-State Tuition and Fees: $7,414. Required Financial Aid Forms: FAFSA, institutional application.

Northern Illinois University

Admissions Office, Northern Illinois University, DeKalb, IL 60115-2857. Phone: (815) 753-0446. Fax: (815) 753-1783. E-mail: admissions-info@niu.edu. Web Site: niu.edu. In-State Tuition and Fees: $4,100. Out-of-State Tuition and Fees: $7,160. Room and Board: $4,416. Required Financial Aid Forms: FAFSA. Deadline to Apply for Financial Aid: May 1.

Northwestern University

Office of Undergraduate Admissions, 1801 Hinman Avenue, Box 3060, Evanston, IL 60204-3060. Phone: (847) 491-7271. E-mail: ug-admission@northwestern.edu. Web Site: northwesterm.edu. Tuition and Fees: $23,496. Room and Board: $6,847. Students Receiving Some Form of Aid: 47%. Average Aid Package: $20,455. Required Financial Aid Forms: Profile. Deadline to Apply for Financial Aid: February 1.

Quincy University

Admissions Office, 1800 College Avenue, Quincy, IL 62301-2699. Phone: (217) 228-5210, (800) 688-4295. Fax: (217) 228-5479. E-mail: admissions@quincy.edu. Web Site: quincy.edu. Tuition and Fees: $14,700. Room and Board: $4,780. Students Receiving Some Form of Aid: 80%. Students Receiving Non-Need-Based Aid: 26%. Average Aid Package: $12,389. Required Financial Aid Forms: FAFSA. Deadline to Apply for Financial Aid: rolling.

Rockford College

Admissions Office, Nelson Hall, 5050 East State Street, Rockford, IL 61108-2393. Phone: (815) 226-4050, (800) 892-2984. Fax: (815) 226-2822. E-mail: admission@rockford.edu. Web Site: rockford.edu. Tuition and Fees: $16,800. Room and Board: $5,430. Required Financial Aid Forms: FAFSA, institution's own financial aid form. Deadline to Apply for Financial Aid: rolling.

Roosevelt University*

Admissions Office, 430 South Michigan Avenue, Chicago, IL 60605. Phone: (312) 341-3515, (877) APPLYRU. Fax: (312) 341-3523. E-mail: applyru@roosevelt.edu. Web Site: roosevelt.edu. Tuition and Fees: $12,260. Room and Board: $5,850. Students Receiving Some Form of Aid: 22%. Students Receiving Non-Need-Based Aid: 4%. Average Aid Package: $11,397. Required Financial Aid Forms: FAFSA, institutional form. Deadline to Apply for Financial Aid: May 1.

School of the Art Institute of Chicago

Admissions Office, 37 South Wabash Avenue, Chicago, IL 60603. Phone: (312) 899-5219, (800) 232-7242. Fax: (312) 899-1840. E-mail: admiss@artic.edu. Web Site: artic.edu/saic/saichome.html. Tuition and Fees: $19,140. Room and Board: $6,950. Students Receiving Some Form of Aid: 66%. Students Receiving Non-Need-Based Aid: 25%. Average Aid Package: $9,080. Required Financial Aid Forms: FAFSA, income tax forms. Deadline to Apply for Financial Aid: March 15 (priority).

Southern Illinois University—Carbondale

Admissions Office, SIUC, Admissions and Records, Carbondale, IL 62901-4701. Phone: (618) 453-4381. Fax: (618) 453-3250. E-mail: admrec@siu.edu. Web Site: siu.edu/oar. In-State Tuition and Fees: $4,113. Out-of-State Tuition and Fees: $7,123. Room and Board: $4,104. Students Receiving Some Form of Aid: 50%. Students Receiving Non-Need-Based Aid: 11%. Average Aid Package: $6,217. Required Financial Aid Forms: institutional form. Deadline to Apply for Financial Aid: April 1 (priority).

Southern Illinois University—Edwardsville

Admissions Counseling, Campus Box 1600, Edwardsville, IL 62026. Phone: (618) 650-3705, (800) 447-SIUE. Fax: (618) 650-2081. E-mail: admis@siue.edu. Web Site: siue.edu. In-State Tuition and Fees: $2,827. Out-of-State Tuition and Fees: $5,035. Room and Board: $4,290. Required Financial Aid Forms: FAFSA. Deadline to Apply for Financial Aid: March 1.

University of Chicago

Admissions Office, 1116 East 59th Street, Chicago, IL 60637. Phone: (773) 702-8650. Fax: (773) 702-4199. Web Site: uchicago.edu. Tuition and Fees: $24,234. Room and Board: $7,834. Required Financial Aid Forms: FAFSA. Deadline to Apply for Financial Aid: February 1.

University of Illinois—Chicago

Admissions Office, Box 5220, Chicago, IL 60680-5220. Phone: (312) 996-4350. Fax: (312) 413-7628. E-mail: uicadmit@uic.edu. Web Site: uic.edu. In-State Tuition and Fees: $4,648. Out-of-State Tuition and Fees: $10,924. Room and Board: $5,856. Students Receiving Some Form of Aid: 53%. Students Receiving Non-Need-Based Aid: 9%. Average Aid Package: $11,500. Required Financial Aid Forms: FAFSA. Deadline to Apply for Financial Aid: March 1.

University of Illinois—Urbana-Champaign

Admissions Office, 901 West Illinois, Urbana, IL 61801. Phone: (217) 333-0302. Fax: (217) 244-0903. E-mail: admissions@oar.uiuc.edu. Web Site: uiuc.edu. In-State Tuition and Fees: $4,744. Out-of-State Tuition and Fees: $12,192. Room and Board: $5,424. Average Aid Package: $7,500. Required Financial Aid Forms: FAFSA. Deadline to Apply for Financial Aid: March 15.

University of Saint Francis

Office of Admissions, 500 Wilcox Street, Joliet, IL 60435. Phone: (800) 735-7500. Fax: (815) 740-4285. E-mail: admissions@stfrancis.edu. Web Site: stfrancis.edu. Tuition and Fees: $14,300. Room and Board: $5,350. Students Receiving Some Form of Aid: 47%. Students Receiving Non-Need-Based Aid: 32%. Average Aid Package: $11,127. Required Financial Aid Forms: FAFSA, institutional form. Deadline to Apply for Financial Aid: rolling.

Western Illinois University

Admissions Office, 1 University Circle, 115 Sherman Hall, Macomb, IL 61455. Phone: (309) 298-3157. Fax: (309) 298-3111. E-mail: wiuadm@wiu.edu. Web Site: wiu.edu. In-State Tuition and Fees: $3,960. Out-of-State Tuition and Fees: $6,772. Room and Board: $4,506. Students Receiving Some Form of Aid: 46%. Average Aid Package: $6,526. Required Financial Aid Forms: FAFSA. Deadline to Apply for Financial Aid: rolling; February 15 (priority).

Wheaton College

Admissions Office, 501 College Avenue, Wheaton, IL 60187. Phone: (630) 752-5005, (800) 222-2419. Fax: (630) 752-5285. E-mail: admissions@wheaton.edu. Web Site: wheaton.edu. Tuition and Fees: $15,540. Room and Board: $5,260. Students Receiving Some Form of Aid: 50%. Students Receiving Non-Need-Based Aid: 16%. Average Aid Package: $13,109. Required Financial Aid Forms: FAFSA, institutional form. Deadline to Apply for Financial Aid: February 15 (priority).

INDIANA

Anderson University

Admissions Office, 1100 East Fifth Street, Anderson, IN 46012-3462. Phone: (765) 641-4080, (800) 428-6414. Fax: (765) 641-4091. E-mail: info@anderson.edu. Web Site: anderson.edu. Tuition and Fees: $14,680. Room and Board: $4,750. Students Receiving Some Form of Aid: 64%. Students Receiving Non-Need-Based Aid: 41%. Average Aid Package: $7,159. Required Financial Aid Forms: FAFSA. Deadline to Apply for Financial Aid: March 1.

Ball State University

Office of Admissions, Ball State University, Muncie, IN 47306-0855. Phone: (765) 285-8300, (800) 482-4278. Fax: (765) 285-1632. E-mail: askus@gw.bsu.edu. Web Site: bsu.edu. In-State Tuition and Fees: $3,576. Out-of-State Tuition and Fees: $9,736. Room and Board: $4,520. Average Aid Package (excluding student loans): $4,568. Required Financial Aid Forms: FAFSA. Deadline to Apply for Financial Aid: March 1.

Butler University

Admissions Office, 4600 Sunset Avenue, Indianapolis, IN 46208. Phone: (317) 940-8100, (800) 368-6852. Fax: (317) 940-8150. E-mail: admission@butler.edu. Web Site: butler.edu. Tuition and Fees: $18,320. Room and Board: $6,140. Students Receiving Some Form of Aid: 42%. Students Receiving Non-Need-Based Aid: 23%. Average Aid Package (excluding student loans): $15,080. Required Financial Aid Forms: FAFSA. Deadline to Apply for Financial Aid: March 1 (priority).

DePauw University

Office of Admission, 101 East Seminary St., Greencastle, IN 46135. Phone: (765) 658-4006, (800) 447-2495. Fax: (765) 658-4007. E-mail: admission@depauw.edu. Web Site: depauw.edu. Tuition and Fees: $18,840. Room and Board: $6,080. Students Receiving Some Form of Aid: 53%. Students Receiving Non-Need-Based Aid: 45%. Average Aid Package: $17,960. Required Financial Aid Forms:

FAFSA, institutional aid form. Deadline to Apply for Financial Aid: March 1 (in-state residents); April 1 (out-of-state residents); February 15 (priority).

Earlham College

Admissions Office, 801 National Road West, Richmond, IN 47374. Phone: (765) 983-1600, (800) 327-5426. Fax: (765) 983-1560. E-mail: admission@earlham.edu. Web Site: earlham.edu. Tuition and Fees: $21,070. Room and Board: $4,936. Students Receiving Some Form of Aid: 66%. Students Receiving Non-Need-Based Aid: 30%. Average Aid Package: $19,634. Required Financial Aid Forms: FAFSA, institutional form. Deadline to Apply for Financial Aid: March 1 (priority).

Hanover College

Admissions Office, P.O. Box 108, Hanover, IN 47243. Phone: (812) 866-7021, (800) 213-2178. Fax: (812) 866-7098. E-mail: admissions@hanover.edu. Web Site: hanover.edu. Tuition and Fees: $11,045. Room and Board: $4,655. Students Receiving Some Form of Aid: 51%. Students Receiving Non-Need-Based Aid: 6%. Average Aid Package: $10,287. Required Financial Aid Forms: FAFSA, Profile. Deadline to Apply for Financial Aid: March 1.

Indiana Institute of Technology

Admissions Office, 1600 East Washington Boulevard, Fort Wayne, IN 46803. Phone: (219) 422-5561, (800) 937-2448. Fax: (219) 422-7696. E-mail: admissions@indtech.edu. Web Site: indtech.edu. Tuition and Fees: $12,300. Room and Board: $4,564. Students Receiving Some Form of Aid: 28%. Required Financial Aid Forms: FAFSA, institutional form.

Indiana State University

Admissions Office, Tirey Hall, Terre Haute, IN 47809. Phone: (812) 237-2121, (800) 742-0891. Fax: (812) 237-8023. E-mail: admisu@amber.indstate.edu. Web Site: web.indstate.edu. In-State Tuition and Fees: $3,426. Out-of-State Tuition and Fees: $8,554. Room and Board: $4,434. Students Receiving Some Form of Aid: 43%. Students Receiving Non-Need-Based Aid: 12%. Average Aid Package: $5,573. Required Financial Aid Forms: FAFSA, institutional forms. Deadline to Apply for Financial Aid: March 1 (priority).

Indiana University-Purdue University—Fort Wayne

Admissions Office, 2101 E. Coliseum Boulevard, Fort Wayne, IN 46805. Phone: (219) 481-6812. Fax: (219) 481-6880. E-mail: ipfwadms@ipfw.edu. Web Site: ipfw.edu. In-State Tuition and Fees: $3,063. Out-of-State Tuition and Fees: $7,072. Students Receiving Some Form of Aid: 18%. Students Receiving Non-Need-Based Aid: less than 1%. Average Aid Package: $4,484. Required Financial Aid Forms: FAFSA. Deadline to Apply for Financial Aid: March 1 (priority).

Indiana University-Purdue University—Indianapolis

Admissions Office, 425 N. University Blvd., Cavanaugh Hall, Room 129, Indianapolis, IN 46202-5143. Phone: (317) 274-4591. Fax: (317) 278-1862. E-mail: apply@iupui.edu. Web Site: iupui.edu. In-State Tuition and Fees: $3,713. Out-of-State Tuition and Fees: $10,961. Room and Board: $4,590. Students Receiving Some Form of Aid: 31%. Students Receiving Non-Need-Based Aid: 6%. Average Aid Package: $5,754. Required Financial Aid Forms: FAFSA, institutional form. Deadline to Apply for Financial Aid: March 1 (priority).

Indiana University—Bloomington

Office of Admissions, 300 North Jordan Avenue, Bloomington, IN 47405-1106. Phone: (812) 855-0661. Fax: (812) 855-5102. E-mail: iuadmit@indiana.edu. Web Site: indiana.edu. In-State Tuition and Fees: $4,212. Out-of-State Tuition and Fees: $12,920. Room and Board: $5,492. Students Receiving Some Form of Aid: 34%. Students Receiving Non-Need-Based Aid: 11%. Average Aid Package: $6,335. Required Financial Aid Forms: FAFSA, institutional form. Deadline to Apply for Financial Aid: March 1 (priority).

Indiana University—East

Office of Admissions, 2325 Chester Boulevard, WZ 116, Richmond, IN 47374-1289. Phone: (765) 973-8208, (800) 959-EAST. Fax: (765) 973-8288. E-mail: eaadmit@indiana.edu. Web Site: indiana.edu. In-State Tuition and Fees: $3,104. Out-of-State Tuition and Fees: $7,874. Students Receiving Some Form of Aid: 33%. Students Receiving Non-Need-Based Aid: 11%. Average Aid Package: $6,115. Required Financial Aid Forms: FAFSA, institutional form. Deadline to Apply for Financial Aid: March 1 (priority).

Indiana University—Kokomo

Office of Admissions, KC 200, P.O. Box 9003, KC 230A, Kokomo, IN 46904-9003. Phone: (765) 455-9510, 1-888-875-4485. Fax: (765) 455-9537. E-mail: iuadmis@iuk.edu. Web Site: indiana.edu. In-State Tuition and Fees: $3,104. Out-of-State Tuition and Fees: $7,874. Students Receiving Some Form of Aid: 19%. Students Receiving Non-Need-Based Aid: 6%. Average Aid Package: $4,437. Required Financial Aid Forms: FAFSA, institutional form. Deadline to Apply for Financial Aid: March 1 (priority).

Indiana University—Northwest

Office of Admissions, 3400 Broadway, Hawthorn 100, Gary, IN 46408. Phone: (219) 980-6991, (888) 968-7486. Fax: (219) 981-4219. E-mail: wlee@iunhawl.iun.indiana.edu. Web Site: indiana.edu. In-State Tuition and Fees: $3,128. Out-of-State Tuition and Fees: $7,898. Students Receiving Some Form of Aid: 30%. Students Receiving Non-Need-Based Aid: 3%. Average Aid Package: $5,105. Required Financial Aid Forms: FAFSA, institutional form. Deadline to Apply for Financial Aid: March 1 (priority).

Indiana University—South Bend

Office of Admissions, 1700 Mishawaka Avenue, P.O. Box 7111, A169, South Bend, IN 46634-7111. Phone: (219) 237-4839. Fax: (219) 237-4834. E-mail: admissions@iusb.edu. Web Site: indiana.edu. In-State Tuition and Fees: $3,197. Out-of-State Tuition and Fees: $8,481. Room and Board: $6,564. Students Receiving Some Form of Aid: 27%. Students Receiving Non-Need-Based Aid: 6%. Average Aid Package: $4,887. Required Financial Aid Forms: FAFSA, institutional form, state aid form. Deadline to Apply for Financial Aid: March 1 (priority).

Indiana University—Southeast

Office of Admissions, 4201 Grant Line Road, UC-100, New Albany, IN 47150. Phone: (812) 941- 2212, (800) 852-8835 (IN or KY). Fax: (812) 941-2595. E-mail: admissions@ius.edu. Web Site: indiana.edu. In-State Tuition and Fees: $3,092. Out-of-State Tuition and Fees: $7,862. Room and Board: $6,670. Students

Receiving Some Form of Aid: 25%. Students Receiving Non-Need-Based Aid: 8%. Average Aid Package: $4,449. Required Financial Aid Forms: FAFSA, institutional form. Deadline to Apply for Financial Aid: March 1 (priority).

Purdue University—West Lafayette

Office of Admissions, 1080 Schleman Hall, West Lafayette, IN 47907-1080. Phone: (765) 494-1776. Fax: (765) 494-0544. E-mail: admissions@purdue.edu. Web Site: purdue.edu. In-State Tuition and Fees: $3,724. Out-of-State Tuition and Fees: $12,348. Room and Board: $5,500. Students Receiving Some Form of Aid: 36%. Students Receiving Non-Need-Based Aid: 4%. Average Aid Package: $6,356. Required Financial Aid Forms: FAFSA. Deadline to Apply for Financial Aid: March 1 (priority).

Rose-Hulman Institute of Technology

Admissions Office, 5500 Wabash Avenue-CM 1, Terre Haute, IN 47803-3999. Phone: (812) 877-8213, (800) 248-7448. Fax: (812) 877-8941. E-mail: Admis.Ofc@Rose-Hulman.Edu. Web Site: rose-hulman.edu. Tuition and Fees: $19,948. Room and Board: $5,751. Students Receiving Some Form of Aid: 75%. Students Receiving Non-Need-Based Aid: 61%. Average Aid Package: $12,274. Required Financial Aid Forms: FAFSA. Deadline to Apply for Financial Aid: March 1 (priority).

Taylor University

Admissions Office, 236 W. Reade Avenue, Upland, IN 46989-1001. Phone: (800) 882-3456. Fax: (765) 998-4925. E-mail: admissions_u@tayloru.edu. Web Site: tayloru.edu. Tuition and Fees: $15,820. Room and Board: $4,740. Students Receiving Some Form of Aid: 57%. Average Aid Package: $11,906. Required Financial Aid Forms: FAFSA, Taylor University FAF. Deadline to Apply for Financial Aid: March 1.

Tri-State University

Admissions Office, 1 University Avenue, Angola, IN 46703. Phone: (219) 665-4132, (800) 347-4878. Fax: (219) 665-4578. E-mail: admit@tristate.edu. Web Site: tristate.edu. Tuition and Fees: $13,900. Room and Board: $4,950. Students Receiving Some Form of Aid: 70%. Students Receiving Non-Need-Based Aid: 70%. Average Aid Package: $11,453. Required Financial Aid Forms: FAFSA. Deadline to Apply for Financial Aid: June 1; March 1 (priority).

University of Evansville

Admissions Office, 1800 Lincoln Avenue, Evansville, IN 47722. Phone: (812) 479-2468, (800) 423-8633. Fax: (812) 474-4076. E-mail: admissions@evansville.edu. Web Site: evansville.edu. Tuition and Fees: $15,500. Room and Board: $5,000. Students Receiving Some Form of Aid: 60%. Students Receiving Non-Need-Based Aid: 48%. Average Aid Package: $11,843. Required Financial Aid Forms: FAFSA, Univof Evansville form. Deadline to Apply for Financial Aid: March 1.

University of Indianapolis

Admissions Office, 1400 E. Hanna Avenue, Indianapolis, IN 46227-3697. Phone: (317) 788-3216, (800) 232-8634, ext. 3216. Fax: (317) 788-3300. E-mail: admissions@uindy.edu. Web Site: uindy.edu. Tuition and Fees: $14,630. Room and Board: $5,225. Students Receiving Some Form of Aid: 33%. Students Receiving Non-Need-Based Aid: 27%. Average Aid Package: $12,118. Required Financial Aid Forms: FAFSA, institutional form. Deadline to Apply for Financial Aid: March 1 (priority).

University of Notre Dame

Undergraduate Admissions, 220 Main Building, Notre Dame, IN 46556. Phone: (219) 631-7505. Fax: (219) 631-8865. E-mail: admissions.admissio.1@nd.edu. Web Site: nd.edu. Tuition and Fees: $23,357. Room and Board: $5,920. Students Receiving Some Form of Aid: 43%. Students Receiving Non-Need-Based Aid: 10%. Average Aid Package: $17,992. Required Financial Aid Forms: FAFSA, CSS Profile, previous year's tax return and W2. Deadline to Apply for Financial Aid: February 15 (priority).

University of Southern Indiana

Admissions Office, 8600 University Boulevard, Evansville, IN 47712-3598. Phone: (812) 464-1765, (800) 467-1965. Fax: (812) 465-7154. E-mail: enroll@usi.edu. Web Site: usi.edu. In-State Tuition and Fees: $2,800. Out-of-State Tuition and Fees: $7,000. Room and Board: $4,586. Average Aid Package: $3,052. Required Financial Aid Forms: FAFSA, USI data sheet. Deadline to Apply for Financial Aid: March 1.

Valparaiso University

Office of Admissions, Kretzmann Hall, Valparaiso, IN 46383. Phone: (219) 464-5011, (888) 468-2576. Fax: (219) 464-6878. E-mail: undergrad_admissions@valpo.edu. Web Site: valpo.edu. Tuition and Fees: $17,636. Room and Board: $4,660. Students Receiving Some Form of Aid: 59%. Students Receiving Non-Need-Based Aid: 28%. Average Aid Package: $16,640. Required Financial Aid Forms: FAFSA. Deadline to Apply for Financial Aid: March 1 (priority).

Wabash College

Admissions Office, P.O. Box 352, Crawfordsville, IN 47933. Phone: (765) 361-6225, (800) 345-5385. Fax: (765) 361-6437. E-mail: admissions@wabash.edu. Web Site: wabash.edu. Tuition and Fees: $17,275. Room and Board: $5,435. Students Receiving Some Form of Aid: 70%. Students Receiving Non-Need-Based Aid: 25%. Average Aid Package: $16,872. Required Financial Aid Forms: FAFSA, CSS/Profile. Deadline to Apply for Financial Aid: March 1.

IOWA

Central College

Office of Admissions, 812 University, Pella, IA 50219. Phone: (877) 462-3687. Fax: (515) 628-5316. E-mail: admission@central.edu. Web Site: central.edu. Tuition and Fees: $14,186. Room and Board: $4,944. Students Receiving Some Form of Aid: 84%. Students Receiving Non-Need-Based Aid: 9%. Average Aid Package: $13,978. Required Financial Aid Forms: FAFSA. Deadline to Apply for Financial Aid: March 1 (priority).

Coe College

Office of Admissions, 1220 First Avenue NE, Cedar Rapids, IA 52402. Phone: (319) 399-8500, (877) CALL-COE. Fax: (319) 399-8816. E-mail: admissions@coe.edu. Web Site: coe.edu. Tuition and Fees: $17,540. Room and Board: $5,020. Students Receiving Some Form of Aid: 73%. Students Receiving Non-Need-Based Aid: 59%. Average Aid Package:

$18,048. Required Financial Aid Forms: FAFSA. Deadline to Apply for Financial Aid: March 1.

Cornell College

Office of Enrollment Services, 600 First Street West, Mount Vernon, IA 52314-1098. Phone: (319) 895-4477, (800) 747-1112. Fax: (319) 895-4451. E-mail: admissions@cornell-iowa.edu. Web Site: cornell-iowa.edu. Tuition and Fees: $19,570. Room and Board: $5,410. Students Receiving Some Form of Aid: 85%. Students Receiving Non-Need-Based Aid: 78%. Average Aid Package: $17,500. Required Financial Aid Forms: FAFSA. Deadline to Apply for Financial Aid: March 1 (priority).

Drake University

Admissions Office, 2507 University Ave., Des Moines, IA 50311-4505. Phone: (515) 271-3181, (800) 44-DRAKE. Fax: (515) 271-2831. E-mail: admitinfo@acad.drake.edu. Web Site: drake.edu. Tuition and Fees: $17,090. Room and Board: $4,870. Students Receiving Some Form of Aid: 56%. Students Receiving Non-Need-Based Aid: 5%. Average Aid Package: $13,630. Required Financial Aid Forms: FAFSA. Deadline to Apply for Financial Aid: March 1 (priority).

Grinnell College

Office of Admission, P.O. Box 805, Grinnell, IA 50112. Phone: (515) 269-3600, (800) 247-0113. Fax: (515) 269-4800. E-mail: askgrin@grinnell.edu. Web Site: grinnell.edu. Tuition and Fees: $20,500. Room and Board: $5,820. Students Receiving Some Form of Aid: 64%. Students Receiving Non-Need-Based Aid: 4%. Average Aid Package: $17,122. Required Financial Aid Forms: FAFSA, institutional form. Deadline to Apply for Financial Aid: February 1.

Iowa State University

Office of Admissions, 100 Alumni Hall, Ames, IA 50011-2011. Phone: (515) 294-5836, (800) 262-3810. Fax: (515) 294-2592. E-mail: admissions@iastate.edu. Web Site: iastate.edu. In-State Tuition and Fees: $3,132. Out-of-State Tuition and Fees: $9,974. Room and Board: $4,171. Students Receiving Some Form of Aid: 55%. Students Receiving Non-Need-Based Aid: 13%. Average Aid Package: $6,032. Required Financial Aid Forms: FAFSA. Deadline to Apply for Financial Aid: March 1 (priority).

Loras College

Admissions Office, 1450 Alta Vista, P.O. Box 178, Dubuque, IA 52001-0178. Phone: (319) 588-7236, (800) 245-6727. Fax: (319) 588-7964. E-mail: adms@loras.edu. Web Site: loras.edu. Tuition and Fees: $15,314. Room and Board: $5,345. Required Financial Aid Forms: FAFSA. Deadline to Apply for Financial Aid: April 15.

Luther College

Admissions Office, 700 College Dr., Descorah, IA 52101. Phone: (319) 387-1287, (800) 458-8437. Fax: (319) 387-2159. E-mail: admissions@luther.edu. Web Site: luther.edu. Tuition and Fees: $17,290. Room and Board: $2,010. Students Receiving Some Form of Aid: 62%. Students Receiving Non-Need-Based Aid: 39%. Average Aid Package: $14,316. Required Financial Aid Forms: FAFSA, Instform. Deadline to Apply for Financial Aid: March 1.

Northwestern College of Iowa

Admissions Office, 101 College Lane, Orange City, IA 51041. Phone: (712) 737-7130, (800) 747-4757. Fax: (712) 737-7164. E-mail: admissions@nwciowa.edu. Web Site: nwciowa.edu. Tuition and Fees: $13,000. Room and Board: $3,650. Students Receiving Some Form of Aid: 94%. Students Receiving Non-Need-Based Aid: 60%. Average Aid Package: $12,243. Required Financial Aid Forms: FAFSA, institutional form. Deadline to Apply for Financial Aid: April 1.

Saint Ambrose University

Admissions Office, 518 West Locust, Davenport, IA 52803-2898. Phone: (319) 333-6300, (800) 383-2627. Fax: (319) 333-6297. E-mail: mflahery@saunix.sau.edu, admit@saunix.sau.edu. Web Site: sau.edu. Tuition and Fees: $13,890. Room and Board: $5,160. Students Receiving Some Form of Aid: 61%. Students Receiving Non-Need-Based Aid: 34%. Average Aid Package: $11,200. Required Financial Aid Forms: FAFSA, institutional form. Deadline to Apply for Financial Aid: March 15 (priority).

University of Dubuque

Admissions Office, Van Vliet Hall, 2000 University Avenue, Dubuque, IA 52001. Phone: (319) 589-3000, (800) 722-5583. Fax: (319) 589-3690. E-mail: admssns@dbq.edu. Web Site: dbq.edu. Tuition and Fees: $14,130. Room and Board: $4,820. Students Receiving Some Form of Aid: 93%. Students Receiving Non-Need-Based Aid: 9%. Average Aid Package: $12,434. Required Financial Aid Forms: FAFSA. Deadline to Apply for Financial Aid: April 1.

University of Iowa

Admissions Office, 107 Calvin Hall, Iowa City, IA 52242-1396. Phone: (319) 335-3847, (800) 553-4692. Fax: (319) 335-1535. E-mail: admissions@uiowa.edu. Web Site: uiowa.edu. In-State Tuition and Fees: $3,128. Out-of-State Tuition and Fees: $10,890. Room and Board: $4,594. Students Receiving Some Form of Aid: 37%. Students Receiving Non-Need-Based Aid: 26%. Average Aid Package: $5,981. Required Financial Aid Forms: FAFSA. Deadline to Apply for Financial Aid: January 1 (priority).

University of Northern Iowa

Office of Admissions, 120 Gilchrist Hall, Cedar Falls, IA 50614-0018. Phone: (319) 273-2281, (800) 772-2037. Fax: (319) 273-2885. E-mail: admissions@uni.edu. Web Site: uni.edu. In-State Tuition and Fees: $3,130. Out-of-State Tuition and Fees: $8,094. Room and Board: $4,200. Students Receiving Some Form of Aid: 47%. Students Receiving Non-Need-Based Aid: 13%. Average Aid Package: $4,771. Required Financial Aid Forms: FAFSA. Deadline to Apply for Financial Aid: February 15 (priority).

Wartburg College

Admissions Office, 222 Ninth Street NW , PO Box 1003, Waverly, IA 50677. Phone: (319) 352-8264, (800) 772-2085. Fax: (319) 352-8579. E-mail: admissions@wartburg.edu. Web Site: wartburg.edu. Tuition and Fees: $15,765. Room and Board: $4,400. Students Receiving Some Form of Aid: 61%. Average Aid Package: $14,306. Required Financial Aid Forms: FAFSA. Deadline to Apply for Financial Aid: March 1 (priority).

KANSAS

Bethel College

Admissions Office, 300 East 27th Street, North Newton, KS 67117. **Phone:** (316) 284-5230, (800) 522-1887. **Fax:** (316) 284-5870. **E-mail:** admissions@bethelks.edu. **Web Site:** bethelks.edu. **Tuition and Fees:** $11,800. **Room and Board:** $4,700. **Students Receiving Some Form of Aid:** 69%. **Students Receiving Non-Need-Based Aid:** 51%. **Average Aid Package:** $12,780. **Required Financial Aid Forms:** FAFSA. **Deadline to Apply for Financial Aid:** March 15 (priority).

Emporia State University

Admissions Office, 1200 Commercial, Emporia, KS 66801. **Phone:** (316) 341-5465, (877) GO-TO-ESU. **Fax:** (316) 341-5599. **E-mail:** gotoesu@emporia.edu. **Web Site:** emporia.edu. **In-State Tuition and Fees:** $2,598. **Out-of-State Tuition and Fees:** $7,064. **Room and Board:** $3,656. **Students Receiving Some Form of Aid:** 49%. **Students Receiving Non-Need-Based Aid:** 24%. **Average Aid Package:** $4,929. **Required Financial Aid Forms:** FAFSA, institution's own financial aid form. **Deadline to Apply for Financial Aid:** rolling.

Fort Hays State University

Office of Admissions, 600 Park Street, Hays, KS 67601. **Phone:** (785) 628-5666, (800) 432-0248. **E-mail:** tigers@fhsu.edu. **Web Site:** fhsu.edu. **In-State Tuition and Fees:** $2,063. **Out-of-State Tuition and Fees:** $6,531. **Room and Board:** $3,770. **Required Financial Aid Forms:** FAFSA. **Deadline to Apply for Financial Aid:** July 2.

Kansas State University

Office of Admissions, 119 Anderson Hall, Manhattan, KS 66506. **Phone:** (785) 532-6250, (800) 432-8270 (in-state). **Fax:** (785) 532-6393. **E-mail:** kstate@ksu.edu. **Web Site:** ksu.edu. **In-State Tuition and Fees:** $2,592. **Out-of-State Tuition and Fees:** $9,195. **Room and Board:** $3,950. **Students Receiving Some Form of Aid:** 49%. **Students Receiving Non-Need-Based Aid:** 14%. **Average Aid Package:** $7,615. **Required Financial Aid Forms:** FAFSA. **Deadline to Apply for Financial Aid:** rolling; March 1 (priority).

Kansas Wesleyan University

Admissions Office, 100 East Claflin Avenue, Salina, KS 67401. **Phone:** (785) 827-5541, ext. 1285, (800) 874-1154. **Fax:** (785) 827-0927. **E-mail:** admissions@diamond.kwu.edu. **Web Site:** kwu.edu. **Tuition and Fees:** $11,800. **Room and Board:** $4,200. **Students Receiving Some Form of Aid:** 70%. **Students Receiving Non-Need-Based Aid:** 70%. **Average Aid Package:** $10,970. **Required Financial Aid Forms:** FAFSA. **Deadline to Apply for Financial Aid:** March 15.

Pittsburg State University

Office of Admissions, 1701 South Broadway, Pittsburg, KS 66762-5880. **Phone:** (316) 235-4251, (800) 854-PITT. **Fax:** (316) 235-6003. **E-mail:** psuadmit@pittstate.edu. **Web Site:** pittstate.edu. **In-State Tuition and Fees:** $2,142. **Out-of-State Tuition and Fees:** $6,464. **Room and Board:** $3,670. **Students Receiving Some Form of Aid:** 48%. **Students Receiving Non-Need-Based Aid:** 3%. **Average Aid Package:** $5,553. **Required Financial Aid Forms:** FAFSA. **Deadline to Apply for Financial Aid:** March 1 (priority).

Saint Mary College

Admissions Office, 4100 South Fourth Street, Leavenworth, KS 66048. **Phone:** (913) 758-6118, (800) 752-7043. **Fax:** (913) 758-6140. **E-mail:** admiss@hub.smcks.edu. **Web Site:** smcks.edu. **Tuition and Fees:** $11,390. **Room and Board:** $4,600. **Students Receiving Some Form of Aid:** 21%. **Students Receiving Non-Need-Based Aid:** 9%. **Average Aid Package:** $9,406. **Required Financial Aid Forms:** FAFSA. **Deadline to Apply for Financial Aid:** March 15.

Southwestern College

Office of Admission, 100 College Street, Winfield, KS 67156-2499. **Phone:** (316) 221-8236, (800) 846-1543. **Fax:** (316) 221-8344. **E-mail:** scadmit@sckans.edu. **Web Site:** sckans.edu. **Tuition and Fees:** $11,300. **Room and Board:** $4,320. **Students Receiving Some Form of Aid:** 51%. **Students Receiving Non-Need-Based Aid:** 43%. **Average Aid Package:** $11,123. **Required Financial Aid Forms:** FAFSA, institutional form. **Deadline to Apply for Financial Aid:** August 1; July 1 (priority).

University of Kansas

Office of Admissions and Scholarships, KU Visitor Center, 1502 Iowa Street, Lawrence, KS 66045. **Phone:** (785) 864-3911. **Fax:** (785) 864-5006. **E-mail:** adm@ukans.edu. **Web Site:** ukans.edu. **In-State Tuition and Fees:** $2,725. **Out-of-State Tuition and Fees:** $9,493. **Room and Board:** $4,114. **Students Receiving Some Form of Aid:** 33%. **Average Aid Package:** $5,067. **Required Financial Aid Forms:** FAFSA. **Deadline to Apply for Financial Aid:** March 1.

Washburn University

Admissions Office, 1700 SW College, Topeka, KS 66621. **Phone:** (785) 231-1030, (800) 332-0291. **E-mail:** zzhansen@washburn.edu. **Web Site:** washburn.edu. **In-State Tuition and Fees:** $3,140. **Out-of-State Tuition and Fees:** $7,010. **Room and Board:** $3,950. **Students Receiving Some Form of Aid:** 32%. **Average Aid Package:** $4,381. **Required Financial Aid Forms:** FAFSA. **Deadline to Apply for Financial Aid:** March 1.

Wichita State University

Admissions Office, 1845 Fairmount Street, Wichita, KS 67260-0124. **Phone:** (316) 978-3085, (800) 362-2594. **Fax:** (316) 978-3174. **E-mail:** wsuadmis@twsuvm.uc.twsu.edu. **Web Site:** wichita.edu. **In-State Tuition and Fees:** $2,572. **Out-of-State Tuition and Fees:** $8,429. **Room and Board:** $4,070. **Students Receiving Some Form of Aid:** 26%. **Students Receiving Non-Need-Based Aid:** 12%. **Average Aid Package:** $4,966. **Required Financial Aid Forms:** FAFSA. **Deadline to Apply for Financial Aid:** March 15 (priority).

KENTUCKY

Asbury College

Admissions Office, 1 Macklem Drive, Wilmore, KY 40390. **Phone:** (606) 858-3511 ext. 2142, (800) 888-1818. **Fax:** (606) 858-3921. **E-mail:** admissions@asbury.edu. **Web Site:** asbury.edu. **Tuition and Fees:** $14,056. **Room and Board:** $3,566. **Students Receiving Some Form of Aid:** 64%. **Students Receiving Non-Need-Based Aid:** 16%. **Average Aid Package:** $10,010. **Required Financial Aid Forms:** FAFSA, institutional form. **Deadline to Apply for Financial Aid:** March 1 (priority).

Bellarmine College

Office of Admission, 2001 Newburg Road, Louisville, KY 40205. Phone: (502) 452-8131, (800) 274-4723, ext. 8131. Fax: (502) 452-8002. E-mail: admissions@bellarmine.edu. Web Site: bellarmine.edu. Tuition and Fees: $13,760. Room and Board: $4,160. Required Financial Aid Forms: FAFSA. Deadline to Apply for Financial Aid: March 1 (priority).

Berea College

Admissions Office, CPO 2220, Berea, KY 40404. Phone: (606) 985-3500, (800) 326-5948. Fax: (859) 985-3512. E-mail: admissions@berea.edu. Web Site: berea.edu. Tuition and Fees: $15,899. Room and Board: $3,686. Students Receiving Some Form of Aid: 97%. Average Aid Package: $19,042. Required Financial Aid Forms: FAFSA. Deadline to Apply for Financial Aid: May 1.

Brescia University

Office of Admissions, 717 Frederica Street, Owensboro, KY 42301. Phone: , (800) 264-1234. Fax: (270) 686-4201. E-mail: admissions@brescia.edu. Web Site: brescia.edu. Tuition and Fees: $9,545. Room and Board: $4,240. Students Receiving Some Form of Aid: 59%. Students Receiving Non-Need-Based Aid: 9%. Average Aid Package: $8,720. Required Financial Aid Forms: FAFSA. Deadline to Apply for Financial Aid: March 1.

Campbellsville University

Office of Admissions, 1 University Drive, Campbellsville, KY 42178-2799. Phone: (270) 789-5220, (800) 264-6014. Fax: (270) 789-5071. E-mail: admissions@campbellsvil.edu. Web Site: campbellsvil.edu. Tuition and Fees: $8,930. Room and Board: $4,360. Required Financial Aid Forms: FAFSA.

Centre College

Admission Office, 600 West Walnut Street, Danville, KY 40422. Phone: (606) 238-5350, (800) 423-6236. Fax: (606) 238-5373. E-mail: admission@centre.edu. Web Site: centre.edu. Tuition and Fees: $21,350. Room and Board: $5,300. Students Receiving Some Form of Aid: 57%. Students Receiving Non-Need-Based Aid: 34%. Average Aid Package: $15,120. Required Financial Aid Forms: FAFSA, institutional form. Deadline to Apply for Financial Aid: March 1.

Cumberland College

Admissions Office, 6178 College Station Drive, Williamsburg, KY 40769-1372. Phone: (606) 539-4241, (800) 343-1609. Fax: (606) 531-4303. E-mail: admiss@cc.cumber.edu. Web Site: cc.cumber.edu. Tuition and Fees: $9,920. Room and Board: $4,276. Required Financial Aid Forms: FAFSA. Deadline to Apply for Financial Aid: August 15.

Eastern Kentucky University

EKU Admissions, Coates CPO2A, 521 Lancaster Avenue, Richmond, KY 40475-3102. Phone: (859) 622-2106, (800) 465-9191. Web Site: eku.edu. In-State Tuition and Fees: $2,590. Out-of-State Tuition and Fees: $7,030. Room and Board: $4,432. Students Receiving Some Form of Aid: 43%. Students Receiving Non-Need-Based Aid: 15%. Average Aid Package: $7,053. Required Financial Aid Forms: FAFSA, institutional form. Deadline to Apply for Financial Aid: March 1.

Georgetown College

Office of Admissions, 400 East College Street, Georgetown, KY 40324. Phone: (502) 863-8009, (800) 788-9985. Fax: (502) 868-8891. E-mail: admissions@georgetowncollege.edu. Web Site: georgetowncollege.edu. Tuition and Fees: $12,390. Room and Board: $4,600. Students Receiving Some Form of Aid: 57%. Students Receiving Non-Need-Based Aid: 35%. Average Aid Package: $11,821. Required Financial Aid Forms: FAFSA. Deadline to Apply for Financial Aid: February 15 (priority).

Kentucky State University

Admissions Office, 400 East Main Street, Frankfort, KY 40601. Phone: (502) 227-6813, (800) 325-1716. Fax: (502) 227-6713. E-mail: ldyson@gwmail.kysu.edu. In-State Tuition and Fees: $2,300. Out-of-State Tuition and Fees: $6,340. Room and Board: $3,446. Required Financial Aid Forms: FAFSA, institutional form. Deadline to Apply for Financial Aid: April 15.

Kentucky Wesleyan College

Admissions Office, 3000 Frederica Street, P.O. Box 1039, Owensboro, KY 42301-1039. Phone: (270) 926-3111, (800) 999-0592, ext. 5747. Fax: (270) 926-3196. E-mail: admitme@kwa.edu. Web Site: kwc.edu. Tuition and Fees: $10,120. Room and Board: $4,220. Students Receiving Some Form of Aid: 77%. Students Receiving Non-Need-Based Aid: 71%. Average Aid Package: $12,250.

Morehead State University

Office of Admissions, HM 301, Morehead, KY 40351-1689. Phone: (606) 783-2000, (800) 585-6781. Fax: (606) 783-5038. E-mail: admissions@moreheadstate.edu. Web Site: moreheadstate.edu. In-State Tuition and Fees: $2,440. Out-of-State Tuition and Fees: $6,480. Room and Board: $3,600. Students Receiving Some Form of Aid: 59%. Students Receiving Non-Need-Based Aid: 21%. Average Aid Package: $5,252. Required Financial Aid Forms: FAFSA, institutional form. Deadline to Apply for Financial Aid: March 15.

Murray State University

Admissions Office, Murray State University, Murray, KY 42071. Phone: (270) 762-3741. Fax: (270) 762-3050. E-mail: phil.bryan@murraystate.edu. Web Site: murraystate.edu. In-State Tuition and Fees: $2,556. Out-of-State Tuition and Fees: $6,900. Room and Board: $3,570. Students Receiving Some Form of Aid: 51%. Students Receiving Non-Need-Based Aid: 22%. Average Aid Package: $4,670. Required Financial Aid Forms: FAF. Deadline to Apply for Financial Aid: April 1.

Northern Kentucky University*

Office of Admissions, AC 400, Nunn Drive, Highland Heights, KY 41099-7010. Phone: (606) 572-5220, (800) 637-9948. Fax: (606) 572-5566. E-mail: admit@nku.edu. Web Site: nku.edu. In-State Tuition and Fees: $2,442. Out-of-State Tuition and Fees: $6,482. Room and Board: $3,866. Students Receiving Some Form of Aid: 47%. Students Receiving Non-Need-Based Aid: less than 1%. Average Aid Package: $4,632. Required Financial Aid Forms: FAFSA, institutional form. Deadline to Apply for Financial Aid: none.

Spalding University

Office of Admissions, 851 South Fourth Street, Louisville, KY 40203. Phone: (502) 585-7111, (800) 896-8941. Fax: (502) 585-7128. E-mail: admissions@spalding.edu. Web Site: spalding.edu. Tuition and Fees: $10,948. Room and Board: $2,810. Students Receiving Some Form of Aid: 49%. Students Receiving Non-Need-Based Aid: 13%. Average Aid Package:

$9,312. Required Financial Aid Forms: FAFSA, institutional form. Deadline to Apply for Financial Aid: March 1 (priority).

Thomas More College

Admissions Office, 333 Thomas More Parkway, Crestview Hills, KY 41017. Phone: (606) 344-3332, (800) 825-4557. Fax: (606) 344-3444. E-mail: mcdermor@thomasmore.edu. Web Site: thomasmore.edu. Tuition and Fees: $12,440. Room and Board: $5,236. Students Receiving Some Form of Aid: 58%. Students Receiving Non-Need-Based Aid: 60%. Average Aid Package: $10,865. Required Financial Aid Forms: FAFSA. Deadline to Apply for Financial Aid: March 1 (priority).

Union College

Admissions Office, 310 College St., Barbourville, KY 40906. Phone: (606) 546-1220, (800) 489-8646. Fax: (606) 546-1667. E-mail: enroll@unionky.edu. Web Site: unionky.edu. Tuition and Fees: $10,565. Room and Board: $3,450. Average Aid Package: $5,896. Required Financial Aid Forms: FAFSA. Deadline to Apply for Financial Aid: May 1.

University of Kentucky

Admissions Office, 100 W.D. Funkhouser Building, Lexington, KY 40506. Phone: (606) 257-2000. Fax: (606) 257-4000. E-mail: admissio@pop.uky.edu. Web Site: uky.edu. In-State Tuition and Fees: $3,782. Out-of-State Tuition and Fees: $10,002. Room and Board: $3,722. Students Receiving Some Form of Aid: 35%. Average Aid Package: $7,259. Required Financial Aid Forms: FAFSA. Deadline to Apply for Financial Aid: rolling.

University of Louisville

Admissions Office, University of Louisville, Louisville, KY 40292. Phone: (502) 852-6531, (800) 334-8635. Fax: (502) 852-4776. E-mail: admitme@gwise.louisville.edu. Web Site: louisville.edu. In-State Tuition and Fees: $3,298. Out-of-State Tuition and Fees: $9,597. Room and Board: $3,500. Students Receiving Some Form of Aid: 55%. Students Receiving Non-Need-Based Aid: 5%. Average Aid Package: $5,778. Required Financial Aid Forms: FAFSA. Deadline to Apply for Financial Aid: July 31.

Western Kentucky University

Admissions Office, Potter Hall, 1 Big Red Way, Bowling Green, KY 42101-3576. Phone: (270) 745-2551. Fax: (270) 745-6133. E-mail: admission@wku.edu. Web Site: wku.edu. In-State Tuition and Fees: $2,534. Out-of-State Tuition and Fees: $6,834. Room and Board: $3,550. Students Receiving Some Form of Aid: 36%. Students Receiving Non-Need-Based Aid: 19%. Average Aid Package: $4,283. Required Financial Aid Forms: FAFSA. Deadline to Apply for Financial Aid: April 1.

LOUISIANA

Centenary College of Louisiana

Admissions Office, 2911 Centenary Boulevard, P.O. Box 41188, Shreveport, LA 71134-1188. Phone: (318) 869-5131, (318) 869-5190. Fax: (318) 869-5005. Web Site: centenary.edu. Tuition and Fees: $13,550. Room and Board: $4,210. Students Receiving Some Form of Aid: 52%. Students Receiving Non-Need-Based Aid: 14%. Average Aid Package: $10,502. Required Financial Aid Forms: FAFSA. Deadline to Apply for Financial Aid: March 15 (priority).

Grambling State University

Admissions Office, P.O. Box 864, Grambling, LA 71245. Phone: (318) 274-6308, (318) 274-2657. Fax: (318) 274-3292. E-mail: Blakelyp@Medgar.gram.edu. Web Site: gram.edu. In-State Tuition and Fees: $4,937. Out-of-State Tuition and Fees: $10,287. Room and Board: $2,612. Students Receiving Some Form of Aid: 15%. Students Receiving Non-Need-Based Aid: 13%. Average Aid Package: $3,373. Required Financial Aid Forms: FAFSA, SAR. Deadline to Apply for Financial Aid: four months before the beginning of the semester.

Louisiana College

Admissions Office, 1140 College Drive, P.O Box 560, Pineville, LA 71359. Phone: (800) 487-1906. Fax: (318) 487-7550. E-mail: admissions@lacollege.edu. Web Site: lacollege.edu. Tuition and Fees: $6,750. Room and Board: $1,580. Students Receiving Some Form of Aid: 67%. Students Receiving Non-Need-Based Aid: 66%. Average Aid Package: $3,500. Required Financial Aid Forms: FAFSA, LC data form. Deadline to Apply for Financial Aid: rolling.

Louisiana State University and A&M College

Admissions Office, 110 Thomas Boyd Hall, Baton Rouge, LA 70803. Phone: (225) 388-1175. Fax: (225) 388-4433. E-mail: lsuadmit@lsu.edu. Web Site: lsu.edu. In-State Tuition and Fees: $2,881. Out-of-State Tuition and Fees: $7,081. Room and Board: $4,130. Students Receiving Some Form of Aid: 31%. Students Receiving Non-Need-Based Aid: 18%. Average Aid Package: $5,876. Required Financial Aid Forms: FAFSA. Deadline to Apply for Financial Aid: April 1 (priority).

Louisiana State University in Shreveport*

Office of Admissions and Records, One University Place, Shreveport, LA 71115. Phone: (318) 797-5115, (800) 797-5112. Fax: (318) 797-5286. E-mail: admissions@pilot.lsus.edu. Web Site: lsus.edu. In-State Tuition and Fees: $2,230. Out-of-State Tuition and Fees: $6,390. Required Financial Aid Forms: FAFSA. Deadline to Apply for Financial Aid: rolling.

Louisiana Tech University*

Admissions Office, P.O. Box 3178, Ruston, LA 71272. Phone: (800) LA TECH 1. Fax: (318) 257-2499. E-mail: bulldog@latech.edu. Web Site: latech.edu. In-State Tuition and Fees: $2,651. Out-of-State Tuition and Fees: $8,092. Room and Board: $3,030.

Loyola University New Orleans

Admissions Office, 6363 St. Charles Avenue, P.O. Box 18, New Orleans, LA 70118-6195. Phone: (504) 865-3240, (800) 4-LOYOLA. Fax: (504) 865-3383. E-mail: admit@loyno.edu. Web Site: loyno.edu. Tuition and Fees: $15,481. Room and Board: $6,116. Students Receiving Some Form of Aid: 46%. Students Receiving Non-Need-Based Aid: 35%. Average Aid Package: $13,122. Required Financial Aid Forms: FAFSA. Deadline to Apply for Financial Aid: May 1 (priority).

McNeese State University*

Admissions Office, 4205 Ryan Street, Lake Charles, LA 70609-2495. Phone: (318) 475-5356, (800) 622-3352. Fax: (318) 475-5189. Web Site: mcneese.edu. In-State Tuition and

Fees: $2,113. Out-of-State Tuition and Fees: $7,983. Room and Board: $2,310. Required Financial Aid Forms: FAFSA. Deadline to Apply for Financial Aid: May 1.

Nicholls State University

Office of Admissions, P.O. Box 2004-NSU, Thibodaux, LA 70310. Phone: (504) 448-4507, (877) NICHOLLS. Fax: (504) 448-4929. E-mail: nicholls@mail.nich.edu. Web Site: nich.edu. In-State Tuition and Fees: $2,589. Out-of-State Tuition and Fees: $6,861. Room and Board: $2,850. Students Receiving Some Form of Aid: 34%. Students Receiving Non-Need-Based Aid: 3%. Average Aid Package: $4,718. Required Financial Aid Forms: FAFSA, institutional form, state aid form.

Northwestern State University of Louisiana

Office of Admissions, Northwestern State University of Louisiana, Natchitoches, LA 71497-9990. Phone: (318) 357-4503. Fax: (318) 357-5567. E-mail: luckj@alpha.nsula.edu. Web Site: nsula.edu/default-net(82).htm. In-State Tuition and Fees: $2,624. Out-of-State Tuition and Fees: $7,850. Room and Board: $2,596. Students Receiving Some Form of Aid: 70%. Students Receiving Non-Need-Based Aid: 9%. Average Aid Package: $4,321.

Our Lady of Holy Cross College

Admissions Office, 4123 Woodland Drive, New Orleans, LA 70131. Phone: (504) 394-7744, ext. 175, 126, (800) 259-7744. Fax: (504) 391-2421. E-mail: studentaffairs@olhcc.edu. Web Site: olhcc.edu. In-State Tuition and Fees: $2,405. Out-of-State Tuition and Fees: $125. Students Receiving Some Form of Aid: 64%. Students Receiving Non-Need-Based Aid: 12%. Average Aid Package: $8,625. Required Financial Aid Forms: student aid report, promissory notes, institution's own form, loan information sheet. Deadline to Apply for Financial Aid: April 15.

Southeastern Louisiana University

Admissions Office, SLU 10752, Hammond, LA 70402. Phone: (504) 549-2066, (800) 222-7358. Fax: (504) 549-5632. E-mail: ssoutullo@selu.edu. Web Site: selu.edu. In-State Tuition and Fees: $2,210. Out-of-State Tuition and Fees: $7,358. Room and Board: $2,620. Required Financial Aid Forms: FAFSA. Deadline to Apply for Financial Aid: May 1 (priority).

Southern University and A&M College

Office of Admissions. , Baton Rouge, LA 70813. Phone: (225) 771-5115, (225) 771-2430. Fax: (225) 771-2500. Web Site: subr.edu. In-State Tuition and Fees: $2,286. Out-of-State Tuition and Fees: $8,078. Room and Board: $3,410. Required Financial Aid Forms: FAFSA. Deadline to Apply for Financial Aid: April 15.

Tulane University

Office of Undergraduate Admission, 6823 St. Charles Avenue, New Orleans, LA 70118-5680. Phone: (504) 865-5731, (800) 873-9283. Fax: (504) 862-8715. E-mail: undergrad.admission@tulane.edu. Web Site: tulane.edu. Tuition and Fees: $25,390. Room and Board: $6,908. Students Receiving Some Form of Aid: 35%. Students Receiving Non-Need-Based Aid: 6%. Average Aid Package: $22,948. Required Financial Aid Forms: FAFSA, CSS Profile. Deadline to Apply for Financial Aid: January 15 (priority).

University of Louisiana—Lafayette

Admissions Office, Box 41210, Lafayette, LA 70504. Phone: (318) 482-6467. Fax: (318) 482-6195. E-mail: admissions@louisiana.edu. Web Site: louisiana.edu. In-State Tuition and Fees: $2,013. Out-of-State Tuition and Fees: $7,245. Room and Board: $2,656. Students Receiving Some Form of Aid: 54%. Average Aid Package: $3,490. Required Financial Aid Forms: FAFSA. Deadline to Apply for Financial Aid: March 1.

University of Louisiana—Monroe*

Director of Admissions, 700 University Avenue, Monroe, LA 71209-1115. Phone: (318) 342-5252, (800) 372-5127. Fax: (318) 342-5274. Web Site: ulm.edu. In-State Tuition and Fees: $2,052. Out-of-State Tuition and Fees: $6,360. Room and Board: $3,660. Required Financial Aid Forms: FAFSA. Deadline to Apply for Financial Aid: April 1.

University of New Orleans

Admissions Office, Administration 103, New Orleans, LA 70148-2135. Phone: (504) 280-6595, (800) 256-5UNO. Fax: (504) 280-5522. E-mail: admissions@uno.edu. Web Site: uno.edu. In-State Tuition and Fees: $2,532. Out-of-State Tuition and Fees: $8,058. Room and Board: $3,175.

Xavier University of Louisiana

Office of Admissions, 7325 Palmetto Street, New Orleans, LA 70125. Phone: (504) 483-7388. Fax: (504) 485-7941. E-mail: apply@xula.edu. Web Site: xula.edu. Tuition and Fees: $9,700. Room and Board: $5,100. Required Financial Aid Forms: FAFSA. Deadline to Apply for Financial Aid: April 1.

MAINE

Bates College

Admissions Office, 23 Campus Avenue, Lewiston, ME 04240-6098. Phone: (207) 786-6000. Fax: (207) 786-6125. E-mail: admissions@bates.edu. Web Site: bates.edu. Total Annual Expenses (1999–2000): $32,650. Students Receiving Some Form of Aid: 43%. Average Aid Package: $20,487. Required Financial Aid Forms: profile, FAFSA, tax returns. Deadline to Apply for Financial Aid: January 15 (November 15 for early decision).

Bowdoin College

Admissions Office, 5000 College Station, Brunswick, ME 04011. Phone: (207) 725-3100. Fax: (207) 725-3101. E-mail: admissions-lit@polar.bowdoin.edu. Web Site: bowdoin.edu. Tuition and Fees: $25,890. Room and Board: $6,760. Students Receiving Some Form of Aid: 40%. Average Aid Package: $19,647. Required Financial Aid Forms: FAFSA, institutional form, CSS Profile, noncustodial parent's statement, Business/Farm Supplement. Deadline to Apply for Financial Aid: February 15.

Colby College

Admissions Office, 4800 Mayflower Hill, Lunder House, Waterville, ME 04901. Phone: (207) 872-3168, (800) 723-3032. Fax: (207) 872-3474. E-mail: admissions@colby.edu. Web Site: colby.edu. Total Annual Expenses

(1999–2000): $32,750. Average Aid Package: $20,100. Required Financial Aid Forms: FAFSA or Colby Aid Application. Deadline to Apply for Financial Aid: February 1.

College of the Atlantic

Office of Admissions, 105 Eden Street, Bar Harbor, ME 04609. Phone: (207) 288-5015, (800) 528-0025. Fax: (207) 288-4126. E-mail: inquiry@ecology.coa.edu. Web Site: coa.edu. Tuition and Fees: $19,485. Room and Board: $5,400. Students Receiving Some Form of Aid: 70%. Students Receiving Non-Need-Based Aid: 5%. Average Aid Package: $14,705. Required Financial Aid Forms: FAFSA, institutional form. Deadline to Apply for Financial Aid: February 15.

Husson College

Admissions Office, One College Circle, Bangor, ME 04401-7935. Phone: (207) 941-7100, (800) 448-7766. Fax: (207) 941-7935. E-mail: admit@husson.edu. Web Site: husson.edu. Tuition and Fees: $9,210. Room and Board: $4,990. Required Financial Aid Forms: FAFSA. Deadline to Apply for Financial Aid: April 1 (priority).

Maine Maritime Academy

Admissions Office, Box C-3, Castine, ME 04420-5000. Phone: (207) 326-2206, (800) 464-6565. Fax: (207) 326-2515. E-mail: admissions@bell.mma.edu. Web Site: mainemaritime.edu. In-State Tuition and Fees: $5,790. Out-of-State Tuition and Fees: $9,445. Room and Board: $5,022. Students Receiving Some Form of Aid: 72%. Students Receiving Non-Need-Based Aid: 17%. Average Aid Package: $75. Required Financial Aid Forms: FAFSA. Deadline to Apply for Financial Aid: April 1.

Saint Joseph's College*

Admissions Office, 278 White's Bridge Road, Standish, ME 04084-5263. Phone: (207) 893-7746, (800) 338-7057. Fax: (207) 893-7862. E-mail: admissions@stcme.edu. Web Site: sjcme.edu. Tuition and Fees: $13,735. Room and Board: $5,950. Required Financial Aid Forms: FAFSA, Profile. Deadline to Apply for Financial Aid: March 1.

Thomas College*

Admissions Office, 180 West River Road, Waterville, ME 04901. Phone: (207) 859-1101, (800) 339-7001. Fax: (207) 859-1114. E-mail: admiss@host2.thomas.edu. Web Site: thomas.edu. Tuition and Fees: $12,290. Room and Board: $5,550. Students Receiving Some Form of Aid: 60%. Students Receiving Non-Need-Based Aid: 12%. Average Aid Package: $14,050. Required Financial Aid Forms: FAFSA. Deadline to Apply for Financial Aid: none.

Unity College

Office of Admissions, P.O. Box 532, Unity, ME 04988-0532. Phone: (207) 948-3131. Fax: (207) 948-6277. E-mail: admissions@unity.edu. Web Site: unity.edu. Tuition and Fees: $12,890. Room and Board: $5,300. Students Receiving Some Form of Aid: 73%. Students Receiving Non-Need-Based Aid: 18%. Average Aid Package: $10,242. Required Financial Aid Forms: FAFSA, institutional form, tax returns/W-2's. Deadline to Apply for Financial Aid: April 15; March 1 (priority).

University of Maine

Admissions Office, 5713 Chadbourne Hall, Orono, ME 04469-5713. Phone: (207) 581-1561, (877) 4UM-ADMIT. Fax: (207) 581-1213. E-mail: um-admit@maine.edu. Web Site: umaine.edu. In-State Tuition and Fees: $4,656. Out-of-State Tuition and Fees: $11,946. Room and Board: $5,256. Students Receiving Some Form of Aid: 62%. Students Receiving Non-Need-Based Aid: 4%. Average Aid Package: $7,745. Required Financial Aid Forms: FAFSA. Deadline to Apply for Financial Aid: March 1.

University of Maine—Augusta

Admissions Office, 46 University Drive, Augusta, ME 04330. Phone: (207) 621-3185, (877) 862-1234. Fax: (207) 621-3116. E-mail: ketcham@maine.edu. Web Site: uma.maine.edu. In-State Tuition and Fees: $3,605. Out-of-State Tuition and Fees: $8,105. Students Receiving Some Form of Aid: 25%. Students Receiving Non-Need-Based Aid: less than 1%. Average Aid Package: $6,923. Required Financial Aid Forms: FAFSA. Deadline to Apply for Financial Aid: March 1.

University of Maine—Farmington

Admissions Office, 102 Main Street, Farmington, ME 04938. Phone: (207) 778-7050. Fax: (207) 778-8182. E-mail: umfadmit@maine.edu. Web Site: umf.maine.edu. In-State Tuition and Fees: $3,776. Out-of-State Tuition and Fees: $8,666. Room and Board: $4,500. Required Financial Aid Forms: FAFSA. Deadline to Apply for Financial Aid: March 1 (recommended).

University of Maine—Machias

Admissions Office, 9 O'Brien Avenue, Machias, ME 04654. Phone: (207) 255-1318, (888) 468-6866. Fax: (207) 255-1363. E-mail: admissions@acad.umm.maine.edu. Web Site: umm.maine.edu. In-State Tuition and Fees: $3,425. Out-of-State Tuition and Fees: $7,955. Room and Board: $4,330. Students Receiving Some Form of Aid: 41%. Students Receiving Non-Need-Based Aid: 8%. Average Aid Package: $7,300. Required Financial Aid Forms: FAFSA. Deadline to Apply for Financial Aid: March 1.

University of Maine—Presque Isle

Admissions Office, 181 Main Street, Presque Isle, ME 04769. Phone: (207) 768-9532. Fax: (207) 768-9608. E-mail: infoumpi@polaris.umpi.maine.edu. Web Site: umpi.maine.edu. In-State Tuition and Fees: $3,390. Out-of-State Tuition and Fees: $7,860. Room and Board: $4,048. Students Receiving Some Form of Aid: 46%. Students Receiving Non-Need-Based Aid: 2%. Average Aid Package: $5,848. Required Financial Aid Forms: FAFSA. Deadline to Apply for Financial Aid: April 1, priority.

University of New England

Admissions Office, Hills Beach Road, Biddeford, ME 04005. Phone: (207) 283-0171, (800) 477-4UNE. Fax: (207) 286-3678. E-mail: mmitchelle@mailbox.une.edu. Web Site: une.edu. Tuition and Fees: $15,500. Room and Board: $6,200. Students Receiving Some Form of Aid: 65%. Students Receiving Non-Need-Based Aid: 20%. Average Aid Package: $9,101. Required Financial Aid Forms: institutional form. Deadline to Apply for Financial Aid: April 1.

University of Southern Maine*

Admissions Office, 37 College Avenue, Gorham, ME 04038. Phone: (207) 780-5670, (800) 800-4USM. Fax: (207) 780-5640. E-mail: usmadm@maine.maine.edu. Web Site: usm.maine.edu. In-State Tuition and Fees: $3,616. Out-of-State Tuition and Fees: $9,180. Room and Board: $4,926. Students Receiving Some Form of Aid: 31%. Students Receiving Non-Need-Based Aid: 2%. Average Aid Package: $6,464. Required Financial Aid Forms: FAFSA. Deadline to Apply for Financial Aid: February 15 for Fall, October 15 for Spring.

MARYLAND

Bowie State University

Admissions Office, 14000 Jericho Park Road, Bowie, MD 20715-9465. Phone: (301) 464-6570. Fax: (301) 464-7521. E-mail: dkiah@bowiestate.edu. Web Site: bowiestate.edu. In-State Tuition and Fees: $3,358. Out-of-State Tuition and Fees: $8,930. Room and Board: $3,915. Average Aid Package: $2,863. Required Financial Aid Forms: FAFSA, institutional application. Deadline to Apply for Financial Aid: March 1.

Capitol College

Admissions Office, 11301 Springfield Road, Laurel, MD 20708. Phone: (301) 953-3200, (800) 950-1992. Fax: (301) 953-1442. E-mail: admissions@capitol-college.edu. Web Site: capitol-college.edu. Tuition and Fees: $12,308. Room and Board: $1,620. Required Financial Aid Forms: FAFSA, scholarship information. Deadline to Apply for Financial Aid: March 1; priority.

College of Notre Dame—Maryland*

Admissions Office, 4701 North Charles Street, Baltimore, MD 21210-2476. Phone: (800) 435-0200 (in-state), (800) 435-0300 (out-of-state). Fax: (410) 435-6287. E-mail: admiss@ndm.edu. Web Site: ndm.edu. Tuition and Fees: $14,930. Room and Board: $6,330. Required Financial Aid Forms: FAFSA and CND form. Deadline to Apply for Financial Aid: February 15.

Coppin State College*

Admissions Office, 2500 West North Avenue, Baltimore, MD 21216-3698. Phone: (410) 383-5995, (800) 635-3674. Fax: (410) 523-7238. Web Site: coppin.umd.edu. In-State Tuition and Fees: $3,272. Out-of-State Tuition and Fees: $8,104. Room and Board: $5,274. Required Financial Aid Forms: FAFSA. Deadline to Apply for Financial Aid: July 15.

Frostburg State University

Admissions Office, 101 Braddock Road, Frostburg, MD 21532. Phone: (301) 687-4201. Fax: (301) 687-7074. E-mail: fsuadmissions@frostburg.edu. Web Site: fsu.umd.edu. In-State Tuition and Fees: $4,132. Out-of-State Tuition and Fees: $9,282. Room and Board: $5,214. Students Receiving Some Form of Aid: 48%. Students Receiving Non-Need-Based Aid: 7%. Average Aid Package: $5,819. Required Financial Aid Forms: FAFSA. Deadline to Apply for Financial Aid: March 1.

Goucher College

Admissions Office, 1021 Dulaney Valley Road, Baltimore, MD 21204-2794. Phone: (410) 337-6100, (800) 468-2437. Fax: (410) 337-6354. E-mail: admission@goucher.edu. Web Site: goucher.edu. Tuition and Fees: $20,485. Room and Board: $7,380. Students Receiving Some Form of Aid: 58%. Students Receiving Non-Need-Based Aid: 8%. Average Aid Package: $16,292. Required Financial Aid Forms: FAFSA, Profile. Deadline to Apply for Financial Aid: February 15.

Hood College

Office of Admissions, 401 Rosemont Avenue, Frederick, MD 21701-8575. Phone: (301) 696-3400, (800) 922-1599. Fax: (301) 696-3819. E-mail: admissions@hood.edu. Web Site: hood.edu. Tuition and Fees: $18,620. Room and Board: $6,900. Students Receiving Some Form of Aid: 66%. Students Receiving Non-Need-Based Aid: 18%. Average Aid Package: $18,283. Required Financial Aid Forms: FAFSA. Deadline to Apply for Financial Aid: February 15.

Johns Hopkins University

Admissions Office, 3400 North Charles Street, Baltimore, MD 21218. Phone: (410) 516-8171. E-mail: gotojhu@jhu.edu. Web Site: jhu.edu. Tuition and Fees: $24,930. Room and Board: $7,870. Students Receiving Some Form of Aid: 43%. Students Receiving Non-Need-Based Aid: 19%. Average Aid Package: $22,436. Required Financial Aid Forms: FAFSA, JHU application. Deadline to Apply for Financial Aid: February 1 (priority).

Loyola College

Admissions Office, 4501 North Charles Street, Baltimore, MD 21210-2699. Phone: (410) 617-5012, (800) 221-9107. Fax: (410) 617-2176. Web Site: loyola.edu. Tuition and Fees: $20,180. Room and Board: $6,850. Students Receiving Some Form of Aid: 43%. Students Receiving Non-Need-Based Aid: 18%. Average Aid Package: $13,650. Required Financial Aid Forms: FAFSA, CSS Profile, non-custodial parent statement, Business Farm Supplement. Deadline to Apply for Financial Aid: February 1.

Maryland Institute—College of Art

Office of Undergraduate Admission, 1300 Mt. Royal Avenue, Baltimore, MD 21217. Phone: (410) 225-2222. Fax: (410) 225-2337. E-mail: admissions@mica.edu. Web Site: mica.edu. Tuition and Fees: $18,710. Room and Board: $6,300. Required Financial Aid Forms: FAFSA, institutional form. Deadline to Apply for Financial Aid: March 1.

Morgan State University

Admissions Office, 1700 Cold Spring Lane, Baltimore, MD 21251. Phone: (443) 885-3000, (800) 332-6674. Fax: (443) 885-3684. E-mail: admissions@morgan.edu. Web Site: morgan.edu. In-State Tuition and Fees: $1,937. Out-of-State Tuition and Fees: $4,729. Room and Board: $2,859. Required Financial Aid Forms: FAFSA. Deadline to Apply for Financial Aid: April 1.

Mount Saint Mary's College

Admissions Office, 16300 Old Emmitsburg Road, Emmitsburg, MD 21727. Phone: (301) 447-5214, (800) 448-4347. Fax: (301) 447-5860. E-mail: admissions@msmary.edu. Web Site: msmary.edu. Tuition and Fees: $16,520. Room and Board: $6,650. Students Receiving Some Form of Aid: 68%. Students Receiving Non-Need-Based Aid: 9%. Average Aid

Package: $12,856. Required Financial Aid Forms: FAFSA, FAF, CSS Profile. Deadline to Apply for Financial Aid: February 15.

Saint John's College

Admissions Office, P.O. Box 2800, Annapolis, MD 21404. Phone: (800) 727-9238, (410) 626-2522. Fax: (410) 629-7916. E-mail: admissions@sjca.edu. Web Site: sjca.edu. Tuition and Fees: $24,770. Room and Board: $6,576. Average Aid Package: $20,546. Required Financial Aid Forms: FAFSA, profile. Deadline to Apply for Financial Aid: February 15.

Saint Mary's College of Maryland

Admissions Office, 18952 E. Fisher Road, St. Mary's City, MD 20686-3001. Phone: (301) 862-0292, (800) 492-7181. Fax: (301) 862-0906. E-mail: admissions@honors.smcm.edu. Web Site: smcm.edu. In-State Tuition and Fees: $7,175. Out-of-State Tuition and Fees: $11,875. Room and Board: $5,970. Students Receiving Some Form of Aid: 37%. Students Receiving Non-Need-Based Aid: 3%. Average Aid Package: $5,455. Required Financial Aid Forms: FAFSA. Deadline to Apply for Financial Aid: March 1.

Salisbury State University

Admissions Office, 1101 Camden Avenue, Salisbury, MD 21801-6862. Phone: (410) 543-6161, (888) 543-0148. Fax: (410) 548-4248. E-mail: admissions@ssu.edu. Web Site: ssu.edu. In-State Tuition and Fees: $4,312. Out-of-State Tuition and Fees: $9,048. Room and Board: $5,790. Students Receiving Some Form of Aid: 71%. Students Receiving Non-Need-Based Aid: 47%. Average Aid Package: $7,500. Required Financial Aid Forms: FAFSA. Deadline to Apply for Financial Aid: March 1.

Towson University

Admissions Office, 8000 York Road, Towson, MD 21252-0001. Phone: (410) 830-2113, (888) 4-TOWSON. Fax: (410) 830-3030. E-mail: admissions@towson.edu. Web Site: towson.edu. In-State Tuition and Fees: $4,710. Out-of-State Tuition and Fees: $11,140. Room and Board: $5,800. Students Receiving Some Form of Aid: 37%. Students Receiving Non-Need-Based Aid: 14%. Average Aid Package: $7,851. Required Financial Aid Forms: FAFSA. Deadline to Apply for Financial Aid: February 15 (priority).

United States Naval Academy

Admissions Office, 117 Decatur Road, Annapolis, MD 21402-5017. Phone: (410) 293-4361. Fax: (410) 293-4348. Web Site: usna.edu. Tuition, Fees, Room and Board: Paid for by the U.S. Government. Midshipmen also receive monthly stipend.

University of Maryland—Baltimore County

Admissions Office, 1000 Hilltop Circle, Baltimore, MD 21250. Phone: (410) 455-2291, (800) UMBC-4U2. Fax: (410) 455-1094. E-mail: admissions@umbc.edu. Web Site: umbc.edu. In-State Tuition and Fees: $5,160. Out-of-State Tuition and Fees: $9,632. Room and Board: $5,694. Students Receiving Some Form of Aid: 53%. Students Receiving Non-Need-Based Aid: 20%. Average Aid Package: $6,000. Required Financial Aid Forms: FAFSA. Deadline to Apply for Financial Aid: March 1 (priority).

University of Maryland—College Park

Admissions Office, Mitchell Building, College Park, MD 20742-5235. Phone: (301) 314-8385, (800) 422-5867. Fax: (301) 314-9693. E-mail: um-admit@uga.umd.edu. Web Site: maryland.edu. In-State Tuition and Fees: $4,939. Out-of-State Tuition and Fees: $11,827. Room and Board: $6,076. Students Receiving Some Form of Aid: 42%. Students Receiving Non-Need-Based Aid: 10%. Average Aid Package: $7,019. Required Financial Aid Forms: FAFSA. Deadline to Apply for Financial Aid: rolling.

University of Maryland—Eastern Shore

Office of Admissions & Registrations, Bird Hall, Princess Anne, MD 21853-1299. Phone: (410) 651-6178, (410) 651-8410. Fax: (410) 651-7670. E-mail: rpeoples@mail.umes.edu. Web Site: umd.edu. In-State Tuition and Fees: $3,833. Out-of-State Tuition and Fees: $8,443. Room and Board: $4,730. Required Financial Aid Forms: FAFSA. Deadline to Apply for Financial Aid: March 1.

Villa Julie College

Admissions Office, 1525 Greenspring, Stevenson, MD 21153. Phone: (410) 486-7001. Fax: (410) 602-6600. E-mail: admissions@vjc.edu. Web Site: vjc.edu. Tuition and Fees: $10,980. Students Receiving Some Form of Aid: 59%. Students Receiving Non-Need-Based Aid: 23%. Average Aid Package: $9,101. Required Financial Aid Forms: FAFSA. Deadline to Apply for Financial Aid: March 1.

Washington College

Admissions Office, 300 Washington Avenue, Chestertown, MD 21620. Phone: (410) 778-7700, (800) 422-1782. Fax: (410) 778-7287. E-mail: adm.off@washcoll.edu. Web Site: washcoll.edu. Tuition and Fees: $20,200. Room and Board: $5,740. Students Receiving Some Form of Aid: 51%. Students Receiving Non-Need-Based Aid: 23%. Average Aid Package: $17,977. Required Financial Aid Forms: FAFSA. Deadline to Apply for Financial Aid: February 15 (priority).

Western Maryland College

Admissions Office, 2 College Hill, Westminster, MD 21157-4390. Phone: (410) 857-2230, (800) 638-5005. Fax: (410) 857-2757. E-mail: admissio@wmdc.edu. Web Site: wmdc.edu. Tuition and Fees: $19,600. Room and Board: $5,350. Students Receiving Some Form of Aid: 66%. Average Aid Package: $16,132. Required Financial Aid Forms: FAFSA, WMC financial aid application. Deadline to Apply for Financial Aid: March 1.

MASSACHUSETTS

Amherst College

Office of Admission, Campus Box 2231, P.O. Box 5000, Amherst, MA 01002. Phone: (413) 542-2328. Fax: (413) 542-2040. E-mail: admissions@amherst.edu. Web Site: amherst.edu. Tuition and Fees: $25,222. Room and Board: $6,560. Students Receiving Some Form of Aid: 43%. Average Aid Package: $22,705. Required Financial Aid Forms: FAFSA, profile. Deadline to Apply for Financial Aid: February 1.

Assumption College

Admissions Office, 500 Salisbury Street, Worcester, MA 01609. Phone: (508) 767-7285, (888) 882-7786. Fax: (508) 799-4412. E-mail: admiss@assumption.edu. Web Site: assumption.edu. Tuition and Fees: $18,120. Room and Board: $6,980. Students Receiving Some Form of Aid: 58%. Students Receiving Non-Need-Based Aid: 6%. Average Aid Package: $13,065. Required Financial Aid Forms: FAFSA, institutional form, Profile. Deadline to Apply for Financial Aid: March 1; February 1 (priority).

Babson College

Admissions Office, Mustard Hall, Babson Park, MA 02457-0310. Phone: (781) 239-5522, (800) 488-3696. Fax: (781) 239-4006. E-mail: ugradadmission@babson.edu. Web Site: babson.edu. Tuition and Fees: $21,952. Room and Board: $8,746. Students Receiving Some Form of Aid: 40%. Students Receiving Non-Need-Based Aid: 4%. Average Aid Package: $16,903. Required Financial Aid Forms: FAFSA, CSS Profile, tax returns. Deadline to Apply for Financial Aid: February 15.

Bentley College

Admissions Office, 175 Forest Street, Waltham, MA 02452-4705. Phone: (781) 891-2244, (800) 523-2354. Fax: (781) 891-3414. E-mail: ugadmission@bentley.edu. Web Site: bentley.edu. Tuition and Fees: $18,910. Room and Board: $8,600. Students Receiving Some Form of Aid: 43%. Students Receiving Non-Need-Based Aid: 3%. Average Aid Package: $16,899. Required Financial Aid Forms: FAFSA, FAF. Deadline to Apply for Financial Aid: February 1.

Berklee College of Music

Office of Admissions, 1140 Boylston Street, Boston, MA 02215-3693. Phone: (617) 266-1400, (800) 421-0084. Fax: (617) 536-2623. E-mail: admissions@berklee.edu. Web Site: berklee.edu. Tuition and Fees: $16,087. Room and Board: $8,090. Required Financial Aid Forms: FAFSA. Deadline to Apply for Financial Aid: March 31 (priority).

Boston College

Office of Undergraduate Admissions, 140 Commonwealth Avenue, Devlin Hall 208, Chestnut Hill, MA 02467-3809. Phone: (617) 552-3100, (800) 360-2522. Fax: (617) 552-0798. E-mail: ugadmis@bc.edu. Web Site: bc.edu. Tuition and Fees: $23,520. Room and Board: $8,510. Average Aid Package: $18,793. Required Financial Aid Forms: FAFSA, CSS Profile. Deadline to Apply for Financial Aid: February 1.

Boston Conservatory

Admissions Office, 8 The Fenway, Boston, MA 02215. Phone: (617) 912-9153. Fax: (617) 247-3159. E-mail: admissions@bostonconservatory.edu. Web Site: unifiedapps.org. Tuition and Fees: $18,250. Room and Board: $8,800. Required Financial Aid Forms: FAFSA. Deadline to Apply for Financial Aid: March 1.

Boston University

Office of Undergraduate Admissions, 121 Bay State Road, Boston, MA 02215. Phone: (617) 353-2300. Fax: (617) 353-9695. E-mail: admissions@bu.edu, intadmis@bu.edu (Int.). Web Site: bu.edu. Tuition and Fees: $25,044. Room and Board: $8,450. Students Receiving Some Form of Aid: 48%. Students Receiving Non-Need-Based Aid: 14%. Average Aid Package: $21,654. Required Financial Aid Forms: FAFSA, CSS Profile. Deadline to Apply for Financial Aid: February 15 (priority).

Brandeis University

Admissions Office, 415 South Street, Waltham, MA 02454. Phone: (781) 736-3500, (800) 622-0622. Fax: (781) 736-3536. E-mail: sendinfo@brandeis.edu. Web Site: brandeis.edu. Tuition and Fees: $25,174. Room and Board: $7,040. Students Receiving Some Form of Aid: 51%. Students Receiving Non-Need-Based Aid: 4%. Average Aid Package: $19,589. Required Financial Aid Forms: FAFSA, CSS Profile. Deadline to Apply for Financial Aid: January 31.

Bridgewater State College

Admissions Office, Gates House, Bridgewater, MA 02325. Phone: (508) 531-1237. Fax: (508) 531-1746. E-mail: admissions@bridgew.edu. Web Site: bridegew.edu. In-State Tuition and Fees: $2,123. Out-of-State Tuition and Fees: $8,141. Room and Board: $4,704. Students Receiving Some Form of Aid: 52%. Students Receiving Non-Need-Based Aid: 6%. Average Aid Package: $3,470. Required Financial Aid Forms: FAFSA. Deadline to Apply for Financial Aid: March 1 (priority).

Clark University

Office of Undergraduate Admissions, 950 Main Street, Worcester, MA 01610-1477. Phone: (508) 793-7431, (800) GO-CLARK. Fax: (508) 793-8821. E-mail: admissions@admissions.clarku.edu. Web Site: clarku.edu. Tuition and Fees: $22,620. Room and Board: $4,350. Students Receiving Some Form of Aid: 60%. Average Aid Package: $18,138. Required Financial Aid Forms: Profile, FAFSA. Deadline to Apply for Financial Aid: February 1.

College of the Holy Cross

Admissions Office, 1 College Street, Worcester, MA 01610-2395. Phone: (508) 793-2443, (800) 442-2421. Fax: (508) 793-3888. E-mail: admissions@holycross.edu. Web Site: holycross.edu. Tuition and Fees: $23,815. Room and Board: $7,540. Students Receiving Some Form of Aid: 50%. Average Aid Package: $17,236. Required Financial Aid Forms: FAFSA, Profile, noncustodial parents' statement. Deadline to Apply for Financial Aid: February 1.

Curry College

Admissions Office, 1071 Blue Hill Avenue, Milton, MA 02186. Phone: (617) 333-2210, (800) 669-0686. Fax: (617) 333-2114. E-mail: curryadm@curry.edu. Web Site: curry.edu:8080. Tuition and Fees: $16,500. Room and Board: $6,560.

Elms College

Office of Admission, 291 Springfield Street, Chicopee, MA 01013. Phone: (413) 592-3189, (800) 255-ELMS. Fax: (413) 594-2781. E-mail: admissions@elms.edu. Web Site: elms.edu. Tuition and Fees: $14,720. Room and Board: $5,566. Students Receiving Some Form of Aid: 49%. Students Receiving Non-Need-Based Aid: 5%. Average Aid Package: $11,892. Required Financial Aid Forms: FAFSA, Elms application. Deadline to Apply for Financial Aid: March 1 (priority).

Emerson College

Office of Admission, 100 Beacon Street, Boston, MA 02116-1596. Phone: (617) 824-8600. Fax: (617) 824-8609. E-mail:

admiss@emerson.edu. Web Site: emerson.edu. Tuition and Fees: $19,206. Room and Board: $8,734. Students Receiving Some Form of Aid: 45%. Students Receiving Non-Need-Based Aid: 10%. Average Aid Package: $12,600. Required Financial Aid Forms: FAFSA, CSS Profile, institutional form. Deadline to Apply for Financial Aid: March 1.

Emmanuel College

Admissions Office, 400 The Fenway, Boston, MA 02115. Phone: (617) 735-9715. Fax: (617) 735-9801. E-mail: enroll@emmanuel.edu. Web Site: emmanuel.edu. Tuition and Fees: $15,788. Students Receiving Some Form of Aid: 22%. Students Receiving Non-Need-Based Aid: 12%. Average Aid Package: $19,350. Required Financial Aid Forms: FAFSA, institutional financial aid form. Deadline to Apply for Financial Aid: April 15.

Fitchburg State College

Admissions Office, 160 Pearl Street, Fitchburg, MA 01420-2697. Phone: (978) 665-3144. Fax: (978) 665-4540. E-mail: admissions@fsc.edu. Web Site: fsc.edu. In-State Tuition and Fees: $3,018. Out-of-State Tuition and Fees: $8,978. Room and Board: $4,540. Required Financial Aid Forms: FAFSA, institutional form. Deadline to Apply for Financial Aid: March 1.

Framingham State College

Admissions Office, 100 State Street, P.O. Box 9101, Framingham, MA 01701-9101. Phone: (508) 626-4500. Fax: (508) 626-4017. E-mail: admiss@frc.mass.edu. Web Site: framingham.edu. In-State Tuition and Fees: $2,830. Out-of-State Tuition and Fees: $8,850. Room and Board: $4,154. Students Receiving Some Form of Aid: 31%. Students Receiving Non-Need-Based Aid: 2%. Average Aid Package: $5,273. Required Financial Aid Forms: FAFSA. Deadline to Apply for Financial Aid: March 1 (priority).

Gordon College

Admissions Office, 255 Grapevine Road, Wenham, MA 01984-1899. Phone: (978) 927-2300 ext.4218, (800) 343-1379. Fax: (978) 524-3722. E-mail: admissions@hope.gordon.edu. Web Site: gordon.edu. Tuition and Fees: $17,270. Room and Board: $5,250. Students Receiving Some Form of Aid: 67%. Students Receiving Non-Need-Based Aid: 45%. Average Aid Package: $11,992. Required Financial Aid Forms: FAFSA, tax forms. Deadline to Apply for Financial Aid: March 1.

Hampshire College

Admissions Office, 893 West Street, Amherst, MA 01002. Phone: (413) 559-5471. Fax: (413) 559-5631. E-mail: admissions@hampshire.edu. Web Site: hampshire.edu. Tuition and Fees: $25,400. Room and Board: $6,622. Students Receiving Some Form of Aid: 60%. Students Receiving Non-Need-Based Aid: 14%. Average Aid Package: $21,500. Required Financial Aid Forms: FAFSA, CSS Profile, institutional form. Deadline to Apply for Financial Aid: February 1.

Harvard College

Harvard College Admssions, Byerly Hall, 8 Garden Street, Cambridge, MA 02138. Phone: (617) 495-1551. Fax: (617) 495-8821. E-mail: college@fas.harvard.edu. Web Site: fas.harvard.edu. Tuition and Fees: $25,128. Room and Board: $7,982. Students Receiving Some Form of Aid: 50%. Average Aid Package: $22,010. Required Financial Aid Forms: FAFSA, CSS Profile, federal income tax returns. Deadline to Apply for Financial Aid: February 1 (priority).

Lesley College

Undergraduate Admissions, 29 Everett Street, Cambridge, MA 02138. Phone: (800) 999-1959, (617) 349-8800. Fax: (617) 349-8810. E-mail: ugadm@mail.lesley.edu. Web Site: lesley.edu. Tuition and Fees: $17,280. Room and Board: $7,520. Students Receiving Some Form of Aid: 67%. Students Receiving Non-Need-Based Aid: 14%. Average Aid Package: $11,200. Required Financial Aid Forms: FAFSA, college form, tax returns. Deadline to Apply for Financial Aid: February 1 (priority).

Massachusetts College of Art

Admissions Office, 621 Huntington Avenue, Boston, MA 02115. Phone: (617) 232-1555. Fax: (617) 739-9744. E-mail: admissions@massart.edu. Web Site: massart.edu. In-State Tuition and Fees: $3,853. Out-of-State Tuition and Fees: $11,793. Room and Board: $7,006. Students Receiving Some Form of Aid: 55%. Students Receiving Non-Need-Based Aid: 9%. Average Aid Package: $8,440. Required Financial Aid Forms: FAFSA. Deadline to Apply for Financial Aid: March 15 (priority).

Massachusetts College of Liberal Arts

Admissions Office, 375 Church Street, North Adams, MA 01247. Phone: (413) 662-5410, (800) 292-6632. Fax: (413) 662-5179. E-mail: admissions@mcla.mass.edu. Web Site: mcla.mass.edu. In-State Tuition and Fees: $3,357. Out-of-State Tuition and Fees: $9,317. Room and Board: $4,290. Students Receiving Some Form of Aid: 56%. Students Receiving Non-Need-Based Aid: 23%. Average Aid Package: $6,217. Required Financial Aid Forms: FAFSA, institutional form. Deadline to Apply for Financial Aid: April 1 (priority).

Massachusetts College of Pharmacy and Allied Health Sciences*

Office of Admission, 179 Longwood Avenue, Boston, MA 02115. Phone: (617) 732-2850, (800) 225-5506. Fax: (617) 732-2801. E-mail: admissions@mcp.edu. Web Site: mcp.edu. Tuition and Fees: $16,958. Room and Board: $7,900. Students Receiving Some Form of Aid: 67%. Students Receiving Non-Need-Based Aid: 1%. Average Aid Package: $14,050. Required Financial Aid Forms: FAFSA, school application, tax returns. Deadline to Apply for Financial Aid: March 15.

Massachusetts Institute of Technology

MIT Admissions Office, 77 Massachusetts Avenue Room 3-108, Cambridge, MA 02139. Phone: (617) 253-4791. Fax: (617) 258-8304. E-mail: admissions@mit.edu. Web Site: web.mit.edu. Tuition and Fees: $26,746. Room and Board: $7,175. Required Financial Aid Forms: FAFSA, school form, profile, tax forms, divorced parent form. Deadline to Apply for Financial Aid: January 17.

Massachusetts Maritime Academy

Admissions Office, 101 Academy Drive, Buzzards Bay, MA 02532. Phone: (508) 830-5000, (800) 544-3411. Fax: (508) 830-5077. E-mail: admissions@mma.mass.edu. Web Site: mma.mass.edu. In-State Tuition and Fees: $2,873. Out-of-State Tuition and Fees:

$10,956. Room and Board: $4,560. Students Receiving Some Form of Aid: 49%. Students Receiving Non-Need-Based Aid: 3%. Average Aid Package: $6,700. Required Financial Aid Forms: FAFSA. Deadline to Apply for Financial Aid: May 1.

Merrimack College

Office of Admission, Austin Hall, North Andover, MA 01845. Phone: (978) 837-5100. Fax: (978) 837-5222. E-mail: admission@merrimack.edu. Web Site: merrimack.edu. Tuition and Fees: $15,710. Room and Board: $7,500. Students Receiving Some Form of Aid: 67%. Students Receiving Non-Need-Based Aid: 9%. Average Aid Package: $13,800. Required Financial Aid Forms: FAFSA. Deadline to Apply for Financial Aid: February 15.

Mount Holyoke College

Office of Admissions, 50 College Street, South Hadley, MA 01075. Phone: (413) 538-2023. Fax: (413) 538-2409. E-mail: admissions@mtholyoke. edu. Web Site: mtholyoke.edu. Tuition and Fees: $24,354. Room and Board: $7,110. Students Receiving Some Form of Aid: 76%. Average Aid Package: $21,130. Required Financial Aid Forms: FAFSA, tax returns, non-custodial parent statement. Deadline to Apply for Financial Aid: January 15.

New England Conservatory of Music

Admissions Office, 290 Huntington Avenue, Boston, MA 02115. Phone: (617) 585-1101. Fax: (617) 585-1115. E-mail: admissions@newenglandconservatory.edu. Web Site: newenglandconservatory.edu. Tuition and Fees: $19,800. Room and Board: $8,500. Students Receiving Some Form of Aid: 79%. Students Receiving Non-Need-Based Aid: 6%. Average Aid Package: $12,115. Required Financial Aid Forms: FAFSA, institutional form. Deadline to Apply for Financial Aid: February 2.

Nichols College

Office of Admissions, P.O. Box 5000, Dudley, MA 01571. Phone: (800) 470-3379, (508) 943-2055. Fax: (508) 943-9885. E-mail: admissions@nichols.edu. Web Site: nichols.edu. Tuition and Fees: $15,650. Room and Board: $7,810. Students Receiving Some Form of Aid: 52%. Students Receiving Non-Need-Based Aid: 8%. Average Aid Package: $11,500. Required Financial Aid Forms: FAFSA. Deadline to Apply for Financial Aid: rolling, March 1 priority.

Northeastern University

Office of Undergraduate Admissions, 360 Huntington Avenue, 150 Richards Hall, Boston, MA 02115. Phone: (617) 373-2200, (617) 373-3100 (TTY). Fax: (617) 373-8780. E-mail: admissions@neu.edu. Web Site: neu.edu. Tuition and Fees: $15,688. Room and Board: $5,740. Students Receiving Some Form of Aid: 69%. Students Receiving Non-Need-Based Aid: 5%. Average Aid Package: $10,737. Required Financial Aid Forms: FAFSA , Profile. Deadline to Apply for Financial Aid: February 15 (priority).

Pine Manor College

Office of Admissions, 400 Heath Street, Chestnut Hill, MA 02467. Phone: (617) 731-7000, (800) 762-1357. Fax: (617) 731-7199. Web Site: pmc.edu. Tuition and Fees: $11,440. Room and Board: $7,160. Students Receiving Some Form of Aid: 62%. Students Receiving Non-Need-Based Aid: 25%. Average Aid Package: $14,492. Deadline to Apply for Financial Aid: none.

Regis College

Admission Office, 235 Wellesley Street, Weston, MA 02493-1571. Phone: (781) 768-7100, (800) 456-1820. Fax: (781) 768-7071. E-mail: admission@regiscollege.edu. Web Site: regiscollege.edu. Tuition and Fees: $16,860. Room and Board: $7,870. Average Aid Package: $15,817. Required Financial Aid Forms: FAFSA, CSS Profile. Deadline to Apply for Financial Aid: March 1 (priority).

Salem State College

Admissions Office, 352 Lafayette Street, Salem, MA 01970. Phone: (978) 542-6200. Fax: (978) 542-6895. E-mail: admissions@salem-mass.edu. Web Site: salem.mass.edu. In-State Tuition and Fees: $2,904. Out-of-State Tuition and Fees: $8,924. Room and Board: $5,625. Required Financial Aid Forms: FAFSA. Deadline to Apply for Financial Aid: April 15.

Simmons College

Admission Office, 300 The Fenway, Boston, MA 02115. Phone: (617) 521-2051, (800) 345-8468. Fax: (617) 521-3190. E-mail: ugadm@simmons.edu. Web Site: simmons.edu. Tuition and Fees: $20,134. Room and Board: $8,046. Students Receiving Some Form of Aid: 68%. Students Receiving Non-Need-Based Aid: 16%. Average Aid Package: $19,059. Required Financial Aid Forms: FAFSA, CSS Profile,non-custodial parents statement, business/farm supplement, federal tax returns. Deadline to Apply for Financial Aid: February 1.

Smith College

Admission Office, 7 College Lane, Northampton, MA 01063. Phone: (413) 585-2500. Fax: (413) 585-2527. E-mail: admission@smith.edu. Web Site: smith.edu. Tuition and Fees: $22,622. Room and Board: $7,820. Students Receiving Some Form of Aid: 59%. Students Receiving Non-Need-Based Aid: 2%. Average Aid Package: $21,548. Required Financial Aid Forms: FAFSA, CSS financial aid profile, institutional form. Deadline to Apply for Financial Aid: February 1.

Springfield College

Office of Undergraduate Admissions, 263 Alden Street, Springfield, MA 01109-3707. Phone: (413) 748-3136. Fax: (413) 748-3694. Web Site: spfldcol.edu. Tuition and Fees: $16,898. Room and Board: $5,865. Required Financial Aid Forms: FAFSA, Profile, tax return. Deadline to Apply for Financial Aid: March 15.

Stonehill College

Admissions Office, 320 Washington Street, Easton, MA 02357-5610. Phone: (508) 565-1373. Fax: (508) 565-1545. E-mail: admissions@stonehill.edu. Web Site: stonehill.edu. Tuition and Fees: $17,320. Room and Board: $8,166. Students Receiving Some Form of Aid: 53%. Students Receiving Non-Need-Based Aid: 7%. Average Aid Package: $12,129. Required Financial Aid Forms: FAFSA and CSS/financial aid profile. Deadline to Apply for Financial Aid: February 1.

Suffolk University

Admissions Office, 8 Ashburton Place, Boston, MA 02108. **Phone:** (617) 573-8460, (800) 6-SUFFOLK. **Fax:** (617) 742-4291. **E-mail:** admission@admin.suffolk.edu. **Web Site:** suffolk.edu. **Tuition and Fees:** $14,620. **Room and Board:** $9,210. **Students Receiving Some Form of Aid:** 44%. **Students Receiving Non-Need-Based Aid:** 12%. **Average Aid Package:** $11,402. **Required Financial Aid Forms:** FAFSA, institutional form. **Deadline to Apply for Financial Aid:** March 1 (priority).

Tufts University

Undergraduate Admissions, Bendetson Hall, Medford, MA 02155. **Phone:** (617) 627-3170. **Fax:** (617) 627-3860. **E-mail:** uadmiss_inquiry@infonet.tufts.edu. **Web Site:** tufts.edu. **Tuition and Fees:** $24,751. **Room and Board:** $7,375. **Students Receiving Some Form of Aid:** 37%. **Average Aid Package:** $19,785. **Required Financial Aid Forms:** FAFSA, Profile, federal tax returns. **Deadline to Apply for Financial Aid:** February 1.

University of Massachusetts—Amherst

Undergraduate Admissions Office, University Admissions Center, Amherst, MA 01003-0120. **Phone:** (413) 545-0222. **Fax:** (413) 545-4312. **E-mail:** mail@admissions.umass.edu. **Web Site:** umass.edu. **In-State Tuition and Fees:** $5,212. **Out-of-State Tuition and Fees:** $13,254. **Room and Board:** $4,790. **Students Receiving Some Form of Aid:** 48%. **Students Receiving Non-Need-Based Aid:** less than 1%. **Average Aid Package:** $8,069. **Required Financial Aid Forms:** FAFSA. **Deadline to Apply for Financial Aid:** March 1.

University of Massachusetts—Boston

Office of Undergraduate Admissions, 100 Morrissey Boulevard, Boston, MA 02125-3393. **Phone:** (617) 287-6100. **Fax:** (617) 287-6242. **E-mail:** bos.admiss@umassp.edu. **Web Site:** umb.edu. **In-State Tuition and Fees:** $4,307. **Out-of-State Tuition and Fees:** $12,437. **Students Receiving Some Form of Aid:** 35%. **Students Receiving Non-Need-Based Aid:** 4%. **Average Aid Package:** $7,447. **Required Financial Aid Forms:** FAFSA. **Deadline to Apply for Financial Aid:** March 1 (priority).

University of Massachusetts—Dartmouth

Admissions Office, 285 Old Westport Road, North Dartmouth, MA 02747-2300. **Phone:** (508) 999-8605. **Fax:** (508) 999-8755. **E-mail:** admissions@umassd.edu. **Web Site:** umassd.edu. **In-State Tuition and Fees:** $4,129. **Out-of-State Tuition and Fees:** $11,783. **Room and Board:** $4,992. **Students Receiving Some Form of Aid:** 31%. **Average Aid Package:** $6,912. **Required Financial Aid Forms:** FAFSA. **Deadline to Apply for Financial Aid:** March 1 (priority).

University of Massachusetts—Lowell

Office of Undergraduate Admissions, 883 Broadway St., Rm. 110, Lowell, MA 01854-5104. **Phone:** (978) 934-3931, (800) 410-4607. **Fax:** (978) 934-3086. **E-mail:** admissions@uml.edu. **Web Site:** uml.edu. **In-State Tuition and Fees:** $4,179. **Out-of-State Tuition and Fees:** $10,816. **Room and Board:** $4,836. **Required Financial Aid Forms:** FAFSA. **Deadline to Apply for Financial Aid:** March 1.

Wellesley College

Admissions Office, 106 Central Street, Wellesley, MA 02481-8203. **Phone:** (781) 283-2270. **Fax:** (781) 283-3678. **E-mail:** admission@wellesley.edu. **Web Site:** wellesley.edu. **Tuition and Fees:** $23,320. **Room and Board:** $7,234. **Students Receiving Some Form of Aid:** 51%. **Average Aid Package:** $18,704. **Required Financial Aid Forms:** FAFSA. **Deadline to Apply for Financial Aid:** February 1 (priority).

Wentworth Institute of Technology*

Admissions Office, 550 Huntingdon Avenue, Boston, MA 02115-5998. **Phone:** (617) 989-4000, (800) 556-0610. **Fax:** (617) 989-4010. **E-mail:** admissions@wit.edu. **Web Site:** wit.edu. **Tuition and Fees:** $12,450. **Room and Board:** $6,500. **Required Financial Aid Forms:** FAFSA. **Deadline to Apply for Financial Aid:** March 1 (priority).

Western New England College

Admissions Office, 1215 Wilbraham Road, Springfield, MA 01119-9920. **Phone:** (413) 782-1321, (800) 325-1122. **Fax:** (413) 782-1777. **Web Site:** wnec.edu. **Tuition and Fees:** $15,504. **Room and Board:** $7,050. **Required Financial Aid Forms:** FAFSA, institutional form. **Deadline to Apply for Financial Aid:** rolling; April 1 (priority).

Westfield State College

Admissions Office, Western Avenue, Westfield, MA 01086. **Phone:** (413) 572-5218, (800) 322-8401. **Fax:** (413) 562-3613. **E-mail:** admission@wsc.mass.edu. **Web Site:** wsc.mass.edu. **In-State Tuition and Fees:** $2,974. **Out-of-State Tuition and Fees:** $8,934. **Room and Board:** $4,174. **Required Financial Aid Forms:** FAFSA. **Deadline to Apply for Financial Aid:** rolling; March 1 (priority).

Wheaton College

Office of Admission, Wheaton College, Norton, MA 02766. **Phone:** (508) 286-8251, (800) 394-6003. **Fax:** (508) 286-8271. **E-mail:** admissions@wheatoncollege.edu. **Web Site:** wheatoncollege.edu. **Tuition and Fees:** $23,150. **Room and Board:** $6,730. **Students Receiving Some Form of Aid:** 61%. **Students Receiving Non-Need-Based Aid:** less than 1%. **Average Aid Package:** $17,949. **Required Financial Aid Forms:** FAFSA, Profile. **Deadline to Apply for Financial Aid:** February 1.

Wheelock College

Admissions Office, 200 The Riverway, Boston, MA 02215-4176. **Phone:** (617) 879-2206, (800) 734-5212. **Fax:** (617) 566-4453. **E-mail:** undergrad@wheelock.edu. **Web Site:** wheelock.edu. **Tuition and Fees:** $16,740. **Room and Board:** $6,615. **Students Receiving Some Form of Aid:** 75%. **Students Receiving Non-Need-Based Aid:** 1%. **Average Aid Package:** $13,557. **Required Financial Aid Forms:** FAFSA, CSS Profile, institutional form. **Deadline to Apply for Financial Aid:** March 1.

Williams College

Admissions Office, 988 Main Street, P.O. Box 487, Williamstown, MA 01267. **Phone:** (413) 597-2211. **E-mail:** admissions@williams.edu. **Web Site:** williams.edu. **Tuition and Fees:** $24,790. **Room and Board:** $6,730. **Students Receiving Some Form of Aid:** 44%. **Average Aid Package:** $21,837. **Required Financial Aid Forms:** FAFSA, Profile, tax forms. **Deadline to Apply for Financial Aid:** February 1.

Worcester Polytechnic Institute

Admissions Office, 100 Institute Road, Worcester, MA 01609. Phone: (508) 831-5286. Fax: (508) 831-5875. E-mail: admissions@wpi.edu. Web Site: wpi.edu. Tuition and Fees: $22,158. Room and Board: $6,912. Students Receiving Some Form of Aid: 71%. Students Receiving Non-Need-Based Aid: 6%. Average Aid Package: $17,428. Required Financial Aid Forms: FAP, FAFSA, Profile. Deadline to Apply for Financial Aid: March 1.

Worcester State College

Office of Admissions, 486 Chandler Street, Worcester, MA 01602-2597. Phone: (508) 929-8040. Fax: (508) 929-8183. E-mail: admissions@worcester.edu. Web Site: worcester.edu. In-State Tuition and Fees: $2,476. Out-of-State Tuition and Fees: $8,436. Room and Board: $4,214. Students Receiving Some Form of Aid: 13%. Students Receiving Non-Need-Based Aid: 5%. Average Aid Package: $4,550. Required Financial Aid Forms: FAFSA, institution's own forms. Deadline to Apply for Financial Aid: March 1 (priority).

MICHIGAN

Adrian College*

Admissions Office, 110 South Madison Street, Adrian, MI 49221. Phone: (517) 265-5161, (800) 877-2246. Fax: (517) 264-3331. E-mail: admissions@adrian.edu. Web Site: adrian.edu. Tuition and Fees: $13,750. Room and Board: $4,460. Students Receiving Some Form of Aid: 78%. Students Receiving Non-Need-Based Aid: 49%. Average Aid Package: $12,877. Required Financial Aid Forms: FAFSA. Deadline to Apply for Financial Aid: February 21.

Albion College

Admissions Office, 611 East Porter Street, Albion, MI 49224. Phone: (800) 858-6770, (517) 629-0321. Fax: (517) 629-0569. E-mail: admissions@albion.edu. Web Site: albion.edu. Tuition and Fees: $18,952. Room and Board: $5,404. Students Receiving Some Form of Aid: 64%. Students Receiving Non-Need-Based Aid: 28%. Average Aid Package: $15,969. Required Financial Aid Forms: FAFSA. Deadline to Apply for Financial Aid: February 15.

Alma College

Admissions Office, 614 West Superior Street, Alma, MI 48801. Phone: (517) 463-7139, (800) 321-ALMA. Fax: (517) 463-7057. E-mail: admissions@alma.edu. Web Site: alma.edu. Tuition and Fees: $21,748. Room and Board: $5,726. Students Receiving Some Form of Aid: 76%. Students Receiving Non-Need-Based Aid: 9%. Average Aid Package: $13,635. Required Financial Aid Forms: FAFSA. Deadline to Apply for Financial Aid: February 15.

Calvin College

Calvin College Admissions Office, 3201 Burton Street S.E., Grand Rapids, MI 49546. Phone: (616) 957-6106, (800) 688-0122. Fax: (616) 957-8513. E-mail: admissions@calvin.edu. Web Site: calvin.edu. Tuition and Fees: $14,040. Room and Board: $4,890. Students Receiving Some Form of Aid: 62%. Students Receiving Non-Need-Based Aid: 2%. Average Aid Package: $10,350. Required Financial Aid Forms: FAFSA, institutional application. Deadline to Apply for Financial Aid: February 15 (priority).

Central Michigan University

Admissions Office, Warriner Hall, 102, Mount Pleasant, MI 48859. Phone: (517) 774-3076. Fax: (517) 774-7267. E-mail: cmuadmit@cmich.edu. Web Site: cmich.edu. In-State Tuition and Fees: $3,630. Out-of-State Tuition and Fees: $8,655. Room and Board: $4,620. Students Receiving Some Form of Aid: 43%. Students Receiving Non-Need-Based Aid: 2%. Average Aid Package: $7,121. Required Financial Aid Forms: FAFSA. Deadline to Apply for Financial Aid: February 1 (priority).

Eastern Michigan University

Admissions Office, 400 Pierce Hall, Ypsilanti, MI 48197. Phone: (734) 487-3060, (800) GO-TO-EMU. Fax: (734) 487-1484. Web Site: emich.edu. In-State Tuition and Fees: $3,753. Out-of-State Tuition and Fees: $8,822. Room and Board: $4,842. Students Receiving Some Form of Aid: 19%. Students Receiving Non-Need-Based Aid: 10%. Average Aid Package: $8,300. Required Financial Aid Forms: FAFSA. Deadline to Apply for Financial Aid: rolling; March 15 (priority).

Ferris State University

Admissions Office, 420 Oak Street, PRK 101, Big Rapids, MI 49307-2020. Phone: (231) 591-2100, (800) 433-7747. Fax: (231) 591-3944. E-mail: admissions@ferris.edu. Web Site: ferris.edu. In-State Tuition and Fees: $4,193. Out-of-State Tuition and Fees: $8,801. Room and Board: $5,110. Average Aid Package: $5,500. Required Financial Aid Forms: FAFSA. Deadline to Apply for Financial Aid: April 1.

Grand Valley State University

Student Services Building, 1 Campus Drive, Allendale, MI 49401. Phone: (616) 895-2025, (800) 748-0246. Fax: (616) 895-2000. E-mail: go2gvsu@gvsu.edu. Web Site: gvsu.edu. In-State Tuition and Fees: $4,108. Out-of-State Tuition and Fees: $8,890. Room and Board: $4,840. Students Receiving Some Form of Aid: 40%. Students Receiving Non-Need-Based Aid: 6%. Average Aid Package: $5,415. Required Financial Aid Forms: FAFSA. Deadline to Apply for Financial Aid: February 1(priority).

Hillsdale College

Admissions Office, 33 East College Street, Hillsdale, MI 49242. Phone: (517) 437-7341. Fax: (517) 437-7241. E-mail: admissions@ac.hillsdale.edu. Web Site: hillsdale.edu. Tuition and Fees: $13,840. Room and Board: $5,700. Students Receiving Some Form of Aid: 65%. Students Receiving Non-Need-Based Aid: 20%. Average Aid Package: $13,500. Required Financial Aid Forms: FAFSA, institutional form. Deadline to Apply for Financial Aid: March 1 (priority).

Hope College

Admissions Office, 69 E. 10th Street, Holland, MI 49423. Phone: (616) 395-7850, (800) 968-7850. Fax: (616) 395-7130. E-mail: admissions@hope.edu. Web Site: hope.edu. Tuition and Fees: $16,644. Room and Board: $5,224. Students Receiving Some Form of Aid: 51%. Students Receiving Non-Need-Based Aid: 31%. Average Aid Package: $14,202. Required Financial Aid Forms: FAFSA, CSS Profile. Deadline to Apply for Financial Aid: February 15.

Kalamazoo College

Office of Admissions, 1200 Academy Street, Kalamazoo, MI 49006. **Phone:** (616) 337-7166, (800) 253-3602. **Fax:** (616) 337-7390. **E-mail:** admission@kzoo.edu. **Web Site:** kzoo.edu. **Tuition and Fees:** $19,834. **Room and Board:** $5,961. **Students Receiving Some Form of Aid:** 54%. **Students Receiving Non-Need-Based Aid:** 9%. **Average Aid Package:** $15,408. **Required Financial Aid Forms:** FAFSA, profile, institutional form. **Deadline to Apply for Financial Aid:** February 15 (priority).

Kettering University

Admissions Office, 1700 West Third Avenue, Flint, MI 48504. **Phone:** (810) 762-7865, (800) 955-4464. **Fax:** (810) 762-9837. **E-mail:** admissions@kettering.edu. **Web Site:** kettering.edu. **Tuition and Fees:** $16,185. **Room and Board:** $4,100. **Required Financial Aid Forms:** FAFSA. **Deadline to Apply for Financial Aid:** none.

Lake Superior State University

Admissions Office, 650 W. Easterday Avenue, Sault Ste. Marie, MI 49783-1699. **Phone:** (888) 800-LSSU, ext. 2231, (906) 635-2231. **Fax:** (906) 635-6669. **E-mail:** ADMISSIONS@GW.LSSU.EDU. **Web Site:** LSSU.EDU. **In-State Tuition and Fees:** $4,034. **Out-of-State Tuition and Fees:** $7,738. **Room and Board:** $4,930. **Students Receiving Some Form of Aid:** 67%. **Students Receiving Non-Need-Based Aid:** 30%. **Average Aid Package:** $3,382. **Required Financial Aid Forms:** FAFSA. **Deadline to Apply for Financial Aid:** rolling; February 21 (priority).

Marygrove College

Admissions Office, 8425 W. McNichols Rd., Detroit, MI 48221. **Phone:** (313) 927-1240. **Fax:** (313) 927-1345. **E-mail:** cmathews@marygrove.edu. **Web Site:** marygrove.edu. **Tuition and Fees:** $10,375. **Room and Board:** $5,200. **Required Financial Aid Forms:** FAFSA, institutional forms. **Deadline to Apply for Financial Aid:** 3/15.

Michigan State University

Admissions Office, 250 Administration Building, MSU, East Lansing, MI 48824. **Phone:** (517) 355-8332, (800) 496-4678. **Fax:** (517) 353-1647. **E-mail:** admis@msu.edu. **Web Site:** msu.edu. **In-State Tuition and Fees:** $5,590. **Out-of-State Tuition and Fees:** $12,992. **Room and Board:** $4,298. **Students Receiving Some Form of Aid:** 35%. **Students Receiving Non-Need-Based Aid:** less than 1%. **Average Aid Package:** $7,142. **Required Financial Aid Forms:** FAFSA, institutional form. **Deadline to Apply for Financial Aid:** Jue 30; February 21 (priority).

Michigan Technological University

Admissions Office, 1400 Townsend Drive, Houghton, MI 49931. **Phone:** (906) 487-2335. **Fax:** (906) 487-2125. **E-mail:** mtu4u@mtu.edu. **Web Site:** mtu.edu. **In-State Tuition and Fees:** $4,698. **Out-of-State Tuition and Fees:** $11,106. **Room and Board:** $4,726. **Students Receiving Some Form of Aid:** 47%. **Students Receiving Non-Need-Based Aid:** 22%. **Average Aid Package:** $6,397. **Required Financial Aid Forms:** FAFSA. **Deadline to Apply for Financial Aid:** rolling; February 21 (priority).

Northern Michigan University

Admissions Office, 1401 Presque Isle Avenue, 304 Cohodas Administrative Center, Marquette, MI 49855. **Phone:** (906) 227-2650, (800) 682-9797. **Fax:** (906) 227-1747. **E-mail:** admiss@nmu.edu. **Web Site:** nmu.edu. **In-State Tuition and Fees:** $3,055. **Out-of-State Tuition and Fees:** $5,407. **Room and Board:** $4,468. **Students Receiving Some Form of Aid:** 43%. **Students Receiving Non-Need-Based Aid:** 18%. **Average Aid Package:** $5,266. **Required Financial Aid Forms:** FAFSA. **Deadline to Apply for Financial Aid:** February 21 (priority).

Oakland University

Office of Admissions, 101 North Foundation Hall, Rochester, MI 48309-4401. **Phone:** (800) OAK-UNIV, (248) 370-3360. **Fax:** (248) 370-4462. **E-mail:** ouinfo@oakland.edu. **Web Site:** oakland.edu. **In-State Tuition and Fees:** $4,292. **Out-of-State Tuition and Fees:** $11,686. **Room and Board:** $4,715. **Students Receiving Some Form of Aid:** 27%. **Students Receiving Non-Need-Based Aid:** 5%. **Average Aid Package:** $5,750. **Required Financial Aid Forms:** FAFSA, institutional form. **Deadline to Apply for Financial Aid:** April 1 (priority).

Saginaw Valley State University

Admissions Office, 7400 Bay Road, University Center, MI 48710. **Phone:** (517) 790-4200, (800) 968-9500. **Fax:** (517) 790-0180. **E-mail:** admissions@svsu.edu. **Web Site:** svsu.edu. **In-State Tuition and Fees:** $3,512. **Out-of-State Tuition and Fees:** $7,051. **Room and Board:** $4,800. **Students Receiving Some Form of Aid:** 33%. **Students Receiving Non-Need-Based Aid:** 10%. **Average Aid Package:** $5,565. **Required Financial Aid Forms:** FAFSA. **Deadline to Apply for Financial Aid:** ASAP after January 1.

University of Detroit Mercy

Admissions Office, PO Box 19900, Detroit, MI 48219-0900. **Phone:** (313) 993-1245, (800) 635-5020. **Fax:** (313) 993-3326. **E-mail:** admissions@udmercy.edu. **Web Site:** udmercy.edu. **Tuition and Fees:** $15,000. **Room and Board:** $5,760. **Students Receiving Some Form of Aid:** 48%. **Average Aid Package:** $13,602. **Required Financial Aid Forms:** FAFSA. **Deadline to Apply for Financial Aid:** April 1 (priority).

University of Michigan—Ann Arbor

Office of Undergraduate Admissions, 1220 Student Activities Building, Ann Arbor, MI 48109-1316. **Phone:** (734) 764-7433. **Fax:** (734) 936-0740. **E-mail:** ugadmiss@umich.edu. **Web Site:** umich.edu. **In-State Tuition and Fees:** $6,735. **Out-of-State Tuition and Fees:** $20,455. **Room and Board:** $5,614. **Students Receiving Some Form of Aid:** 37%. **Students Receiving Non-Need-Based Aid:** 22%. **Average Aid Package:** $10,405. **Required Financial Aid Forms:** FAFSA, parent/student 1040 forms. **Deadline to Apply for Financial Aid:** February 15.

University of Michigan—Dearborn*

Admissions Office, 220 SSC, 4901 Evergreen Road, Dearborn, MI 48128-1491. **Phone:** (313) 593-5100. **Fax:** (313) 436-9167. **E-mail:** umdgoblu@umd.umich.edu. **Web Site:** umd.umich.edu. **In-State Tuition and Fees:** $4,664. **Out-of-State Tuition and Fees:** $12,162. **Students Receiving Some Form of Aid:** 20%. **Students Receiving Non-Need-Based Aid:** 3%. **Average Aid Package:** $8,767.

Required Financial Aid Forms: FAFSA. Deadline to Apply for Financial Aid: April 1 (priority).

University of Michigan—Flint

Admissions Office, 303 East Kearsley, Flint, MI 48502-1950. **Phone:** (810) 762-3300. **Fax:** (810) 762-3272. **E-mail:** admissions@flint.umich.edu. **Web Site:** flint.umich.edu. **In-State Tuition and Fees:** $3,800. **Out-of-State Tuition and Fees:** $10,990. **Required Financial Aid Forms:** FAFSA. **Deadline to Apply for Financial Aid:** rolling.

Wayne State University

University Admissions, 3 East Helen N. Joy Building, Detroit, MI 48202. **Phone:** (313) 577-3577. **Fax:** (313) 577-7536. **E-mail:** Admissions@wayne.edu. **Web Site:** wayne.edu. **In-State Tuition and Fees:** $3,818. **Out-of-State Tuition and Fees:** $8,249. **Students Receiving Some Form of Aid:** 34%. **Students Receiving Non-Need-Based Aid:** 17%. **Average Aid Package:** $4,804. **Required Financial Aid Forms:** FAFSA, W2 forms, Federal tax forms. **Deadline to Apply for Financial Aid:** March 1 (priority).

Western Michigan University

Admissions and Orientation, 1201 Oliver Street, Kalamazoo, MI 49009. **Phone:** (616) 387-2000, (800) 400-4968. **Fax:** (616) 387-2096. **E-mail:** ask-wmu@wmich.edu. **Web Site:** wmich.edu. **In-State Tuition and Fees:** $3,944. **Out-of-State Tuition and Fees:** $8,990. **Room and Board:** $4,831. **Students Receiving Some Form of Aid:** 73%. **Students Receiving Non-Need-Based Aid:** 20%. **Average Aid Package:** $4,078. **Required Financial Aid Forms:** FAFSA. **Deadline to Apply for Financial Aid:** January 31 (priority).

MINNESOTA

Augsburg College

Undergraduate Admissions, Campus Box 143, 2211 Riverside Ave., Minneapolis, MN 55454. **Phone:** (612) 330-1001, (800) 788-5678. **Fax:** (612) 330-1590. **E-mail:** admissions@augsburg.edu. **Web Site:** augsburg.edu. **Tuition and Fees:** $16,340. **Room and Board:** $5,320. **Students Receiving Some Form of Aid:** 54%. **Students Receiving Non-Need-Based Aid:** 29%. **Average Aid Package:** $9,428. **Required Financial Aid Forms:** institutional form, FAFSA. **Deadline to Apply for Financial Aid:** August 1; April 15 (priority).

Carleton College

Admissions Office, 100 South College Street, Northfield, MN 55057. **Phone:** (507) 646-4190, (800) 995-2275. **Fax:** (507) 646-4526. **E-mail:** admissions@acs.carleton.edu. **Web Site:** carleton.edu. **Tuition and Fees:** $23,469. **Room and Board:** $4,761. **Students Receiving Some Form of Aid:** 51%. **Students Receiving Non-Need-Based Aid:** 19%. **Average Aid Package:** $18,824. **Required Financial Aid Forms:** FAFSA, CSS Profile, Noncustodial Parent's Statement. **Deadline to Apply for Financial Aid:** February 15.

College of Saint Benedict

Office of Admissions, 37 South College Avenue, Saint Joseph, MN 56374. **Phone:** (320) 363-5308, (800) 544-1489. **Fax:** (320) 363-5010. **E-mail:** admissions@csbsju.edu. **Web Site:** csbsju.edu. **Tuition and Fees:** $16,687. **Room and Board:** $5,272. **Students Receiving Some Form of Aid:** 75%. **Students Receiving Non-Need-Based Aid:** 29%. **Average Aid Package:** $14,488. **Required Financial Aid Forms:** FAFSA, institutional forms, tax forms. **Deadline to Apply for Financial Aid:** rolling.

Concordia College—Moorhead

Admissions Office, 901 South Eightth Street, Moorhead, MN 56562-9981. **Phone:** (218) 299-3004, (800) 699-9897. **Fax:** (218) 299-3947. **E-mail:** admissions@cord.edu. **Web Site:** cord.edu. **Tuition and Fees:** $14,020. **Room and Board:** $3,900. **Students Receiving Some Form of Aid:** 72%. **Students Receiving Non-Need-Based Aid:** 12%. **Average Aid Package:** $11,209. **Required Financial Aid Forms:** FAFSA, Concordia Supplement. **Deadline to Apply for Financial Aid:** May 1 (priority).

Gustavus Adolphus College

Admissions Office, 800 West College Avenue, St. Peter, MN 56082-1498. **Phone:** (507) 933-7676, (800) 487-8288. **Fax:** (507) 933-7474. **E-mail:** admission@gac.edu. **Web Site:** gac.edu. **Tuition and Fees:** $18,250. **Room and Board:** $4,605. **Students Receiving Some Form of Aid:** 65%. **Students Receiving Non-Need-Based Aid:** 22%. **Average Aid Package:** $13,549. **Required Financial Aid Forms:** FAFSA. **Deadline to Apply for Financial Aid:** May 1.

Macalester College

Admissions Office, 1600 Grand Avenue, St. Paul, MN 55105-1899. **Phone:** (651) 696-6357, (800) 231-7974. **Fax:** (651) 696-6724. **E-mail:** admissions@macalester.edu. **Web Site:** macalester.edu. **Tuition and Fees:** $20,688. **Room and Board:** $5,760. **Students Receiving Some Form of Aid:** 77%. **Average Aid Package:** $16,006. **Required Financial Aid Forms:** FAFSA, Financial Aid Profile. **Deadline to Apply for Financial Aid:** April 15.

Minnesota State University—Mankato

Admissions Office, 209 Wigley, Mankato, MN 56001. **Phone:** (507) 389-1822, (800) 722-0544. **Fax:** (507) 389-5114. **E-mail:** admissions@mankato.msus.edu. **Web Site:** mankato.msus.edu. **In-State Tuition and Fees:** $2,996. **Out-of-State Tuition and Fees:** $5,796. **Room and Board:** $3,344. **Students Receiving Some Form of Aid:** 68%. **Students Receiving Non-Need-Based Aid:** 15%. **Average Aid Package:** $5,365. **Required Financial Aid Forms:** FAFSA. **Deadline to Apply for Financial Aid:** rolling; mid-March (priority).

Minnesota State University—Moorhead

Admissions Office, 1104 7th Avenue South, Owens Hall, Moorhead, MN 56563. **Phone:** (218) 236-2161, (800) 593-7246. **Fax:** (218) 236-2168. **E-mail:** dragon@mnscu1.mnstate.edu. **Web Site:** mnstate.edu. **In-State Tuition and Fees:** $2,908. **Out-of-State Tuition and Fees:** $6,020. **Room and Board:** $3,256. **Required Financial Aid Forms:** FAFSA. **Deadline to Apply for Financial Aid:** March 1 (priority).

Northwestern College

Admissions Office, 3003 Snelling Avenue North, St. Paul, MN 55113-1598. **Phone:** (651) 631-5111, (800) 827-6827. **Fax:** (651) 631-5680. **E-mail:** admissions@nwc.edu. **Web Site:** nwc.edu. **Tuition and Fees:** $14,982. **Room and Board:** $4,448. **Students Receiving Some Form of Aid:** 60%. **Students Receiving Non-Need-Based Aid:** 53%. **Average Aid Package:** $12,641. **Required Financial Aid**

Forms: FAFSA, institutional financial aid form. Deadline to Apply for Financial Aid: March 1 (priority).

Saint Cloud State University

Admissions Office, 720 4th Ave. So., St. Cloud, MN 56301-4498. Phone: (320) 255-2244, (800) 369-4260. Fax: (320) 255-2243. E-mail: scsu4u@stcloudstate.edu. Web Site: stcloudstate.edu. In-State Tuition and Fees: $3,555. Out-of-State Tuition and Fees: $6,036. Room and Board: $3,422. Students Receiving Some Form of Aid: 42%. Students Receiving Non-Need-Based Aid: 10%. Average Aid Package: $4,801. Required Financial Aid Forms: FAFSA, institutional forms, FA profile, state aid form, noncustodial parent's statement. Deadline to Apply for Financial Aid: rolling; June 1 (priority).

Saint John's University

Office of Admissions, P.O. Box 7155, Collegeville, MN 56321-7155. Phone: (320) 363-2196, (800) 245-6467. Fax: (320) 363-3206. E-mail: admissions@csbsju.edu. Web Site: csbsju.edu. Tuition and Fees: $16,687. Room and Board: $4,930. Students Receiving Some Form of Aid: 57%. Students Receiving Non-Need-Based Aid: 31%. Average Aid Package: $13,677. Required Financial Aid Forms: FAFSA, institutional forms, tax forms. Deadline to Apply for Financial Aid: March 1 (priority).

Saint Olaf College

Admissions Office, 1520 St. Olaf Avenue, Northfield, MN 55057-1098. Phone: (507) 646-3025, (800) 800-3025. Fax: (507) 646-3832. E-mail: admissions@stolaf.edu. Web Site: stolaf.edu. Tuition and Fees: $19,400. Room and Board: $4,500. Students Receiving Some Form of Aid: 59%. Students Receiving Non-Need-Based Aid: 21%. Average Aid Package: $14,481. Required Financial Aid Forms: FAFSA, StOlaf financial aid form. Deadline to Apply for Financial Aid: March 1 (priority).

Southwest State College

Admissions Office, 1501 State Street, Marshall, MN 56258. Phone: (507) 537-6286. Fax: (507) 537-7154. E-mail: shearerr@southwest.msus.edu. Web Site: southwest.msus.edu. In-State Tuition and Fees: $3,428. Out-of-State Tuition and Fees: $6,924. Room and Board: $3,588. Students Receiving Some Form of Aid: 48%. Required Financial Aid Forms: FAFSA, institution's own form. Deadline to Apply for Financial Aid: rolling.

University of Minnesota—Duluth

Admissions Office, 23 Campus Center, 10 University Drive, Duluth, MN 55812. Phone: (218) 726-7171, (800) 232-1339. Fax: (218) 726-6394. E-mail: umdadmis@d.umn.edu. Web Site: d.umn.edu. In-State Tuition and Fees: $4,054. Out-of-State Tuition and Fees: $10,270. Room and Board: $4,132. Students Receiving Some Form of Aid: 58%. Students Receiving Non-Need-Based Aid: 22%. Average Aid Package: $6,979. Required Financial Aid Forms: FAFSA. Deadline to Apply for Financial Aid: last day of term.

University of Minnesota—Morris

Admissions and Financial Aid, 600 East Fourth Street,105 Behmler Hall, Morris, MN 56267. Phone: (320) 589-6035, (800) 992-8863. Fax: (320) 589-1673. E-mail: admissions@mrs.umn.edu. Web Site: mrs.umn.edu. In-State Tuition and Fees: $5,312. Out-of-State Tuition and Fees: $10,014. Room and Board: $3,910. Students Receiving Some Form of Aid: 72%. Students Receiving Non-Need-Based Aid: 48%. Average Aid Package: $6,496. Required Financial Aid Forms: FAFSA. Deadline to Apply for Financial Aid: March 1.

University of Minnessota—Twin Cities

Office of Admissions, 240 Williamson Hall, 231 Pillsbury Drive SE, Minneapolis, MN 55455-0115. Phone: (612) 625-2008, (800) 752-1000, TTY: (612) 625-9051. Fax: (612) 626-1693. E-mail: admissions@tc.umn.edu. Web Site: umn.edu/tc. In-State Tuition and Fees: $4,649. Out-of-State Tuition and Fees: $12,789. Room and Board: $4,494. Students Receiving Some Form of Aid: 41%. Students Receiving Non-Need-Based Aid: 4%. Average Aid Package: $7,854. Required Financial Aid Forms: FAFSA. Deadline to Apply for Financial Aid: rolling.

University of Saint Thomas

Admissions Office, 2115 Summit Avenue, Mail #32-F1, St. Paul, MN 55105-1096. Phone: (651) 962-6150, (800) 328-6819, ext. 2-6150. Fax: (651) 962-6160. E-mail: admissions@stthomas.edu. Web Site: stthomas.edu. Tuition and Fees: $17,313. Room and Board: $5,407. Students Receiving Some Form of Aid: 52%. Students Receiving Non-Need-Based Aid: 3%. Average Aid Package: $13,310. Required Financial Aid Forms: FAFSA. Deadline to Apply for Financial Aid: April 1 (priority).

Winona State University

Admissions Office, P.O. Box 5838, Winona, MN 55987-5838. Phone: (507) 457-5100, (800) DIAL-WSU, ext. 5100. Fax: (507) 457-5620. E-mail: admissions@vax2.winona.msus.edu. Web Site: winona.msus.edu. In-State Tuition and Fees: $3,300. Out-of-State Tuition and Fees: $6,800. Room and Board: $3,600. Students Receiving Some Form of Aid: 50%. Students Receiving Non-Need-Based Aid: 22%. Average Aid Package: $4,868. Required Financial Aid Forms: FAFSA. Deadline to Apply for Financial Aid: March 1(priority).

MISSISSIPPI

Alcorn State University*

Admissions Office, 1000 ASU Drive #300, Lorman, MS 39096-7500. Phone: (601) 877-6147/6148, (800) 222-6790. Fax: (601) 877-6347. E-mail: ebarnes@alcorn.lorman.edu. Web Site: alcorn.edu. Room and Board: $2,627. Students Receiving Some Form of Aid: 94%. Students Receiving Non-Need-Based Aid: 72%. Average Aid Package: $8,087. Required Financial Aid Forms: FAFSA, institutional form. Deadline to Apply for Financial Aid: April 1.

Delta State University

Admissions Office, Kethley 105, Highway 8, Cleveland, MS 38733. Phone: (662) 846-4018, (800) 468-6378. Fax: (662) 846-4016. E-mail: dheslep@dsu.deltast.edu. Web Site: deltast.edu. In-State Tuition and Fees: $2,596. Out-of-State Tuition and Fees: $5,546. Room and Board: $2,600. Students Receiving Some Form of Aid: 50%. Students Receiving Non-Need-Based Aid: 25%. Average Aid Package: $4,785. Required Financial Aid Forms: FAFSA. Deadline to Apply for Financial Aid: May 1.

Jackson State University

Office of Admissions, 1400 J.R. Lynch Street, P.O. Box 17330, Jackson, MS 39217. **Phone:** (601) 979-2100, (800) 848-6817. **Fax:** (601) 979-3445. **E-mail:** schatman@ccaix.jsums.edu. **Web Site:** jsums.edu. **In-State Tuition and Fees:** $2,688. **Out-of-State Tuition and Fees:** $5,546. **Room and Board:** $3,566. **Required Financial Aid Forms:** FAFSA. **Deadline to Apply for Financial Aid:** rolling.

Millsaps College

Admissions Office, 1701 North State Street, Jackson, MS 39210. **Phone:** (601) 974-1050, (800) 352-1050. **Fax:** (601) 974-1059. **E-mail:** admissions@millsaps.edu. **Web Site:** millsaps.edu. **Tuition and Fees:** $15,029. **Room and Board:** $6,106. **Students Receiving Some Form of Aid:** 57%. **Students Receiving Non-Need-Based Aid:** 14%. **Average Aid Package:** $15,692. **Required Financial Aid Forms:** FAFSA, Institutional form, state aid form. **Deadline to Apply for Financial Aid:** March 1 (priority).

Mississippi College

Admissions Office, P.O. Box 4026, Clinton, MS 39058. **Phone:** (800) 738-1236, (601)925-3240. **Fax:** (601) 925-3804. **E-mail:** admissions@mc.edu. **Web Site:** mc.edu. **Tuition and Fees:** $9,614. **Room and Board:** $4,176. **Students Receiving Some Form of Aid:** 42%. **Students Receiving Non-Need-Based Aid:** 37%. **Average Aid Package:** $12,369. **Required Financial Aid Forms:** FAFSA. **Deadline to Apply for Financial Aid:** March 1 (priority).

Mississippi State University

Admissions Office, P.O. Box 6305, Mississippi State, MS 39762. **Phone:** (662) 325-2224. **Fax:** (662) 325-7360. **E-mail:** admit@admissions.msstate.edu. **Web Site:** msstate.edu. **In-State Tuition and Fees:** $3,017. **Out-of-State Tuition and Fees:** $6,119. **Room and Board:** $4,835. **Students Receiving Some Form of Aid:** 54%. **Students Receiving Non-Need-Based Aid:** 5%. **Average Aid Package:** $5,440. **Required Financial Aid Forms:** FAFSA, scholarship application, state grant/scholarship application. **Deadline to Apply for Financial Aid:** April 1.

Rust College

Admissions Office, 150 Rust Avenue, Holly Springs, MS 38635. **Phone:** (662) 252-8000, ext. 4070, (888) 886-8492, ext. 4065. **Fax:** (662) 252-8895. **E-mail:** ibmcdonald@rustcollege.edu. **Web Site:** rustcollege.edu. **Tuition and Fees:** $5,200. **Room and Board:** $2,400. **Required Financial Aid Forms:** FAFSA, institutional form, FAid transcript-transfer. **Deadline to Apply for Financial Aid:** May 1.

University of Mississippi

Office of Admissions, 145 Martindale Center, PO Box 1848, University, MS 38677. **Phone:** (662) 915-7226, (800) OLE-MISS. **Fax:** (662) 915-5869. **Web Site:** olemiss.edu. **In-State Tuition and Fees:** $3,053. **Out-of-State Tuition and Fees:** $6,155. **Room and Board:** $3,414. **Students Receiving Some Form of Aid:** 35%. **Students Receiving Non-Need-Based Aid:** 22%. **Average Aid Package:** $6,523. **Required Financial Aid Forms:** FAFSA. **Deadline to Apply for Financial Aid:** March 15 (priority).

University of Southern Mississippi*

Admissions Office, Southern Station, Box 5011, Hattiesburg, MS 39406. **Phone:** (601) 266-5000, (601) 266-5006. **Fax:** (601) 266-5816. **Web Site:** usm.edu. **In-State Tuition and Fees:** $2,870. **Out-of-State Tuition and Fees:** $5,972. **Average Aid Package:** $10,361. **Required Financial Aid Forms:** FAFSA. **Deadline to Apply for Financial Aid:** March 15.

MISSOURI

Avila College

Office of Admissions, 11901 Wornall Road, Kansas City, MO 64145. **Phone:** (816) 942-8400, ext. 3500, (800) GO-AVILA. **Fax:** (816) 942-3362. **E-mail:** admissions@mail.avila.edu. **Web Site:** avila.edu. **Tuition and Fees:** $12,720. **Room and Board:** $5,000. **Required Financial Aid Forms:** FAFSA. **Deadline to Apply for Financial Aid:** none.

Central Missouri State University

Admissions Office, Administration Building, Room 104, Warrensburg, MO 64093. **Phone:** (660) 543-4290, (800) SAY-CMSU. **Fax:** (660) 543-8517. **E-mail:** admit@cmsuvmb.cmsu.edu. **Web Site:** cmsu.edu. **In-State Tuition and Fees:** $3,210. **Out-of-State Tuition and Fees:** $6,360. **Room and Board:** $4,230. **Students Receiving Some Form of Aid:** 44%. **Students Receiving Non-Need-Based Aid:** 21%. **Average Aid Package:** $7,975. **Required Financial Aid Forms:** FAFSA, institutional form. **Deadline to Apply for Financial Aid:** rolling.

College of the Ozarks

Office of Admissions, College of the Ozarks, Point Lookout, MO 65726. **Phone:** (417) 334-6411, (800) 222-0525. **Fax:** (417) 335-2618. **E-mail:** admiss4@cofo.edu. **Web Site:** cofo.edu. **Tuition and Fees:** $150 (work study required). **Room and Board:** $2,500. **Students Receiving Some Form of Aid:** 82%. **Students Receiving Non-Need-Based Aid:** 19%. **Average Aid Package:** $10,200. **Required Financial Aid Forms:** FAFSA. **Deadline to Apply for Financial Aid:** March 15 (priority).

Columbia College

Columbia College Admissions, 1001 Rogers Street, Columbia, MO 65216. **Phone:** (573) 875-7352, (800) 231-2391, ext. 7352. **Fax:** (573) 875-7506. **E-mail:** admissions@email.ccis.edu. **Web Site:** ccis.edu. **Tuition and Fees:** $10,102. **Room and Board:** $4,400. **Students Receiving Some Form of Aid:** 24%. **Students Receiving Non-Need-Based Aid:** 13%. **Average Aid Package:** $6,193. **Required Financial Aid Forms:** FAFSA, institutional form.

Culver-Stockton College

Admissions Office, One College Hill, Canton, MO 63435. **Phone:** (217) 231-6331, (800) 537-1883. **Fax:** (217) 231-6611. **E-mail:** enrollment@culver.edu. **Web Site:** culver.edu. **Tuition and Fees:** $10,650. **Room and Board:** $4,750. **Students Receiving Some Form of Aid:** 72%. **Students Receiving Non-Need-Based Aid:** 27%. **Average Aid Package:** $8,378. **Required Financial Aid Forms:** FAFSA. **Deadline to Apply for Financial Aid:** June 15.

Drury University

Office of Admissions, 900 North Benton Avenue, Springfield, MO 65802. **Phone:** (417) 873-7205, (800) 922-2274. **Fax:** (417) 866-3873. **E-mail:** druryad@drury.edu. **Web Site:** drury.edu. **Tuition and Fees:** $10,795. **Room and Board:** $4,004. **Students Receiving Some

Form of Aid: 84%. Students Receiving Non-Need-Based Aid: 82%. Average Aid Package: $7,983. Required Financial Aid Forms: FAFSA, Drury financial aid form. Deadline to Apply for Financial Aid: February.

Lindenwood College*

Office of Admissions, 209 S. Kings Highway, St. Charles, MO 63301. Phone: (636) 949-4949. E-mail: admissions@lindenwood.edu. Web Site: lindenwood.edu. Tuition and Fees: $10,200. Room and Board: $5,000. Required Financial Aid Forms: FAFSA. Deadline to Apply for Financial Aid: April 1.

Maryville University of Saint Louis

Office of Admissions, 13550 Conway Road, St. Louis, MO 63141-7299. Phone: (314) 529-9350, (800) 627-9855. Fax: (314) 529-9927. E-mail: admissions@maryville.edu. Web Site: maryville.edu. Tuition and Fees: $13,000. Room and Board: $5,600. Students Receiving Some Form of Aid: 33%. Students Receiving Non-Need-Based Aid: 17%. Average Aid Package: $10,279. Required Financial Aid Forms: institutional form. Deadline to Apply for Financial Aid: April 1 (priority).

Missouri Southern State College

Admissions Office, 3950 East Newman Road, Joplin, MO 64801-1595. Phone: (417) 782-6772, (800) 606-MSSC. Fax: (417) 659-4429. E-mail: admissions@mail.mssc.edu. Web Site: mssc.edu. In-State Tuition and Fees: $2,496. Out-of-State Tuition and Fees: $4,866. Room and Board: $3,610. Students Receiving Some Form of Aid: 52%. Students Receiving Non-Need-Based Aid: 18%. Average Aid Package: $3,354. Required Financial Aid Forms: FAFSA. Deadline to Apply for Financial Aid: February 15 (priority).

Missouri Valley College

Admissions Office, 500 East College, Marshall, MO 65340. Phone: (660) 831-4114. Fax: (660) 831-4039. E-mail: naylorj@moval.edu. Web Site: moval.edu. Tuition and Fees: $11,950. Room and Board: $5,000. Required Financial Aid Forms: FAFSA. Deadline to Apply for Financial Aid: March 1 (priority).

Missouri Western State College

Admissions Office, 4525 Downs Drive, St. Joseph, MO 64507. Phone: (816) 271-4266, (800) 622-7041. E-mail: admissn@giffon.mwsc.edu. Web Site: mwsc.edu. In-State Tuition and Fees: $2,774. Out-of-State Tuition and Fees: $4,982. Room and Board: $3,600. Required Financial Aid Forms: FAFSA. Deadline to Apply for Financial Aid: April 1.

Northwest Missouri State University

Mabel Cook Admissions and Visitor's Center, 800 University Drive, Maryville, MO 64468. Phone: (660) 562-1562, (800) 633-1175. Fax: (660) 562-1121. E-mail: admissions@mail.nwmissouri.edu. Web Site: nwmissouri.edu. In-State Tuition and Fees: $3,285. Out-of-State Tuition and Fees: $5,543. Room and Board: $4,150. Students Receiving Some Form of Aid: 78%. Students Receiving Non-Need-Based Aid: 23%. Average Aid Package: $5,000. Required Financial Aid Forms: FAFSA. Deadline to Apply for Financial Aid: rolling.

Rockhurst University

Admissions Office, 1100 Rockhurst Road, Kansas City, MO 64110-2561. Phone: (816) 501-4100. Fax: (816) 501-4241. E-mail: admissions@rockhurst.edu. Web Site: rockhurst.edu. Tuition and Fees: $12,940. Room and Board: $4,870. Students Receiving Some Form of Aid: 9%. Students Receiving Non-Need-Based Aid: 8%. Average Aid Package: $13,277. Required Financial Aid Forms: FAFSA, Institutional form. Deadline to Apply for Financial Aid: April 1.

Saint Louis College of Pharmacy

Admissions Office, 4588 Parkview Place, St. Louis, MO 63110. Phone: (314) 367-8700, ext. 1065, (800) 278-5267. Fax: (314) 367-2784. E-mail: admissions@stlcop.edu. Web Site: stlcop.edu. Tuition and Fees: $12,935. Room and Board: $5,110. Students Receiving Some Form of Aid: 87%. Students Receiving Non-Need-Based Aid: 42%. Average Aid Package: $13,580. Required Financial Aid Forms: FAFSA, institutional application. Deadline to Apply for Financial Aid: May 1.

Saint Louis University

Admissions Office, 221 North Grand Boulevard, St. Louis, MO 63103. Phone: (314) 977-2500, (800) SLU -4-U. Fax: (314) 977-7136. E-mail: admitme@slu.edu. Web Site: slu.edu. Tuition and Fees: $17,268. Room and Board: $5,900. Students Receiving Some Form of Aid: 45%. Students Receiving Non-Need-Based Aid: 33%. Average Aid Package: $23,224. Required Financial Aid Forms: FAFSA. Deadline to Apply for Financial Aid: June 1.

Southeast Missouri State University

Office of Admissions, One University Plaza, Mailstop 3550, Cape Girardeau, MO 63701. Phone: (573) 651-2590. Fax: (573) 651-2255. E-mail: s333rec@stmovm.stmo.edu. Web Site: stmo.edu. In-State Tuition and Fees: $2,345. Out-of-State Tuition and Fees: $5,805. Room and Board: $4,267. Students Receiving Some Form of Aid: 44%. Students Receiving Non-Need-Based Aid: 11%. Average Aid Package: $5,268. Required Financial Aid Forms: FAFSA. Deadline to Apply for Financial Aid: March 1 (priority).

Southwest Missouri State University

Admissions Office, 901 South National, Springfield, MO 65804-0094. Phone: (417) 836-5517, (800) 492-7900. Fax: (417) 836-6334. E-mail: smsuinfo@mail.smsu.edu. Web Site: smsu.edu. In-State Tuition and Fees: $3,564. Out-of-State Tuition and Fees: $6,744. Room and Board: $3,846. Students Receiving Some Form of Aid: 42%. Students Receiving Non-Need-Based Aid: 12%. Average Aid Package: $7,000. Required Financial Aid Forms: FAFSA. Deadline to Apply for Financial Aid: March 31 (priority).

Truman State University

Office of Admission, McClain Hall 205, 100 East Normal, Kirksville, MO 63501. Phone: (660) 785-4114, (800) 892-7792 (in-state). Fax: (660) 785-7456. E-mail: admissions@truman.edu. Web Site: truman.edu. In-State Tuition and Fees: $3,712. Out-of-State Tuition and Fees: $6,696. Room and Board: $4,452. Students Receiving Some Form of Aid: 33%. Students Receiving Non-Need-Based Aid: 20%. Average Aid Package: $5,200.

Required Financial Aid Forms: FAFSA. Deadline to Apply for Financial Aid: April 1 (priority).

University of Missouri—Columbia

Admissions Office, 230 Jesse Hall, Columbia, MO 65211. Phone: (573) 882-7786, (800) 225-6075. Fax: (573) 882-7887. E-mail: MU4U@missouri.edu. Web Site: missouri.edu. In-State Tuition and Fees: $4,726. Out-of-State Tuition and Fees: $12,895. Room and Board: $3,815. Required Financial Aid Forms: FAFSA. Deadline to Apply for Financial Aid: March 1.

University of Missouri—Kansas City*

Admissions Office, 5100 Rockhill Road, 101 AC, Kansas City, MO 64110. Phone: (816) 235-1111. Fax: (816) 235-5544. E-mail: admit@umkc.edu. Web Site: umkc.edu. In-State Tuition and Fees: $3,852. Out-of-State Tuition and Fees: $10,387. Room and Board: $4,865. Students Receiving Some Form of Aid: 38%. Students Receiving Non-Need-Based Aid: 19%. Average Aid Package: $11,920. Required Financial Aid Forms: FAFSA. Deadline to Apply for Financial Aid: March 15 (priority).

University of Missouri—Rolla

Admissions Office, 106 Parker Hall, 1870 Miner Circle, Rolla, MO 65409-1060. Phone: (573) 341-4164, (800) 522-0938. Fax: (573) 341-4082. E-mail: umrolla@umr.edu. Web Site: umr.edu. In-State Tuition and Fees: $4,805. Out-of-State Tuition and Fees: $12,974. Room and Board: $4,838. Students Receiving Some Form of Aid: 50%. Students Receiving Non-Need-Based Aid: 8%. Average Aid Package: $8,067. Required Financial Aid Forms: FAFSA. Deadline to Apply for Financial Aid: March 1 (priority).

University of Missouri—St. Louis

Office of Admissions, 8001 Natural Bridge Road, St. Louis, MO 63121-4499. Phone: (314) 516-5451, (314) 516-5000. Fax: (314) 516-5310. E-mail: curt_coonrod@ccmail.umsl.edu. Web Site: umsl.edu. In-State Tuition and Fees: $4,796. Out-of-State Tuition and Fees: $12,710. Room and Board: $4,000. Required Financial Aid Forms: FAFSA. Deadline to Apply for Financial Aid: April 1.

Washington University in St. Louis

Admissions Office, Campus Box 1089, One Brookings Drive, St. Louis, MO 63130-4899. Phone: (314) 935-6000, (800) 638-0700. Fax: (314) 935-4290. E-mail: admissions@wustl.edu. Web Site: wustl.edu. Tuition and Fees: $24,745. Room and Board: $7,724. Students Receiving Some Form of Aid: 46%. Students Receiving Non-Need-Based Aid: 11%. Average Aid Package: $20,679. Required Financial Aid Forms: FAFSA, CSS, 1040 tax return. Deadline to Apply for Financial Aid: February 15; November 1 (early decision).

Webster University

Admissions Office, 8356 Big Bend Boulevard, St. Louis, MO 63119-3194. Phone: (314) 968-6991, (800) 75-ENROL. Fax: (314) 968-7115. E-mail: admit@websteruniv.edu. Web Site: webster.edu. Tuition and Fees: $12,150. Room and Board: $5,440. Students Receiving Some Form of Aid: 41%. Students Receiving Non-Need-Based Aid: 24%. Average Aid Package: $12,709. Required Financial Aid Forms: FAFSA, institutional form. Deadline to Apply for Financial Aid: April 1 (priority).

Westminster College

Office of Enrollment Services, 501 Westminster Avenue, Fulton, MO 65251-1299. Phone: (573) 592-5251, (800) 475-3361. Fax: (573) 592-5255. E-mail: admissions@jaynet.wcmo.edu. Web Site: wcmo.edu. Tuition and Fees: $14,300. Room and Board: $5,020. Students Receiving Some Form of Aid: 55%. Students Receiving Non-Need-Based Aid: 9%. Average Aid Package: $12,400. Required Financial Aid Forms: FAFSA. Deadline to Apply for Financial Aid: February 28 (priority).

William Jewell College

Admission Office, 500 College Hill, Liberty, MO 64068. Phone: (816) 781-7700 ext. 5137, (800) 753-7009. Fax: (816) 415-5027. E-mail: admissions@william.jewell.edu. Web Site: jewell.edu. Tuition and Fees: $13,020. Room and Board: $4,010. Students Receiving Some Form of Aid: 55%. Required Financial Aid Forms: FAFSA, institutional forms. Deadline to Apply for Financial Aid: March 1 (priority).

William Woods University

Office of Admission, 200 West Twelfth Street, Fulton, MO 65251-1098. Phone: (573) 592-4221, (800) 995-3159. Fax: (573) 592-1146. E-mail: admissions@iris.wmwoods.edu. Web Site: williamwoods.edu. Tuition and Fees: $13,350. Room and Board: $5,600. Average Aid Package: $9,000. Required Financial Aid Forms: FAFSA. Deadline to Apply for Financial Aid: March 1 (preferred).

MONTANA

Carroll College

Admissions Office, 1601 North Benton Avenue, Helena, MT 59625. Phone: (406) 447-4384. Fax: (406) 447-4533. E-mail: enroll@carroll.edu. Web Site: carroll.edu. Tuition and Fees: $11,978. Room and Board: $4,716. Students Receiving Some Form of Aid: 54%. Students Receiving Non-Need-Based Aid: 44%. Average Aid Package: $10,696. Required Financial Aid Forms: FAFSA. Deadline to Apply for Financial Aid: July 1.

Montana State University

New Student Services, P.O. Box 172190, Bozeman, MT 59717-2190. Phone: (406) 994-2452, (888) 678-2287. Fax: (406) 994-1923. E-mail: admissions@montana.edu. Web Site: montana.edu. In-State Tuition and Fees: $2,965. Out-of-State Tuition and Fees: $8,715. Room and Board: $4,650. Students Receiving Some Form of Aid: 44%. Students Receiving Non-Need-Based Aid: 2%. Average Aid Package: $6,141. Required Financial Aid Forms: FAFSA. Deadline to Apply for Financial Aid: rolling; March 1 (priority).

Montana State University—Billings

Admissions Office, 1500 North 30th Street, Billings, MT 59101-2302. Phone: (406) 657-2158, (800) 656-MSU-B. Fax: (406) 657-2302. E-mail: keverett@msubillings.edu. Web Site: msubillings.edu. In-State Tuition and Fees: $2,922. Out-of-State Tuition and Fees: $7,885. Room and Board: $4,200. Required Financial

Aid Forms: FAFSA, institutional forms, federal tax forms. Deadline to Apply for Financial Aid: March 1.

Rocky Mountain College

Office of Admissions, 1511 Poly Drive, Billings, MT 59102-1796. Phone: (406) 657-1026, (800) 877-6259. Fax: (406) 259-9751. E-mail: admissions@rocky.edu. Web Site: rocky.edu. Tuition and Fees: $12,243. Room and Board: $4,147. Students Receiving Some Form of Aid: 72%. Students Receiving Non-Need-Based Aid: 5%. Average Aid Package: $10,387. Required Financial Aid Forms: FAFSA, institutional forms. Deadline to Apply for Financial Aid: rolling; April 1 (priority).

University of Montana—Missoula

Admissions and New Student Services, Lodge 103, Missoula, MT 59812-0002. Phone: (406) 243-6266, (800) 462-8636. Fax: (406) 243-5711. E-mail: admiss@selway.umt.edu. Web Site: umt.edu. In-State Tuition and Fees: $2,910. Out-of-State Tuition and Fees: $8,020. Room and Board: $4,400. Students Receiving Some Form of Aid: 41%. Students Receiving Non-Need-Based Aid: 2%. Required Financial Aid Forms: FAFSA, UMinformation. Deadline to Apply for Financial Aid: March 1.

Western Montana College of the University of Montana

Admissions Office, 710 South Atlantic, Dillon, MT 59725. Phone: (406) 683-7331, (800) 962-6668. Fax: (406) 683-7493. E-mail: admissions@wmc.edu. Web Site: wmc.edu. In-State Tuition and Fees: $2,460. Out-of-State Tuition and Fees: $7,426. Room and Board: $3,960. Students Receiving Some Form of Aid: 62%. Students Receiving Non-Need-Based Aid: 36%. Average Aid Package: $5,728. Required Financial Aid Forms: FAFSA. Deadline to Apply for Financial Aid: March 1.

NEBRASKA

Bellevue University

Admissions Office, 1000 Galvin Road South, Bellevue, NE 68005-3098. Phone: (402) 293-3766, (800) 756-7920, ext. 2030. Fax: (402) 293-3730. E-mail: bellevue-u@scholars.bellevue.edu. Web Site: bellevue.edu. Tuition and Fees: $3,990. Students Receiving Some Form of Aid: 75%. Students Receiving Non-Need-Based Aid: 56%. Average Aid Package: $7,131. Required Financial Aid Forms: FAFSA. Deadline to Apply for Financial Aid: rolling.

Chadron State College

Admissions Office, 1000 Main Street, Chadron, NE 69337. Phone: , (800) 242-3766. Fax: (308) 432-6229. E-mail: inquire@csc.edu. Web Site: csc.edu. In-State Tuition and Fees: $2,263. Out-of-State Tuition and Fees: $4,138. Room and Board: $3,300. Required Financial Aid Forms: FAFSA. Deadline to Apply for Financial Aid: July 1.

Concordia University

Admissions Office, 800 North Columbia Avenue, Seward, NE 68434. Phone: (402) 643-7233, (800) 535-5494. Fax: (402) 643-4073. E-mail: admiss@seward.cune.edu. Web Site: cune.edu. Tuition and Fees: $11,876. Room and Board: $3,938. Students Receiving Some Form of Aid: 25%. Students Receiving Non-Need-Based Aid: 4%. Average Aid Package: $13,133. Required Financial Aid Forms: FAFSA, institutional form. Deadline to Apply for Financial Aid: rolling.

Creighton University

Admissions Office, 2500 California Plaza, Omaha, NE 68178-0055. Phone: (402) 280-2703, (800) 282-5835. Fax: (402) 280-2685. E-mail: admissions@creighton.edu. Web Site: creighton.edu. Tuition and Fees: $14,910. Room and Board: $5,782. Students Receiving Some Form of Aid: 12%. Students Receiving Non-Need-Based Aid: 5%. Average Aid Package: $11,979. Required Financial Aid Forms: FAFSA. Deadline to Apply for Financial Aid: April 1.

Doane College

Admissions Office, 1014 Boswell Avenue, Crete, NE 68333. Phone: (402) 826-8222, (800) 333-6263. Fax: (402) 826-8600. E-mail: dkunzman@doane.edu. Web Site: doane.edu. Tuition and Fees: $12,280. Room and Board: $3,730. Students Receiving Some Form of Aid: 51%. Average Aid Package: $11,161. Required Financial Aid Forms: institutional form. Deadline to Apply for Financial Aid: March 1 (priority).

Hastings College

Admissions Office, 800 N. Turner Ave., Hastings, NE 68901. Phone: (402) 461-7316, (800) 532-7642. Fax: (402) 461-7490. E-mail: admissions@hastings.edu. Web Site: hastings.edu. Tuition and Fees: $12,418. Room and Board: $3,986. Students Receiving Some Form of Aid: 73%. Students Receiving Non-Need-Based Aid: 67%. Average Aid Package: $10,292. Required Financial Aid Forms: FAFSA, institutional form. Deadline to Apply for Financial Aid: September 1.

Midland Lutheran College

Admissions Office, 900 North Clarkson, Fremont, NE 68025. Phone: (402) 721-5480, (800) 642-8382. Fax: (402) 721-0250. Web Site: mlc.edu. Tuition and Fees: $13,940. Room and Board: $3,760. Required Financial Aid Forms: FAFSA. Deadline to Apply for Financial Aid: April 1.

Nebraska Wesleyan University

Admissions Office, 5000 St. Paul Avenue, Lincoln, NE 68504. Phone: (402) 466-2371, (800) 541-3818. Fax: (402) 465-2179. E-mail: admissions@nebrwesleyan.edu. Web Site: nebrwesleyan.edu. Tuition and Fees: $12,906. Room and Board: $3,890. Students Receiving Some Form of Aid: 64%. Students Receiving Non-Need-Based Aid: 4%. Average Aid Package: $9,822. Required Financial Aid Forms: FAFSA.

Peru State College

Office of Admissions, P.O. Box 10, Peru, NE 68421-0010. Phone: (402) 872-2221, (800) 742-4412. Fax: (402) 872-2296. E-mail: admissions@bobcat.peru.edu. Web Site: peru.edu. In-State Tuition and Fees: $2,251. Out-of-State Tuition and Fees: $4,126. Room and Board: $3,192. Required Financial Aid Forms: FAFSA, institutional forms. Deadline to Apply for Financial Aid: March 1.

University of Nebraska—Kearney

Admissions Office, MSAB, Kearney, NE 68849. Phone: (308) 865-8526. Fax: (308) 865-8987. E-mail: admissionsug@unk.edu. Web Site: unk.edu. In-State Tuition and Fees: $2,728. Out-of-State Tuition and Fees: $4,581. Room and Board: $3,430. Required Financial Aid Forms: FAFSA, institutional form. Deadline to Apply for Financial Aid: March 1.

University of Nebraska—Lincoln

Office of Admissions, 1410 Q Street, Lincoln, NE 68588-0417. **Phone:** (402) 472-2023, (800) 742-8800. **Fax:** (402) 472-0670. **E-mail:** nuhusker@unl.edu. **Web Site:** unl.edu. **In-State Tuition and Fees:** $3,278. **Out-of-State Tuition and Fees:** $7,785. **Room and Board:** $4,070. **Students Receiving Some Form of Aid:** 40%. **Students Receiving Non-Need-Based Aid:** 2%. **Average Aid Package:** $5,394. **Required Financial Aid Forms:** FAFSA. **Deadline to Apply for Financial Aid:** rolling.

University of Nebraska—Omaha

Admissions Office, 60th and Dodge Streets, Omaha, NE 68182. **Phone:** (402) 554-2393. **Fax:** (402) 554-3472. **E-mail:** unoadm@unomaha.edu. **Web Site:** unomaha.edu. **In-State Tuition and Fees:** $2,823. **Out-of-State Tuition and Fees:** $6,888. **Students Receiving Some Form of Aid:** 24%. **Students Receiving Non-Need-Based Aid:** 17%. **Required Financial Aid Forms:** FAFSA. **Deadline to Apply for Financial Aid:** March 1 (priority date).

Wayne State College

Admissions Office, 1111 Main Street, Wayne, NE 68787. **Phone:** (402) 375-7234, (800) 228-9972. **Fax:** (402) 375-7204. **E-mail:** wscadmit@wscgate.wsc.edu. **Web Site:** wsc.edu. **In-State Tuition and Fees:** $2,265. **Out-of-State Tuition and Fees:** $4,140. **Room and Board:** $3,310. **Students Receiving Some Form of Aid:** 52%. **Students Receiving Non-Need-Based Aid:** 7%. **Average Aid Package:** $3,066. **Required Financial Aid Forms:** FAFSA. **Deadline to Apply for Financial Aid:** rolling.

NEVADA

University of Nevada—Las Vegas

Admissions Office, 4505 Maryland Parkway, Las Vegas, NV 89154. **Phone:** (702) 895-3443. **Fax:** (702) 895-1118. **E-mail:** unrgradadmision@ccmail.nevada.edu. **Web Site:** unlv.edu. **In-State Tuition and Fees:** $2,386. **Out-of-State Tuition and Fees:** $9,366. **Room and Board:** $5,694. **Students Receiving Some Form of Aid:** 26%. **Students Receiving Non-Need-Based Aid:** 11%. **Average Aid Package:** $6,765. **Required Financial Aid Forms:** FAFSA. **Deadline to Apply for Financial Aid:** February 1 (priority).

University of Nevada—Reno

Admissions and Records, Mail Stop 120, Reno, NV 89557. **Phone:** (775) 784-6865. **Fax:** (775) 784-4283. **E-mail:** unrug@unr.edu. **Web Site:** unr.edu. **In-State Tuition and Fees:** $2,454. **Out-of-State Tuition and Fees:** $9,434. **Room and Board:** $5,400. **Students Receiving Some Form of Aid:** 18%. **Students Receiving Non-Need-Based Aid:** 9%. **Average Aid Package:** $9,500. **Required Financial Aid Forms:** FAFSA. **Deadline to Apply for Financial Aid:** February 1.

NEW HAMPSHIRE

Dartmouth College

Office of Undergraduate Admissions, 6016 McNutt Hall, Hanover, NH 03755. **Phone:** (603) 646-2875. **Fax:** (603) 646-1216. **E-mail:** admissions.office@dartmouth.edu. **Web Site:** dartmouth.edu. **Tuition and Fees:** $25,653. **Room and Board:** $7,557. **Students Receiving Some Form of Aid:** 48%. **Average Aid Package:** $23,331. **Required Financial Aid Forms:** FAFSA, CSS Profile, Parent's 1999 federal income tax return, Student's 1999 federal income tax return, Noncustodial Parent's Statement and 1999 federal income tax return if parents are divorced, Business/Farm supplement if parents own a farm or business. **Deadline to Apply for Financial Aid:** February 1.

Franklin Pierce College

Admissions Office, College Road, Box 60, Rindge, NH 03461-0060. **Phone:** (603) 899-4050, (800) 437-0048. **Fax:** (603) 899-4394. **E-mail:** admissions@fpc.edu. **Web Site:** fpc.edu. **Tuition and Fees:** $18,985. **Room and Board:** $6,250. **Students Receiving Some Form of Aid:** 92%. **Students Receiving Non-Need-Based Aid:** 6%. **Average Aid Package:** $14,769. **Required Financial Aid Forms:** FAFSA. **Deadline to Apply for Financial Aid:** rolling.

Keene State College

KSC Admissions, Elliot Hall, 229 Main Street, Keene, NH 03435-2604. **Phone:** (603) 358-2276, (800) KSC-1909. **Fax:** (603) 358-2767. **E-mail:** admissions@keene.edu. **Web Site:** keene.edu. **In-State Tuition and Fees:** $5,026. **Out-of-State Tuition and Fees:** $10,336. **Room and Board:** $4,938. **Students Receiving Some Form of Aid:** 53%. **Students Receiving Non-Need-Based Aid:** 13%. **Average Aid Package:** $6,923. **Required Financial Aid Forms:** FAFSA, income tax forms. **Deadline to Apply for Financial Aid:** March 1 (priority).

New England College*

Office of Admission, 26 Bridge Street, Henniker, NH 03242-3297. **Phone:** (603) 428-2223, (800) 521-7642. **Fax:** (603) 428-7230. **E-mail:** admis@nec1.nec.edu. **Web Site:** nec.edu. **Tuition and Fees:** $17,040. **Room and Board:** $3,110. **Required Financial Aid Forms:** FAFSA. **Deadline to Apply for Financial Aid:** March 1.

New Hampshire College

Office of Admissions, 2500 North River Road, Manchester, NH 03106. **Phone:** (603) 645-9611, (800) NHC-4YOU. **Fax:** (603) 645-9693. **E-mail:** admission@nhc.edu. **Web Site:** nhc.edu. **Tuition and Fees:** $15,848. **Room and Board:** $6,790. **Required Financial Aid Forms:** FAFSA. **Deadline to Apply for Financial Aid:** December 15 (priority).

Plymouth State College

Admission Office, MSC #52, 17 High Street, Plymouth, NH 03264-1595. **Phone:** (800) 842-6900, (603) 535-2237. **Fax:** (603) 535-2714. **E-mail:** pscadmit@mail.plymouth.edu. **Web Site:** plymouth.edu. **In-State Tuition and Fees:** $5,032. **Out-of-State Tuition and Fees:** $10,342. **Room and Board:** $5,030. **Students Receiving Some Form of Aid:** 58%. **Students Receiving Non-Need-Based Aid:** 5%. **Average Aid Package:** $7,005. **Required Financial Aid Forms:** FAFSA. **Deadline to Apply for Financial Aid:** March 1.

Saint Anselm College

Admissions Office, 100 Saint Anselm Drive, Manchester, NH 03102-1310. **Phone:** (603) 641-7500, (888) 426-7356. **Fax:** (603) 641-7550. **E-mail:** admissions@anselm.edu. **Web Site:** anselm.edu. **Tuition and Fees:** $18,950. **Room and Board:** $7,000. **Students Receiving Some Form of Aid:** 83%. **Students Receiving Non-Need-Based Aid:** 33%. **Average Aid Package:** $13,048. **Required Financial Aid Forms:** FAFSA Profile. **Deadline to Apply for Financial Aid:** April 15; March 1 (priority).

University of New Hampshire

Admissions Office, Grant House, 4 Garrison Avenue, Durham, NH 03824. Phone: (603) 862-1360. Fax: (603) 862-0077. E-mail: admissions@unh.edu. Web Site: unh.edu. In-State Tuition and Fees: $7,395. Out-of-State Tuition and Fees: $16,465. Room and Board: $5,154. Students Receiving Some Form of Aid: 51%. Students Receiving Non-Need-Based Aid: 2%. Average Aid Package: $10,405. Required Financial Aid Forms: FAFSA. Deadline to Apply for Financial Aid: March 1 (priority).

NEW JERSEY

Bloomfield College

Admissions Office, One Park Place, Bloomfield, NJ 07003. Phone: (973) 748-9000, ext. 230, (800) 848-4555. Fax: (973) 748-0916. E-mail: admission@bloomfield.edu. Web Site: bloomfield.edu. Tuition and Fees: $10,450. Room and Board: $5,150. Students Receiving Some Form of Aid: 62%. Students Receiving Non-Need-Based Aid: 4%. Average Aid Package: $9,841. Required Financial Aid Forms: FAFSA, institutional form. Deadline to Apply for Financial Aid: June 1 (priority).

College of New Jersey

Office of Admissions, P.O. Box 7718, Ewing, NJ 08628-0718. Phone: (609) 771-2131, (800) 624-0967. Fax: (609) 637-5174. E-mail: admiss@vm.tcnj.edu. Web Site: tcnj.edu. In-State Tuition and Fees: $5,685. Out-of-State Tuition and Fees: $9,002. Room and Board: $6,330. Students Receiving Some Form of Aid: 70%. Students Receiving Non-Need-Based Aid: 27%. Average Aid Package: $6,000. Required Financial Aid Forms: FAFSA, institutional form. Deadline to Apply for Financial Aid: April 1.

Drew University

Office of College Admissions. , Madison, NJ 07940-1493. Phone: (973) 408-DREW. Fax: (973) 408-3068. E-mail: cadm@drew.edu. Web Site: drew.edu. Tuition and Fees: $23,008. Room and Board: $6,564. Students Receiving Some Form of Aid: 51%. Students Receiving Non-Need-Based Aid: 7%. Average Aid Package: $20,137. Required Financial Aid Forms: FAFSA and CSS Profile. Deadline to Apply for Financial Aid: February 15.

Fairleigh Dickinson University*

Admissions Office, 1000 River Road, Teaneck, NJ 07666. Phone: (201) 692-2000, (800) 338-8803. Fax: (201) 692-7319. E-mail: info@admit.fdu.edu. Web Site: fdu.edu. Tuition and Fees: $15,800. Room and Board: $6,536. Required Financial Aid Forms: FAFSA. Deadline to Apply for Financial Aid: March 15.

Kean University

Admissions Office, Kean University, Union, NJ 07083. Phone: (908) 527-2195. Fax: (908) 355-5143. Web Site: kean.edu. In-State Tuition and Fees: $4,383. Out-of-State Tuition and Fees: $6,080. Room and Board: $5,530. Required Financial Aid Forms: FAFSA. Deadline to Apply for Financial Aid: rolling.

Monmouth University

Office of Admission, 400 Cedar Avenue, West Long Branch, NJ 07764-1898. Phone: (732) 571-3456, (800) 543-9671. Fax: (732) 263-5166. E-mail: admission@monmouth.edu. Web Site: monmouth.edu. Tuition and Fees: $15,686. Room and Board: $6,682. Students Receiving Some Form of Aid: 56%. Students Receiving Non-Need-Based Aid: 47%. Average Aid Package: $11,181. Required Financial Aid Forms: FAFSA. Deadline to Apply for Financial Aid: rolling.

Montclair State University*

Admissions Office, Russ Hall, Upper Montclair, NJ 07043-1624. Phone: (973) 655-4444, (800) 331-9205. Fax: (973) 655-7700. E-mail: msuadm@saturn.montclair.edu. Web Site: montclair.edu. In-State Tuition and Fees: $4,050. Out-of-State Tuition and Fees: $5,846. Room and Board: $6,054. Students Receiving Some Form of Aid: 35%. Students Receiving Non-Need-Based Aid: 19%. Average Aid Package: $7,495. Required Financial Aid Forms: FAFSA. Deadline to Apply for Financial Aid: March 1.

New Jersey City University

Admissions Office, 2039 Kennedy Memorial Boulevard, Jersey City, NJ 07305-1597. Phone: (201) 200-3234, (888) 441-JCSC. Fax: (201) 200-2044. E-mail: admissions@njcu.edu. Web Site: njcu.edu. In-State Tuition and Fees: $3,893. Out-of-State Tuition and Fees: $7,081. Room and Board: $5,200. Required Financial Aid Forms: FAFSA. Deadline to Apply for Financial Aid: April 15.

New Jersey Institute of Technology

Admissions Office, University Heights, Newark, NJ 07102-9938. Phone: (973) 596-3300, (800) 222-NJIT. Fax: (973) 802-1854. E-mail: admissions@admin.njit.edu. Web Site: njit.edu. In-State Tuition and Fees: $6,472. Out-of-State Tuition and Fees: $10,816. Room and Board: $7,050. Students Receiving Some Form of Aid: 60%. Students Receiving Non-Need-Based Aid: 21%. Average Aid Package: $9,445. Required Financial Aid Forms: FAFSA. Deadline to Apply for Financial Aid: March 15 (priority).

Princeton University

Admissions Office, Princeton University, Princeton, NJ 08544-0430. Phone: (609) 258-3060. Fax: (609) 258-6743. Web Site: princeton.edu. Tuition and Fees: $25,805. Room and Board: $7,206. Students Receiving Some Form of Aid: 39%. Average Aid Package: $21,800. Required Financial Aid Forms: FAFSA, institutional form, CSS Profile. Deadline to Apply for Financial Aid: February 1.

Ramapo College of New Jersey

Office of Admissions, 505 Ramapo Valley Road, Mahwah, NJ 07430-1680. Phone: (201) 684-7300, (800) 9 RAMAPO. Fax: (201) 684-7508. E-mail: admissions@ramapo.edu. Web Site: ramapo.edu. In-State Tuition and Fees: $5,180. Out-of-State Tuition and Fees: $8,046. Room and Board: $6,624. Students Receiving Some Form of Aid: 27%. Students Receiving Non-Need-Based Aid: 3%. Average Aid Package: $5,594. Required Financial Aid Forms: FAFSA. Deadline to Apply for Financial Aid: rolling.

Richard Stockton College of New Jersey

Admissions Office, Jim Leeds Road, P.O. Box 195, Pomona, NJ 08240. Phone: (609) 652-4261. Fax: (609) 748-5541. E-mail: admissions@pollux.stockton.edu. In-State Tuition and Fees: $4,400. Out-of-State Tuition and Fees: $6,432. Room and Board: $5,368.

Students Receiving Some Form of Aid: 55%. Students Receiving Non-Need-Based Aid: 9%. Average Aid Package: $7,980. Required Financial Aid Forms: FAFSA. Deadline to Apply for Financial Aid: March 1 (priority).

Rider University

Admissions Office, 2083 Lawrenceville Road, Lawrenceville, NJ 08648-3099. Phone: (609) 896-5042, (800) 257-9026. Fax: (609) 895-6645. E-mail: admissions@rider.edu. Web Site: rider.edu. Tuition and Fees: $17,450. Room and Board: $7,080. Students Receiving Some Form of Aid: 57%. Students Receiving Non-Need-Based Aid: 25%. Average Aid Package: $14,637. Required Financial Aid Forms: FAFSA. Deadline to Apply for Financial Aid: June 1; March 1 (priority).

Rowan University

Admissions Office, 201 Mullica Hill Road, Glassboro, NJ 08028. Phone: (856) 256-4200, (800) 447-1165. Fax: (856) 256-4430. Web Site: rowan.edu. In-State Tuition and Fees: $4,921. Out-of-State Tuition and Fees: $8,671. Room and Board: $5,766. Students Receiving Some Form of Aid: 58%. Students Receiving Non-Need-Based Aid: 16%. Average Aid Package: $5,235. Required Financial Aid Forms: FAFSA. Deadline to Apply for Financial Aid: March 15.

Rutgers University—Camden College of Arts and Sciences

Admissions Office, 406 Penn Street, Camden, NJ 08102. Phone: (856) 225-6104. Fax: (856) 225-6498. E-mail: admissions@asb-ugadm.rutgers.edu. Web Site: rutgers.edu. In-State Tuition and Fees: $5,874. Out-of-State Tuition and Fees: $10,804. Room and Board: $5,548. Students Receiving Some Form of Aid: 47%. Students Receiving Non-Need-Based Aid: 6%. Average Aid Package: $7,720. Required Financial Aid Forms: FAFSA. Deadline to Apply for Financial Aid: March 15.

Rutgers University—College of Nursing

Admissions Office, 249 University Avenue, Newark, NJ 07102-1896. Phone: (973) 353-5205. Fax: (973) 353-1440. E-mail: admissions@asb_ugadm.rutgers.edu. Web Site: rutgers.edu. In-State Tuition and Fees: $5,792. Out-of-State Tuition and Fees: $10,722. Room and Board: $6,110. Students Receiving Some Form of Aid: 44%. Students Receiving Non-Need-Based Aid: 8%. Average Aid Package: $8,444. Required Financial Aid Forms: FAFSA. Deadline to Apply for Financial Aid: rolling; March 15 (priority).

Rutgers University—College of Pharmacy

University Undergraduate Admissions, 65 Davidson Road, Room 202,, Piscataway, NJ 08854-8097. Phone: (732) 932-INFO. Fax: (732) 445-0237. E-mail: admissions@asb-ugadm.rutgers.edu. Web Site: rutgers.edu. In-State Tuition and Fees: $6,576. Out-of-State Tuition and Fees: $12,044. Room and Board: $6,098. Students Receiving Some Form of Aid: 47%. Students Receiving Non-Need-Based Aid: 20%. Average Aid Package: $8,611. Required Financial Aid Forms: FAFSA. Deadline to Apply for Financial Aid: March 15 (priority).

Rutgers University—Cook College

University Undergraduate Admissions, 65 Davidson Road #202, Piscataway, NJ 08854-8097. Phone: (732) 932-INFO. Fax: (732) 445-0237. E-mail: admissions@asb-ugadm.rutgers.edu. Web Site: rutgers.edu. In-State Tuition and Fees: $6,544. Out-of-State Tuition and Fees: $12,012. Room and Board: $6,098. Students Receiving Some Form of Aid: 44%. Students Receiving Non-Need-Based Aid: 11%. Average Aid Package: $8,198. Required Financial Aid Forms: FAFSA. Deadline to Apply for Financial Aid: March 15 (priority).

Rutgers University—Douglass College

University Undergraduate Admissions, 65 Davidson Road, Room #202, Piscataway, NJ 08854-8097. Phone: (732) 932-INFO. Fax: (732) 445-0237. E-mail: admissions@asb-ugadm.rutgers.edu. Web Site: rutgers.edu. In-State Tuition and Fees: $6,017. Out-of-State Tuition and Fees: $10,947. Room and Board: $6,098. Students Receiving Some Form of Aid: 46%. Students Receiving Non-Need-Based Aid: 10%. Average Aid Package: $8,541. Required Financial Aid Forms: FAFSA. Deadline to Apply for Financial Aid: March 15 (priority).

Rutgers University—Livingston College

University Undergraduate Admissions, 65 Davidson Road #202, Piscataway, NJ 08854-8097. Phone: (732) 932-INFO. Fax: (732) 445-0237. E-mail: admissions@asb-ugadm.rutgers.edu. Web Site: rutgers.edu. In-State Tuition and Fees: $6,038. Out-of-State Tuition and Fees: $10,968. Room and Board: $6,098. Students Receiving Some Form of Aid: 46%. Students Receiving Non-Need-Based Aid: 6%. Average Aid Package: $8,392. Required Financial Aid Forms: FAFSA. Deadline to Apply for Financial Aid: rolling; March 15 (priority).

Rutgers University—Mason Gross School of the Arts

University Undergraduate Admissions, 65 Davidson Road, Room #202, Piscataway, NJ 08854-8097. Phone: (732) 932-INFO. Fax: (732) 445-0237. E-mail: admissions@asb-ugadm.rutgers.edu. Web Site: rutgers.edu. In-State Tuition and Fees: $6,052. Out-of-State Tuition and Fees: $10,982. Room and Board: $6,098. Students Receiving Some Form of Aid: 41%. Students Receiving Non-Need-Based Aid: 8%. Average Aid Package: $7,817. Required Financial Aid Forms: FAFSA. Deadline to Apply for Financial Aid: rolling; March 15 (priority).

Rutgers University—Newark College of Arts and Sciences

Admissions Office, 249 University Avenue, Newark, NJ 07102-1896. Phone: (973) 353-5205. Fax: (973) 353-1440. E-mail: admissions@asb-ugadm.rutgers.edu. Web Site: rutgers.edu. In-State Tuition and Fees: $5,814. Out-of-State Tuition and Fees: $10,744. Room and Board: $6,110. Students Receiving Some Form of Aid: 50%. Students Receiving Non-Need-Based Aid: 8%. Average Aid Package: $7,876. Required Financial Aid Forms: FAFSA. Deadline to Apply for Financial Aid: March 15 (priority).

Rutgers University—Rutgers College

University Undergraduate Admissions, 65 Davidson Road #202, Piscataway, NJ 08854-8097. Phone: (732) 932-INFO. Fax: (732) 445-0237. E-mail: admissions@asb-ugadm.rutgers.edu. Web Site: rutgers.edu. In-

State Tuition and Fees: $6,052. Out-of-State Tuition and Fees: $10,982. Room and Board: $6,098. Students Receiving Some Form of Aid: 42%. Students Receiving Non-Need-Based Aid: 11%. Average Aid Package: $8,586. Required Financial Aid Forms: FAFSA. Deadline to Apply for Financial Aid: March 15 (priority).

Rutgers University—School of Engineering

University Undergraduate Admissions, 65 Davidson Road, Room #202, Piscataway, NJ 08854-8097. Phone: (732) 932-INFO. Fax: (732) 445-0237. E-mail: admissions@asb-ugadm.rutgers.edu. Web Site: rutgers.edu. In-State Tuition and Fees: $6,576. Out-of-State Tuition and Fees: $12,044. Room and Board: $6,098. Students Receiving Some Form of Aid: 43%. Students Receiving Non-Need-Based Aid: 12%. Average Aid Package: $8,988. Required Financial Aid Forms: FAFSA. Deadline to Apply for Financial Aid: rolling; March 15 (priority).

Saint Peter's College

Admissions Office, 2627 Kennedy Boulevard, Jersey City, NJ 07306. Phone: (201) 915-9213, (888) SPC-9933. Fax: (201) 432-5860. E-mail: admissions@spcvxa.spc.edu. Web Site: spc.edu. Tuition and Fees: $14,886. Room and Board: $5,165. Students Receiving Some Form of Aid: 71%. Students Receiving Non-Need-Based Aid: 44%. Average Aid Package: $11,638. Required Financial Aid Forms: FAFSA. Deadline to Apply for Financial Aid: March 15 (recommended).

Seton Hall University

Enrollment Services Office, 400 South Orange Avenue, South Orange, NJ 07079. Phone: (973) 761-9332, (800) THE-HALL (out-of-state). Fax: (973) 275-2040. E-mail: thehall@shu.edu. Web Site: shu.edu. Tuition and Fees: $18,290. Room and Board: $7,722. Students Receiving Some Form of Aid: 62%. Students Receiving Non-Need-Based Aid: 3%. Average Aid Package: $11,608. Required Financial Aid Forms: FAFSA. Deadline to Apply for Financial Aid: April 1.

Stevens Institute of Technology

Office of Undergraduate Admissions, Castle Point on Hudson, Hoboken, NJ 07030. Phone: (201) 216-5194, (800) 458-5323. Fax: (201) 216-8348. E-mail: admissions@stevens-tech.edu. Web Site: stevens-tech.edu. Tuition: $20,890. Room and Board: $7,280. Students Receiving Some Form of Aid: 49%. Students Receiving Non-Need-Based Aid: 14%. Average Aid Package: $16,936. Required Financial Aid Forms: FAFSA. Deadline to Apply for Financial Aid: February 15 preferred.

William Paterson University

Office of Admissions, 300 Pompton Road, Wayne, NJ 07470. Phone: (973) 720-2125, (877) WPU-EXEL. Fax: (973) 720-2910. E-mail: admissions@wpunj.edu. Web Site: wpunj.edu. In-State Tuition and Fees: $4,690. Out-of-State Tuition and Fees: $7,360. Room and Board: $5,760. Students Receiving Some Form of Aid: 47%. Students Receiving Non-Need-Based Aid: 8%. Average Aid Package: $6,675. Required Financial Aid Forms: FAFSA. Deadline to Apply for Financial Aid: April 1.

NEW MEXICO

Eastern New Mexico University

Admissions Office, Station 7, ENMU, Portales, NM 88130. Phone: (505) 562-2178, (800) 367-3668. Fax: (505) 562-2566. E-mail: Douglas.Dobbins@enmu.edu. Web Site: enmu.edu. In-State Tuition and Fees: $1,752. Out-of-State Tuition and Fees: $6,510. Room and Board: $2,818. Students Receiving Some Form of Aid: 61%. Students Receiving Non-Need-Based Aid: 4%. Average Aid Package: $5,862. Required Financial Aid Forms: FAFSA. Deadline to Apply for Financial Aid: March 1 (priority).

New Mexico State University

Office of Admissions, Box 30001, MSC 3A, Las Cruces, NM 88003-8001. Phone: (505) 646-3121, (800) 662-6678. Fax: (505) 646-6330. E-mail: admissions@nmsu.edu. Web Site: nmsu.edu. In-State Tuition and Fees: $2,502. Out-of-State Tuition and Fees: $8,166. Room and Board: $3,726. Required Financial Aid Forms: FAFSA. Deadline to Apply for Financial Aid: March 1.

Saint John's College

Admissions Office, 1160 Camino Cruz Blanca, Santa Fe, NM 87501. Phone: (800) 331-5232, (505) 984-6060. Fax: (505) 984-6003. E-mail: admissions@mail.sjcsf.edu. Web Site: sjcsf.edu. Tuition and Fees: $22,200. Room and Board: $6,386. Students Receiving Some Form of Aid: 46%. Students Receiving Non-Need-Based Aid: 3%. Average Aid Package: $17,512. Required Financial Aid Forms: CSS Profile, FAFSA. Deadline to Apply for Financial Aid: February 15.

University of New Mexico

Office of Admissions, Student Services Center 150, Albuquerque, NM 87131-2046. Phone: (505) 277-2446, (800) CALL-UNM. Fax: (505) 277-6686. E-mail: apply@unm.edu. Web Site: unm.edu. In-State Tuition and Fees: $2,430. Out-of-State Tuition and Fees: $9,172. Room and Board: $4,800. Students Receiving Some Form of Aid: 37%. Students Receiving Non-Need-Based Aid: 2%. Average Aid Package: $8,074. Required Financial Aid Forms: FAFSA. Deadline to Apply for Financial Aid: March 1 (priority).

Western New Mexico University

Office of Admissions, P.O. Box 680, Silver City, NM 88061. Phone: (505) 538-6105, (800) 872-9668. Fax: (505) 538-6127. E-mail: admstudnt@iron.wnmu.edu. Web Site: wnmu.edu. In-State Tuition and Fees: $1,768. Out-of-State Tuition and Fees: $6,456. Room and Board: $3,080. Students Receiving Some Form of Aid: 100%. Students Receiving Non-Need-Based Aid: 32%. Average Aid Package: $3,468. Required Financial Aid Forms: FAFSA. Deadline to Apply for Financial Aid: April 1.

NEW YORK

Albany College of Pharmacy*

Admissions Office, 106 New Scotland Avenue, Albany, NY 12208-3492. Phone: (518) 445-7221. Fax: (518) 445-7202. Web Site: panther.acp.edu. Tuition and Fees: $12,173. Room and Board: $5,100. Students Receiving Some Form of Aid: 93%. Students Receiving Non-Need-Based Aid: 13%. Average Aid Package: $10,993. Required Financial Aid Forms: FAFSA, institutional form. Deadline to Apply for Financial Aid: February 1.

Alfred University

Admissions Office, Saxon Drive, Alfred, NY 14802-1205. Phone: (607) 871-2115, (800) 541-9229. Fax: (607) 871-2198. E-mail: admwww@alfred.edu. Web Site: alfred.edu. Tuition and Fees: $21,036. Room and Board: $7,582. Students Receiving Some Form of Aid: 16%. Students Receiving Non-Need-Based Aid: 6%. Average Aid Package: $21,472. Required Financial Aid Forms: FAFSA and AU financial aid form. Deadline to Apply for Financial Aid: rolling.

Bard College

Admissions Office, Hopson Cottage, Bard College, Annandale-On-Hudson, NY 12504. Phone: (914) 758-7472. Fax: (914) 758-5208. E-mail: admissions@bard.edu. Web Site: bard.edu. Tuition and Fees: $24,000. Room and Board: $7,220. Required Financial Aid Forms: FAFSA, CSS Profile. Deadline to Apply for Financial Aid: March 15.

Barnard College—Columbia University

Admissions Office, 3009 Broadway, New York, NY 10027. Phone: (212) 854-2014. Fax: (212) 854-6220. E-mail: admissions@barnard.edu. Web Site: barnard.edu. Tuition and Fees: $23,056. Room and Board: $9,358. Students Receiving Some Form of Aid: 46%. Average Aid Package: $21,706. Required Financial Aid Forms: FAFSA, profile, Barnard application, tax forms, state aid, business farms supplement, noncustodial parent statement. Deadline to Apply for Financial Aid: February 1.

Canisius College

Admissions Office, 2001 Main Street, Buffalo, NY 14208. Phone: (716) 888-2200, (800) 843-1517. Fax: (716) 888-2377. E-mail: inquiry@canisius.edu. Web Site: canisius.edu. Tuition and Fees: $16,386. Room and Board: $6,730. Students Receiving Some Form of Aid: 46%. Students Receiving Non-Need-Based Aid: 8%. Average Aid Package: $13,396. Required Financial Aid Forms: FAFSAFFAFSA, institutional form. Deadline to Apply for Financial Aid: February 1, recommended.

Cazenovia College

Admissions Office, Cazenovia College, Cazenovia, NY 13035. Phone: (315) 655-7208, (800) 654-3210. Fax: (315) 655-4860. E-mail: admission@cazcollege.edu. Web Site: cazcollege.edu. Tuition and Fees: $11,730. Room and Board: $4,053. Students Receiving Some Form of Aid: 62%. Students Receiving Non-Need-Based Aid: 43%. Average Aid Package: $11,159. Required Financial Aid Forms: FAFSA, TAP application. Deadline to Apply for Financial Aid: March 15.

City University of New York—Baruch College

Undergraduate Admissions, 17 Lexington Avenue, Box H0720, New York, NY 10010. Phone: (212) 802-2300. Fax: (212) 802-2310. Web Site: baruch.cuny.edu. In-State Tuition and Fees: $3,350. Out-of-State Tuition and Fees: $6,950. Required Financial Aid Forms: FAFSA. Deadline to Apply for Financial Aid: June 1.

City University of New York—Brooklyn College

Admissions Office, 2900 Bedford Avenue, Brooklyn, NY 11210. Phone: (718) 951-5001. Fax: (718) 951-4506. E-mail: adminqry@brooklyn.cuny.edu. Web Site: brooklyn.cuny.edu. In-State Tuition and Fees: $3,393. Out-of-State Tuition and Fees: $6,993. Students Receiving Some Form of Aid: 52%. Students Receiving Non-Need-Based Aid: 5%. Average Aid Package: $7,600. Required Financial Aid Forms: FAFSA. Deadline to Apply for Financial Aid: May 1 (priority).

City University of New York—City College

Admission Office, 160 Convent Avenue, New York, NY 10031. Phone: (212) 650-6977. Fax: (212) 650-6417. E-mail: admissions@admin.ccny.cuny.edu. Web Site: ccny.cuny.edu. In-State Tuition and Fees: $3,402. Out-of-State Tuition and Fees: $7,002.

City University of New York—College of Staten Island

Office of Recruitment and Admissions, North Administration Building 2A, 2800 Victory Boulevard, Staten Island, NY 10314. Phone: (718) 982-2010, (718) 982-2259. Fax: (718) 982-2500. Web Site: csi.cuny.edu. In-State Tuition and Fees: $3,358. Out-of-State Tuition and Fees: $5,964. Required Financial Aid Forms: FAFSA, CUNY TAP/APTS. Deadline to Apply for Financial Aid: May 27.

City University of New York—Hunter College

Office of Undergraduate Admissions, 695 Park Avenue, New York, NY 10021. Phone: (212) 772-4490. Fax: (212) 650-3336. E-mail: admissions@hunter.cuny.edu. Web Site: hunter.cuny.edu. In-State Tuition and Fees: $3,347. Out-of-State Tuition and Fees: $6,547. Room and Board: $1,900. Students Receiving Some Form of Aid: 44%. Students Receiving Non-Need-Based Aid: 10%. Average Aid Package: $4,491. Required Financial Aid Forms: FAFSA , State form. Deadline to Apply for Financial Aid: April 1 (FAFSA); May 1 (State form).

City University of New York—John Jay College of Criminal Justice

Admissions Office, 445 West 59th Street, Room 4205 N, New York, NY 10019. Phone: (212) 237-8865. E-mail: admiss @jjay.cuny.edu. Web Site: jjcj.cuny.edu. In-State Tuition and Fees: $3,251. Out-of-State Tuition and Fees: $6,851. Students Receiving Some Form of Aid: 69%. Students Receiving Non-Need-Based Aid: 6%. Average Aid Package: $3,600. Required Financial Aid Forms: FAFSA. Deadline to Apply for Financial Aid: rolling.

City University of New York—Lehman College

Office of Admissions, 250 Bedford Park Boulevard West, Bronx, NY 10468. Phone: (718) 960-8131. Web Site: lehman.edu. In-State Tuition and Fees: $3,320. Out-of-State Tuition and Fees: $6,920. Required Financial Aid Forms: FAFSA. Deadline to Apply for Financial Aid: rolling.

City University of New York—Medgar Evers College

Admissions Office, 1150 Carroll Street, Brooklyn, NY 11225-2201. Phone: (718) 270-6023, (718) 270-6024. Fax: (718) 270-6198. Web Site: mec.cuny.edu. In-State Tuition and Fees: $3,241. Out-of-State Tuition and Fees: $6,841. Average Aid Package: $3,003. Deadline to Apply for Financial Aid: August 15.

City University of New York—Queens College

Admissions Office, 65-30 Kissena Boulevard, Kiely Hall, Room 217, Flushing, NY 11367-1597. **Phone:** (718) 997-5614. **Fax:** (718) 997-5617. **Web Site:** qc.edu. **In-State Tuition and Fees:** $3,393. **Out-of-State Tuition and Fees:** $6,993. **Students Receiving Some Form of Aid:** 42%. **Students Receiving Non-Need-Based Aid:** 6%. **Average Aid Package:** $4,500. **Required Financial Aid Forms:** FAFSA, institutional form. **Deadline to Apply for Financial Aid:** rolling.

City University of New York—York College

Admissions Office, 94-20 Guy R. Brewer Boulevard, Jamaica, NY 11451. **Phone:** (718) 262-2165. **Fax:** (718) 262-2730. **Web Site:** york.cuny.edu. **In-State Tuition and Fees:** $3,292. **Out-of-State Tuition and Fees:** $6,892. **Required Financial Aid Forms:** FAFSA. **Deadline to Apply for Financial Aid:** rolling.

Clarkson University

Admissions Office, Box 5605, Potsdam, NY 13699. **Phone:** (315) 268-6479, (800) 527-6577. **Fax:** (315) 268-7647. **E-mail:** admissions@clarkson.edu. **Web Site:** clarkson.edu. **Tuition and Fees:** $20,225. **Room and Board:** $7,484. **Students Receiving Some Form of Aid:** 77%. **Students Receiving Non-Need-Based Aid:** 17%. **Average Aid Package:** $14,647. **Required Financial Aid Forms:** FAFSA. **Deadline to Apply for Financial Aid:** March 1 (priority).

Colgate University

Admissions Office, 13 Oak Drive, Hamilton, NY 13346-1383. **Phone:** (315) 228-7401. **Fax:** (315) 228-7544. **E-mail:** admission@mail.colgate.edu. **Web Site:** colgate.edu. **Tuition and Fees:** $25,740. **Room and Board:** $6,330. **Students Receiving Some Form of Aid:** 42%. **Average Aid Package:** $21,543. **Required Financial Aid Forms:** FAFSA , Profile. **Deadline to Apply for Financial Aid:** February 1.

College of Mount Saint Vincent*

Admissions Office, 6301 Riverdale Avenue, Bronx, NY 10471-1093. **Phone:** (718) 405-3267, (800) 665-CMSV. **Fax:** (718) 549-7945. **E-mail:** admissions@cmsv.edu. **Web Site:** cmsv.edu. **Tuition and Fees:** $15,070. **Room and Board:** $7,020. **Required Financial Aid Forms:** FAFSA, TAP for NY state residents. **Deadline to Apply for Financial Aid:** none.

College of New Rochelle—The School of Arts and Sciences and The School of Nursing

Office of Admissions, 29 Castle Place, New Rochelle, NY 10805-2339. **Phone:** (800) 933-5923, (914) 654-5452. **Fax:** (914) 654-5554. **E-mail:** admission@cnr.edu. **Web Site:** cnr.edu. **Tuition and Fees:** $11,700. **Room and Board:** $6,000. **Average Aid Package:** $11,878. **Deadline to Apply for Financial Aid:** rolling.

Columbia University—Columbia College

Office of Undergraduate Admissions, 1130 Amsterdam Avenue MC 2807, New York, NY 10027. **Phone:** (212) 854-2522. **Fax:** (212) 854-1209. **E-mail:** ugrad-admiss@columbia.edu. **Web Site:** columbia.edu. **Tuition and Fees:** $24,974. **Room and Board:** $7,732. **Required Financial Aid Forms:** FAFSA. **Deadline to Apply for Financial Aid:** January 1.

Columbia University—School of Engineering and Applied Science

Office of Undergraduate Admissions, 1130 Amsterdam Avenue, MC 2807, New York, NY 10027. **Phone:** (212) 854-2522. **Fax:** (212) 854-1209. **E-mail:** ugrad-admiss@columbia.edu. **Web Site:** columbia.edu. **Tuition and Fees:** $24,974. **Room and Board:** $7,732. **Required Financial Aid Forms:** FAFSA, Profile, tax forms. **Deadline to Apply for Financial Aid:** February 10.

Columbia University—School of General Studies

Admissions Office, 408 B. Lewisohn Hall, Mail Code 4100, 2970 Broadway, New York, NY 10027. **Phone:** (212) 854-2772. **Fax:** (212) 854-6316. **E-mail:** gsdegree@columbia.edu. **Web Site:** gs.columbia.edu. **Tuition and Fees:** $28,672. **Room and Board:** $10,000. **Required Financial Aid Forms:** FAFSA, General Studies Scholarship Form. **Deadline to Apply for Financial Aid:** July 1, only for General Studies form.

Concordia College

Admissions Office, 171 White Plains Road, Bronxville, NY 10708. **Phone:** (914) 337-9300, (800) 937-2655. **Fax:** (914) 395-4500. **E-mail:** admission@concordia-ny.edu. **Web Site:** concordia-ny.edu. **Tuition and Fees:** $14,350. **Room and Board:** $6,200. **Required Financial Aid Forms:** FAFSA. **Deadline to Apply for Financial Aid:** April 15 (recommended).

Cooper Union for the Advancement of Science and Art

Admissions Office, 30 Cooper Square, New York, NY 10003. **Phone:** (212) 353-4120. **Fax:** (212) 353-4342. **E-mail:** admissions@cooper.edu. **Web Site:** cooper.edu. **Tuition and Fees:** $8,800. **Room and Board:** $10,000. **Students Receiving Some Form of Aid:** 100%. **Students Receiving Non-Need-Based Aid:** 100%. **Average Aid Package:** $5,920. **Required Financial Aid Forms:** FAFSA, state aid form, income tax form. **Deadline to Apply for Financial Aid:** May 1.

Cornell University

Undergraduate Admissions, 410 Thurston Avenue, Ithaca, NY 14850-2488. **Phone:** (607) 255-0659, (607) 255-2000. **E-mail:** admissions@cornell.edu. **Web Site:** cornell.edu. **Tuition and Fees:** $23,848. **Room and Board:** $7,827. **Students Receiving Some Form of Aid:** 11%. **Average Aid Package:** $18,400. **Required Financial Aid Forms:** FAFSA, divorced parents form, CSS Profile, state aid, tax. **Deadline to Apply for Financial Aid:** February 14.

D'Youville College

Admissions Office, 320 Porter Avenue, Buffalo, NY 14201. **Phone:** (716) 881-7600. **Fax:** (716) 881-7790. **E-mail:** admiss@dyc.edu. **Web Site:** dyc.edu. **Tuition and Fees:** $11,930. **Room and Board:** $5,270. **Required Financial Aid Forms:** FAFSA. **Deadline to Apply for Financial Aid:** April 15.

Daemen College

Admissions Office, 4380 Main Street, Amherst, NY 14226. **Phone:** (716) 839-8225, (800) 462-7652 (USA and Canada). **Fax:** (716) 839-8370. **E-mail:** admissions@daemen.edu. **Web Site:** daemen.edu. **Tuition and Fees:** $12,220. **Room and Board:** $6,100. **Students Receiving Some Form of Aid:** 69%. **Students Receiving**

Non-Need-Based Aid: 26%. Average Aid Package: $7,686. Required Financial Aid Forms: FAFSA, Daemen financial aid application. Deadline to Apply for Financial Aid: February 15.

Dominican College

Office of Admissions, 470 Western Highway, Orangeburg, NY 10962-1299. Phone: (914) 359-7800, ext. 208. Fax: (914) 365-3150. E-mail: admissions@dc.edu. Web Site: dc.edu. Tuition and Fees: $13,160. Room and Board: $7,000. Required Financial Aid Forms: FAFSA, college application. Deadline to Apply for Financial Aid: March 15.

Dowling College*

Enrollment Services, Idle Hour Boulevard, Rm. 228, Oakdale, NY 11769-1999. Phone: (631) 244-3030, (800) DOWLING. Fax: (516) 563-3827. E-mail: macdonar@dowling.edu. Web Site: dowling.edu. Tuition and Fees: $12,489. Room and Board: $7,546. Students Receiving Some Form of Aid: 52%. Students Receiving Non-Need-Based Aid: 17%. Average Aid Package: $9,363. Required Financial Aid Forms: FAFSA. Deadline to Apply for Financial Aid: May 30 (priority).

Elmira College

Admissions Office, One Park Place, Elmira, NY 14901. Phone: (607) 735-1724, (800) 9-ELMIRA. Fax: (607) 735-1718. E-mail: admissions@elmira.edu. Web Site: elmira.edu. Tuition and Fees: $22,540. Room and Board: $7,280. Students Receiving Some Form of Aid: 56%. Students Receiving Non-Need-Based Aid: 44%. Average Aid Package: $17,373. Required Financial Aid Forms: FAFSA, Profile. Deadline to Apply for Financial Aid: March 1.

Eugene Lang College*

Admissions Office, 65 West 11th Street, New York, NY 10011. Phone: (212) 229-5665. Fax: (212) 229-5355. E-mail: lang@newschool.edu. Web Site: newschool.edu. Tuition and Fees: $19,104. Room and Board: $9,005. Students Receiving Some Form of Aid: 73%. Average Aid Package: $13,125. Required Financial Aid Forms: FAFSA. Deadline to Apply for Financial Aid: March 1 (priority).

Fordham University

Office of Undergraduate Admission, Thebaud Hall, Bronx, NY 10458-9993. Phone: (718) 817-1000, (800) FORDHAM. Fax: (718) 367-9404. E-mail: enroll@fordham.edu. Web Site: fordham.edu. Tuition and Fees: $20,660. Room and Board: $8,310. Students Receiving Some Form of Aid: 61%. Students Receiving Non-Need-Based Aid: 3%. Average Aid Package: $16,351. Required Financial Aid Forms: FAFSA, CSS Profile. Deadline to Apply for Financial Aid: February 1.

Hamilton College

Admissions Office, 198 College Hill Road, Clinton, NY 13323. Phone: (315) 859-4421, (800) 843-2655. Fax: (315) 859-4457. E-mail: admission@hamilton.edu. Web Site: hamilton.edu. Tuition and Fees: $25,050. Room and Board: $6,200. Students Receiving Some Form of Aid: 57%. Average Aid Package: $19,490. Required Financial Aid Forms: FAFSA, Profile. Deadline to Apply for Financial Aid: February 1.

Hartwick College

Admissions Office, P.O. Box 4020, Oneonta, NY 13820-4020. Phone: (607) 431-4200, (888) 427-8942. Fax: (607) 431-4154. E-mail: admissions@hartwick.edu. Web Site: hartwick.edu. Tuition and Fees: $24,070. Room and Board: $6,340. Students Receiving Some Form of Aid: 70%. Students Receiving Non-Need-Based Aid: 40%. Average Aid Package: $17,200. Required Financial Aid Forms: FAFSA, institutional form, state aid form, foreign student aid form. Deadline to Apply for Financial Aid: February 1.

Hobart and William Smith Colleges

Admissions Office, 629 South Main Street, Geneva, NY 14456. Phone: (800) 852-2256 (Hobart), (800) 245-0100 (William Smith). Fax: (315) 781-3471. E-mail: hoadm@hws.edu. Web Site: hws.edu. Tuition and Fees: $24,342. Room and Board: $6,882. Students Receiving Some Form of Aid: 66%. Students Receiving Non-Need-Based Aid: 2%. Average Aid Package: $21,368. Required Financial Aid Forms: FAFSA, Profile. Deadline to Apply for Financial Aid: March 15.

Hofstra University

Admissions Office, Admissions Center, Bernon Hall, 100 Hofstra University, Hempstead, NY 11549. Phone: (516) 463-6700, (800) HOFSTRA. Fax: (516) 560-7660. E-mail: hofstra@hofstra.edu. Web Site: hofstra.edu. Tuition and Fees: $14,512. Room and Board: $7,060. Students Receiving Some Form of Aid: 61%. Students Receiving Non-Need-Based Aid: 42%. Average Aid Package: $7,839. Required Financial Aid Forms: FAFSA. Deadline to Apply for Financial Aid: February 15 (priority).

Houghton College

Office of Admission, Willard Avenue, Houghton, NY 14744. Phone: (716) 567-9353, (800) 777-2556. Fax: (716) 567-9522. E-mail: admission@houghton.edu. Web Site: houghton.edu. Tuition and Fees: $15,140. Room and Board: $5,400. Students Receiving Some Form of Aid: 67%. Students Receiving Non-Need-Based Aid: 48%. Average Aid Package: $12,340. Required Financial Aid Forms: FAFSA, NYS TAP, college forms. Deadline to Apply for Financial Aid: March 1 (priority); as funds are available.

Iona College

Office of Undergraduate Admissions, 715 North Avenue, New Rochelle, NY 10801-1890. Phone: (914) 633-2622, (800) 231-IONA. Fax: (914) 633-2642. E-mail: icad@iona. Web Site: iona.edu. Tuition and Fees: $15,070. Room and Board: $8,430. Students Receiving Some Form of Aid: 60%. Students Receiving Non-Need-Based Aid: 7%. Average Aid Package: $14,955. Required Financial Aid Forms: FAFSA, institutional form, state aid form. Deadline to Apply for Financial Aid: none.

Ithaca College

Office of Admission, 100 Job Hall, Ithaca, NY 14850-7020. Phone: (607) 274-3124, (800) 429-4274. Fax: (607) 274-1900. E-mail: admission@ithaca.edu. Web Site: ithaca.edu. Tuition and Fees: $18,410. Room and Board: $7,956. Students Receiving Some Form of Aid: 66%. Students Receiving Non-Need-Based Aid: 13%. Average Aid Package: $16,634. Required Financial Aid Forms: FAFSA, tax forms, College Scholarship Service Profile (for early decision). Deadline to Apply for Financial Aid: February 1 (priority).

Juilliard School

Admissions Office, 60 Lincoln Center Plaza, New York, NY 10023-6588. **Phone:** (212) 799-5000, ext. 223. **Fax:** (212) 724-0263. **Tuition and Fees:** $16,600. **Room and Board:** $6,850. **Required Financial Aid Forms:** FAFSA, institutional forms, tax forms. **Deadline to Apply for Financial Aid:** March 1.

Keuka College

Admissions Office, Keuka Park, Keuka Park, NY 14478. **Phone:** (315) 536-5254. **Fax:** (315) 536-5386. **E-mail:** admissions@mail.keuka.edu. **Web Site:** keuka.edu. **Tuition and Fees:** $12,970. **Room and Board:** $6,370. **Students Receiving Some Form of Aid:** 87%. **Average Aid Package:** $11,262. **Required Financial Aid Forms:** FAFSA, NYS Tuition Assistance, Keuka Resource Application. **Deadline to Apply for Financial Aid:** March 1.

Le Moyne College

Admissions Office, 1419 Salt Springs Road, Syracuse, NY 13214-1399. **Phone:** (315) 445-4300, (800) 333-4733. **Fax:** (315) 445-4711. **E-mail:** admsoffc@maple.lemoyne.edu. **Web Site:** lemoyne.edu. **Tuition and Fees:** $14,980. **Room and Board:** $6,320. **Students Receiving Some Form of Aid:** 80%. **Students Receiving Non-Need-Based Aid:** 4%. **Average Aid Package:** $12,578. **Required Financial Aid Forms:** FAFSA, institutional form. **Deadline to Apply for Financial Aid:** February 1 (priority).

Long Island University—Brooklyn Campus

Office of Admissions, One University Plaza, Brooklyn, NY 11201. **Phone:** (718) 488-1011, (800) 548-7526. **Fax:** (718) 797-2399. **E-mail:** admissions@brooklyn.liu.edu. **Web Site:** liu.edu. **Tuition and Fees:** $12,207. **Room and Board:** $5,610. **Students Receiving Some Form of Aid:** 69%. **Students Receiving Non-Need-Based Aid:** 8%. **Average Aid Package:** $13,307. **Required Financial Aid Forms:** FAFSA. **Deadline to Apply for Financial Aid:** rolling.

Long Island University—C.W. Post Campus*

Admissions Office, 720 Northern Boulevard, Brookville, NY 11548-1300. **Phone:** (516) 299-2900, (800) 548-7526. **Fax:** (516) 299-2137. **E-mail:** enroll@cwpost.liu.edu. **Web Site:** liu.edu. **Tuition and Fees:** $15,340. **Room and Board:** $6,540. **Students Receiving Some Form of Aid:** 57%. **Students Receiving Non-Need-Based Aid:** 38%. **Deadline to Apply for Financial Aid:** varies.

Long Island University—Southampton College

Admissions Office, 239 Montauk Highway, Southampton, NY 11968. **Phone:** (631) 287-8200, (800) 548-7526. **Fax:** (516) 287-8130. **E-mail:** admissions@southampton.liunet.edu. **Web Site:** southampton.liu.edu. **Tuition and Fees:** $16,120. **Room and Board:** $7,390. **Students Receiving Some Form of Aid:** 70%. **Students Receiving Non-Need-Based Aid:** 57%. **Average Aid Package:** $12,874. **Required Financial Aid Forms:** FAFSA, institutional form. **Deadline to Apply for Financial Aid:** rolling.

Manhattan College*

Admissions Office, 4513 Manhattan College Parkway, Riverdale, NY 10471. **Phone:** (718) 862-7200, (800) MC2-XCEL. **Fax:** (718) 862-8019. **E-mail:** admit@manhattan.edu. **Web Site:** manhattan.edu. **Tuition and Fees:** $16,600. **Room and Board:** $7,450. **Students Receiving Some Form of Aid:** 79%. **Students Receiving Non-Need-Based Aid:** 31%. **Average Aid Package:** $3,200. **Required Financial Aid Forms:** FAFSA. **Deadline to Apply for Financial Aid:** February 15.

Manhattanville College

Admissions Office, 2900 Purchase Street, Purchase, NY 10577. **Phone:** (914) 323-5464, (800) 456-6000. **Fax:** (914) 694-1732. **E-mail:** admissions@mville.edu. **Web Site:** manhattanville.edu. **Tuition and Fees:** $18,860. **Room and Board:** $8,000. **Students Receiving Some Form of Aid:** 80%. **Students Receiving Non-Need-Based Aid:** 72%. **Average Aid Package:** $14,936. **Required Financial Aid Forms:** FAFSA. **Deadline to Apply for Financial Aid:** March 1.

Mannes College of Music

Office of Admissions, 150 West 85th Street, New York, NY 10024. **Phone:** (212) 580-0210, ext. 246 or 247, (800) 292-3040. **Fax:** (212) 580-1738. **E-mail:** mannesadmissions@newschool.edu. **Web Site:** mannes.edu. **Tuition and Fees:** $18,200. **Room and Board:** $6,600. **Required Financial Aid Forms:** FAFSA. **Deadline to Apply for Financial Aid:** March 1.

Marist College

Admissions Office, Marist College, Poughkeepsie, NY 12601-1387. **Phone:** (914) 575-3226, (800) 436-5483, ext. 2. **Fax:** (914) 575-3215. **E-mail:** admissions@marist.edu. **Web Site:** marist.edu. **Tuition and Fees:** $14,758. **Room and Board:** $7,418. **Students Receiving Some Form of Aid:** 56%. **Students Receiving Non-Need-Based Aid:** 11%. **Average Aid Package:** $10,302. **Required Financial Aid Forms:** FAFSA, Marist Application. **Deadline to Apply for Financial Aid:** March 1.

Marymount Manhattan College

Admissions Office, 221 East 71st Street, New York, NY 10021. **Phone:** (212) 517-0430, (800) MARYMOUNT. **Fax:** (212) 517-0413. **E-mail:** admissions@mmm.edu. **Web Site:** marymount.mmm.edu/home.htm. **Tuition and Fees:** $14,070. **Room and Board:** $7,000. **Students Receiving Some Form of Aid:** 42%. **Students Receiving Non-Need-Based Aid:** 25%. **Average Aid Package:** $11,377. **Required Financial Aid Forms:** FAFSA. **Deadline to Apply for Financial Aid:** Febuary 15 (priority).

Molloy College

Admissions Office, 1000 Hempstead Avenue, P.O Box 5002, Rockville Centre, NY 11571. **Phone:** (516) 678-5000, ext. 6230, (888) 4-MOLLOY. **Fax:** (516) 256-2247. **Web Site:** molloy.edu. **Tuition and Fees:** $12,545. **Required Financial Aid Forms:** FAFSA, institution's own financial aid form. **Deadline to Apply for Financial Aid:** rolling.

Mount Saint Mary College

Admissions Office, 330 Powell Avenue, Newburgh, NY 12550. **Phone:** (914) 569-3248, (888) YES-MSMC. **Fax:** (914) 562-6762. **E-mail:** ogrady@msmc.edu. **Web Site:** msmc.edu. **Tuition and Fees:** $11,485. **Room and Board:** $5,670. **Students Receiving Some Form of Aid:** 67%. **Students Receiving Non-Need-Based Aid:** 17%. **Average Aid Package:** $8,200. **Required Financial Aid Forms:** FAFSA and NY TAP for NY residents, MSMC FA form. **Deadline to Apply for Financial Aid:** February 15 (priority).

Nazareth College of Rochester

Admissions Office, 4245 East Avenue, Rochester, NY 14618-3790. Phone: (716) 389-2860, (800) 462-3944. Fax: (716) 389-2826. E-mail: admissions@naz.edu. Web Site: naz.edu. Tuition and Fees: $14,146. Room and Board: $6,376. Students Receiving Some Form of Aid: 71%. Students Receiving Non-Need-Based Aid: 4%. Average Aid Package: $13,245. Required Financial Aid Forms: FAFSA, Profile (for early decision only). Deadline to Apply for Financial Aid: May 1; February 15 (priority).

New York Institute of Technology—Old Westbury

Admissions Office, P.O. Box 8000, Old Westbury, NY 11568-8000. Phone: (516) 686-7520, (800) 345-NYIT. Fax: (516) 626-0419. E-mail: admissions@nyit.edu. Web Site: nyit.edu. Tuition and Fees: $11,900. Room and Board: $6,360. Students Receiving Some Form of Aid: 41%. Students Receiving Non-Need-Based Aid: 26%. Average Aid Package: $7,298. Required Financial Aid Forms: FAFSA. Deadline to Apply for Financial Aid: rolling.

New York University

Office of Undergraduate Admissions, 22 Washington Square North, New York, NY 10011-9191. Phone: (212) 998-4500. Fax: (212) 995-4902. Web Site: nyu.edu. Tuition and Fees: $23,456. Room and Board: $8,676. Students Receiving Some Form of Aid: 50%. Average Aid Package: $15,999. Required Financial Aid Forms: FAFSA. Deadline to Apply for Financial Aid: February 15.

Niagara University

Admissions Office, Bailo Hall, Niagara University, NY 14109-2011. Phone: (716) 286-8700, (800) 462-2111. Fax: (716) 286-8710. E-mail: admissions@niagara.edu. Web Site: niagara.edu. Tuition and Fees: $13,940. Room and Board: $6,330. Students Receiving Some Form of Aid: 79%. Students Receiving Non-Need-Based Aid: 6%. Average Aid Package: $12,284. Required Financial Aid Forms: FAFSA. Deadline to Apply for Financial Aid: February 15.

Nyack College

Admissions Office, 1 South Boulevard, Nyack, NY 10960-3698. Phone: (914) 358-1710, ext. 350, (800) 33-NYACK. Fax: (914) 358-3047. E-mail: enroll@nyack.edu. Web Site: nyackcollege.edu. Tuition and Fees: $12,740. Room and Board: $5,800. Required Financial Aid Forms: FAFSA. Deadline to Apply for Financial Aid: March 1 (priority).

Pace University—New York

Office of Undergraduate Admissions, 1 Pace Plaza, New York, NY 10038. Phone: (212) 346-1323, (800) 874-PACE. Fax: (212) 346-1040. E-mail: infoctr@pace.edu. Web Site: pace.edu. Tuition and Fees: $15,490. Room and Board: $6,550. Students Receiving Some Form of Aid: 58%. Students Receiving Non-Need-Based Aid: 13%. Average Aid Package: $10,800. Required Financial Aid Forms: FAFSA, State Aid Form. Deadline to Apply for Financial Aid: February 15 (priority).

Pace University—Pleasantville/Briarcliff

Admissions Office, 861 Bedford Road, Pleasantville, NY 10570. Phone: (914) 773-3321, (800) 874-PACE. Fax: (914) 773-3851. E-mail: infoctr@pace.edu. Web Site: pace.edu. Tuition and Fees: $15,490. Room and Board: $6,550. Students Receiving Some Form of Aid: 58%. Students Receiving Non-Need-Based Aid: 13%. Average Aid Package: $11,200. Required Financial Aid Forms: FAFSA, state aid form. Deadline to Apply for Financial Aid: February15 (priority).

Parsons School of Design

Admissions Office, 66 Fifth Avenue, New York, NY 10011-8878. Phone: (212) 229-8910, (800) 252-0852. Fax: (212) 229-8975. E-mail: parsadm@newschool.edu. Web Site: parsons.edu. Tuition and Fees: $21,420. Room and Board: $8,857. Required Financial Aid Forms: FAFSA. Deadline to Apply for Financial Aid: April 1.

Polytechnic University*

Admissions Office, 6 Metrotech Center, Brooklyn, NY 11201-2999. Phone: (718) 260-3100, (800) POLYTEC. Fax: (718) 260-3446. E-mail: admitme@poly.edu. Web Site: poly.edu. Tuition and Fees: $20,810. Room and Board: $5,000. Students Receiving Some Form of Aid: 72%. Students Receiving Non-Need-Based Aid: 54%. Average Aid Package: $17,262. Required Financial Aid Forms: FAFSA. Deadline to Apply for Financial Aid: March 19.

Pratt Institute

Office of Admissions, 200 Willoughby Avenue, Brooklyn, NY 11205. Phone: (718) 636-3588, (800) 331-0834. Fax: (718) 636-3670. E-mail: admissions@pratt.edu. Web Site: pratt.edu. Tuition and Fees: $20,074. Room and Board: $7,900. Required Financial Aid Forms: FAFSA. Deadline to Apply for Financial Aid: February 1.

Rensselaer Polytechnic Institute

Office of Undergraduate Admissions, 110 8th Street, Troy, NY 12180-3590. Phone: (518) 276-6216, (800) 448-6562. Fax: (518) 276-4072. E-mail: admissions@rpi.edu. Web Site: rpi.edu. Tuition and Fees: $22,955. Room and Board: $4,250. Students Receiving Some Form of Aid: 72%. Students Receiving Non-Need-Based Aid: 24%. Average Aid Package: $17,537. Required Financial Aid Forms: FAFSA, state aid form. Deadline to Apply for Financial Aid: February 15 (priority).

Roberts Wesleyan College

Admissions Office, 2301 Westside Drive, Rochester, NY 14624-1997. Phone: (716) 594-6400, (800) 777-4792. Fax: (716) 594-6371. E-mail: admissions@roberts.edu. Web Site: roberts.edu. Tuition and Fees: $13,630. Room and Board: $4,614. Required Financial Aid Forms: FAFSA. Deadline to Apply for Financial Aid: June 15.

Rochester Institute of Technology

Admissions Office, 60 Lomb Memorial Drive, Rochester, NY 14623. Phone: (716) 475-6631. Fax: (716) 475-7424. E-mail: admissions@rit.edu. Web Site: rit.edu. Tuition and Fees: $17,637. Room and Board: $6,852. Students Receiving Some Form of Aid: 62%. Students Receiving Non-Need-Based Aid: 14%. Average Aid Package: $14,700. Required Financial Aid Forms: FAFSA. Deadline to Apply for Financial Aid: March 15 (priority).

Russell Sage College

Admissions Office, 45 Ferry Street, Troy, NY 12180-4115. Phone: (518) 244-2217, (888) 837-9724. Fax: (518) 244-6880. E-mail: rscadm@sage.edu. Web Site: sage.edu. Tuition and Fees: $15,200. Room and Board: $5,950. Students Receiving Some Form of Aid: 76%. Students Receiving Non-Need-Based Aid: 7%.

Required Financial Aid Forms: FAFSA. Deadline to Apply for Financial Aid: rolling; March 1 (priority).

Saint Bonaventure University

Admissions Office, P.O. Box D, St. Bonaventure, NY 14778. Phone: (716) 375-2400, (800) 462-5050. Fax: (716) 375-2005. E-mail: admissions@sbu.edu. Web Site: sbu.edu. Tuition and Fees: $15,140. Room and Board: $5,790. Students Receiving Some Form of Aid: 71%. Average Aid Package: $12,811. Required Financial Aid Forms: FAFSA, institutional form. Deadline to Apply for Financial Aid: February 1.

Saint Francis College

Admissions Office, 180 Remsen Street, Brooklyn, NY 11201. Phone: (718) 489-5200. Fax: (718) 522-1274. E-mail: admissions@stfranciscollege.edu. Web Site: stfranciscollege.edu. Tuition and Fees: $8,510. Average Aid Package: $6,750. Required Financial Aid Forms: FAFSA. Deadline to Apply for Financial Aid: rolling.

Saint John Fisher College

Admissions Office, 3690 East Avenue, Rochester, NY 14618. Phone: (716) 385-8064, (800) 444-4640. Fax: (716) 385-8129. Web Site: sjfc.edu. Tuition and Fees: $14,000. Room and Board: $6,000. Required Financial Aid Forms: FAFSA. Deadline to Apply for Financial Aid: March 1.

Saint John's University

Admissions Office, 8000 Utopia Parkway, Jamaica, NY 11439. Phone: (718) 990-2000, (888) 9 ST JOHNS. Fax: (718) 990-5728. E-mail: admissions@stjohns.edu. Web Site: stjohns.edu. Tuition and Fees: $14,420. Room and Board: $8,550. Students Receiving Some Form of Aid: 69%. Students Receiving Non-Need-Based Aid: 21%. Average Aid Package: $10,517. Required Financial Aid Forms: FAFSA. Deadline to Apply for Financial Aid: February 1 (priority).

Saint Joseph's College—Brooklyn

Admissions Office, 245 Clinton Avenue, Brooklyn, NY 11205. Phone: (718) 636-6868. Fax: (718) 636-7242. E-mail: mrohan@sjcny.edu. Web Site: sjcny.edu. Tuition and Fees: $9,352. Students Receiving Some Form of Aid: 32%. Students Receiving Non-Need-Based Aid: 21%. Average Aid Package: $7,000. Required Financial Aid Forms: FAFSA. Deadline to Apply for Financial Aid: February 25 (priority).

Saint Joseph's College—Patchogue

Admissions Office, 155 West Roe Boulevard, Patchogue, NY 11772. Phone: (631) 447-3219. Fax: (631) 447-1734. Web Site: sjcny.edu. Tuition and Fees: $9,182. Average Aid Package: $5,000. Required Financial Aid Forms: FAFSA, institution's own form. Deadline to Apply for Financial Aid: February 25 (priority).

Saint Lawrence University

Admissions Office, St. Lawrence University, Canton, NY 13617. Phone: (315) 229-5261, (800) 285-1856. Fax: (315) 229-5818. E-mail: admissions@stlawu.edu. Web Site: stlawu.edu. Tuition and Fees: $23,095. Room and Board: $7,205. Students Receiving Some Form of Aid: 64%. Students Receiving Non-Need-Based Aid: 23%. Average Aid Package: $22,736. Required Financial Aid Forms: FAFSA. Deadline to Apply for Financial Aid: February 15.

Saint Thomas Aquinas College

Office of Admissions and Financial Aid, 125 Route 340, Sparkill, NY 10976-1050. Phone: (845) 398-4100, (800) 999-STAC. Fax: (845) 359-8136. E-mail: admissions@stac.edu. Web Site: stac.edu. Tuition and Fees: $12,700. Room and Board: $7,400. Required Financial Aid Forms: FAFSA. Deadline to Apply for Financial Aid: April 1.

Sarah Lawrence College

Admission Office, One Mead Way, Bronxville, NY 10708-5999. Phone: (914) 395-2510, (800) 888-2858. Fax: (914) 395-2676. E-mail: slcadmit@slc.edu. Web Site: slc.edu. Tuition and Fees: $25,406. Room and Board: $7,991. Students Receiving Some Form of Aid: 54%. Students Receiving Non-Need-Based Aid: 5%. Average Aid Package: $17,957. Required Financial Aid Forms: FAFSA, Profile, state aid and non-custodial divorced (separated) parent's statement. Deadline to Apply for Financial Aid: February 1.

School of Visual Arts

Admissions Office, 209 East 23rd Street, New York, NY 10010. Phone: (212) 592-2100, (800) 436-4204. Fax: (212) 592-2116. E-mail: admissions@adm.schoolofvisualarts.edu. Web Site: schoolofvisualarts.edu. Tuition and Fees: $15,320. Room and Board: $8,200. Students Receiving Some Form of Aid: 39%. Students Receiving Non-Need-Based Aid: 5%. Average Aid Package: $9,400. Required Financial Aid Forms: FAFSA. Deadline to Apply for Financial Aid: February 12.

Siena College

Admissions Office, 515 Loudon Road, Loudonville, NY 12211. Phone: (518) 783-2423, (888) AT-SIENA. Fax: (518) 783-2436. E-mail: admit@siena.edu. Web Site: siena.edu. Tuition and Fees: $14,835. Room and Board: $6,445. Students Receiving Some Form of Aid: 66%. Students Receiving Non-Need-Based Aid: 26%. Average Aid Package: $10,440. Required Financial Aid Forms: FAFSA, institutional form. Deadline to Apply for Financial Aid: February 1.

Skidmore College

Admissions Office, 815 North Broadway, Saratoga Springs, NY 12866. Phone: (800) 867-6007. Fax: (518) 580-5584. E-mail: admissions@skidmore.edu. Web Site: skidmore.edu. Tuition and Fees: $25,475. Room and Board: $7,270. Students Receiving Some Form of Aid: 36%. Students Receiving Non-Need-Based Aid: 7%. Average Aid Package: $18,355. Required Financial Aid Forms: FAFSA, profile. Deadline to Apply for Financial Aid: January 15.

State University of New York—Albany

Admissions Office, 1400 Washington Avenue, Albany, NY 12222. Phone: (518) 442-5435, (800) 293-7869. Fax: (518) 442-5383. E-mail: ugadmissions@albany.edu. Web Site: albany.edu. In-State Tuition and Fees: $4,338. Out-of-State Tuition and Fees: $9,238. Room and Board: $5,828. Students Receiving Some Form of Aid: 51%. Students Receiving Non-Need-Based Aid: 3%. Average Aid Package: $6,962. Required Financial Aid Forms: FAFSA. Deadline to Apply for Financial Aid: March 15 (priority).

State University of New York—Binghamton University

Admissions Office, P.O. Box 6000, Binghamton, NY 13902-6001. Phone: (607) 777-2171. Fax: (607) 777-4445. E-mail: admit@binghamton.edu. Web Site: binghamton.edu. In-State Tuition and Fees: $4,416. Out-of-State Tuition and Fees: $9,316. Room and Board: $5,516. Students Receiving Some Form of Aid: 49%. Students Receiving Non-Need-Based Aid: 6%. Average Aid Package: $9,573. Required Financial Aid Forms: FAFSA, TAP application if student desires NYS aid, CSS Profile (for early action only). Deadline to Apply for Financial Aid: March 1 (priority).

State University of New York—Buffalo State College

Admissions Office, 1300 Elmwood Avenue, Buffalo, NY 14222. Phone: (716) 878-4017. Fax: (716) 878-6100. E-mail: admissio@buffalostate.edu. Web Site: buffalostate.edu. Tuition and Fees: $3,909. Room and Board: $5,170. Students Receiving Some Form of Aid: 58%. Students Receiving Non-Need-Based Aid: 4%. Average Aid Package: $3,037. Required Financial Aid Forms: FAFSA. Deadline to Apply for Financial Aid: March 15 (priority).

State University of New York—College at Brockport

Admissions Office, 350 New Campus Drive, Brockport, NY 14420. Phone: (716) 395-2751, (800) 382-8447. Fax: (716) 395-5452. E-mail: admit@brockport.edu. Web Site: brockport.edu. In-State Tuition and Fees: $4,014. Out-of-State Tuition and Fees: $8,914. Room and Board: $5,410. Students Receiving Some Form of Aid: 55%. Students Receiving Non-Need-Based Aid: 5%. Average Aid Package: $7,017. Required Financial Aid Forms: FAFSA, Brockport application. Deadline to Apply for Financial Aid: February 15.

State University of New York—College at Geneseo

Office of Admissions, 1 College Circle, Geneseo, NY 14454-1401. Phone: (716) 245-5571. Fax: (716) 245-5550. E-mail: admissions@geneseo.edu. Web Site: geneseo.edu. In-State Tuition and Fees: $4,221. Out-of-State Tuition and Fees: $9,121. Room and Board: $4,880. Students Receiving Some Form of Aid: 45%. Students Receiving Non-Need-Based Aid: 10%. Average Aid Package: $6,730. Required Financial Aid Forms: FAFSA. Deadline to Apply for Financial Aid: February 15.

State University of New York—College at Oneonta

Office of Admissions, SUNY Oneonta, Oneonta, NY 13820-4016. Phone: (607) 436-2524, (800) SUNY-123. Fax: (607) 436-3074. E-mail: admissions@oneonta.edu. Web Site: oneonta.edu. In-State Tuition and Fees: $4,123. Out-of-State Tuition and Fees: $9,023. Room and Board: $5,456. Students Receiving Some Form of Aid: 59%. Average Aid Package: $7,997. Required Financial Aid Forms: FAFSA. Deadline to Apply for Financial Aid: rolling.

State University of New York—College at Potsdam

Admissions Office, 44 Pierrepont Avenue, Potsdam, NY 13676-2294. Phone: (315) 267-2180. Fax: (315) 267-2163. E-mail: admissions@potsdam.edu. Web Site: potsdam.edu. In-State Tuition and Fees: $3,935. Out-of-State Tuition and Fees: $8,835. Room and Board: $5,750. Students Receiving Some Form of Aid: 67%. Students Receiving Non-Need-Based Aid: 15%. Average Aid Package: $9,198. Required Financial Aid Forms: FAFSA. Deadline to Apply for Financial Aid: rolling.

State University of New York—College of Agriculture and Technology at Cobleskill

Office of Admissions, SUNY Cobleskill, Cobleskill, NY 12043. Phone: (518) 255-5525, (800) 295-8988. Fax: (518) 255-6769. E-mail: admissions@cobleskill.edu. Web Site: cobleskill.edu. In-State Tuition and Fees: $3,851. Out-of-State Tuition and Fees: $5,651. Room and Board: $5,620. Average Aid Package: $4,700. Required Financial Aid Forms: FAFSA. Deadline to Apply for Financial Aid: rolling.

State University of New York—Cortland

Admissions Office, P.O. Box 2000, Cortland, NY 13045-0900. Phone: (607) 753-4711. Fax: (607) 753-5998. E-mail: admssn_info@snycorva.cortland.edu. Web Site: cortland.edu. In-State Tuition and Fees: $4,104. Out-of-State Tuition and Fees: $9,004. Room and Board: $5,560. Average Aid Package: $6,630. Required Financial Aid Forms: FAFSA. Deadline to Apply for Financial Aid: March 31.

State University of New York—Empire State College*

Admissions Office, 2 Union Avenue, Saratoga Springs, NY 12866. Phone: (518) 587-2100, ext. 223, (800) 847-3000, ext. 223. Fax: (518) 587-5404. E-mail: admissions@esc.edu. Web Site: esc.edu. In-State Tuition and Fees: $3,545. Out-of-State Tuition and Fees: $8,445. Students Receiving Some Form of Aid: 45%. Required Financial Aid Forms: FAFSA. Deadline to Apply for Financial Aid: May 1.

State University of New York—Fredonia

Office of Admissions, 178 Central Ave, Fredonia, NY 14063. Phone: (716) 673-3251, (800) 252-1212. Fax: (716) 673-3249. E-mail: admissionsinq@fredonia.edu. Web Site: fredonia.edu. In-State Tuition and Fees: $4,175. Out-of-State Tuition and Fees: $9,075. Room and Board: $5,190. Students Receiving Some Form of Aid: 57%. Students Receiving Non-Need-Based Aid: 10%. Average Aid Package: $5,480. Required Financial Aid Forms: FAFSA, state aid form. Deadline to Apply for Financial Aid: February 15 (priority).

State University of New York—New Paltz

Admissions Office, 75 South Manheim Boulevard, New Paltz, NY 12561-2499. Phone: (914) 257-3200, (888) 639-7589. Fax: (914) 257-3209. E-mail: admissions@newpaltz.edu. Web Site: newpaltz.edu. In-State Tuition and Fees: $3,915. Out-of-State Tuition and Fees: $8,815. Room and Board: $5,246. Students Receiving Some Form of Aid: 58%. Students Receiving Non-Need-Based Aid: 6%. Average Aid Package: $7,500. Required Financial Aid Forms: FAFSA, TAP. Deadline to Apply for Financial Aid: March 15.

State University of New York—Old Westbury

Admissions Office, P.O. Box 307, Old Westbury, NY 11568. Phone: (516) 876-3073. Fax: (516) 876-3307. E-mail: bellm@oldwestbury.edu. Web Site:

oldwestbury.edu. In-State Tuition and Fees: $3,946. Out-of-State Tuition and Fees: $8,846. Room and Board: $5,286. Required Financial Aid Forms: FAFSA. Deadline to Apply for Financial Aid: rolling.

State University of New York—Oswego

Office of Admissions, 201 Culkin Hall, Oswego, NY 13126. Phone: (315) 341-2250. Fax: (315) 341-3260. E-mail: admiss@oswego.edu. Web Site: oswego.edu. In-State Tuition and Fees: $3,975. Out-of-State Tuition and Fees: $8,875. Room and Board: $5,888. Students Receiving Some Form of Aid: 59%. Students Receiving Non-Need-Based Aid: 7%. Average Aid Package: $7,049. Required Financial Aid Forms: FAFSA. Deadline to Apply for Financial Aid: April 1.

State University of New York—Plattsburgh State University

Admissions Office, Kehoe 1011, 101 Broad Street, Plattsburgh, NY 12901. Phone: (518) 564-2040, (888) 673-0012. Fax: (518) 564-2045. In-State Tuition and Fees: $3,957. Out-of-State Tuition and Fees: $8,857. Room and Board: $4,850. Students Receiving Some Form of Aid: 61%. Students Receiving Non-Need-Based Aid: 5%. Average Aid Package: $6,701. Required Financial Aid Forms: FAFSA. Deadline to Apply for Financial Aid: March 1 (priority).

State University of New York—Purchase College

Admissions Office, 735 Anderson Hill Road, Purchase, NY 10577-1400. Phone: (914) 251-6300. Fax: (914) 251-6314. E-mail: admissn@purchase.edu. Web Site: purchase.edu. In-State Tuition and Fees: $4,044. Out-of-State Tuition and Fees: $8,944. Room and Board: $5,942. Students Receiving Some Form of Aid: 55%. Students Receiving Non-Need-Based Aid: 18%. Average Aid Package: $8,510. Required Financial Aid Forms: FAFSA, Purchase's financial aid form, state aid form. Deadline to Apply for Financial Aid: March 15 (priority).

State University of New York—Stony Brook

Admissions Office, University at Stony Brook, Stony Brook, NY 11794. Phone: (631) 632-6868. Fax: (631) 632-9898. E-mail: admiss@mail.vpsa.sunysb.edu. Web Site: sunysb.edu. In-State Tuition and Fees: $3,975. Out-of-State Tuition and Fees: $8,875. Room and Board: $6,222. Average Aid Package: $7,157. Required Financial Aid Forms: FAFSA. Deadline to Apply for Financial Aid: March 1.

State University of New York—University at Buffalo

Admissions Office, 17 Capen Hall, Buffalo, NY 14260. Phone: (716) 645-6900, (800) 822-3648. Fax: (716) 645-6411. E-mail: ub-admissions@admissions.buffalo.edu. Web Site: buffalo.edu. In-State Tuition and Fees: $4,655. Out-of-State Tuition and Fees: $9,555. Room and Board: $5,904. Students Receiving Some Form of Aid: 49%. Students Receiving Non-Need-Based Aid: 2%. Average Aid Package: $5,940. Required Financial Aid Forms: FAFSA. Deadline to Apply for Financial Aid: March 1.

Syracuse University

Admissions Office, 201 Tolley Administration Building, Syracuse, NY 13244. Phone: (315) 443-3611. E-mail: orange@syr.edu. Web Site: syracuse.edu. Tuition and Fees: $20,816. Room and Board: $8,750. Students Receiving Some Form of Aid: 60%. Students Receiving Non-Need-Based Aid: 16%. Average Aid Package: $15,700. Required Financial Aid Forms: FAFSA. Deadline to Apply for Financial Aid: February 15.

Union College

Admissions Office, Stanley R. Becker Hall, Schenectady, NY 12308. Phone: (518) 388-6112, (888) 843-6688. Fax: (518) 388-6986. E-mail: admissions@union.edu. Web Site: union.edu. Tuition and Fees: $24,099. Room and Board: $6,474. Students Receiving Some Form of Aid: 55%. Average Aid Package: $21,084. Required Financial Aid Forms: FAFSA, CSS Profile. Deadline to Apply for Financial Aid: February 1.

United States Merchant Marine Academy*

Admissions Office, Steamboat Road, Kings Point, NY 11024-1699. Phone: (516) 773-5391, (800) 732-6267. Fax: (516) 773-5390. E-mail: admissions@usmma.edu. Web Site: usmma.edu. Tuition, Fees, Room and Board: Paid for by the U.S. Government. Required Financial Aid Forms: Application for Federal Student Aid, FAFSA. Deadline to Apply for Financial Aid: March 1- year of application.

United States Military Academy—West Point*

Director of Admissions, 606 Thayer Road, West Point, NY 10996-1797. Phone: (914) 938-4041. Fax: (914) 938-3021. E-mail: admissions@usma.edu. Web Site: usma.edu. Tuition, Fees, Room and Board: Paid for by the U.S. Government.

University of Rochester

Office of Admissions, P.O. Box 270251, Rochester, NY 14627-0001. Phone: (716) 275-3221, (888) 822-2256. Fax: (716) 461-4595. E-mail: admit@admissions.rochester.edu. Web Site: rochester.edu. Tuition and Fees: $23,730. Room and Board: $7,740. Students Receiving Some Form of Aid: 53%. Students Receiving Non-Need-Based Aid: 39%. Average Aid Package: $21,103. Required Financial Aid Forms: FAFSA, Profile, State aid form, Noncustodial Parent's Statement and Business/Farm Supplement. Deadline to Apply for Financial Aid: February 1.

Utica College of Syracuse University

Admissions Office, 1600 Burrstone Road, Utica, NY 13502. Phone: (315) 792-3006, (800) 782-8884. Fax: (315) 792-3003. E-mail: admiss@utica.ucsu.edu. Web Site: ucsu.edu. Tuition and Fees: $17,144. Room and Board: $6,660. Students Receiving Some Form of Aid: 59%. Students Receiving Non-Need-Based Aid: 12%. Average Aid Package: $17,517. Required Financial Aid Forms: FAFSA. Deadline to Apply for Financial Aid: February 15.

Vassar College

Office of Admission, Vassar College, Box 10, 124 Raymond Ave, Poughkeepsie, NY 12604. Phone: (914) 437-7300, (800) 827-7270. Fax: (914) 437-7063. E-mail: admissions@vassar.edu. Web Site: vassar.edu. Tuition and Fees: $24,030. Room and Board: $6,770. Students Receiving Some Form of Aid: 59%. Average Aid Package: $19,662. Required Financial Aid Forms: Profile, FAFSA, institutional form. Deadline to Apply for Financial Aid: January 10.

Wagner College

Admissions Office, One Campus Road, Staten Island, NY 10301. Phone: (718) 390-3411, (800) 221-1010. Fax: (718) 390-3105. E-mail: admissions@wagner.edu. Web Site: wagner.edu. Tuition and Fees: $18,000. Room and Board: $6,500. Students Receiving Some Form of Aid: 90%. Students Receiving Non-Need-Based Aid: 20%. Average Aid Package: $12,064. Required Financial Aid Forms: FAFSA. Deadline to Apply for Financial Aid: April 1.

Webb Institute

Admissions Office, Crescent Beach Road, Glen Cove, NY 11542. Phone: (516) 671-2213. Fax: (516) 674-9838. E-mail: admissions@webb-institute.edu. Web Site: webb-institute.edu. Room and Board: $6,250. Required Financial Aid Forms: FAFSA. Deadline to Apply for Financial Aid: July 5.

Wells College

Office of Admissions, Route 90, Aurora, NY 13026. Phone: (315) 364-3264, (800) 952-9355. Fax: (315) 364-3327. E-mail: admissions@wells.edu. Web Site: wells.edu. Tuition and Fees: $12,300. Room and Board: $6,100. Students Receiving Some Form of Aid: 79%. Students Receiving Non-Need-Based Aid: 37%. Average Aid Package: $13,807. Required Financial Aid Forms: FAFSA, CSS profile (for early decision candidates). Deadline to Apply for Financial Aid: February 15 (priority).

Yeshiva University*

Admissions Office, 500 West 185th Street, New York, NY 10033-3201. Phone: (212) 960-5277. Fax: (212) 960-0086. E-mail: admission@yu1.yu.edu. Web Site: yu.edu. Tuition and Fees: $14,920. Required Financial Aid Forms: institutional form, FAFSA, state form, income tax form. Deadline to Apply for Financial Aid: April 15.

NORTH CAROLINA

Appalachian State University

Office of Admissions. , Boone, NC 28608. Phone: (828) 262-2120. Fax: (828) 262-3296. E-mail: admissions@appstate.edu. Web Site: appstate.edu. In-State Tuition and Fees: $2,088. Out-of-State Tuition and Fees: $9,358. Room and Board: $3,560. Students Receiving Some Form of Aid: 32%. Students Receiving Non-Need-Based Aid: 7%. Average Aid Package: $5,235. Required Financial Aid Forms: free application for Federal Student Aid. Deadline to Apply for Financial Aid: March 15 (priority).

Barber-Scotia College*

Admissions Office, 145 Cabarrus Avenue W., Concord, NC 28025. Phone: (704) 789-2902, (704) 789-2900. Fax: (714) 789-2624. Web Site: barber-scotia.edu. Tuition and Fees: $7,866. Room and Board: $3,500. Required Financial Aid Forms: FAFSA.

Barton College

Office of Admissions, P.O. Box 5000, Wilson, NC 27893-7000. Phone: (252) 399-6317, (800) 345-4973. Fax: (252) 399-6572. E-mail: enroll@barton.edu. Web Site: barton.edu. Tuition and Fees: $10,834. Room and Board: $3,892. Average Aid Package: $9,100. Required Financial Aid Forms: FAFSA. Deadline to Apply for Financial Aid: July 1.

Belmont Abbey College

Admissions Office, 100 Belmont- Mt. Holly Road, Belmont, NC 28012-1802. Phone: (704) 825-6665. Fax: (704) 825-6220. E-mail: admissions@crusader.bac.edu. Web Site: belmontabbeycollege.edu. Tuition and Fees: $12,712. Room and Board: $6,528. Deadline to Apply for Financial Aid: March 1.

Campbell University

Admissions Office, P.O. Box 546, Buies Creek, NC 27506. Phone: (910) 893-1200, ext. 1290, (800) 334-4111, ext. 1320. Fax: (910) 893-1288. E-mail: adm@mailcenter.campbell.edu. Web Site: campbell.edu/cuindex.html. Tuition and Fees: $11,000. Room and Board: $3,926. Students Receiving Some Form of Aid: 72%. Students Receiving Non-Need-Based Aid: 66%. Average Aid Package: $16,342. Required Financial Aid Forms: FAFSA.

Catawba College

Admissions Office, 2300 West Innes Street, Salisbury, NC 28144. Phone: (704) 637-4402, (800) CATAWBA. Fax: (704) 637-4444. E-mail: admissions@catawba.edu. Web Site: catawba.edu. Tuition and Fees: $13,275. Room and Board: $4,980. Students Receiving Some Form of Aid: 82%. Students Receiving Non-Need-Based Aid: 82%. Required Financial Aid Forms: FAFSA. Deadline to Apply for Financial Aid: March 1 (priority).

Davidson College

Admissions Office, P.O. Box 1737, Davidson, NC 28036. Phone: (704) 892-2230, (800) 768-0380. Fax: (704) 892-2016. E-mail: admissions@davidson.edu. Web Site: davidson.edu. Tuition and Fees: $22,228. Room and Board: $6,340. Average Aid Package: $13,889. Required Financial Aid Forms: FAFSA, CSS Profile, noncustodial parent's statement, business/farm supplement. Deadline to Apply for Financial Aid: February 15.

Duke University

Admissions Office, 2138 Campus Drive, Durham, NC 27708. Phone: (919) 684-3214. Fax: (919) 683-8941. E-mail: askduke@admiss.duke.edu. Web Site: duke.edu. Tuition and Fees: $25,630. Room and Board: $7,387. Students Receiving Some Form of Aid: 38%. Students Receiving Non-Need-Based Aid: less than 1%. Average Aid Package: $19,563. Required Financial Aid Forms: FAFSA, CSS Profile, Business/Farm Supplement, noncustodial parent's statement. Deadline to Apply for Financial Aid: February 1.

East Carolina University

Admissions Office, 106 Whichard, Greenville, NC 27858. Phone: (252) 328-6640. Fax: (252) 328-6945. Web Site: ecu.edu. In-State Tuition and Fees: $1,998. Out-of-State Tuition and Fees: $9,564. Students Receiving Some Form of Aid: 26%. Students Receiving Non-Need-Based Aid: 5%. Required Financial Aid Forms: FAFSA. Deadline to Apply for Financial Aid: April 15 (priority).

Elizabeth City State University

Admissions Office, 1704 Weeksville Road, Campus Box 901, Elizabeth City, NC 27909. Phone: (252) 335-3305, (800) 347-3278. Fax: (252) 335-3537. Web Site: ecsu.edu. In-State Tuition and Fees: $1,631. Out-of-State Tuition and Fees: $8,049. Room and Board: $3,898. Students Receiving Some Form of Aid: 78%. Required Financial Aid Forms: FAFSA. Deadline to Apply for Financial Aid: March 1.

Elon College

Admissions Office, 2700 Campus Box, Elon College, NC 27244-2010. Phone: (336) 584-2370, (800) 334-8448. Fax: (336) 538-3986. E-mail: admissions@elon.edu. Web Site: elon.edu. Tuition and Fees: $12,671. Room and Board: $4,551. Students Receiving Some Form of Aid: 38%. Students Receiving Non-Need-Based Aid: 2%. Average Aid Package: $9,365. Required Financial Aid Forms: FAFSA, CSS Profile, institutional form. Deadline to Apply for Financial Aid: February 15 (priority).

Fayetteville State University*

Admissions Office, 1200 Murchison Rd, Fayetteville, NC 28301-4298. Phone: (910) 486-1371, (800) 222-2594. Fax: (910) 486-6024. E-mail: CAD@adml.uncfsu.edu. Web Site: uncfsu.edu. In-State Tuition and Fees: $1,770. Out-of-State Tuition and Fees: $9,046. Room and Board: $3,800. Required Financial Aid Forms: FAFSA. Deadline to Apply for Financial Aid: March 1, April 1, October 1.

Guilford College

Admission Office, 5800 West Friendly Avenue, Greensboro, NC 27410. Phone: (336) 316-2100, (800) 992-7759. Fax: (336) 316-2954. E-mail: admission@guilford.edu. Web Site: guilford.edu. Tuition and Fees: $16,970. Room and Board: $5,610. Students Receiving Some Form of Aid: 40%. Students Receiving Non-Need-Based Aid: 27%. Average Aid Package: $14,420. Required Financial Aid Forms: FAFSA, CSS Profile. Deadline to Apply for Financial Aid: March 1 (priority).

High Point University

Undergraduate Admissions, University Station 3598, High Point, NC 27262-3598. Phone: (336) 841-9216, (800) 345-6993. Fax: (336) 888-6382. E-mail: admiss@highpoint.edu. Web Site: highpoint.edu. Tuition and Fees: $12,440. Room and Board: $5,770. Students Receiving Some Form of Aid: 45%. Students Receiving Non-Need-Based Aid: 19%. Average Aid Package: $14,430. Required Financial Aid Forms: FAFSA. Deadline to Apply for Financial Aid: rolling.

Johnson C. Smith University

Office of Admissions, 100 Beatties Ford Road, Charlotte, NC 28216. Phone: (704) 378-1010, (800) 782-7303. Fax: (704) 378-1242. Web Site: jcsu.edu. Tuition and Fees: $9,974. Room and Board: $3,875. Students Receiving Some Form of Aid: 85%. Students Receiving Non-Need-Based Aid: 59%. Average Aid Package: $6,200. Required Financial Aid Forms: FAFSA. Deadline to Apply for Financial Aid: May 1.

Lees-McRae College

Admissions Office, P.O. Box 128, Banner Elk, NC 28604. Phone: (828) 898-8723. Fax: (828) 898-4310. E-mail: admissions@lmc.edu. Web Site: lmc.edu. Tuition and Fees: $10,720. Room and Board: $3,900. Students Receiving Some Form of Aid: 62%. Students Receiving Non-Need-Based Aid: 46%. Average Aid Package: $8,790. Required Financial Aid Forms: FAFSA. Deadline to Apply for Financial Aid: April 1.

Lenoir-Rhyne College

Admissions House, Lenoir-Rhyne College, Hickory, NC 28603. Phone: (828) 328-7300. Fax: (828) 328-7378. E-mail: admission@lrc.edu. Web Site: lrc.edu. Tuition and Fees: $13,356. Room and Board: $4,920. Students Receiving Some Form of Aid: 60%. Students Receiving Non-Need-Based Aid: 54%. Average Aid Package: $10,432. Required Financial Aid Forms: FAFSA, institution's own form. Deadline to Apply for Financial Aid: March 1 (priority).

Meredith College

Office of Admissions, 3800 Hillsborough Street, Raleigh, NC 27607-5298. Phone: (800) MEREDITH, (919) 760-8581. Fax: (919) 760-2348. E-mail: admissions@meredith.edu. Web Site: meredith.edu. Tuition and Fees: $9,840. Room and Board: $4,260. Students Receiving Some Form of Aid: 39%. Students Receiving Non-Need-Based Aid: 4%. Average Aid Package: $8,649. Required Financial Aid Forms: FAFSA, institutional form; CSS/financial aid profile for Early Decision. Deadline to Apply for Financial Aid: February 15 (priority).

Methodist College

Admissions Office, 5400 Ramsey Street, Fayetteville, NC 28311-1420. Phone: (910) 630-7027, (800) 488-7110. Fax: (910) 630-7285. Tuition and Fees: $13,300. Room and Board: $5,080. Students Receiving Non-Need-Based Aid: 20%. Average Aid Package: $8,700. Required Financial Aid Forms: FAFSA. Deadline to Apply for Financial Aid: May 1.

Mount Olive College

Admissions Office, 634 Henderson Street, Mount Olive, NC 28365. Phone: (919) 658-7164, (800) 653-0854. Fax: (919) 658-7180. E-mail: bkornegay@exchange.moc.edu. Web Site: mountolivecollege.edu. Tuition and Fees: $9,210. Room and Board: $4,000. Students Receiving Some Form of Aid: 51%. Students Receiving Non-Need-Based Aid: 4%. Average Aid Package: $6,627. Required Financial Aid Forms: FAFSA. Deadline to Apply for Financial Aid: March 1 (priority).

North Carolina A&T State University*

Admissions Office, 1601 East Market Street, Greensboro, NC 27411. Phone: (336) 334-7946, (800) 443-8964. Fax: (336) 334-7478. E-mail: uadmit@ncat.edu. Web Site: ncat.edu. In-State Tuition and Fees: $1,889. Out-of-State Tuition and Fees: $9,159. Room and Board: $4,010. Students Receiving Some Form of Aid: 67%. Students Receiving Non-Need-Based Aid: 18%. Average Aid Package: $8,643. Required Financial Aid Forms: FAFSA. Deadline to Apply for Financial Aid: March 15.

North Carolina Central University*

Undergraduate Admissions, #1 McDougald House, 1801 Fayetteville St., Durham, NC 27707. Phone: (919) 560-6326. Fax: (919) 530-7625. E-mail: ebridges@wpo.nccu.edu. Web Site: nccu.edu. In-State Tuition and Fees: $2,182. Out-of-State Tuition and Fees: $9,452. Room and Board: $3,904. Students Receiving Some Form of Aid: 62%. Students Receiving Non-Need-Based Aid: 33%. Average Aid Package: $6,301. Required Financial Aid Forms: FAFSA. Deadline to Apply for Financial Aid: March 31, April 1 (priority).

North Carolina School of the Arts

Office of Admissions, 1533 South Main Street, Winston-Salem, NC 27117. Phone: (336) 770-3291. Fax: (336) 770-3370. E-mail: admissions@ncarts.edu. Web Site: ncarts.edu. In-State Tuition and Fees: $2,655. Out-of-State Tuition and Fees: $11,283. Room and

Board: $4,686. Students Receiving Some Form of Aid: 49%. Students Receiving Non-Need-Based Aid: 1%. Average Aid Package: $6,476. Required Financial Aid Forms: FAFSA. Deadline to Apply for Financial Aid: March 1 (priority).

North Carolina State University

Undergraduate Admissions Office, Box 7103, Raleigh, NC 27695. Phone: (919) 515-2434. Fax: (919) 515-5039. E-mail: undergrad_admissions@ncsu.edu. Web Site: ncsu.edu. In-State Tuition and Fees: $2,414. Out-of-State Tuition and Fees: $11,580. Room and Board: $4,540. Students Receiving Some Form of Aid: 40%. Students Receiving Non-Need-Based Aid: 8%. Average Aid Package: $5,661. Required Financial Aid Forms: FAFSA, Institutional form. Deadline to Apply for Financial Aid: March 1 (priority).

Pfeiffer University

Admissions Office, P.O. Box 960, Misenheimer, NC 28109. Phone: (800) 338-2060. Fax: (704) 463-1363. E-mail: admiss@pfeiffer.edu. Web Site: pfeiffer.edu. Tuition and Fees: $11,380. Room and Board: $4,560. Students Receiving Non-Need-Based Aid: 71%. Average Aid Package: $7,315. Required Financial Aid Forms: FAFSA. Deadline to Apply for Financial Aid: March 1.

Queens College

Admissions Office, 1900 Selwyn Avenue, Charlotte, NC 28274. Phone: (704) 337-2212, (800) 849-0202. Fax: (704) 337-2403. E-mail: cas@queens.edu. Web Site: queens.edu. Tuition and Fees: $10,680. Room and Board: $5,890. Students Receiving Some Form of Aid: 30%. Students Receiving Non-Need-Based Aid: 10%. Average Aid Package: $11,440. Required Financial Aid Forms: FAFSA. Deadline to Apply for Financial Aid: March 1 (priority).

Saint Andrews Presbyterian College

Admissions Office, 1700 Dogwood Mile, Laurinburg, NC 28352. Phone: (910) 277-5555, (800) 763-0198. E-mail: admissions@sapc.edu. Web Site: sapc.edu. Tuition and Fees: $14,040. Room and Board: $5,300. Students Receiving Some Form of Aid: 59%. Students Receiving Non-Need-Based Aid: 53%. Average Aid Package: $11,310. Required Financial Aid Forms: FAFSA.

Saint Augustine's College

Admissions Office, 1315 Oakwood Avenue, Raleigh, NC 27610. Phone: , (800) 948-1126. Fax: (919) 516-4415. E-mail: admissions@es.st-aug.edu. Web Site: st-aug.edu. Tuition and Fees: $7,182. Room and Board: $4,508. Students Receiving Some Form of Aid: 91%. Students Receiving Non-Need-Based Aid: 70%. Average Aid Package: $8,762. Required Financial Aid Forms: FAFSA, institutional form. Deadline to Apply for Financial Aid: June 1, April 15 (priority).

Salem College

Admissions Office, P.O. Box 10548, Winston-Salem, NC 27108. Phone: (336) 721-2621, (800) 327-2536. Fax: (336) 917-5572. E-mail: admissions@salem.edu. Web Site: salem.edu. Tuition and Fees: $13,585. Room and Board: $8,255. Required Financial Aid Forms: FAFSA. Deadline to Apply for Financial Aid: March 1.

Shaw University

Office of Admissions, 118 East South Street, Raleigh, NC 27601. Phone: (919) 546-8275, (800) 214-6683. Fax: (919) 546-8271. E-mail: ksmith@shawu.edu. Web Site: shawuniversity.edu. Tuition and Fees: $6,854. Room and Board: $4,342. Students Receiving Some Form of Aid: 60%. Students Receiving Non-Need-Based Aid: 51%. Average Aid Package: $5,775. Required Financial Aid Forms: FAFSA, institutional form. Deadline to Apply for Financial Aid: April 1 (priority).

University of North Carolina—Asheville

Office of Admissions, CPO #2210, 117 Lipinsky Hall, Asheville, NC 28804-8510. Phone: (828) 251-6481, (800) 531-9842. Fax: (828) 251-6482. E-mail: admissions@unca.edu. Web Site: unca.edu. In-State Tuition and Fees: $1,960. Out-of-State Tuition and Fees: $8,580. Room and Board: $4,179. Students Receiving Some Form of Aid: 34%. Students Receiving Non-Need-Based Aid: 9%. Average Aid Package: $6,014. Required Financial Aid Forms: FAFSA. Deadline to Apply for Financial Aid: March 1.

University of North Carolina—Chapel Hill

Office of Undergraduate Admissions, Campus Box 2200, Jackson Hall, Chapel Hill, NC 27599. Phone: (919) 966-3621. Fax: (919) 962-3045. E-mail: uadm@email.unc.edu. Web Site: unc.edu. In-State Tuition and Fees: $2,364. Out-of-State Tuition and Fees: $11,530. Room and Board: $5,740. Students Receiving Some Form of Aid: 28%. Students Receiving Non-Need-Based Aid: 27%. Average Aid Package: $6,772. Required Financial Aid Forms: FAFSA, CSS Profile. Deadline to Apply for Financial Aid: March 1.

University of North Carolina—Charlotte

Admissions Office, 9201 University City Blvd., Charlotte, NC 28223-0001. Phone: (704) 547-2213. Fax: (704) 510-6483. E-mail: unccadm@email.uncc.edu. Web Site: uncc.edu. In-State Tuition and Fees: $1,920. Out-of-State Tuition and Fees: $9,190. Room and Board: $3,816. Students Receiving Some Form of Aid: 33%. Students Receiving Non-Need-Based Aid: 4%. Average Aid Package: $6,629. Required Financial Aid Forms: FAFSA. Deadline to Apply for Financial Aid: April 1 (priority).

University of North Carolina—Greensboro

Admissions Office, 123 Mossman Bldg., Greensboro, NC 27402-6710. Phone: (336) 334-5243. Fax: (336) 334-4180. E-mail: undergrad_admissions.uncg.edu. Web Site: uncg.edu. In-State Tuition and Fees: $2,189. Out-of-State Tuition and Fees: $10,643. Room and Board: $4,186. Students Receiving Some Form of Aid: 37%. Students Receiving Non-Need-Based Aid: 10%. Average Aid Package: $6,128. Required Financial Aid Forms: FAFSA. Deadline to Apply for Financial Aid: March 1.

University of North Carolina—Pembroke

Admissions Office, P.O. Box 1510, Pembroke, NC 28372. Phone: (910) 521-6262, (800) 949-8627. Fax: (910) 521-6497. E-mail: admissions@papa.uncp.edu. Web Site: uncp.edu. In-State Tuition and Fees: $1,706. Out-of-State Tuition and Fees: $8,976. Room and Board: $3,358. Students Receiving Some

Form of Aid: 38%. Students Receiving Non-Need-Based Aid: 7%. Average Aid Package: $4,630. Required Financial Aid Forms: FAFSA. Deadline to Apply for Financial Aid: March 15.

University of North Carolina—Wilmington

Admissions Office, 601 South College Road, Wilmington, NC 28403. Phone: (910) 962-3243, (800) 228-5571. Fax: (910) 962-3038. E-mail: admission@uncwil.edu. Web Site: uncwil.edu. In-State Tuition and Fees: $2,068. Out-of-State Tuition and Fees: $9,338. Room and Board: $4,656. Students Receiving Some Form of Aid: 31%. Students Receiving Non-Need-Based Aid: 2%. Average Aid Package: $7,282. Required Financial Aid Forms: FAFSA. Deadline to Apply for Financial Aid: rolling.

Wake Forest University

Admissions Office, Reynolda Station, Winston-Salem, NC 27109. Phone: (336) 758-5201. Fax: (336) 758-4324. Web Site: wfu.edu. Tuition and Fees: $21,420. Room and Board: $5,900. Students Receiving Some Form of Aid: 32%. Students Receiving Non-Need-Based Aid: 5%. Average Aid Package: $17,451. Required Financial Aid Forms: FAFSA, CSS Profile, state aid form, Noncustodial Parent's Sstatement. Deadline to Apply for Financial Aid: February 1 (priority).

Western Carolina University

Admissions Office, HFR Administration building, Cullowhee, NC 28723. Phone: (828) 227-7317, (800) 928-2369. Fax: (828) 227-7319. E-mail: cauley@wcu.edu. Web Site: wcu.edu. In-State Tuition and Fees: $2,082. Out-of-State Tuition and Fees: $9,352. Room and Board: $2,534. Required Financial Aid Forms: FAFSA. Deadline to Apply for Financial Aid: March 31 (priority).

Wingate University

Admissions Office, Campus Box 3059, Wingate, NC 28174. Phone: (704) 233-8200, (800) 755-5550. Fax: (704) 233-8110. E-mail: admit@wingate.edu. Web Site: wingate.edu. Tuition and Fees: $12,850. Room and Board: $5,200. Students Receiving Some Form of Aid: 62%. Students Receiving Non-Need-Based Aid: 59%. Average Aid Package: $11,500. Required Financial Aid Forms: FAFSA, institutional form. Deadline to Apply for Financial Aid: March 1 (priority).

Winston-Salem State University

Admissions Office, Campus Box 19413, Winston-Salem, NC 27110. Phone: (336) 750-2070. Fax: (336) 750-2079. Web Site: wssu.edu. In-State Tuition and Fees: $2,142. Out-of-State Tuition and Fees: $8,560. Room and Board: $3,403. Required Financial Aid Forms: FAFSA. Deadline to Apply for Financial Aid: April 1.

NORTH DAKOTA

Dickinson State University

Office of Admissions and Academic Records. , Dickinson, ND 58601-4896. Phone: (483) 227-2175, (800) 279-HAWK. E-mail: dsuhawks@eagle.dsu.nodak.edu. Web Site: dickinsonstate.com. In-State Tuition and Fees: $1,906. Out-of-State Tuition and Fees: $5,090. Room and Board: $2,610. Required Financial Aid Forms: FAFSA. Deadline to Apply for Financial Aid: rolling.

Jamestown College

Admissions Office, 6081 College Lane, Jamestown, ND 58405. Phone: (701) 252-3467, ext. 2562, (800) 336-2554. Fax: (701) 253-4318. E-mail: admissions@acc.jc.edu. Web Site: acc.jc.edu. Tuition and Fees: $7,150. Room and Board: $3,200. Required Financial Aid Forms: FAFSA. Deadline to Apply for Financial Aid: August 1.

Mayville State University

Admissions Office, 330 Third Street NE, Mayville, ND 58257. Phone: (701) 786-4842, (800) 437-4104, ext. 34774. Fax: (701) 786-4748. E-mail: admit@mail.masu.nodak.edu. Web Site: masu.nodak.edu. In-State Tuition and Fees: $3,182. Out-of-State Tuition and Fees: $6,492. Room and Board: $3,026. Students Receiving Some Form of Aid: 41%. Students Receiving Non-Need-Based Aid: 6%. Average Aid Package: $5,394. Required Financial Aid Forms: FAFSA. Deadline to Apply for Financial Aid: April 15 (priority).

Minot State University

Enrollment Services, 500 University Avenue West, Minot, ND 58707. Phone: (701) 858-3350, (701) 858-3351. Fax: (701) 858-3386. E-mail: askmsu@misu.nodak.edu. Web Site: misu.nodak.edu. In-State Tuition and Fees: $2,425. Out-of-State Tuition and Fees: $6,005. Room and Board: $2,800. Students Receiving Some Form of Aid: 88%. Average Aid Package: $7,500. Required Financial Aid Forms: FAFSA. Deadline to Apply for Financial Aid: April 15 (priority).

North Dakota State University

Admission Office, University Station P.O. Box 5454, Fargo, ND 58105. Phone: (701) 231-8643, (800) 488-6378. Fax: (701) 231-8802. E-mail: nuadmiss@plains.nodak.edu. Web Site: ndsu.edu. In-State Tuition and Fees: $3,010. Out-of-State Tuition and Fees: $7,359. Room and Board: $3,542. Students Receiving Some Form of Aid: 48%. Students Receiving Non-Need-Based Aid: 8%. Average Aid Package: $4,926. Required Financial Aid Forms: FAFSA and verification form. Deadline to Apply for Financial Aid: April 15 (priority).

University of Mary

Admissions Office, 7500 University Drive, Bismarck, ND 58504-9652. Phone: (701) 255-7500, (800) 288-6279. Fax: (701) 255-7687. E-mail: marauder@umary.edu. Web Site: umary.edu. Tuition and Fees: $8,700. Room and Board: $3,600. Students Receiving Some Form of Aid: 77%. Students Receiving Non-Need-Based Aid: 60%. Average Aid Package: $6,000. Required Financial Aid Forms: FAFSA. Deadline to Apply for Financial Aid: rolling.

University of North Dakota

Enrollment Services, Box 8135, Grand Forks, ND 58202. Phone: (701) 777-4463, (800) 225-5863. Fax: (701) 777-4857. E-mail: enrolser@sage.und.nodak.edu. Web Site: und.edu. In-State Tuition and Fees: $2,956. Out-of-State Tuition and Fees: $7,098. Room and Board: $3,406. Students Receiving Some Form of Aid: 74%. Students Receiving Non-Need-Based Aid: 19%. Average Aid Package: $7,511. Required Financial Aid Forms: FAFSA. Deadline to Apply for Financial Aid: rolling, April 15 (priority).

OHIO

Antioch College

Admissions and Financial Aid Office, 795 Livermore Street, Yellow Springs, OH 45387. **Phone:** (937) 754-5100, (800) 543-9436. **E-mail:** admissions@antioch-college.edu. **Web Site:** antioch-college.edu. **Tuition and Fees:** $19,521. **Room and Board:** $4,876. **Students Receiving Some Form of Aid:** 88%. **Students Receiving Non-Need-Based Aid:** 45%. **Average Aid Package:** $17,594. **Deadline to Apply for Financial Aid:** rolling.

Ashland University

Admissions Office, 401 College Avenue, Ashland, OH 44805. **Phone:** (419) 289-5052, (800) 882-1548. **Fax:** (419) 289-5999. **E-mail:** auadmsn@ashland.edu. **Web Site:** ashland.edu. **Tuition and Fees:** $15,534. **Room and Board:** $5,610. **Students Receiving Some Form of Aid:** 54%. **Average Aid Package:** $14,415. **Required Financial Aid Forms:** institution's own form. **Deadline to Apply for Financial Aid:** March 15 (priority).

Baldwin-Wallace College

Admission Office, 275 Eastland Road, Berea, OH 44017. **Phone:** (440) 826-2222, (877) BW-APPLY. **Fax:** (440) 826-6522. **E-mail:** admission@bw.edu. **Web Site:** bw.edu. **Tuition and Fees:** $15,340. **Room and Board:** $5,460. **Average Aid Package:** $11,828. **Required Financial Aid Forms:** FAFSA. **Deadline to Apply for Financial Aid:** May 1.

Bluffton College

Office of Admissions, 280 West College Avenue, Bluffton, OH 45817. **Phone:** (419) 358-3257, (800) 488-3257. **Fax:** (419) 358-3232. **E-mail:** admissions@bluffton.edu. **Web Site:** bluffton.edu. **Tuition and Fees:** $14,326. **Room and Board:** $5,122. **Students Receiving Some Form of Aid:** 77%. **Students Receiving Non-Need-Based Aid:** 7%. **Average Aid Package:** $12,395. **Required Financial Aid Forms:** FAFSA.

Bowling Green State University

Office of Admissions, 110 McFall Center, Bowling Green, OH 43403. **Phone:** (419) 372-2086. **Fax:** (419) 372-6955. **E-mail:** admissions@bgnet.bgsu.edu. **Web Site:** bgsu.edu/welcome. **In-State Tuition and Fees:** $4,874. **Out-of-State Tuition and Fees:** $10,422. **Room and Board:** $4,612. **Students Receiving Some Form of Aid:** 44%. **Students Receiving Non-Need-Based Aid:** 14%. **Average Aid Package:** $5,688. **Required Financial Aid Forms:** FAFSA. **Deadline to Apply for Financial Aid:** rolling.

Capital University

Admission Office, Capital University, Columbus, OH 43209. **Phone:** (614) 236-6101, (800) 289-6289. **Fax:** (614) 236-6926. **E-mail:** admissions@capital.edu. **Web Site:** capital.edu. **Tuition and Fees:** $16,000. **Room and Board:** $4,900. **Students Receiving Some Form of Aid:** 54%. **Students Receiving Non-Need-Based Aid:** 54%. **Average Aid Package:** $14,406. **Required Financial Aid Forms:** FAFSA. **Deadline to Apply for Financial Aid:** August 1.

Case Western Reserve University

Office of Undergraduate Admission, 103 Tomlinson Hall, 10900 Euclid Avenue, Cleveland, OH 44106-7055. **Phone:** (216) 368-4450, (800) 967-8898. **Fax:** (216) 368-5111. **E-mail:** admission@po.cwru.edu. **Web Site:** cwru.edu. **Tuition and Fees:** $20,260. **Room and Board:** $5,815. **Students Receiving Some Form of Aid:** 54%. **Students Receiving Non-Need-Based Aid:** 47%. **Average Aid Package:** $18,549. **Required Financial Aid Forms:** FAFSA, Profile. **Deadline to Apply for Financial Aid:** February 1 (priority); April 1 (deadline).

Cedarville College

Admissions Office, 251 North Main Street, Cedarville, OH 45314. **Phone:** (937) 766-7700, (800) 233-2784. **Fax:** (937) 766-7575. **E-mail:** admiss@cedarville.edu. **Web Site:** cedarville.edu. **Tuition and Fees:** $10,740. **Room and Board:** $4,788. **Students Receiving Some Form of Aid:** 55%. **Students Receiving Non-Need-Based Aid:** 35%. **Average Aid Package:** $9,867. **Required Financial Aid Forms:** FAFSA. **Deadline to Apply for Financial Aid:** February 10 (priority).

Central State University

Admissions Office, 1400 Brush Row Road, Wilberforce, OH 45384. **Phone:** (937) 376-6348, (800) 388-2781. **Fax:** (937) 376-6530. **E-mail:** admissions@csu.ces.edu. **Web Site:** ces.edu. **In-State Tuition and Fees:** $3,453. **Out-of-State Tuition and Fees:** $7,566. **Room and Board:** $4,860. **Average Aid Package:** $11,710. **Required Financial Aid Forms:** FAFSA. **Deadline to Apply for Financial Aid:** August 1.

Cleveland State University

Office of Admission, 1983 East 24th Street ft 109, Cleveland, OH 44115-2440. **Phone:** (216) 687-2100, (888) CSU-OHIO. **Fax:** (216) 687-9210. **E-mail:** admissions@csuohio.edu. **Web Site:** csuohio.edu. **In-State Tuition and Fees:** $3,864. **Out-of-State Tuition and Fees:** $7,728. **Room and Board:** $5,194. **Required Financial Aid Forms:** FAFSA. **Deadline to Apply for Financial Aid:** April 15 (recommended).

College of Wooster

Office of Admission, 1189 Beall Avenue, Wooster, OH 44691. **Phone:** (330) 263-2322, (800) 877-9905. **Fax:** (330) 263-2621. **E-mail:** admissions@acs.wooster.edu. **Web Site:** wooster.edu. **Tuition and Fees:** $20,530. **Room and Board:** $5,420. **Students Receiving Some Form of Aid:** 65%. **Students Receiving Non-Need-Based Aid:** 8%. **Average Aid Package:** $17,365. **Required Financial Aid Forms:** FAFSA, Profile. **Deadline to Apply for Financial Aid:** rolling; February 15 (priority).

Denison University

Admissions Office, 1 Southridge Road, Granville, OH 43023. **Phone:** (740) 587-6276, (800) DENISON. **Fax:** (740) 587-6306. **E-mail:** admissions@denison.edu. **Web Site:** denison.edu. **Tuition and Fees:** $22,210. **Room and Board:** $6,300. **Students Receiving Some Form of Aid:** 48%. **Students Receiving Non-Need-Based Aid:** 45%. **Average Aid Package:** $9,772. **Required Financial Aid Forms:** FAFSA. **Deadline to Apply for Financial Aid:** February 15 (priority).

Heidelberg College*

Admissions Office, 310 East Market Street, Tiffin, OH 44883. **Phone:** (419) 448-2330, (800) 434-3352. **Fax:** (419) 448-2334. **E-mail:** adminfo@mail.heidelberg.edu. **Web Site:** heidelberg.edu. **Tuition and Fees:** $16,422. **Room and Board:** $5,264. **Required Financial Aid Forms:** FAFSA. **Deadline to Apply for Financial Aid:** rolling.

John Carroll University

Office of Admission, 20700 North Park Blvd., University Heights, OH 44118. Phone: (216) 397-4294. Fax: (216) 397-3098. E-mail: admission@jcu.edu. Web Site: jcu.edu. Tuition and Fees: $15,474. Room and Board: $5,950. Students Receiving Some Form of Aid: 88%. Students Receiving Non-Need-Based Aid: 83%. Average Aid Package: $12,025. Required Financial Aid Forms: FAFSA. Deadline to Apply for Financial Aid: March 1.

Kent State University

Admissions Office, P.O. Box 5190, Kent, OH 44242-0001. Phone: (330) 672-2444, (800) 988-KENT. Fax: (330) 672-2499. E-mail: kentadm@admissions.kent.edu. Web Site: kent.edu/admissions/app_opt.html. In-State Tuition and Fees: $5,014. Out-of-State Tuition and Fees: $9,918. Room and Board: $4,530. Students Receiving Some Form of Aid: 58%. Students Receiving Non-Need-Based Aid: 4%. Average Aid Package: $5,604. Required Financial Aid Forms: FAFSA. Deadline to Apply for Financial Aid: March 1 (priority).

Kenyon College

Office of Admissions, Ransom Hall, Kenyon College, Gambier, OH 43022. Phone: (740) 427-5776, (800) 848-2468. Fax: (740) 427-5770. E-mail: admissions@kenyon.edu. Web Site: kenyon.edu. Tuition and Fees: $24,680. Room and Board: $4,160. Students Receiving Some Form of Aid: 41%. Students Receiving Non-Need-Based Aid: 23%. Average Aid Package: $19,401. Required Financial Aid Forms: FAFSA, Profile. Deadline to Apply for Financial Aid: February 15.

Marietta College

Admissions Office, 215 Fifth Street, Marietta, OH 45750-4005. Phone: (740) 376-4600, (800) 331-7896. Fax: (740) 376-8888. E-mail: admit@marietta.edu. Web Site: marietta.edu. Tuition and Fees: $18,244. Room and Board: $5,196. Students Receiving Some Form of Aid: 66%. Students Receiving Non-Need-Based Aid: 52%. Average Aid Package: $15,643. Required Financial Aid Forms: FAFSA. Deadline to Apply for Financial Aid: March 1.

Miami University

Office of Admission, Campus Avenue Building, Oxford, OH 45056. Phone: (513) 529-2531. Fax: (513) 529-1550. E-mail: admission@muohio.edu. Web Site: muohio.edu. In-State Tuition and Fees: $6,112. Out-of-State Tuition and Fees: $12,766. Room and Board: $5,330. Students Receiving Some Form of Aid: 36%. Students Receiving Non-Need-Based Aid: 10%. Average Aid Package: $5,889. Required Financial Aid Forms: FAFSA. Deadline to Apply for Financial Aid: rolling; February 15 (priority).

Notre Dame College of Ohio

Admissions Office, 4545 College Road, South Euclid, OH 44121. Phone: (216) 381-1680, (800) NDC-1680. Fax: (216) 381-3802. E-mail: admissions@ndc.edu. Web Site: ndc.edu. Tuition and Fees: $13,618. Room and Board: $5,248. Average Aid Package: $11,044. Required Financial Aid Forms: FAFSA. Deadline to Apply for Financial Aid: April 1 (priority).

Oberlin College

Admissions Office. , Oberlin, OH 44074. Phone: (800) 622-OBIE. Fax: (440) 775-6905. E-mail: admissions@oberlin.edu. Web Site: oberlin.edu. Tuition and Fees: $24,264. Room and Board: $6,178. Students Receiving Some Form of Aid: 52%. Students Receiving Non-Need-Based Aid: 11%. Average Aid Package: $22,758. Required Financial Aid Forms: FAFSA, Profile. Deadline to Apply for Financial Aid: January 15.

Ohio Northern University

Admissions Office, 525 South Main Street, Ada, OH 45810. Phone: (419) 772-2260, (888) 408-4668. Fax: (419) 772-2313. E-mail: admissions-ug@onu.edu. Web Site: onu.edu. Tuition and Fees: $21,435. Room and Board: $5,265. Average Aid Package: $17,100. Required Financial Aid Forms: FAFSA, institutional form. Deadline to Apply for Financial Aid: rolling.

Ohio State University

Admissions Office, Third Floor Lincoln Tower, 1800 Cannon Drive, Columbus, OH 43210. Phone: (614) 292-3980. Fax: (614) 292-4818. E-mail: telecounseling@fa.adm.ohio-state.edu. Web Site: osu.edu. In-State Tuition and Fees: $4,137. Out-of-State Tuition and Fees: $12,087. Room and Board: $5,328. Students Receiving Some Form of Aid: 40%. Students Receiving Non-Need-Based Aid: 18%. Average Aid Package: $7,043. Required Financial Aid Forms: FAFSA. Deadline to Apply for Financial Aid: February 15 (priority).

Ohio University

Office of Undergraduate Admissions, 120 Chubb Hall, Athens, OH 45701-2979. Phone: (740) 593-4100. Fax: (740) 593-0560. E-mail: frshinfo@ohiou.edu. Web Site: ohiou.edu. In-State Tuition and Fees: $4,800. Out-of-State Tuition and Fees: $10,101. Room and Board: $5,484. Students Receiving Some Form of Aid: 40%. Students Receiving Non-Need-Based Aid: 16%. Average Aid Package: $6,528. Required Financial Aid Forms: FAFSA. Deadline to Apply for Financial Aid: March 15 (priority).

Ohio Wesleyan University

Office of Admissions, 61 S. Sandusky Street, Delaware, OH 43015. Phone: (740) 368-3020, (800) 922-8953. Fax: (740) 368-3314. E-mail: owuadmit@cc.owu.edu. Web Site: owu.edu. Tuition and Fees: $21,880. Room and Board: $6,610. Students Receiving Some Form of Aid: 57%. Students Receiving Non-Need-Based Aid: 53%. Average Aid Package: $19,285. Required Financial Aid Forms: FAFSA, institutional form. Deadline to Apply for Financial Aid: March 15 (priority); May 15.

University of Akron

Office of Admissions, 302 Buchtel Mall, Akron, OH 44398-0413. Phone: (330) 972-7077, (800) 655-4884. Fax: (330) 972-7022. E-mail: admissions@uakron.edu. Web Site: uakron.edu. In-State Tuition and Fees: $4,152. Out-of-State Tuition and Fees: $10,353. Room and Board: $5,010. Students Receiving Some Form of Aid: 10%. Students Receiving Non-Need-Based Aid: 4%. Average Aid Package: $4,834. Required Financial Aid Forms: FAFSA. Deadline to Apply for Financial Aid: February 1.

University of Cincinnati

Office of Admissions, P.O. Box 210091, Cincinnati, OH 45221-0091. Phone: (513) 556-1100. Fax: (513) 556-1105. E-mail: admissions@uc.edu. Web Site: uc.edu. In-State Tuition and Fees: $4,998. Out-of-State Tuition and Fees: $12,879. Room and Board: $6,282. Students Receiving Some Form of Aid: 30%. Students Receiving Non-Need-Based Aid: 2%. Average Aid Package: $5,087. Required Financial Aid Forms: FAFSA. Deadline to Apply for Financial Aid: ASAP after January 1.

University of Dayton

Admission Office, 300 College Park, Dayton, OH 45469-1300. Phone: (937) 229-4411, (800) 837-7433. Fax: (937) 229-4729. E-mail: admission@udayton.edu. Web Site: udayton.edu. Tuition and Fees: $16,070. Room and Board: $5,080. Average Aid Package: $11,032. Required Financial Aid Forms: FAFSA. Deadline to Apply for Financial Aid: March 31 (priority).

University of Toledo

Admissions Office, 2801 West Bancroft Street, Toledo, OH 43606. Phone: (419) 530-8888, (800) 586-5336. Fax: (419) 530-4504. E-mail: enroll@utnet.utoledo.edu. Web Site: utoledo.edu. In-State Tuition and Fees: $3,496. Out-of-State Tuition and Fees: $9,660. Room and Board: $5,096. Students Receiving Some Form of Aid: 42%. Students Receiving Non-Need-Based Aid: 6%. Average Aid Package: $5,571. Required Financial Aid Forms: FAFSA. Deadline to Apply for Financial Aid: rolling.

Urbana University

Admissions Office, 579 College Way, Urbana, OH 43078. Phone: (937) 484-1356, (800) 787-2262. Fax: (937) 484-1389. E-mail: admiss@urbana.edu. Web Site: urbana.edu. Tuition and Fees: $11,488. Room and Board: $5,000. Required Financial Aid Forms: FAS.

Wittenberg University

Admissions Office, P.O. Box 720, Springfield, OH 45501. Phone: (937) 327-6314, (800) 677-7558. Fax: (937) 327-6379. E-mail: admissions@wittenberg.edu. Web Site: wittenberg.edu. Tuition and Fees: $21,640. Room and Board: $5,374. Students Receiving Some Form of Aid: 68%. Students Receiving Non-Need-Based Aid: 64%. Average Aid Package: $19,361. Required Financial Aid Forms: FAFSA. Deadline to Apply for Financial Aid: March 15.

Wright State University

Office of Admissions, E148 Student Union, 3640 Colonel Glenn Hwy., Dayton, OH 45435-0001. Phone: (937) 775-5700, (800) 247-1770 (Ohio only). Fax: (937) 775-3301. E-mail: Cathy.Davis@Wright.edu. Web Site: Wright.edu. In-State Tuition and Fees: $4,128. Out-of-State Tuition and Fees: $8,256. Room and Board: $4,545. Average Aid Package: $8,271. Required Financial Aid Forms: FAFSA. Deadline to Apply for Financial Aid: March 1.

Xavier University

Office of Admission, 3800 Victory Parkway, Cincinnati, OH 45207-5311. Phone: (513) 745-3301, (800) 344-4698. Fax: (513) 745-4319. E-mail: xuadmit@admin.xu.edu. Web Site: xu.edu. Tuition and Fees: $15,930. Room and Board: $6,680. Students Receiving Some Form of Aid: 41%. Students Receiving Non-Need-Based Aid: 7%. Average Aid Package: $11,619. Required Financial Aid Forms: FAFSA. Deadline to Apply for Financial Aid: February 15 (priority).

Youngstown State University*

Undergraduate Recruitment and Admissions, Dana Hall, One University Plaza, Youngstown, OH 44555-0001. Phone: (330) 742-2000, (877) 468-6978. Fax: (330) 742-3674. E-mail: enroll@ysu.edu. Web Site: ysu.edu. In-State Tuition and Fees: $3,762. Out-of-State Tuition and Fees: $5,526. Room and Board: $4,695. Students Receiving Some Form of Aid: 95%. Required Financial Aid Forms: FAFSA, institutional aid request. Deadline to Apply for Financial Aid: March 1.

OKLAHOMA

Cameron University

Admissions Office, 2800 West Gore Boulevard, Lawton, OK 73505. Phone: (580) 581-2289. Fax: (580) 581-5514. E-mail: zoed@cameron.edu. Web Site: cameron.edu. In-State Tuition and Fees: $2,060. Out-of-State Tuition and Fees: $4,849. Room and Board: $2,850. Required Financial Aid Forms: FAFSA. Deadline to Apply for Financial Aid: rolling.

Northeastern State University

Admissions Office, 601 N. Grand, Tahlequah, OK 74464. Phone: (918) 456-5511, ext. 2200, (800) 722-9614. Fax: (918) 458-2342. E-mail: nsuadmis@nsuok.edu. Web Site: nsuok.edu. In-State Tuition and Fees: $1,940. Out-of-State Tuition and Fees: $4,460. Room and Board: $3,260. Average Aid Package: $5,500. Required Financial Aid Forms: FAFSA, institutional form. Deadline to Apply for Financial Aid: rolling.

Northwestern Oklahoma State University

Admissions Office, 709 Oklahoma Boulevard, Alva, OK 73717. Phone: (580) 327-8546, (580) 327-8547. Fax: (580) 327-1881. E-mail: krschrock@nwosu.edu. Web Site: nwalva.edu. In-State Tuition and Fees: $1,986. Out-of-State Tuition and Fees: $4,674. Room and Board: $2,316. Students Receiving Some Form of Aid: 36%. Students Receiving Non-Need-Based Aid: 23%. Average Aid Package: $565. Required Financial Aid Forms: FAFSA, institutional form. Deadline to Apply for Financial Aid: rolling.

Oklahoma City University

Office of Undergraduate Admissions, 2501 N. Blackwelder, Oklahoma City, OK 73106. Phone: (405) 521-5050, (800) 633-7242. Fax: (405) 521-5916. E-mail: uadmissions@okcu.edu. Web Site: okcu.edu. Tuition and Fees: $9,558. Room and Board: $4,400. Students Receiving Some Form of Aid: 27%. Students Receiving Non-Need-Based Aid: 22%. Average Aid Package: $8,968. Required Financial Aid Forms: FAFSA, Institutional form. Deadline to Apply for Financial Aid: March 1 (priority).

Oklahoma State University

Office of Admissions, 324 Student Union, Stillwater, OK 74078. Phone: (405) 744-6858, (800) 233-5019 (in-state). Fax: (405) 744-5285. E-mail: admit@okstate.edu. Web Site: okstate.edu. In-State Tuition and Fees: $2,578. Out-of-State Tuition and Fees: $7,168. Room and Board: $4,536. Students Receiving Some Form of Aid: 41%. Students Receiving Non-Need-Based Aid: 19%. Average Aid Package: $7,292. Required Financial Aid Forms: FAFSA. Deadline to Apply for Financial Aid: ASAP.

Oral Roberts University

Admissions Office, 7777 South Lewis Ave., Tulsa, OK 74171. Phone: (918) 496-6518, (800) 678-8876. Fax: (918) 495-6222. E-mail: admissions@oru.edu. Web Site: oru.edu. Tuition and Fees: $11,650. Room and Board: $5,076. Students Receiving Some Form of Aid: 62%. Students Receiving Non-Need-Based Aid: 24%. Average Aid Package: $11,612. Required Financial Aid Forms: FAFSA. Deadline to Apply for Financial Aid: August 1; March 15 (priority).

Southeastern Oklahoma State University

Admissions Office, Southeastern Oklahoma State University, Durant, OK 74701. Phone: (580) 924-0121, ext. 2060, (800) 435-1327. Fax: (580) 745-7472. E-mail: rmanley@sosu.edu. Web Site: sosu.edu. In-State Tuition and Fees: $1,964. Out-of-State Tuition and Fees: $4,394. Room and Board: $2,689. Students Receiving Some Form of Aid: 85%. Students Receiving Non-Need-Based Aid: 31%. Average Aid Package: $2,433. Required Financial Aid Forms: FAFSA. Deadline to Apply for Financial Aid: April 1.

Southwestern Oklahoma State University—Weatherford

Admissions Office, 100 Campus Drive, Weatherford, OK 73096-3098. Phone: (580) 774-3009. Fax: (580) 774-3795. E-mail: phillic@swosu.edu. Web Site: swosu.edu. In-State Tuition and Fees: $1,888. Out-of-State Tuition and Fees: $4,543. Room and Board: $2,440. Students Receiving Some Form of Aid: 55%. Students Receiving Non-Need-Based Aid: 48%. Average Aid Package: $948. Required Financial Aid Forms: FAFSA. Deadline to Apply for Financial Aid: March 1.

University of Central Oklahoma

Admissions Office, 100 North University Drive, Edmond, OK 73034-5209. Phone: (405) 974-2338, (800) 254-4215. Fax: (405) 341-4964. Web Site: ucok.edu. In-State Tuition and Fees: $1,936. Out-of-State Tuition and Fees: $4,456. Room and Board (In-state students): $2,783. Students Receiving Some Form of Aid: 31%. Students Receiving Non-Need-Based Aid: 13%. Average Aid Package: $4,750. Required Financial Aid Forms: FAFSA, Institutional Form. Deadline to Apply for Financial Aid: April 1.

University of Oklahoma

Office of Admissions, 1000 Asp Avenue, Norman, OK 73019-4076. Phone: (800) 234-6868. Fax: (405) 325-7124. E-mail: admrec@ouou.edu. Web Site: ou.edu. In-State Tuition and Fees: $2,456. Out-of-State Tuition and Fees: $6,791. Room and Board: $4,384. Students Receiving Some Form of Aid: 43%. Students Receiving Non-Need-Based Aid: 14%. Average Aid Package: $5,991. Required Financial Aid Forms: FAFSA. Deadline to Apply for Financial Aid: June 1; March 1 (priority).

University of Science and Arts of Oklahoma

Admissions Office, P.O. Box 82345, Chickasha, OK 73018. Phone: (405) 574-1204. Fax: (405) 574-1220. E-mail: jwevans@usao.edu. Web Site: usao.edu. In-State Tuition and Fees: $1,893. Out-of-State Tuition and Fees: $4,548. Room and Board: $2,320. Students Receiving Some Form of Aid: 53%. Students Receiving Non-Need-Based Aid: 27%. Average Aid Package: $6,946. Required Financial Aid Forms: FAFSA, institution's own form. Deadline to Apply for Financial Aid: March 15 (priority).

University of Tulsa

Admissions Office, 600 South College Avenue, Tulsa, OK 74104. Phone: (918) 631-2307, (800) 331-3050. Fax: (918) 631-5003. E-mail: admission@utulsa.edu. Web Site: utulsa.edu. Tuition and Fees: $13,480. Room and Board: $4,660. Students Receiving Some Form of Aid: 52%. Students Receiving Non-Need-Based Aid: 30%. Average Aid Package: $14,439. Required Financial Aid Forms: FAFSA, institutional form. Deadline to Apply for Financial Aid: April 1 (priority).

OREGON

Eastern Oregon University

Office of Admissions, One University Boulevard, La Grande, OR 97850. Phone: (541) 962-3393, (800) 452-8639. Fax: (541) 962-3418. E-mail: admissions@eou.edu. Web Site: eou.edu. Tuition and Fees: $3,366. Room and Board: $4,565. Students Receiving Some Form of Aid: 56%. Students Receiving Non-Need-Based Aid: 19%. Average Aid Package: $5,540. Required Financial Aid Forms: FAFSA. Deadline to Apply for Financial Aid: rolling; March 1 (priority).

Lewis and Clark College

Office of Admissions, 0615 S.W. Palatine Hill Road, Portland, OR 97219. Phone: (503) 768-7040, (800) 444-4111. Fax: (503) 768-7055. E-mail: admissions@lclark.edu. Web Site: lclark.edu. Tuition and Fees: $20,326. Room and Board: $6,220. Students Receiving Some Form of Aid: 54%. Students Receiving Non-Need-Based Aid: 20%. Average Aid Package: $19,060. Required Financial Aid Forms: FAFSA. Deadline to Apply for Financial Aid: March 1.

Linfield College

Office of Admissions, 900 S.E. Baker Street, McMinnville, OR 97128. Phone: (503) 434-2213, (503) 434-2214. Fax: (503) 434-2472. E-mail: admissions@linfield.edu. Web Site: linfield.edu. Tuition and Fees: $18,080. Room and Board: $5,300. Students Receiving Some Form of Aid: 69%. Students Receiving Non-Need-Based Aid: 17%. Average Aid Package: $14,800. Required Financial Aid Forms: FAFSA. Deadline to Apply for Financial Aid: February 1.

Marylhurst University

Office of the Registrar, 17600 Pacific Highway (Hwy 43), Marylhurst, OR 97036-0261. Phone: (503) 699-6268, (800) 634-9982. Fax: (503) 636-9526. E-mail: wbird@marylhurst.edu. Web Site: marylhurst.edu. Tuition and Fees: $10,770. Room and Board: $5,928. Average Aid Package: $13,100. Required Financial Aid Forms: FAFSA, institutional form. Deadline to Apply for Financial Aid: rolling.

Oregon Institute of Technology

Admissions Office, 3201 Campus Drive, Klamath Falls, OR 97601-8801. Phone: (541) 885-1000, (800) 422-2017. Fax: (541) 885-1115. E-mail: oit@oit.edu. Web Site: oit.edu. In-State Tuition and Fees: $3,309. Out-of-State Tuition and Fees: $10,539. Room and Board: $4,865. Required Financial Aid Forms: FAFSA. Deadline to Apply for Financial Aid: March 1.

Oregon State University

Admissions Office, 104 Kerr Administration Building, Corvallis, OR 97331-2106. **Phone:** (541) 737-4411, (800) 291-4192. **Fax:** (541) 737-2482. **E-mail:** osuadmit@orst.edu. **Web Site:** osu.orst.edu. **In-State Tuition and Fees:** $3,549. **Out-of-State Tuition and Fees:** $12,393. **Room and Board:** $5,394. **Required Financial Aid Forms:** FAFSA. **Deadline to Apply for Financial Aid:** May 1; February 1 (priority).

Pacific University

Admissions Office, 2043 College Way, Forest Grove, OR 97116. **Phone:** (503) 359-2218, (800) 677-6712. **Fax:** (503) 359-2975. **E-mail:** admissions@pacificu.edu. **Web Site:** pacificu.edu. **Tuition and Fees:** $17,800. **Room and Board:** $5,295. **Students Receiving Some Form of Aid:** 73%. **Students Receiving Non-Need-Based Aid:** 7%. **Average Aid Package:** $15,832. **Required Financial Aid Forms:** FAFSA. **Deadline to Apply for Financial Aid:** rolling.

Portland State University

Office of Admissions and Records, P.O. Box 751, Portland, OR 97207-0751. **Phone:** (503) 725-3511, (800) 547-8887. **Fax:** (503) 725-5525. **E-mail:** askadm@ess.pdx.edu. **Web Site:** pdx.edu. **In-State Tuition and Fees:** $3,468. **Out-of-State Tuition and Fees:** $11,661. **Room and Board:** $6,150. **Students Receiving Some Form of Aid:** 36%. **Students Receiving Non-Need-Based Aid:** 10%. **Average Aid Package:** $6,229. **Required Financial Aid Forms:** FAFSA, institutional form, CSS/Financial Aid PROFILE. **Deadline to Apply for Financial Aid:** rolling.

Reed College

Office of Admission, 3203 Southeast Woodstock Boulevard, Portland, OR 97202-8199. **Phone:** (503) 777-7511, (800) 547-4750. **Fax:** (503) 777-7769. **E-mail:** admission@reed.edu. **Web Site:** reed.edu. **Tuition and Fees:** $24,990. **Room and Board:** $6,820. **Students Receiving Some Form of Aid:** 42%. **Average Aid Package:** $19,999. **Required Financial Aid Forms:** FAFSA, Profile, institutional form, parent tax forms, W-2. **Deadline to Apply for Financial Aid:** February 1.

Southern Oregon University

Admissions Office, 1250 Siskiyou Boulevard, Ashland, OR 97520. **Phone:** (541) 552-6411, (800) 482-7672 (Oregon only). **Fax:** (541) 552-6614. **E-mail:** admissions@sou.edu. **Web Site:** sou.edu. **In-State Tuition and Fees:** $2,758. **Out-of-State Tuition and Fees:** $9,421. **Room and Board:** $5,484. **Students Receiving Some Form of Aid:** 54%. **Students Receiving Non-Need-Based Aid:** 1%. **Average Aid Package:** $6,892. **Required Financial Aid Forms:** FAFSA. **Deadline to Apply for Financial Aid:** March 1 (priority).

University of Oregon

Admissions Office, 240 Oregon Hall, Eugene, OR 97403. **Phone:** (541) 346-3201, (800) BE A DUCK. **Fax:** (541) 346-5815. **E-mail:** darkwing.uoregon.edu/admit. **Web Site:** uoregon.edu. **In-State Tuition and Fees:** $3,810. **Out-of-State Tuition and Fees:** $13,197. **Room and Board:** $5,350. **Students Receiving Some Form of Aid:** 65%. **Students Receiving Non-Need-Based Aid:** 16%. **Average Aid Package:** $8,204. **Required Financial Aid Forms:** FAFSA. **Deadline to Apply for Financial Aid:** February 1.

University of Portland

Admissions Office, 5000 North Willamette Boulevard, Portland, OR 97203. **Phone:** (503) 943-7147, (888) 627-5601. **Fax:** (503) 943-7315. **E-mail:** admissio@up.edu. **Web Site:** up.edu. **Tuition and Fees:** $17,299. **Room and Board:** $5,190. **Students Receiving Some Form of Aid:** 57%. **Students Receiving Non-Need-Based Aid:** 24%. **Average Aid Package:** $15,143. **Required Financial Aid Forms:** FAFSA, institutional form. **Deadline to Apply for Financial Aid:** March 1 (priority).

Western Oregon University

Admissions Office, 345 North Monmouth Avenue, Monmouth, OR 97361. **Phone:** (503) 838-8211, (877) 877-1593. **Fax:** (503) 838-8067. **E-mail:** wolfgram@wou.edu. **Web Site:** wou.edu. **In-State Tuition and Fees:** $3,222. **Out-of-State Tuition and Fees:** $10,062. **Room and Board:** $5,004. **Students Receiving Some Form of Aid:** 54%. **Students Receiving Non-Need-Based Aid:** 9%. **Average Aid Package:** $7,221. **Required Financial Aid Forms:** FAFSA. **Deadline to Apply for Financial Aid:** February 1 (priority).

Willamette University

Undergraduate Admission Office, 900 State Street, Salem, OR 97301. **Phone:** (503) 370-6303, (877) 542-2787. **E-mail:** undergrad-admission@willamette.edu. **Web Site:** willamette.edu. **Tuition and Fees:** $21,821. **Room and Board:** $5,700. **Students Receiving Some Form of Aid:** 65%. **Students Receiving Non-Need-Based Aid:** 14%. **Average Aid Package:** $18,285. **Required Financial Aid Forms:** FAFSA, CSS Profile. **Deadline to Apply for Financial Aid:** February 1 (priority).

PENNSYLVANIA

Albright College*

Admissions Office, P.O. Box 15234, 13th and Bern Streets, Reading, PA 19612-5234. **Phone:** (610) 921-7512, (800) 252-1856. **Fax:** (610) 921-7294. **E-mail:** albright@joe.alb.edu. **Web Site:** albright.edu. **Tuition and Fees:** $25,240. **Room and Board:** $5,612. **Students Receiving Some Form of Aid:** 79%. **Students Receiving Non-Need-Based Aid:** 55%. **Average Aid Package:** $17,402. **Required Financial Aid Forms:** FAFSA. **Deadline to Apply for Financial Aid:** May 1 (March 1 priority).

Allegheny College

Admissions Office, P.O. Box 5, 520 N. Main Street, Meadville, PA 16335. **Phone:** (814) 332-4351, (800) 521-5293. **Fax:** (814) 337-0431. **E-mail:** admiss@admin.alleg.edu. **Web Site:** alleg.edu. **Tuition and Fees:** $21,570. **Room and Board:** $5,100. **Students Receiving Some Form of Aid:** 76%. **Students Receiving Non-Need-Based Aid:** 9%. **Average Aid Package:** $17,415. **Required Financial Aid Forms:** FAFSA. **Deadline to Apply for Financial Aid:** February 15.

Alvernia College

Admissions Office, 400 St. Bernardine Street, Reading, PA 19607. **Phone:** (610) 796-8220, (888) ALVERNIA. **Fax:** (610) 796-8336. **Web Site:** alvernia.edu. **Tuition and Fees:** $13,180. **Room and Board:** $5,840. **Required Financial Aid Forms:** FAFSA. **Deadline to Apply for Financial Aid:** April 1.

Beaver College

Office of Enrollment Management, 450 South Easton Road, Glenside, PA 19038. **Phone:** (215) 572-2910, (888) BEAVER-3. **Fax:** (215) 572-4049. **E-mail:** admiss@beaver.edu. **Web Site:** beaver.edu. **Tuition and Fees:** $18,030. **Room and Board:** $7,740. **Students Receiving Some Form of Aid:** 68%. **Students Receiving Non-Need-Based Aid:** 48%. **Average Aid Package:** $16,433. **Required Financial Aid Forms:** FAFSA, institutional form. **Deadline to Apply for Financial Aid:** March 1.

Bloomsburg University of Pennsylvania

Admissions Office, 10 Ben Franklin Hall, 400 East Second Street, Bloomsburg, PA 17815. **Phone:** (570) 389-4316. **Fax:** (570) 389-4741. **E-mail:** buadmiss@bloomu.edu. **Web Site:** bloomu.edu. **In-State Tuition and Fees:** $4,455. **Out-of-State Tuition and Fees:** $9,883. **Room and Board:** $3,784. **Students Receiving Some Form of Aid:** 58%. **Students Receiving Non-Need-Based Aid:** 13%. **Average Aid Package:** $6,872. **Required Financial Aid Forms:** FAFSA, PHEAA. **Deadline to Apply for Financial Aid:** March 15 (priority).

Bryn Mawr College

Admissions Office, Ely House, 101 N. Merion Avenue, Bryn Mawr, PA 19010-2899. **Phone:** (610) 526-5152. **Fax:** (610) 526-7471. **E-mail:** admissions@brynmawr.edu. **Web Site:** brynmawr.edu. **Tuition and Fees:** $23,360. **Room and Board:** $8,100. **Students Receiving Some Form of Aid:** 58%. **Average Aid Package:** $20,802. **Required Financial Aid Forms:** FAFSA, CSS/Financial Aid Profile. **Deadline to Apply for Financial Aid:** January 15.

Bucknell University

Admissions Office, Freas Hall, Lewisburg, PA 17837. **Phone:** (570) 577-1101. **Fax:** (570) 577-3760. **E-mail:** admissions@bucknell.edu. **Web Site:** bucknell.edu. **Tuition and Fees:** $22,881. **Room and Board:** $5,469. **Students Receiving Some Form of Aid:** 53%. **Average Aid Package:** $17,241. **Required Financial Aid Forms:** FAFSA, CSS Profile. **Deadline to Apply for Financial Aid:** January 1.

Cabrini College*

Admissions Office, 610 King of Prussia Road, Radnor, PA 19087-3698. **Phone:** (610) 902-8559, (800) 848-1003. **Fax:** (610) 902-8508. **E-mail:** admit@cabrini.edu. **Web Site:** cabrini.edu. **Tuition and Fees:** $14,650. **Room and Board:** $6,900. **Students Receiving Some Form of Aid:** 46%. **Average Aid Package:** $11,601.

California University of Pennsylvania*

Admissions Office, 250 University Avenue, California, PA 15419-1394. **Phone:** (724) 938-4404, (888) 412-0479. **Fax:** (724) 938-4564. **Web Site:** cup.edu. **In-State Tuition and Fees:** $4,741. **Out-of-State Tuition and Fees:** $10,169. **Room and Board:** $4,526. **Required Financial Aid Forms:** FAFSA. **Deadline to Apply for Financial Aid:** April 1.

Carnegie Mellon University

Admissions Office, 5000 Forbes Avenue, Pittsburgh, PA 15213. **Phone:** (412) 268-2082. **Fax:** (412) 268-7838. **E-mail:** undergraduate-admissions+@andrew.cmu.edu. **Web Site:** cmu.edu. **Tuition and Fees:** $23,056. **Room and Board:** $7,028. **Students Receiving Some Form of Aid:** 52%. **Students Receiving Non-Need-Based Aid:** 22%. **Average Aid Package:** $15,789. **Required Financial Aid Forms:** FAFSA, institutional form, parent's tax form. **Deadline to Apply for Financial Aid:** February 15 (priority), May 1.

Cedar Crest College

Admissions Office, 100 College Drive, Allentown, PA 18104-6196. **Phone:** (610) 740-3780, (800) 360-1222. **Fax:** (610) 606-4647. **E-mail:** cccadmis@cedarcrest.edu. **Web Site:** cedarcrest.edu. **Tuition and Fees:** $17,790. **Room and Board:** $6,465. **Students Receiving Some Form of Aid:** 51%. **Students Receiving Non-Need-Based Aid:** 4%. **Average Aid Package:** $15,198. **Required Financial Aid Forms:** FAFSA, institutional form. **Deadline to Apply for Financial Aid:** rolling.

Chatham College

Admissions Office, Woodland Road, Pittsburgh, PA 15232. **Phone:** (412) 365-1290, (800) 837-1290. **Fax:** (412) 365-1209. **E-mail:** admissions@chatham.edu. **Web Site:** chatham.edu. **Tuition and Fees:** $17,544. **Room and Board:** $6,120. **Students Receiving Some Form of Aid:** 69%. **Students Receiving Non-Need-Based Aid:** 65%. **Average Aid Package:** $17,247. **Required Financial Aid Forms:** FAFSA. **Deadline to Apply for Financial Aid:** May 1.

Chestnut Hill College

Admissions Office, 9601 Germantown Avenue, Philadelphia, PA 19118-2693. **Phone:** (215) 248-7001, (800) 248-0052 (out-of-state). **Fax:** (215) 248-7082. **E-mail:** chcapply@chc.edu. **Web Site:** chc.edu. **Tuition and Fees:** $16,900. **Room and Board:** $6,840. **Required Financial Aid Forms:** FAFSA. **Deadline to Apply for Financial Aid:** April 15 (priority).

Clarion University of Pennsylvania

Admissions Office, 840 Wood Street, Clarion, PA 16214. **Phone:** (814) 393-2306. **Fax:** (814) 393-2030. **E-mail:** smcmille@mail.clarion.edu. **Web Site:** clarion.edu. **In-State Tuition and Fees:** $4,600. **Out-of-State Tuition and Fees:** $6,410. **Room and Board:** $3,984. **Required Financial Aid Forms:** FAFSA. **Deadline to Apply for Financial Aid:** May 1.

College Misericordia

Office of Admissions, 301 Lake Street, Dallas, PA 18612. **Phone:** (570) 674-6460, (800) 852-7675. **Fax:** (570) 675-2441. **E-mail:** admiss@miseri.edu. **Web Site:** miseri.edu. **Tuition and Fees:** $15,250. **Room and Board:** $6,340. **Students Receiving Some Form of Aid:** 80%. **Students Receiving Non-Need-Based Aid:** 76%. **Average Aid Package:** $13,000. **Required Financial Aid Forms:** FAFSA. **Deadline to Apply for Financial Aid:** March 1.

Delaware Valley College

Admissions Office, 700 East Butler Avenue, Doylestown, PA 18901. **Phone:** (215) 489-2211, (800) 233-5825. **Fax:** (215) 230-2968. **Web Site:** devalcol.edu. **Tuition and Fees:** $17,048. **Room and Board:** $6,339. **Students Receiving Some Form of Aid:** 58%. **Students Receiving Non-Need-Based Aid:** 15%. **Average Aid Package:** $13,935. **Required Financial Aid Forms:** FAFSA. **Deadline to Apply for Financial Aid:** May 1.

Dickinson College

Admissions Office, P.O. Box 1773, Carlisle, PA 17013-2896. Phone: (717) 245-1231, (800) 644-1773. Fax: (717) 245-1442. E-mail: admit@dickinson.edu. Web Site: dickinson.edu. Tuition and Fees: $24,475. Room and Board: $6,450. Students Receiving Some Form of Aid: 68%. Students Receiving Non-Need-Based Aid: 9%. Average Aid Package: $20,228. Required Financial Aid Forms: FAFSA, CSS Profile. Deadline to Apply for Financial Aid: February 1.

Drexel University

Office of Admissions, 3141 Chestnut Street, Philadelphia, PA 19104-2875. Phone: (215) 895-2400, (800) 237-3935. Fax: (215) 895-5939. E-mail: enroll@drexel.edu. Web Site: drexel.edu. Tuition and Fees: $16,867. Room and Board: $8,320. Students Receiving Some Form of Aid: 56%. Students Receiving Non-Need-Based Aid: 29%. Average Aid Package: $13,622. Required Financial Aid Forms: FAFSA. Deadline to Apply for Financial Aid: February 15.

Duquesne University

Admissions Office, 600 Forbes Avenue, Pittsburgh, PA 15282-0201. Phone: (412) 396-5000, (800) 456-0590. Fax: (412) 396-5644. E-mail: admissions@duq2.cc.duq.edu. Web Site: duq.edu. Tuition and Fees: $15,579. Room and Board: $6,314. Students Receiving Some Form of Aid: 62%. Students Receiving Non-Need-Based Aid: 32%. Average Aid Package: $13,982. Required Financial Aid Forms: FAFSA, institutional form. Deadline to Apply for Financial Aid: May 1.

East Stroudsburg University of Pennsylvania

Admissions Office, 200 Prospect Street, East Stroudsburg, PA 18301-2999. Phone: (570) 422-3542, (877) 230-5547. Fax: (570) 422-3933. E-mail: undergrads@po-box.esu.edu. Web Site: esu.edu. In-State Tuition and Fees: $4,492. Out-of-State Tuition and Fees: $9,920. Room and Board: $3,938. Students Receiving Some Form of Aid: 48%. Students Receiving Non-Need-Based Aid: 2%. Average Aid Package: $4,455. Required Financial Aid Forms: FAFSA. Deadline to Apply for Financial Aid: March 1.

Eastern College

Office of Admissions, 1300 Eagle Rd., St. Davids, PA 19087-3696. Phone: (610) 341-5967, (800) 452-0996. Fax: (610) 341-1723. E-mail: ugadm@eastern.edu. Web Site: eastern.edu. Tuition and Fees: $14,590. Room and Board: $6,240. Required Financial Aid Forms: FAFSA, institutional form. Deadline to Apply for Financial Aid: rolling.

Elizabethtown College

Admissions Office, One Alpha Drive, Elizabethtown, PA 17022. Phone: (717) 361-1400. Fax: (717) 361-1365. E-mail: admissions@etown.edu. Web Site: etown.edu. Tuition and Fees: $19,100. Room and Board: $5,600. Students Receiving Some Form of Aid: 67%. Students Receiving Non-Need-Based Aid: 5%. Average Aid Package: $15,036. Required Financial Aid Forms: FAFSA, CSS Profile, institutional form. Deadline to Apply for Financial Aid: March 15 (priority).

Franklin and Marshall College

Admissions Office, P.O. Box 3003, Lancaster, PA 17604-3003. Phone: (717) 291-3953. Fax: (717) 291-4389. E-mail: admission@fandm.edu. Web Site: fandm.edu. Tuition and Fees: $24,816. Room and Board: $5,994. Students Receiving Some Form of Aid: 48%. Students Receiving Non-Need-Based Aid: 7%. Average Aid Package: $17,860. Required Financial Aid Forms: FAFSA, Profile. Deadline to Apply for Financial Aid: February 1.

Gannon University

Office of Admissions, 109 University Square, Erie, PA 16541-0001. Phone: (814) 871-7240, (800) GANNON U. Fax: (814) 871-5803. E-mail: admissions@gannon.edu. Web Site: gannon.edu. Tuition and Fees: $13,954. Room and Board: $5,300. Students Receiving Some Form of Aid: 70%. Students Receiving Non-Need-Based Aid: 70%. Average Aid Package: $11,825. Required Financial Aid Forms: FAFSA. Deadline to Apply for Financial Aid: rolling (March 15 priority).

Geneva College

Admissions Office, 3200 College Avenue, Beaver Falls, PA 15010. Phone: (724) 847-6500, (800) 847-8255 (out-of-state). Fax: (724) 847-6776. E-mail: admissions@geneva.edu. Web Site: geneva.edu. Tuition and Fees: $13,350. Room and Board: $5,690. Students Receiving Some Form of Aid: 57%. Students Receiving Non-Need-Based Aid: 40%. Average Aid Package: $9,000. Required Financial Aid Forms: FAFSA. Deadline to Apply for Financial Aid: (April 15 priority date).

Gettysburg College

Director of Admissions, Eisenhower House, Gettysburg, PA 17325-1484. Phone: (800) 431-0803, (717) 337-6100. Fax: (717) 337-6145. E-mail: admiss@gettysburg.edu. Web Site: gettysburg.edu. Tuition and Fees: $24,032. Room and Board: $5,644. Students Receiving Some Form of Aid: 59%. Students Receiving Non-Need-Based Aid: 13%. Average Aid Package: $19,800. Required Financial Aid Forms: FAFSA, CSS Profile. Deadline to Apply for Financial Aid: March 15.

Grove City College

Admissions Office, 100 Campus Drive, Grove City, PA 16127. Phone: (724) 458-2100. Fax: (724) 458-3395. E-mail: admissions@gcc.edu. Web Site: gcc.edu. Tuition and Fees: $7,220. Room and Board: $4,206. Students Receiving Some Form of Aid: 30%. Students Receiving Non-Need-Based Aid: 2%. Average Aid Package: $5,950. Required Financial Aid Forms: institutional form. Deadline to Apply for Financial Aid: April 15.

Gwynedd-Mercy College

Admissions Office, P.O. Box 901, Sumneytown Pike, PA 19437-0901. Phone: (215) 646-7300, (800) DIAL-GMC (in-state). Fax: (215) 641-5556. E-mail: admissions@gmc.edu. Web Site: gmc.edu. Tuition and Fees: $13,540. Room and Board: $6,500. Students Receiving Some Form of Aid: 40%. Students Receiving Non-Need-Based Aid: 14%. Average Aid Package: $12,720. Required Financial Aid Forms: FAFSA, federal tax forms, institutional form. Deadline to Apply for Financial Aid: March 15 (priority).

Haverford College

Admissions Office, 370 Lancaster Avenue, Haverford, PA 19041-1392. Phone: (610) 896-1350. Fax: (610) 896-1338. E-mail: Admitme@haverford.edu. Web Site: haverford.edu. Tuition and Fees: $24,940. Room and Board: $7,910. Students Receiving Some Form of Aid: 44%. Average Aid

Package: $19,984. Required Financial Aid Forms: FAFSA, CSS Profile. Deadline to Apply for Financial Aid: January 31.

Holy Family College

Admissions Office, Grant and Frankford Avenues, Philadelphia, PA 19114. Phone: (215) 637-3050, (800) 637-1191. Fax: (215) 281-1022. E-mail: rnolan@hfc.edu. Web Site: hfc.edu. Tuition and Fees: $11,760. Average Aid Package: $8,600. Required Financial Aid Forms: FAFSA, institution's own form. Deadline to Apply for Financial Aid: February 15 (priority).

Immaculata College

Office of Admission, P.O. Box 642, Immaculata, PA 19345. Phone: (877) 428-6329, (610) 647-4400, ext. 3015. Fax: (610) 251-1668. E-mail: admiss@immaculata.edu. Web Site: immaculata.edu. Tuition and Fees: $13,400. Room and Board: $6,500. Students Receiving Some Form of Aid: 14%. Students Receiving Non-Need-Based Aid: 14%. Average Aid Package: $13,689. Required Financial Aid Forms: FAFSA. Deadline to Apply for Financial Aid: May 1; February 15 (priority).

Indiana University of Pennsylvania

Office of Admissions, 216 Pratt Hall, Indiana, PA 15705. Phone: (724) 357-2230, (800) 442-6830. Fax: (724) 357-6281. E-mail: admissions_inquiry@grove.iup.edu. Web Site: iup.edu. In-State Tuition and Fees: $4,419. Out-of-State Tuition and Fees: $9,847. Room and Board: $3,782. Students Receiving Some Form of Aid: 73%. Students Receiving Non-Need-Based Aid: 12%. Average Aid Package: $6,483. Required Financial Aid Forms: FAFSA, state aid form. Deadline to Apply for Financial Aid: April 15.

Juniata College

Enrollment Center, 1700 Moore Street, Huntingdon, PA 16652. Phone: (814) 641-3420, (877) JUNIATA. Fax: (814) 641-3100. E-mail: info@juniata.edu. Web Site: juniata.edu. Tuition and Fees: $19,360. Room and Board: $5,290. Students Receiving Some Form of Aid: 81%. Students Receiving Non-Need-Based Aid: 71%. Average Aid Package: $16,697. Required Financial Aid Forms: FAFSA. Deadline to Apply for Financial Aid: March 1 (priority).

King's College

Admissions Office, 113 North River Street, Wilkes-Barre, PA 18711. Phone: (570) 208-5858, (888) 546-4772. Fax: (570) 208-5971. E-mail: admssns@kings.edu. Web Site: kings.edu. Tuition and Fees: $16,700. Room and Board: $6,890. Students Receiving Some Form of Aid: 68%. Students Receiving Non-Need-Based Aid: 29%. Average Aid Package: $12,439. Required Financial Aid Forms: FAFSA, state aid form, institutional form. Deadline to Apply for Financial Aid: March 1 (priority).

Kutztown University

Admissions Office, 15200 Kutztown Road, Kutztown, PA 19530. Phone: (610) 683-4060, (877) 628-1915. Fax: (610) 683-1375. E-mail: admission@kutztown.edu. Web Site: kutztown.edu. In-State Tuition and Fees: $3,618. Out-of-State Tuition and Fees: $9,046. Room and Board: $3,620. Students Receiving Some Form of Aid: 50%. Students Receiving Non-Need-Based Aid: 6%. Average Aid Package: $5,072. Required Financial Aid Forms: FAFSA. Deadline to Apply for Financial Aid: February 15 (priority).

La Salle University

Office of Admission, 1900 W. Olney Drive, Philadelphia, PA 19141. Phone: (215) 951-1500, (800) 328-1910. Fax: (215) 951-1656. E-mail: admiss@lasalle.edu. Web Site: lasalle.edu. Tuition and Fees: $17,260. Room and Board: $6,702. Required Financial Aid Forms: FAFSA. Deadline to Apply for Financial Aid: February 15.

Lafayette College

Office of Admissions, Lafayette College, Easton, PA 18042. Phone: (610) 330-5100. Fax: (610) 330-5355. E-mail: admissions@lafayette.edu. Web Site: lafayette.edu. Tuition and Fees: $23,846. Room and Board: $7,413. Students Receiving Some Form of Aid: 46%. Students Receiving Non-Need-Based Aid: 4%. Average Aid Package: $19,556. Required Financial Aid Forms: FAFSA, CSS Profile, Noncustodial Parent's Statement, Business/Farm Supplement, student's and parents' prior year tax returns along with all schedules and W-2's. Deadline to Apply for Financial Aid: February 1.

Lebanon Valley College

Admissions Office, 101 North College Avenue, Annville, PA 17003-0501. Phone: (717) 867-6181, (800) 445-6181. Fax: (717) 867-6026. E-mail: admiss@lvc.edu. Web Site: lvc.edu. Tuition and Fees: $18,420. Room and Board: $5,680. Students Receiving Some Form of Aid: 59%. Students Receiving Non-Need-Based Aid: 44%. Average Aid Package: $13,762. Required Financial Aid Forms: FAFSA, LVC form. Deadline to Apply for Financial Aid: March 1 (priority).

Lehigh University

Admissions Office, 27 Memorial Drive West, Bethlehem, PA 18015. Phone: (610) 758-3100. Fax: (610) 758-4361. E-mail: inado@lehigh.edu. Web Site: lehigh.edu. Tuition and Fees: $24,280. Room and Board: $6,860. Students Receiving Some Form of Aid: 50%. Students Receiving Non-Need-Based Aid: 8%. Average Aid Package: $18,100. Required Financial Aid Forms: FAFSA, profile, institutional form. Deadline to Apply for Financial Aid: February 1.

Lincoln University

Admissions Office, Lincoln Hall, P.O. Box 179, Lincoln University, PA 19352. Phone: (610) 932-8300, ext. 3993, (800) 790-0191. Fax: (610) 932-1209. E-mail: admiss@lu.lincoln.edu. Web Site: lincoln.edu. In-State Tuition and Fees: $4,824. Out-of-State Tuition and Fees: $7,716. Room and Board: $5,034. Students Receiving Some Form of Aid: 314%. Students Receiving Non-Need-Based Aid: 27%. Average Aid Package: $4,800. Required Financial Aid Forms: FAFSA, state aid form. Deadline to Apply for Financial Aid: rolling.

Lock Haven University of Pennsylvania

Admissions Office, Akeley Hall, Lock Haven, PA 17745. Phone: (570) 893-2027, (800) 332-8900. Fax: (570) 893-2201. E-mail: admissions@lhup.edu. Web Site: lhup.edu. In-State Tuition and Fees: $4,072. Out-of-State Tuition and Fees: $7,428. Room and Board: $3,676. Students Receiving Some Form of Aid: 61%. Students Receiving Non-Need-Based Aid: 13%. Average Aid Package: $5,414. Required Financial Aid Forms: FAFSA. Deadline to Apply for Financial Aid: May 1; April 1 (priority).

Lycoming College

Drum Admission House, 700 College Place, Williamsport, PA 17701. Phone: (800) 345-3920, (570) 321-4026. Fax: (570) 321-4317. E-mail: admissions@lycoming.edu. Web Site: lycoming.edu. Tuition and Fees: $18,540. Room and Board: $5,145. Students Receiving Some Form of Aid: 80%. Students Receiving Non-Need-Based Aid: 18%. Average Aid Package: $14,900. Required Financial Aid Forms: FAFSA, institutional form. Deadline to Apply for Financial Aid: April 15.

Mansfield University

Office of Admission, Mansfield University, Mansfield, PA 16933. Phone: (570) 662-4243, (800) 577-6826. Fax: (570) 662-4121. E-mail: admissns@mnsfld.edu. Web Site: mansfield.edu. In-State Tuition and Fees: $4,578. Out-of-State Tuition and Fees: $10,006. Room and Board: $3,852. Required Financial Aid Forms: FAFSA, institutional form. Deadline to Apply for Financial Aid: March 1, April 1.

Marywood University

Office of Admissions, 2300 Adams Avenue, Scranton, PA 18509. Phone: (570) 348-6234, (800) 346-5014. Fax: (570) 961-4763. E-mail: ugadm@ac.marywood.edu. Web Site: marywood.edu. Tuition and Fees: $15,623. Room and Board: $6,540. Students Receiving Some Form of Aid: 72%. Students Receiving Non-Need-Based Aid: 72%. Average Aid Package: $13,000. Required Financial Aid Forms: FAFSA, institutional form. Deadline to Apply for Financial Aid: rolling.

Mercyhurst College

Admissions Office, Mercyhurst College, Erie, PA 16546. Phone: (814) 824-2241, (800) 825-1926. Fax: (814) 824-2071. E-mail: admug@mercyhurst.edu. Web Site: mercyhurst.edu. Tuition and Fees: $14,090. Room and Board: $5,364. Students Receiving Some Form of Aid: 41%. Students Receiving Non-Need-Based Aid: 24%. Average Aid Package: $8,152. Required Financial Aid Forms: FAFSA. Deadline to Apply for Financial Aid: rolling, May 1 (priority).

Messiah College

Admissions Office, College Avenue, Grantham, PA 17027-0800. Phone: (717) 691-6000, (800) 233-4220 (out-of-state), (800) 342-1349 (in-state). Fax: (717) 796-5374. E-mail: admiss@messiah.edu. Web Site: messiah.edu. Tuition and Fees: $15,096. Room and Board: $5,580. Students Receiving Some Form of Aid: 72%. Students Receiving Non-Need-Based Aid: 51%. Average Aid Package: $11,909. Required Financial Aid Forms: FAFSA. Deadline to Apply for Financial Aid: April 1 (priority).

Millersville University of Pennsylvania

Admissions Office, P.O. Box 1002, Millersville, PA 17551-0302. Phone: (717) 872-3371, (800) 682-3648. Fax: (717) 871-2147. E-mail: muadmit@marauder.millersv.edu. Web Site: millersv.edu. In-State Tuition and Fees: $4,595. Out-of-State Tuition and Fees: $10,023. Room and Board: $4,730. Students Receiving Some Form of Aid: 32%. Average Aid Package: $5,866. Required Financial Aid Forms: FAFSA, PHEAA, institutional forms. Deadline to Apply for Financial Aid: March 15.

Moore College of Art and Design

Admissions Office, 20th Street and the Parkway, Philadelphia, PA 19103. Phone: (215) 568-4515, ext. 1105, (800) 523-2025. Fax: (215) 568-3547. E-mail: admiss@moore.edu. Web Site: moore.edu. Tuition and Fees: $15,975. Room and Board: $6,100. Required Financial Aid Forms: FAFSA. Deadline to Apply for Financial Aid: April 1.

Moravian College

Admissions Office, 1200 Main Street, Bethlehem, PA 18018. Phone: (610) 861-1320. Fax: (610) 861-3956. E-mail: admissions@moravian.edu. Web Site: moravian.edu. Tuition and Fees: $18,575. Room and Board: $5,920. Students Receiving Some Form of Aid: 68%. Students Receiving Non-Need-Based Aid: 6%. Average Aid Package: $15,040. Required Financial Aid Forms: FAFSA, CSS Profile, tax forms. Deadline to Apply for Financial Aid: April 1; February 15 (priority).

Muhlenberg College

Admissions Office, 2400 Chew Street, Allentown, PA 18104-5586. Phone: (610) 821-3245. Web Site: muhlenberg.edu. Tuition and Fees: $20,085. Room and Board: $5,390. Required Financial Aid Forms: FAFSA, CSS Profile. Deadline to Apply for Financial Aid: February 15.

Neumann College

Office of Admissions and Financial Aid, One Neumann Drive, Aston, PA 19014-1298. Phone: (800) 9-NEUMAN. Fax: (610) 558-5652. E-mail: neumann@neumann.edu. Web Site: neumann.edu. Tuition and Fees: $14,320. Room and Board: $6,640. Students Receiving Some Form of Aid: 52%. Students Receiving Non-Need-Based Aid: 9%. Required Financial Aid Forms: FAFSA. Deadline to Apply for Financial Aid: rolling.

Peirce College

Admissions Office, 1420 Pine Street, Philadelphia, PA 19102. Phone: (215) 545-6400, ext. 9214, (800) GO-PEIRCE. Fax: (215) 893-4346. E-mail: sales@peirce.edu. Web Site: peirce.edu. Tuition and Fees: $8,220. Students Receiving Some Form of Aid: 30%. Students Receiving Non-Need-Based Aid: 13%. Average Aid Package: $3,500. Required Financial Aid Forms: FAFSA, institutional form. Deadline to Apply for Financial Aid: February 15.

Pennsylvania State University

Undergraduate Admissions Office, 201 Shields Building, University Park, PA 16802. Phone: (814) 865-5471. Fax: (814) 863-7590. E-mail: admissions@psu.edu. Web Site: psu.edu. In-State Tuition and Fees: $6,436. Out-of-State Tuition and Fees: $13,552. Room and Board: $4,690. Required Financial Aid Forms: FAFSA. Deadline to Apply for Financial Aid: February 15.

Pennsylvania State University—Erie, Behrend College

Admissions Office, Glenhill Farmhouse, Erie, PA 16563. Phone: (814) 898-6100. Fax: (814) 898-6044. E-mail: behrend.admissions@psu.edu. Web Site: pserie.psu.edu. In-State Tuition and Fees: $6,436. Out-of-State Tuition and Fees: $12,110. Room and Board: $4,690. Required Financial Aid Forms: FAFSA. Deadline to Apply for Financial Aid: February 15.

Philadelphia University

Admissions Office, School House Lane and Henry Avenue, Philadelphia, PA 19144-5497. **Phone:** (215) 951-2800, (800) 951-7287. **Fax:** (215) 951-2907. **E-mail:** admissions@PhilaU.edu. **Web Site:** PhilaU.edu. **Tuition and Fees:** $14,738. **Room and Board:** $6,576. **Students Receiving Some Form of Aid:** 54%. **Students Receiving Non-Need-Based Aid:** 4%. **Average Aid Package:** $11,719. **Required Financial Aid Forms:** FAFSA. **Deadline to Apply for Financial Aid:** April 15.

Point Park College

Admissions Office, 201 Wood Street, Pittsburgh, PA 15222. **Phone:** (412) 392-3430, (800) 321-0129. **Fax:** (412) 391-1980. **E-mail:** enroll@ppc.edu. **Web Site:** ppc.edu. **Tuition and Fees:** $12,454. **Room and Board:** $5,334. **Students Receiving Some Form of Aid:** 47%. **Students Receiving Non-Need-Based Aid:** 34%. **Average Aid Package:** $8,553. **Required Financial Aid Forms:** FAFSA. **Deadline to Apply for Financial Aid:** May 1.

Robert Morris College*

Enrollment Management, 881 Narrows Run Road, Moon Township, PA 15108-1189. **Phone:** (412) 262-8206, (800) 762-0097. **Fax:** (412) 299-2425. **E-mail:** budzisze@robert-morris.edu. **Web Site:** robert-morris.edu. **Tuition and Fees:** $9,472. **Room and Board:** $5,828. **Students Receiving Some Form of Aid:** 55%. **Students Receiving Non-Need-Based Aid:** 7%. **Average Aid Package:** $3,600. **Required Financial Aid Forms:** FAFSA. **Deadline to Apply for Financial Aid:** May 1.

Rosemont College

Office of Admissions and Financial Aid, 1400 Montgomery Avenue, Rosemont, PA 19010. **Phone:** (800) 331-0708. **E-mail:** admissions@rosemont.edu. **Web Site:** rosemont.edu. **Tuition and Fees:** $14,670. **Room and Board:** $7,030. **Students Receiving Some Form of Aid:** 28%. **Students Receiving Non-Need-Based Aid:** 17%. **Average Aid Package:** $15,600. **Required Financial Aid Forms:** FAFSA. **Deadline to Apply for Financial Aid:** March 1.

Saint Francis College

Admissions Office, Box 600, Loretto, PA 15940. **Phone:** (814) 472-3044. **E-mail:** admission@sfcpa.edu. **Web Site:** sfcpa.edu. **Tuition and Fees:** $15,040. **Room and Board:** $6,480. **Students Receiving Some Form of Aid:** 75%. **Students Receiving Non-Need-Based Aid:** 38%. **Average Aid Package:** $1,556. **Required Financial Aid Forms:** FAFSA. **Deadline to Apply for Financial Aid:** May 1.

Saint Joseph's University

Admissions Office, 5600 City Avenue, Philadelphia, PA 19131. **Phone:** (610) 660-1300. **Fax:** (610) 660-1314. **E-mail:** admi@sju.edu. **Web Site:** sju.edu. **Tuition and Fees:** $18,430. **Room and Board:** $7,514. **Students Receiving Some Form of Aid:** 51%. **Students Receiving Non-Need-Based Aid:** 20%. **Average Aid Package:** $11,150. **Required Financial Aid Forms:** FAFSA. **Deadline to Apply for Financial Aid:** February 15 (priority).

Saint Vincent College

Office of Admission and Financial Aid, 300 Fraser Purchase Road, Latrobe, PA 15650-2690. **Phone:** (724) 537-4540, (800) SVC-5549. **Fax:** (724) 532-5069. **E-mail:** admission@stvincent.edu. **Web Site:** stvincent.edu. **Tuition and Fees:** $14,955. **Room and Board:** $5,114. **Students Receiving Some Form of Aid:** 47%. **Students Receiving Non-Need-Based Aid:** 10%. **Average Aid Package:** $11,420. **Required Financial Aid Forms:** FAFSA. **Deadline to Apply for Financial Aid:** February 15 (priority).

Seton Hill College

Admissions Office, Seton Hill Drive, Greensburg, PA 15601. **Phone:** (724) 838-4255, (800) 826-6234. **Fax:** (724) 830-1294. **E-mail:** admit@setonhill.edu. **Web Site:** setonhill.edu. **Tuition and Fees:** $14,500. **Room and Board:** $5,050. **Students Receiving Some Form of Aid:** 69%. **Students Receiving Non-Need-Based Aid:** 17%. **Average Aid Package:** $17,200. **Required Financial Aid Forms:** FAFSA, institutional form. **Deadline to Apply for Financial Aid:** rolling; April 1 (priority).

Shippensburg University of Pennsylvania

Admissions Office, Old Main 105, 1871 Old Main Drive, Shippensburg, PA 17257-2299. **Phone:** (717) 477-1231. **Fax:** (717) 477-4016. **E-mail:** admiss@ship.edu. **Web Site:** ship.edu. **In-State Tuition and Fees:** $4,550. **Out-of-State Tuition and Fees:** $9,978. **Room and Board:** $4,126. **Students Receiving Non-Need-Based Aid:** 7%. **Average Aid Package:** $4,962. **Required Financial Aid Forms:** FAFSA. **Deadline to Apply for Financial Aid:** May 1; March 15 (priority).

Slippery Rock University

Office of Admissions, Maltby Center, Slippery Rock, PA 16057. **Phone:** (724) 738-2015, (800) SRU-9111. **Fax:** (724) 738-2913. **E-mail:** apply@sru.edu. **Web Site:** sru.edu. **In-State Tuition and Fees:** $4,484. **Out-of-State Tuition and Fees:** $9,912. **Room and Board:** $3,810. **Students Receiving Some Form of Aid:** 60%. **Students Receiving Non-Need-Based Aid:** 10%. **Average Aid Package:** $5,619. **Required Financial Aid Forms:** FAFSA. **Deadline to Apply for Financial Aid:** May 1 (priority).

Susquehanna University

Admissions Office, 514 University Avenue, Selinsgrove, PA 17870-1001. **Phone:** (570) 372-4260, (800) 326-9672. **Fax:** (570) 372-2722. **E-mail:** suadmiss@susqu.edu. **Web Site:** susqu.edu. **Tuition and Fees:** $19,670. **Room and Board:** $5,550. **Students Receiving Some Form of Aid:** 64%. **Students Receiving Non-Need-Based Aid:** 7%. **Average Aid Package:** $16,518. **Required Financial Aid Forms:** FAFSA, CSS Profile, tax returns. **Deadline to Apply for Financial Aid:** May 1 (March 1 priority deadline).

Swarthmore College

Office of Admissions, 500 College Avenue, Swarthmore, PA 19081. **Phone:** (610) 328-8300, (800) 667-3110. **Fax:** (610) 328-8580. **E-mail:** admissions@swarthmore.edu. **Web Site:** swarthmore.edu. **Tuition and Fees:** $24,190. **Room and Board:** $7,500. **Students Receiving Some Form of Aid:** 48%. **Average Aid Package:** $23,515. **Required Financial Aid Forms:** FAFSA, institutional form, CSS Profile, tax returns (parent and student). **Deadline to Apply for Financial Aid:** early February.

Temple University

Undergraduate Admissions, 1801 N. Broad Street (041-09), Philadelphia, PA 19122-6096. **Phone:** (215) 204-7200, (888) 340-2222. **Fax:** (215) 204-5694. **E-mail:** tuadm@vm.temple.edu. **Web Site:** temple.edu. **In-State Tuition and Fees:** $6,622. **Out-of-State Tuition and Fees:** $11,740. **Room and Board:** $6,302. **Students Receiving Some Form of Aid:** 50%. **Students Receiving Non-Need-Based Aid:** 14%. **Average Aid Package:** $8,947. **Required Financial Aid Forms:** FAFSA. **Deadline to Apply for Financial Aid:** March 1.

Thiel College*

Admissions Office, 75 College Avenue, Greenville, PA 16125. **Phone:** (724) 589-2345, (800) 24-THIEL. **Fax:** (724) 589-2021. **E-mail:** admissio@thiel.edu. **Web Site:** thiel.edu. **Tuition and Fees:** $10,785. **Room and Board:** $5,490. **Required Financial Aid Forms:** FAFSA. **Deadline to Apply for Financial Aid:** March 15 (priority).

University of Pennsylvania

Admissions Office, 1 College Hall, Philadelphia, PA 19104-6376. **Phone:** (215) 898-7507. **Fax:** (215) 898-9670. **E-mail:** info@admissions.ugao.upenn.edu. **Web Site:** upenn.edu. **Tuition and Fees:** $24,230. **Room and Board:** $4,592. **Students Receiving Some Form of Aid:** 44%. **Average Aid Package:** $21,660. **Required Financial Aid Forms:** FAF, insititutional form. **Deadline to Apply for Financial Aid:** February 15.

University of Pittsburgh

Office of Admissions and Financial Aid, Second Floor, Bruce Hall, 4200 Fifth Avenue, Pittsburgh, PA 15260. **Phone:** (412) 624-PITT. **Fax:** (412) 648-8815. **E-mail:** oafa@pitt.edu. **Web Site:** pitt.edu. **In-State Tuition and Fees:** $6,698. **Out-of-State Tuition and Fees:** $14,014. **Room and Board:** $5,766. **Students Receiving Some Form of Aid:** 51%. **Students Receiving Non-Need-Based Aid:** 17%. **Average Aid Package:** $7,922. **Required Financial Aid Forms:** FAFSA, institutional form. **Deadline to Apply for Financial Aid:** March 1 (priority).

University of Pittsburgh—Bradford

Admissions Office, 300 Campus Drive, Bradford, PA 16701. **Phone:** (800) 872-1787, (814) 362-7555. **Fax:** (814) 362-7578. **Web Site:** upb.edu. **In-State Tuition and Fees:** $6,814. **Out-of-State Tuition and Fees:** $14,426. **Room and Board:** $5,138. **Required Financial Aid Forms:** FAFSA. **Deadline to Apply for Financial Aid:** March 1 (priority).

University of Pittsburgh—Greensburg

Office of Admissions, 1150 Mount Pleasant Road, Greensburg, PA 15601. **Phone:** (724) 836-9880. **Fax:** (724) 836-7160. **E-mail:** upgadmit@pitt.edu. **Web Site:** pitt.edu/~upg. **In-State Tuition and Fees:** $6,582. **Out-of-State Tuition and Fees:** $13,898. **Room and Board:** $4,850. **Students Receiving Some Form of Aid:** 87%. **Required Financial Aid Forms:** FAFSA. **Deadline to Apply for Financial Aid:** March 1.

University of Pittsburgh—Johnstown

Admissions Office, 157 Blackington Hall, Johnstown, PA 15904-1200. **Phone:** (814) 269-7050, (800) 765-4875. **Fax:** (814) 269-7044. **Web Site:** pitt.edu/~upjweb. **In-State Tuition and Fees:** $6,630. **Out-of-State Tuition and Fees:** $13,946. **Room and Board:** $5,190. **Required Financial Aid Forms:** FAFSA. **Deadline to Apply for Financial Aid:** April 1.

University of Scranton

Admissions Office, 800 Linden Street, Scranton, PA 18510-4699. **Phone:** (570) 941-7540, (800) 888-SCRANTON. **Fax:** (570) 941-5928. **E-mail:** admissions@scranton.edu. **Web Site:** scranton.edu. **Tuition and Fees:** $17,740. **Room and Board:** $7,710. **Students Receiving Some Form of Aid:** 51%. **Students Receiving Non-Need-Based Aid:** 5%. **Average Aid Package:** $12,759. **Required Financial Aid Forms:** FAFSA, institutional form or CSS profile. **Deadline to Apply for Financial Aid:** February 15 (priority).

University of the Arts

Office of Admissions, 320 South Broad Street, Philadelphia, PA 19102. **Phone:** (215) 717-6030, (800) 616-ARTS. **Fax:** (215) 717-6045. **E-mail:** admissions@uarts.edu. **Web Site:** uarts.edu. **Tuition and Fees:** $16,800. **Room and Board:** $4,500. **Students Receiving Some Form of Aid:** 70%. **Students Receiving Non-Need-Based Aid:** 70%. **Average Aid Package:** $13,182. **Required Financial Aid Forms:** FAFSA. **Deadline to Apply for Financial Aid:** March15.

University of the Sciences in Philadelphia

Admission Office, 600 S. 43rd Street, Philadelphia, PA 19104-4495. **Phone:** (215) 596-8810, (888) 996-8747. **Fax:** (215) 596-8821. **E-mail:** admit@usip.edu. **Web Site:** usip.edu. **Tuition and Fees:** $14,680. **Room and Board:** $6,500. **Students Receiving Some Form of Aid:** 72%. **Students Receiving Non-Need-Based Aid:** 19%. **Average Aid Package:** $10,600. **Required Financial Aid Forms:** FAFSA. **Deadline to Apply for Financial Aid:** March 15.

Ursinus College

Admissions Office, P.O. Box 1000, Collegeville, PA 19426. **Phone:** (610) 409-3200. **Fax:** (610) 489-3662. **E-mail:** admissions@ursinus.edu. **Web Site:** ursinus.edu. **Tuition and Fees:** $23,460. **Room and Board:** $6,140. **Students Receiving Some Form of Aid:** 86%. **Students Receiving Non-Need-Based Aid:** 7%. **Average Aid Package:** $14,859. **Required Financial Aid Forms:** FAFSA, CSS Profile. **Deadline to Apply for Financial Aid:** February 15.

Villanova University*

Office of University Admission, 800 Lancaster Avenue, Villanova, PA 19085-1672. **Phone:** (610) 519-4000, 800 338-7927. **Fax:** (610) 519-6450. **E-mail:** gotovu@email.villanova.edu. **Web Site:** villanova.edu. **Tuition and Fees:** $20,670. **Room and Board:** $7,830. **Students Receiving Some Form of Aid:** 5%. **Students Receiving Non-Need-Based Aid:** 5%. **Average Aid Package:** $14,033. **Required Financial Aid Forms:** FAFSA, institutional forms. **Deadline to Apply for Financial Aid:** February 15.

Washington and Jefferson College

Admissions Office, 60 South Lincoln Street, Washington, PA 15301. **Phone:** (724) 223-6025, (888) 926-3529. **Fax:** (724) 223-6534. **E-mail:** admission@washjeff.edu. **Web Site:** washjeff.edu. **Tuition and Fees:** $19,650. **Room and Board:** $5,160. **Students Receiving Some**

Form of Aid: 72%. Students Receiving Non-Need-Based Aid: 1%. Average Aid Package: $14,489. Required Financial Aid Forms: FAFSA, state aid form. Deadline to Apply for Financial Aid: February 15.

West Chester University of Pennsylvania

Admissions Office, Messikoner Hall, West Chester, PA 19383. Phone: (610) 436-3411. Fax: (610) 436-3540. E-mail: ugadmiss@wcupa.edu. Web Site: wcupa.edu. In-State Tuition and Fees: $4,312. Out-of-State Tuition and Fees: $9,740. Room and Board: $4,636. Average Aid Package: $5,085. Required Financial Aid Forms: FAFSA. Deadline to Apply for Financial Aid: March 1.

Widener University

Admissions Office, One University Place, Chester, PA 19013. Phone: (610) 499-4126, (888) WIDENER. Fax: (610) 499-4676. E-mail: admissions.office@widener.edu. Web Site: widener.edu. Tuition and Fees: $16,750. Room and Board: $6,810. Students Receiving Some Form of Aid: 44%. Students Receiving Non-Need-Based Aid: 7%. Average Aid Package: $14,388. Required Financial Aid Forms: FAFSA. Deadline to Apply for Financial Aid: rolling; February 15 (priority).

York College of Pennsylvania

Office of Admissions, Country Club Road, York, PA 17405-7199. Phone: (717) 849-1600, (800) 455-8018. Fax: (717) 849-1607. E-mail: admissions@ycp.edu. Web Site: ycp.edu. Tuition and Fees: $6,630. Room and Board: $4,670. Students Receiving Some Form of Aid: 39%. Students Receiving Non-Need-Based Aid: 6%. Average Aid Package: $5,655. Required Financial Aid Forms: FAFSA, institutional form. Deadline to Apply for Financial Aid: April 15.

RHODE ISLAND

Brown University

College Admissions Office, Box 1876, Providence, RI 02912. Phone: (401) 863-2378. Fax: (401) 863-9300. E-mail: admission_undergraduate@brown.edu. Web Site: brown.edu. Tuition and Fees: $26,184. Room and Board: $7,346. Students Receiving Some Form of Aid: 38%. Students Receiving Non-Need-Based Aid: 6%. Average Aid Package: $20,745. Required Financial Aid Forms: FAFSA, Financial Aid Form, parent and student tax returns. Deadline to Apply for Financial Aid: January 20 (Financial Aid Form), March 1 (income tax returns), April 15 (FAFSA).

Bryant College

Office of Admission and Financial Aid, 1150 Douglas Pike, Smithfield, RI 02917-1284. Phone: (401) 232-6100, (800) 622-7001. Fax: (401) 232-6741. E-mail: admissions@bryant.edu. Web Site: bryant.edu. Tuition and Fees: $17,330. Room and Board: $7,250. Students Receiving Some Form of Aid: 61%. Students Receiving Non-Need-Based Aid: 14%. Average Aid Package: $12,519. Required Financial Aid Forms: FAFSA, CSS Profile. Deadline to Apply for Financial Aid: February 15.

Johnson & Wales University

Admissions Office, 8 Abbott Park Place, Providence, RI 02903-3703. Phone: (401) 598-2310, (800) 342-5598. Fax: (401) 598-2948. E-mail: admissions@jwu.edu. Web Site: jwu.edu. Tuition and Fees: $13,850. Room and Board: $5,970. Students Receiving Some Form of Aid: 55%. Students Receiving Non-Need-Based Aid: 30%. Average Aid Package: $10,407. Required Financial Aid Forms: FAFSA. Deadline to Apply for Financial Aid: rolling.

Providence College

Office of Admissions, River Avenue and Eaton Street, Providence, RI 02918. Phone: (401) 865-2535, (800) 721-6444. Fax: (401) 865-2826. E-mail: pcadmiss@providence.edu. Web Site: providence.edu. Tuition and Fees: $18,750. Room and Board: $7,625. Students Receiving Some Form of Aid: 54%. Students Receiving Non-Need-Based Aid: 5%. Average Aid Package: $14,350. Required Financial Aid Forms: FAFSA, Profile. Deadline to Apply for Financial Aid: February 1.

Rhode Island College

Office of Undergraduate Admissions, 600 Mt. Pleasant Avenue, Providence, RI 02908. Phone: (401) 456-8234, (800) 669-5760. Fax: (401) 456-8817. E-mail: admissions@ric.edu. Web Site: ric.edu. In-State Tuition and Fees: $3,371. Out-of-State Tuition and Fees: $8,471. Room and Board: $5,715. Required Financial Aid Forms: FAFSA, institutional form. Deadline to Apply for Financial Aid: March 1.

Rhode Island School of Design*

Admissions Office, 2 College Street, Providence, RI 02903. Phone: (401) 454-6300. Fax: (401) 454-6309. E-mail: admissions@risd.edu. Web Site: risd.edu. Tuition and Fees: $21,405. Room and Board: $6,490. Students Receiving Some Form of Aid: 59%. Students Receiving Non-Need-Based Aid: 2%. Average Aid Package: $11,250. Required Financial Aid Forms: FAFSA, CSS Profile. Deadline to Apply for Financial Aid: February 15.

Roger Williams University

Admissions Office, One Old Ferry Road, Bristol, RI 02809. Phone: (401) 254-3500, (800) 458-7144, ext. 3500. Fax: (401) 254-3557. E-mail: admit@alpha.rwu.edu. Web Site: rwu.edu. Tuition and Fees: $17,855. Room and Board: $7,770. Students Receiving Some Form of Aid: 43%. Students Receiving Non-Need-Based Aid: 16%. Average Aid Package: $14,462. Required Financial Aid Forms: FAFSA, Profile. Deadline to Apply for Financial Aid: March 1.

University of Rhode Island

Undergraduate Admissions Office, 8 Ranger Road, Suite 1, Kingston, RI 02881-2020. Phone: (401) 874-7000. Fax: (401) 874-5523. E-mail: uriadmit@uri.edu. Web Site: uri.edu. In-State Tuition and Fees: $4,928. Out-of-State Tuition and Fees: $13,148. Room and Board: $6,378. Students Receiving Some Form of Aid: 61%. Students Receiving Non-Need-Based Aid: 23%. Average Aid Package: $8,149. Required Financial Aid Forms: FAFSA. Deadline to Apply for Financial Aid: rolling; March 1 (priority).

SOUTH CAROLINA

Charleston Southern University

Admissions Office, 9200 University Boulevard, Charleston, SC 29423. Phone: (843) 863-7050, (800) 947-7474. Fax: (843) 863-7070. E-mail: enroll@csuniv.edu. Web Site: csuniv.edu. Tuition and Fees: $11,346. Room and Board: $4,362. Students Receiving Some Form of Aid: 72%. Students Receiving Non-Need-

Based Aid: 11%. Average Aid Package: $7,700. Required Financial Aid Forms: FAFSA. Deadline to Apply for Financial Aid: April 15.

Citadel

Office of Admissions, 171 Moultrie Street, Charleston, SC 29409-0204. Phone: (843) 953-5230, (800) 868-1842. Fax: (843) 953-7630. E-mail: admissions@citadel.edu. Web Site: citadel.edu. In-State Tuition and Fees: $4,258. Out-of-State Tuition and Fees: $9,854. Room and Board: $4,340. Students Receiving Some Form of Aid: 39%. Students Receiving Non-Need-Based Aid: 28%. Average Aid Package: $7,406. Required Financial Aid Forms: FAFSA. Deadline to Apply for Financial Aid: March 15.

Clemson University

UG Admissions, 105 Sikes Hall, Clemson, SC 29634-5124. Phone: (864) 656-2287. Fax: (864) 656-2464. Web Site: clemson.edu. In-State Tuition and Fees: $3,470. Out-of-State Tuition and Fees: $9,456. Room and Board: $4,122. Students Receiving Some Form of Aid: 34%. Students Receiving Non-Need-Based Aid: 17%. Average Aid Package: $7,123. Required Financial Aid Forms: FAFSA. Deadline to Apply for Financial Aid: April 1 (priority).

Coastal Carolina University

Admissions Office, P.O. Box 261954, Conway, SC 29528-6054. Phone: (843) 349-2026, (800) 277-7000. Fax: (843) 349-2127. E-mail: admissions@coastal.edu. Web Site: coastal.edu. In-State Tuition and Fees: $3,340. Out-of-State Tuition and Fees: $9,280. Room and Board: $4,970. Students Receiving Some Form of Aid: 40%. Students Receiving Non-Need-Based Aid: 3%. Average Aid Package: $6,281. Required Financial Aid Forms: FAFSA. Deadline to Apply for Financial Aid: April 1 (priority).

Coker College

Office of Admissions, 300 East College Avenue, Hartsville, SC 29550. Phone: (843) 383-8050, (800) 950-1908. Fax: (843) 383-8056. E-mail: admissions@coker.edu. Web Site: coker.edu. Tuition and Fees: $14,666. Room and Board: $4,720. Required Financial Aid Forms: FAFSA. Deadline to Apply for Financial Aid: August 1.

College of Charleston

Admissions Office, 66 George Street, Charleston, SC 29424. Phone: (843) 953-5670. Fax: (843) 953-6322. E-mail: admissions@cofc.edu. Web Site: cofc.edu. In-State Tuition and Fees: $3,520. Out-of-State Tuition and Fees: $7,210. Room and Board: $4,070. Students Receiving Some Form of Aid: 35%. Students Receiving Non-Need-Based Aid: 4%. Average Aid Package: $5,644. Required Financial Aid Forms: FAFSA. Deadline to Apply for Financial Aid: March 15 (priority).

Columbia College

Admissions Office, 1301 Columbia College Drive, Columbia, SC 29203. Phone: (800) 277-1301, (803) 786-3871. Fax: (803) 786-3674. Web Site: columbiacollegesc.edu. Tuition and Fees: $14,260. Room and Board: $4,790. Average Aid Package: $12,356. Required Financial Aid Forms: FAFSA. Deadline to Apply for Financial Aid: April1.

Francis Marion University

Admissions Office, P.O. Box 100547, Florence, SC 29501-0547. Phone: (800) 368-7551, (843) 661-1231. Fax: (843) 661-4635. E-mail: admission@fmarion.edu. Web Site: fmarion.edu. In-State Tuition and Fees: $3,590. Out-of-State Tuition and Fees: $6,850. Room and Board: $3,550. Required Financial Aid Forms: FAFSA , institutional, scholarship application. Deadline to Apply for Financial Aid: March 1.

Furman University

Office of Admissions, 3300 Poinsett Highway, Greenville, SC 29613. Phone: (864) 294-2034. Fax: (864) 294-3127. E-mail: admissions@furman.edu. Web Site: furman.edu. Tuition and Fees: $19,152. Room and Board: $5,144. Students Receiving Some Form of Aid: 46%. Students Receiving Non-Need-Based Aid: 4%. Average Aid Package: $14,200. Required Financial Aid Forms: FAFSA, institutional form. Deadline to Apply for Financial Aid: February 1 (priority).

Johnson & Wales University—South Carolina

Admissions Office, 701 East Bay Street, Charleston, SC 29403. Phone: (843) 727-3000, (800) 868-1522. Fax: (843) 763-0318. E-mail: admissions@jwu.edu. Web Site: jwu.edu. Tuition and Fees: $12,390. Room Only: $4,200. Students Receiving Some Form of Aid: 65%. Students Receiving Non-Need-Based Aid: 31%. Average Aid Package: $9,028. Required Financial Aid Forms: FAFSA. Deadline to Apply for Financial Aid: rolling.

University of South Carolina

Admissions Office, University of South Carolina, Columbia, SC 29208. Phone: (803) 777-7700, (800) 868-5872. Fax: (803) 777-0101. E-mail: admissions-ugrad@sc.edu. Web Site: sc.edu. In-State Tuition and Fees: $3,740. Out-of-State Tuition and Fees: $9,814. Room and Board: $4,167. Students Receiving Some Form of Aid: 48%. Students Receiving Non-Need-Based Aid: 15%. Average Aid Package: $3,211. Required Financial Aid Forms: FAFSA. Deadline to Apply for Financial Aid: April 15 (priority).

University of South Carolina—Aiken*

Admissions Office, 471 University Parkway, Aiken, SC 29801. Phone: (803) 641-3366, (888) 969-8722. Fax: (803) 641-3727. E-mail: admit@sc.edu. Web Site: usca.sc.edu. In-State Tuition and Fees: $3,318. Out-of-State Tuition and Fees: $7,844. Room and Board: $3,490. Required Financial Aid Forms: FAFSA. Deadline to Apply for Financial Aid: March 15.

University of South Carolina—Spartanburg

Admissions Office, Admin. 208, 800 University Way, Spartanburg, SC 29303. Phone: (864) 503-5246, (800) 277-8727. Fax: (864) 503-5727. E-mail: uscs.admissions@sc.edu. Web Site: uscs.edu. In-State Tuition and Fees: $3,428. Out-of-State Tuition and Fees: $7,954. Room and Board: $3,950. Students Receiving Some Form of Aid: 38%. Students Receiving Non-Need-Based Aid: 8%. Average Aid Package: $3,507. Required Financial Aid Forms: FAFSA, institutional form. Deadline to Apply for Financial Aid: March 1 (priority).

Winthrop University

Office of Admissions, Stewart House, Rock Hill, SC 29733. Phone: (803) 323-2191. Fax: (803) 323-2137. E-mail: admissions@winthrop.edu. Web Site: winthrop.edu. In-State Tuition and Fees:

$4,126. **Out-of-State Tuition and Fees:** $7,434. **Room and Board:** $4,022. **Students Receiving Some Form of Aid:** 47%. **Students Receiving Non-Need-Based Aid:** 12%. **Average Aid Package:** $6,061. **Required Financial Aid Forms:** FAFSA and school form. **Deadline to Apply for Financial Aid:** March 1 (priority).

Wofford College

Admissions Office, 429 North Church Street, Spartanburg, SC 29303-3663. **Phone:** (864) 597-4130. **Fax:** (864) 597-4149. **E-mail:** admissions@wofford.edu. **Web Site:** wofford.edu. **Tuition and Fees:** $17,730. **Room and Board:** $5,235. **Students Receiving Some Form of Aid:** 62%. **Students Receiving Non-Need-Based Aid:** 18%. **Average Aid Package:** $14,278. **Required Financial Aid Forms:** FAFSA, institutional form, CSS/Financial Aid Profile. **Deadline to Apply for Financial Aid:** March 15 (priority).

SOUTH DAKOTA

Black Hills State University

The Enrollment Center, 1200 University, USB 9502, Spearfish, SD 57799-9502. **Phone:** (605) 642-6343, (800) 255-2478. **Fax:** (605) 642-6024. **E-mail:** jberry@mystic.bhsu.edu. **Web Site:** bhsu.edu. **In-State Tuition and Fees:** $3,363. **Out-of-State Tuition and Fees:** $7,437. **Room and Board:** $2,785. **Required Financial Aid Forms:** FAFSA. **Deadline to Apply for Financial Aid:** April 1.

Dakota State University

Enrollment Services, Dakota State University 820 N. Washington, Madison, SD 57042. **Phone:** (605) 256-5139, (888) DSU-9988. **Fax:** (605) 256-5020. **E-mail:** dsuinfo@pluto.dsu.edu. **Web Site:** dsu.edu. **In-State Tuition and Fees:** $3,588. **Out-of-State Tuition and Fees:** $7,661. **Room and Board:** $2,800. **Students Receiving Some Form of Aid:** 49%. **Students Receiving Non-Need-Based Aid:** 2%. **Average Aid Package:** $4,873. **Required Financial Aid Forms:** FAFSA, Institutional form. **Deadline to Apply for Financial Aid:** March 1.

Northern State University

Admissions Office, Northern State University, Aberdeen, SD 57401. **Phone:** (605) 626-2544, (800) 678-5330. **Fax:** (605) 626-2587. **E-mail:** admission1@wolf.northern.edu. **Web Site:** northern.edu. **In-State Tuition and Fees:** $3,075. **Out-of-State Tuition and Fees:** $6,894. **Room and Board:** $2,575. **Required Financial Aid Forms:** FAFSA. **Deadline to Apply for Financial Aid:** March 1.

South Dakota School of Mines and Technology

Admissions Office, 501 East St. Joseph, Rapid City, SD 57701-3995. **Phone:** (605) 394-2414, (800) 544-8162, ext. 2414. **Fax:** (605) 394-1268. **Web Site:** sdsmt.edu. **In-State Tuition and Fees:** $1,867. **Out-of-State Tuition and Fees:** $5,941. **Room and Board:** $3,122. **Required Financial Aid Forms:** FAFSA. **Deadline to Apply for Financial Aid:** March 15.

South Dakota State University

Admissions Office, Box 2201, Brookings, SD 57007. **Phone:** (605) 688-4121, (800) 952-3541. **Fax:** (605) 688-6384. **Web Site:** sdstate.edu. **In-State Tuition and Fees:** $3,560. **Out-of-State Tuition and Fees:** $7,379. **Room and Board:** $2,594. **Students Receiving Some Form of Aid:** 76%. **Students Receiving Non-Need-Based Aid:** 32%. **Average Aid Package:** $4,922. **Required Financial Aid Forms:** FAFSA. **Deadline to Apply for Financial Aid:** rolling.

University of South Dakota*

Admissions Office, 414 East Clark Street, Vermillion, SD 57069. **Phone:** (877) 677-5206. **Fax:** (605) 677-6753. **E-mail:** admiss@usd.edu. **Web Site:** usd.edu. **In-State Tuition and Fees:** $3,460. **Out-of-State Tuition and Fees:** $7,533. **Room and Board:** $2,946. **Required Financial Aid Forms:** FAFSA. **Deadline to Apply for Financial Aid:** March 1.

TENNESSEE

Austin Peay State University

Admissions Office, P.O. Box 4548, Clarksville, TN 37044. **Phone:** (931) 221-7661, (800) 844-2778. **Fax:** (931) 221-6168. **E-mail:** admissions@apsu01.apsu.edu. **Web Site:** apsu.edu. **In-State Tuition and Fees:** $2,584. **Out-of-State Tuition and Fees:** $7,700. **Room and Board:** $3,230. **Students Receiving Some Form of Aid:** 39%. **Students Receiving Non-Need-Based Aid:** 19%. **Average Aid Package:** $6,924. **Required Financial Aid Forms:** FAFSA. **Deadline to Apply for Financial Aid:** April 1 (priority).

Belmont University

Office of Admissions, 1900 Belmont Boulevard, Nashville, TN 37212-3757. **Phone:** (615) 460-6785, (800) 56-ENROLL. **Fax:** (615) 460-5434. **E-mail:** buadmission@belmont.edu. **Web Site:** belmont.edu. **Tuition and Fees:** $11,550. **Room and Board:** $5,000. **Students Receiving Some Form of Aid:** 42%. **Students Receiving Non-Need-Based Aid:** 21%. **Average Aid Package:** $10,913. **Required Financial Aid Forms:** Federal Application. **Deadline to Apply for Financial Aid:** March 1.

Carson-Newman College

Admissions Office, 1646 South Russell, Jefferson City, TN 37760. **Phone:** (865) 471-3223, (800) 678-9061. **Fax:** (865) 471-3502. **E-mail:** cnadmiss@cncacc.cn.edu. **Web Site:** cn.edu. **Tuition and Fees:** $11,640. **Room and Board:** $3,910. **Students Receiving Some Form of Aid:** 64%. **Students Receiving Non-Need-Based Aid:** 8%. **Average Aid Package:** $10,643. **Required Financial Aid Forms:** FAFSA, institutional form. **Deadline to Apply for Financial Aid:** April 1 (priority).

Christian Brothers University

Admissions Office, 650 East Parkway South, Memphis, TN 38104. **Phone:** (901) 321-3205, (800) 288-7576. **Fax:** (901) 321-3202. **E-mail:** admissions@cbu.edu. **Web Site:** cbu.edu. **Tuition and Fees:** $13,490. **Room and Board:** $4,080. **Required Financial Aid Forms:** FAFSA. **Deadline to Apply for Financial Aid:** March 1 (preferred).

East Tennessee State University

Admissions Office, P.O. Box 70731, Johnson City, TN 37614-0731. **Phone:** (423) 439-4213, (800) 462-3878. **Fax:** (423) 461-7156. **E-mail:** go2etsu@etsu.edu. **Web Site:** etsu.edu. **In-State Tuition and Fees:** $2,552. **Out-of-State Tuition and Fees:** $7,648. **Room and Board:** $3,000. **Students Receiving Some Form of Aid:** 58%. **Students Receiving Non-Need-Based Aid:** 18%. **Average Aid Package:** $7,075. **Required Financial Aid Forms:** FAFSA. **Deadline to Apply for Financial Aid:** April 15 (priority).

Fisk University

Enrollment Management Office, 1000 17th Ave North, Nashville, TN 37208-3051. **Phone:** (615) 329-8565, (800) 443-3475. **Fax:** (615) 329-8774. **E-mail:** admissions@dubois.fisk.edu. **Web Site:** fisk.edu. **Tuition and Fees:** $8,770. **Room and Board:** $4,930. **Students Receiving Some Form of Aid:** 88%. **Students Receiving Non-Need-Based Aid:** 19%. **Average Aid Package:** $12,500. **Required Financial Aid Forms:** FAFSA. **Deadline to Apply for Financial Aid:** March 15 (deadline).

Freed-Hardeman University

Admissions Office, 158 East Main Street, Henderson, TN 38340. **Phone:** (901) 989-6651, (800) 630-3480. **Fax:** (901) 989-6775. **E-mail:** admissions@fhu.edu. **Web Site:** fhu.edu. **Tuition and Fees:** $8,558. **Room and Board:** $4,400. **Students Receiving Some Form of Aid:** 63%. **Students Receiving Non-Need-Based Aid:** 52%. **Average Aid Package:** $11,372. **Required Financial Aid Forms:** FAFSA. **Deadline to Apply for Financial Aid:** April 1.

Lee University

Office of Admissions, P.O. Box 3450, Cleveland, TN 37320-3450. **Phone:** (423) 614-8500, (800) 533-9930. **Fax:** (423) 614-8533. **E-mail:** admissions@leeuniversity.edu. **Web Site:** leeuniversity.edu. **Tuition and Fees:** $11,132. **Room and Board:** $4,020. **Students Receiving Some Form of Aid:** 55%. **Students Receiving Non-Need-Based Aid:** 2%. **Average Aid Package:** $6,644. **Required Financial Aid Forms:** FAFSA, institutional form. **Deadline to Apply for Financial Aid:** April 15 (priority).

Lincoln Memorial University

Admissions Office, Cumberland Gap Parkway, Harrogate, TN 37752. **Phone:** (423) 869-6280, (800) 325-0900. **Fax:** (423) 869-6250. **E-mail:** admissions@inetlmu.lmunet.edu. **Web Site:** lmunet.edu. **Tuition and Fees:** $9,600. **Room and Board:** $3,900. **Students Receiving Some Form of Aid:** 65%. **Students Receiving Non-Need-Based Aid:** 38%. **Average Aid Package:** $7,201. **Required Financial Aid Forms:** FAFSA. **Deadline to Apply for Financial Aid:** April 1 (priority).

Lipscomb University

Admissions Office, 3901 Granny White Pike, Nashville, TN 37204-3951. **Phone:** (615) 269-1776, (800) 333-4358. **Fax:** (615) 269-1804. **E-mail:** admissions@lipscomb.edu. **Web Site:** lipscomb.edu. **Tuition and Fees:** $10,268. **Room and Board:** $4,792. **Required Financial Aid Forms:** FAFSA.

Middle Tennessee State University

Admissions Office, Cope Administration Building, Suite 208, Murfreesboro, TN 37132. **Phone:** (615) 898-2111, (800) 331-MTSU (in-state), (800) 433-MTSU (out-of-state). **Fax:** (615) 898-5478. **E-mail:** admissions@mtsu.edu. **Web Site:** mtsu.edu. **In-State Tuition and Fees:** $2,516. **Out-of-State Tuition and Fees:** $7,632. **Room and Board:** $5,596. **Students Receiving Some Form of Aid:** 11%. **Students Receiving Non-Need-Based Aid:** 4%. **Average Aid Package:** $5,845. **Required Financial Aid Forms:** FAFSA. **Deadline to Apply for Financial Aid:** March 15.

Rhodes College

Office of Admissions, 2000 North Parkway, Memphis, TN 38112. **Phone:** (901) 843-3700, (800) 844-5969. **E-mail:** adminfo@rhodes.edu. **Web Site:** rhodes.edu. **Tuition and Fees:** $18,719. **Room and Board:** $5,454. **Students Receiving Some Form of Aid:** 42%. **Students Receiving Non-Need-Based Aid:** 10%. **Average Aid Package:** $18,024. **Required Financial Aid Forms:** FAFSA, profile. **Deadline to Apply for Financial Aid:** March 1.

Tennessee State University

Admissions Office, 3500 John A. Merritt Boulevard, Nashville, TN 37209-1561. **Phone:** (615) 963-5100. **Fax:** (615) 963-5108. **E-mail:** jcade@picard.tnstate.edu. **Web Site:** tnstate.edu. **In-State Tuition and Fees:** $2,308. **Out-of-State Tuition and Fees:** $7,134. **Room and Board:** $3,600. **Students Receiving Some Form of Aid:** 53%. **Students Receiving Non-Need-Based Aid:** 9%. **Average Aid Package:** $8,366. **Required Financial Aid Forms:** FAF. **Deadline to Apply for Financial Aid:** April 1.

Tennessee Technological University

Admissions Office, Box 5006, Cookeville, TN 38505. **Phone:** (931) 372-3888, (800) 255-8881. **Fax:** (931) 372-6250. **E-mail:** u_admissions@tntech.edu. **Web Site:** tntech.edu. **In-State Tuition and Fees:** $2,390. **Out-of-State Tuition and Fees:** $7,506. **Room and Board:** $4,170. **Students Receiving Some Form of Aid:** 35%. **Students Receiving Non-Need-Based Aid:** 10%. **Average Aid Package:** $3,198. **Required Financial Aid Forms:** FAFSA, income tax form. **Deadline to Apply for Financial Aid:** March 15 (priority).

Union University

Office of Enrollment Services, 1050 Union University Drive, Jackson, TN 38305. **Phone:** (901) 661-5000, (800) 338-6466. **Fax:** (901) 661-5187. **E-mail:** info@uu.edu. **Web Site:** uu.edu. **Tuition and Fees:** $11,900. **Room and Board:** $3,830. **Students Receiving Some Form of Aid:** 49%. **Students Receiving Non-Need-Based Aid:** 36%. **Average Aid Package:** $7,800. **Required Financial Aid Forms:** FAFSA, institutional form. **Deadline to Apply for Financial Aid:** February 15 (priority).

University of Memphis

Admissions Office, 229 Administration Building, Memphis, TN 38152. **Phone:** (901) 678-2111, (800) 669-2678. **Fax:** (901) 678-3053. **E-mail:** bhellums@cc.memphis.edu. **Web Site:** memphis.edu. **In-State Tuition and Fees:** $2,818. **Out-of-State Tuition and Fees:** $8,078. **Room and Board:** $3,320. **Required Financial Aid Forms:** FAFSA. **Deadline to Apply for Financial Aid:** April 1.

University of Tennessee—Chattanooga

Admissions Office, 131 Hooper Hall, Chattanooga, TN 37403. **Phone:** (423) 755-4662, (800) UTC-MOCS. **Fax:** (423) 755-4157. **Web Site:** utc.edu. **In-State Tuition and Fees:** $2,660. **Out-of-State Tuition and Fees:** $7,870. **Room and Board:** $4,547. **Students Receiving Some Form of Aid:** 43%. **Students Receiving Non-Need-Based Aid:** 16%. **Average Aid Package:** $8,300. **Required Financial Aid Forms:** FAFSA. **Deadline to Apply for Financial Aid:** March 1.

University of Tennessee—Knoxville

Admissions Office, 320 Student Services Building, Knoxville, TN 37996-0230. **Phone:** (865) 974-2184, (800) 221-8657. **Fax:** (865) 974-6341. **E-mail:** admissions@utk.edu. **Web Site:** utk.edu. **In-State Tuition and Fees:** $3,104. **Out-of-State Tuition and Fees:** $9,172. **Room and Board:** $4,430. **Students Receiving Some Form of Aid:** 30%. **Average Aid Package:** $5,892. **Required Financial Aid Forms:** FAFSA, institutional forms. **Deadline to Apply for Financial Aid:** March 1.

University of Tennessee—Martin

Admissions Office, 200 Hall-Moody Administration Building, Martin, TN 38238. **Phone:** (901) 587-7020, (800) 829-8861. **Fax:** (901) 587-7029. **E-mail:** admit.me@utm.edu. **Web Site:** utm.edu. **In-State Tuition and Fees:** $2,656. **Out-of-State Tuition and Fees:** $7,916. **Room and Board:** $3,606. **Students Receiving Some Form of Aid:** 41%. **Students Receiving Non-Need-Based Aid:** 14%. **Average Aid Package:** $5,867. **Required Financial Aid Forms:** FAFSA. **Deadline to Apply for Financial Aid:** March 1.

University of the South

Admissions Office, 735 University Avenue, Sewanee, TN 37383-1000. **Phone:** (800) 522-2234, (931) 598-1238. **Fax:** (931) 538-3248. **E-mail:** collegeadmission@sewanee.edu. **Web Site:** sewanee.edu. **Tuition and Fees:** $19,080. **Room and Board:** $5,230. **Students Receiving Some Form of Aid:** 39%. **Average Aid Package:** $16,600. **Required Financial Aid Forms:** FAFSA, income tax form, institutional form. **Deadline to Apply for Financial Aid:** March 1.

Vanderbilt University

Admissions Office, 2305 West End Avenue, Nashville, TN 37203. **Phone:** (615) 322-2561, (800) 288-0432. **Fax:** (615) 343-7765. **E-mail:** admissions@vanderbilt.edu. **Web Site:** vanderbilt.edu. **Tuition and Fees:** $23,598. **Room and Board:** $8,032. **Students Receiving Some Form of Aid:** 37%. **Students Receiving Non-Need-Based Aid:** 14%. **Average Aid Package:** $23,905. **Required Financial Aid Forms:** FAFSA, CSS Profile. **Deadline to Apply for Financial Aid:** February 1 (priority).

TEXAS

Abilene Christian University

Admissions Office, ACU Box 29000, Abilene, TX 79699. **Phone:** (915) 674-2650, (800) 460-6228. **Fax:** (915) 674-2130. **E-mail:** info@admissions.acu.edu. **Web Site:** acu.edu. **Tuition and Fees:** $10,290. **Room and Board:** $4,020. **Students Receiving Some Form of Aid:** 58%. **Students Receiving Non-Need-Based Aid:** 50%. **Average Aid Package:** $10,694. **Required Financial Aid Forms:** FAFSA, institutional form. **Deadline to Apply for Financial Aid:** March 1(priority).

Angelo State University

Office of Admissions and Retention, P.O. Box 11014, ASU Station, San Angelo, TX 76909. **Phone:** (915) 942-2041. **Fax:** (915) 942-2078. **E-mail:** admissions@angelo.edu. **Web Site:** angelo.edu. **Tuition and Fees:** $2,560. **Room and Board:** $4,080. **Required Financial Aid Forms:** FAFSA, university forms. **Deadline to Apply for Financial Aid:** June 1.

Austin College

Office of Admissions, 900 North Grand Avenue, Sherman, TX 75090-4400. **Phone:** (800) 442-5363. **Fax:** (903) 813-3198. **E-mail:** admission@austinc.edu. **Web Site:** austinc.edu. **Tuition and Fees:** $15,219. **Room and Board:** $5,891. **Students Receiving Some Form of Aid:** 64%. **Students Receiving Non-Need-Based Aid:** 62%. **Average Aid Package:** $15,654. **Required Financial Aid Forms:** FAFSA, institutional form. **Deadline to Apply for Financial Aid:** April 1 (priority).

Baylor University

Admissions Office, P.O. Box 97056, Waco, TX 76798-7056. **Phone:** (254) 710-3435, 800-299-5678. **Fax:** (254) 710-3436. **E-mail:** Admission_Serv_Office@Baylor.edu. **Web Site:** baylor.edu. **Tuition and Fees:** $11,988. **Room and Board:** $5,238. **Students Receiving Some Form of Aid:** 44%. **Students Receiving Non-Need-Based Aid:** 19%. **Average Aid Package:** $8,805. **Required Financial Aid Forms:** FAFSA, Baylor financial aid scholarship application. **Deadline to Apply for Financial Aid:** March 1 (priority).

Hardin-Simmons University

Office of Enrollment Services, Box 16050, Abilene, TX 79698. **Phone:** (915) 670-1206, (800) 568-2692. **Fax:** (915) 671-1527. **E-mail:** enroll@hsutx.edu. **Web Site:** hsutx.edu. **Tuition and Fees:** $9,950. **Room and Board:** $3,336. **Students Receiving Some Form of Aid:** 64%. **Students Receiving Non-Need-Based Aid:** 44%. **Average Aid Package:** $10,773. **Required Financial Aid Forms:** FAFSA. **Deadline to Apply for Financial Aid:** March 15 (priority).

Lamar University

Admissions Office, P.O. Box 10009, Beaumont, TX 77710. **Phone:** (409) 880-8888. **Fax:** (409) 880-8463. **E-mail:** admissions@hal.lamar.edu. **Web Site:** lamar.edu. **In-State Tuition and Fees:** $2,024. **Out-of-State Tuition and Fees:** $7,208. **Room and Board:** $3,726. **Students Receiving Some Form of Aid:** 88%. **Students Receiving Non-Need-Based Aid:** 16%. **Required Financial Aid Forms:** FAFSA, Lamar supplement. **Deadline to Apply for Financial Aid:** April 1.

Le Tourneau University

Office of Admissions, P.O. Box 7001, Longview, TX 75607-7001. **Phone:** (903) 233-3400, (800) 759-8811. **Fax:** (903) 233-3411. **E-mail:** admissions@letu.edu. **Web Site:** letu.edu. **Tuition and Fees:** $12,240. **Room and Board:** $5,250. **Students Receiving Some Form of Aid:** 65%. **Students Receiving Non-Need-Based Aid:** 19%. **Average Aid Package:** $11,748. **Required Financial Aid Forms:** FAFSA. **Deadline to Apply for Financial Aid:** February 15 (priority).

McMurry University

Admissions Office, McMurry Station Box 278, Abilene, TX 79697. **Phone:** (915) 793-4700, (800) 460-2392. **Fax:** (915) 793-4718. **E-mail:** mstrang@mcm.edu. **Web Site:** mcm.edu. **Tuition and Fees:** $9,695. **Room and Board:** $4,244. **Required Financial Aid Forms:** FAFSA. **Deadline to Apply for Financial Aid:** rolling.

Midwestern State University

Admissions Office, 3410 Taft Boulevard, Wichita Falls, TX 76308. **Phone:** (940) 397-4321. **Fax:** (940) 397-4672. **E-mail:** school.relations@nexus.mwsu.edu. **Web Site:** mwsu.edu. **In-State Tuition and Fees:** $2,596. **Out-of-State Tuition and Fees:** $7,400. **Room** and Board: $3,700. Required Financial Aid Forms: school's own form. Deadline to Apply for Financial Aid: April 1.

Our Lady of the Lake University

Admissions Office, 411 S.W. 24th Street, San Antonio, TX 78207-4689. Phone: (210) 434-6711, ext. 314, (800) 436-6558. Fax: (210) 431-4036. E-mail: admission@lake.ollusa.edu. Web Site: ollusa.edu. Tuition and Fees: $11,408. Room and Board: $4,352. Students Receiving Some Form of Aid: 52%. Students Receiving Non-Need-Based Aid: 47%. Average Aid Package: $12,060. Required Financial Aid Forms: FAFSA. Deadline to Apply for Financial Aid: rolling.

Rice University*

Office of Admission MS 17, Post Office Box 1892, Houston, TX 77251-1892. Phone: (713) 348-4036, (800) 527-OWLS. E-mail: admission@rice.edu. Web Site: rice.edu. Tuition and Fees: $15,796. Room and Board: $6,600. Required Financial Aid Forms: FAFSA, institutional form. Deadline to Apply for Financial Aid: rolling.

Saint Edward's University

Office of Undergraduate Admission, 3001 South Congress Avenue, Austin, TX 78704-6489. Phone: (512) 448-8500, (800) 555-0164. Fax: (512) 464-8877. E-mail: seu.admit@admin.stedwards.edu. Web Site: stedwards.edu. Tuition and Fees: $11,438. Room and Board: $5,000. Students Receiving Some Form of Aid: 37%. Students Receiving Non-Need-Based Aid: 15%. Average Aid Package: $9,587. Required Financial Aid Forms: FAFSA. Deadline to Apply for Financial Aid: April 15 (priority).

Saint Mary's University

Admissions Office, One Camino Santa Maria, San Antonio, TX 78228. Phone: (210) 436-3126, (800) 367-7868. Fax: (210) 431-6742. E-mail: uadm@stmarytx.edu. Web Site: stmarytx.edu. Tuition and Fees: $12,615. Room and Board: $4,850. Students Receiving Some Form of Aid: 61%. Students Receiving Non-Need-Based Aid: 23%. Average Aid Package: $12,100. Required Financial Aid Forms: FAFSA. Deadline to Apply for Financial Aid: rolling; February 15 (priority).

Sam Houston State University

Admissions Office, 1700 Sam Houston Avenue, Huntsville, TX 77341. Phone: (409) 294-1828. Fax: (409) 294-3758. Web Site: shsu.edu. In-State Tuition and Fees: $1,988. Out-of-State Tuition and Fees: $7,172. Room and Board: $3,390. Students Receiving Some Form of Aid: 32%. Students Receiving Non-Need-Based Aid: 6%. Average Aid Package: $5,178. Required Financial Aid Forms: FAFSA. Deadline to Apply for Financial Aid: June 30; March 31 (priority).

Southern Methodist University

Admissions Office, P.O. Box 750296, Dallas, TX 75275-0296. Phone: (214) 768-2058, (800) 323-0672. Fax: (214) 768-2507. E-mail: ugadmission@smu.edu. Web Site: smu.edu. Tuition and Fees: $18,510. Room and Board: $6,901. Students Receiving Some Form of Aid: 45%. Students Receiving Non-Need-Based Aid: 29%. Average Aid Package: $19,298. Required Financial Aid Forms: FAFSA. Deadline to Apply for Financial Aid: February 1 (priority).

Southwest Texas State University

Admissions Office, 129 Guadalupe, San Marcos, TX 78666. Phone: (512) 245-2364. Fax: (512) 245-8044. E-mail: admissions@swt.edu. Web Site: swt.edu. In-State Tuition and Fees: $3,296. Out-of-State Tuition and Fees: $9,776. Room and Board: $4,564. Students Receiving Some Form of Aid: 36%. Students Receiving Non-Need-Based Aid: 5%. Average Aid Package: $6,217. Required Financial Aid Forms: FAFSA. Deadline to Apply for Financial Aid: April 1 (priority).

Southwestern University

Admissions Office, 1001 E. University, Georgetown, TX 78626. Phone: (512) 863-1200, (800) 252-3166. Fax: (512) 863-9601. E-mail: admission@southwestern.edu. Web Site: southwestern.edu. Tuition and Fees: $15,700. Room and Board: $5,518. Students Receiving Some Form of Aid: 55%. Students Receiving Non-Need-Based Aid: 13%. Average Aid Package: $12,454. Required Financial Aid Forms: FAFSA, institutional form. Deadline to Apply for Financial Aid: March 1.

Stephen F. Austin State University

Admissions Office, P.O. Box 13051, SFA Station, Nacogdoches, TX 75962. Phone: (936) 468-2504, (800) 731-2902. Fax: (936) 468-3849. E-mail: mbsmith@sfasu.edu. Web Site: sfasu.edu. In-State Tuition and Fees: $3,298. Out-of-State Tuition and Fees: $9,778. Room and Board: $4,194. Students Receiving Some Form of Aid: 37%. Students Receiving Non-Need-Based Aid: 8%. Average Aid Package: $2,277. Required Financial Aid Forms: FAFSA, general application. Deadline to Apply for Financial Aid: November 1.

Sul Ross State University

Office of Admissions and Records, C-2 SRSU, Alpine, TX 79832. Phone: (915) 837-8050. Fax: (915) 837-8431. E-mail: rcullins@sulross.edu. Web Site: sulross.edu. In-State Tuition and Fees: $2,150. Out-of-State Tuition and Fees: $8,630. Room and Board: $3,530. Students Receiving Some Form of Aid: 69%. Students Receiving Non-Need-Based Aid: 21%. Average Aid Package: $4,207. Required Financial Aid Forms: FAFSA, institutional forms. Deadline to Apply for Financial Aid: May 1.

Texas A&M University

Office of Admissions and Records, Mail Stop 1265, College Station, TX 77843-1265. Phone: (409) 845-3741. Fax: (409) 847-8737. E-mail: admissions@tamu.edu. Web Site: tamu.edu. In-State Tuition and Fees: $3,167. Out-of-State Tuition and Fees: $9,647. Room and Board: $4,898. Students Receiving Some Form of Aid: 29%. Students Receiving Non-Need-Based Aid: 13%. Average Aid Package: $6,959. Required Financial Aid Forms: FAFSA. Deadline to Apply for Financial Aid: April 1 (priority).

Texas A&M University—Commerce

Admissions Office, Box 3011, Commerce, TX 75429-3011. Phone: (903) 886-5081, (800) 868-2682. Fax: (903) 886-5888. E-mail: robert.hodges@tamu-commerce.edu. Web Site: tamu-commerce.edu. In-State Tuition and Fees: $2,526. Out-of-State Tuition and Fees: $9,006. Room and Board: $4,550. Required Financial Aid Forms: FAFSA. Deadline to Apply for Financial Aid: rolling.

Texas A&M University—Galveston

Admissions and Records Office, P.O. Box 1675, Galveston, TX 77553-1675. Phone: (409) 740-4415, (877) 322-4443. Fax: (409) 740-4731. E-mail: seaggie@tamug.tamu.edu. Web Site: tamug.tamu.edu. In-State Tuition and Fees: $2,854. Out-of-State Tuition and Fees: $9,334. Room and Board: $3,476. Students Receiving Some Form of Aid: 38%. Average Aid Package: $5,455. Required Financial Aid Forms: FAFSA, institutional forms. Deadline to Apply for Financial Aid: rolling.

Texas A&M University—Kingsville

Admissions Office, MSC 105, Kingsville, TX 78363. Phone: (361) 593-2315, (800) 687-6000. Fax: (361) 593-2195. Web Site: tamuk.edu. In-State Tuition and Fees: $2,542. Out-of-State Tuition and Fees: $8,962. Room and Board: $3,484. Average Aid Package: $6,492. Required Financial Aid Forms: FAFSA. Deadline to Apply for Financial Aid: April 15 (priority).

Texas Christian University

Office of Admissions, TCU Box 297013, Fort Worth, TX 76129. Phone: (817) 257-7490, (800) TCU-FROG. Fax: (817) 257-7268. E-mail: frogmail@tcu.edu. Web Site: tcu.edu. Tuition and Fees: $13,125. Room and Board: $4,240. Required Financial Aid Forms: FAFSA, income tax forms. Deadline to Apply for Financial Aid: May 1.

Texas Lutheran University

Admissions Office, 1000 West Court Street, Seguin, TX 78155. Phone: (830) 372-8050, (800) 771-8521. Fax: (830) 372-8096. E-mail: admissions@txlutheran.edu. Web Site: txlutheran.edu. Tuition and Fees: $11,444. Room and Board: $4,366. Students Receiving Some Form of Aid: 67%. Students Receiving Non-Need-Based Aid: 49%. Average Aid Package: $11,045. Required Financial Aid Forms: FAFSA. Deadline to Apply for Financial Aid: June 1.

Texas Southern University

Admissions Office, 3100 Cleburne Avenue, Houston, TX 77004. Phone: (713) 313-7472. Fax: (713) 313-7070. Web Site: tsu.edu. In-State Tuition and Fees: $1,451. Out-of-State Tuition and Fees: $4,043. Room and Board: $4,000. Deadline to Apply for Financial Aid: April 1.

Texas Tech University

New Students Relations, Box 45005, Lubbock, TX 79409-5005. Phone: (806) 742-1482. Fax: (806) 742-0980. E-mail: nsr@ttu.edu. Web Site: texastech.edu. In-State Tuition and Fees: $3,107. Out-of-State Tuition and Fees: $9,587. Room and Board: $4,787. Students Receiving Some Form of Aid: 36%. Students Receiving Non-Need-Based Aid: 8%. Average Aid Package: $5,322. Required Financial Aid Forms: FAFSA. Deadline to Apply for Financial Aid: May 1 (priority).

Texas Wesleyan University

Freshman Admission, 1201 Wesleyan Street, Fort Worth, TX 76105-1536. Phone: (817) 531-4422, (800) 580-8980. Fax: (817) 531-4231. E-mail: freshman@txwesleyan.edu. Web Site: txwesleyan.edu. Tuition and Fees: $9,250. Room and Board: $3,886. Required Financial Aid Forms: FAFSA, university application. Deadline to Apply for Financial Aid: none (April 15, priority).

Texas Woman's University

Undergraduate Admissions, P.O. Box 425589, Denton, TX 76204. Phone: (940) 898-3040, (888) 948-9984. Fax: (940) 898-3081. E-mail: admissions@twu.edu. Web Site: twu.edu. In-State Tuition and Fees: $2,072. Out-of-State Tuition and Fees: $7,256. Room and Board: $3,873. Average Aid Package: $5,969. Required Financial Aid Forms: FAFSA, institutional form. Deadline to Apply for Financial Aid: April 1.

Trinity University

Admissions Office, 715 Stadium Drive, San Antonio, TX 78212-7200. Phone: (210) 999-7207, (800) TRINITY. Fax: (210) 999-8164. E-mail: admissions@trinity.edu. Web Site: trinity.edu. Tuition and Fees: $15,804. Room and Board: $6,330. Students Receiving Some Form of Aid: 44%. Students Receiving Non-Need-Based Aid: 15%. Average Aid Package: $15,745. Required Financial Aid Forms: CSS Profile, FAFSA, non-custodial parent's statement. Deadline to Apply for Financial Aid: February 1 (priority).

University of Dallas

Admissions Office, 1845 East Northgate, Irving, TX 75062-4799. Phone: (972) 721-5266, (800) 628-6999. Fax: (972) 721-5017. E-mail: undadmis@acad.udallas.edu. Web Site: udallas.edu. Tuition and Fees: $14,420. Room and Board: $5,416. Students Receiving Some Form of Aid: 64%. Students Receiving Non-Need-Based Aid: 11%. Average Aid Package: $13,365. Required Financial Aid Forms: FAF, institutional form. Deadline to Apply for Financial Aid: February 15 (priority).

University of Houston

Office of Admissions, University of Houston, Houston, TX 77204-2161. Phone: (713) 743-1010. Fax: (713) 743-9633. E-mail: admissions@uh.edu. Web Site: uh.edu. In-State Tuition and Fees: $2,444. Out-of-State Tuition and Fees: $7,604. Room and Board: $4,513. Students Receiving Some Form of Aid: 16%. Students Receiving Non-Need-Based Aid: 1%. Average Aid Package: $6,352. Required Financial Aid Forms: FAFSA. Deadline to Apply for Financial Aid: April 1.

University of North Texas

Office of Admissions, P.O. Box 311277, Denton, TX 76203-1277. Phone: (940) 565-2681, (800) UNT-8211. Fax: (940) 565-2408. E-mail: undergrad@unt.edu. Web Site: unt.edu. In-State Tuition and Fees: $2,762. Out-of-State Tuition and Fees: $9,242. Room and Board: $8,193. Students Receiving Some Form of Aid: 28%. Students Receiving Non-Need-Based Aid: 5%. Average Aid Package: $5,145. Required Financial Aid Forms: FAFSA. Deadline to Apply for Financial Aid: June 1 (priority).

University of Texas—Arlington

Admissions Office, Box 19111, Arlington, TX 76019-0111. Phone: (817) 272-6287. Fax: (817) 272-3435. E-mail: admissions@uta.edu. Web Site: uta.edu. In-State Tuition and Fees: $2,670. Out-of-State Tuition and Fees: $7,854. Room Only: $1,686. Students Receiving Some Form of Aid: 27%. Students Receiving Non-Need-Based Aid: 7%. Average Aid Package: $7,149. Required Financial Aid Forms: FAFSA. Deadline to Apply for Financial Aid: June 1 (priority).

University of Texas—Austin

Admissions Office, John Hargis Hall, Campus Mail Code D0700, Austin, TX 78712-1111. **Phone:** (512) 475-7440. **Fax:** (512) 475-7475. **E-mail:** frmn@uts.cc.utexas.edu. **Web Site:** utexas.edu. **In-State Tuition and Fees:** $3,128. **Out-of-State Tuition and Fees:** $9,608. **Room and Board:** $4,854. **Students Receiving Some Form of Aid:** 38%. **Average Aid Package:** $7,452. **Required Financial Aid Forms:** FAFSA. **Deadline to Apply for Financial Aid:** April 1 (priority).

University of Texas—El Paso

Admissions Office, 500 W. University, Academic Services Building, Room 104, El Paso, TX 79968. **Phone:** (915) 747-5576. **Fax:** (915) 747-5848. **E-mail:** admission@utep.edu. **Web Site:** utep.edu. **In-State Tuition and Fees:** $2,652. **Out-of-State Tuition and Fees:** $9,132. **Room Only:** $2,150. **Students Receiving Some Form of Aid:** 34%. **Students Receiving Non-Need-Based Aid:** 5%. **Average Aid Package:** $6,741. **Required Financial Aid Forms:** FAFSA, institutional forms. **Deadline to Apply for Financial Aid:** March 15.

University of Texas—San Antonio

Admissions Office, UTSA, 6900 North Loop, 1604 West, San Antonio, TX 78249-0617. **Phone:** (210) 458-4530, (800) 669-0919. **Web Site:** utsa.edu. **In-State Tuition and Fees:** $2,974. **Out-of-State Tuition and Fees:** $9,454. **Room and Board:** $5,876. **Students Receiving Some Form of Aid:** 36%. **Students Receiving Non-Need-Based Aid:** 7%. **Required Financial Aid Forms:** FAFSA. **Deadline to Apply for Financial Aid:** March 1.

West Texas A&M University

Admissions Office, P.O. Box 60907, Canyon, TX 79016. **Phone:** (806) 651-2020, (800) 999-8268. **Fax:** (806) 651-2017. **E-mail:** lvars@mail.wtamu.edu. **Web Site:** wtamu.edu. **In-State Tuition and Fees:** $2,028. **Out-of-State Tuition and Fees:** $7,164. **Room and Board:** $3,310. **Students Receiving Some Form of Aid:** 30%. **Students Receiving Non-Need-Based Aid:** 10%. **Average Aid Package:** $7,425. **Required Financial Aid Forms:** FAFSA. **Deadline to Apply for Financial Aid:** May 1 (priority).

UTAH

Brigham Young University

Admissions Office, A-153 ASB, Provo, UT 84602. **Phone:** (801) 378-2507, (801) 378-2500. **Fax:** (801) 378-4264. **E-mail:** admissions@byu.edu. **Web Site:** byu.edu. **Tuition and Fees (members of the Church of Latter Day Saints):** $2,830. **Tuition and Fees (non-members of the Church of Latter Day Saints):** $4,250. **Room and Board:** $4,350. **Students Receiving Some Form of Aid:** 54%. **Students Receiving Non-Need-Based Aid:** 44%. **Average Aid Package:** $4,890. **Required Financial Aid Forms:** FAFSA, school's own aid form. **Deadline to Apply for Financial Aid:** June 1.

Southern Utah University

Admissions Office, 351 West Center, Cedar City, UT 84720. **Phone:** (435) 586-7740. **Fax:** (435) 865-8223. **E-mail:** adminfo@suu.edu. **Web Site:** suu.edu. **In-State Tuition and Fees:** $2,011. **Out-of-State Tuition and Fees:** $6,368. **Room and Board:** $2,790. **Students Receiving Some Form of Aid:** 52%. **Students Receiving Non-Need-Based Aid:** 16%. **Average Aid Package:** $5,148. **Required Financial Aid Forms:** FAFSA. **Deadline to Apply for Financial Aid:** rolling.

University of Utah

Admissions Office, 201 South 1460 East Room 250S, Salt Lake City, UT 84112-9057. **Phone:** (801) 581-7281. **Fax:** (801) 585-7864. **Web Site:** acs.utah.edu. **In-State Tuition and Fees:** $2,790. **Out-of-State Tuition and Fees:** $8,495. **Room and Board:** $4,890. **Required Financial Aid Forms:** FAFSA, institutional form. **Deadline to Apply for Financial Aid:** February 15 (priority).

Utah State University

Admissions Office, 1600 Old Main Hill, Logan, UT 84322-1600. **Phone:** (435) 797-1079. **Fax:** (435) 797-4077. **E-mail:** admit@admissions.usu.edu. **Web Site:** usu.edu. **In-State Tuition and Fees:** $2,314. **Out-of-State Tuition and Fees:** $7,004. **Room and Board:** $4,038. **Students Receiving Some Form of Aid:** 36%. **Students Receiving Non-Need-Based Aid:** 8%. **Average Aid Package:** $5,400. **Required Financial Aid Forms:** FAFSA. **Deadline to Apply for Financial Aid:** rolling.

Weber State University

Admissions Office, 1137 University Circle, Ogden, UT 84408-1137. **Phone:** (801) 626-6747, (800) 257-3219. **Fax:** (801) 626-6744. **E-mail:** admissions@weber.edu. **Web Site:** weber.edu. **In-State Tuition and Fees:** $2,104. **Out-of-State Tuition and Fees:** $6,240. **Room and Board:** $3,196. **Students Receiving Some Form of Aid:** 38%. **Average Aid Package:** $5,200. **Required Financial Aid Forms:** FAFSA, institutional form. **Deadline to Apply for Financial Aid:** March 1 (priority).

Westminster College

Admissions Office, 1840 South 1300 East, Salt Lake City, UT 84105. **Phone:** (801) 832-2200, (800) 748-4753. **Fax:** (801) 484-3252. **E-mail:** admispub@wcslc.edu. **Web Site:** wcslc.edu. **Tuition and Fees:** $12,726. **Room and Board:** $4,500. **Students Receiving Some Form of Aid:** 54%. **Students Receiving Non-Need-Based Aid:** 3%. **Average Aid Package:** $10,686. **Required Financial Aid Forms:** FAFSA, institutional form. **Deadline to Apply for Financial Aid:** rolling.

VERMONT

Bennington College

Office of Admissions, The First Year, Bennington, VT 05201. **Phone:** (800) 833-6845. **Fax:** (802) 440-4320. **E-mail:** admissions@bennington.edu. **Web Site:** bennington.edu. **Tuition and Fees:** $22,500. **Room and Board:** $5,650. **Students Receiving Some Form of Aid:** 78%. **Students Receiving Non-Need-Based Aid:** 23%. **Average Aid Package:** $17,200. **Required Financial Aid Forms:** Institutional, FAFSA, noncustodial parent's statement, parent and student tax returns. **Deadline to Apply for Financial Aid:** March 1.

Castleton State College

Admissions Office, Castleton State College, Castleton, VT 05735. **Phone:** (802) 468-1214, (800) 639-8521. **Fax:** (802) 468-1476. **E-mail:** info@castleton.edu. **Web Site:** castleton.edu. **In-State Tuition and Fees:** $4,870. **Out-of-State Tuition and Fees:** $10,366. **Room and Board:** $5,298. **Students Receiving Some Form of**

Aid: 72%. Required Financial Aid Forms: FAFSA. Deadline to Apply for Financial Aid: March 15 (priority).

Champlain College

Admissions Office, 163 South Willard Street, Burlington, VT 05401. Phone: , (800) 570 5858. Fax: (802) 860-2767. E-mail: admission@champlain.edu. Web Site: champlain.edu. Tuition and Fees: $11,205. Room and Board: $7,765. Students Receiving Some Form of Aid: 62%. Students Receiving Non-Need-Based Aid: 5%. Required Financial Aid Forms: FAFSA, Institutional Form. Deadline to Apply for Financial Aid: May preference (rolling).

Marlboro College

Admissions Office. , Marlboro, VT 05344. Phone: (802) 258-9236, (800) 343-0049. Fax: (802) 257-4154. E-mail: admissions@marlboro.edu. Web Site: marlboro.edu. Tuition and Fees: $19,585. Room and Board: $6,750. Students Receiving Some Form of Aid: 100%. Students Receiving Non-Need-Based Aid: 18%. Required Financial Aid Forms: FAFSA, Profile. Deadline to Apply for Financial Aid: March 1.

Middlebury College

Office of Admissions, The Emma Willard House, Middlebury, VT 05753-6002. Phone: (802) 443-3000. Fax: (802) 443-2056. E-mail: admissions@middlebury.edu. Web Site: middlebury.edu. Total Annual Expenses (1999–2000): $32,600. Students Receiving Some Form of Aid: 36%. Average Aid Package: $23,538. Required Financial Aid Forms: FAFSA, CSS Profile. Deadline to Apply for Financial Aid: December 31.

Norwich University*

Admissions. , Northfield, VT 05663. Phone: (802) 485-2001, (800) 468-6679. Fax: (802) 485-2580. E-mail: nuadmin@norwich.edu. Web Site: norwich.edu. Tuition and Fees: $15,156. Room and Board: $5,718. Average Aid Package: $11,364. Required Financial Aid Forms: FAFSA, profile. Deadline to Apply for Financial Aid: March 1 (priority).

Saint Michael's College

Office of Admission, One Winooski Park, Colchester, VT 05439. Phone: (802) 654-3000, (800) SMC-8000. Fax: (802) 654-2591. E-mail: admission@smcvt.edu. Web Site: smcvt.edu. Tuition and Fees: $17,662. Room and Board: $7,253. Students Receiving Some Form of Aid: 68%. Students Receiving Non-Need-Based Aid: 16%. Average Aid Package: $13,259. Required Financial Aid Forms: FAFSA, institutional form. Deadline to Apply for Financial Aid: March 15.

Southern Vermont College*

Admissions Office, 982 Foothills Road, Bennington, VT 05201. Phone: (800) 378-2782. Fax: (802) 447-4695. E-mail: admis@svc.edu. Web Site: svc.edu. Tuition and Fees: $10,990. Room and Board: $5,350. Students Receiving Some Form of Aid: 52%. Average Aid Package: $9,512. Required Financial Aid Forms: FAFSA, school's financial aid form. Deadline to Apply for Financial Aid: May 1 (recommended).

University of Vermont

Office of Admissions, 194 S. Prospect Street, Burlington, VT 05401-3596. Phone: (802) 656-3370. Fax: (802) 656-8611. E-mail: admissions@uvm.edu. Web Site: uvm.edu. In-State Tuition and Fees: $8,044. Out-of-State Tuition and Fees: $19,252. Room and Board: $5,620. Students Receiving Some Form of Aid: 48%. Average Aid Package: $14,677. Required Financial Aid Forms: FAFSA, institutional form. Deadline to Apply for Financial Aid: February 10 (priority).

VIRGINIA

Bridgewater College

Admissions Office, 402 East College Street, Bridgewater, VA 22812-1599. Phone: (540) 828-5375. Fax: (540) 828-5481. E-mail: admissions@bridgewater.edu. Web Site: bridgewater.edu. Tuition and Fees: $14,970. Room and Board: $6,970. Students Receiving Some Form of Aid: 74%. Students Receiving Non-Need-Based Aid: 59%. Average Aid Package: $14,900. Required Financial Aid Forms: FAFSA. Deadline to Apply for Financial Aid: March 1.

Christopher Newport University

CNU Admissions, One University Place, Newport News, VA 23608. Phone: (757) 594-7015, (800) 333-4268. Fax: (757) 594-7333. E-mail: admit@cnu.edu. Web Site: cnu.edu. In-State Tuition and Fees: $3,048. Out-of-State Tuition and Fees: $8,816. Room and Board: $4,950. Students Receiving Some Form of Aid: 49%. Students Receiving Non-Need-Based Aid: 8%. Average Aid Package: $4,645. Required Financial Aid Forms: FAFSA. Deadline to Apply for Financial Aid: March 1 (priority).

College of William and Mary

Office of Admission, P.O. Box 8795, Williamsburg, VA 23187-8795. Phone: (757) 221-4223. Fax: (757) 221-1242. E-mail: admiss@facstaff.wm.edu. Web Site: wm.edu. In-State Tuition and Fees: $4,687. Out-of-State Tuition and Fees: $16,904. Room and Board: $5,096. Students Receiving Some Form of Aid: 30%. Students Receiving Non-Need-Based Aid: 2%. Average Aid Package: $7,965. Required Financial Aid Forms: FAFSA. Deadline to Apply for Financial Aid: March 15.

Emory and Henry College

Admissions Office, P.O. Box 947, Emory, VA 24327-0947. Phone: (540) 944-6134, (800) 848-5493. Fax: (540) 944-6935. E-mail: ehadmiss@ehc.edu. Web Site: ehc.edu. Tuition and Fees: $13,150. Room and Board: $5,322. Students Receiving Some Form of Aid: 72%. Students Receiving Non-Need-Based Aid: 40%. Average Aid Package: $11,729. Required Financial Aid Forms: FAFSA, state aid form. Deadline to Apply for Financial Aid: April 1.

Ferrum College

Admissions Office, Spilman House, P.O. Box 1000, Ferrum, VA 24088. Phone: (540) 365-4290, (800) 868-9797. Fax: (540) 365-4366. E-mail: admissions@ferrum.edu. Web Site: ferrum.edu. Tuition and Fees: $10,990. Room and Board: $5,000. Students Receiving Some Form of Aid: 74%. Average Aid Package: $10,022. Required Financial Aid Forms: FAFSA, state aid form. Deadline to Apply for Financial Aid: March 1 (priority).

George Mason University*

Undergraduate Admissions Office, 4400 University Drive, MSN 3A4, Fairfax, VA 22030-4444. Phone: (703) 993-2400. Fax: (703) 993-2392. E-mail: admissions@gmu.edu. Web Site: gmu.edu. In-State Tuition and Fees: $3,756. Out-of-State Tuition and Fees: $12,516. Room and Board: $5,080. Students Receiving Some Form of Aid: 39%. Students Receiving Non-Need-Based Aid: 5%. Average

Aid Package: $6,114. Required Financial Aid Forms: FAFSA. Deadline to Apply for Financial Aid: March 1.

Hampden-Sydney College

Office of Admissions, P.O. Box 667, Hampden-Sydney, VA 23943. Phone: (804) 223-6120, (800) 755-0733. Fax: (804) 223-6346. E-mail: hsapp@tiger.hsc.edu. Web Site: hsc.edu. Tuition and Fees: $16,531. Room and Board: $5,898. Students Receiving Some Form of Aid: 82%. Students Receiving Non-Need-Based Aid: 13%. Average Aid Package: $14,217. Required Financial Aid Forms: FAFSA, CSS Profile. Deadline to Apply for Financial Aid: March 1.

Hampton University

Office of Admissions. , Hampton, VA 23668. Phone: (757) 727-5328, (800) 624-3328. Fax: (757) 727-5095. E-mail: admit@hamptonu.edu. Web Site: hamptonu.edu. Tuition and Fees: $10,580. Room and Board: $4,754. Students Receiving Some Form of Aid: 61%. Students Receiving Non-Need-Based Aid: 29%. Average Aid Package: $19,760. Required Financial Aid Forms: FAFSA. Deadline to Apply for Financial Aid: March 31.

Hollins University

Admissions Office, P.O. Box 9707, Roanoke, VA 24020-1707. Phone: (540) 362-6401, (800) 456-9595. Fax: (540) 362-6218. E-mail: huadm@hollins.edu. Web Site: hollins.edu. Tuition and Fees: $16,710. Room and Board: $6,125. Students Receiving Some Form of Aid: 53%. Students Receiving Non-Need-Based Aid: 42%. Average Aid Package: $14,846. Required Financial Aid Forms: FAFSA. Deadline to Apply for Financial Aid: February 15.

James Madison University

Office of Admission, Sonner Hall MSC 0101, Harrisonburg, VA 22807. Phone: (540) 568-6211. Fax: (540) 568-3332. E-mail: gotojmu@jmu.edu. Web Site: jmu.edu. In-State Tuition and Fees: $3,926. Out-of-State Tuition and Fees: $9,532. Room and Board: $5,182. Students Receiving Some Form of Aid: 28%. Students Receiving Non-Need-Based Aid: 1%. Average Aid Package: $5,036. Required Financial Aid Forms: FAFSA. Deadline to Apply for Financial Aid: February 15.

Liberty University

Office of Admissions, 1971 University Blvd., Lynchburg, VA 24502-2269. Phone: (800) 543-5317. Fax: (804) 582-2421. E-mail: admissions@liberty.edu. Web Site: liberty.edu. Tuition and Fees: $8,750. Room and Board: $4,800. Required Financial Aid Forms: FAFSA. Deadline to Apply for Financial Aid: April 15.

Longwood College

Admissions Office, 201 High Street, Farmville, VA 23909-1898. Phone: (804) 395-2060, (800) 281-4677. Fax: (804) 395-2332. E-mail: lcadmit@longwood.lwc.edu. Web Site: lwc.edu. In-State Tuition and Fees: $3,924. Out-of-State Tuition and Fees: $9,370. Room and Board: $4,620. Students Receiving Some Form of Aid: 46%. Students Receiving Non-Need-Based Aid: 20%. Average Aid Package: $2,045. Required Financial Aid Forms: FAFSA. Deadline to Apply for Financial Aid: March 1.

Lynchburg College

Admissions Office, 1501 Lakeside Drive, Lynchburg, VA 24501-3199. Phone: (804) 544-8300, (800) 426-8101. Fax: (804) 544-8653. E-mail: admissions@lynchburg.edu. Web Site: lynchburg.edu. Tuition and Fees: $18,105. Room and Board: $4,400. Students Receiving Some Form of Aid: 55%. Students Receiving Non-Need-Based Aid: 9%. Average Aid Package: $13,127. Required Financial Aid Forms: FAFSA. Deadline to Apply for Financial Aid: March 1.

Mary Baldwin College

Office of Admissions, POB 1500, Staunton, VA 24401. Phone: (540) 887-7019, (800) 468-2262. Fax: (540) 886-6634. E-mail: admit@mbc.edu. Web Site: mbc.edu. Tuition and Fees: $14,645. Room and Board: $7,450. Students Receiving Some Form of Aid: 63%. Students Receiving Non-Need-Based Aid: 4%. Average Aid Package: $11,164. Deadline to Apply for Financial Aid: June.

Mary Washington College

Office of Admissions, 1301 College Avenue, Fredricksburg, VA 22401. Phone: (540) 654-2000, (800) 468-5614. Fax: (540) 654-1857. E-mail: admit@mwc.edu. Web Site: mwc.edu. In-State Tuition and Fees: $3,204. Out-of-State Tuition and Fees: $9,634. Room and Board: $5,298. Students Receiving Some Form of Aid: 39%. Students Receiving Non-Need-Based Aid: 8%. Average Aid Package: $4,690. Required Financial Aid Forms: FAFSA. Deadline to Apply for Financial Aid: March 1.

Marymount University

Admissions Office, 2807 North Glebe Road, Arlington, VA 22207. Phone: (703) 284-1500, (800) 548-7638. Fax: (703) 522-0349. E-mail: admissions@marymount.edu. Web Site: marymount.edu. Tuition and Fees: $13,870. Room and Board: $6,160. Students Receiving Some Form of Aid: 44%. Students Receiving Non-Need-Based Aid: 23%. Average Aid Package: $14,975. Required Financial Aid Forms: FAFSA, institutional form, state aid form. Deadline to Apply for Financial Aid: March 1 (priority).

Norfolk State University

Admissions Office, 700 Park Avenue, Norfolk, VA 23504. Phone: (757) 823-8396. Fax: (757) 823-9435. E-mail: Admissions@nsu.edu. Web Site: nsu.edu. In-State Tuition and Fees: $2,754. Out-of-State Tuition and Fees: $7,554. Room and Board: $5,267. Students Receiving Some Form of Aid: 95%. Students Receiving Non-Need-Based Aid: 76%. Average Aid Package: $8,285. Required Financial Aid Forms: FAFSA. Deadline to Apply for Financial Aid: March 15.

Old Dominion University

Admissions Office, 108 Rollins Hall, 5215 Hampton Boulevard, Norfolk, VA 23529-0050. Phone: (800) 348-7926. Fax: (757) 683-3255. E-mail: admit@odu.edu. Web Site: odu.edu. In-State Tuition and Fees: $3,796. Out-of-State Tuition and Fees: $11,386. Room and Board: $5,114. Students Receiving Some Form of Aid: 41%. Students Receiving Non-Need-Based Aid: 7%. Average Aid Package: $6,550. Required Financial Aid Forms: FAFSA. Deadline to Apply for Financial Aid: April 1; February 15 (priority).

Radford University

Office of Admissions, Box 6903, Radford, VA 24142-6903. Phone: (540) 831-5371, (800) 890-4265. Fax: (540) 831-5038. E-mail: ruadmiss@runet.edu. Web Site: runet.edu. In-State Tuition and Fees: $2,887. Out-of-State Tuition and Fees: $8,642. Room and Board: $4,770. Students Receiving Some Form of Aid: 41%. Students Receiving Non-Need-

Based Aid: 10%. Average Aid Package: $6,660. Required Financial Aid Forms: FAFSA. Deadline to Apply for Financial Aid: March 1 (priority).

Randolph-Macon College

Admissions Office, P.O. Box 5005, Ashland, VA 23005-5505. Phone: (804) 752-7305, (800) 888-1762. Fax: (804) 752-4707. E-mail: admissions_office@rmc.edu. Web Site: rmc.edu. Tuition and Fees: $18,350. Room and Board: $4,905. Students Receiving Some Form of Aid: 86%. Students Receiving Non-Need-Based Aid: 38%. Average Aid Package: $13,627. Required Financial Aid Forms: FAFSA. Deadline to Apply for Financial Aid: February 1 (priority).

Randolph-Macon Woman's College

Admissions Office, 2500 Rivermont Avenue, Lynchburg, VA 24503. Phone: (804) 947-8100, (800) 745-7692. Fax: (804) 947-8996. E-mail: admissions@rmwc.edu. Web Site: rmwc.edu. Tuition and Fees: $17,080. Room and Board: $7,010. Students Receiving Some Form of Aid: 57%. Students Receiving Non-Need-Based Aid: 11%. Average Aid Package: $15,515. Required Financial Aid Forms: FAFSA, state aid form. Deadline to Apply for Financial Aid: March 1; February 1 (priority).

Roanoke College

Admissions Office, 221 College Lane, Salem, VA 24153-3794. Phone: (540)375-2270, (800) 388-2276. Fax: (540) 375-2267. E-mail: admissions@roanoke.edu. Web Site: roanoke.edu. Tuition and Fees: $17,095. Room and Board: $5,540. Students Receiving Some Form of Aid: 59%. Students Receiving Non-Need-Based Aid: 55%. Average Aid Package: $14,784. Required Financial Aid Forms: FAFSA, state aid form. Deadline to Apply for Financial Aid: March 1 (priority).

Shenandoah University

Admissions Office, 1460 University Drive, Winchester, VA 22601. Phone: (540) 665-4581, (800) 432-2266. Fax: (540) 665-4627. E-mail: admit@su.edu. Web Site: su.edu. Tuition and Fees: $15,700. Room and Board: $5,300. Students Receiving Some Form of Aid: 71%. Students Receiving Non-Need-Based Aid: 63%. Average Aid Package: $10,544. Required Financial Aid Forms: FAFSA. Deadline to Apply for Financial Aid: March 15 (priority).

Sweet Briar College

Office of Admissions, P.O. Box B, Sweet Briar, VA 24595. Phone: (804) 381-6142, (800) 381-6142. Fax: (804) 381-6152. E-mail: admissions@sbc.edu. Web Site: sbc.edu. Tuition and Fees: $17,324. Room and Board: $7,016. Students Receiving Some Form of Aid: 53%. Students Receiving Non-Need-Based Aid: 9%. Average Aid Package: $14,621. Required Financial Aid Forms: FAFSA, institutional form. Deadline to Apply for Financial Aid: March 1 (priority).

University of Richmond

Office of Admission, 28 Westhampton Way, University of Richmond, VA 23173. Phone: (804) 289-8640, (800) 700-1662. Fax: (804) 287-6003. E-mail: Admissions@richmond.edu. Web Site: Richmond.edu. Tuition and Fees: $20,430. Room and Board: $4,240. Students Receiving Some Form of Aid: 32%. Students Receiving Non-Need-Based Aid: 23%. Average Aid Package: $15,111. Required Financial Aid Forms: FAFSA, institutional form. Deadline to Apply for Financial Aid: February 25.

University of Virginia

Office of Undergraduate Admission, P.O. Box 400160, Charlottesville, VA 22904-4160. Phone: (804) 982-3200. Fax: (804) 924-3587. E-mail: Undergrad-Admission@Virginia.edu. Web Site: Virginia.EDU. In-State Tuition and Fees: $4,130. Out-of-State Tuition and Fees: $16,603. Room and Board: $4,589. Students Receiving Some Form of Aid: 23%. Students Receiving Non-Need-Based Aid: 3%. Average Aid Package: $10,042. Required Financial Aid Forms: FAFSA, institutional form. Deadline to Apply for Financial Aid: March 1 (priority).

Virginia Commonwealth University

Admissions Office, 821 West Franklin Street, Box 842526, Richmond, VA 23284-2526. Phone: (804) 831-3638 (in-state), (800) 841-3638 (out-of-state). Fax: (804) 828-1899. E-mail: vcuinfo@vcu.edu. Web Site: vcu.edu. In-State Tuition and Fees: $3,587. Out-of-State Tuition and Fees: $13,041. Room and Board: $4,839. Students Receiving Some Form of Aid: 48%. Students Receiving Non-Need-Based Aid: 10%. Average Aid Package: $5,377. Required Financial Aid Forms: FAFSA. Deadline to Apply for Financial Aid: April 1 (priority).

Virginia Intermont College

Office of Admissions, 1013 Moore Street, Bristol, VA 24201. Phone: (540) 669-6101. Fax: (540) 466-7855. E-mail: viadmit@vic.edu. Web Site: vic.edu. Tuition and Fees: $11,750. Room and Board: $5,200. Students Receiving Some Form of Aid: 88%. Students Receiving Non-Need-Based Aid: 45%. Average Aid Package: $4,963. Required Financial Aid Forms: FAFSA. Deadline to Apply for Financial Aid: June 1.

Virginia Military Insititute

VMI Office of Admissions. , Lexington, VA 24450-0304. Phone: (800) 767-4207, (540) 464-7211. Fax: (540) 464-7746. E-mail: admissions@mail.vmi.edu. Web Site: vmi.edu. In-State Tuition and Fees: $5,014. Out-of-State Tuition and Fees: $14,454. Room and Board: $4,376. Students Receiving Some Form of Aid: 40%. Students Receiving Non-Need-Based Aid: 3%. Average Aid Package: $8,873. Required Financial Aid Forms: FAFSA, institutional form. Deadline to Apply for Financial Aid: April 1; March 1 (priority).

Virginia Polytechnic Institute and State University

Office of Undergraduate Admissions, 201 Burruss Hall, Blacksburg, VA 24061. Phone: (540) 231-6267. Fax: (540) 231-3242. E-mail: vtadmiss@vt.edu. Web Site: vt.edu. In-State Tuition and Fees: $3,620. Out-of-State Tuition and Fees: $11,844. Room and Board: $3,865. Required Financial Aid Forms: FAFSA. Deadline to Apply for Financial Aid: March 1 (priority).

Virginia State University*

Admissions Office, P.O. Box 9018, Petersburg, VA 23806. Phone: (804) 524-5902. Fax: (804) 524-5055. E-mail: lwinn@vsu.edu. Web Site: vsu.edu. In-State Tuition and Fees: $3,086. Out-of-State Tuition and Fees: $8,630. Room and Board: $5,096. Students Receiving Some Form of Aid: 69%. Students Receiving Non-Need-Based Aid: 7%. Average Aid Package: $2,369. Required Financial Aid Forms: FAFSA. Deadline to Apply for Financial Aid: March 31.

Virginia Wesleyan College*

Admissions Office, 1584 Wesleyan Drive, Norfolk, VA 23502-5599. **Phone:** (757) 455-3208, (800) 737-8684. **Fax:** (757) 461-5238. **E-mail:** admissions@vwc.edu. **Web Site:** vwc.edu. **Tuition and Fees:** $14,050. **Room and Board:** $5,650. **Students Receiving Some Form of Aid:** 56%. **Students Receiving Non-Need-Based Aid:** 40%. **Average Aid Package:** $12,789. **Required Financial Aid Forms:** FAFSA. **Deadline to Apply for Financial Aid:** March 1 (priority).

Washington and Lee University*

Office of Admissions, Letcher Avenue, Lexington, VA 24450-0303. **Phone:** (540) 463-8710. **Fax:** (540) 463-8062. **E-mail:** admissions@wlu.edu. **Web Site:** wlu.edu. **Tuition and Fees:** $17,105. **Room and Board:** $5,547. **Students Receiving Some Form of Aid:** 26%. **Students Receiving Non-Need-Based Aid:** 6%. **Average Aid Package:** $13,560. **Required Financial Aid Forms:** FAFSA, CSS Profile. **Deadline to Apply for Financial Aid:** February 1 (priority).

WASHINGTON

Central Washington University

Admissions Office, 400 E. 8th Avenue, Ellensburg, WA 98926-7463. **Phone:** (509) 963-3001. **Fax:** (509) 963-3022. **E-mail:** cwuadmis@cwu.edu. **Web Site:** cwu.edu. **In-State Tuition and Fees:** $3,063. **Out-of-State Tuition and Fees:** $10,062. **Room and Board:** $5,122. **Students Receiving Some Form of Aid:** 37%. **Students Receiving Non-Need-Based Aid:** 4%. **Average Aid Package:** $8,218. **Required Financial Aid Forms:** FAFSA.

Eastern Washington University

Admissions Office, 526 Fifth Street, MS 148, Cheney, WA 99004. **Phone:** (509) 359-2397, (888) 740-1914. **Fax:** (509) 359-6692. **E-mail:** admissions@mail.ewu.edu. **Web Site:** ewu.edu. **In-State Tuition and Fees:** $2,907. **Out-of-State Tuition and Fees:** $9,801. **Room and Board:** $4,399. **Students Receiving Some Form of Aid:** 47%. **Students Receiving Non-Need-Based Aid:** 5%. **Average Aid Package:** $13,003. **Required Financial Aid Forms:** FAFSA. **Deadline to Apply for Financial Aid:** February 15 (priority).

Evergreen State College

Admissions Office, 2700 Evergreen Parkway NW, Olympia, WA 98505. **Phone:** (360) 866-6000, ext. 6170. **Fax:** (360) 866-6680. **E-mail:** admissions@evergreen.edu. **Web Site:** evergreen.edu. **In-State Tuition and Fees:** $2,792. **Out-of-State Tuition and Fees:** $9,794. **Room and Board:** $5,136. **Students Receiving Some Form of Aid:** 55%. **Students Receiving Non-Need-Based Aid:** 5%. **Average Aid Package:** $9,300. **Required Financial Aid Forms:** FAFSA, institutional form. **Deadline to Apply for Financial Aid:** February 15.

Gonzaga University

Admissions Office, 502 East Boone Avenue, Spokane, WA 99258-0001. **Phone:** (509) 323-6572, (800) 986-9585. **Fax:** (509) 323-5780. **E-mail:** ballinger@gu.gonzaga.edu. **Web Site:** zagweb.gonzaga.edu. **Tuition and Fees:** $16,860. **Room and Board:** $5,350. **Students Receiving Some Form of Aid:** 57%. **Students Receiving Non-Need-Based Aid:** 27%. **Average Aid Package:** $11,510. **Required Financial Aid Forms:** FAFSA. **Deadline to Apply for Financial Aid:** February 1 (priority).

Pacific Lutheran University

Office of Undergraduate Admissions. , Tacoma, WA 98447. **Phone:** (253) 535-7151, (800) 274-6758. **Fax:** (253) 536-5136. **E-mail:** admissions@plu.edu. **Web Site:** plu.edu. **Tuition and Fees:** $16,800. **Room and Board:** $5,300. **Students Receiving Some Form of Aid:** 62%. **Students Receiving Non-Need-Based Aid:** 26%. **Average Aid Package:** $15,083. **Required Financial Aid Forms:** FAFSA. **Deadline to Apply for Financial Aid:** January 31 (priority).

Seattle Pacific University

Admissions Office, 3307 Third Avenue West, Seattle, WA 98119-1997. **Phone:** (800) 366-3344, (206) 281-2021. **Fax:** (206) 281-2669. **E-mail:** admissions@spu.edu. **Web Site:** spu.edu. **Tuition and Fees:** $15,381. **Room and Board:** $5,895. **Students Receiving Some Form of Aid:** 62%. **Average Aid Package:** $12,576. **Required Financial Aid Forms:** FAFSA. **Deadline to Apply for Financial Aid:** January 1.

Seattle University

Admissions Office, 900 Broadway, Seattle, WA 98122-4340. **Phone:** (206) 296-5800, (800) 426-7123. **Fax:** (206) 296-5656. **E-mail:** admissions@seattleu.edu. **Web Site:** seattleu.edu. **Tuition and Fees:** $17,010. **Room and Board:** $6,075. **Students Receiving Some Form of Aid:** 57%. **Students Receiving Non-Need-Based Aid:** 19%. **Average Aid Package:** $17,567. **Required Financial Aid Forms:** FAFSA. **Deadline to Apply for Financial Aid:** February 1 (priority).

University of Puget Sound

Admissions Office, 1500 North Warner Street, Tacoma, WA 98416-0062. **Phone:** (253) 879-3211, (800) 396-7191. **Fax:** (253) 879-3993. **E-mail:** admission@ups.edu. **Web Site:** ups.edu. **Tuition and Fees:** $20,605. **Room and Board:** $5,270. **Students Receiving Some Form of Aid:** 57%. **Students Receiving Non-Need-Based Aid:** 36%. **Average Aid Package:** $16,939. **Required Financial Aid Forms:** FAFSA. **Deadline to Apply for Financial Aid:** February 1.

University of Washington

Admissions Office, 1410 NE Campus Parkway, 320 Schmitz Hall Box 355840, Seattle, WA 98195-5840. **Phone:** (206) 543-9686. **E-mail:** askuwadm@u.washington.edu. **Web Site:** u.washington.edu. **In-State Tuition and Fees:** $3,638. **Out-of-State Tuition and Fees:** $12,029. **Room and Board:** $5,844. **Students Receiving Some Form of Aid:** 38%. **Students Receiving Non-Need-Based Aid:** 3%. **Average Aid Package:** $8,167. **Required Financial Aid Forms:** FAFSA. **Deadline to Apply for Financial Aid:** February 28.

Washington State University

Office of Admissions, Washington State University, Pullman, WA 99164-1067. **Phone:** (509) 335-5586. **Fax:** (509) 335-4902. **E-mail:** admiss@wsu.edu. **Web Site:** wsu.edu. **In-State Tuition and Fees:** $3,662. **Out-of-State Tuition and Fees:** $10,696. **Room and Board:** $4,618. **Students Receiving Some Form of Aid:** 41%. **Students Receiving Non-Need-Based Aid:** 14%. **Average Aid Package:** $10,500. **Required Financial Aid Forms:** FAFSA. **Deadline to Apply for Financial Aid:** March 1.

Western Washington University

Office of Admissions, Old Main 200, 516 High Street, Bellingham, WA 98225-9009. **Phone:** (360) 650-3440. **Fax:** (360) 650-7369. **E-mail:** admit@cc.wwu.edu. **Web Site:** ac.wwu.edu. **In-State Tuition and Fees:** $2,994. **Out-of-State Tuition and Fees:** $9,996. **Room and Board:** $4,810. **Students Receiving Some Form of Aid:** 38%. **Students Receiving Non-Need-Based Aid:** less than 1%. **Average Aid Package:** $6,320. **Required Financial Aid Forms:** FAFSA. **Deadline to Apply for Financial Aid:** February 15.

Whitman College

Admissions Office, 345 Boyer Avenue, Walla Walla, WA 99362-2083. **Phone:** (509) 527-5176. **Fax:** (509) 527-4967. **E-mail:** admission@whitman.edu. **Web Site:** whitman.edu. **Tuition and Fees:** $21,742. **Room and Board:** $6,090. **Students Receiving Some Form of Aid:** 51%. **Students Receiving Non-Need-Based Aid:** 36%. **Average Aid Package:** $13,533. **Required Financial Aid Forms:** FAFSA, FAP. **Deadline to Apply for Financial Aid:** February 1.

WEST VIRGINIA

Bluefield State College

Admissions Office, 219 Rock Street, Bluefield, WV 24701. **Phone:** (304) 327-4065, (800) 654-7796. **Fax:** (304) 325-7747. **E-mail:** bscadmit@bscvax.wvnet.edu. **Web Site:** bluefield.wvnet.edu. **In-State Tuition and Fees:** $2,178. **Out-of-State Tuition and Fees:** $5,290. **Students Receiving Some Form of Aid:** 26%. **Students Receiving Non-Need-Based Aid:** 5%. **Average Aid Package:** $4,500. **Required Financial Aid Forms:** FAFSA, institutional form. **Deadline to Apply for Financial Aid:** March 1.

Concord College

Admissions Office, 1000 Vermillion Street, Athens, WV 24712. **Phone:** (304) 384-5248, (888) 384-5249. **Fax:** (304) 384-9044. **E-mail:** admissions@concord.edu. **Web Site:** concord.edu. **In-State Tuition and Fees:** $2,578. **Out-of-State Tuition and Fees:** $5,620. **Room and Board:** $4,018. **Students Receiving Some Form of Aid:** 73%. **Students Receiving Non-Need-Based Aid:** 34%. **Average Aid Package:** $4,800. **Required Financial Aid Forms:** FAFSA. **Deadline to Apply for Financial Aid:** April 15 (FAFSA); March 1 (State).

Fairmont State College

Admissions Office, 1201 Locust Avenue, Fairmont, WV 26554-2470. **Phone:** (304) 367-4141, (304) 367-4142. **Fax:** (304) 367-4789. **E-mail:** admit@mail.fscwv.edu. **Web Site:** fairmont.wvnet.edu. **In-State Tuition and Fees:** $2,244. **Out-of-State Tuition and Fees:** $5,228. **Room and Board:** $3,822. **Students Receiving Some Form of Aid:** 18%. **Students Receiving Non-Need-Based Aid:** 2%. **Average Aid Package:** $4,090. **Deadline to Apply for Financial Aid:** March 1.

Glenville State College

Enrollment Services, 200 High Street, Glenville, WV 26351. **Phone:** (304) 462-4117, (800) 924-2010. **Fax:** (304) 462-8619. **Web Site:** glenville.edu. **In-State Tuition and Fees:** $1,104. **Out-of-State Tuition and Fees:** $2,604. **Room and Board:** $1,855. **Students Receiving Some Form of Aid:** 53%. **Students Receiving Non-Need-Based Aid:** 5%. **Average Aid Package:** $5,885. **Required Financial Aid Forms:** FAFSA. **Deadline to Apply for Financial Aid:** March 1.

Marshall University

Admissions Office, 400 Hal Greer Boulevard, Huntington, WV 25755. **Phone:** (800) 642-3499. **Fax:** (304) 696-3135. **E-mail:** admissions@marshall.edu. **Web Site:** marshall.edu. **In-State Tuition and Fees:** $2,886. **Out-of-State Tuition and Fees:** $6,958. **Room and Board:** $4,652. **Students Receiving Some Form of Aid:** 38%. **Students Receiving Non-Need-Based Aid:** 11%. **Average Aid Package:** $5,273. **Required Financial Aid Forms:** FAFSA, state aid form. **Deadline to Apply for Financial Aid:** March 1.

Shepherd College

Office of Admissions, Shepherd College, Shepherdstown, WV 25443-3210. **Phone:** (304) 876-5212, (800) 344-5231, ext. 5212. **Fax:** (304) 876-5165. **E-mail:** admoff@shepherd.edu. **Web Site:** shepherd.edu. **In-State Tuition and Fees:** $2,430. **Out-of-State Tuition and Fees:** $5,784. **Room and Board:** $4,112. **Students Receiving Some Form of Aid:** 28%. **Students Receiving Non-Need-Based Aid:** 3%. **Average Aid Package:** $6,609. **Required Financial Aid Forms:** FAFSA. **Deadline to Apply for Financial Aid:** March 1.

University of Charleston

Admissions Office, 2300 MacCorkle Avenue, Charleston, WV 25304-1099. **Phone:** (304) 357-4750, (800) 995-4682. **Fax:** (304) 357-4781. **E-mail:** admissions@uchaswv.edu. **Web Site:** uchaswv.edu. **Tuition and Fees:** $13,200. **Room and Board:** $4,480. **Required Financial Aid Forms:** FAFSA. **Deadline to Apply for Financial Aid:** rolling, March 1 for WV.

West Liberty State College

Admissions Office, P.O. Box 295, West Liberty, WV 26074-0295. **Phone:** (304) 336-8076, (800) 732-6204. **Fax:** (304) 336-8403. **E-mail:** wladmsn1@wlsc.wvnet.edu. **Web Site:** wlsc.wvnet.edu. **In-State Tuition and Fees:** $2,320. **Out-of-State Tuition and Fees:** $5,760. **Room and Board:** $3,200. **Students Receiving Some Form of Aid:** 47%. **Students Receiving Non-Need-Based Aid:** 4%. **Average Aid Package:** $2,686. **Required Financial Aid Forms:** FAFSA. **Deadline to Apply for Financial Aid:** March 1 (priority).

West Virginia State College*

Admissions Office, P.O. Box 1000, Institute, WV 25112-1000. **Phone:** (304) 766-3221, (800) 987-2112. **Fax:** (304) 768-9842. **Web Site:** wvsc.wvnet.edu/wvsc.html. **In-State Tuition and Fees:** $2,386. **Out-of-State Tuition and Fees:** $5,588. **Room and Board:** $3,600. **Required Financial Aid Forms:** FAF, institutional form. **Deadline to Apply for Financial Aid:** March 1, November 15.

West Virginia University

Admissions and Records, P.O. Box 6009, Morgantown, WV 26506-6009. **Phone:** (304) 293-2121, (800) 344-9881. **Fax:** (304) 293-3080. **E-mail:** WVUAdmissions@arc.wvu.edu. **Web Site:** wvu.edu. **In-State Tuition and Fees:** $2,748. **Out-of-State Tuition and Fees:** $8,100. **Room and Board:** $4,990. **Students Receiving Some Form of Aid:** 59%. **Students Receiving Non-Need-Based Aid:** 18%. **Average Aid Package:** $4,590. **Required Financial Aid Forms:** FAFSA. **Deadline to Apply for Financial Aid:** February (priority); March 1.

West Virginia University Institute of Technology*

Admissions Office, Box 10 Old Main, Montgomery, WV 25136. Phone: (304) 442-3167, (888) 554-8324. Fax: (304) 442-3097. E-mail: wvutech@wvit.wvnet.edu. Web Site: wvit.wvnet.edu. In-State Tuition and Fees: $2,546. Out-of-State Tuition and Fees: $6,458. Room and Board: $4,498. Students Receiving Some Form of Aid: 37%. Students Receiving Non-Need-Based Aid: 5%. Average Aid Package: $5,397. Required Financial Aid Forms: FAFSA. Deadline to Apply for Financial Aid: April 1.

West Virginia Wesleyan College

Admissions Office, 59 College Avenue, Buckhannon, WV 26201. Phone: (304) 473-8510, (800) 722-9933. Fax: (304) 473-8108. E-mail: admission@wvwc.edu. Web Site: wvwc.edu. Tuition and Fees: $18,050. Room and Board: $4,350. Students Receiving Some Form of Aid: 73%. Students Receiving Non-Need-Based Aid: 49%. Average Aid Package: $16,796. Required Financial Aid Forms: FAFSA. Deadline to Apply for Financial Aid: February 15 (priority).

WISCONSIN

Alverno College

Admissions Office, 3400 South 43rd Street, P.O. Box 343922, Milwaukee, WI 53234. Phone: (414) 382-6100, (800) 933-3401. Fax: (414) 382-6354. E-mail: admissions@alverno.edu. Web Site: alverno.edu. Tuition and Fees: $10,900. Room and Board: $4,250. Required Financial Aid Forms: FAFSA, institutional form, Tax Returns, verification form. Deadline to Apply for Financial Aid: April 15.

Beloit College

Admissions Office, 700 College Avenue, Beloit, WI 53511. Phone: (608) 363-2500, (800) 356-0751. Fax: (608) 363-2075. E-mail: admiss@beloit.edu. Web Site: beloit.edu. Tuition and Fees: $21,550. Room and Board: $4,882. Students Receiving Some Form of Aid: 62%. Students Receiving Non-Need-Based Aid: 28%. Average Aid Package: $14,773. Required Financial Aid Forms: school's form, state aid, FAFSA. Deadline to Apply for Financial Aid: March 1 (priority), January for merit programs.

Lawrence University

Admissions Office, P.O. Box 599, Appleton, WI 54912. Phone: (920) 832-6500, (800) 227-0982. Fax: (920) 832-6782. E-mail: excel@lawrence.edu. Web Site: lawrence.edu. Tuition and Fees: $21,849. Room and Board: $4,791. Students Receiving Some Form of Aid: 72%. Students Receiving Non-Need-Based Aid: 4%. Average Aid Package: $19,143. Required Financial Aid Forms: FAFSA, Lawrence aid application. Deadline to Apply for Financial Aid: March 1.

Marquette University

Office of Undergraduate Admissions, P.O. Box 1881, Milwaukee, WI 53201-1881. Phone: (414) 288-7302, (800) 222-6544. Fax: (414) 288-3764. E-mail: admissions@marquette.edu. Web Site: Marquette.edu. Tuition and Fees: $17,336. Room and Board: $6,086. Students Receiving Some Form of Aid: 56%. Students Receiving Non-Need-Based Aid: 3%. Average Aid Package: $15,461. Required Financial Aid Forms: FAFSA. Deadline to Apply for Financial Aid: rolling.

Milwaukee School of Engineering

Admission Office, 1025 North Broadway, Milwaukee, WI 53202-3109. Phone: (414) 277-7200, (800) 332-6763. Fax: (414) 277-7475. E-mail: explore@msoe.edu. Web Site: msoe.edu. Tuition and Fees: $19,845. Room and Board: $4,530. Students Receiving Some Form of Aid: 65%. Students Receiving Non-Need-Based Aid: 3%. Average Aid Package: $12,400. Required Financial Aid Forms: FAFSA. Deadline to Apply for Financial Aid: March 15 (priority).

Saint Norbert College

Admissions Office, 100 Grant Street, De Pere, WI 54115-2099. Phone: (800) 236-4878. Fax: (920) 403-4072. E-mail: Admit@mail.snc.edu. Web Site: snc.edu. Tuition and Fees: $16,770. Room and Board: $5,162. Students Receiving Some Form of Aid: 64%. Students Receiving Non-Need-Based Aid: 8%. Average Aid Package: $13,045. Required Financial Aid Forms: FAFSA, institutional form. Deadline to Apply for Financial Aid: March 1 (priority).

University of Wisconsin—Eau Claire

Admissions Office, 105 Garfield Avenue, Eau Claire, WI 54702-4004. Phone: (715) 836-5415, (888) 463-6893. Fax: (715) 836-2409. E-mail: ask-uwec@uwec.edu. Web Site: uwec.edu. In-State Tuition and Fees: $3,210. Out-of-State Tuition and Fees: $10,074. Room and Board: $3,301. Students Receiving Some Form of Aid: 42%. Students Receiving Non-Need-Based Aid: 2%. Average Aid Package: $5,225. Required Financial Aid Forms: FAFSA. Deadline to Apply for Financial Aid: April 15 (priority).

University of Wisconsin—Green Bay

Admissions Office, 2420 Nicolet Drive, Green Bay, WI 54311-7001. Phone: (920) 465-2111, (888) 367-8942 (out-of-state). Fax: (920) 465-5754. E-mail: uwgb@uwgb.edu. Web Site: uwgb.edu. In-State Tuition and Fees: $3,150. Out-of-State Tuition and Fees: $10,014. Room and Board: $3,500. Students Receiving Some Form of Aid: 37%. Students Receiving Non-Need-Based Aid: 7%. Average Aid Package: $5,317. Required Financial Aid Forms: FAFSA. Deadline to Apply for Financial Aid: April 15.

University of Wisconsin—La Crosse

Admissions Office, 1725 State Street, La Crosse, WI 54601. Phone: (608) 785-8939. Fax: (608) 785-8940. E-mail: admissions@uwlax.edu. Web Site: uwlax.edu. In-State Tuition and Fees: $3,240. Out-of-State Tuition and Fees: $10,104. Room and Board: $3,350. Students Receiving Some Form of Aid: 53%. Students Receiving Non-Need-Based Aid: 2%. Average Aid Package: $5,370. Required Financial Aid Forms: FAFSA. Deadline to Apply for Financial Aid: March 15 (priority).

University of Wisconsin—Madison

Admissions Office, 3rd Floor, Red Gym, 716 Langdon Street, Madison, WI 53706-1400. Phone: (608) 262-3961. Fax: (608) 262-1429. E-mail: on.wisconsin@mail.admin.wisc.edu. Web Site: wisc.edu. In-State Tuition and Fees: $3,650. Out-of-State Tuition and Fees: $12,400. Room and Board: $5,250. Students Receiving Some Form of Aid: 28%. Students

Receiving Non-Need-Based Aid: 10%. Average Aid Package: $2,753. Required Financial Aid Forms: institutional form, FAFSA. Deadline to Apply for Financial Aid: rolling.

University of Wisconsin—Milwaukee

Admissions Office, P.O. Box 413, Milwaukee, WI 53201. **Phone:** (414) 229-3800. **Fax:** (414) 229-6940. **E-mail:** uwmlook@des.uwm.edu. **Web Site:** uwm.edu. **In-State Tuition and Fees:** $3,741. **Out-of-State Tuition and Fees:** $12,361. **Room and Board:** $4,566. **Students Receiving Some Form of Aid:** 34%. **Students Receiving Non-Need-Based Aid:** less than 1%. **Required Financial Aid Forms:** FAFSA. **Deadline to Apply for Financial Aid:** March 1 (priority).

University of Wisconsin—Oshkosh

Admissions Office, 800 Algoma Blvd., Oshkosh, WI 54901-8602. **Phone:** (920) 424-0202, (920) 424-0416. **Fax:** (920) 424-1098. **E-mail:** oshadmuw@uwosh.edu. **Web Site:** uwosh.edu. **In-State Tuition and Fees:** $2,950. **Out-of-State Tuition and Fees:** $9,606. **Room and Board:** $3,130. **Required Financial Aid Forms:** FAFSA. **Deadline to Apply for Financial Aid:** March 15.

University of Wisconsin—Platteville

Admissions Office, 1 University Plaza, Platteville, WI 53818. **Phone:** (608) 342-1125, (800) 362-5515. **Fax:** (608) 342-1122. **E-mail:** admit@uwplatt.edu. **Web Site:** uwplatt.edu. **In-State Tuition and Fees:** $3,132. **Out-of-State Tuition and Fees:** $9,996. **Room and Board:** $3,338. **Required Financial Aid Forms:** FAFSA. **Deadline to Apply for Financial Aid:** March 15 (priority).

University of Wisconsin—River Falls

Admissions Office, 112 South Hall, River Falls, WI 54022. **Phone:** (715) 425-3500. **Fax:** (715) 425-0676. **E-mail:** admit@uwrf.edu. **Web Site:** uwrf.edu. **In-State Tuition and Fees:** $3,746. **Out-of-State Tuition and Fees:** $10,626. **Room and Board:** $3,036. **Required Financial Aid Forms:** standard. **Deadline to Apply for Financial Aid:** February 1.

University of Wisconsin—Stevens Point

Admissions Office, University of Wisconsin/Stevens Point, Stevens Point, WI 54481-3897. **Phone:** (715) 346-2441. **Fax:** (715) 346-2561. **E-mail:** admiss@uwsp.edu. **Web Site:** uwsp.edu. **In-State Tuition and Fees:** $3,140. **Out-of-State Tuition and Fees:** $10,004. **Room and Board:** $3,524. **Students Receiving Some Form of Aid:** 46%. **Students Receiving Non-Need-Based Aid:** 5%. **Average Aid Package:** $5,034. **Required Financial Aid Forms:** FAFSA. **Deadline to Apply for Financial Aid:** rolling.

University of Wisconsin—Stout

Admissions Office, UW-Stout, Menomonie, WI 54751. **Phone:** (715) 232-1411, (800) HI-STOUT. **Fax:** (715) 232-1667. **E-mail:** admissions@uwstout.edu. **Web Site:** uwstout.edu. **In-State Tuition and Fees:** $3,256. **Out-of-State Tuition and Fees:** $10,120. **Room and Board:** $3,382. **Required Financial Aid Forms:** FAFSA. **Deadline to Apply for Financial Aid:** April 1.

University of Wisconsin—Superior

Admissions Office, Belknap & Catlin, P.O. Box 2000, Superior, WI 54880. **Phone:** (715) 394-8230. **Fax:** (715) 394-8407. **E-mail:** admissions@uwsuper.edu. **Web Site:** uwsuper.edu. **In-State Tuition and Fees:** $3,323. **Out-of-State Tuition and Fees:** $10,187. **Room and Board:** $3,464. **Students Receiving Some Form of Aid:** 57%. **Students Receiving Non-Need-Based Aid:** 8%. **Average Aid Package:** $5,211. **Required Financial Aid Forms:** FAFSA. **Deadline to Apply for Financial Aid:** April 15.

University of Wisconsin—Whitewater

Office of Admissions. , Whitewater, WI 53190-1790. **Phone:** (262) 472-1440. **Fax:** (262) 472-1515. **E-mail:** Uwwadmit@mail.uww.edu. **Web Site:** uww.edu. **In-State Tuition and Fees:** $3,425. **Out-of-State Tuition and Fees:** $10,289. **Room and Board:** $3,164. **Required Financial Aid Forms:** FAFSA. **Deadline to Apply for Financial Aid:** March 15.

WYOMING

University of Wyoming

Admissions Office, P.O. Box 3434, Laramie, WY 82071. **Phone:** (307) 766-5160, (800) 342-5996. **Fax:** (307) 766-4042. **E-mail:** undergraduate.admissions@uwyo.edu. **Web Site:** uwyo.edu. **In-State Tuition and Fees:** $2,575. **Out-of-State Tuition and Fees:** $7,693. **Room and Board:** $4,568. **Students Receiving Some Form of Aid:** 43%. **Students Receiving Non-Need-Based Aid:** 13%. **Average Aid Package:** $5,814. **Required Financial Aid Forms:** FAFSA. **Deadline to Apply for Financial Aid:** March 1 (priority).

NOTES

NOTES

How Did We Do? Grade Us.

Thank you for choosing a Kaplan book. Your comments and suggestions are very useful to us. Please answer the following questions to assist us in our continued development of high-quality resources to meet your needs.

The Kaplan book I read was: ______________________________

My name is: ______________________________

My address is: ______________________________

____

My e-mail address is: ______________________________

What overall grade would you give this book? (A) (B) (C) (D) (F)

How relevant was the information to your goals? (A) (B) (C) (D) (F)

How comprehensive was the information in this book? (A) (B) (C) (D) (F)

How accurate was the information in this book? (A) (B) (C) (D) (F)

How easy was the book to use? (A) (B) (C) (D) (F)

How appealing was the book's design? (A) (B) (C) (D) (F)

What were the book's strong points? ______________________________

How could this book be improved? ______________________________

Is there anything that we left out that you wanted to know more about?

Would you recommend this book to others? ☐ YES ☐ NO

Other comments: ______________________________

____

____

Do we have permission to quote you? ☐ YES ☐ NO

Thank you for your help. Please tear out this page and mail it to:

Dave Chipps, Managing Editor
Kaplan Educational Centers
888 Seventh Avenue
New York, NY 10106

Or, you can submit your comments electronically by using Kaplan's online feedback form at http://www.kaptest.com/customer-service/lvl5_comments.jhtml

Thanks!

About KAPLAN

Kaplan, Inc. is one of the nation's leading providers of education and career services. Kaplan is a wholly owned subsidiary of The Washington Post Company.

KAPLAN TEST PREPARATION & ADMISSIONS

Kaplan's nationally recognized test prep courses cover more than 20 standardized tests, including secondary school, college and graduate school entrance exams, as well as foreign language and professional licensing exams. In addition, Kaplan offers a college admissions course, private tutoring, and a variety of free information and services for students applying to college and graduate programs. Kaplan also provides information and guidance on the financial aid process. Students can enroll in online test prep courses and admissions consulting services at www.kaptest.com.

Kaplan K12 Learning Services partners with schools, universities, and teachers to help students succeed, providing customized assessment, education, and professional development programs.

SCORE! EDUCATIONAL CENTERS

SCORE! after-school learning centers help K–10 students build confidence along with academic skills in a motivating, sports-oriented environment.

SCORE! Prep provides in-home, one-on-one tutoring for high school academic subjects and standardized tests.

eSCORE.com is the first educational services Web site to offer parents and kids newborn to age 18 personalized child development and educational resources online.

KAPLANCOLLEGE.COM

KaplanCollege.com, Kaplan's distance learning platform, offers an array of online educational programs for working professionals who want to advance their careers. Learners will find nearly 500 professional development, continuing education, certification, and degree courses and programs in Nursing, Education, Criminal Justice, Real Estate, Legal Professions, Law, Management, General Business, and Computing/Information Technology.

KAPLAN PUBLISHING

Kaplan Publishing produces retail books and software. Kaplan Books, published by Simon & Schuster, include titles in test preparation, admissions, education, career development, and life skills; Kaplan and *Newsweek* jointly publish guides on getting into college, finding the right career, and helping children succeed in school.

KAPLAN PROFESSIONAL

Kaplan Professional provides assessment, training, and certification services for corporate clients and individuals seeking to advance their careers. Member units include:

- Dearborn, a leading supplier of licensing training and continuing education for securities, real estate, and insurance professionals
- Perfect Access/CRN, which delivers software education and consultation for law firms and businesses
- Kaplan Professional Call Center Services, a total provider of services for the call center industry
- Self Test Software, a world leader in exam simulation software and preparation for technical certifications
- Schweser's Study Program/AIAF, which provides preparation services for the CFA examination

KAPLAN INTERNATIONAL PROGRAMS

Kaplan assists international students and professionals in the United States through a series of intensive English language and test preparation programs. These programs are offered at campus-based centers across the United States. Specialized services include housing, placement at top American universities, fellowship management, academic monitoring and reporting, and financial administration.

COMMUNITY OUTREACH

Kaplan provides educational career resources to thousands of financially disadvantaged students annually, working closely with educational institutions, not-for-profit groups, government agencies and grass roots organizations on a variety of national and local support programs. These programs help students and professionals from a variety of backgrounds achieve their educational and career goals.

BRASSRING

BrassRing Inc., the premier business-to-business hiring management and recruitment services company, offers employers a vertically integrated suite of online and offline solutions. BrassRing, created in September 1999, combined Kaplan Career Services, Terra-Starr, Crimson & Brown Associates, thepavement.com, and HireSystems. In March 2000, BrassRing acquired Career Service Inc./Westech. Kaplan is a shareholder in BrassRing, along with Tribune Company, Central Newspapers, and Accel Partners.